VICTORIA R. I.

'The circumstances of Queen Victoria's birth are strangely at variance with the legendary propriety of her long life and reign. A double crisis, in the British monarchy and in the private fortunes of the man destined to be her father, must be held responsible. But for these two unedifying events, there would have been no Victoria to stamp a great age with the royal cypher. The nineteenth century would have been great without her. It would not have been "Victorian", as we understand it.'

This brilliantly detailed, engrossing biography brings to life a young Queen tormented by an unhappy childhood, enraptured by a love match which led to an all too brief marriage, restricted by nine pregnancies, then driven by the shock of the Prince Consort's death into a long retirement.

Then, impelled by an iron sense of duty, the secluded widow emerges at last — to rule her vast Empire as a mother, and her large, high-spirited family as a Queen.

A whole galaxy of notable personalities from Melbourne and Flora Hastings, to Gladstone and Disraeli cross these pages, freshly portrayed and assessed. Lady Longford's widely acclaimed biography of Queen Victoria recaptures the fascinating interplay of State affairs and private life which went to make up the Queen's unparalleled career.

VICTORIA R.I.

ELIZABETH LONGFORD

UNABRIDGED

PAN BOOKS LTD · LONDON

First published 1964 by Weidenfeld & Nicolson Ltd.
This edition published 1966 by Pan Books Ltd.,
33 Tothill Street, London, S.W.1

ISBN 0 330 83121 6

2nd Printing 1970

To Frank

*Printed in Great Britain by Richard Clay (The Chaucer Press), Ltd.,
Bungay, Suffolk*

CONTENTS

PART ONE

PART TWO

ILLUSTRATIONS

between pages 288 and 289

between pages 368 and 369

Queen Victoria by Loch Muick. Painting by Landseer. *Reproduced by gracious permission of HM The Queen*

Lord Melbourne. Painting by William Hayter (*Photo: Radio Times Hulton Picture Library*)

Lord John Russell (*Photo: Radio Times Hulton Picture Library*)

Sir Robert Peel (*Photo: Radio Times Hulton Picture Library*)

Lord Palmerston. Painting by John Partridge. National Portrait Gallery (*Photo: National Portrait Gallery*)

Osborne. Watercolour by Leitch, drawing master to Queen Victoria. *Reproduced by gracious permission of HM The Queen* (*Photo: John Freeman*)

Portrait of a child, probably the Princess Royal, drawn by Queen Victoria, etched by Prince Albert.

The Royal Family at Osborne. Photographic portrait, Windsor Castle (*Photo: John Freeman*)

Wedding photograph of the Princess Royal and her parents. Photographic portrait, Windsor Castle

Buckingham Palace, 1846. Watercolour by Joseph Nash. *Reproduced by gracious permission of HM The Queen*

The Corridor, Windsor Castle. Watercolour by Joseph Nash. *Reproduced by gracious permission of HM The Queen*

Queen Victoria in State Robes, 1859. Painting by Winterhalter. *Reproduced by gracious permission of HM The Queen*

Queen Victoria and the Prince Consort. Photographic portrait by Mayall, Windsor Castle.

between pages 432 and 433

The Blue Room. Photographic portrait, Windsor Castle

Queen Victoria and Princess Alice on either side of the bust of the Prince Consort, 1862. Photographic portrait by Prince Alfred, Windsor Castle. *Reproduced by kind permission of Helmut Gernsheim, Esq.*

Balmoral (*Photo: Radio Times Hulton Picture Library*)

Queen Victoria with John Brown (*Photo: Radio Times Hulton Picture Library*)

Sir Henry Ponsonby. *Photograph reproduced by kind permission of Lord Ponsonby of Shulbrede*

Bust of John Brown by Sir Edgar Boehm. *Reproduced by kind permission of James Forbes, Esq. (Photo: Derrick Witty)*

William Ewart Gladstone (*Photo:* Radio Times *Hulton Picture Library*)

The Marquess of Salisbury (*Photo:* Radio Times *Hulton Picture Library*)

Benjamin Disraeli, Earl of Beaconsfield. Painting by Millais. National Portrait Gallery (*Photo: National Portrait Gallery*)

The Earl of Rosebery (*Photo:* Radio Times *Hulton Picture Library*)

Queen Victoria and her family. A composite photograph, c. 1875 (*Photo: R. A. Reuter*)

The Royal Mausoleum, Frogmore. Watercolour by Brewer. *Reproduced by gracious permission of HM The Queen*

between pages 512 and 513

The Blot on the Queen's Head. *Reproduced by kind permission of Nicolas Bentley, Esq.*

'Moving the Royal Thumb', from *John Brown's Legs. Reproduced by kind permission of Nicolas Bentley, Esq.*

Victoria R.I., 1875. Painting by Joachim von Angeli. National Portrait Gallery (*Photo: National Portrait Gallery*)

Four Generations (*Photo:* Radio Times *Hulton Picture Library*)

A family group photographed by Gustav Mullins

The Golden Jubilee official photograph by Gustav Mullins, 1887 (*Photo:* Illustrated London News)

Queen Victoria and the Munshi with Sir Arthur Bigge. Watercolour by Begg. *Reproduced by gracious permission of HM The Queen (Photo: John Freeman)*

The Diamond Jubilee, 1897 (*Photo:* Radio Times *Hulton Picture Library*)

Queen Victoria in old age. Photographic portrait, Windsor Castle

AUTHOR'S NOTE

QUEEN VICTORIA reigned for nearly sixty-four years and died nearly sixty-four years ago. She once remarked upon the quantity of books which had been written about her, most of them bad. Since then the number and, it must be admitted, the standard have risen. Lytton Strachey, despite the limited sources at his disposal, has left a portrait which in its own way is inimitable. My excuse for adding to the number is twofold.

Just when interesting, new material was beginning to be published the stream of biographies began to dry up. This was part of the inevitable reaction against all things Victorian. The time now seems to have arrived when a more sympathetic generation can see Queen Victoria in the round, neither with the early sentimental adulation which she herself would have been the first to deride, nor with the impatience which succeeded it. Broad hints of a new approach have already appeared in distinguished biographies of her contemporaries and descendants. In any case, a complete portrait of Queen Victoria was never possible without recourse to the copious material in the Royal Archives at Windsor Castle.

By gracious permission of Her Majesty the Queen I have been given unhindered access to all the relevant papers. My very grateful thanks are due to Sir Michael Adeane, Her Majesty the Queen's Private Secretary and Keeper of the Archives, for his unfailing generosity in advice and criticism; to Mr Robert Mackworth-Young, librarian at Windsor Castle, for lavish help with information and suggestions; and to his staff, especially Miss Price-Hill and Miss Langton. At the same time I offer my warm thanks to the Hon. Mrs H. Adeane, Sir Martin and Lady Charteris, Lady Adeane, Surgeon Rear Admiral E. T. S. Rudd, House Governor of Osborne, and Mrs Rudd for so agreeably illuminating the past of Windsor, Balmoral and Osborne.

11

For access to or information about family papers I am greatly indebted to Lord Ponsonby of Shulbrede (Ponsonby Letters), the Duke of Wellington and his librarian, Mr Francis Needham (Stratfield Saye MSS), the Marquess of Salisbury and Dr John Mason, the librarian of Christ Church (Salisbury Papers), the Hon. Leo Russell and Miss Gladys Scott-Thompson (Russell Papers), Mr Rupert Gunnis and the Tunbridge Wells Public Library (Knollys Papers), Mrs Naomi Mitchison (Mrs J. S. Haldane's Papers), Mr Robert Blake (Disraeli MS), Viscount Astor (Cliveden Papers), Lord David Cecil (Beerbohm Papers), Dr Joseph Baylen (Stead Papers), Mr Merritt Abrash of the Rensselaer Polytechnic Institute, Mr Valentine Logue, the Earl of Rosslyn, the Earl of Lytton, the Earl of Dunraven, and Mrs Wroughton's executor (Lady Simmons' diary).

I have to thank the staff of the India Office Library, Hughenden Manor, the British Museum, Public Records Office, Chelsea Public Library, the London Library, the Library of Congress, the Royal College of Obstetrics & Gynaecology, the British Medical Association, the Haemophilia Association, the *Eugenics Review*, the Salvation Army, the Society for Psychical Research, the London College of Psychic Science, the *Psychic News* and Mr Mostyn Gilbert, Miss Eva Lees, and Mr Gerd Ludemann. I am also obliged to 'Burke's Peerage', Sotheby & Co. and Bernard Quaritch Ltd.

Among others whom I must thank individually are Sir John Wheeler-Bennett, Sir Arthur Bell, FROG, Mr Harold Jordan Malkin, FROG, my brother, Dr John Bishop Harman, FRCP, Mr Roger Fulford, Sir Philip Magnus, Mr James Pope-Hennessy, Mr Hector Bolitho, Mr Frank Eyck, Mr Christopher Sykes, Mr Osbert Lancaster, Mr Arthur Calder-Marshall, the Earl of Birkenhead, Mr Peter Coats, Mr Frank Hardie, Mr Fred Leventhal, Dr Ann Dally and Mr Frank Bywater.

I am grateful to the following authors, editors and publishers for permission to quote from their books: John Murray Ltd for *The Girlhood* and *Letters of Queen Victoria* and *The Life of Benjamin Disraeli*; Evans Brothers Ltd for

Dearest Child edited by Roger Fulford; Macmillan and Co Ltd for *Letters of Empress Frederick* edited by Sir Frederick Ponsonby, *Further Letters of Queen Victoria* edited by Hector Bolitho and *The Greville Memoirs* edited by Lytton Strachey and Roger Fulford; Cassell & Co Ltd for *The English Empress* by Egon Caesar Conte Corti; B. T. Batsford Ltd for *The Greville Memoirs* edited by Roger Fulford.

My gratitude is indeed profound to those who have read and corrected the proofs: my sister-in-law, Lady Violet Powell, Mr Robert Rhodes James and Mr Harold Kurtz to whom I am also most grateful for massive assistance of all kinds and for new material. Lastly I must thank Mrs Angela Lambert and Mrs Elaine Moss for help with cutting and shaping, Mrs Agnes Fenner for her impeccable typing, and my family for invaluable criticism and support.

ELIZABETH LONGFORD

London, June 26th, 1964

ACKNOWLEDGEMENTS

I owe a great deal to Miss Scott-Elliot for her help in achieving a balanced collection of illustrations. Photographs of Queen Victoria present a special problem. As Disraeli wrote to her from Berlin in 1878 on being shown her latest photograph: 'Lord Beaconsfield protested against the photograph, which is always serious and sometimes severe and never gives the inspiring smile and inimitable grace which often charm and encourage him'. My thanks are also due to Miss Prudence Molesworth St Aubyn for her care and skill in collecting the pictures.

E.L.

Part One

CHAPTER I

BORN TO SUCCEED
1815–19

THE CIRCUMSTANCES of Queen Victoria's birth are strangely at variance with the legendary propriety of her long life and reign. A double crisis, in the British Monarchy and in the private fortunes of the man destined to be her father, must be held responsible. But for these two unedifying events, there would have been no Victoria to stamp a great age with the royal cypher. The nineteenth century would have been great without her. It would not have been 'Victorian', as we understand it.

The man was Prince Edward, Duke of Kent, fourth son of King George III. In September 1815, the year of Waterloo, he told his friends that he had reached the parting of the ways. Without a career since 1803 when he had been retired from the Army on a charge of disciplinary fanaticism amounting to brutality, he had sunk into graver and graver debt. Now, at the age of nearly forty-eight, he resolved to exile himself in Brussels for four years. As he told a penurious friend with a large family, General Knollys, you could educate five children there for the price of one anywhere else. Not that the Duke had any children to educate; he would merely be living 'in retirement and *very much reduced*'. When self-denial had done its work he hoped to return for good, safe and solvent.[1]

At his side, sharing his exile, would be a dear friend. Already the companion of twenty-five years, she was referred to indulgently as 'Edward's French lady'. Her name was Julie, Madame de St Laurent. She was now nearing the age of fifty though still charming. Her past is wrapped in mystery. All we know for certain is that a *Mademoiselle* (not Madame) de St Laurent was shipped by Prince Edward from Marseilles to Malaga in 1790. Engaged as a *chanteuse* for the sake of appearances, she was actually intended to share his home, as he explained to her in one of three letters, all written in French, which survive. 'Talent is not the first object.' Since her life with him would be spent in a soldier's cottage carrying a haversack, she must not expect 'the embroidered coverlets' of kings.[2] On these unambiguous terms Mademoiselle de St Laurent entered upon an assignment which was to become a sedate partnership, resembling marriage, of nearly twenty-eight years' duration.

Many legends were later to embellish or contradict the meagre facts. That she was married, that she and her husband were aristocratic refugees from the French Revolution, that the Duke smuggled them on forged papers from Geneva to Gibraltar, that the husband conveniently vanished and that Edward eventually made Julie his morganatic wife. Furthermore, that Julie bore him a son or sons, who were adopted by others at birth, and that Queen Victoria assisted them with funds or alternatively that she repudiated the claim and had Julie's marriage lines stolen from Quebec by two masked men.*

So luxuriantly grows the ivy on the bare wall.

Prince Edward duly retreated to Brussels. At the end of the allotted four years he was indeed safe home again, but with a different lady at his side and in his arms the future Queen of England.

In February 1816, not long after the Duke of Kent's arrival in Brussels, a young German Prince, Leopold of Saxe-Coburg, landed at Dover as the guest of the Duke's brother, the Prince Regent, and suitor for the hand of his only child, the Princess Charlotte of Wales. Within three months Prince Leopold and Princess Charlotte, a popular and handsome pair, were married. The year before, Princess Charlotte's father had violently opposed the match; her helpful Uncle Edward allowed his equerry to carry letters between the lovers. Perhaps in return, they devised a plan for rescuing him from exile.

---

* If the Duke of Kent did have any children by his acknowledged partner, Madame de St Laurent, it is hard to see why he should have wanted to conceal them; this was not the practice of his brothers. It is more likely, in fact, that the Duke's illegitimate children — assuming that he had some — were the result of other youthful liaisons.

18

There was one certain way, as all royal personages knew, of acquiring a substantial income from Parliament. This was to marry. In the tiny German principality of Leiningen a suitable bride for the Duke of Kent was to be found. Victoria of Saxe-Coburg, Princess of Leiningen, was the widow of Prince Emich Charles of Leiningen and, more important, sister of Prince Leopold of Saxe-Coburg. Young Leopold and Charlotte urged their uncle to pay a visit to Princess Victoria's remote castle of Wald-Leiningen, near Amorbach. No question arose of the English succession. Princess Charlotte was the heir, desperately in love and hoping to be married. It was simply that the Duke of Kent needed an income and thirty-year-old Princess Victoria needed a husband.

The Duke's flying visit accordingly took place during the autumn of 1816, discreetly sandwiched between visits to numerous other small German courts. He was clearly taken with the handsome widow and her attractive children, Charles and Feodore, for he pressed his suit. His courtship, however, hung fire. Afterwards he came to the conclusion that he had rushed it. Meanwhile winter passed into spring and he heard that his niece, Princess Charlotte, was pregnant. All thoughts were fixed on the happy event, due in October 1817.

Round about the official date for Princess Charlotte's confinement the Duke discovered that there had been a leak over his secret romance. He wrote uneasily to his friend Mr Putnam in London. Would he get Prince Leopold to bring his sister, the Princess of Leiningen, to a decision as soon as Princess Charlotte's accouchement was safely over and he was free to travel? Twelve days after that letter was written Prince Leopold was free enough: all that bound him to a life of warm, spontaneous affection had expired for ever with his still-born infant son and young wife, dead in childbirth.

If the husband was desolate so was the country. As the appalling news circulated on that dismal morning of November 6th, 1817, people realized with horror that there was no one left to whom they could give their hearts. The Monarch, George III, had a little longer to live but he was piteously insane. Of his fifteen children, twelve ageing Princes and Princesses still remained. They inspired the nation about as

19

much as the procession of Banquo's descendants inspired Macbeth. All five Princesses were spinsters or childless. The seven Princes could not boast between them a single offspring who was not either a bastard or otherwise debarred from the throne.

Only three of the Princes were validly married. These three were George, the Prince Regent, Frederick, Duke of York (childless) and Ernest, Duke of Cumberland. The dead Princess's father, the Prince Regent, abhorred his wife and would never breed from her again. Ernest, Duke of Cumberland, had allied himself to a twice widowed German Princess who was rumoured to have murdered her previous husbands. He himself, with his horribly scarred face, looked like a murderer. Scandal-mongers said that he had cut his valet's throat as well as being vicious, incestuous, perverted, disgusting, tyrannical, reactionary and un-British. No one regretted the fact that their union, up to the death of Princess Charlotte, had not been blessed. All the same, it deepened the fear that King George III's huge family was heading for extinction.

In this crisis Parliament demanded an appropriate return from the four unmarried Royal Dukes who had for years been receiving steady, if inadequate, incomes from the public coffers. To the altar with them all.

Augustus, Duke of Sussex, let the call go unheeded. Nothing could tear this faithful Hanoverian from the Lady Cecilia Underwood who shared with him everything but a marriage certificate.* William, Duke of Clarence, Adolphus, Duke of Cambridge, and Edward, Duke of Kent, were prepared to obey.

Up till now Julie de St Laurent had known nothing of Edward's secret courtship for he had been careful not to let his left hand know what his right was doing. He dared not risk losing Julie before Victoria was his. No doubt he planted responsibility for this deception on his nephew and niece. It was their plan. Besides, royal mistresses went into these things with their eyes open. Nevertheless, various agitated letters written to friends show that he felt guilty. His sisters

* He was permitted to marry morganatically by Queen Victoria.

had nicknamed him 'Joseph Surface' – the hypocrite – but he was a hypocrite with a conscience. He handed on his conscience to his daughter Victoria much improved and having been miraculously divested of guile.

An accident first disclosed to Madame de St Laurent how the land lay. The exiled pair were sitting over their Sunday breakfast table like any Darby and Joan. In answer to a casual request the Duke passed Madame the London paper; a minute later an extraordinary noise brought him to his feet. Madame was on the floor in convulsions, the newspaper lying open at an editorial recommending the Duke of Kent and his brothers to get married forthwith.

During the ensuing weeks the Duke hoped to deal gradually and tenderly with Madame's position. He began unveiling the truth to those of his friends who might help her in the sad times to come, including General Knollys and the Duke of Orleans (afterwards King Louis Philippe). Suddenly Adolphus, Duke of Cambridge, forced the pace. News reached Brussels that this brother, the youngest, had been accepted by Princess Augusta of Hesse-Cassel and would marry her without delay. The Duke of Kent snatched up his pen and on January 10th, 1818, asked the Princess Victoria of Leiningen for a 'positive' answer. This time maternal and other scruples were overborne. A chaste double sheet of white paper, with a wreath of small embossed leaves framing the first page, reached the Duke of Kent from Amorbach: '25 January, 1818, . . . *Je quitte une situation indépendente et agréable dans l'espoir que votre amitié m'en dédomagera.*' She would hope to find compensation in the Duke's love.[3]

Forty years on, when the Duke was long dead and the Duchess near her end, it would be possible to decide whether she had done so. Against the loss of her 'agreeable and independent position' in a castle which might have lain east of the sun and west of the moon for all its importance on the political map, she could put a few months of true affection springing from a marriage of convenience, followed by an intense though sometimes turbulent mother–daughter relationship with England's Queen.

The Princess of Leiningen, as she pointed out to the Duke,

21

would forfeit by remarriage the sum of *'Zwanzig Tausend Gulden'*. Edward, however, would be marrying for the succession and expected to receive an additional allowance from Parliament of £25,000 a year. 'As for the payment of my debts,' he told a friend, 'I don't call them great. The nation, on the contrary, is greatly my debtor.'

Spendthrift jauntiness was so pronounced a characteristic of the House of Hanover, that one is again astonished at Queen Victoria's good fortune in inheriting neither this nor any other of her father's besetting sins. When people remarked that she resembled her royal father she would claim with a tightening of the lips to have inherited 'more from my dear Mother'.

Nothing became Madame de St Laurent in her position as royal mistress like the leaving of it. With unobtrusive dignity she removed from Brussels into a Paris convent, where the thoughts of her remorseful friend still turned to her for many months to come. In November 1818 Edward was encouraging General Knollys to call on her while entreating him to make an allusion to 'my position *now*, and to my *present partner*'; some such recent remark by a tactless friend had very nearly killed her. Finally, on April 22nd of the following year, Edward thanked Knollys for his well-intentioned visit and apologized for Julie having declined to receive him. As the Duke of Orleans rightly pointed out, the shock to her nerves had been so great that she could not yet meet anyone connected with 'the happy times of our intimacy'.[4]

A month before the birth of Queen Victoria, the Duke's anxious letters come to an end. It is said that Julie's seclusion eventually ended also and that she finished her life in Canada as the Princess Prospero Colonna, second wife of a nobleman.

By the spring of 1818 letters were flying merrily from London to Amorbach in the Duke's neat, legible hand. He wrote in French but with lover-like ardour proposed a 'double plan' to learn each other's language, which would beyond everything increase their 'mutual attachment'.[5] At length came the day of their formal betrothal: May 27th, 1818. He dispatched a little note to his 'Victoire', touchingly reminiscent of one his daughter was to send to her Albert on their wedding morning, twenty-two years later.

He brought his bride to Kew for the English marriage ceremony on July 11th, 1818, where his elder brother William was simultaneously united to Princess Adelaide of Saxe-Meiningen. The service was printed with German alongside the English, even down to the operative words, *Ich will*. For Edward's 'double plan' was proceeding very slowly: 'Victoire' had become Victoria but that was about all. When the time came for making speeches at official functions the Duchess of Kent had to depend on someone putting her words into phonetics.

> 'Ei hoeve tu regrétt, biing *aes yiett* so littl cônversent in this Inglisch lênguetsch, uitsch obleitschës – miy, tu seh, in *averi fiú words*, theat ei em môhst grêtful for yur congratu-leschens end gud uishes, *end heili*, flatterd, bei yur allucheon, to mei brother . . .'[6]

During the battles that were later to take place between the Duchess on one side and Lord Melbourne and her daughter on the other, the cynical old man always affirmed that the Duchess had perfect command of English but kept up a pretence of ignorance for diplomatic reasons.

Language was not the Kents' only problem. Financial anxieties had not been lifted by the magic act of marriage. A mere £6,000 of the extra allowance which Edward had counted upon materialized. They were pigging it in Kensington Palace by reluctant permission of the Prince Regent, who disapproved of the marriage, or visiting the widower at Clare-mont, Prince Leopold. Here they were constantly reminded of Princess Charlotte's death by her cloak hung up in the hall, exactly as she had left it at the end of her last walk. In October Edward finally gathered up his wife's manifold chattels – hats, mantles, shawls, furniture, lady-in-waiting, maids, dogs and bird-cages – and swept them off to Germany. The marriage for the succession already showed signs of fulfilling its purpose and the Duchess was pregnant. Boldly ignoring the fact that she was only in her second month, they rumbled away. New

Year's Eve came at Amorbach and with it another tender note from Edward to Victoria. This time it was in English. 'God bless you. Love me as I love you.'[7]

The great matrimonial marathon of the four Royal Dukes was singularly meagre in its results. True, 1819 was a bumper year with four royal births. The Clarences and Cambridges led off in March. William, Duke of Clarence, was already the father of ten lusty illegitimate children. Two weakly girls who did not survive infancy followed by still-born twins were his total contribution to the succession. Adolphus, Duke of Cambridge, produced a son, George, in the marathon year and later two daughters. The second pair of 'succession babies' made their appearance in May, both doomed to be only children. The younger, born on the 27th, was another George, son of the Duke of Cumberland. He became the sad, blind King of Hanover and lost his throne. The Duke of Kent's daughter had arrived three days earlier and again it seemed that many brothers and sisters must follow her to reinforce the succession, for the Duchess was young and the Duke had never suffered from a day's illness. Eight months after presenting Princess Victoria to the nation he died.

It was from this low ebb, both physical and moral, that his daughter rescued the royal line. Many years later, as an old, revered matriarch, she was moved to comment in her private Journal on the physical defects of a certain ruler, the Prince of Naples. His fine, large head tailed off into a puny trunk and wretched little legs. She hoped he would marry a 'strong Princess', otherwise the race would 'dwindle away'.[8] The House of Hanover appeared to be in a similar condition when she was born. Victoria was their strong Princess who replenished not only the nurseries of Windsor but also the thrones of Europe.

The Duke of Kent always intended to leave Germany before the Duchess gave birth. Had not a gipsy in Malta prophesied that he would beget a great Queen? This child of fortune must at whatever cost first open her eyes on English soil. The cost to the Duchess might have been high, for she was nearing

24

her time before the Duke could beg or borrow enough money to get them there. Stuffed to the roof with humanity and belongings, their huge shabby coach was driven by the Duke himself to save the expense of a coachman. The 'unbelievably odd caravan', as an eyewitness called it, reached Dover in a gale on St George's Day, April 23rd. Fortunately, if the child had arrived prematurely at one of the seven squalid halting-places which broke their heroic journey, there would have been a doctor at hand, for packed in among the lap-dogs and song-birds was Fräulein Siebold, a famous German midwife who had the distinction, almost unique even in Germany, of being also a qualified doctor. Thus Queen Victoria who abhorred the very idea of lady doctors was herself brought into the world by one – a piece of pleasant irony. To do her justice, she made an exception of female obstetricians.*

On May 24th, 1819, the event which the Duke's arrangements had made somewhat precarious took place. The birds' chorus had begun and the scent of lilac and may was drifting up from the shrubberies of Kensington Palace when Princess Victoria gave her first gusty cry at a quarter past four in the morning. A strong cry from a strong baby. The Duke's 'unfeeling' family might consider the little creature too healthy and therefore 'an intruder'; the Duke himself might remember for an instant that his amiable Duchess had promised him a son; but nothing must cloud the joy of this spring dawn. 'The decrees of Providence,' he reflected, 'are at all times wisest and best.' 'The English like Queens,' announced the baby's Coburg grandmother firmly. The little 'May blossom' might be destined to play a great part.

The Duchess of Kent was determined to give her child 'maternal nutriment', as the Duke called it, benignly contemplating 'an office most interesting in its nature'. When the 'office' was over the baby would be lulled to sleep by German cradle songs. Hearing only German spoken, Princess Victoria spoke nothing else until she was three, when she began to learn English. With her good ear she soon mastered it, speaking without a trace of German accent. There was a precision and clarity about her pronunciation, however, which some

* The Duchess's confinement was attended also by Dr Daniel Davis.

25

people found exquisite while others called it refined.

The belief of this conscientious pair in natural feeding did not prevent them from giving their child all the benefits of modern science. Vaccination against smallpox was coming in among advanced parents. Princess Victoria was the first member of the Royal Family to be vaccinated. In later life she would have agreed most heartily that this was also the first occasion on which she set a good example to the country.

As the days lengthened and the dawn chorus began to subside, another chorus of German voices broke into subdued raptures over the baby's cradle. Fräulein Siebold brought up the baby's twelve-year-old half-sister, Princess Feodore of Leiningen, to have a peep, while behind stood the Duchess's lady-in-waiting, Fräulein Späth. After a few weeks Fräulein Siebold returned to Germany for the confinement of the Duke of Coburg's fascinating wife, Princess Louise. She was expecting her second child.

The baby, Prince Albert, was born on August 26th, a date which was to become one of the most precious in Queen Victoria's calendar.

Another German voice later came to join the worshippers round Princess Victoria's cot. This newcomer was Fräulein Lehzen, Princess Feodore's governess. Lehzen craned her thin neck to get a good view, her sharp nose and nutcracker chin twitching with excitement and the caraway seeds which she loved to chew tucked away for the moment in her pocket.

A cheerful family group, almost middle-class in sentiment and certainly Germanic, was thus in process of settling itself into the southeast wing of Kensington Palace. It offered warmth and security to the new baby. Suddenly, when the Princess was a month old the harmony of her family circle suffered a brutal disturbance.

CHAPTER II

'*I WILL BE GOOD*'
1819–30

ON JUNE 24TH, 1819, the Cupola Room at Kensington Palace was prepared for the Princess Victoria's christening, a golden font in the centre. Over it hovered the traditional bad fairy. He was Victoria's 'wicked uncle', the Prince Regent. He had been invited to stand as the child's godfather and also to approve of her being christened Georgiana Charlotte Augusta Alexandrina Victoria. Alexander I, Tsar of Russia, had consented to be the other godfather: hence 'Alexandrina'. No answer whatever had been received from the Prince Regent until the evening before the ceremony, when a curt message at last reached the affronted parents,

'that the name of Georgiana could not be used, – as He did not chuse to place His name before the Emperor of Russia's, – and He could not allow it to follow.'[1]

As for the other names, he would speak to the Duke about them at the christening. And so the Archbishop of Canterbury, baby in arms, stood waiting for the Prince Regent to pronounce the first name.

Determined to give pain the Prince remained silent. At length he gruffly proposed 'Alexandrina'. (Lord Melbourne was to tell Queen Victoria shortly before her Coronation that she had been called after the Tsar expressly to annoy the Prince Regent, who 'HATED him; God damn him!'[2].) Then he stopped. Again the Archbishop waited. One name was enough for the little intruder, thought the Prince Regent, but his brother prompted him with 'Charlotte'. At the mention of Charlotte the Prince Regent fiercely shook his head. They should not use the name of his dead child. Deeply wounded, the Duke nevertheless went on to propose 'Augusta'. No, certainly not. The Prince resented its suggestion of grandeur. What name? What name? 'Let her be called after her mother,' he thundered, glaring at the poor Duchess of Kent whose

27

elaborate curls and enormous hat shook with tempestuous sobs.

So dramatic a scene was not likely to escape the gossips, and in fact Princess Lieven, wife of the Russian Ambassador who stood proxy for the Tsar, passed on one of several variants to her crony, the famous diarist, Charles Greville. Some heard that the Prince Regent turned down 'Georgiana' at the baptism, not beforehand, others that it was he who wished the Princess to be given the second name of 'Georgiana', in his honour, and Edward who refused. The above account, however, which is derived from a letter to Lord Grey written by the Duchess of Kent herself, must be regarded as authentic. All agree that it was the Prince Regent's distinction to have settled on 'Victoria', adding rudely that the Tsar's name must always come first. Thus the child born fifth in succession to the throne of England was called for the first nine years of her life by the foreign diminutive 'Drina'. (When she was eleven the claims of 'Charlotte' were again unsuccessfully canvassed, 'Elizabeth' being also advanced: 'Victoria', it was said, did not accord with the feelings of the English people. Even the Duchess of Kent reluctantly admitted, in her letter to Lord Grey already mentioned, that 'the two foreign names She bears are not suited to our national feeling, and that they should be laid aside', despite her daughter's 'great attachment' to Victoria.[3] King William IV, on the other hand, felt the sailors would like it and would tattoo Victoria's face on their arms, imagining she was called after Nelson's flagship.)

Baptized and vaccinated, baby Drina was now prepared to meet the world, the flesh and the devil.

Two months after the baptism, Edward decided to parade his daughter again in front of her 'unfeeling' uncle. He took her to a military review. 'What business has that infant here?' bellowed the enraged Prince Regent. It was the first of countless reviews which Victoria attended during her long life. Edward also planned to introduce her to his Radical friends. Early in the new year, 1820, she was to accompany him to New Lanark Mills, where Robert Owen conducted experiments in practical socialism; Edward's death in January prevented this visit.

'Look at her well,' he would say to his friends, 'for she will be Queen of England.'

Owing to financial stringency the Kents were again guests of Prince Leopold for a time at Claremont. It seemed unjust that Edward's nephew should be granted a spacious home by Parliament and an equally spacious £50,000 a year; when Leopold advised the Kents to accept his offer of the fare back to Germany, Edward decided it was time to move.

He accepted the suggestion of Dr Fisher, Bishop of Salisbury, that the family should spend Christmas in Devon at the seaside town of Sidmouth. Like Brussels, Sidmouth would be cheap and the salt breezes would invigorate his wife and child who had just been weaned. Edward arranged that one of the breaks in their long journey should be at Salisbury. He toured the icy Cathedral and caught a bad cold. Having frequently boasted that he would outlive all his brothers, he felt no undue anxiety but settled his family into the small white house called Woolbrook Cottage and stalked outdoors to draw the sea breezes into his congested lungs. There was a moment when his baby daughter's life seemed to be in greater danger than her father's. A boy shooting sparrows in the road sent a shower of pellets against the Princess's windows, breaking the glass and tearing the sleeve of her nightgown. It was Victoria's first but by no means last experience of fire. She stood it as befitted a soldier's daughter, observed the Duke with pride.

Out on the sea-front the air was not doing him the good he expected. His cold grew worse, his breathing more difficult; he was forced to take to his bed. Suddenly it became obvious to all that the burly soldier with dyed brown hair and whiskers was not going to recover. Only Prince Leopold, attended by his friend young Dr Stockmar, arrived to say goodbye. Stockmar urged the Duke to make his will and appoint executors. One of those whom Edward named was his equerry, John Conroy.

His wife nursed him with devotion and as she leaned over him at the last she had the satisfaction of hearing him whisper, 'Do not forget me.' To forget a deathbed wish was unthinkable in Queen Victoria's mother. After the Duchess's own death, Queen Victoria went through her mother's diaries and was deeply touched to find so many tender references to the father she had never known.

The Duke of Kent died of pneumonia on January 23rd, 1820. Six days later his father, George III, was released from a phantom existence. They were both buried by night in the family vault at Windsor, into which the Duke's enormous coffin, fitfully illuminated by smoky torches, was with difficulty manoeuvred after becoming jammed in the entrance.

The Duchess of Kent and her child found themselves in a miserable predicament. There was no ready money to get them home. The Duke's legacy to his family consisted of a mountain of debt. Prince Leopold came to their rescue and on February 12th, 1820, a raw bitter day, they made their sad return journey to Kensington at his expense, while out of the plenitude of his £50,000 annuity he further allowed his sister £2,000 and later £3,000 a year. According to Lehzen, at last summoning up courage to 'look into that little blooming face'[4] he braced the Duchess to resist the call of Amorbach. Edward's decision that the English Princess should be brought up in England was the wisest he ever made and it was faithfully obeyed.

How serious was this loss of a father? To Victoria the security of belonging to a family and having possessions of her own, came late. She spent much of her life looking for father-figures. The first was her Uncle Leopold. Unfortunately the comfort he gave was counteracted by an anti-figure, Sir John Conroy. She may well have noticed as she looked at portraits of the Duke of Kent that Sir John Conroy was not unlike him in appearance.

Queen Victoria often spoke of her dull, sad childhood but there is a sparkle in many of the earlier, fragmentary pictures which have survived. While her 'Uncle King', as she called George IV, was steadily ridding himself of all his better qualities except good taste; while the London mob was howling at somebody's carriage wheels or breaking somebody else's windows; while Roman Catholics were clamouring for emancipation and Protestants for the freeing of African slaves, her earliest childhood passed serenely enough in the old, red brick Palace of Kensington, between Hyde Park and the small market gardens of Fulham.

Her first memory was of her aunt, the Duchess of Gloucester, being painted by Sir Thomas Lawrence. She watched them intently, her lips just parted showing her perfect baby teeth. Something unusual in so young a child was the slight downward curve of the nose. Her expression was determined even though the very small chin sloped gently away. Her arms and neck were bare. She wore a plain, high-waisted dress down to her ankles, white socks and slippers.

There were half memories even before this.[5] Of a yellow carpet in the room where visitors were received; of terrifying bishops in strange wigs and aprons getting down on their hands and knees to play with her – she never could abide bishops; of her father's little tortoise-shell clock ticking in her mother's bedroom, where she lay in her cot and afterwards in a white-painted French bed with chintz hangings. Kensington Palace was full of clocks belonging to her father or to her eccentric uncle, the Duke of Sussex. She was a little afraid of her uncle. Aunt Sophia, her father's youngest surviving sister, was another inmate of the Palace. She had once been beautiful; Princess Victoria distrusted her without at first knowing why. When Victoria was eight the Duke of York died. She remembered people running down the garden to Kensington Road to see his funeral go by.

Portraits of herself at every age recalled the past. There was little three-year-old Drina clinging round her Mama's neck, painted by Beechey in 1822. Drina was all curves and curls, a cupid-bow mouth slightly opened in a smile, hair waving away from a centre parting, dimples everywhere. There was an interesting picture of her at seven. The blue eyes were larger than ever, there were no curls and her hair was smooth and darker. Her tightly closed mouth was secretive. On her left shoulder she wore a miniature of 'Uncle King', which he had given her to mark one of the happiest days of her childhood.

It was in the summer of 1826. King George IV was living at Royal Lodge, Windsor, with his favourite, Lady Conyngham, her husband, the Lord Steward and their children. To this strange family party were summoned the Duchess of Kent and her two daughters, Feodore and Victoria. For the first time Drina faced the preposterous, ageing figure of the King – swollen, gouty, bewigged, bedaubed – as he roared out in coarse affection, 'Give me your little paw.' Out shot the child's hand, very tiny now and destined to become famous for its diminutive size even when it was older and plumper and covered with rings. Lady Conyngham brazenly pinned the King's miniature on Drina's chaste dress; then the little one was hauled on to the royal knee so that she might kiss the rouged cheek. Despite that dreadful kiss the Princess could appreciate regal grandeur when she saw it: in later years she recalled not only her uncle's dissolute appearance but also his wonderful dignity and charm. He, too, warmed to his small niece; for there is no reason to believe Madame de Lieven. 'In spite of the caresses the king lavished on her,' she wrote, 'I could see that he did not like dandling on his sixty-four knee this little bit of the future.'

The ordeal over, Princess Victoria relaxed in the cottage of a royal page, Mr Whiting, stuffing herself with peaches and cramming the ones she had no room for into the mouth of Mr Whiting's little girl. Next day the King's superb phaeton overtook the Princess and her family out walking. 'Pop her in!' the King shouted, as his magnificent horses were brought to a slithering halt. Between huge 'Uncle King' and Aunt Mary of Gloucester a space was made for Drina and away they dashed – the child exhilarated beyond words by the brilliant liveries and whirlwind speed. Remembering it, she wrote afterwards with characteristic simplicity: 'I was greatly pleased.' She remembered also the terror on Mama's face as she vanished from sight, clutched by her aunt round the waist. Mama is afraid I will fall out, thought little Drina. In reality the Duchess feared the King intended to kidnap her.

Every day there was some new entertainment to please Drina: Tyrolese dancers creating a 'gay uproar' or a party in the conservatory with coloured lights and music drifting in on the scented air. Princess Drina knew how to please. 'What would you like the band to play next?' asked her uncle. She replied at once in her clear, clipped voice: 'Oh, Uncle King, I should like them to play "God Save the King"!' Having seen the grease-paint cracked by smiles, Drina was quick to repeat her success. 'Tell me what you enjoyed most of your visit?' inquired His Majesty at the end. 'The drive with you,' said Drina, as truthful as she was clever.

In the glittering summer weather she was allowed to breakfast with her mother in the garden. When she felt like it she could jump down from her chair and dash across the garden to pick a flower. Early one sunshiny morning old Lord Albemarle happened to look over the hedge into the garden of Kensington Palace. There he saw a little girl watering her flowers. A straw hat kept the sun off her round, rosy, intent face and she wore a plain white cotton dress with no trimming but a coloured fichu.

For all her simplicity there was sophistication too. She was once overheard saying to a child about to play with her toys: 'You must not touch those, they are mine; and I may call you Jane, but you must not call me Victoria.' When she was very young she thought all the gentlemen looked at her to see if she was being a good girl. Later on she began to wonder why they raised their hats to her and not to her sister Feodore.

Nature intended her to be a merry, mischievous child. She possessed a gift for mimicry and repartee which Lord Melbourne afterwards said was 'in the Family'. The pithy retorts with which, as Queen, she silenced her Ministers were learnt at her mother's knee. 'When you are naughty,' said the Duchess of Kent after one of her tantrums, 'you make me and yourself very unhappy.' 'No Mama,' corrected Drina, who honestly enjoyed a good set-to, 'not *me*, not myself, but *you*!'

Honesty and truthfulness went as so often with a hot temper. Drina did not care to sail under false colours and made sure that her mentors always knew the worst. At four years old she was already learning her letters off printed cards and finding it tedious to sit still so long. One morning as her tutor was about to begin her reading lesson he asked the

33

Duchess if she had been good. 'Yes, she has been good this morning,' the Duchess replied, 'but yesterday there was a little storm.' Drina chipped in. 'Two storms – one at dressing and one at washing.' This engaging mixture of self-depreciation and complacency remained with Queen Victoria to the end of her life.

Victoria's grandmother, the Dowager Duchess of Saxe-Coburg, visited Claremont when she was five to take Princess Feodore back with her for a holiday in Germany; her looks were attracting too much attention. In the rabbit warren of Kensington Palace there were a number of unattached males, some of them problem members of the Royal Family. Plans were laid at Claremont to marry Feodore as soon as possible to Prince Hohenlohe-Langenburg.

The old Duchess next reported on the 'little cousin' at Coburg, five-year-old Prince Albert. He was a marvellously beautiful child whose intense seriousness contrasted with Victoria's sociability. The three Coburg relatives, led by Prince Leopold, came to the conclusion that a marriage between Victoria and Albert must be their aim. Albert would be another Leopold to Victoria's Charlotte and the first ill-starred union of the Houses of Hanover and Coburg would be brilliantly resurrected in the next generation.

There is a glimpse of the ten-year-old Princess at a children's ball given by King George IV during a State visit of the child Queen of Portugal, Maria da Gloria. Unfortunately this picture of the English Princess is seen through the film of malice which the earlier diaries of Charles Greville always spread. The two little girls were exactly the same age and Greville compared the good looks and 'sensible Austrian countenance' of Maria with Victoria's inadequacies. 'Our little princess is a short, vulgar-looking child, and not near so good-looking as the Portuguese.'[6] It was Donna Maria, however, who fell down at the ball, hurt herself and went home early.

Another picture of Victoria at Claremont comes from the not altogether reliable pen of a young German actress with whom Prince Leopold had sought brief consolation – Caroline

Bauer, niece of his friend Dr Stockmar. Caroline and her mother ventured to trespass one May evening in Claremont Park. Suddenly they heard a girl's clear voice. Out of the dappled shade trotted a child of eleven on a grey pony followed by a large white dog. Her hair was long and flowing, her eyes shone and she looked at the strangers with inquisitive surprise. In a moment she had wheeled her pony, galloped off and returned with a portly lady whose eyes slid severely over Caroline's blushing face. The Duchess of Kent had known the Bauers in childhood. She cut them dead.

Family visits to Windsor and Claremont or health visits to Ramsgate and Broadstairs were welcome breaks in what was to become the lonely monotony of Princess Victoria's schoolroom. It would have mattered less if she had had a companion of her own age. Her half-sister Feodore was twelve years older than herself and married when Victoria was only nine, leaving her 'poor darling sister' to endure 'imprisonment' alone. There was indeed Victoire Conroy, a child of the Princess's own age who came over once a week to play with her. But she was the daughter of the man who poisoned the Princess's childhood, Sir John Conroy, Comptroller of the Duchess's Household.

When Drina was five she passed out of the hands of her nurse, Mrs Brock, into those of Fräulein Lehzen. Louise Lehzen, created a German baroness in 1827, was the daughter of a Lutheran pastor in Coburg. Her family were socially unassuming. One of her sisters worked in England as a maid. Louise came in for her full share of the ridicule reserved for everything German. Germans were reputed to scratch their heads with their forks. Later on, malicious gossip fastened upon Princess Victoria's table manners: she picked her bones and did unmentionable things with her asparagus. Lehzen was constantly reminded that her passion for caraway seeds was vulgar.

The German governess had no gift for passing off this treatment lightly. Though she was kind-hearted and later popular with Queen Victoria's maids-of-honour, her talents did not lie in delicate human relations. She was highly strung and subject to headaches, cramps and occasional migraines.

35

Insensitive to the feelings of her mistress's friends as well as of her enemies, Lehzen responded fully to one thing only: the supposed needs of Victoria. Her instinct was to give Victoria everything she wanted, always. Support against Sir John Conroy? She was ready with it. A mother-substitute? She would play the part. There was a touch of the blue stocking about her which showed itself in a taste for intellectual gossip and in her clever, mobile nose, her straight brows, deep-set eyes and hideous cap stuck with flowers and frills. It was she who later defended the reading of novels against Lord Melbourne and Queen Victoria.

Lehzen's new pupil showed not the slightest bent in a high-brow direction but was immensely lively, quick and energetic. By a shrewd mixture of discipline and ingenuity Lehzen managed to lay the foundations in Princess Victoria of a real interest in history. At first Lehzen would read little stories aloud to her while she was being dressed by Mrs Brock, partly to prevent her from talking in front of servants. Sometimes the child invented her own plot, and from these 'beautiful stories' Lehzen discovered what went on in her pupil's mind. After Mrs Brock's departure Lehzen changed the 'little stories' into history books for the Princess to enjoy while she was having her hair brushed. As Queen, Victoria did not allow this improving habit to be dropped.

She held her governess in awe but she adored her. Lehzen's severity, like everything else, sprang from devotion. Indeed, Lehzen drew up a régime for herself even more strict than the one she imposed on Princess Victoria. She must never see her own friends in the rooms where she lived with the Princess. She must never, never keep a journal: it would be imprudent. In the light of that grand renunciation it is amusing to think that the best thing Lehzen ever did for Princess Victoria was to teach her to keep a diary every day of her life.

Lehzen's rule was not all iron. It was due to her versatility that Princess Victoria acquired her famous collection of dolls.[7] She and Lehzen dressed one hundred and thirty-two tiny wooden puppets, copying them from stars of the opera or Court. *Kenilworth* inspired one of the most dashing couples: the Earl of Leicester in slashed breeches, tabbed tunic, a lace ruffle, the Garter ribbon and a black velvet hat with sweeping white and yellow plumes; the Countess in the white, pink and green dress of the grotto scene.* The Countess of Rothesay held twin babies in her arms, the heir in satin, the younger in cotton. There are no villains among them into whom Lehzen might stick her pins, unless Queen Elizabeth, whom Victoria disliked for her immodesty, was one. This silken, feathered tinselled family with their high-flown names and empty wooden faces turned out to be a substitute for the brothers and sisters the Princess lacked. Her childhood friends were grown-up people or dolls.

Education did little to fill the gap in Princess Victoria's life. She disliked learning and suffered from too few of what she called 'holly days'. In another sense there was too much holly, for a sprig was often pinned to the front of her dress to keep her chin up. Her first teacher was the Reverend George Davys, a young Evangelical clergyman whose academic qualifications came second to co-operation with Conroy. At seven Victoria was reading, among other classics, Mrs Trimmer's illustrated volumes of scripture and history, and moral tales written by authors who delicately signed themselves 'A Lady' or 'A Mother'. In French she was always more advanced than children of her age. German lessons were her only chance of speaking her mother's tongue until she was eighteen; so firm was the Duchess's resolve to bring her up as an English woman. From St Margaret's, Westminster, came John Sale to train her voice at the age of seven. It was always her most beautiful possession. Piano lessons were not so successful. 'There is no royal road to music, Princess,' expostulated her master one day. 'You must practise like everybody else.' Victoria shut the piano with a bang. 'There! You see there is no *must* about it.' Drawing she learnt from Mr Westall and dancing from Madame Boudin who equipped a naturally graceful child with the

* Lehzen and Princess Victoria repeated the mistake which Scott probably originated in his *Kenilworth*. Amy Robsart was never Countess of Leicester, but died as Lady Robert Dudley.

unselfconscious dignity of a queen.

Princess Victoria's gift for languages was encouraged by her intense love of the opera and ballet. She learnt Italian under this stimulus and the pages of her Journal were spattered with operatic ejaculations, especially in moments of rage. It was through the opera, rather than formal education, that she saw into the world of art and poetry. She liked poetry but the sentimental, pious and moralistic rhymes offered to girls of her age and class did nothing to develop a taste in literature. Her writing was said to have 'great legibility with much freedom';[8] it was never elegant and in time, as it gathered speed and volume, the freedom increased while the legibility declined. She had an excellent head for figures. Over Latin she made no effort though she started it at eight with a book used by the Eton boys. In 1830 Mr Davys was obliged to report: 'We are not far advanced.'[9] In the teaching of religion Davys was scrupulously honest. He did not try to push the Princess in the direction of his own Evangelicalism (Victoria disliked Evangelicals when she grew up) but taught her to avoid bigotry and to revere tolerance, as befitted the probable Sovereign of many races holding different creeds. She inherited a simple piety from her Lutheran mother and governess which rarely failed her.

With all her childish wilfulness, smart retorts and inattention, her teachers loved her. 'I am afraid of saying too much,' wrote Davys in a report to the Duchess, 'because my feelings towards the Princess may prevent me from being an impartial judge.'[10]

On March 11th, 1830, after Mr Davys had gone home, Princess Victoria opened *Howlett's Tables* of the Kings and Queens of England, to begin her history lesson with Lehzen. She found to her surprise that an extra page had been slipped into the book. 'I never saw that before,' she exclaimed. 'No, Princess,' said Lehzen. 'It was not thought necessary that you should.' Victoria studied the genealogical table. So many possible heirs to the throne but each one with the date of death written after the name, until she came to the names of her two uncles, George and William, and then her own. She drew the deduction. 'I am nearer to the throne than I thought.' Then she burst into tears. After the 'little storm' had subsided she pointed out to her dear Lehzen that whereas many children might boast of the splendour they would not realize the difficulties. Lifting up the forefinger of her right hand she spoke the famous words: 'I will be good.'

Lehzen recalled in 1867 that the Princess next proceeded to explain what she meant. 'I understand now why you urged me so much to learn, even Latin. My cousins Augusta and Mary never did; but you told me Latin is the foundation of the English grammar and of all the elegant expressions; and I learnt it, as you wished it, but I understand all better now' – and she put her right hand into Lehzen's repeating solemnly, 'I will be good.' A good girl who learnt her lessons was what she meant, but the thought at the back of her mind of sometime becoming a good queen gave the words their gravity.[11]

Queen Victoria afterwards corrected one glaring mistake in Lehzen's story. Her cousin Princess Augusta of Cambridge was a child of only seven at the time and Princess Mary was not born. 'How could I say that?' she commented, referring to her alleged remark about the differences in their education.*

Some people have thought that Princess Victoria realized her destiny long before she was eleven. Walter Scott, having met her during the celebrations for her ninth birthday, came to the conclusion that though no servant was permitted to whisper in her ear, 'a little bird' had carried the truth into her heart. He was mistaken. The Princess knew no more than that her rank was high until the disclosure of March 1830. After her mother's death in March 1861 she read an account of the incident in the Duchess's diary. She did not dispute it. 'The Queen perfectly recollects this circumstance,' noted Prince Albert in the following May, 'and says the discovery made her very unhappy.' It was a traumatic turning-point in her life. She rightly guessed that the tensions at Kensington were about to increase. Her first storm of tears, often repeated when she thought of the future, testified to the shock.

* The Queen did not reject the whole 'I will be good' story, as some writers have assumed.

Behind this scene so dramatically sprung upon the eleven-year-old child lay an ingenious adult plan. Conceived by Conroy, it was carried out by the Duchess and two bishops, the object being to strengthen Kensington in their struggle against the Royal Family.

CHAPTER III

ROYAL PROGRESS
1830–4

BY THE SPRING OF 1830 the exacting pleasures and
pains of King George IV's life were drawing to a close. For
Kensington Palace this meant unqualified relief and a burst
of diplomatic activity. King George would be succeeded by his
brother William whose health was uncertain. If King William
died before Princess Victoria reached her majority at the age
of eighteen, a Regency would be necessary. Both Prince
Leopold of Coburg and Sir John Conroy had no doubt that
the Duchess of Kent must be Regent.

How could Parliament be persuaded to choose her? Surely
by proving that Princess Victoria's education under the Kensington system was not only in advance of girls of her age
but also perfectly suited to her exalted destiny. With this in
view, the Duchess described her system to the Bishops of
London and Lincoln on March 1st, 1830. She expressed
herself aware that to give a child of Victoria's sex a liberal
education invited criticism. The Duchess of Northumberland (Victoria's official Governess), therefore, was present in
the room during all lessons, and she herself during most.*
Deportment and dancing were taught by mistresses for reasons
of delicacy. Finally, it was not part of the system to tell the
Princess as yet about her glittering prospects.[1]

The last point was the only one on which the Bishops
demurred. When was the Princess to be told? they asked. The
Duchess replied that she preferred it to happen by accident,
during Victoria's studies. A fortnight later she was able to
inform the Bishop of London that the accident had taken
place. 'It was not possible for anything to occur more

---

* At eighteen Queen Victoria described to Lord Melbourne the
'excessive' tyranny of this system. Her Prime Minister warmly agreed:
'A heap of people in the room' would impede learning. Royal
Archives. Queen Victoria's Journal, March 24th, 1838.

naturally,' she wrote: 'what accident has done I feel no art could have done half so well. . . . We have everything to hope from this Child.'[2]

When King George IV died on June 26th, 1830, and Parliament debated the Regency Bill, the Duchess and Conroy reaped their reward. Notwithstanding scraps with both political parties – the Tory Duke of Wellington refused to have her created Dowager Princess of Wales and the Liberal Lord Grey called her 'a tiresome devil' – Parliament duly appointed her Regent in case of need, with an additional £10,000 a year at once for the Princess's education.

With this advance in status the Duchess's relations with the world should have improved. Thanks to Conroy, they did not do so. Unfortunately the one person who might have guided her prudently, Leopold of Saxe-Coburg, had recently become inaccessible.

For many years Princess Victoria's handsome Uncle Leopold had visited Kensington every Wednesday afternoon. He had become a hypochondriac under the strain of his grief but none of his eccentricities – wig, 3-inch soles, feather boa – damaged his excellent judgement. He had made a study of statecraft in a spirit at once serious and faintly cynical which gave his advice a rare detachment. His advice to the Duchess, however, was defective in one respect. He himself had fallen out with the Royal Family after Princess Charlotte's death and so he took no immediate steps to improve their relations with his sister. By the time Princess Victoria was ten his affair with the actress Caroline Bauer reached its zenith, alienating him from Kensington. In addition, he was tortured by the problem of whether to accept the throne of Greece. One of his weaknesses was an inability to make up his mind – he was known as *Monsieur Peu-à-Peu* – a failing which was not transmitted to his niece. When George IV was seen to be dying, Prince Leopold declined the Greek crown in order, it was said, to become Regent of England, through his sister. To Conroy's relief, this scheme also was rapidly superseded. After the European revolutions of July 1830, the Belgian people broke away from Holland and invited Leopold to become their first king. England did not see him again for over four years and Sir John Conroy stepped into his shoes as the Duchess of Kent's first counsellor.

'Mama [the Duchess of Kent] would never have fallen into the hands of Conroy,' wrote the Prince Consort after her death, 'if Uncle Leopold had taken the trouble to guide her.' Instead, King Leopold merely told Lord Grey to keep a sharp eye on Sir John. That was not enough.

The Comptroller of the Duchess of Kent's Household, Sir John Conroy, was two months her senior. He was a man of extravagant ambitions, an intriguer, a vulgarian and a scamp. He had brains and like most villains was not as black as he was painted. In his own fashion he was attached to those whom he disastrously misled and whose finances passed through his hands like water. Though he had a familiar manner with women highly unsuitable in one determined to weave his way among royal entanglements, he was not a Don Juan. In some respects a closer parallel would be with Sir John Falstaff, especially in Conroy's final rejection, with its authentic touch of outrageous pathos. As he lay dying, he fixed his gaze on William Fowler's portrait of little Drina, aged five, opposite his bed. If his daughter-in-law, Mrs Henry Conroy, is to be believed, he then sank back with a happy smile as if to say, 'Ah! there – I did my duty'.[3]

A career in the Army was young Conroy's first choice but having reached the rank of captain he abandoned it for the Duke of Kent's service. His family were of Anglo-Irish descent, Sir John owning a small estate in Ireland which brought him in £100 a year even in bad times. Having married into the Fisher family – the 'loaves and Fishers', they were called – Conroy made it his object to increase the loaves. Reckless greed and desire for power dominated him. His wife was a weak woman whom Queen Victoria rather liked. Her only fault in the whole business, as the Duchess of Kent later observed, was 'indolence', which prevented her from noticing what her husband was up to. His financial transactions ultimately damaged his own family far more than Queen Victoria's.

Conroy's manner, though overbearing, possessed a swashbuckling charm. Prince Charles Leiningen, Victoria's half-brother, found him a boon companion. In the melancholy days for Conroy's family which set in after his death in 1854, his family managed to unearth a tribute or two from men as various as Lord Melbourne, Lord Liverpool and the Duke of Wellington. That the Duke of Kent on his deathbed seized Conroy's hand entreating him never to desert the Duchess and her child, Queen Victoria emphatically denied.

In the year that Conroy was created a baronet (1827) he was painted by Fowler who admirably caught his subject's personality. The lips are curled but not in a smile and he wears a military uniform to which King William IV constantly said he was not entitled. Despite the thinning hair and strangely cleft chin, there is a *panache* about the whole which must have had its effect.

The Duchess of Kent, as we have seen, had no reason to love her English relations. It was Conroy's aim to stoke up her fears until they became obsessional. As he saw things, a complete rift between Kensington and the Court would deliver the future Sovereign into his hands. The bogy was already there in Princess Victoria's Uncle Ernest, the Duke of Cumberland.

It was known that Cumberland's influence over George IV was immense. It was feared that Cumberland's designs upon Princess Victoria were horrific. Conroy fed every ugly rumour to the trembling Duchess: that Cumberland was hatching a devilish plot to remove the only life which stood between himself and the throne; that he would weaken the little Princess's health with small doses of poison introduced by a bribed servant into her bread-and-milk, so that the public would become used to the idea of her being a sickly child; that at the critical moment Cumberland would get the King to have her kidnapped; that she would survive at Court for a few weeks in a decline and then, to no one's surprise, perish.

Conroy's propaganda to the Duchess was facilitated by reports in the newspapers that the Princess's childish ailments were signs of precarious health. Her legs and feet were said to be so diseased that walking was almost impossible. Conroy urged the Duchess to counteract these rumours by taking exercise in public: from the gate of Kensington Gardens right to Apsley House at Hyde Park she and her daughter must walk and walk in full view of the people.

Forty years later Queen Victoria poured scorn on the whole idea of a 'Cumberland plot'. When the Greville *Memoirs* were coming out in the 1870s, Conroy's family tried to justify his past actions on the ground that they were counter measures against Cumberland. Every one of their statements was slashed by the Queen. 'A total untruth' – 'Utterly false' – 'I don't believe it' – 'I never was delicate as a child & had only *one* illness' – 'Sir John's invention'. She defended Cumberland staunchly. It was 'mere gossip' that he put lies about her ill-health into the newspapers; he never showed 'the slightest symptom' of wanting to do away with her. The report that she had weak legs was entirely due to 'something Victoire Conroy said'.[4]

The 'Cumberland plot' culminated in a scandal which still lives while the rest is forgotten. Soon after Cumberland returned from Germany to England in 1829 a whisper began to circulate that the Duchess of Kent was too fond of her Comptroller. Who started it? Cumberland, came the answer pat from the Conroy circle; Cumberland started it in order to make the King remove Princess Victoria from the care of her 'immoral' mother. The plot, they said, was thwarted only by the intervention of the Duke of Wellington followed by the King's death.

Again, Queen Victoria fiercely rejected every aspersion on her Uncle Ernest. She did not deny, however, that until death removed the King he intended to remove her from the guardianship of her mother. Nor did she deny that the scandal concerning her mother and Conroy had decided the King to remove her. But what caused the scandal? 'Sir John's OWN* behaviour & invention', was the Queen's answer, scrawled in pencil with the indignation which half a century was not long enough to mitigate. 'All Sir John's invention & Princess Sophia's fearful falseness.'[5]

* The word 'OWN', printed above in block capitals, is underlined three times by Queen Victoria in her Journal. See also the entry for February 10th, 1840, p. 178.

It is now generally accepted that Queen Victoria was right, at least about Cumberland. He did not plot to kill her. Conroy, however, may have genuinely believed some of the rumours with which he terrified the Duchess. Others besides his dupes believed him. Baroness Lehzen recognized a need to guard Victoria every hour of the day and night. Though Lehzen did not sleep with her charge in the same room – this duty was performed by the Duchess – she sat in the Princess's bedroom each evening until the Duchess came to bed, to the detriment of her own health. Queen Adelaide also advised the Duchess never to leave her daughter. As for the Duchess of Kent, her credulity was painfully obvious. She did not allow Victoria to sleep alone until she herself, having become Queen, insisted. She did not allow Victoria to walk downstairs without someone holding her hand, until that hand had been kissed in homage by her Ministers. The backstairs connecting the two floors of the Kent's apartments were narrow, dark and winding, with an oval skylight far above. Perhaps it is significant that Amy Robsart, whom legend disposed of by breaking her neck in a fall downstairs, occupied an important place among Princess Victoria's dolls.

The exploitation of this situation benefited no one but Sir John Conroy at the time; in the end it damaged him disastrously. Because it was he who cut off Princess Victoria from her 'Uncle King', who caused her life to be dull and overprotected and who made rude remarks about her royal relations, she began to hate him. He went out of his way to humiliate her, teasing her for looking like 'Silly Billy', the Duke of Gloucester, rather than her 'Uncle King' as Victoria herself fancied, and ridiculing her for saving up her pocket money in a manner unworthy of a princess. Did she also notice as a child that Conroy flirted with Mama and Aunt Sophia?* The inference from her later comments on Conroy's 'behaviour' during this period is that she did. It would be surprising if one whose observation was as keen as her memory was retentive, missed anything of Conroy's technique for obtaining the mastery of Kensington.

* A permanent inmate of Kensington Palace, daughter of King George III.

The death of King George IV brought an end to the Cumberland bogy but not to the breach with Princess Victoria's royal relations. New divisions quickly developed to make her childhood more than ever sad.

This time the cause of friction lay in the Sovereign's illegitimate children, the Fitzclarences – the *bâtards* as they were called in the smart world. William IV was determined that the relations between Windsor and Kensington should be put on a new footing. Kensington must come to Windsor and on occasion Windsor to Kensington. Equally firm was the Duchess's opposition. Victoria should remain on friendly terms with their Majesties but there must be no interference and no association with the illegitimate members of the Royal Family. How else could the child learn the difference between vice and virtue?

The Duchess's case was not as good as it sounded. There were complicating factors which later caused her daughter to side with King William and 'vice' against the 'virtue' of Kensington. A letter written by her aunt, Princess Sophia, to Sir John Conroy on October 14th, 1830, lifts the veil for a moment from a scene of gossip, intrigue and spite which must have been a commonplace in Kensington Palace and could not fail to disgust a child like Victoria for whom a frank atmosphere was the breath of life.

It was nearly midnight when Princess Sophia sat down to write a report for Sir John Conroy of a conversation which she had just held with 'Mrs Aquatic' (Queen Adelaide) on the subject of changes in the Duchess of Kent's Household. Baroness Späth, the Duchess's lady-in-waiting, was to be dismissed.

'You know about poor Späth's going?' began Queen Adelaide; 'it will make a great noise in the world.'

'Noise?' interrupted Princess Sophia. 'Why?' The dismissal would kill her, replied Queen Adelaide; Lehzen would go next; the Duchess intended to get rid of all foreigners and have only English ladies.

Princess Sophia again broke in with a telling rejoinder: the Court had long criticized the Duchess's German entourage, sighing for 'nice English ladies'. Now they would get them

One of the gentlemen, Mr Paget, insisted Queen Adelaide, burst into tears when he heard Späth was going and cried, 'Going! Impossible! Oh! who has done this?'

Princess Sophia at once challenged the innuendo against Conroy.

'Pray did Mr Paget not *name anyone* as the person to force Victoria [the Duchess of Kent] for that is the most wonderful attack I ever heard.'

Queen Adelaide retreated. No one had been named, she said. Then she continued:

'How impossible it will be to find a second Lehzen!'

'A second is not wanted,' retorted Princess Sophia.

Next they bickered about Princess Victoria's upbringing. Princess Sophia tartly contradicted rumours that she was kept up too late shaking hands with visitors – 'making a child of such consequence' – and at the same time locked up too closely by her mother. It was said that 'no Boy after 7 years old was allowed to see the Child'; the Countess of Munster [wife of William IV's illegitimate son] had had to leave her little boy behind when visiting Kensington Palace.

Though Princess Sophia ridiculed this tale it was probably true. She then brought her letter to Conroy to a close:

'I dare not keep this any longer as it is striking 12 & the Gazelle [Lady Conyngham] will be here in a few minutes. We shall see what I have to report tomorrow, but unless [you are] named I shall say nothing. God bless you! I hope this is legible. Your *name carefully avoided* . . .'[6]

The facts behind Princess Sophia's letter constituted another step in Conroy's ruthless campaign to isolate the Duchess of Kent and her daughter. Späth was banished to Princess Feodore's Household in Germany. Both she and Lehzen had resented Conroy's airs, assumed after his baronetcy; he insisted on Lady Conroy taking precedence over the German baronesses and when Späth tried to put his daughter Victoire in her place, the axe fell. It was also rumoured that Späth had remonstrated with the Duchess about 'familiarities' with Conroy, witnessed by Princess Victoria.

The second part of Conroy's scheme – the ousting of Lehzen – failed. That intelligent woman played her cards too well, allying herself firmly with the Court.

Victoria loved Baroness Späth; she doted on Baroness Lehzen. In this attempt to separate her from Lehzen is to be found a clue to the dramatic events which were to disturb the early years of her reign. The 'Bedchamber Plot' and the Flora Hastings scandal of 1839 were direct results of struggles which preceded them. Similarly, the strength and weakness of character which Queen Victoria was to show had taken shape during the hard years when she was manipulated by rival factions like one of her own puppets.

The new régime by which the Sovereign was to see more of his heir did not prosper. Princess Victoria attended a Garter ceremony at St James's Palace in July 1830, and the German Ambassador picked out her small, withdrawn figure by its intolerable load of mourning: black veil and weepers reaching to the ground. Next month Queen Adelaide's birthday brought another summons to the Court. This should have been a happy occasion: Victoria felt no jealousy and always hoped her aunt would have another child. Unhappily she was too much frightened of her mother's wrath to bestow on anyone her entrancing smiles. King William complained afterwards that she had stared at him stonily.

Another even stonier rebuff from Kensington soon followed. Princess Victoria and her mother were commanded to attend the King's Coronation on September 3rd, 1831. They were staying at Norris Castle, near Cowes on the Isle of Wight, where Conroy's regal arrangements had already driven the King into a frenzy. Conroy had ordered the ships at Portsmouth to fire their guns in a royal salute. William commanded this 'popping', as he called it, to stop. Conroy refused. Later, when the Duchess toured Britain with her daughter in tow, to 'pop' or not to 'pop' became a cause of endless wrangling. Greville and his circle heartily agreed that the King must 'whip her into line'.

Over the Princess's attendance at the Coronation the Duchess and Conroy were not to be whipped. After dragging

49

their feet interminably they seized upon the question of precedence – always a fertile source of trouble – as an excuse to break off negotiations. Because the Princess Victoria was incorrectly assigned a place in the procession behind the Royal Dukes instead of immediately after the King, she was not allowed to attend. The prisoner of Norris Castle, shut up in the 'little Lobby' at the top of the stairs, cried and cried and then, still crying, watched the royal procession from Marlborough House.

A few days after the Coronation, Greville dined with the Duke of Wellington and was informed by his host that Sir John Conroy was the cause of the Duchess of Kent's hostility to the King. 'I said I concluded he was her lover,' wrote Greville in his diary, 'and he said "he supposed so".'[7]

In 1832, when Princess Victoria was thirteen, her mother's Comptroller instituted a series of annual, semi-royal tours during which she was formally presented to the nation. Such publicity directed on a child could scarcely be justified and certainly not without the consent of the reigning Monarch. The Duchess's impresario, on the contrary, went out of his way to foster the idea of rival royalty. At Eaton Hall a jewelled crown held the bread at breakfast and at Torquay a procession of girls carrying a crown in their midst met the Princess. Conroy exploited the emotions aroused by the year of the great Reform Bill. Citizens were encouraged to present loyal addresses containing references to the Duchess's support for the 'free people' of England – a tribute to the fact that Victoria's entourage was predominantly Whig, while William IV's was Tory. In theory Princess Victoria was being brought up non-party: she slept impartially at great Whig houses like Chatsworth, Woburn and Plas Newydd or Tory strongholds like Belvoir and Euston; but there was no doubt that the sympathies of Kensington lay on the opposite side to the King.

Properly conducted, the Princess's 'Royal Progresses', as the King sarcastically called them, could have done good. Even as it was, William's mood of senile excitement led him to exaggerate the harm. He became 'so indecent in his wrath', wrote Greville, that people abroad believed that he was 'cracked'.

Queen Victoria was indebted to these 'Royal Progresses' for two things of inestimable value: her knowledge of the country and her talent as a diarist.

The Princess's knowledge of the country was usefully supplemented by the country's knowledge of her. As the Duchess wrote to her daughter later, it was essential for Victoria to get herself known and admired before it was too late.

'Avoid stepping out of your room an unknown and untried person . . . Shew a promise of character – let the People hope for something worth having, free from all the faults of former reigns.'[8]

A small notebook with mottled covers and leather back was presented to Princess Victoria. In an unformed, round hand she wrote:

'This book, Mama gave me, that I might write the journal of my journey to Wales in it. Victoria, Kensington Palace, July 31st.'

At six minutes past seven, wrote the Princess on the first page with the exactitude insisted upon by dearest Lehzen, they left for an extensive tour of the Midlands and Wales lasting for over three months. Day after day the diary would begin strenuously, 'I awoke at ½ past 6 & got up at 7.' Sometimes it would be 5. Not surprisingly the long days ended with an exhausted, 'I was soon in bed & asleep.'

Up through the Midlands dashed the royal carriage, 'at a tremendous rate'. It rained incessantly. 'The men, women, children, country & houses are all black.' She snatched up her pencil to describe her first furnace: 'I just now see an extraordinary building flaming with fire.' Among the coal heaps were wretched huts, ragged children. But all was so extraordinary she gave up the attempt and put her diary away until they reached Powis Castle.

Anglesey welcomed her with troops of yeomanry, bands and guns – the King could not stop the Pagets from 'popping' in their own park. Galloping about their fields on her pony Rosa, who 'literally *flew*', was the happiest experience of this

51

tour. She had to leave 'dear Plas Newydd' for the grandeurs of Chatsworth and the painted ceiling of the Sheldonian Theatre, Oxford. Here Sir John Conroy was made a Doctor of Civil Law and received the Freedom of the City. In the Bodleian Library Victoria was shown Queen Elizabeth's Latin exercise book, written 'when she was of my age [13]'. Roger Ascham, Elizabeth's tutor, never had to say, like Mr Davys, 'we are not far advanced'.

Next year Conroy arranged for a 'Royal Progress' through the South and West. The holiday began with a visit to Norris Castle. The Conroy family had taken Osborne Lodge close by. (Years later, when Queen Victoria and Prince Albert were living at Osborne House, they pulled down the Lodge and built Osborne Cottage on the site.) A voyage down the coast followed, the Duchess being 'dreadfully sick', which proved a serious 'drawback' to Victoria's 'amusement'. At Portsmouth she explored Nelson's flagship, the Victory, sampling the men's rations. She pronounced their beef, potatoes and grog 'excellent'.[9]

In 1834 she spent a long holiday in Tunbridge Wells, riding with Mama, Lehzen and the Conroys to the surrounding villages and rejoicing when she was allowed to canter 'almost the whole way back'. At a public dinner she was toasted with musical honours, Sir John being curiously acclaimed in a song entitled 'The Wolf'. They left 'dear Tunbridge Wells with GREAT REGRET' and amid cries of 'Welcome, welcome Royal visitors', they moved to St Leonards-on-Sea and Hastings.

> 'Six fishermen in rough blue jackets,
> red caps and coarse white aprons,
> preceded by a band, bore a basket
> ornamented with flowers, full of fish
> as a present for us.'[10]

This is one of the word pictures from which Victoria would afterwards make her water-colour sketches. At St Leonards occurred one of those accidents so common in the days of the horse. The fifteen-year-old Princess took command like a true soldier's daughter in the moment of crisis. With the carriage overturned and two kicking horses on the ground, she first called for her dog to be rescued from the rumble and then 'ran on with him in my arms calling Mama to follow, Lehzen and Lady Flora [Hastings] followed us also'. Princess Victoria ordered her party to take cover behind a wall when one of the horses chased them down the road. She created Mr Peckham Micklethwaite of Iridge, Sussex, a baronet in her Coronation Honours for having sat on its head.

The Princess's entry into her teens marked the beginning of a general tightening of the reins. Her tutor filled the whole morning with lessons, including more history and natural philosophy. Victoria was *very MUCH amused* by a lecture on alchemy but squeamishness always rendered anatomical descriptions 'very disagreeable'.[11] Her Governess, the Duchess of Northumberland, stated positively that her courses of reading went far beyond the Lucys and Harriets of her own age. The list gradually expanded to include Pope, Gray, Cowper, Goldsmith, 'parts of' Virgil in Latin and all Scott's poems. The last was the only item she really enjoyed. The magical simplicity of Maria Edgeworth's *Tales* still pleased her more than 'many a novel'.[12] This phrase was a *façon de parler* for Queen Victoria had read few novels before marriage, and at this date only Fenimore Cooper's *Last of the Mohicans*, which she found 'very interesting' and 'very horrible'.[13] On January 9th, 1837, she began reading aloud to Lehzen what she described in her Journal as her first novel – Scott's *Bride of Lammermoor*.

She praised simplicity in all the arts, affecting to despise exaggeration of style or feeling. An actress who raged was criticized as *'outré'* – a sinister word in Princess Victoria's vocabulary. She sketched industriously but only subjects of innocent charm: ships and trees, animals and ballet dancers, peasants, babies and cousins. Preachers were judged according to their naturalness. She could not endure mannerisms. Over-emphasis, a nasal twang or heavy breathing were ruthlessly condemned. All her life she showed a highly articulate interest in sermons, from which she expected to derive the week's spiritual sustenance. Those with a cheerful message suited her best. 'Behold, now is the day of salvation' was a text the young Princess particularly liked. Perhaps it made her dream of Conroy's downfall.

Humble life drew her increasingly. At Claremont she designated an encampment of gipsies 'the chief ornament of the Portsmouth Road'.[14] She sent them blankets and soup, longing to have their children instructed. The contrast between their affection for one another and her own domestic strife shocked her, especially when her charitable efforts were met with frigid scepticism at home. She and Lehzen read Crabbe's *Gipsies' Advocate*. This book convinced them that poor folk would respond to kindness: one should not be ashamed to speak to them. Conroy did not agree. 'All this, & more, Lehzen & I have urged to some people, but in vain.'[15]

Washington Irving's book, *The Conquest of Granada*, set her wandering in imagination through the mysterious Orient – 'But these are all Phantom Castles,' she added sadly, 'which I love to form!'[16] The magnetism of the East continued to draw her whether she read about the Moors or admired the olive complexions of Indian and Persian visitors to Kensington Palace. The same spell was at work when she succumbed years later to the shining ringlets of Disraeli and the turbans of her Indian servants.

Princess Victoria's romantic susceptibilities seem to make nonsense of her own claim to abhor the *outré* and admire only simplicity. Her baroque tastes are also incompatible with the theory of some of her biographers that her nature was crystal clear, uncompromisingly sensible and utterly lacking in imagination. She is frequently denied the gift of introspection, though her Journals, after the age of sixteen, are by no means devoid of self-analysis. Victoria's character was in fact neither simple nor crystalline. Indeed, part of her fascination lies in her contradictions and inconsistencies – one way in which a rich nature presents itself to the spectator.

At the beginning of February 1832 the Duchess of Kent appointed additional ladies to her Household, among them Lady Flora Hastings, in order that Princess Victoria might be able to choose new friends from a wide but approved circle. There were other additions to Victoria's social life more congenial than the chance to have Lady Flora as a friend. She was brought downstairs by Lehzen, hand in hand, to meet increasing numbers of distinguished people and knew by sight, when she came to the throne, such intimidating characters as Princess Lieven and Sir Robert Peel or that paragon, Lord Palmerston, 'so very agreeable, clever, amusing & gentleman-like'.

Almost anything arranged by their Majesties delighted the Princess as much as it annoyed her mother. The King gave a juvenile ball at St James's Palace on her fourteenth birthday. The whole day was a touching mixture of childhood and adolescence. At one end of the scale Uncle Leopold sent her a serious letter recommending self-examination and a soul above trifles, at the other, she had a reunion with her old nurse, Mrs Brock. She opened the ball with her first cousin, George Cambridge, whom the King intended her eventually to marry, and rounded it off by 'one more quadrille with Lord Emlyn'. Madame Boudin, the Princess's dancing mistress, was present to see that no mistakes were made. 'I was *VERY* much amused.'

Her delight in the opera and ballet knew no bounds and it was the increase in this kind of entertainment which brought most happiness to the later years of her childhood. Like any teenage girl, she had her idol of idols, Giulia Grisi, nineteen years old with a mild expression, fine long lashes, sweet mouth and dark hair lying flat in front under an amethyst bandeau. She looked *'quite beautiful'* off stage and on the stage was 'all-ways smiling'. Princess Victoria studied with minute care everything she wore: the white flowered silk, the corals, the blonde; she lamented on the day that Grisi did not look as pretty as usual, having combed her hair 'too low into her face'; she went into ecstasies when Grisi sang at Kensington Palace to celebrate her sixteenth birthday. Grisi's concert was her best birthday present – better than the print of Taglioni from Lehzen, the brooch made of Mama's hair, the earrings from the King, the writing-case from Sir J. Conroy, the paper-knife from sharp-tongued Lady Flora, the prayer book from a 'bookseller of the name of Hatchard' and the 'two small oil pictures from an old Mrs Pakenham . . .' .

Lablache, the great tenor, was engaged to teach her singing; at first she trembled so much that no sound came out. Tamburini, Rubini, Ivanhoff, Madame Malibran – '*O cara rimembranza!*' Dear memories were all she had to live on when the London season ended and she was bundled off in a stifling post-chaise to the seaside.

Entwined in Victoria's heart with the glamour of Drury Lane was the inexpressible joy of her relations' visits to England. Her cousins Ernest and Alexander Württemberg came over in 1833 for the London season. Like Miranda in *The Tempest*, she drank in their astonishing masculinity and found them perfection – until another, more wonderful pair arrived three years later, Ferdinand and Augustus, and four months after them a pair more marvellous still, Albert and Ernest.

An older visitor, who came in 1834, was Prince Ferdinand of Saxe-Coburg-Kohary, her mother's second brother. Uncle Ferdinand at once became her father-figure. He seems to have relieved her of many emotional burdens by touching on Conroy's designs during a *diner à trois* with her and Lehzen. She found his conversation so '*useful*' and 'so *extremely clever in seeing through everything*'.[17] When he too departed, taking with him a packet of geranium seeds, bitter and copious were her tears. Sir John was back again at dinner and Princess Victoria wrote in her Journal: 'I do not remember passing *so* sad a day for a *long* time.'

There was a moment when Sir John Conroy redeemed himself in Victoria's eyes. He presented her mother on January 14th, 1833, with a King Charles's spaniel called Dash. Three months later Princess Victoria had adopted '*DEAR SWEET LITTLE DASH*' and was dressing him up in scarlet jacket and blue trousers. She gave him for Christmas three india-rubber balls and two bits of gingerbread decorated with holly and candles. Dash showed his devotion by jumping into the sea and swimming after her yacht; when she was ill he spent 'his little life' in her room.

Animals became the Princess's companions after her dolls

were put away. There was Mama's new parakeet which laughed and coughed and the old canary, so tame that it came out of its cage to peck Dashy's fur. When her throat was too sore to go sightseeing on the Isle of Wight she found the strength to come down to the pier and see 'the dear horses' land.

The Duchess of Kent was not entirely satisfied with Victoria's development. On New Year's Eve 1834 she warned her that simplicity of character was all very well but she should not overdo it nor under-estimate her station. Conroy cherished grandiose plans for 1835. It was a year which Queen Victoria never forgot.

CHAPTER IV

'SHE MUST BE COERCED'
1835–7

PRINCESS VICTORIA'S GIFT for predicting her future was never more apparent than on her sixteenth birthday. '. . . I feel that the 2 years to come till I attain my 18th,' she wrote on May 24th, 1835, 'are the most important of any almost . . .' A wave of energy had swept over her at the beginning of this year. 'I *love* to be *employed*; I *hate* to be *idle*.'[1] It was just as well, for during the following two years her battle against Conroy was fought out.

The Princess's Confirmation took place on July 30th, 1835, at the Chapel Royal, St James's, and was attended by members of the Royal Family. The day opened with a homily from the Duchess of Kent: Victoria should behave with 'friendliness' to those around and always 'confide in me'.[2] Friendliness to Conroy was too much to ask of the resolute young Princess, looking so deceptively meek in her white lace dress and rose-trimmed bonnet. Nevertheless she entered the Chapel with 'a firm determination' to become a true Christian. Immediately a shocking dispute broke out. The King counted her mother's retinue, found it too large and ordered her Comptroller out of the Chapel. For the poor Duchess, this was Victoria's christening over again. For Victoria, it was a horror of embarrassment in no way alleviated by the Archbishop of Canterbury's formidable sermon. Misery, religious awe and July heat overwhelmed her. She returned to Kensington and cried bitterly. Her Journal, which the Duchess always read, recorded simply: 'I was very much affected indeed when we came home.'

A month later her trials began anew with a grand tour of the North. She implored her mother to cancel it: she *knew* it would make her ill and these 'Royal Progresses' only upset the King. The Duchess replied with a little note (she found she could write more 'quietly' than she could speak). The

King was merely jealous; Victoria must cherish an 'Honourable ambition' in these critical times and not give way. So on September 3rd, in heat and dust, with headache and backache, Princess Victoria set forth again.

The tour began with the York Musical Festival. After a week the Princess was wilting. She felt too sick to eat but, as on all other similar occasions during her childhood, her rigorous time-table remained unaltered. Going through Leeds, Wakefield and Barnsley she was quite overcome. She revived a little at the Doncaster races and the Belvoir mausoleum, where a stained-glass window threw beautiful lights on to the faces of four dead Rutland infants. In East Anglia the people of Lynn insisted on dragging the carriage right round the town, thus adding one hour and a quarter to the journey and incidentally running over a poor man. They reached Holkham in darkness and pouring rain. Princess Victoria was so exhausted she nearly fell asleep over dinner. At last, after a visit to Euston, which was neither imposing nor handsomely furnished, the ordeal was over.

'Here is an end to our journey, I am happy to say. Though I liked some of the places very well, I was much tired by the long journeys & the great crowds we had to encounter. We cannot travel like other people, quietly & pleasantly, but we go through towns & crowds & when one arrives at any nobleman's seat, one must instantly dress for dinner & consequently I could never rest properly.'[3]

At the end of September the Kents moved to Ramsgate where they were joined by Princess Victoria's uncle, the King of the Belgians, and her new aunt Louise, his wife, whom she was meeting for the first time. Victoria fell madly in love with both of them.

She had not seen Uncle Leopold for four years. Of course there had been letters; King Leopold would not ignore a niece who had written to him when she was nine: 'I am very angry with you, Uncle, for you have never written to me once since you went, and that is a long while.'[4] So many letters had passed between them – 'My dearest Uncle,' 'My Dearest Love' – but a letter however full of wise advice was not the same as meeting. 'What happiness was it for me,' she wrote on September 29th, 1835, 'to throw myself in the arms of that *dearest* of Uncles, who has always been to me like a father . . .'

Ten months before, Princess Victoria had sent her uncle 'a very clever sharp little letter', as he called it, asking what a Queen *ought to be* – he had already used the example of Queen Anne to show her what a Queen ought *not* to be. Now he would be able to answer this and many other questions. Sure enough, on a Sunday night the Princess recorded that her uncle had given her 'very valuable & important advice.'[5] It is probable that King Leopold spoke mainly about English politics and Society, whose chief denizens were 'wolves in sheep's clothes'; but he may well have included a few words on the wolf of Kensington. His advice would have been to do nothing hastily, stick to Lehzen and keep on good terms with Mama.

Louise of Orleans, Queen of the Belgians, was the favourite child of Louis Philippe, King of the French, and it was the intimate family life of this new young aunt, blessed with so many brothers, which held Victoria spellbound. Aunt Louise quickly adopted her lonely niece and putting her arm through Victoria's told her to treat her as an elder sister. The sisterly bond was sealed by a raid on Aunt Louise's wardrobe. Chattering and laughing, Victoria tried on her aunt's Parisian clothes: brown silk, white moiré and a rose for the hair. Meanwhile King Leopold took a walk with Sir John Conroy on the sands. After hearing about the troubles at Kensington he assured Sir John that with tact he might still win himself 'a very good position'.[6]

On October 5th, two days before the beloved visitors were due to depart, Princess Victoria woke up feeling sick. Next morning she was no better although Aunt Louise loaded her with presents – ribbons, bonnets, a *pélérine* and a fan. Dr Clark, the Duchess of Kent's resident physician who had joined her Household in April that year, ordered the Princess to take a dose of physic at noon.

The last day came and Victoria wished the steamer waiting for her uncle and aunt would carry her away too. She cried bitterly. All seemed 'terribly *fade* & dull without them'. Dr Clark hovered around offering her cocoa. She was too ill and wretched to eat.

Next day the diary went blank. No entries were made between October 7th and 31st. When Victoria began to write again she was only just convalescent after a severe attack of typhoid. She still took a quinine draught at 7.30 am, had nothing but potato soup for luncheon, a little boiled mutton, rice and orange jelly for dinner; no occupation but knitting. She could not walk more than a few steps, she was thin and had lost so much hair that she was 'litterally [*sic*] now getting *bald*'.[7] As a last desperate measure Lehzen cut off most of what hair remained, leaving just enough to make a small puff. It was once so thick, sighed Princess Victoria plaintively, that Lehzen could hardly grasp it in her hand. Towards the middle of November she felt strong enough to draw herself in the mirror. Pinched cheeks, sharp chin – what a sad spectacle. The face in the mirror looked extraordinarily young but it had the anxious eyes of an old woman. After nearly five weeks of imprisonment she went downstairs. Lehzen had to rub her ice-cold feet at least once a day. She was still rubbing them in January. It was not till February that lessons were once more in full swing.

Sir John Conroy had not missed his opportunity to strike. He decided to confront the Princess, while still on her sick bed, with a fateful decision. Those large blue eyes staring out of the sunken face must be forced to look into the future. She would soon be Queen. She would need a private secretary. Who better equipped to fill this post than her mother's majordomo? Backed up by the deluded Duchess, Conroy applied every conceivable pressure to obtain a pledge in his favour, finally thrusting paper and pencil before the helpless invalid and commanding her to sign.

There was a fearful duel. Conroy had not banked on Princess Victoria's stubborn will. Had not Uncle Leopold recently warned her against wolves in sheep's clothing? When she saw the wolf at her own door she knew she must speak or for ever hold her peace. Faithful Lehzen never left her side though lashed by Conroy's fury. (Afterwards she often referred to what dearest Lehzen had '*endured*'.) Princess Victoria utterly refused to sign under duress.

Not a breath of this horrifying episode disturbed the calm pages of her Journal. The story, however, reached the ears of King Leopold. Because of the 'sad incident' at Ramsgate, he turned against Sir John. And when Queen Victoria's reign had begun Lord Melbourne was told the story.

> 'I resisted in spite of my illness.'
> 'What a blessing!'[8]

Her words were matter-of-fact but her experience had been a nightmare.

Many of Princess Victoria's contemporaries felt that one thing alone could explain her loathing of Conroy: she must have seen her mother in his arms. Conroy's 'behaviour' was indeed execrated by Queen Victoria, as we have seen, but familiarity is not the same thing as adultery. Whatever Conroy's relations with the Duchess – and this question must be left till later – Victoria now knew enough of his methods towards herself to hate him like poison.

At Ramsgate the iron entered into her soul. If Sir John could not defeat her, worn down as she was by the tour and the ravages of typhoid, what chance had Ministers like Sir Robert Peel and Gladstone? Victoria was trained in a hard school. A sprig of holly had taught her to keep her chin up. At sixteen she knew how to say 'No'.

The year 1836 began well. Princess Victoria was profoundly thankful to return from Ramsgate to London. Dr Clark ordered her extra bread-and-butter, a standing desk, exercises for her extremities, Indian clubs, no singing directly after meals and regular drives to Finchley, Hampstead and Harrow. All the same, '*pleasure*' did one more good, as she once reminded Uncle Leopold, than all the driving in the world. And now there were pleasures too. It was delightful to explore the spacious new suite at Kensington Palace which Dr Clark had insisted upon for the sake of her enfeebled health. But she would never again, as in the past, visit the Conroys in their house next door.

At the beginning of February Dr Clark allowed her to visit St James's Palace wearing her grey satin *broché* coat trimmed with roses which Aunt Louise had sent from Paris. She looked so bewitching that young Lord Elphinstone sketched her in church; the Duchess secured his banishment to Madras. Next month her cousins Ferdinand and Augustus of Saxe-Coburg-Kohary visited England.

On St Valentine's Day Uncle Leopold had sent her a thumbnail sketch of these young Germans. They were handsome and clever but 'very *new* in the world'. Princess Victoria copied this phrase into the Journal, perhaps because she also felt 'new', though less new since her baptism of fire at Ramsgate. Ferdinand was on his way to Portugal to marry Victoria's young contemporary, Queen Maria de Gloria. Since the day when Greville had compared young Victoria unfavourably with Queen Maria, the latter had grown enormously stout. Nevertheless, Princess Victoria felt that Maria was perhaps well suited to dear good 'Fernando', with his slow way of talking through his nose, his singular high singing voice and his funny German habit of shaking hands every time one met. Augustus helped her to seal her letters. Then, suddenly, they were gone. She missed them every moment of the day but especially as partners in the waltz and gallop, which etiquette forbade her to perform except with royalty. 'Now they are quite quite gone,' she wrote on April 2nd, '& no one can replace them.' Six weeks later they had been replaced.

It was not without difficulty that King Leopold got his second pair of Coburg nephews to the shores of England. Ernest and Albert, sons of the Duchess of Kent's eldest brother, Duke Ernest of Saxe-Coburg-Gotha, were far from welcome at Court. Prince Ernest, nearly eighteen, mattered less, since he would succeed his father as Duke and settle in Coburg. But his brother Albert, seventeen on August 26th, three months after Victoria, was being groomed for her consort. The Duchess of Kent sent a personal invitation to her nephews on the occasion of Princess Victoria's seventeenth birthday.

King William, who had other ideas for his niece, was furious. First he tried forbidding the Saxe-Coburg family to land, a threat which drove his rival match-maker, King Leopold, into paroxysms of sarcasm. 'Now that slavery is abolished in the British Colonies,' he wrote to Victoria, 'I do not comprehend *why your lot alone should be to be kept a white little slavey in England,* for the pleasure of the Court . . .'[9] William's high-handed action having finally been stopped by the Prime Minister, he concentrated on catching his niece's fancy with rival suitors. His choice was singularly inept. Young Prince George of Cambridge did not interest Victoria at all; among her cousins she preferred blind Prince George of Cumberland, a match which Wellington is said to have favoured. The Duke of Brunswick, a Byronic desperado, might have stood a chance, but not Prince Alexander of Orange, who, strangely enough, had been rejected by Princess Charlotte. Victoria found him 'lumbering'.

Princess Feodore of Hohenlohe had prepared her half-sister for Uncle Leopold's nephews. 'You will like our two Coburg cousins,' she wrote to Victoria in March: they were more manly than the Saxe-Coburg-Kohary cousins. Though Albert was the cleverer and handsomer she preferred Ernest for his good nature. (Here Princess Feodore was less than tactful.) 'I shall be very curious to hear your opinion of them,' she ended.

Princess Victoria's opinion was not revealed to chance spectators. Trained by the rigours of life at Kensington to hide her feelings under an expressionless mask, she dispensed her favours with polite impartiality at her birthday ball. Beneath this impassive exterior she was adjusting her heart to Uncle Leopold's head. With all her native buoyancy she set to work at once to see the best in Albert.

The Coburg cousins arrived on an early afternoon in May 1836. That evening Princess Victoria's Journal gave Albert pride of place. Albert was as tall as Ernest but broader and extremely handsome. Ernest had not got a good nose or mouth; Albert's nose was beautiful, his mouth sweet and his teeth fine; 'but the charm of his countenance is his expression, which is most delightful; *c'est à la fois* full of goodness and sweetness, and very clever and intelligent.'[10] Princess Victoria wanted 'expression' above all, and just as she had found it in Grisi among her stage idols, so among her tall cousins she found it in Albert.

Like herself, Prince Albert had large blue eyes and hair 'about the same colour as mine' – a light brown. Ernest was altogether dark. Both were delightfully accomplished: they played well on the piano and appreciated prints, sitting on either side of her on the sofa; they drew well, 'particularly Albert'. They were both naturally clever, 'particularly Albert, who is the most reflective of the two.' Speaking with all the maturity of her sex, she praised both cousins for being so serious and yet '*so very very* merry and gay and happy, like young people ought to be'[11]; but it was Albert who kept the breakfast table in a roar with his witty remarks and played so funnily with Dash.

The visit was not all roses. Princess Victoria knew that the King was in a rage and strife with His Majesty always pained her. Prince Albert suffered tortures of sleepiness and for a time completely collapsed. Late hours were hitherto unknown to him and his little cousin's resolute attitude towards pleasure appalled him. He became unwell on the eve of her birthday and went to bed early. On the great day he was still very poorly. He took the floor at St James's Palace, turned pale as ashes, almost fainted and went straight home. Next day he wisely remained 'a prisoner' in his room and on the next could eat nothing at breakfast though he bravely came downstairs. Several days later he left another ball early.

Fortunately all was bliss during the last week and when, on June 10th, these dearest cousins departed, all was wretchedness. Victoria analysed her feelings with the new authority of her seventeen years. Comparing this parting with the earlier one, she wrote:

'I feel this separation more deeply, though I do not lament so much as I did then; which came from my nerves

65

not being strong then. I can bear more now. I shall always love dear Ferdinand & dear Augustus very much, but dear Ernest & dear Albert I greatly prefer to the latter (A); they are so much more sensible & grown up & are so delightful to be with & talk to.'[12]

Knowing what was expected of her, she particularly praised Albert to King Leopold. 'He possesses every quality that could be desired to make me perfectly happy.' Then, remembering his early beds and untouched breakfasts, she added: 'I have only now to beg you, my dearest Uncle, to take care of the health of one, now *so dear* to me . . .'[13]

The Princess returned to her normal routine. Paley, Blackstone and Racine in the mornings, Aunt Sophia in the evenings, correspondence with Uncle Leopold on politics, charitable visits with Mama. In the summer there were more invitations from Windsor for the Duchess to handle. She allowed Princess Victoria to join in the royal procession at Ascot for the first time, where she was observed by an American visitor listening, characteristically, to a ballad-singer. The republican from overseas found her 'quite unnecessarily pretty and interesting' for one who was destined 'to be sold in marriage for political purposes'.

The celebration of Queen Adelaide's birthday started up a new round of hostilities between the Court and Kensington. The Duchess of Kent began it by declining to attend. A few days later came His Majesty's birthday, on August 21st, which could not be ignored. When Princess Victoria and her mother left Kensington for Windsor the King basely seized his chance to inspect the royal apartments at Kensington Palace in the absence of the tenants. He was already in a temper when he reached Kensington: a marine whom he wished to have executed had been reprieved. He saw the Duchess's new suite, including the King's Gallery which, though disused, he had forbidden her to occupy. Boiling with rage he clattered into the Quadrangle of Windsor Castle on the eve of his birthday. After pointedly telling Princess Victoria how delighted he was to see *her*, he accused the Duchess of steal-

66

ing seventeen rooms. Lord Adolphus Fitzclarence felt his father's excitement augured ill for the morrow.

Sure enough the King publicly insulted his sister-in-law at his birthday dinner in front of a hundred guests. The Duchess sat on his right, Princess Victoria opposite. King William rose to respond to the toast and at the end of a rambling speech suddenly pointed his finger at his terrified niece. He hoped that the royal authority would pass to 'that Young Lady' and not to 'the person now near me, who is surrounded by evil advisers' – a solution which he himself meant to promote by living another nine months until Princess Victoria came of age. The Duchess, he thundered, had grossly insulted him by keeping the said young lady from Court; in future he would *insist* on her appearing *always*. Princess Victoria burst into tears. The Duchess of Kent ordered their carriage forthwith but was prevailed upon to remain for another day for the sake of appearances, when she took a partial revenge by keeping their Majesties waiting interminably for dinner.[14]

The case of the seventeen rooms remains something of a mystery. It is probable that there was a genuine misunderstanding. No mystery, however, attaches to the result of this episode. The King's behaviour caused a resounding scandal and his remarks about the Duchess's 'evil advisers' gave new life to the moribund rumour that she was Sir John Conroy's mistress.

Princess Victoria noted on her uncle's birthday that he was seventy-one; she hoped he would live 'many more years'. She wanted a Regency no more than he did. Before the fatal dinner-party she had visited the family tombs at Windsor, including her 'poor dear Father's'. Melancholy thoughts swept over her: so many near and dear ones lying under the stones she walked upon, so many walking above who would soon be underneath.[15] As she put it a month later, how dreadful it was to lose those we loved and to be 'encumbered' by those we disliked.

The months slipped by between the autumn of 1836 and the following spring. For Christmas, 'dearest best Lehzen' gave her a button decorated with an angel's head and Mama

67

a gold buckle in the shape of two serpents. In February she watched her first train.

'We went to see the Railroad near Hersham, & saw the steam carriage pass with surprising quickness, striking sparks as it flew along the railroad, enveloped in clouds of smoke & making a loud noise. It is a curious thing indeed!'[16]

The railway struck sparks from Victoria. A year later, when Melbourne was damning it – 'Oh! none of these modern inventions consider human life' – Queen Victoria only waited the chance to get on board.

On an April day the little fair-haired Princess caught sight of a wild, handsome fellow riding in the Park, with dark mustachios and fur-timmed coat – her second cousin, Duke Charles of Brunswick. At the theatre she could not help admiring the singular way in which he and his gentleman did their hair:

'it is divided all down the head (parted in the middle) & hangs I should say about two inches below the ear all round. It may not suit ugly people, that's true, but it certainly becomes these handsome ones.'[17]

A month later two ladies brought her the thrilling news that they had seen Duke Charles close to. His expression was 'dreadful, so very fierce & desperate'.[18] Princess Victoria had already observed him occasionally looking at her, though he never spoke. Supposing this lost soul who had gone to the bad in Vienna were to address her with just one fierce, desperate word? Baroness Lehzen and the Duchess, working together for once, saw to it that the desperate word was never uttered.

The Princess's health, thanks to prolonged walking about indoors and outdoors, was back to normal; indeed she had to return some smart gaiters sent by Aunt Louise from Paris because they were too small. As her eighteenth birthday approached, each side at Kensington was assembling its forces for the last round.

Those who subscribed to the Kensington 'system'* included the Duchess of Kent, Lady Flora Hastings, Princess Sophia, Prince Charles Leiningen (Victoria's half-brother who visited England in March) and the Duke of Sussex. Conroy sometimes thought that the Duke had designs on the Crown himself but he was confident of leading the old gentleman by the nose.

Princess Sophia's place in the 'system' was peculiar. Conroy called her his 'spy' at Court; among other things she repeated to the Duchess all the King's unkind remarks. Every evening after dinner she would come to the Duchess's apartments. She had, wrote Leiningen, 'a close-linked friendship'[19] with Conroy – a fact which the tone of her correspondence supports. Sir John was her Comptroller also, and she seems to have promised him a large gift of money with which to buy an estate. When she died her affairs were in no better order than those of the Duchess. In the political world, Conroy counted among others upon Mr Abercromby, Speaker of the House, Lord Liverpool, Lord Durham, sometimes the erratic Lord Brougham, and Baron Stockmar.

On the other side, Princess Victoria's only effective supporter was Baroness Lehzen. Her Governess, the Duchess of Northumberland, had begun latterly to co-operate with Lehzen and was 'treated accordingly', said Leiningen, by Conroy. But she never saw Princess Victoria alone nor got to know her. She resigned in protest against the 'system' shortly before the King died. As for political counsellors, Stockmar remarked that Princess Victoria's misfortune was in having no English adviser at all.

Charles Leiningen found the situation at Kensington had greatly deteriorated compared with two years ago. His step-sister no longer concealed her coolness towards her mother and complained vehemently of Sir John's affronts. Shocked

* The 'system' developed into something much wider than Princess Victoria's education. Charles Leiningen summed it up as (1) to win Victoria popularity by cutting her off from the Court's morals and politics, (2) to ensure a Regency for the Duchess, (3) to achieve the position of private secretary for Conroy. Prince Leiningen wrote (in German) at the Prince Consort's request a long account of these events, going back to 1819. (R. A. M.7/67.)

by these discoveries, Leiningen implored Conroy to beg Princess Victoria's forgiveness. Conroy, however, got no further than drafting a letter of apology and then burning it. All his calculations depended on a Regency. If the King survived until Princess Victoria attained her legal majority at eighteen, he would throw in the sponge, consoling himself with the thought that Parliament would surely banish Lehzen, 'in disgrace and shame'. Leiningen strongly opposed this pusillanimity. In April he met King Leopold and urged him to intervene. Let him persuade his niece voluntarily to ask for a Regency, even if the King survived. Sir John, explained Leiningen, was indispensable; Victoria would be 'a young lady of 18' incapable of ruling England by herself.[20]

As a result of Leiningen's mission King Leopold sent his confidential agent, Baron Stockmar, to England late in May.

Meanwhile Conroy was ready to present the Duchess's case in a lengthy financial memorandum to Parliament. It dwelt on her poverty, emphasizing her generous patronage of British industry, arts and charities and concluding with an unctuous allusion to the future:

> 'When the Great Governor of all things shall appoint the time, there is a cheering prospect that the Duchess will reap the sweet reward of Her Maternal Counsels and Example.'[21]

But the Great Governor of all things seemed in no hurry to appoint the time for the King's death. Instead, King William anticipated Conroy's memorandum with a financial bombshell of his own.

May 19 seemed like any other day. Princess Victoria romped with her two little Leiningen nephews in the nursery. Suddenly she was sent for, to receive a letter from the King. William IV had instructed his messenger, Lord Conyngham, to deliver it into her own hands, a task which he accomplished only after a brush with Conroy. 'By what authority?' demanded the majordomo, stepping forward. 'His Majesty's,' replied Conyngham. The Duchess next put out her hand to intercept the letter but was equally unsuccessful.[22]

Princess Victoria read it before showing it to her mother.

70

The King offered her three things: £10,000 a year of her own entirely free from her mother's control; an independent Privy Purse under Sir Benjamin Stephenson; and the right to appoint her own ladies. Each item was a blow in Conroy's vitals. He himself intended to administer Princess Victoria's affairs as Keeper of her Privy Purse, her conscience, her body and soul; and he intended that prominent among her new ladies should be his own daughter, Victoire Conroy. The Duchess added her execrations to Sir John's, for Sir Benjamin Stephenson belonged to the Fitzclarence set and had once been reprimanded for insulting her.

As the storm rose, the Princess retired to her room. 'Felt very miserable & agitated. Did not go down to dinner.'[23] In her absence Conroy furiously set to work to thwart the King. Victoria must be forced to renounce her rights, ask for a Regency and promise Sir John his appointment as private secretary. He had failed at Ramsgate; now he must succeed.

Next day the Princess found a draft reply to the King's letter ready for her to sign. At first she refused, for the draft, while gratefully accepting the £10,000, pleaded her youth and inexperience as a reason for remaining 'in every respect as I am now'.[24] Her income was not to be 'mother-free'. She tried to amend the draft, to consult Lord Melbourne or Mr Abercromby, the Speaker. All in vain. They browbeat her into signing. Immediately she returned to her room and dictated to Lehzen a statement that the draft was not her own – a fact which did not escape the King's notice. 'Victoria has not written that letter,' he growled when he received it.[25]

By May 21st the quarrel had involved Lord Melbourne who, as head of the Whig Government, was terrified lest the Tories should make capital out of Conroy's collision with the King. 'God! I don't like this man; there seems to be something very odd about him,' Melbourne burst out to the Speaker.[26] But he knew nothing of Princess Victoria's 'torments' – if he had, there would have been a 'blow up', he told her afterwards[27] – and so in a series of calming notes he entreated His Majesty not to attack the Duchess's entrenched position until Princess Victoria was twenty-one. The King would not be soothed. 'The real point,' he dictated to his scribe, 'is the Duchess and king John want money'; she had 'thrown off the mask' and he would defeat her.[28]

The Duchess was no less intransigent. When, on May 27th, Melbourne offered her a compromise – £6,000 for herself and £4,000 for her daughter – she sent a rejection in Princess Victoria's name without consulting her.

Nothing but a surface politeness was maintained. The Princess still sang duets with her mother but would not speak to her; even strangers noticed her coldness. One man who presented a loyal address on her birthday was struck by the Duchess's excited demeanour which seemed to him beautiful, whereas something was lacking in Princess Victoria's face. In fact he was witnessing her determination to give nothing away. It was ironic that her birthday should coincide with the peak of Conroy's power. The white and gold banner which floated over Kensington Palace bearing the name VICTORIA celebrated the victory of Sir John rather than that of the young Princess. The King gave her a grand piano and a grand ball;* great crowds stood in the streets to see 'poor stupid me' go by. But the ballroom itself became a centre of intrigue. Baroness Lehzen exchanged some conspiratorial words on the ballroom floor with the Duchess of Northumberland, though, as she said, 'Sir John watched me the whole evening'.[29] Princess Victoria's formula for a happy day – 'I was *very much amused*' – was conspicuously absent from her Journal on May 24th, 1837. It opened sombrely: 'Today is my 18th birthday! How old! and yet how far am I from being what I should be.'[30]

Towards the end of May Baron Stockmar arrived on the scene, warmly welcomed at first by both sides – a sign, incidentally, that King Leopold was out of touch with his niece's situation. Indeed, he had admitted as much when he wrote to her on May 25th: 'My Dearest Child – You have had some battles and difficulties of which I am completely in the dark.'[31]

Victoria quickly convinced Stockmar of her case, so that

* There is some doubt about the exact status of the piano; it seems that the King's personal present was a dressing-case. (Una Pope-Hennessy, *Agnes Strickland*, p. 76.)

Conroy emerged exasperated from his first interview with the umpire. Stockmar had informed him that nothing would induce Princess Victoria to have him for her private secretary; Lehzen was not to blame, it was Sir John's own personality. At the same time some agreement must be reached to reconcile mother and daughter.

Day after day the Duchess, Stockmar and Charles Leiningen tried to batter the eighteen-year-old girl into accepting a compromise. She would not budge an inch. As for her half-brother Charles, she refused to answer his letters, requiring him to be silent about a matter which did not concern him.

The Duchess and Conroy became ever more desperate as the sands of the King's life ran out. 'You are still very young,' wrote the Duchess to her daughter, abandoning the last shreds of tact, 'and all your success so far has been due to your *Mother*'s reputation. Do not be *too sanguine* in *your* own *talents* and *understanding*.'[32] Victoria, though bruised and anxious, still felt her talents sufficient to defeat the cabal.

On June 15th, five days before the King's death, both sides made their last throw. Lord Liverpool, a much-respected Tory and family friend, was summoned to Kensington. Afterwards he wrote a detailed memorandum of his conversations. He saw Conroy first. Conroy promptly started a long, false trail about Victoria's mental instability. She could not do without a private secretary, he argued: she was 'younger in intellect than in years', had frivolous tastes and was much taken with dress and fashion. Would Lord Liverpool advise her to make no changes in Ministers or Majordomos except to 'clear out entirely' her Household? (This meant ousting Lehzen and instating his daughter Victoire.) Lord Liverpool retorted that Victoria must have 'no private secretary', such as William IV and George IV had; he would suggest, however, that Conroy should be Keeper of the Privy Purse with no political power and only 'small duties'. Lord Liverpool then opened negotiations with the other side.[33]

The interview with Princess Victoria was remarkable. She saw him, as she emphasized, 'alone'. Immediately producing a paper with headings for their discussion, she accepted Lord Liverpool's advice that she should do without a private secretary and instead put herself in Lord Melbourne's hands. As for making Sir John Conroy even Keeper of the Privy Purse, this was out of the question. Did not Lord Liverpool know of the 'many slights and incivilities' she had suffered? His own daughter, Lady Catherine Jenkinson, could vouch for them. Besides this, 'she knew things of him which rendered it totally impossible for her to place him in any confidential situation near her . . . which entirely took away her confidence in him . . . she knew this of herself without any other person informing her'.[34] She showed Liverpool a letter (dictated by Lehzen and referred to in Princess Victoria's Journal by the single word '*Wrote!!*')[35] which he agreed was respectful to the Duchess and firm to Sir John, refusing to bind herself by any promise whatever. The interview closed with a pathetic appeal from the Princess to 'open their eyes to the difficulty of the situation in which they place me'. Lord Liverpool, like Stockmar, was convinced.

For the next few days Princess Victoria remained in her room, seeing no one but Lehzen, taking her meals alone. Sir John consulted one more friend, Mr Speaker Abercromby, who declared that if Princess Victoria would not listen to reason '*she must be coerced*'.[36] Charles Leiningen, however, speaking hurriedly in German so that Sir John should not understand, begged his mother not to lock her up. Sir John afterwards confided to Leiningen that he abandoned coercion only because 'he did not credit the Duchess of Kent with enough strength for such a step'.

The news from Windsor was critical. Conroy's 'spy', Princess Sophia, reported that the doctors gave the King only a few more hours. Almost suffocated with asthma, he whispered on Waterloo Day his last earthly desire. 'This is the 18th of June; I should like to live to see the sun of Waterloo set.' The Duke of Wellington sent to his bedside the tricolour flag. 'Right, right . . .' he murmured to Lord Munster; 'Unfurl it and let me feel it . . . Glorious day . . .' At twelve minutes past two on the morning of June 20th his own sun set.[37]

Archbishop Howley, accompanied by the Lord Chamberlain, Lord Conyngham, and the King's physician, travelled straight from the royal deathbed to Kensington Palace, where the young Queen lay asleep in her mother's bedroom. Excited by the hour and the circumstances, they galloped the whole way, only to find the lodge gates shut and the porter snoring. It was about five o'clock. The midsummer dawn lit up the lion and unicorn over the gate as they rang and rang the bell. At last they were admitted and their carriage rolled on up the drive to the Clock Court and the Palace door. Again there was delay. The Duchess would not admit Lord Conyngham to Princess Victoria's presence saying that she was still asleep. It was only when he demanded to see 'the Queen' that at six o'clock she 'awoke the dear Child with a kiss'[38] and led her through the anteroom to the King's Backstairs.

Together they descended the awkward flight hand in hand for the last time, the Duchess carrying a silver candlestick and Lehzen hastening behind with a bottle of smelling salts. A cotton dressing-gown covered Victoria's nightdress and her long, light hair streamed down her back. At the door of her sitting-room she parted from her mother and Lehzen, entering the apartment, as she noted in her Journal, '*alone*'. She saw her visitors fall on their knees; she heard Lord Conyngham's first explanatory phrases. When he reached the word 'Queen', she shot out her hand for him to kiss even more swiftly than she had given 'Uncle King' her 'little paw'. It was not merely the efficient performance of a well-rehearsed act. Victoria would have stretched out both hands if etiquette had allowed. After so much travail she was grasping the glorious future.

CHAPTER V

LITTLE VICTORY
1837

STILL IN HER dressing-gown and slippers, Queen Victoria laid her head on her mother's shoulder and wept briefly for the old King to whom she had been unable to say goodbye. 'I then went to my room and dressed.' In putting on her plain black dress that morning she marked the beginning of a new life as surely as a nun in the ceremony of Clothing.*

'I am very young,' continued the entry in Queen Victoria's Journal, 'and perhaps in many, though not in all things, inexperienced, but I am sure, that very few have more real good will and more real desire to do what is fit and right than I have.'[1] Her modest confidence was justified. All her life she was buoyed up not only by a sense of duty but also by the knowledge that she possessed it. As for her inexperience, it existed in regard to the joys of life rather than its trials.

The qualities which introspection had revealed to Queen Victoria about herself were still hidden from the public. What was she like? How would she behave? Nobody knew. Those who guessed, guessed wrong. From an invalid couch the poetess Elizabeth Barrett prettily misinterpreted the young Queen's first tears:

> The Maiden wept;
> She wept to wear a crown!

Fanny Kemble, the actress whose memoirs had alternately shocked and delighted the Princess during hair-brushing hours,

* The dress is now in the very place where Queen Victoria wore it – Kensington Palace (the London Museum). During the 1939–45 war, when it had to be stored without the necessary warmth and humidity, it turned brown, having been inky black. One must assume that the dress was an old one which the economical Duchess of Kent had had dipped at home when King William's mother-in-law died. The dye was not fast but was no doubt considered good enough by the Duchess who, as well as being economical, disliked the King and Queen intensely.

was no nearer the truth. 'Poor young creature!' was her refrain; 'all that grandeur' would drive her into a melancholy and she would soon long to retire on a small pension. Another writer, Thomas Carlyle, was 'heartily sorry for the poor bairn' when he saw her driving in the Park. Though a 'sonsy lassie', her comeliness could not disguise her timidity. 'Little Victory' he called her, with gentle irony. William IV had gone out, in Disraeli's words, 'like an old lion'; they expected Victoria to come in like a lamb.

Within a few hours of the poor bairn's Accession, a large gathering of Ministers formed a different opinion of their young Sovereign.

Queen Victoria had already seen Stockmar once and Melbourne twice and written three letters when she came downstairs into the Red Saloon at Kensington Palace for her first Council. The Council met at eleven. Notwithstanding the short notice there was a record attendance of Privy Counsellors, all eager to see the unknown Queen. The hopes of a new reign of England had been successively occupied, in the words of Sir Sidney Lee, by 'an imbecile, a profligate and a buffoon'. It was hardly possible to visualize a greater change.

As the Privy Counsellors waited in the Red Saloon one question in particular interested them. Would she come accompanied by the great officers of State? There was a momentary hush as the doors flew open and a small black figure entered, in her own words, 'quite alone'. The Royal Dukes, Cumberland and Sussex, came forward to meet her and lead her to her throne, the bizarre trio resembling, it was said, Beauty and the Beasts or Bel and the Dragons. The Queen read her Declaration in the celebrated silver voice whose extreme clarity and precision always concealed any nervousness she might be feeling. Then came the swearing-in. Blushing up to the eyes, she received the humble obeisances of her uncles; she approached the Duke of Sussex instead of waiting for him to approach her, a kindness towards the infirm which she was to repeat with effect at her Coronation. Charles Greville, Clerk of the Council, described her as bewildered by the multitude who had to be sworn but after the first blush not a sign of emotion clouded her bright smooth face. Occasionally she glanced inquiringly at Lord Melbourne for instructions but when he and other great personages – Peel, Palmerston and Wellington, all of whom she knew – kissed her hand, not a word nor a smile escaped her. All agreed that the royal hand was 'remarkably sweet and soft'.

After she had retired, the Red Saloon echoed to an astonished chorus of praise. It was her unexpected exhibition of agreeable opposites which struck them all. Sir Robert Peel marvelled at her modesty and firmness, others at her perfect self-possession combined with graceful diffidence. At her second Council, Greville was even more moved than at the first. The cynicism with which he had regarded the new reign melted away: *'nothing* will happen', he had written on June 18th, 'because in this Country, *nothing* ever does'. Though she was handed the wrong papers she continued to hold the Council as if she had been doing it all her life. She was tiny, she was unpretentious; yet her good nature together with her youth, continued Greville, 'inspire an excessive interest in all who approach her, and which I can't help feeling myself.'

A large composition representing Queen Victoria's first Council was executed by Sir David Wilkie at her command. All the likenesses were excellent, she wrote at the time. There is a stiff charm in this conversation piece, though some of the glances are curiously side-long, even furtive, the artist being obliged to depict every eye glued on Her Majesty. Moreover his zeal for the pure young innocent betrayed him into painting the Queen's gown white. When she examined the picture again, ten years later, she decided it was one of the worst she had ever seen.[2]

Victoria's first day as Queen of England was a crowded one. Complete satisfaction of that craving for employment which she had discovered on her sixteenth birthday, had come at last. After the Council she saw her Prime Minister, Lord Melbourne, twice more; also the Archbishop of Canterbury, the Home Secretary, the Master of the Horse and two of her relations. She wrote another letter and her Journal, saw Stockmar twice after dinner, appointed Dr Clark to be her physician and dismissed Conroy from her Household. (She could not remove him from her mother's.)

> Conroy goes not to Court, the reason's plain,
> King John has played his part and ceased to reign.

Another appointment was that of Baroness Lehzen to the airy title of Lady Attendant on the Queen. It was safest to give the German confidante a post which did not officially exist. 'My *dear* Lehzen will *always* remain with me as my friend,' ran the last entry in the Journal for June 20th, 'but will take no situation about me, and I think she is right.' Just above this tender sentence Queen Victoria wrote with harsh brevity, 'Went down & said good night to Mama, etc.' This was the only mention of Mama, apart from her mother's having woken her up at six o'clock. When Queen Victoria wished her Mama goodnight, darkness descended on the Duchess of Kent for three mournful years.

The first letter, dashed off by the Queen at half past eight on that busy morning, was addressed to her 'Dearest, Most Beloved Uncle'. It gave King Leopold the news of William IV's death. King Leopold had wisely decided not to rush over the moment his niece ascended the throne. 'People might fancy I came to enslave you,' he wrote. So, for the first fifteen months of her reign, he left Stockmar in England as his *alter ego*, contenting himself with sending advice. Much of it influenced the Queen as long as she lived.

King Leopold wrote that she could not cultivate too much discretion; those around her observed that her discretion was preternaturally great, almost unpleasing in so young a girl. Leopold advised her never to give an immediate answer to Ministers; Greville heard that she always said 'I will think it over', even to Melbourne. Leopold advocated strict business habits such as seeing Ministers between 11 am and 1.30 pm each day; the Queen always saw Lord Melbourne between those hours. Leopold urged her to form her own opinions on all questions and stick to them; her reign was not two months old before people noticed 'slight signs of a peremptory disposition' and 'a strong will of her own'.[3] Leopold insisted that if people spoke to her uninvited on personal matters she should change the subject 'and make the individual feel that he has made a mistake'; no one could deliver more effectively than Queen Victoria the look that froze or the phrase that made men and women shrivel: 'We are not amused.'

The King further emphasized that his niece could never be too 'national' in politics nor too vocal about the Established Church. On the first count, he was speaking to the converted; on the second, Queen Victoria's relations with the Church were not unclouded but its 'establishment' aspect always appealed to her.

Was it possible that the King was trying to guide the young Queen a shade too masterfully, even from a distance? If he could have seen her Journal for the first day of her reign, one word, five times repeated, would have caught his eye: 'alone . . . & of COURSE quite ALONE . . . quite alone . . . & alone . . . alone'. Beginning with Lord Conyngham at 6 am, she saw all her visitors alone. Over Melbourne's first audience she was most explicit: 'At 9 came Lord Melbourne, whom I saw in my room, & of COURSE quite ALONE as I shall always do all my Ministers.'[4] It was a sign of independence not of loneliness; for an essential part of Conroy's coercive policy – fortunately thwarted – was to insist on the Duchess of Kent being present at all the Queen's audiences. She might have added in her Journal that her bed was removed that same day from her mother's room. The experience of a lifetime was reversed. Her waking hours were deliciously sociable and for the first time she slept alone.

Baron Christian Frederick Stockmar, the man whom King Leopold sent to England in his stead, was fifty years old. His knowledge of the Royal Family was extensive. He had been Prince Leopold's physician, held Princess Charlotte's hand as she died, superintended the Duke of Kent's will and drawn up for King Leopold the Belgian Constitution. Stockmar's sagacity tended to obscure the fact that he made mistakes. His interpretation of the British Constitution was one. Unfortunately he had studied this illusive organism in books, unaware that it resembled in no way the logical, synthetic Constitution of Belgium. His researches into what historians had written about an unwritten Constitution gave him many erroneous ideas regarding the British Monarchy which he passed on to Queen Victoria and Prince Albert.

Like so many eminent Victorians, Stockmar suffered from hypochondria. It is amusing to find his employer, King Leopold, himself a victim, expressing the hope that his *useful occupation* at the English Court would keep his mind off his own health. He had begun his practice as a doctor during the Napoleonic wars and credited himself with exceptional psychological insight – more than he in fact possessed, when it came to a young woman like Victoria. He employed this gift in directing the lives of rulers, his principles being three: honesty in giving unwelcome advice, courage in bearing periods of coldness from offended Majesty and self-control in refraining from saying afterwards, 'I told you so'. He shared with Melbourne, though unofficially, a position amounting to private secretary.

Stockmar, having arrived in England in 1837, flitted for the next twenty years to and fro between Coburg and Windsor unheralded but never unwanted. With his wizened features, small stature and shrunken legs, too chilly to be exposed in Court hose to the rigours of Windsor Castle, he combined the qualities of Puck and Merlin. The mysterious descents of the Welsh wizard upon the Court of King Arthur were deemed to be no more essential to royal welfare than the little doctor's visits to the Court of Queen Victoria.

As Lord Melbourne emerged from the Queen's first Council he was stopped by Baron Stockmar who was waiting to unburden himself of the whole Conroy story up to that morning.

Sir John, he said, had waylaid him and confessed himself beaten. 'I must submit,' he announced, pressing into the Baron's hand his 'terms' for retirement from the Duchess of Kent's service and demanding that they be shown to Lord Melbourne immediately.

Melbourne, who knew something of Conroy's ambitions

81

from his own negotiations over the King's £10,000 annuity for Princess Victoria, was nevertheless astounded by what he read. Nothing short of a pension of £3,000 a year, the Grand Cross of the Bath, a peerage and a seat on the Privy Council would satisfy the Duchess of Kent's majordomo. A Minister of the Crown would have been offered less. The paper trembled in the Prime Minister's hand; he dropped it more than once, ejaculating, 'This is really too bad! Have you ever heard such impudence!'[5] Nevertheless, anxiety to get rid of Conroy drove Melbourne into granting a substantial part of his demands. In the autumn of 1837 Melbourne recommended the Queen to pay Conroy a pension of £3,000 and to confer on him a baronetcy. He was further promised an Irish peerage as soon as a vacancy occurred, this honour depending, according to Stockmar, on Melbourne still being Prime Minister.

Both sides had negotiated under pressure and each accused the other afterwards of playing false. When the Irish vacancy occurred, Peel was Prime Minister; he refused to recognize an undertaking given by his predecessor. Conroy 'sneeringly' kept telling Stockmar that he would not fulfil his part of the bargain until the Queen fulfilled hers. In Stockmar's words, he intrigued more and more violently against the Queen in a 'spirit of feminine revenge'.[6] There is no doubt that Melbourne and Stockmar between them advised the Queen badly. Anything for a quiet life had always been Melbourne's motto and he hoped to secure Conroy's retirement at once while paying for it by instalments. The magnitude of his miscalculation is shown by the fatal part Conroy later played in the Flora Hastings affair.

Meanwhile Queen Victoria was only too pleased to have in Melbourne an adviser who would take most of this *disagreeable business* out of her hands. True, she spent a large part of her first day in discussing Conroy's affairs. She also received some disturbing notes from her mother, the first begging that she might take Lady Flora and Conroy with her *'just'* this first day, the last warning her daughter against disclosing her dislike of Conroy to Melbourne:

'Lord Melbourne will find it out very quickly that you are not gracious to Sir John – and you will find him not very pliant to your order [to reward Conroy]: take care Victoria you know your Prerogative! Take care that Lord Melbourne is not King . . .'[7]

The warning fell on deaf ears for Queen Victoria already called him 'the best-hearted, kindest & most feeling man in the world.'

The three-year partnership between Queen Victoria and Lord Melbourne is one of the romances of history. If King Leopold was her second father, Melbourne was her third; but since her association with him began when she had ceased to be a child it was that much more intense than anything which had gone before. Melbourne's fatherly devotion was enriched in her eyes with the wisdom of a political genius, the detachment of a philosopher, the brilliance of a scholar, the fascination of a man of the world, the melancholy appeal of a bitterly disappointed husband and father and the glamour of one who had miraculously come unscathed through two divorce suits in both of which he was co-respondent.* To Queen Victoria, Melbourne was the first vista outside the prison gates; to Melbourne, she was the blind he would teach to see, the dumb who would learn through him to speak.

She gloried in Melbourne's 'stores' of knowledge. His conversation always 'improved' her. He gilded all his excellent advice with wit, scepticism, paradox. No opinion was too bizarre, no judgement too cynical to serve in rousing the young Queen from her beauty sleep: 'it is a source of great amusement to me to collect his "sayings".' She was never shocked. For one thing, she had made up her mind that Melbourne was 'good'. For another, Melbourne's 'dashing' conversation, as Greville called it, appealed to the submerged side of her own temperament. No doubt she neutralized his absurdities with her loud, sensible laughter, but underneath it did her

* The second case concerned Caroline Norton, one of the three lovely Sheridan sisters, and had occurred only the year before Queen Victoria's Accession.

good to indulge her own taste for the *outré* in company so respectable as that of the Prime Minister. On one subject only was the Prime Minister invariably serious, even sentimental, and that was Queen Victoria herself. Whenever he talked about her, she noticed, his eyes filled with tears.

The tragic past of the Prime Minister similarly filled the Queen with a tender interest. She was too discreet to question him but she discussed it with the Duchess of Sutherland much as she had discussed the Duke of Brunswick with her ladies a year ago. Thus she found out about Melbourne's dead wife, Caroline Lamb, who had been mad, and his son who had died the year before her Accession, an epileptic. The bonds between herself and Melbourne drew closer for she, too, had been till lately very much alone.

Melbourne lectured the Queen on the duties of a constitutional monarch. His views, despite their seasoning of irony, were given and received most earnestly. Political education was Victoria's greatest need. Her sudden liberation from bondage, her own headstrong temperament and her inevitable contacts with the undemocratic ideas of Continental royalty, made her vulnerable to dangerous thoughts. With Lord Melbourne as Minister it was sheer pleasure for the Queen to accept the full rigour of the Constitution. There was nothing she wanted more than to take her Minister's advice. At eighteen one did not look too far ahead; there could, there *must* be no other adviser than the present one. When the inevitable change of government came and Melbourne fell, her temperament, combined with the force of the Conroy feud and the weakness of Melbourne in practice, temporarily defeated Melbourne's excellent teaching.

The list of Melbourne's gifts to the Queen are a tribute to the generosity of his nature. He gave her self-confidence through affection and praise; sophistication through inimitable table-talk; enthusiasm for her work through the delight with which he invested it. Her lack of height had always been a source of anxiety. Queen Victoria was under five feet tall and constantly lamented this fact. Once in despair she complained: 'Everybody grows but me.' Kind Lord Melbourne replied, laughing, 'I think you are grown.' Generally he would smile at her complaint, saying her height was no misfortune. He was right. The contrast between her lack of inches and dignity only heightened the queenly effect. Her nervousness, said Melbourne, was the sign of a 'sensitive and susceptible temperament'; her shyness meant that she had 'high and right feelings'. People who had small features and 'Squeeny noses' – Victoria's nose if not quite hooked was certainly not squeeny – 'never did anything'.

Part of Melbourne's charm lay in a carefree quality that was rare among Englishmen in public life; at any rate it was often described in foreign phrases. Greville drew attention to his *insouciance*, King Leopold to his being *poco curante*. He was slack; he did not care. Melbourne was incapable of over-dramatizing a situation and this was of great use to Victoria who tended to see things in terms of her favourite Italian opera. But when the situation was already pulsating with drama, as in the Flora Hastings affair, Melbourne's *insouciance* became negligence, his imperturbability, drifting.

One question remains. Was Melbourne's sophisticated adult approach the best training for a young impressionable queen? Certainly it provided a new standard by which she might correct her inherited effusiveness. On the other hand, her own common sense was quite capable of doing it for her and she paid a high price for her glimpse into Melbourne's cool world. He was the first of a long line of advisers to assure Queen Victoria that things were better than they seemed. The bringer of bad news is never popular and it has always needed courage to inform royalty that some of the people are starving. Queen Victoria's naturally warm sympathies, however, would have made her exceptionally responsive to the sad truth. Melbourne did not dry up the wells of her pity – that would have been impossible – but he did blunt her social conscience by starting the evil legend that all discontent was due to a handful of agitators. Particularly was this so in Ireland, where Melbourne himself had recently applied coercion and martial law against the advice of his own Lord-Lieutenant. At seventeen Victoria had studied Irish history with Lehzen: 'How ill treated that poor Country & Nation has been!' she exclaimed in her Journal.[8] When, as Queen, she asked Melbourne what happened to the 'poor Irish' who were evicted by their landlords, Melbourne replied, 'They become *absorbed* somehow or other' – which made them all laugh amazingly. He added that 'they ate too much and there was not enough for them and you'.[9] Under Melbourne's callous tuition she gradually came to believe that every rebellious Irishman was 'a low Irishman'. It is fair to add that he strongly advocated royal visits both to Ireland and Scotland. The young Victoria, however, only wanted to see the Continent, which was impossible.

Melbourne profoundly distrusted social change. Nothing could be changed for the better, he felt, whether it was the factory system, the Church of England or the ventilation of Buckingham Palace. Nothing that had stood the test of time should be abolished, not even the flogging of men, women and boys; only animals should be exempt since they did not know what it was for. Dogs liked dragging carts in the coalmines; factory children ought to work rather than starve. As for Lord Shaftesbury's championship of the young, why, the hypocrite disliked his own children! Nevertheless, Melbourne held liberal views about children. Solitary confinement and '*silence*', Victoria thought from personal experience, were good punishments; Melbourne wrote them off as 'very stupifying'.

The epigrams with which he entertained the young Queen had a Johnsonian ring. Of wife-beating: 'Why, it is almost worthwhile for a woman to be beat, considering the exceeding pity she excites.' Of euthanasia: 'If they get the habit of doing such a thing when a person is in a hopeless state, why, they *may* do it when a person is *not* in a hopeless state.' Of large families: 'if there are many, they have seldom anything the matter with them.' Of the Derby horse-race: it was 'not perfect without somebody killing himself'. Of cheating: 'No people cheat like the English.' Of doctors: 'English physicians kill you, the French let you die.' Of female friends: 'It's very rare that women are kind to one another.'

One day the Duke of Richmond said how disgraceful it was that people often came out of prison worse than they went in. 'I am afraid there are many places one comes out of

86

worse than one went in,' said Melbourne; 'one often comes out worse of a ballroom than one went in.' The Queen shouted with laughter. Another day she observed that there were not very many good preachers. Lord Melbourne agreed, adding, 'But there are not *many very good* anything' – 'which is *very true*,' wrote the Queen: 'I'm sure *he is* one of the *very* good.'[10]

They talked about Christian names. Melbourne thought 'Alice' beautiful and 'Louise' fastidious; the Queen chose them for two of her daughters. They talked about teeth and poor little chimney-sweeps and pronunciation. (Melbourne used the old-fashioned forms of 'goold' for gold and 'Proosia' for Prussia.) Best of all Melbourne told her endless tales of George II, George III and all her uncles, filling the gaps in her knowledge and making her feel at last that she was part of a family. Her father, he told her, was as agreeable as George IV and more *posé* than William IV with none of his talkativeness: 'from all what I heard,' noted Queen Victoria, whose grammar often fell short of her enthusiasm, 'my father was the best of all.'[11]

Lord Melbourne was fifty-eight when he became Victoria's first Prime Minister. He had lost the dazzling looks which captured Caroline Ponsonby but he could still race a lady-in-waiting down the Corridor at Windsor. His eyes, grey-blue, large and expressive with dark lashes, recalled something of the past. Queen Victoria often commented in her Journal on his physical attractions, especially when wearing the 'Windsor uniform' of dark blue and red, or when his hair was ruffled by the wind. A twelve-inch marble bust of Melbourne stood on the press in her sitting-room. To her he was more than a father but less than a lover. In spite of the Duchess of Kent's disapproval of their relationship, in spite of Greville's opinion that Victoria's feelings were unconsciously sexual, in spite of malicious gossip that they were about to be married, no mud has stuck.

What Queen Victoria meant to Lord Melbourne was perceived early on by Greville and summed up with rare accuracy:

'I have no doubt he is passionately fond of her as he might be of his daughter if he had one; and the more because he is a man with a capacity for loving without having anything in the world to love. It is become his province to educate, instruct and form the most interesting mind and character in the world.'[12]

As a politician, Melbourne was the head of a weak Whig Government, holding Tory views himself and feeling no sympathy for the Radicals among his followers. Queen Victoria, therefore, became a rabid Whig with little comprehension of what Liberalism stood for. In more ways than one she would have fared better had she started with a Tory, such as Wellington or Peel. The Tories themselves thoroughly agreed:

'The Queen is with us,' Whigs insulting say;
'For when she found us in she let us stay.'
It may be so, but give me leave to doubt
How long she'll keep you when she finds you out.

The Queen rejoiced exceedingly when the Whigs won the first general election of her reign by 38 seats. With equal pleasure she received the news that Joseph Hume, one of their Radical supporters, was out. 'It is a fact,' wrote a young Tory, Benjamin Disraeli, 'that the little Queen clapped her hands . . .'

CHAPTER VI

THE WONDERFUL YEAR
1837–8

THE QUEEN WAS proclaimed from an open window in St James's Palace on June 21st, 1837. As the trumpets sounded, the names 'Alexandrina Victoria' floated over the crowds – but for the last time. By the Queen's express command, her first name was removed from all official papers and never used again. George IV's joke was over and little Drina had vanished for ever.

Three days later she went to the House of Lords where the Duke of Argyll read his speech so 'schockingly' (one of the young Queen's agreeable Germanisms) that he put her off her stroke: she herself came to a temporary halt in the middle of her own speech. But when she prorogued Parliament on July 17th Lord Melbourne told her with tears in his eyes how well she had done. She was not at all tired after it, she wrote to Uncle Leopold, but felt 'quite frisky'.

The delightful business of reigning had begun. She chose a Household considerably more economical than Queen Anne's (the last Queen Regnant) and with her interest in lovely women appointed the Duchess of Sutherland to be her Mistress of the Robes. This exquisite creature, whose fashion sense Conroy had once condemned for leading Princess Victoria astray, had a burning social conscience and later kept the Queen in touch, sometimes to the latter's annoyance, with the kind of causes which found no place in Melbourne's cynical world. Among the maids-of-honour, Queen Victoria preferred those who were merry. Melbourne took no pains to balance her Whig Household with a sprinkling of Tories, though his majority in Parliament was so slender. As a result the Queen most unwisely surrounded herself with Whig ladies. When criticism reached her ears she and Melbourne were much amused. By the end of July a little of the gilt was already beginning to flake from the Queen's image. The Tories resented having an exclusively Whig Queen and their disgruntlement was fed by reports of domestic wrangling inside Buckingham Palace.

The Queen had moved on July 13th from Kensington – 'this poor old Palace' – to Buckingham Palace, where 'dear *Dashy*' her spaniel was quite happy in the garden. The Duchess of Kent, however, was far from happy in the house. She was accommodated in a separate suite where she complained of not having enough room for her belongings. No structural alterations were undertaken to facilitate communication between mother and daughter; on the contrary, she was put as far away as possible. A hole, however, was quickly thumped in Her Majesty's bedroom wall to give access to Lehzen. She confided to Melbourne that 'formerly' she had been nervous of robbers at night. Indeed, though she did not see ghosts like Lord Melbourne, she was superstitious and frequently woke up in a fright. Now she had Lehzen's room on one side and her maid's on the other.[1]

It looks as though the escape from her Mama's company at night had brought its own punishment.

About this time Princess Lieven dined at the Palace and found the Queen very tongue-tied and the Duchess very vexed. Queen Victoria had been warned by Uncle Leopold not to discuss her affairs with strangers. The Duchess of Kent, however, loudly bewailed Conroy's dismissal by the Queen, adding that she herself was now '*nothing*'.[2] When Princess Lieven suggested that the Duchess ought to rejoice in her child's prodigious success, she only shook her head with its burden of ostrich feathers and smiled dolefully. A month later it was known that the Duchess could not see her daughter without special permission and often got a note back saying, 'Busy'. At other times the Queen was advised by Melbourne not to answer her mother's notes at all but to let him send a formal reply. 'My appeal was to *you* as my Child,' replied the Duchess after one of these frigid letters drafted by Melbourne, '– not to the Queen'.[3]

The magnificent dinner given in honour of Queen Victoria at the Guildhall on November 9th was the occasion for special pangs and recriminations. Up to three days before the great event the Duchess was still vainly imploring her daughter to allow Sir John to attend her: 'the Queen should forget what *displeased* the Princess'.[4] The Duchess went on to drop a hint which Melbourne decided to ignore. Victoria's coldness, she said, was causing all kinds of talk. Only if she took Sir John back would the talk stop. By her obstinacy she was hurting herself and her Mama more than Sir John:

> 'Really dearest Angel we have made too much of this affair . . . I have the greatest regard for Sir John. I cannot forget what he has done for me and for you! although he had the misfortune to displease you!'[5]

The Duchess had a point. The world read only one meaning into the Queen's displeasure: that Conroy and her mother were lovers.

The Queen rode alone to the City in her golden coach drawn by eight cream ponies bred in Hanover, the Lord Mayor riding before her with the Elizabethan Pearl Sword carried point upwards in his right hand. One of the sheriffs whom she knighted was Mr Montefiore, a Jew; she was very glad to be the first person to do 'what *I* think quite right'. The youthful Victoria was admirably free of prejudice.

After the dinner was over another letter of complaint arrived from the Duchess, some of it written in Sir John's hand. She had not been given proper precedence, she said. She had had the Queen's aunt above her and immediately below her the Queen's aunt-in-law, first cousin and cousin-once-removed. Would this recur at the Coronation procession?

Queen Victoria saw the Duchess a week later – 'and oh! what a scene did she make!'[6] Life in Kensington had acclimatized Victoria to scenes and instead of melting she proceeded to sever herself even more completely from the Duchess and her Household. Hitherto the Duchess had always accompanied her daughter at official functions for the sake of appearances. Henceforth the Queen frequently went without her.

Shortly afterwards, in December, Queen Victoria received her first independent income and the Duchess an extra annuity of £8,000, bringing her income up to £30,000 a year. Melbourne hoped this grant would meet with some opposition in Parliament; the Duchess and Conroy would then see that their vaunted popularity was not so great after all. Two Radicals in the Commons and Lord Brougham in the Lords had already opposed the Queen's own grant but a move to reduce the Civil List by £50,000 found only 19 supporters. Queen Victoria heard from Lord Duncannon that Brougham was 'prompted by that fiend J.C. to make all this fuss'.[7]

Parliament voted a Civil List of £385,000 a year for the Queen's life, divided into £60,000 for her Privy Purse, £131,260 for Household salaries and £172,500 for Household expenses, £13,200 for the Royal Bounty and £8,040 unappropriated. The Queen also enjoyed the Crown revenues from the Duchies of Lancaster and Cornwall, amounting to over £60,000 each at the end; Cornwall, however, passed to the Prince of Wales in 1841.

Queen Victoria's state thus changed in the first four months of her reign from penury to affluence, from the necessity to borrow from Messrs Coutts the bankers, to the ability to pay off all her father's debts. She plunged at once into this filial enterprise, setting aside £50,000 for the purpose – the whole of her Privy Purse for one year, apart from £10,000. Affluence never tempted Queen Victoria from her ingrained carefulness. Seven years' training by Lehzen in strict accountancy were not to be wiped out by sixty-three years a wealthy queen.

On December 14th Melbourne with tears in his eyes told her that the Duchess's annuity had been granted only out of respect for herself. Nine days later and with tears again in his eyes he admitted that getting the Civil List through had been hard work but Peel had kept the fractious Tories in order for her sake. Melbourne, the good, the kind, was wrapping her in a cocoon of sentiment from which in a year's time she would be roughly torn. At present there was still plenty of warm feeling and people were delighted with the generosity of 'our little Vic' towards her own relatives, whether legitimate or otherwise, as well as to her father's creditors. She astonished the world by her thoughtfulness towards Queen Adelaide, whom she addressed on the first day of her own reign as 'Queen' instead of 'Dowager Queen', allowing her to take away her favourite furniture from Windsor. She pleasantly surprised the '*bâtards*' by retaining them in their jobs.

The joys of this *annus mirabilis* at times took little Victoria's breath away: 'the pleasantest summer I *EVER* passed in *my life*, & I shall never forget this first summer of my Reign.' Her fascinated subjects watched with amazement the girlish figure slipping, as Greville put it, into her new role as if she had been ruling all her life. Princess Lieven commented on the extraordinary impression made by her aplomb and air of command combined with her childish face, slim build and sweet smile. The pressure of business she found greatly to her taste:

'June 24th . . . I received so many communications from my Ministers, but I like it very much.' 'July 1st . . . I *delight* in this work.'[8]

She had her hand kissed nearly three thousand times at a levée and a Quaker gentleman, Joseph Sturge of Birmingham, who kissed it on behalf of the Society of Friends found the experience no hardship. In August, with the season over, she reluctantly left London – 'the *greatest* Metropolis in the *World*' – for Windsor, whose cawing rooks and striking clock made her feel melancholy. But soon, with her gay Court around her, Uncle Leopold and Aunt Louise staying for the first time under her own roof and Lord Melbourne nearly always in attendance, Windsor began to look less gloomy. She 'ventured' to admit Dashy to her *tête-à-têtes* with the Prime Minister; he behaved very well, licking Lord Melbourne's hand. 'All dogs like me,' said the statesman.[9]

The little Blue Closet where these audiences always took place became one of Queen Victoria's favourite rooms: it was so 'cosy' and 'cheerful'. The great Corridor, 550 feet long, was a fine place for a game of ball with visiting children or battledore and shuttlecock with her ladies. Queen Victoria loved to entertain children, especially the little Conynghams who had curving black lashes and called her 'the Tween'. Babies were another matter: she sprained her wrist one day lifting Lady Portman's. In the Corridor were portraits of the Royal Family by Zoffany and scenes by Canaletto; on a lonely afternoon she and Lehzen passed the time counting Canalettos; they counted 43 in all, besides busts and screens and gilt

93

clocks, some of which appeared again in the background to family portraits.

Every evening the Duchess of Kent was planted at her own whist table – the only way of keeping her awake till half past eleven – while the Queen and her ladies sat round a large mahogany table, Victoria drawing, the others working, laughing and talking. When the gentlemen were present the pace would be accelerated to include spilikins, puzzles, draughts and games of 'German Tactics' at which the English Queen twice out-manoeuvred her Coburg uncle. Chess was so serious a pursuit that Lords Melbourne, Palmerston, Conyngham and Sir John Hobhouse hovered over Queen Victoria giving contradictory advice in an effort to checkmate Queen Louise. There being two queens on the chess-board and two at the table, instructions about 'the queen' became very confusing, particularly as Victoria, wearing a crimson velvet dress from Paris, was clearly the Red Queen. 'Between them all,' she wrote, 'I got quite beat, & Aunt Louise triumphed over my Council of Ministers!'

There were walks to Adelaide Cottage and back, and walks on the Terrace above the Slopes, where primroses and cowslips grew in spring. The Terrace was always full of people 'who were civil to their Queen', as Victoria noted with satisfaction, remembering how they used to push and jostle her funny old Uncle William.

Better than all other recreations were the Queen's great cavalcades of up to thirty riders, galloping for miles without once pulling up. Her small stature did not show on horseback: she looked immensely seductive in a black velvet riding habit, top hat and veil, with her bright cheeks and eyes and fair hair. So thought Lord Alfred Paget, one of her gentlemen, a 'handsome young Calmuck-looking fellow' of twenty-one who had once gone on a pilgrimage to the resting place of his father's leg, shot off at Waterloo. He owned a retriever, much admired by the Queen, named Mrs Bumps. Both Lord Alfred and his dog wore her portrait. The Queen professed to find him less attractive than he had promised to be when she first saw him nine years before; he was too boyish in his ideas but had the good sense to look up to Lehzen. Lord Melbourne rode always by the Queen's side, bringing a series of splendid horses with him from London.

Queen Victoria's triumph as a horsewoman reached its peak when in August she reviewed her troops at Windsor wearing an adaptation of the Windsor uniform and the Garter ribbon, sitting 'Leopold' for two-and-a-half hours and then going out again for another hour-and-a-half's canter on 'Barbara'. (She liked riding Barbara because she was often naughty, which gave her something to do.) She had narrowly escaped being forced to review her troops in Hyde Park two months earlier, from a carriage. Not having ridden since her illness at Ramsgate, she could not at first convince them that she would be able to hold her horse. Melbourne and the Duchess opposed the horse for the additional reason of propriety: a carriage could hold a female attendant whereas on horseback she would prance alone between the Duke of Wellington and Lord Hill. This latter idea appealed to the Queen so strongly that at the end of a heated argument she presented Melbourne with an ultimatum: 'Very well, my lord, very well – remember, no horse no review.' So there was no Hyde Park review in June and the reason for its cancellation having leaked into the Press, Victoria's amused subjects celebrated her triumph:

> *I will have a Horse, I'm determined on that,*
> *If there is to be a review,*
> *No horse, no review, my Lord Melbourne, that's flat,*
> *In spite of Mama and of you.*
>
> *You may wonder and blunder, and argue and stare,*
> *But remember that I am your Queen,*
> *And learn that it is not a trifling affair,*
> *To please a young girl of eighteen.*[10]

Suddenly it was autumn. The six weeks in the country had flown like six days – 'how quickly time passes when one is happy' – and now she was off to Brighton for her first visit to the Marine Pavilion where her 'Uncle King' had spent so many unedifying hours. Queen Victoria was not amused by the flying dragons, serpent-entwined pillars, ceilings painted with bamboo rods bound with lilac ribbons, lustres arranged like lotuses, cornices hung with golden bells and pagodas standing fifteen feet high. 'The pavilion is a strange, odd Chinese looking thing, both inside and outside; most rooms low,' she wrote disparagingly. Her bedroom was over the entrance hall; what was the good of living at Brighton if 'I only see a little morsel of the *sea* from one of my sitting-room windows'? Next day her indomitable spirits bounded back to normal. Her sitting-room was now 'pretty & cheerful'; the 'little morsel' had become a 'nice little peep of the sea'. She was nothing if not adaptable and would always enjoy herself if it were at all possible. Mr Creevey, the diarist, met her at the Pavilion and heard her loud uninhibited laughter. Like others, Creevey complained of her opening her mouth too wide when she laughed and showing not very pretty gums. She also gobbled her food. But her voice and expression were perfect. 'She blushes and laughs every instant in so natural a way as to disarm anybody.' The sight of 'the poor little thing' struggling to pull off a tight glove so that he might kiss her hand quite melted his heart.

Then it was back again to London for the season and another birthday and the Coronation.

The Coronation festivities, which included three State balls, two levées, a drawing-room and a State concert, opened with Queen Victoria's first State ball in May. Melbourne affected to be shocked by the number of people who had written for invitations; 'very pushing and very degrading'. It was talked of as the best ball ever to be given in London, he said, because the company was so select. He did not wish the Rothschilds to be asked. Even in this rarefied, aristocratic atmosphere, however, there was still no arm fit to encircle the Queen's waist in a waltz – she had to watch the waltzers dancing to Strauss's band from a dais among her aunts – so she danced quadrilles most beautifully until sunrise. 'It was a lovely ball,' she wrote in her Journal, 'so gay, so nice – I felt so happy & so merry; I had not danced for *so* long & was so glad to do so again!' Her only regret was that Lord Melbourne was prevented by indisposition from sharing her happiness. Greville as usual found something to criticize:

though the Queen was 'perfect' the gallery was ill-lit and the whole thing not a patch on the Tuileries.

On Queen Victoria's nineteenth birthday she counted the 'VERY GREAT BLESSINGS' she had received during her wonderful year, ingenuously balancing the gain of a Prime Minister's friendship against the loss by death of old Louie, Princess Charlotte's former dresser and afterwards the house-keeper at Claremont, who spoilt little Drina so lovingly as a child. It always seemed quite natural to Queen Victoria to speak of servants and Ministers in the same breath. To say that she loved them equally was a compliment to the latter. Old Louie had been the first to show her the astounding effect obtainable by dignity and grace, even when beauty was absent. Queen Victoria saw her in imagination 'standing in my room of an evening, dressed in her best, holding herself so erect, as she always did, & making the low dignified curtsy so peculiar to herself'.

The Duchess of Kent chose for her daughter's nineteenth birthday present a copy of *King Lear*.

> *I prithee, daughter, do not make me mad:*
> *I will not trouble thee, my child; farewell:*
> *We'll no more meet, no more see one another:*
> *But yet thou art my flesh, my blood, my daughter . . .*

What sort of person was emerging from Lord Melbourne's hands at the end of this first year? The boundaries between childhood and maturity had been crossed only in places. The Queen's naïve humility, which was part of her charm, had survived all the months of pomp. 'I said I did not mind being recognized at the theatres,' she wrote in her Journal, 'but that I feared the people would be tired of seeing me.'[11] Melbourne smiled kindly at her artlessness. She had not yet developed her gift for demolishing an erring lady or gentleman with one look. Her adolescent timidity and kind-heartedness made the task of keeping her maids-of-honour in their place, especially the wild Miss Dillon who needed 'much managing', an un-congenial one. Melbourne urged her to 'start right' – either she or they must govern.[12] The difficulty with the male mem-bers of her Household – most of them much older than herself – was even greater. Queen Victoria disliked telling them they were wrong but Lehzen and Melbourne said she must not be afraid of hurting people's feelings.

She was deeply conscious of her own faults. Starting with good, patient Lord Melbourne, she feared she plagued those of whom she was fondest. Now and then she felt compunction even about the Duchess – 'I am sure I often plague my *Mother* (for that she *ever has* BEEN & *is*)'[13] – but more often the growing strife with her mother brought out the side of her character which she herself called 'passionate' and which Melbourne called 'choleric'.[14] They both meant the same thing – hot-tempered.

An uncontrollable temper was Queen Victoria's greatest burden. She often spoke of herself as being, like King George IV, 'naturally very passionate'.[15] Her words have been wrongly interpreted to mean hot-blooded in an exclusively erotic sense. Queen Victoria's passions were robust but she was not in the least troubled with George IV's 'deadly sin' of lust. This limited interpretation of the word 'passionate' has led to another error: the legend that like the female spider she devoured her mate, Prince Albert, and a few years afterwards, insatiable as ever, took another more vigorous partner, John Brown, from the Highland glens.

Apart from Queen Victoria's temper, she was developing a possessiveness which sometimes inconvenienced Melbourne. She grudged every minute of his time spent with the famous Whig hostess, Lady Holland, now nearly seventy, who in turn questioned him suspiciously about what went on in Buckingham Palace. 'Lord Melbourne dines with Lady Holland tonight,' wrote the Queen on February 15th, 1838; 'I WISH he dined with me!' Nevertheless she often asked Melbourne whether he was not bored spending so much time with her, to which he always replied with tears in his eyes, 'Oh! no!'

Hardworking, dutiful, conscientious; full of kindness and animal spirits; still shy and modest, sometimes diffident; capable of loyalty and affection so fierce that there was a danger of jealousy and partisanship – this was the nineteen-year-old girl who went to be crowned in Westminster Abbey on June 28th, 1838.

London was awake most of the night before. For days there had been din of hammers, dust of scaffolding and bits falling on people's heads. The town was all mob, the Park all encampment. People were meeting friends up from the country. 'We are all mad about the Coronation, raving mad,' remarked a Londoner as he welcomed his niece from the country at Charing Cross. At midnight the bells rang in the Coronation and the crowds shouted it in until daybreak. Even those who were not sleeping out rose with the dawn and many ladies in silk and satin, protected only by thin shawls, found themselves at six o'clock in the morning shivering in the windy Abbey cloisters until the doors opened at seven.

Queen Victoria slept badly. Not unnaturally she had spent several days before feeling unwell. 'Oh, you'll like it when you are there,' said Lord Melbourne.[16] He was shown the crown and ordered by Victoria to make sure that the Archbishop of Canterbury put it on firmly. During the homage she understood that each peer had to touch the crown. Lord Melbourne was very funny about this. She heard that one hundred and sixty more peers were coming to her Coronation than had attended the last one; Parliament was making a splash, spending £200,000 compared with £50,000 on King William IV. Melbourne kept up the Queen's spirits with titbits of gossip. One peer had asked whether he'd be missed if he shirked the ceremony. Melbourne replied: 'I can tell you the Queen will certainly miss you and ask why you are not there.' 'Oh! then I'll go,' said the shirker. Only two peers knew how to put on their robes properly, Lords Wilton and Mulgrave; they had both taken part in theatricals.[17]

All the Queen's ladies were in a fuss over their Coronation dresses. The Duchess of Richmond had chosen the design for the young train-bearers without consulting their mamas. Poetically beautiful in white and silver trimmed with roses and crowned with wreaths of silver corn, their gowns unfortunately had trains of their own which impeded them in carrying the Queen's. When the time came they frequently pulled her up short and were severely scolded for their clumsiness by the Mistress of the Robes.

The Queen had been awakened at four o'clock by the guns

in the Park and was kept awake by music and shouting until she rose at seven, 'feeling strong & well'. She took two bites at her breakfast, one before and one after dressing, and at ten o'clock stepped into her State coach. There had been some difficulty about getting the cream ponies from Hanover, but anything else in the State coach, said Melbourne, would look like rats or mice. Those inside the Abbey heard the salute of guns to show that she had started. The wind and rain which had chilled the ladies in the cloisters four hours earlier, vanished. Glorious sunshine – 'Queen's weather' as it came to be called – flooded the route, warming thousands of cheering people, some of whom the Queen feared would be fatally crushed in the vast press. '. . . I really cannot say *how* proud I feel to be Queen of *such* a Nation,' she wrote in her Journal afterwards, needing no Uncle Leopold to teach her patriotism.[18]

Wearing a diamond circlet, the Parliament Robes of crimson velvet furred with ermine, bordered with gold lace and fastened with a tasselled golden cord, Queen Victoria entered the Abbey attended by her eight train-bearers. She was 'gay as a lark', said one observer, 'like a girl on her birthday'. But when she saw the towering pillars hung with crimson and gold, the congregation ten thousand strong with the banks of peers and peeresses glowing and sparkling, she clasped her hands, drew in her breath and trembled, glad to throw herself down on the faldstool. The congregation in its turn was deeply moved by the poignant dignity of the childlike figure in the centre of the great nave, surrounded by a cloud of silver and white train-bearers like the vapours of dawn. Young Arthur Stanley, afterwards Queen Victoria's faithful Dean of Westminster, was sitting in one of the galleries. He felt the rails in front of him quiver in the sudden grip of a hundred hands. More than one onlooker felt that there was something pathetic in this flower-like face, scarcely emerged from childhood, belonging to so great a personage. Slim as a girl of twelve and no taller, she added something unique to the splendour of her Coronation.

The Sovereign took the oath to maintain 'the Protestant reformed religion as it is established by law' – an oath which

Queen Victoria never forgot though she did not mention it in her Journal on that day – and was anointed with the holy oil. Leaving the altar she retired into St Edward's Chapel, 'a dark small place', as she called it, where she took off her Parliament Robes, putting on first a 'singular sort of little gown of linen trimmed with lace' and then the supertunica (which Melbourne afterwards said suited her best of all) woven of cloth of gold and silver embroidered with palms, roses, shamrocks and thistles, trimmed with gold pillow lace and lined with crimson silk, for the Crowning. Bare-headed she returned to the Abbey. The supreme moment had come. Seated in St Edward's Chair, she received the dalmatic robe, stiff with golden eagles, and the rest of the royal regalia. Then with a ray of sunshine falling on her head she was crowned by the Archbishop of Canterbury Queen of England. All the peers and peeresses put on their coronets, the silver trumpets sounded and the Archbishop presented the Queen to the people, turning her to the east, west, south and north. The pageant reached its zenith in a tumult of waving flags and scarves, of huzzas and cheers. The Duchess of Kent burst into tears.

After the Homage, the Queen descended from the throne, took off her royal crown 'very prettily' and humbly received the Sacrament. Throughout the hot summer afternoon the intricate medieval ceremony slowly unwound itself until at last the end came with the *Hallelujah Chorus*. The Queen in her Robes of State prepared to leave: 'the Procession being formed, I replaced my Crown (which I had taken off for a few minutes), took the Orb in my left hand and the Sceptre in my right, and thus *loaded*, proceeded through the Abbey – which resounded with cheers . . . I shall ever remember this day as the *proudest* of my life!'[19]

Queen Victoria was proud of her people but not of all those who played a conspicuous part in the ceremonies. As always, she frankly faced the debit side of the occasion and there was a sizeable list of mistakes. Perhaps it was not altogether disagreeable to her that so many of them were made by the officiating clergy.

'Pray tell me what I am to do,' she had implored Lord

John Thynne, the Sub-Dean at one point, 'for they don't know.' The Bishop of Durham, who stood near the Queen, could not help her for he himself was quite lost. Before the Crowning he and his colleagues began the Litany too soon, and near the end of the service the Bishop of Bath and Wells turned over two pages at once. He did not notice his error, told Her Majesty the service was finished and had to fetch her back from St Edward's Chapel whither she had retired. She was shocked to find that in this chapel 'what was *called* an *Altar* was covered with sandwiches, bottles of wine, etc, etc'. Melbourne was so tired by carrying the enormously heavy Sword of State that he helped himself to a glass. According to Disraeli, who was among the Commons, Melbourne held the sword like a butcher, looking singularly uncouth with his robes under his feet and his coronet over his nose. Lord Ward, added this commentator, was seen after the ceremony with robes disordered and coronet cock-eyed, drinking champagne out of a pewter pot.

The Archbishop of Canterbury crushed the ruby ring on to her fourth finger not noticing that it had inadvertently been made to fit the fifth. She got it off again with great pain and only after bathing it in iced water. The Archbishop tried to give her the orb after she had already got it, 'and he (as usual) was *so* confused and puzzled and knew nothing, & went away'.

The elaborate rehearsals of our own times did not find a place in Queen Victoria's Coronation. Only Melbourne seems to have thought of making her try the height of two thrones when she visited the Abbey the day before. Both were too low. Nor was her Coronation distinguished by today's decorous behaviour. Medals were scattered broadcast, peers wrestling with generals for them on the Abbey floor. Melbourne afterwards inquired of the Queen whether it was true that two of her train-bearers had chattered throughout the service and if so, did Her Majesty hear them? Victoria recorded her answer in her Journal with some asperity: 'I said they did; & I heard them.'[20]

Any unusual incident provoked stormy applause. During the Homage, Lord Rolle, nearly ninety, caught his foot in his robes on the steps of the throne and rolled to the bottom. As he struggled to his feet and prepared again to make the perilous ascent, frantic cheering broke out; it became a perfect tornado when the Queen, anxiously whispering, 'May I not get up and meet him?' leaned down and saved him the risk of another roll. That it was Lord *Rolle* who took the toss delighted everybody. Foreigners were assured it was part of the *droit de seigneur* to demand a roll from this noble family in addition to their homage. Disraeli saw the Queen's courteous action and praised her 'delicate sentiment'. Greville acclaimed her as 'the most unaffected Queen in the world'. A lady from the country, however, turned to her neighbour in the stand and remarked how nice it must be to be a queen: 'You or I might save a dozen old gentlemen from a tumble, but no one would cheer us.' Miss Harriet Martineau, that dyspeptic Radical battle-axe, complained that the service erred both in endowing the Queen with divinity and the Almighty with royalty. The whole thing made her feel tired. Queen Victoria might well have felt the same, but apart from aching feet she remained fresh. The crown had weighed her down cruelly. So had that strange, round object, the orb.

'What am I to do with it?'
'Your Majesty is to carry it, if you please in your hand.'
'Am I? It is very heavy.'[21]

Something in Queen Victoria always shrank from the vibrancy of trumpets and after the Crowning she had turned white and red, looking, as someone said, 'as if she would creep under the Archbishop's wing'. She had been saved, however, by the encouraging tears in Lord Melbourne's eyes and the smile 'of another most dear Being'. Baroness Lehzen was sitting just above the royal box and the enthroned Queen caught her eye. 'We exchanged smiles.' She did not exchange smiles with her mother who had made the last months hideous with grievances about her place in the procession.

No one seemed to have troubled to explain to Queen Victoria the nature of the ancient Coronation service. Perhaps there was no one who understood it clearly enough himself. At any rate, the Queen's kaleidoscopic account in her Journal, though vivid and moving, would not have convinced the formidable Miss Martineau that something was taking place at the Coronation which transcended the pleasures of pageantry.

At the end of five hours in the Abbey, Queen Victoria drove home in State. Some considered she looked 'white and tremulous'; Thomas Carlyle, peering towards the gilded coach, murmured:

> 'Poor little Queen, she is at an age at which a girl can hardly be trusted to choose a bonnet for herself; yet a task is laid upon her from which an archangel might shrink.'

Then the crowds dispersed and began to prepare themselves for fireworks in the Park – a display which one small child afterwards likened to the destruction of Sodom and Gomorrah.

Inside Buckingham Palace the Queen still had one duty to perform. An attendant standing at the foot of the stairs watched her gather her skirts and run up to her room to give Dash his bath.

CHAPTER VII

DISENCHANTMENT
1838–9

TOWARDS THE END OF 1838 word got round that
the Queen was losing her girlish prettiness. Miss Martineau,
said to be the ugliest woman in the world, was one of the
first to declare that she began to look discontented; others
pointed out that she was putting on weight. None of these
strictures could equal the young Queen's increasing load of
self-criticism. Many things combined to destroy her peace.
At the centre of the trouble, exacerbating all the minor miseries, was the old, festering sore – her horror of Sir John
Conroy. They still could not budge him. In March 1838 the
thought crossed their minds of sending the Duchess away
instead; nothing came of the idea. If only she had carried out
her threat to stay at Kensington instead of following the
Queen to Buckingham Palace. But as Lord Melbourne observed, Victoria could not really have lived alone, unmarried,
without a lady of her own rank.

One suggestion for getting rid of Sir John emanated from
the Duchess herself. She approached Stockmar with the
abrupt words: 'There must be an end to this; and Sir John
must be sent abroad.' Stockmar replied shortly, 'Impossible'.
Melbourne, he knew, was determined to resist the Duchess's
plot to get 'J.C.' off abroad 'well endowed'. Next day the
Duchess, in an interview with Melbourne himself, again proposed that Conroy should leave her, half admitting that she
had been wrong in the past. Melbourne told the Queen that
her mother's new humility was all put on. Similarly a wish on
the Duchess's part to write to Lehzen and make it up with
her was treated with contempt. Let her send 'this man' away
first, was Melbourne's stubborn refrain.[1] A letter of appease-
ment from the Duchess to Lehzen did in fact arrive a month
later. Melbourne cynically remarked, 'Ah! then that letter
has been cooking the whole time' and advised Lehzen to do
no more than acknowledge it. This would annoy the Duchess,

he added, but she could not complain.[2]

All this malice was profoundly distasteful to the Queen's open nature. She told Lord Melbourne so, who merely said such situations between mothers and daughters were common. They went on to discuss for the hundredth time the 'torments' of Victoria's childhood. Melbourne summed up the Queen's mother as weak-minded and devoid of real feeling: the first time he met her he had never seen anyone with such a foolish, puzzled look. The Queen in turn could not deny that her mother seemed to find something wrong in everything she did, from riding through the crowds in London which she called 'highly improper' to overeating at luncheon. She only came into Victoria's room nowadays to find fault.

Melbourne's scepticism, his rudeness about the Duchess and method of persistently rebuffing her advances served Queen Victoria ill. The dismissal of Sir John Conroy would have been cheap at any price. Had Melbourne seized the chance offered by the Duchess's evident wish for a reconciliation, the Flora Hastings affair would never have taken the disastrous form it did.

Animosities grew apace. The Queen was shocked to find that contrary to Sir John's assurances, the Duchess of Kent was £70,000 in debt and it was only thanks to Miss Coutts's discretion and generosity, who advanced money without telling her own mother and father, that the Duchess's finances were salvaged. Some of the tradesmen's bills continued to be so enormous that Queen Victoria suspected part of Miss Coutts's loan was still going 'elsewhere'. Why did Conroy tell Parliament there were no debts? For the sake of his own popularity, declared the Queen. To cap all, he put it about that the Duchess's financial difficulties were due to her having paid off the debts left by her late husband, the Duke of Kent. Since Queen Victoria, unknown to her mother, was engaged in paying them off herself, this was a bit too much.*

* The Duchess only heard of her daughter's generosity by accident, eighteen months later. Amazed, Melbourne asked why. 'I didn't like to praise myself,' replied Queen Victoria. (R. A., Journal, November 24th, 1839.)

There were constant squabbles between the Queen's and the Duchess's ladies, the Palace rift cutting right through the two Households. The Duchess was even said to be jealous because one of her ladies, Lady Mary Stopford, did *not* quarrel with the Queen. The Queen's maids-of-honour found Baroness Lehzen a sympathetic, motherly figure, while they confessed themselves afraid to speak to 'Scotty', the Duchess's lady (Lady Flora Hastings), particularly as Sir John was so often in her room. Scotty 'plagued' Lehzen and annoyed the Queen.[3]

Queen Victoria's passion for Lehzen, compact of gratitude, protectiveness and misplaced filial feeling, redoubled. She regularly referred to her now either as her 'mother' or by the pet name of Daisy. A few sentences from the Journal show how the wind was blowing: 'Walked, with my ANGELIC, dearest Mother, *Lehzen*, who I do so love! . . . the most estimable & precious treasure I possess & EVER SHALL POSSESS.' 'Dearest Lehzen, or *Daisy* as *I* generally call her . . .' Lord Alfred Paget, having studied the royal climate, also began calling Lehzen his mother which she at once reciprocated by calling him her son.[4]

As for Lord Melbourne, since the Coronation his name came so frequently into the Queen's Journal that henceforth she referred to him more often than not as 'Lord M'.

The Queen's hatred for 'J.C.' kept pace with her love for Daisy. One day in August she heard that Conroy had met with an accident on the railroad; 'upon which Ld. Melbourne *said* – what Daisy & I *felt*, but scarcely dared *say*, & which I won't repeat here.'[5] Their hopes were not fulfilled, but this incident shows how the Prime Minister acted as a catalyst for the Queen's feelings.

After the Coronation was over the criticisms of 'foreign influence' at Court became so serious that Queen Victoria decided Stockmar must go. She believed that 'Ma.' invented stories against him which were circulated by 'J.C.' through the Duke of Sussex. There was the wicked story, for instance, that Stockmar was once discovered by the Duchess sitting in the Queen's room, 'with all the BOXES *open*!!' With his departure in the early autumn xenophobia abated for a time but the Queen was still liable to be attacked for patronizing foreign industry, decking out her menservants in gold lace made in France or herself following the French fashions. Increasing unemployment at home, particularly among the Spitalfields silk weavers, lent point to popular outcry. Melbourne refused to pay any attention. There was not 'THE SLIGHTEST' foreign influence at Court, he said, and if there was it should be encouraged since foreigners had 'no connections'.[6] When the Duchess objected to Queen Victoria speaking to her maid, Fräulein Singer, in German, Melbourne stoutly exclaimed, 'Nonsense'. As for the Queen's dresses, it was impossible to look well in English clothes – all English women dressed badly. 'Things don't fit well, nor stay on.'

This fanatical, closed society in which the Queen was now living, with its twin pillars of Melbourne and Lehzen, inevitably cut her off from other influences which might have let in fresh air.

King Leopold was the most important outside influence to disappear.

Queen Victoria had only been on the throne a few months when the King of the Belgians noticed a new, sharp note in his niece's correspondence. 'My Dearest Child,' he replied to one of her letters in December 1837, 'You were *somewhat irritable* when you wrote to me!'[7] Prince Albert's future was the subject which happened to provoke Queen Victoria at that moment. Two months later she was telling Lord Melbourne that the Duchess and Conroy had blackened her character with Uncle Leopold and Aunt Louise – 'About the basest thing I knew'. But what could you expect? As Lord Melbourne said, her misguided mother hardly knew what Conroy made her do: 'When a woman gives herself over to someone she will do anything.'[8] By the middle of May Lord Brougham had 'undeceived' Uncle Leopold about 'Ma. & J.C.', but it was too late. Her uncle's behaviour was now 'very wrong' over something else.

The difficulty was political. As Queen of England, Victoria discovered that her Continental relations expected more of her than affectionate letters or occasional visits to Windsor. She was required to lend a helping hand whenever they were in trouble. King Leopold begged her in November 1837 to help her harassed sister-sovereigns in Spain and Portugal. Next June he himself was the suppliant. Would his beloved niece use her influence to win justice for the Belgian people in their territorial dispute with the Dutch over the Treaty of 1831, now reaching a climax? Only *great discretion* had prevented him from touching on his own affairs before. But in this emergency he counted on her kind Majesty *occasionally* telling good Lord Melbourne that she did *not* wish HM Government to take the *lead* in bringing about the *destruction* of her uncle's country.

Queen Victoria knew her constitutional duty. Without a moment's hesitation she turned over the King's letter to good Lord Melbourne, who, in his dual capacity of Prime Minister and private secretary, prepared a rough draft in reply, leaving the final version to the Queen.* In this, Queen Victoria conceded that the Treaty of 1831 was not very advantageous to the Belgians. But was it any more favourable to the Dutch? After some sententious remarks upon the sanctity of treaties delivered with all the authority of an aunt to a nephew, she trusted that her dearest Uncle would at all times believe her to be 'his devoted & most affectionate Niece, Victoria R.' Leopold, stretching his famous sense of humour to the utmost, assured his 'dearest and most beloved Victoria' that her letter had given him '*great pleasure and satisfaction*'. It was a relief to find that he had not after all been put aside 'like a piece of furniture'. In November he was complaining again: her Ministers were 'really very unfair'. His letter began coldly: 'My Dear Victoria', and ended without a thaw: 'I remain, my dear Victoria, your affectionate Uncle, Leopold R.' Queen Victoria responded with an even colder douche: she would in future abstain altogether from

* That the final draft, dated June 10th, 1838, was the work of the incensed Queen herself is proved by Melbourne's criticism of it next day; he was afraid that her uncle might think it 'a little severe' (Queen's Journal). Lytton Strachey in his *Queen Victoria* implies that the finished note was dictated by Melbourne.

discussing politics in their otherwise delightful correspondence.

Abstention was easier promised than maintained. In April 1839, when Queen Victoria's nerves were thoroughly on edge over other matters, she accused him of being 'very unjust' to England. King Leopold resolutely maintained a light touch. 'I am glad,' he wrote, 'I extracted some spark of politics from your dear Majesty, very *kindly* and *nicely* expressed.'[9] Her dear Majesty was not to be drawn. 'Though you seem not to dislike my political sparks,' she retorted, 'I think it is better not to increase them, as they might finally take fire . . .'[10] She had won hands down and when next the King of the Belgians wrote a political letter to the Queen of England it was to congratulate her on the spark she had generated over the Bedchamber crisis. 'I approve very highly of the whole mode in which you proceeded . . .'[11] Anything to recapture his lost influence.

This was not to be. The Queen would in future tolerate no interference from abroad, not even from her *padre secondo*. A week after she sent her 'severe' letter of April to the King she was informing Lord Melbourne that whereas King Leopold's influence over her in the old days had been great it was now '*very* small'.

Politically, Queen Victoria's emancipation from King Leopold marked a step forward in her development. Psychologically, it drove her further and further back upon Lord Melbourne and was a regression towards her childhood pattern of the small, tight circle, to which she clung ever more desperately but with a growing malaise.

A multitude of lesser evils plagued and pestered the Queen as 1838 drew to a close. She was worried about her health. 'Was weighed and to my horror weigh 8 stone 13!!'[12] This calamity was the culmination of fruitless battles over diet and attempts to reduce her weight. Beer did not agree with her, nor tea. She liked sweet ale and negus but Lord M. ruled them out as unwholesome. Highly flavoured food also pleased her but again Lord M. said it must be guarded against. Champagne made her giddy; too little wine, however, was deprecated by her Prime Minister who (wrongly) attributed Princess Charlotte's death to being kept too 'low'. No Hanoverian, he added, could flourish on a low diet. 'Moreover the best figure for a woman was fine and full with a fine bust.' In the autumn a report circulated in Paris that the little Queen was ordering her dresses a size larger. Of course this was true, for she 'couldn't endure tight clothes'. How many resolutions had she not made to eat very little at dinner and only half a biscuit for luncheon? In the summer she decided that no luncheon whatever and a good breakfast suited her best. But the excellent resolves were all broken.

Melbourne developed various techniques for reassuring the anxious Queen about her health. One was to attribute all failings to her royal ancestry: her fears of going blind and her sore eyes came from King George III (she once showed Melbourne a stye 'which made him rather sick') and her tendency to plumpness from her aunts. Playfully he would tell her that she had 'a good chance of getting very fat'. Another was to point out that she was at 'a bad age' and would improve as the season advanced.

A kind of lethargy afflicted her. She hated getting up in the morning, disliked washing and took her bath at night instead of before dinner in order to cut down on the dressing and undressing. She confessed to having become quite lazy about dress, to which Melbourne replied, 'That's the feeling of a sensible person, but I shouldn't encourage you.' On another occasion he denounced married women for not dressing at home among their children – 'nothing is so bad for a woman'. Dressing, he added, 'brushes women up'. She did not want to be brushed up, nor even to brush her own teeth. Teeth, she and Melbourne agreed, were a plague. All the same he quoted to her the 'Four Commandments' which Mrs Sheridan had taught to her children. 'Fear God. Honour the King. Obey your Parents. Brush your Teeth.'

King Leopold and Melbourne both urged her to walk if she did not want to get fat, to which she objected that when she walked she got stones in her shoes. 'Have them made tighter,' said Lord M. while Uncle dragged in poor Princess Charlotte again, saying that she had died through not walking enough. In the end Victoria and Melbourne had quite a set-to about it. She complained of feeling morbid in St George's Chapel, Windsor; all her relations were there and she would 'go there once'. 'Do more walking,' advised her kind friend. 'My feet swell,' retorted Victoria. 'Do more then!' Victoria: 'No!' Melbourne: 'Yes!' Victoria: 'Donna Maria is so fat and yet she took such exercise.' This silenced Lord M.

Apart from health, the Queen was becoming dissatisfied with her appearance. Melbourne, teasingly, kept drawing attention to her hair. It was getting darker and he preferred fair hair – it looked cleaner. She feared she had inadequate eyebrows and intended to shave them to make them grow. Melbourne advised her not to, saying hers were very nice. He also praised her ears for sticking very close to her head, unlike those of the Sultan of Muscat, which were no good for hearing.

In the winter her feet and hands were always cold, swollen and red. She covered her fingers with rings to improve their appearance and then found it extremely uncomfortable to wear gloves. Sometimes she tried to console herself with the thought that it was better not to be handsome; at others, with the fact that she still looked superb on a horse. Landseer painted her more than once, sometimes on Comus, a white horse with pink trappings and a blue rosette. Dressed in black and green velvet she would complete the dashing ensemble with a white plume.

Increasing jealousies were at the bottom of this new self-distrust. Queen Victoria now admitted frankly that she could not bear her own Mistress of the Robes, the Duchess of Sutherland, to sit next to Lord M. at dinner because she monopolized him. At this revelation Lord M. ventured nothing more than a smile. In August she proposed burning incense in the dining-room before dessert as they did at Holland House, until Melbourne said it made a worse smell than the one it was meant to cure. Once she plucked up courage to tell Lord M. that she was jealous of his visits to Holland House and later that her affection for him was greater than Lady Holland's. This was a situation with which the connoisseur of gallantry was well able to deal. He 'smiled kindly', wrote the Queen, 'and bowed assent'. A year later, when her whole life had taken a further downward plunge, she taxed him outright with finding Lady Holland more attractive than herself. Lord Melbourne still had the situation in hand. 'Oh! no,' he said.

New Year's Eve 1838 found the Queen thoroughly out of sorts. Her besetting sins had increased during the past year in spite of unremitting efforts at reform. Her temper was shorter than ever; even poor dear Daisy came under its lash and in turn seemed to have caught the Queen's edginess. Lehzen admitted ruefully to having 'a Devil of a *temper*' and shouting at her maids just like Her Majesty, whose impatience with her dressers had become so extreme that she finally decided to employ only two maids instead of three: the tedious business actually got done quicker. This was after a French maid had been dismissed for nearly giving her mistress ringworm. Would the embittered maid go about denouncing the Queen's temper? Lord Melbourne shrugged and said it couldn't be helped if she did.

The Duchess of Kent attacked her daughter for indulging in light books, the immediate object of her scorn being *Oliver Twist*, which was coming out in instalments. Queen Victoria found it '*too* interesting' and was inclined to agree with Mama on the danger of novels. It was a good thing, she felt, that she had not been allowed as a child to develop a taste for them. On other matters the chasm between them yawned wider than ever, as an incident which took place on January 4th, 1839, showed.

Just before luncheon the Queen and her Prime Minister were sitting in the Blue Closet discussing the speed at which King George III used to consume his meals. 'At this moment (I think) Ma. unceremoniously opened the door, but on my holloaing out, begged pardon & retired.' This kind of thing, added Her Majesty, was becoming a habit. Even the Duchess of Cambridge would come into her room uninvited and take a good look at what lay on the table.[13] During the following week the Queen thrashed the matter out and was able to record on January 9th that she had carried her point about Mama not entering without permission. The Duchess did not willingly accept the new dispensation which led the Queen to say to Lord Melbourne: 'I was obliged sometimes to remind her of *who* I was.' 'Quite right,' said his Lordship: such reminders were disagreeable but necessary.[14] A second disagreeable step was taken five days later when the Queen decided on Lehzen's advice to answer her mother in future only verbally, since all written replies were shown to Sir John.

Queen Victoria's mention of her aunt, the Duchess of Cambridge, revealed another sore spot. The Royal Family were now split from top to bottom. Charles Leiningen changed on to the Queen's side after the Coronation, while the Duchess of Cambridge and her children had been seduced into the ranks of the enemy. Queen Victoria's cousin, Augusta Cambridge, a girl of near her own age, was now seldom allowed to visit her alone for a chat. The Duchess of Kent was suspected of wishing to offer her daughter's hand in marriage to young Prince George of Cambridge. She requested Victoria to invite him to stay. After consideration, Melbourne advised against. Not surprisingly, when the Duchess of Cambridge caught sight of the Prime Minister going down a passage at Windsor, she exclaimed: *'Da geht mein grösster Feind'* – there goes my greatest enemy. 'Infamous woman' wrote the enraged Queen.[15] She rounded off many bitter thoughts with the conclusion that she had had an unloved childhood: 'Ma. never was very fond of me.'[16]

Charles Greville has left a biting tribute to the dullness of the Queen's Court. Invited to a dinner party at Buckingham Palace in January 1838 he found that the men, after only a quarter of an hour for coffee, were shepherded back into the drawing-room where they huddled round the door 'in the sort of half-shy, half-awkward way people do' until the Queen came up to talk to each. What Greville sarcastically called his 'deeply interesting' dialogue with H.M. proceeded as follows:

Queen: 'Have you been riding today, Mr Greville?'
Greville: 'No, Madam, I have not.'
Queen: 'It was a fine day.'

Greville: 'Yes, ma'am, a very fine day.'

Queen: 'It was rather cold though.'

Greville: 'It *was* rather cold, madam.'

Queen: 'Your sister, Lady Francis Egerton, rides I think, does not she?'

Greville: 'She does ride sometimes, madam.' (A pause when I took the lead though adhering to the same topic.)

Greville: 'Has your Majesty been riding today?'

Queen (with animation): 'O yes, a very long ride.'

Greville: 'Has your Majesty got a nice horse?'

Queen: 'O, a very nice horse.'

After this experience Greville said he evaded all further invitations to the Palace. To play shilling whist with the Duchess of Kent was a great honour – 'but le jeu ne vaut pas la chandelle'.[17] Years later, however, the Queen told her private secretary, Sir Henry Ponsonby, that she had in fact never repeated her invitation to Greville, because of his shouting across the dinner-table and talking every one down.

In vain Lord M. tried to cheer the Queen by saying that her Court was much more lively and intellectual than King George III's. By the end of 1838 she herself was in a mood to agree with every word Greville had written. She too was beginning to think that the game was not worth the candle. Even Lehzen and Melbourne, her 'DEAREST *Mother*' and 'Father', were unable to shake her out of her growing distaste for Court life. At first Melbourne suggested it was 'all stomach', though anxiety over public affairs no doubt contributed; but when the Queen persisted in decrying levées and drawing-rooms, Melbourne became alarmed. This rebelliousness must be countered. Kindly but firmly he told her that though the feeling was natural she must fight it. 'A queen's life is very laborious; it's a life of moments, hardly any leisure.' George III did himself harm by 'fidgeting for time'.[18] This was a shrewd dig, for Victoria had often told Melbourne that she had a horror of madness. Even her handwriting had deteriorated; she left out words and sometimes wrote so indistinctly that the Prime Minister finally promised to send back all her notes he could not read.

In December the Queen was near to defeatism. 'I felt *how* unfit I was for my station,' she repeated, not for the first time. 'Never think that,' urged the Prime Minister. She must take courage, do her best and leave the rest to fate.[19] At the beginning of January boredom absolutely engulfed her. She had taken to writing in her Journal the single word, 'Dawdled'. Melbourne was away. She spent the evenings in the company of peers and peeresses whom she described in a manner that Greville himself could not have bettered as deaf, stupid, vulgar bores. Melbourne's absence made her think of the time when he might have to resign. His Government, she knew, was shaky and the good, kind man had given her several hints of coming separation. In a gallant effort to train herself for independence she wrote out Melbourne's explanation of corn prices, eking out his 'lucid words' with a plentiful sprinkling of '&c. &c. &c.'

As Queen Victoria and Lehzen sat upstairs together one day talking in muted voices of the precarious future, they both dissolved into tears, the Queen's fears for the loss of Melbourne mingling with penitence for her wayward and peevish behaviour towards the faithful creature at her side. Into this gloomy atmosphere already laden with anxiety, guilt and remorse, broke the Flora Hastings affair like a freak storm. No stroke could have been more cruel, no human being less prepared to meet it with calm judgement, than the despondent girl who occupied the throne.

CHAPTER VIII

'MAMA'S AMIABLE LADY'
1839

ONCE WHEN THE Duchess of Cambridge was being particularly vexatious, Lord Melbourne begged the Queen not to mind – 'the Duchess of Cambridge must be met by a steady course'.[1] If ever a steady course was needed it was during the extraordinary affair of Lady Flora Hastings. Unfortunately the Queen, as well as being herself on the verge of something like a nervous breakdown, was irretrievably prejudiced against her mother's lady-in-waiting.

Lady Flora had always been on Conroy's side and against Lehzen. The coming of Melbourne only widened the gulf. The Hastings family were Tories. 'I don't think there is an ounce of sense between them all,' said Melbourne a year before the crisis broke. The Queen agreed with operatic vehemence: 'E vero.'[2] Whenever Lady Flora returned to Windsor or Buckingham Palace for a spell of waiting, the Queen would warn Melbourne not to say anything in front of her: 'I said (she) was a Spie of J.C.'[3] Mama and 'her AMIABLE lady', as the Queen called Lady Flora in her Journal, had taken to leaving the drawing-room as soon as possible after dinner. Who cared? Lord M., while agreeing that Lady Flora was plain and disagreeable, nevertheless feared it was awkward and made a bad impression.

In point of fact, Lady Flora was not without talent, though her temperament was somewhat reserved and her manner cool. She was the eldest of the Dowager Marchioness's daughters, still unmarried at thirty-two and much loved by her younger sisters. A graceful figure and a long slender neck supported a neat head and delicate face full of expressive sensibility if not beauty. Thin curls fell on either side of her cheeks, her eyes and mouth were small but intelligent. In youth she had possessed elegance as well as vivacity, and her piety was extreme. She wrote poetry and prose, including a long piece entitled 'The Cross of Constantine', of which the following was the last verse:

> *Conquer in this! – when by thy fever'd bed*
> *Thou sees't the dark-wing'd angel take his stand,*
> *Who soon shall lay thy body with the dead,*
> *And bear thy spirit to the spirit's land.*

Lady Flora had composed these words in 1833. They were soon to be all too apposite.

On January 10th, 1839 Lady Flora Hastings came into waiting, having spent the Christmas holiday at her mother's home, Loudoun Castle, in Scotland. She and Sir John Conroy had shared a post-chaise on the return journey. The unfortunate woman had been ill ever since December, so on the very day she returned to Buckingham Palace she consulted the Duchess's physician, Sir James Clark, who was also the Queen's doctor, for derangement of the bowel, pain in the left side and a protuberance of the stomach.

Clark, fifty-one years old, was a Scot who had qualified at Aberdeen University, practised as a naval surgeon, attended Keats in Rome and had been appointed to Prince Leopold, by whom he was recommended to the Duchess of Kent in 1835. He had published a thesis on climate, and developed a mania for fresh air. He wanted a machine to pump air into Buckingham Palace which he believed to be clogged with moisture from the surrounding trees. The Queen roared with laughter. Clark had once cherished a dream of getting his friend Dr Arnott to make a thorough enquiry into Palace hygiene. When it transpired that Dr Arnott believed people might live for several hundred years, given proper ventilation, his survey was banned.

Clark prescribed what he himself accurately described as 'very simple remedies' – a matter of twelve rhubarb and ipecacuanha pills ('one at bed-time') and a liniment compounded of camphor, soap and opium. As one of his scornful colleagues pointed out afterwards, they could do neither good nor harm. The sickness and pain did not abate. The swelling, however, began to subside. From January 10th to February 16th Clark saw his patient twice a week.

The same evening that Lady Flora first visited Clark (January 10th), the Queen wrote in her Journal, 'Ly. F.H. dined.' Two days later she and Lehzen noticed a suspicious change in Lady Flora's figure. She appeared to be pregnant. There is no clear evidence as to which of them saw it first (Queen Victoria spoke of 'we' in her Journal)[4] but judging by the Queen's acute powers of observation and greater opportunities, it may well have been Her Majesty. Their suspicions were not allayed by a conversation with Lord Melbourne a week later.

Queen Victoria observed to him that Mama disliked staying at home these days and seemed afraid of Lady Flora. Lord M. gave her a sharp look 'as if he *knew* more than he liked to *say*': then he announced that the Duchess was in fact jealous of Lady Flora's intimacy with Sir John.[5]

On January 21st they were discussing Conroy again: how he was constantly visited by the Queen's uncles before her Accession and courted above all by Princess Sophia. 'What an amazing scape of a man he must have been,' said Lord M., 'to have kept three ladies at once in good humour.'[6] He was capable of 'every villainy', added the Queen with meaning.

Lady Tavistock was due back in waiting at the end of January. She found the ladies in a hubbub. Sir James Clark had told someone that Lady Flora appeared to be pregnant; they called upon Lady Tavistock to 'protect their purity from this contamination'.* Accordingly she decided to convey her suspicions officially to Lord Melbourne. Why did she take the unusual course of approaching the Prime Minister instead of speaking first to Lady Flora or the Duchess of Kent? Lady Tavistock, indeed, later said that she herself had wished to take up the matter direct with Lady Flora but 'circumstances' prevented her.[7] What the circumstances were she never disclosed. The Queen's Journal, however, throws light on the reason for this fatal move.

It was made 'with Lehzen's concurrence',[8] which almost certainly means, by Lehzen's advice. And why did Lehzen 'concur' in Lady Tavistock's going to Melbourne rather than

* The senior ladies-of-the-bedchamber were expected to be moral guardians of the Palace flock.

to the Duchess? Because she had reason to believe, as we have seen, that Melbourne already suspected the worst, whereas the Duchess had not observed anything. 'She never does,' wrote the Queen.[9]

There was another, deplorable reason. '*I* had observed it,' noted the Queen, 'but not being on good terms with the Duchess, could not speak to her!'[10] The same iron curtain which prevented the Queen from speaking to Mama or even referring to her by that name, debarred the Queen's lady, Lady Tavistock, from direct communication.

Anna Maria, Marchioness of Tavistock, was the wife of the Duke of Bedford's heir and sister-in-law of Lord John Russell, Home Secretary in Melbourne's Government. Thus the Queen's lady-of-the-bedchamber was intimately connected with the greatest Whig family in the land. Melbourne, however, had no great feeling for Anna Maria personally. Bedizened in finery, she had an inconspicuous, crumpled little face like a dressed-up monkey, and a mischievous tongue. Once the Queen, suffering from cold feet, decided to leave her carriage and walk. Anna Maria, who was in attendance, afterwards complained to Creevey that she had got wet, abusing Her Majesty for being 'a resolute little chit'.

Lady Tavistock's interview with Melbourne was indecisive. He advised her to keep quiet and watch; doctors often made mistakes. But as soon as she had departed Melbourne sent for Clark. What was Clark's opinion of the patient whom he had now been treating with rhubarb and camphor for over three weeks? Clark replied that things looked pretty bad morally but he could not be certain. It was agreed between them that the only policy was to wait and see.

The fact of the Prime Minister having conducted these two interviews seemed to give a validity to the ladies' suspicions which they had not before possessed. From this moment Queen Victoria firmly believed that 'Mama's *amiable & virtuous* Lady' was Conroy's mistress. On February 2nd she decided for the first time 'to divulge' the truth in the pages of her Journal:

'We have no doubt that she is – to use plain words –

120

with child!! Clark cannot deny the suspicion; the horrid cause of all this is the Monster & demon Incarnate, whose name I forbear to mention, but which is the 1st word of the 2nd line of this page.'

The first word on the second line was 'J.C.'

The atmosphere was thunderous. Lehzen, a martyr to violent headaches, suddenly on February 12th had an attack of migraine. For an hour she was struck by what the Queen with unconscious insight described as 'a sort of blindness'. The wait-and-see policy was proving an intolerable strain. Sir James Clark felt pretty certain that his patient's condition was due to pregnancy rather than disease. How otherwise, he asked himself, could she continue to go about her duties 'with apparently little inconvenience to herself'? Nevertheless, he could not be quite sure until he had examined her. Having failed to make a satisfactory diagnosis 'over her dress' he suggested attempting one 'with her stays removed'. Lady Flora declined.

Four days after Lehzen's migraine the wait-and-see policy was dramatically abandoned. Lady Portman, senior lady-of-the-bedchamber after Lady Tavistock, came back into waiting in February. Emma Portman was thirty and a daughter of Lord Harewood. She was described as 'gentler than a swan, livelier than a dove'. She approached Sir James Clark with the request that he should inform Flora Hastings forthwith of the ladies' suspicions. Presumably this move also was made 'with Lehzen's concurrence', for it was Lehzen who, after much discussion, hit upon a delicate and discreet way in which Clark might convey this message to Lady Flora. He was to say to her, 'You must be secretly married.'

The interview took place. Clark dropped his bomb with the delicacy which Lehzen had devised and when his patient, 'lightly' according to one source, denied the charge, he roughly urged her to see a second physician. Lady Flora indignantly refused. Sir James afterwards confessed that this refusal finally convinced him of her guilt. In vain Lady Flora entreated him to look at her dresses. She had had them taken

121

in, for the swelling about which she had consulted him was subsiding rather than increasing. In this Lady Flora was probably right, for during the course of her malady the swelling, due to pressure on the stomach from an enlarged liver, fluctuated considerably. This may also explain why the Duchess had not noticed her condition. The poor victim attributed her temporary recovery not to Clark's rhubarb and camphor but to 'walking and porter'.

Clark, however, was no longer open to conviction. He waved her clothes aside and went on clamouring for a proper examination.

Meanwhile Lady Portman had been instructed to seek an interview with the Duchess. She broke the news of Lady Flora's predicament, adding that for the Queen's sake she was not to appear at Court again until her innocence had been proved. That evening, February 16th, the Queen wrote in her Journal that Lady Flora was 'of course' not at dinner: she herself had also 'seen Ma.', who was 'horror-struck'.

Next day was a Sunday. Lady Flora changed her mind. She boldly and sensibly resolved to have her innocence medically established despite the shocked protests of the Duchess who, said Lady Flora, treated her thoughout with all the tenderness of a mother.

Sir Charles Clarke, a specialist in women's diseases, happened to be in the Palace at that moment. He went at once to Lady Flora accompanied by Sir James and Lady Portman. With her maid as an indignant witness, she submitted herself to a medical examination, Lady Portman standing by the window and hiding her face in her hands. (The maid afterwards swore that Lady Portman pushed up to the bedside.)

From this ordeal Lady Flora emerged triumphant. 'I have the satisfaction of possessing a certificate,' she wrote to her uncle, Hamilton Fitzgerald, a fortnight later, 'signed by my accuser, Sir James Clark and also by Sir Charles Clarke, stating, as strongly as language can state it, that "there are no grounds for believing pregnancy does exist, or ever has existed".' She was a virgin.

It was now Lady Portman's duty to inform Her Majesty of this result. The Queen at once realized the magnitude of

122

her blunder. She sent Lady Portman back to Lady Flora with a message of deep regret at what had happened and an offer to see her that very evening if she so wished. Her Majesty also hoped that Lady Flora would remain long enough in the Palace to convince everyone of the Queen's complete belief in her innocence. The wronged lady expressed her gratitude but begged that the interview might be postponed until next morning. In fact, Lady Flora, overcome by her testing experiences, did not feel up to seeing Her Majesty until February 23rd, a week after Sir James Clark's disastrous visit. During this period the situation again deteriorated.

The two doctors were not as happy about their diagnosis as Lady Flora imagined. Sir Charles, especially, was so uneasy that Sir James suggested they should both see Melbourne. Accordingly they called on him privately the morning after the examination and informed him that the opinion given in the certificate was not cast-iron. Though there were many reasons for believing pregnancy did not exist, it was still possible. Such things could happen.[11]

Sir James Clark wished to quote his colleague's doubts when he published his own defence after Lady Flora's death, for his first, mistaken diagnosis lost him many patients. But someone overrode his wishes, for the public never heard from him of the doctor's dilemma. Lord Melbourne, however, told Queen Victoria and she passed on the information to her mother in a somewhat chaotic note written in mixed German and English:

'Sir C. Clarke had said that though she is a virgin still that it might be possible and one could not tell if such things could not happen. That there was an enlargement in the womb like a child.'[12]

This secret episode is important for the effect it had on the attitude of Melbourne and through him of the Queen. After the second message from the doctors Melbourne never really believed in Lady Flora's innocence, which partly explains the callousness with which the victim was treated even after her official exoneration.

While recovering from her shock, Lady Flora sent an account of the scandal to the head of her family, the thirty-year-old Marquess of Hastings. Her letter reached Lord Hastings on a bed of sickness. He rushed up to London with a high temperature, breathing fire and slaughter. Queen Victoria, still waiting to see the victim of her tragic error, felt the ground beginning to shake under her feet. How many people knew of the scandal? she asked her Prime Minister anxiously. Only those who had been told, Lord John Russell and Lord Lansdowne, he answered, begging the Queen to keep calm and at the same time admitting things were 'very uncomfortable'. He was now sorry, he said, that the examination had not been made sooner. Next day, in reply to troubled inquiries from the Queen as to whether things could not have been handled better, he regretted the haste with which the ultimatum had been delivered on the Sunday. The haste, explained Queen Victoria, was partly accidental. Sir Charles Clarke had come sooner than was expected. Lehzen had wanted to wait for another month. Doubts filled the Queen's mind. Perhaps Sir James should have spoken first to the Duchess, since she herself was not on speaking terms? She began to feel ill. 'Do I look yellow?' she asked Lord M. No, he said; just a little pale. Her pallor was due to sleepless nights. Had she been 'too rough' with Mama in the past? Melbourne advised studious civility in the future – because it made a bad impression if parents were ill-treated.

The Duchess of Kent was determined to champion her slandered friend with all the warmth of her nature. This scandal, she felt, was the culmination of innumerable cruelties to herself; it was an insult to *her* as well as to her lady. Sir James Clark she dismissed from her service within a few hours of the examination. Let her erring daughter do the same. A phrase began to appear in the Duchess's letters which was to sound ever more ominously in Victoria's ears. The Queen had 'made no reparation'.

Fortunately the Duchess turned as she often did when in trouble to a most trusty adviser – the Duke of Wellington. The old hero, his hair white but his mind as trenchant as on the day he fought Waterloo, had come to possess for the Royal

Family the moral authority of a father confessor, the wisdom of a judge and the experience of a family solicitor. On the same day, the Duchess and Lord Hastings independently put the same question to Wellington: how could they vindicate past all doubt Lady Flora's honour? Lord Hastings had burst in upon the Prime Minister demanding to know who had slandered his sister. He had already unsuccessfully consulted Counsel with a view to taking legal action. Melbourne assured him on his word of honour that he himself was quite innocent. No Whig plot was afoot. Nothing but the tittle-tattle of the ladies. He advised Lord Hastings to consult the Duke of Wellington at once. Somewhat mollified, Hastings complied.

The Duke gave the same soothing advice to both his clients. They should obey Melbourne and in the interests of H.M., the public and 'the Young Lady Herself', hush the whole thing up. For various reasons, neither the Duchess nor Lord Hastings were at first prepared to follow Wellington's advice. But his presence in the affair offered the best hope of an ultimate solution.

Meanwhile the suspense increased, as Queen Victoria still awaited her call from Lady Flora. At last the day of reconciliation arrived. On Saturday February 23rd, Lady Flora screwed up her courage to face the Queen. A flood of pity swept over Victoria as the poor woman came towards her, wretchedly ill and trembling with nervousness. The Queen took her hand gently and kissed her, expressing sorrow for the past and a wish that all should be forgotten for the Duchess's sake. For the Duchess's sake, replied Lady Flora, she would suppress her wounded feelings. She thanked the Queen.

Queen Victoria now hoped that reparation had been made. With this scene the curtain did indeed fall on the first part of the tragedy. There were few, however, who dared predict that it would not rise again.

On the very next day the Queen noted that Clark was going about looking pale and ill – 'Clark's scotch blood is up' – and those not yet in the secret asked why. Melbourne advised her to keep Sir James in a good humour by frequently seeing him, otherwise he might make a fuss if abused by his colleagues. There was a danger also that Conroy would not allow Lady Flora to let the matter drop. Rightly Queen Victoria suspected that the basic hatred between Conroy and Lehzen would keep the quarrel alive. And the ladies were beginning to gossip.

Gossip, of which a steady trickle found its way into the Press at the beginning of March, was mainly responsible for the new phase in the Flora Hastings affair. True, the Duke of Wellington attributed the initial failure of his mission to the incurable hostility between the Queen and her mother. The Queen, he told Greville, 'has neither a particle of affection nor of respect for her Mother', while the Duchess, when she did receive an affectionate letter from the Queen, said it was not in her daughter's handwriting. But without the spate of gossip his mission might have succeeded.

One question still had not been answered and until it was, gossip would be busy fabricating a reply. Who had started the slander against Lady Flora? If the culprit was Clark, why was he still the Queen's physician? If the ladies of the Court, as Melbourne had told Lord Hastings, they should be dismissed. But what if it were 'a foreign influence'? Gossip fastened upon Lehzen. At a party given by the Duke of Sussex, the Speaker of the House of Commons told Melbourne that Lehzen was the 'snake in the grass' and the Queen 'a heartless child'. In face of all these rumours, the Hastings family made a sudden concerted effort to get at the truth.

On March 7th, the old Dowager Marchioness of Hastings sent an eight-page letter through the Duchess of Kent to the Queen. Victoria described it as 'violent' and 'foolish'. Melbourne advised her to return it to her mother without comment. The letter called upon Her Majesty, in the interests of her own honour, not to suffer the criminal inventor of the recent slander to remain without discovery. It concluded with a telling sentence:

126

'To a female sovereign especially, women of all ranks in Britain look with confidence for protection and . . . for sympathy.'

On the same day, Lord Hastings asked Lord Portman to name the person who had put the suspicion into Lady Portman's head. What communications had taken place between Lady Portman and the Baroness Lehzen? Three days later, after some preliminary exchanges, Lord Hastings' mother delivered a stinging ultimatum to the Prime Minister. As the Queen's adviser, let Melbourne remove Sir James Clark, the author of 'this atrocious conspiracy', from the Palace.

From now on letters of attack and defence, of horror at the hidden culprit's continued immunity and shocked amazement at the renewal of hostilities, flew between the parties. The Queen was shown everything that anybody sent or received, thereby being kept in a perpetual state of feverish agitation. Melbourne was desperately trying to control his own side; to prevent any of the outraged husbands from rushing into print and so bringing about what Melbourne dreaded and the Hastings family craved – a public exposure.

By the middle of March the Marquess of Hastings extracted from Lady Portman a statement that her suspicions had been in no way due to the Baroness Lehzen. As far as the true culprit's name was concerned, he was no wiser than before. Garbled accounts of the scandal continued to reach the Press and excite the public, but up to March 17th all was speculation and hearsay. Old Dr William Allen, for instance, the librarian at Holland House, noted in his diary on the 17th that he did not yet understand the full story: all he grasped was the general line-up, the good done by Wellington and the harm by newspapers who, secretly instigated by Conroy, were goading Hastings to destroy the Court ladies.[13]

A week after this entry Dr Allen's curiosity and Lord Hastings' desire for a public exposure were both partially satisfied. The letter written by Lady Flora Hastings at the beginning of the month to her uncle, Mr Hamilton Fitzgerald, was published by the latter in *The Examiner*.

Lady Flora's letter astonished the world by its frankness. Sir James Clark, she wrote, had been talked over into a conviction that she was in the family way. She had no doubt who was the talker – 'a certain foreign lady'. She had secured her certificate of innocence and the whole thing was a diabolical conspiracy of the Whig ladies to ruin first herself and then the Duchess. Lady Flora concluded with an assurance to her uncle that public sympathy was on her side.

'Good bye, my dear Uncle, I blush to send you so revolting a letter, but I wish you to know the truth, the whole truth, and nothing but the truth – and you are welcome to tell it right and left.'

Hamilton Fitzgerald took the hint. As a resident in Brussels he was aware that rumours about his niece were circulating all over the Continent. In Brussels they had got hold of a tale launched by Stockmar about a 'previous error' of Lady Flora's and were betting on when she would have to 'bolt'; from Vienna came a report that she had spent an hour on her knees begging her Majesty for mercy. Deeply concerned he returned to England, visiting various clubs and private houses incognito in order to test the temperature. Far from discovering public sympathy for the victim, he heard everywhere a cynical view that though Lady Flora had been harshly used, these things happened in palaces and the sooner she was smuggled away the better.

Fitzgerald forthwith sent his article to *The Examiner*. His intervention ruptured the remaining threads of agreement which Wellington had managed to weave. Henceforth it was war to the death. Melbourne and the Palace party were viciously attacked in the Press and Queen Victoria, who had formerly boasted that she did not care a straw what she read, could no longer bear to see the *Morning Post*, *Spectator* or *Age*.

Her thoughts were in a ferment. How could she live without Lord M.? And yet the Tories were resolved to tear him from her. On March 22nd she heard that Melbourne's Government had been defeated in the Lords by five votes. There was still a chance that the Commons would give him a vote of confidence but the Queen was by now too much broken down to face the future with hope. Melbourne was the best friend she ever possessed:

'But *I* am but a poor helpless girl, who clings to him for support & protection, – & the thought of ALL ALL my happiness being possibly at stake, so completely over-came me that I burst into tears and remained crying for some time.'[14]

The vote of confidence was in fact carried and her 'happiness',* such as it was, returned for another few weeks.

The situation between the Duchess and her daughter was becoming intolerable. Every day Melbourne would provide the Queen with new nourishment for the animosity which she now felt justified in indulging. When the Duchess irritated her by looking unattractive Melbourne would point out un-kindly that she was getting old; when she looked well he said sarcastically: 'All these people are stronger than their daughters; I don't know how it is.'

It was the same with Lady Flora: Melbourne insinuated that her illness was not all that it appeared. She was better in the face, she no longer had a queasy look and should not therefore have absented herself from a drawing-room. After glancing at Lady Flora he said to the Queen: 'I think she has got a new Milliner; her dress is better made, shows her shape . . .'

When Lady Tavistock's turn for waiting came round again at the beginning of April things went from bad to worse. She was terrified of Lady Flora and brought the news that Lord Hast-ings might 'call out' her husband; whereupon it was decided that she must at all costs speak to Lady Flora though with-out attempting any explanations. A macabre scene followed. Lady Tavistock followed the emaciated figure of Lady Flora from apartment to apartment of the Palace until at last, having cornered her victim, she was able to stammer: 'Won't

* After the coming of Prince Albert and the departure of both Melbourne and Lehzen, the Queen repented of this word. See below, p. 207.

you speak to me? Won't you shake hands?' 'That is quite impossible,' whispered the injured woman and glided away, leaving Lady Tavistock to regret that she had not taken the Queen's advice and stuck to indifferent subjects. That evening the Duchess of Kent left her whist-table early in order to avoid sitting by Lady Tavistock and next day Lady Flora again cut her. Should the Queen retaliate? Be less civil? 'Be more distant,' advised Lord M.[15]

From then onwards the Queen cut Lady Flora. This return to the ostracism which she had decreed before the medical examination was duly reported in the papers and damaged the royal reputation still further. Troubles were multiplying. Sir James Clark wanted, in the Queen's words, to 'shove' as much as possible on to Lady Portman; Lord Portman threatened to bring a libel action against *The Age*; Mama and J.C. were rumoured to be producing a pamphlet of their own and just as Lord Hastings made up his quarrel with Lord Tavistock, his mother, the Dowager Marchioness, published her whole correspondence with Melbourne in the *Morning Post*.

Queen Victoria was beside herself with fury. She longed to hang the editor of that infamous Tory organ and the whole Hastings family with him. She still referred to her mother icily in her Journal as 'the Duchess', while the Duchess's lady-in-waiting had once more become that '*nasty* woman', 'that wretched Ly. Flo.'[16] For appearances' sake and in obedience to the Duke of Wellington's urgent representations, the three women were still going about in public together but for Queen Victoria even the opera had lost all its enchantment. Mama never ceased to torment her, first wishing to leave early and then staying on to the bitter end.

The Duke of Wellington had become thoroughly alarmed at the course of events. His old heart cared for one thing only: the safety of the Throne, which this 'slur on the palace' was endangering. The Queen and her mother must make it up. There was one person, called by the Duke 'the greatest rascal',[17] whom he believed he might influence. Wellington told the Queen that he intended to persuade Conroy to quit her mother's service. The Queen rejoiced. Melbourne, however, dashed her hopes. Conroy would never obey the Duke, while the Duchess would never obey anyone but Conroy. In this Melbourne was to prove unduly pessimistic.

Sir James Clark was another whose dismissal would restore harmony, but only the Queen could get rid of him and if she did he would write to the papers. Queen Victoria, enraged by what she believed to be Conroy's secret Press campaign, was barely restrained by Melbourne from writing to the papers herself. Lord Portman wanted a 'Committee of Three' to investigate the ladies' behaviour. It was as bad as Queen Caroline's trial, groaned the Prime Minister.

They had all reached the end of their tether, including the Government, which might fall any moment. The Queen was constantly lamenting her lot, Lehzen scolding her for doing so and Melbourne agreeing that royalty must not complain. One day when Victoria objected to the shooting of old horses, Melbourne burst out that he would shoot old men and women too.

There was one person whose removal, if it could be accomplished, would put an end to Queen Victoria's 'torments'. This was the Duchess of Kent.

On April 17th a significant conversation took place between Queen Victoria and Lord Melbourne. It opened with the customary: 'Said I felt so changed; – this year; that I did not enjoy pleasures so much: "Oh! you will, when they begin," he said, leaning towards me kindly.' (The season did not start until May.) Their talk then passed on as usual to the subject of Mama. It was impossible to live with her and yet impossible to live without her – as long as Queen Victoria was unmarried. Suddenly the solution she had hitherto refused to consider clamoured for recognition. The problem of Mama had a 'schocking alternative' – marriage.

Despite her predicament Queen Victoria was still extremely wary of the subject of marriage. Lord M. must understand that she only wanted to *discuss* it, not to *do* it. Nor did she want even to discuss it now. But one day perhaps he would notice a preoccupied look on her face; then he should ask her what was on her mind and she would tell him.

The very next day Lord M. saw the look. 'Now, ma'am, for this other matter,' he began.

'I felt terrified (foolishly) when it came to the point,' she wrote in her Journal; 'too silly of me to be frightened of talking to him.'

At last she plucked up courage to go into the 'schocking alternative': how Uncle Leopold and Uncle Ernest (Duke of Saxe-Coburg) were both pressing her to marry her cousin Albert but how she could decide nothing until she had seen Albert again: a visit was planned for the autumn.

The Queen's roundabout and inhibited approach to the whole subject seems to have convinced Melbourne that she did not really want to marry and this, added to his own doubts, led him at once to raise objections. The first obstacle was of course Mama. 'How would that be with the Duchess?' he asked, meaning, as Victoria went on to explain in her Journal, 'that if I was to make such a connection & then he was to go with Ma., that would be dreadful for me; I assured him he need have no fear *whatever* on that score . . .'[18]*

Melbourne next argued against the Queen marrying a Coburg. Cousins were not very good things, he said; her Coburg cousins were unpopular abroad and hated by the Russians. 'The Duchess,' he added, 'is a good specimen of the Coburgs.' Queen Victoria burst out laughing but assured him that the men were better. 'I hope so,' said Lord M., joining in the merriment. The more Melbourne criticized the more Victoria warmed to her defence of Albert. By all she heard of him he would be just the person. Melbourne then fired his

* The omission of the middle section of this sentence from the published Journal gives the impression that Melbourne feared the Duchess might not approve of Prince Albert as a son-in-law whereas, as the full text shows, his fear was that Prince Albert and the Duchess might combine against the Queen. In other words, the Duchess might be strengthened instead of weakened by the Queen's marrying. This indirect reference to the Flora Hastings story was no doubt cut out from the published text for the same reason that the story as a whole was excluded. It is questionable whether this policy of exclusion has really enhanced the Queen's reputation. The published Journal at present gives the impression that this terrible tragedy passed over her head without casting a shadow on her young life. In reality she was tortured by the affair for many months.

last shot. 'I don't think a foreigner would be popular,' he said, at the same time agreeing with the Queen that an Englishman would not do either. Marrying a subject, as she said, 'made one so much their equal' and created jealousies.

Consciously or unconsciously Melbourne had made marriage seem impossible.

'I said, Why need I marry at all for 3 or 4 years? did he see the necessity? I did not think so, still this & certainly the present state is dreadful; always, as he says on the verge of a quarrell [sic]; I said I dreaded the thought of marrying; that I was so accustomed to have my own way, that I thought it was 10 to 1 that I shouldn't agree with anybody.'[19]

Melbourne had worked with the Queen for two years and he replied without hesitation, 'Oh! but you would have it still . . .'

Nevertheless Queen Victoria was not convinced. Even if she always got her own way in the end, might it not be after calamitous scenes with her future husband? She did not feel that her quick temper had yet been sufficiently mastered for marriage to be safe. It would be better to wait a few more years until her character had improved. In a letter written to Stockmar during a quarrel with Prince Albert two and a half years later, Queen Victoria explained that this self-mistrust had been her main reason for fearing marriage.

So the 'schocking alternative' was shelved. The present state, which the Queen found so dreadful, had to get worse before it got better.

CHAPTER IX

LADIES OF THE BEDCHAMBER
1839

LORD MELBOURNE'S OPINION that Queen Victoria would get her own way against any male colleague was soon vindicated. But whereas he had visualized her outwitting a mere husband, it was the leading statesmen of the day whom she defeated.

At the beginning of May the catastrophe which she had long dreaded, the resignation of Lord M., was at hand. A week after she had finally abandoned the 'schocking alternative' to life with Mama, her Journal spoke of 'new horrors' ahead.[1] Melbourne's Government was in fatal difficulties over the Jamaica Bill.

At this period of her life the restless young Queen was compiling a formidable list of things which gave her the horrors; among them turtle soup, insects, 'cercléing' (going round the circle of her guests), Madame de Lieven, dying young and going blind. To these she now added the Tories, naïvely informing Lord M. that the British Royal Family ought always to be Whig. Yet here were the Jamaican settlers defying the Whig Government's reform laws on behalf of the sugar workers, and finding enough support in Parliament to bring the Government down. On May 7th Lord John Russell told a weeping Sovereign that Melbourne's Government must resign.

Melbourne arrived with a memorandum suggesting how 'the others' should be handled during the change-over. Her Majesty, he said, should first desire the Duke of Wellington to form an administration. If he declined in favour of Sir Robert Peel, the Queen should agree only on condition that Wellington also served in the Cabinet. Of her late Government, she should speak with praise and regret. Towards 'the others' she should show complete trust once they were in charge of her affairs; at the same time she must be very vigilant and watchful. The extreme confidence she reposed in himself (Lord M.) had perhaps got her into the habit of approving measures and appointments too easily.

One more point arose at the end of the memorandum. What about the Queen's Household? 'Your Majesty had better express your hope,' advised Melbourne, 'that none of your Majesty's Household, except those who are engaged in Politics, may be removed. I think you might ask him for that.' Melbourne was thus the first to put into the Queen's head the idea of retaining her Household intact, apart from those engaged in politics.

No doubt Melbourne had his reasons. The last thing he wanted was a contingent of Tory ladies let loose in the Palace, publicizing and criticizing his handling of the Flora Hastings affair. Apart from this natural concern, he knew Her Majesty was in no fit state for such an ordeal. Indeed, one of Queen Victoria's main reasons for clinging to Melbourne was her terror of facing the Flora Hastings affair alone. He besought her to be strong: 'You must try and be as collected as you can and act with great firmness and decision.'[2]

The time had come for parting. It would be unwise for him to stay for dinner. With an infinitely kind look of pity and grief the Prime Minister kissed the Queen's hand and despite her entreaties to come back after dinner, said he had better remain at Holland House. She followed him to the door, tears running down her cheeks. As nothing would stop them, she spent the evening upstairs with no dinner.

'All ALL my happiness gone! that happy peaceful life destroyed, that dearest kind Lord Melbourne no more my Minister!'[3]

Forgotten were her own storms, the peevishness, the discontent. She remembered only the infinite patience, stimulating frankness and warm humanity of her dear old friend. Melbourne came round next day, May 8th, for one last rehearsal before her audience with the Duke of Wellington. He cautioned her against showing too great a dislike for individual Tories. 'They'll not touch your ladies,' were his last words to which the Queen replied sharply that they dared not; she'd never allow it.[4]

Just before one o'clock the Queen left the dear Blue Closet where she always saw Lord M. and went to the Yellow Closet for her audience with the Duke. Wellington found Her Majesty gracious and civil but unaware of her constitutional obligations. Though she understood that Wellington's age, deafness and lack of contact with the House of Commons were reasons for his not accepting the Premiership, she did not at first see that he could not promise to be Foreign Secretary instead; this appointment, like all others, must be made by the new Prime Minister, Peel. Nor could Wellington make promises about her future Household.

The interview lasted twenty minutes. An hour or so later, the Queen allotted the same time to an audience with Peel. She hated every minute of it. The mannerisms of the Leader of the Opposition were not unknown to her but everything she knew of Peel she disliked. It was not that she minded personal idiosyncrasies; after all, Lord M. had a 'peculiar walk' and laughed in loud hoots. Sir Robert's oddities, she felt, were not those of a gentleman: he reminded her of a dancing master, especially in the mincing way he shuffled his feet and pointed his toes. 'You must try to get over your dislike for Peel,' Melbourne had warned her before the interview; 'he's a close, stiff man.'

Worse than stiff, he was 'embarrassed and put out', as the Queen noticed when he arrived. The Duke's account to Peel of his own interview with the Queen was doubtless responsible for Peel's state, but it was unfortunate. His annoyance at once communicated itself to the Queen. In an effort to conceal her own embarrassment she became, as she boasted to Melbourne afterwards, 'very much collected, civil and high . . .'[5]

Nevertheless, the interview began moderately well. Three of the new Ministers now named by Peel were anathema to her: Lord Lyndhurst, for his championship of her mother, Aberdeen, for saying she was a baby in Melbourne's hands, Graham for looking just like Conroy, but she accepted them after frankly expressing her dislike. She also hoped that Peel would not demand the dissolution of Parliament (the Whigs would have been defeated in a general election) but when he declined to be bound by a promise she accepted this too.

It was only when the Household appointments came up that there was tension. Peel explained that some changes in her Household were necessary to demonstrate her confidence in the new Government. The Queen then repeated the terms suggested by Melbourne: no changes except among the gentlemen of the Household who were also in Parliament. Peel replied that nothing should be done without her agreement. He made no comment on her terms.

After the two interviews were over Queen Victoria again broke down, endlessly pacing her room in a passion of weeping. At the back of her mind, however, a faint hope had begun to glimmer. Her impression of Peel, though his coldness and oddness prevented her from making out exactly what he meant, was not that of a victor determined to exploit his success: 'he is not *happy* and sanguine.'[6] Perhaps a demonstration of firmness would change the whole situation? Melbourne had been urging her for months to be more 'decided'. Now she would show him.

Meanwhile Sir Robert had not found the Queen too 'high' and was well satisfied with his reception.

After a night's rest she received on May 9th a letter from Melbourne praising her conduct at the two interviews (which she had described to him by letter) but sounding a warning note. It was true that the Sovereign's Household, according to precedent, was a private not a political matter; but it would not do to break off negotiations on this issue – nor indeed on any other, such as a dissolution of her own distrust of Peel's motives. Peel was not plotting against Lord Melbourne personally; his ambiguous manner was due to reserve not deceit. In a second letter Melbourne assured the Queen that if she based her demand in regard to her Household on the rights accorded to previous Sovereigns, he did not see how Sir Robert could refuse.

Thus the statesmen on both sides looked forward to an amicable settlement with the young Queen.

For her part, she felt herself again alone save for the support of Lehzen, 'ever kind & good'. The last time she had been in this situation was in Kensington when the King was dying, and before that, at Ramsgate when she had typhoid. On neither occasion had she failed to get her way.

Sir Robert Peel was the most cautious of mankind. He began his second, fateful interview by again discussing the personnel of his Ministry – a subject on which the Queen had already promised to be quite fair. Having then tactfully, as he thought, offered her Lord Ashley, Melbourne's kinsman, as her Treasurer or Comptroller (in fact Queen Victoria disliked Ashley), he thought it safe to tackle the thorny question.

'Now, Ma'am, about the Ladies.'

The Queen put the sequel into her own words:

'. . . I said I could *not* give up *any* of my Ladies, and never had imagined such a thing. He asked if I meant to retain *all*. "*All*," I said. "The Mistress of the Robes and the Ladies of the Bedchamber?" I replied, "*All*"—'[7]

Sir Robert was utterly taken aback. 'I never saw a man so frightened,' wrote Queen Victoria to Melbourne gleefully.[8]

He explained that these ladies were married to Whig opponents of the Government.

They would not interfere in politics, countered the Queen, for she never talked politics with her ladies. Moreover, they had plenty of Tory relatives. She proceeded to enumerate Tories related to her bedchamber women and maids-of-honour.

He didn't mean *all* these lesser ladies, put in Peel; it was only the most prominent ladies who must be changed —

'to which I replied *they* were of more consequence than the others, and that I could *not* consent and that it had never been done before. He said I was a Queen Regnant, and that made the difference. "Not here," I said – and I maintained my right.'[9]

There was deadlock. The little creature glared at the tall, discomforted man. Even when Peel smiled, his smile was said to be like the silver fittings of a coffin; now he was just the coffin.

They finally agreed that he should consult Wellington, after which the two Tory leaders returned separately for further discussion. Queen Victoria was on the top of her form, 'in high passion & excitement', as Wellington said, though dignity was preserved.[10] She shocked and astonished him by her childishness – 'Oh, *He* began it,' she had exclaimed, 'and not me' – but even more by her obstinacy and cleverness. He afterwards attributed her ready arguments to Melbourne's coaching. In fact Queen Victoria's gift for repartee was all her own and apart from the argument based on precedent, she spontaneously dealt Peel her most telling blow. 'Was Sir Robert so weak that *even* the ladies must be of his opinion?'[11]

Baffled, Sir Robert withdrew and after more consultations returned to inform Her Majesty dramatically that unless she surrendered *some* of her ladies, he could not go on. She coolly promised to give him her final decision that evening or next morning. Then, snatching up her pen she described the interview to Lord M., ordering him to stand by for action:

'I was calm but very decided and I think you would have been pleased to see my composure and great firmness. The Queen of England will not submit to such trickery. Keep yourself in readiness for you may soon be wanted.'[12]

A few minutes later she was writing to Melbourne again: they were trying to suggest that her ladies were in place of lords. But as Melbourne advised, she would only allow lords who had seats in Parliament to be removed. 'I should like to know if they mean to give the *Ladies* seats in Parliament?'[13]

And with this triumphant *reductio ad absurdum* she impatiently awaited Lord M.'s arrival.

He was with her at half past six and certainly seemed pleased, Victoria thought, with the day's work. 'Lord M. approved all & saw & said I could not do otherwise.'[14] She herself had no doubts. For she believed that Peel's moves represented, not a serious desire to rule the country (for which she was prepared) but a plot to separate her from her ladies, with whom she had gone through so much. To the Tories, the Queen's stubbornness represented a plot to keep, not her ladies but her lord, while Melbourne's support for the

Queen was seen as a bid to climb back to political power through his Sovereign's infatuation. Both sides thus agreed on one aspect of the Bedchamber crisis. It was a plot.

Melbourne found himself in something of a dilemma. He had been ordered by his royal lady to hold himself in readiness – for what? Perhaps for a split in his own party. He told her that he must summon an emergency meeting for nine-thirty that night.

Queen Victoria sat up in her room long after midnight waiting for the fateful decision. It came at a quarter to two on the morning of May 10th. The debate had been fierce, lasting three and a half hours. Those for standing out against Peel were incomparably strengthened by Melbourne's reading aloud the letters from Queen Victoria. The fiery words delivered in Melbourne's rich voice rallied the waverers: 'it was impossible,' wrote one of those present, 'to abandon such a queen and such a woman.' On a wave of chivalry, Melbourne at last swept his colleagues in behind her. They even supplied her with a formula to send back to Peel: his proposal to remove her ladies was 'contrary to usage and repugnant to her feelings'.

There was to be one more flutter during the following day, before Queen Victoria was able to settle down again to life with Lord M. In answer to her last message Peel made a devastating point. He pinned the breakdown upon the Queen's refusal to allow even '*some* changes'. The effect of these two words – 'some changes' – on Melbourne as he listened to the Queen reading Peel's letter, is vividly reproduced in her Journal:

> 'He started at one part where he (Sir Robert) says, "*some* changes" – but some or all, I said, was the same; & Lord Melbourne said, "I must submit this to the Cabinet".'[15]

The Queen had previously given the impression that Peel wished to remove all her ladies and here he was demanding only some. The 'Cabinet', however, rejected the possibility that Her Majesty had deceived them and accepted her intuitive flash that 'some or all was the same'.

On the evening of May 10th the Queen gave a magnificent

ball in Buckingham Palace in honour of a royal guest, the Tsarevitch Alexander, Hereditary Grand Duke of Russia. Before his arrival she had as usual lamented the trouble involved in Court ceremony but when the ball began it seemed especially devised to celebrate her triumph. She spoke to Melbourne as she made the *cercle*; everybody was whispering about the events of the day, he told her. Peel and Wellington came by looking 'very much put out', while all her own people were 'in such spirits'. Queen Victoria closed her Journal for that night on a serene note: 'I left the Ball-room at a $\frac{1}{4}$ p.3, much pleased, as my mind felt happy.'[16]

Well might her mind feel happy for she had won back, in the teeth of the Tories and the Constitution, Lord Melbourne and his Whig Government.

The Bedchamber Plot is today far more interesting to the student of human nature than of politics. No doubt the Constitution was rent in the course of the Queen's struggle to get her way, but the burning question of 'some changes' versus 'no changes' among the ladies has ceased even to smoulder. The battle of 1839 was the last to be fought on this issue; in future Queen Victoria had to change only her Mistress of the Robes. Today the Queen is not expected to make any changes at all.

What caused the crisis? There were certainly some misunderstandings but these were of motives not of facts. Queen Victoria knew very well that Peel had never threatened to remove *all* her ladies. Yet this rumour got about and she won much popular sympathy for having escaped such a lonely and desolate fate. On the other hand her belief that '*some* changes' were the thin end of the wedge, was quite genuine. Peel's supporters declared that far from intending to remove those of the Queen's ladies who were prominent in the Flora Hastings affair, Peel had had to look up in the 'Red Book' to find out exactly who served the Queen. Victoria did not believe it.[17] Beginning with Lady Tavistock and Lady Portman, she felt sure that Peel would sweep out every friend she possessed down to Baroness Lehzen herself – the 'foreign lady' on whom the Tories blamed Lady Flora's purgatory.

It must not be forgotten that the Flora Hastings affair was the matrix in which the Bedchamber Plot grew; the two did not merely synchronize or overlap; they sustained each other with an interchange of hatred and suspicion. Though Peel denied in Parliament any evil intentions against Lehzen; though Lord Hastings exonerated her in the Press; though even Melbourne gently hinted to Queen Victoria, 'I think you carry that too far,' she remained convinced of the worst. The Tory ladies were already boasting of their 'triumph' over the Queen.[18]

Probably the truth lay somewhere between Peel's denials and Queen Victoria's suspicions. Peel and Wellington honestly wished to make the changes on principle, the latter assuring Lord Tavistock in writing, 'I never thought that there was any trace of malice in these transactions.'[19] The same could not be said of the Tory extremists.

The fairest judgement on Queen Victoria's role was passed by herself, sixty years after. 'Yes, I was very hot about it and so were my ladies,' she said to her private secretary, Sir Arthur Bigge, 'as I had been so brought up under Lord Melbourne; but I was *very* young, only 20, and never should have acted so again – Yes! it was a mistake.'[20]

Lord Melbourne came to regret his part, particularly his failure to warn the Queen that extensive changes would be necessary in her Court. In fact his sin was not only one of omission. He actually encouraged her to hope that no changes at all among the ladies would be demanded. In one respect, however, he did his best to damp down the crisis. Urbane himself, he was disturbed by the raw antagonism developing between the Queen and Peel, both of them sincere and even noble characters who became unnecessarily edgy when in personal difficulties. While the crisis was on, Melbourne tried to soften the Queen's attitude to Peel. Melbourne's chief fault was weakness, his supreme disservice to Queen Victoria in continually urging her to be firm and decided. Her naturally determined character needed no pushing in this direction.

Sir Robert Peel was a curious foretaste of Prince Albert. He had all the strength which Melbourne lacked. After Prince Albert succeeded in interpreting Peel to the Queen, she came to see in him her greatest Prime Minister of all; but his gifts appealed at first sight to men rather than women and his strained, gauche manner was partly responsible for the Bedchamber crisis. Queen Victoria interpreted it as a sign of double-dealing. Apart from Peel's physical limitations, which after all were not his fault, he made a mistake in hurrying the Queen. As Melbourne sagely observed, when a person is angry you must give them time.

The Bedchamber Plot knocked more paint off the Queen's battered image. Stockmar, who was abroad, did not help matters by suggesting that Queen Victoria, like her grandfather King George III, had gone mad. Though there was popular enthusiasm over her fight to keep her friends, Society became more hostile than ever. The Queen felt it deeply. She grew thinner – a slight compensation perhaps for her sufferings – and for weeks went on brooding over the old problems. Did the Tories eventually mean to take *all*? Had she damaged Melbourne's position? She denounced everybody, including the faithful Duke of Wellington, and when Melbourne told her Peel was very hurt, she simply denied it. 'I felt thoroughly upset with my situation,' she wrote in her Journal on May 14th and a few days later she announced to Lord Melbourne that she was going to be ill. 'Oh! no, you won't,' said he.[21] Melbourne was right. It was Flora Hastings who, at the end of the month, was desperately sick.

This first great political crisis of Queen Victoria's reign took place, fantastically, against the gayest possible background. The young Queen's stamina was remarkable. The week of crisis had been crowned by what might be called the Bedchamber Ball; during the following week she entertained the Russian Grand Duke with a theatre, two concerts, a reception and another ball. 'The Queen for ever! Bravo!' shouted the people as she drove through the streets to her parties. Her only complaint of weariness was made on the first day: 'Really all these Fètes in the midst of such very serious & anxious business are quite overwhelming.'

Several things had brought about this new pleasure-loving mood. Revulsion from the memory of her recent ordeal;

another birthday, making her cling to her youth ('this day I *go out of my teens* & become 20!'); above all, Russian gaiety and the Russian Grand Duke. Quite deliberately she watched herself falling in love with him, calmly noted King Leopold's disapproval expressed in a crusty letter and summed up her new feelings in a revealing remark to Lord M.: 'I said all this excitement did me good.' Melbourne, unexpectedly crusty too, pointed out that she might suffer for it afterwards.

Queen Victoria could think only of the sweet smile on her tall visitor's face, his warm 'shake hands' and especially his masterful dancing. At the next ball there was a mazurka, which Queen Victoria had never danced before:

> 'the Grand-duke is so very strong that in running round, you must follow quickly, and after that you are whisked round like in a Valse, which is very pleasant.'[22]

They ended with the *Grossvater*, a German country dance which Victoria had never even seen. It was excessively amusing, with the men jumping over a pocket handkerchief, some of them always falling down and the Grand Duke splitting his sides. When the Queen and her towering partner had to creep under the handkerchief, the Grand Duke caught his hair in her wreath. 'I never enjoyed myself more. We were all so merry; . . . I got to bed by a ¼ to 3 but could not sleep till 5.' Was she thinking of the Grand Duke, trapped by his mane in her toils? 'I really am quite in love with the Grand-duke; he is a dear, delightful young man.' And after he had gone – 'I felt so sad to take leave of this dear amiable young man whom I really think (talking jokingly) I was a little in love with . . .'[23]

The Grand Duke's sad leave-taking coincided with the news of another more welcome departure.

Ever since the Duke of Wellington's failure to hush up the Flora Hastings affair he had been working patiently to get rid of Conroy. At last at the beginning of June he succeeded. Sir John resigned from the Duchess of Kent's Household and prepared to quit the country.

How did His Grace do it? asked the incredulous Greville.

Partly by flattery: he sent Sir John a coveted invitation to a party on May 18th (Queen Victoria thought this 'schocking') where J. C. had the satisfaction of cutting Lord M. dead. When Conroy finally told Wellington he had decided to go, the Duke warmly congratulated him:

> 'I cannot but think that you are quite right in the Course which you have taken, and considering the sacrifices which you make, and that it is liable to misrepresentation it is an Honourable and a Manly course.'[24]

This letter the Duke ironically described to Lord Liverpool as a *'Pont d'Or'* over which Sir John might retire to the Continent.

With the end of Sir John Conroy a chapter in Queen Victoria's life closed. At intervals she was to hear from him or his family again, mostly with pleas for positions or pensions to rescue them from the distress into which his extravagance had plunged them. But from the day in June when he left the Duchess's service, the way was clear for reconciliation between the Queen and her mother.

The Conroy tale did not end happily. During the next ten years Conroy made repeated, angry demands for the Irish peerage promised by Melbourne in 1837. Prince Albert, strongly supported by the Prime Minister of the day, refused; for the peerage would have given Sir John access to the Court, a thing Queen Victoria would never allow. In 1848 Sir John's stewardship came under suspicion: he received a letter from the Cambridges' and Gloucesters' lawyer asking what had happened to Princess Sophia's money. She left only £1,607.19.7 in the bank and yet her savings were enormous, her expenses trifling. Sir John had nothing to say.

Two years later the Duchess of Kent's Comptroller, Sir George Couper, who had taken over from Conroy, went into the Duchess's old accounts which had been locked in two chests in the Clarence House library. A deplorable situation was revealed. The Household accounts had been kept up to 1829 and then no more. Where was the £16,000 given to the Duchess by King Leopold? It was never paid into Coutts's Bank. Conroy, said Couper, could not have presented accounts without condemning himself. The Duchess, alas, had not signed the accounts even when they were kept. She blamed herself. 'I BLAME myself *severely* that I was so blind and so *inactive*.'[25]

Her private accounts were in a locked portmanteau. With a sinking heart she opened it herself. These also ended at 1829, which explained why Sir John had always either denied the Duchess's debts or boasted that she did not apply to Parliament for their payment. If she had applied it would have been necessary to produce accounts. Sir John's dishonesty had prevented the Duchess from getting the help from Parliament which her small allowance would have justified.

In another four years Conroy was dead. Sums given to the Duchess and not accounted for were now found to reach at least £60,000: £50,000 from King Leopold and £10,000 from King William in 1834. Conroy's family, left in sad straits, were assisted by the Duchess until her own death and afterwards by the Queen. The last request came in 1887 from Conroy's third son, Sir Henry. He applied to be Keeper of the Tennis Court. He was seventy and the post had been abolished several years before.

On the death of Sir John on March 1st, 1854, the Duchess of Kent and her daughter exchanged poignant letters. The Duchess made no effort to hide the shock caused by 'the death of this man, who has been for MANY, MANY years with me . . . and who has been of great use to me, but unfortunately has also done great harm!'

Queen Victoria replied with tender understanding of the shock, and concluded with the words:

'I will not speak of the *past* and of the many sufferings he entailed on me by creating divisions between you & me wh. wd. never have existed otherwise; they are buried with him. For his poor wife & Children I am truly sorry. *They are now free* from the *ban* wh. kept them from ever appearing before me!'[26]

When in 1861 the Duchess died, Queen Victoria was overwhelmed with remorse by what she read in her mother's diaries. The extent and depth of the Duchess's devotion to herself took her by surprise. How could she have told Lord Melbourne, as she did in 1838, that Mama never really loved her?

In the light of all these facts, it is doubtful whether the Duke of Wellington would have persisted in his view that the Queen's dislike of Conroy and breach with her mother were 'unquestionably owing to her having witnessed some familiarity between them'. The Duke gave this opinion to Charles Greville on August 15th, 1839, and Greville's diaries have since spread the belief that Conroy and the Duchess were lovers. It is time to look at this question once more.

The Duke's opinion was probably shared by Lord Melbourne. Too well bred to discuss it openly with Queen Victoria, he nevertheless seems to have made insinuations. When, for instance, the Queen once pointed out that King Leopold could have put a stop to Conroy if he had exerted himself, Melbourne objected that the Duchess and King Leopold had power over each other[27] – implying that the existence of Leopold's mistress, Caroline Bauer, created a mutual blackmail. His observation to Victoria, already quoted, that 'when a woman gives herself over to someone she will do anything', is also suggestive; so is Caroline Norton's assumption that Queen Victoria believed in her mother's misconduct.[28] As one of Melbourne's close associates, Mrs Norton probably got this impression from him.

Conroy's coarse, familiar manner with women was a matter of common knowledge. It was this which turned the Leiningens against him. As guests of Queen Victoria at the Palace, they shared a sitting-room with the Duchess and were disgusted by Conroy's 'insolence' in barging in whenever he felt like it. And it was this to which the Queen herself attributed the rumours of the liaison – 'Sir John's own behaviour'. When she read the later Greville diaries in the 'eighties, she was horrified to find that her debarring of Conroy from Court had strengthened the false rumours. She asked the Duchess of Abercorn whether this was indeed the case. The Duchess had to reply that it was. How could such a thing be believed? exclaimed the Queen; Mama's piety alone would have made it impossible.

The evidence against the existence of an immoral union is strong. Queen Victoria afterwards explicitly denied it. This in itself might not be conclusive, though in view of the Queen's regard for truth her denial should be respected. Her extraordinary revulsion against this period of her life may in part be due to her having for a time tacitly accepted the slur put upon her mother.

The Duchess's moral principles were genuine, as Queen Victoria realized as soon as she had emerged from the miasma of 1839. Amid the welter of remorse in which the Duchess indulged after the discovery of Conroy's dishonesty, she never wrote a word to suggest that she repented of anything but her own extreme carelessness, her blind trust in Conroy and his offensiveness to her daughter. The correspondence between the Duchess and the Queen must surely have taken a very different form had the Duchess been repenting of adultery. She would hardly have insisted up to the last that Conroy had been 'very useful to her'. Nor would Queen Victoria have wasted sympathy on her mother's 'shock' at his death.

Again, in the innumerable criticisms of Conroy and the Duchess, many of them exceedingly harsh, which Queen Victoria made between 1837 and 1839 to Lord Melbourne and recorded in her Journals, her anger was exclusively directed against their cruelty to herself, never to their fondness for one another. A *certain wicked person's* conduct to me before I came to the throne' was a typical formula for describing Conroy's sin.[29] Her own sufferings both as Princess and Queen, both in spirit and in pocket, from 'that man' are enough to account for the bitterness which so much impressed Wellington.

The epitaph on Sir John Conroy may be taken from a letter written to Queen Victoria by King Leopold in 1864: 'such an extraordinary character one will not easily find again'.[30]

At the same time as the Duke of Wellington discussed Conroy's resignation with the Duchess of Kent, tactfully praising his contribution to 'the Peace of the Palace', he again entreated her to make up her own quarrel, particularly with 'the Minister' and 'the Favourite'.

The Duchess frowned. 'Am I to court Melbourne?' she asked defiantly. Wellington replied with a touch of diplomatic flattery. 'Ladies know better than we do how to manage these matters . . .' The Duchess was not appeased. She disapproved, she said, of Melbourne's being so much with the Queen. 'Nonsense – all stuff and nonsense,' retorted the Duke. 'He is quite right. I'd have come more; moved into Kensington Palace instantly and then moved to Buckingham Palace.'

The Duchess accepted this but turned her attention to 'the Favourite'. 'What should she do if her daughter said, "Mama! I wish you would shake hands with Lehzen."?' 'Take her into your arms and kiss her!' answered Wellington, hastily adding as he noticed the Duchess's look of horror, 'I don't mean Lehzen but the Queen!'[31] The poor Duchess collapsed in roars of hearty, German laughter.

This time the Duchess made an effort to take Wellington's advice. At first the embittered figure of Lehzen stood in her way. Far from asking Mama to shake hands with her dearest treasure, Queen Victoria was persuaded by Lehzen that the whole thing was a put-up job. Sir John, said Lehzen, was only going away in order to show the Duchess that she could not do without him. Lehzen and the Queen agreed that the Duchess would be no better after Conroy had left: she was 'irredeemable'.[32] The Queen admitted in her Journal to feeling utterly callous about Mama. She told 'stories' to avoid going out with her, a drastic procedure which made the truthful Queen blush. 'I felt I was often in the wrong.'[33] Intermittently even Melbourne advised her to make advances to the Duchess but the Queen said she couldn't.

The Duchess's good intentions were further chilled by the Queen's attitude to a sudden worsening in the condition of Lady Flora Hastings. During May the unhappy woman had gallantly continued to attend public functions, although her condition was clearly desperate, in order to disprove the persistent rumours that she was with child. She was applauded at the opera, at a wedding and elsewhere, while Melbourne and the Queen were hissed.

On June 7th when the Queen inquired why Lady Flora had not appeared for several days, she was told the lady was too ill, her symptoms being acute sickness. Queen Victoria of course passed on this news to Melbourne and recorded his reaction in her Journal:

'"Sick," said Lord M. with a significant laugh.'

The Queen sent kind inquiries only 'after great gulping'. At the same time she felt disgusted with herself – 'weak, low, cross & hot'.[34] Melbourne recommended a good glass of wine. But instead of something to cheer her the Queen was given a hissing at Ascot. As she and the Prime Minister rode up the course two ladies in the grandstand were heard to hiss and when the Queen appeared smiling on a balcony there were cries of 'Mrs Melbourne'. Melbourne's friend, Mrs Norton, afterwards informed him that the offending ladies were the Duchess of Montrose and Lady Sarah Ingestre – two Tories. It was indignantly denied but Lady Lichfield, having sat directly behind them, confirmed the story, adding that she herself had called out 'Order! order!' Queen Victoria went scarlet with rage when Melbourne described the incident to her and wanted to flog them. 'Peel is a stupid, underbred fellow,' said Melbourne of the Tories' leader.[35]

A week after Lady Flora's 'bilious attack' she was no better; 'odd', said Lord M.[36] Then they heard she had a fever and could eat nothing. The Duchess was desperately anxious for her daughter to postpone a forthcoming ball out of respect for the invalid. The Queen agreed to do so and Melbourne approved: 'As you say, ma'am, it would be very awkward if that woman was to die,' but he still seems to have thought she would die in childbed, if at all.[37]

Everything was going wrong again at once. Lord Hastings, having maintained an interval of silence, suddenly demanded from Melbourne an apology for a curt letter he had sent to his mother, the Dowager Marchioness, in March. Lord Rosslyn delivered the ultimatum and there would have been a duel if Melbourne had not climbed down. At the same time Lady Flora's swelling returned – 'a deuced unlucky thing', Lord M. said. It meant a post-mortem if she died, to prove that she was not pregnant. He could not see the point of one; these things happened in families; why make such a fuss?[38]

150

Notwithstanding Melbourne's bravado he and the Queen discussed little else but Lady Flora. As her end drew manifestly nearer, the Queen at last listened to her conscience and did all she could for 'this unfortunate Lady Flora'.[39] On June 26th she suggested a visit, but though her offer was gratefully accepted, Lady Flora was not well enough to see her that day. The Queen hoped she did not suffer but feared she must.

Next day Her Majesty arranged to 'run down' when they knocked to tell her Lady Flora was ready. Her Journal continued:

'I found poor Ly Flora stretched on a couch looking as thin as anybody can be who is still alive; literally a skeleton, but the body *very* much swollen like a person who is with child; a searching look in her eyes, rather like a person who is dying; her voice like usual, a good deal of strength in her hands; she was friendly, said she was very comfortable, & was very grateful for all I had done for her; & that she was glad to see me look well. I said to her, I hoped to see her again when she was better, – upon which she grasped my hand as if to say "I shall not see you again".'[40]

The Queen had always felt a horror of death but also a duty to become accustomed to it. In all the circumstances her visit to Lady Flora, undertaken quite alone and at her own desire, was an act worthy of remembrance.

On July 4th she heard that Lady Flora was unconscious. She put off her dinner guests, dining alone with her Household and Lord Melbourne. At nine o'clock in the morning of the 5th Lehzen came to her bedside with the melancholy news that Lady Flora had died a little after two: 'the poor thing died without a struggle & only just raised her hands & gave one gasp . . .'[41]

The result of this tragic death was another flare-up of public scandal. The post-mortem, which Lady Flora had desired and which her family agreed to have performed by anyone but Sir James Clark, showed that she had been suffering from a tumour on the liver for many months. Nevertheless, her friends went about saying that she had died from a broken heart and indicating who had broken it. Press attacks multiplied. The Hastings family returned to Her Majesty a gift of £50 presented to Lady Flora's maid after the death and also called in two bracelets of Lady Flora's hair given at one time by the Queen to her ladies. A duel was actually fought between the Tory MP for Canterbury, who grossly insulted Her Majesty in a speech, and the Whig MP for Cockermouth. No damage was done, except of course to the Court. The Queen thought it worthwhile to record in her Journal an occasion when she and Melbourne had ridden in Rotten Row *without* one *hiss*.

There were other public occasions when Her Majesty's name was received in silence equally offensive. At a dinner in Nottingham, Sir Charles Napier, the distinguished soldier, reported that only one voice had responded to the loyal toast – his own. So calamitously had the young Queen become embedded in a decaying, partisan cause, Whiggery.

Melbourne was inclined to advise the Queen against sending a carriage to Lady Flora's funeral for fear of hostile demonstrations. Queen Victoria, however, insisted and was rewarded by nothing worse than a few stones thrown at the royal equipage, as with twenty others at four o'clock in the morning it followed the cortège to the wharf. Sophia Hastings, Lady Flora's sister, reported that a man in the crowd exclaimed, 'What is the good of her gilded trumpery after she has killed her?' The Press made much of her funeral. It took place at Loudoun. Five thousand people assembled with tears 'glistening down their cheeks'. Next Sunday the Rev Norman Macleod, the Presbyterian minister, preached to a packed congregation on the shortness of life and especially of Lady Flora's. By a strange coincidence Dr Macleod's sermons later captured the heart of the widowed Queen Victoria at Balmoral.

Many poetic tributes like the following were paid to the departed:

> *She knew that she was dying,*
> *But she dreaded not her doom*

and Lady Flora herself had written some lines before death entitled *Swan Song:*

> *Grieve not that I die young. Is it not well*
> *To pass away ere life hath lost its brightness . . .*[42]

On September 14th the irreconcilable Lord Hastings gave to the Press a mass of new material, including the first prescription Sir James Clark had made out for Lady Flora. It was generally felt that Hastings had now overshot the mark. Sympathy turned to Lady Portman, who had lost a baby through agony of mind. Unfortunately Sir James Clark took this opportunity to defend himself in the Press, whereupon *The Lancet* called him 'at best no better than a go between', while a certain John Fisher Murray, MD, tore his diagnosis and prescriptions to shreds in an analysis entitled *The Court Doctor Dissected.* Had Clark never heard of symptoms resembling pregnancy? – hepatic diseases, diseases of the digestive organs, splenic disease, mesenteric, aneurismal diseases of the abdominal arteries, dropsy, umbilical hernia, abdominal tumours and combinations of two or more of the above? Why did he jump to the conclusion that because Lady Flora's waist was enlarged her morals were relaxed? And so it went on. The Queen's Journal was full of self-distrust. She snapped at poor Lord M., chastising herself afterwards for such shameful behaviour : 'I can't think what possessed me . . .'

The coming of Prince Albert to England two days after the publication of Clark's defence at last turned Queen's thoughts away from a subject which she had come to dread.

How far was Queen Victoria to blame for the most disastrous episode of her early reign? She certainly did not instigate the original inquiries into Lady Flora's condition. She told Melbourne after Lady Flora's death that she and Lehzen had never mentioned their suspicions to anyone. But the fact remained that she was one of the first, if not the first, to entertain false suspicions. In future she promised not to judge by 'people's appearance'. When, as usual, she got stones in her shoes out walking and Melbourne said it was 'a penance', she did not disagree.[43]

153

Between Lady Flora's death and Prince Albert's coming, the Queen dreamt more than once about the dead woman and her *joie de vivre* vanished; perhaps the truest sign of her penitence. She and Lord M. talked about this and that, but the salt had lost its savour. Nothing seemed amusing, not even riding. Politics she longed to get rid of altogether. She hated the country but did not know what to do in London once the opera season was over: 'I couldn't go about like other people, & was always a prisoner.'[44]

Melbourne, too, had a guilty conscience. Why did he ever mention the ladies to Lord Hastings? 'I'm very sorry,' he confessed to the Queen, 'that I didn't say to him, "I'll give no explanation but I'm responsible for it all".' Queen Victoria replied that he had suffered so much already it was much better for the ladies to be blamed.[45] But in spite of the Queen's loyalty, his record was indeed a wretched one. As Greville said, the only justification for his 'domiciliation' in the Palace was to prevent such things happening. He was supine; he was short-sighted if not caddish to drag in the ladies; his uncharitableness kept alive the Conroy feud which was at the bottom of the whole trouble.

The day after Lady Flora died Queen Victoria told Lord Melbourne that when she was out in the Palace garden she longed to roll on the grass. Was it just momentary animal spirits or an irrepressible need to cleanse herself of the past? Two days after Prince Albert arrived in England, Lord Alfred Paget regaled the Queen with a story of 'how the Emperor (Russia) & Empress & all the Grand-duchesses romped'.

A roll and a romp. It was high time for the twenty-year-old Queen to start life afresh.

CHAPTER X

'MY BELOVED ALBERT'
1839–40

QUEEN VICTORIA'S instinctive need for a new life did not mean that she saw at once where to find it. Marriage was certainly not uppermost in her mind. For a few hours in secret conclave with Lord M., she had contemplated it as a 'schocking alternative' to her even more deplorable situation. This was in April 1839. Two months later Sir John left the country and the one after Lady Flora left the world. Ten days later, on July 15th, the Queen wrote to King Leopold warning him that the marriage with Albert was, for the time at any rate, off.

She did not mince her words. She had 'great repugnance' to changing her present state, she was too young and the country showed no anxiety for such an event. She therefore desired her uncle to cancel a proposed visit from Albert and Ernest and demanded a clarification of the position in regard to their 'engagement'. Did Albert know of Uncle Leopold's hopes? (In fact she knew he did.) If so, did he realize there was *'no engagement'*? It was possible, she admitted, that she might like him enough to marry him – 'all the reports of Albert are most favourable' – but then again, 'I might like him as a friend, and as a *cousin*, and as a *brother*, but not *more* . . .' In any case there could be no decision for two or three years ' at the *very earliest*'.[1]

King Leopold was diplomat enough to keep his head and refrain from pressing his niece about her feelings. He held her to one thing only – the visit of his nephews in the autumn. He had taken the precaution over a year ago of summoning Prince Albert to Brussels and telling him how the land lay. Prince Albert had agreed to wait provided his cousin would marry him in the end; for if several years passed and she then refused him, what chance would he stand of winning an eligible wife? All the best princesses would long ago have been snapped up.

Queen Victoria saw the reasonableness of this plea, quoting it later to Melbourne. Melbourne agreed that it wouldn't be right to keep a man dangling, but there was no harm in the Queen just seeing her cousins. As for marriage – 'It is *not* NECESSARY,' said Lord M. emphatically.[2]

The Queen's success with the Russian Tsarevitch had undoubtedly raised her standards. Everything that reminded her of Ascot week was delightful. 'Ah, Lady Lyttelton, this room, this music – ain't it like *old times*?' she exclaimed at a dance in August when they played her favourite tune, *Gays Loisirs*, introduced by the Tsarevitch.[3] Perhaps Lord Alfred Paget also had something to do with this awakening. The number of times that Queen Victoria assured Lord Melbourne she couldn't and wouldn't marry a subject – 'it would never do' – suggests that she was not impervious to her subjects' charms.

What had the colourless companionship shared with Prince Albert for a brief moment at seventeen, to offer her now? One day during Prince Albert's first visit Lord de L'Isle had watched the Princess and her cousin walking together in the garden of Kensington Palace and wondered whether the pair were lovers or just good friends. Far from being lovers, the cousins never even mentioned the possibility of an engagement during the whole visit. Nor had a word on the subject been exchanged between them since. All the approaches were mediated by King Leopold and Stockmar. If ever a marriage was entirely 'arranged', it looked as if this one would be.

Such a conventional procedure, however, had become repugnant to Queen Victoria. When she heard that young Princess Sophie of Württemberg had married the despised Prince of Orange, she was aghast. 'I couldn't understand the wish of getting married,' she wrote, 'amounting to marrying any one.' Melbourne later put the case for arranged marriages. 'Better to be led a little,' he said, adding that such matches did much better than those of choice.[4] The Queen knew his own tragic story of wilful love and tactfully did not argue.

At first the spell of Lord M. had led Queen Victoria to

dream of a man older than herself. Later, her yearning for young partners in the dance and young playmates in the Corridor made her forget the glamour of the old. She even wanted the companionship of 'young relations', which of course meant Germans. Lord M. did his best to put her against the race. For one thing, Germans *smoked*, a crime which both he and the Duchess of Kent agreed in putting down: 'I always make a great row about it,' said he; 'if I smell any tobacco I swear perhaps for half an hour.' For another thing, Germans didn't wash their faces – but the Queen said this would just suit her.

In September the Queen was visited by the 'Ferdinand' Coburgs – her Uncle Ferdinand and her cousins Augustus and Leopold, younger brothers of the King of Portugal, and their sister Victoire. '*Dear dear* young people,' she sighed into the pages of her Journal: how different, how happy life was now. She loved their family jokes and nicknames and soon began calling them 'Vecto' and 'Gusti' instead of Victoire and Augustus. They were all brothers and sisters together, she wrote, Leopold teasing Gusti so funnily and saying to the Queen, when she tearfully lamented her inability to frisk with the old people who surrounded her, '*Nicht mit de[m] Melbourne*' – at which comical picture she broke into laughter.[5]

Another Coburg cousin, Alexander Mensdorff-Pouilly, son of Princess Sophia of Saxe-Coburg and a French émigré, had come with the 'Ferdinands'. The Queen was in ecstasies over this handsome, able, quiet soldier and Lord M. praised his hair, pointing out that no German could have such nice hair. So retiring was Alexander that he could hardly screw himself up to call his little cousin '*du*' instead of 'Majesty'; when he left, he was prepared to set out without a servant in a hired carriage – and he was the Queen's first cousin! Victoria, no snob, was entranced by such modesty.

At last the sad day came for their departure. They rowed out to the *Lightning* from Woolwich and the agile Queen ran lightly up the ship's ladder. 'No help, thank you!' she called to an officer on the way down, 'I am used to this.'[6] On board there had been a great squeezing of hands, kissing and sob-bing. The Queen and Victoire exchanged handkerchiefs and young Leopold was given a little pin decorated with a knight on his knees. When the band played 'The Queen' and the guns fired, Queen Victoria was ready to sink under her grief: 'we were *so* intimate, *so* united, *so* happy!'

King Leopold had thus cleverly set the stage for Prince Albert and a renewal of warm Coburg family life. Melbourne unwittingly assisted. Instead of exerting himself to fill the gap left by the cousins' departure, the ageing man relaxed, showing scant sympathy with Queen Victoria's desolation. He could not understand her cousins' language nor appreciate their boisterous gambols. The Queen roundly accused him of being glad that her cousins had gone. He protested that it was only *young* children he disliked and taunted her in return for being infatuated by Alexander's looks; this she hotly denied though admitting with disarming candour that she was 'not insensible to beauty'.[7]

The Queen's susceptibility to beauty was one of her most interesting characteristics. Whether in men, women, children, animals, landscapes, houses or clothes, she hailed it with an enthusiasm unexpected in one who set such store by sterling worth. Just before her marriage she frequently emphasized her admiration for male beauty, often discussing the handsome figure of one or other of her courtiers. Melbourne tried to damp down this ardour, perhaps because he feared no suitable consort would come up to the Queen's romantic ideals. But she was set on a love-match and beauty was one of the essentials.

The reaction of males to feminine beauty also interested her: the Tsarevitch admired it excessively while Alexander Mensdorff was quite unmoved by it. This was unnatural, said Melbourne disapprovingly, and most unusual. Curiously enough, Queen Victoria was to find that Prince Albert, her chosen lover, shared his cousin Alexander's 'unnatural' immunity. She was well aware of the limitations to her own charms and was fortunate to discover men, who outstandingly handsome themselves, did not demand comparable beauty in ladies.

King Leopold joined Melbourne in deprecating Alexander.

He had no wish to see the Queen falling in love with the wrong cousin at the last moment. Nor did he desire her to develop a taste for courtship without marriage, which Lord M. once told her was the trouble with her ancestor, Queen Elizabeth. The King particularly disapproved of her small dances as being too 'familiar'; moreover, she ought to invite some Tories.[8]

The Queen waited impatiently for letters from her departed cousins, especially Alexander. Melbourne teased her affectionately: they were not as mercurial as she was, with her sudden passions. When Alexander's letter came at last it was tender, sad and realistic. Pleasant times passed, he wrote, never to return and things could not be the same again. He was right. As soon as the 'Ferdinands' and Alexander were safely off the scene King Leopold concluded the arrangements for the visit of Albert and Ernest.

Before their arrival Queen Victoria could think of nothing but how to get through the time with the minimum of Tories and the maximum of gaiety. King Leopold disapproved of gaiety but approved of Tories. How would Albert fit into her new régime of 'Gays Loisirs'? She racked her brains for someone gay and non-Tory to meet him. 'Nobody is gay now,' said Melbourne, 'they are so religious.' Then he pressed her, just as her uncle had, to invite some Tories for Prince Albert. The Queen's temper, which had not been sweetened by the memory of King Leopold's criticisms, suddenly flared up, as it often did these days, especially when she and Melbourne argued about religion or party politics. She swept out of the room and upstairs to see Lady Sandwich's baby but even this pilgrimage could not calm her. She returned to greet Lord Melbourne with frigid stares and cross words. Accustomed to seat himself without waiting for an invitation, he suddenly dared not claim his privilege from this angry girl but stood humbly before her on his weary legs. 'I can't think what possessed me,' she wrote afterwards in shame and sorrow – 'for I love this *dear excellent* man who is kindness & forbearance itself, *most dearly*.'[9]

Next day, in chastened mood, the Queen discussed Prince Albert's need for sleep instead of her own need for gaiety.

Did Lord M. know about Albert's habit of falling asleep after dinner? 'I am very glad to hear it,' said Melbourne.

There was much of interest about Prince Albert which neither the Queen nor her Prime Minister knew.

He kept a diary at only five years old and among the things he entered in it were his many childish ailments. His Gotha grandmother had told his father not to let him take too much medicine or hear his health discussed; it would make him nervous. But he was nervous already, having last seen his mother when he was four. The two brothers, Ernest and Albert, had been shut up in their nursery with whooping-cough when their lovely Mama, in tears, rode out of the courtyard and out of their lives for ever. It was a painful story. Tiny, sprightly, bubbling with spirits, Princess Louise had married at sixteen the much older Duke who neglected her shamefully while continuing to pursue his habitual debaucheries. After the birth of Prince Albert on August 26th, 1819, she consoled herself elsewhere. Duke Ernest separated from her in 1824 and divorced her in 1826. She married again but fell ill and died seven years later.

A story survived late into the reign of Queen Victoria and was believed by many of her Court that Prince Albert was illegitimate, probably with a Jewish father. His extraordinary unlikeness to the two Ernests, father and brother, both in character and looks, may partly account for the insistency of a tradition without apparent foundation. The hair of the Ernests was as black as their morals: Albert was pure and fair, with his mother's gentleness and winning manners. From his mother he also inherited a certain melancholy which, however, never subdued his childish gaiety and love of life.

Despite his angelic, other-worldly appearance, he did not suffer from sentimental piety. Brought up in Coburg where Martin Luther wrote his psalms, Prince Albert was uncompromisingly Lutheran, hardened by the rationalist views of his native Thuringia. His unsatisfied, spiritual longings were expressed in music. The perceptive Lady Lyttelton once heard him, after his marriage, playing the organ: she saw something in his face which made her feel that only the instrument really knew what was in his soul. Music affected Queen Victoria in somewhat the same way: even after she lost her first prettiness observers noticed that her face was transfigured and could still look almost beautiful when listening to music.

She and Albert had their love of music in common. In almost every other way Prince Albert was Queen Victoria's complement. His Coburg grandmother had hailed him at birth as 'the pendant to the little cousin'. Except that Victoria was to hang on Albert rather than vice versa, the two young Coburgs did indeed complete each other like two pieces of Victorian jewellery.

At eleven years old Prince Albert recorded in his diary a great resolution: 'I intend to train myself to be a good and useful man.' How different was this from Princess Victoria's, 'I will be good,' said at the same age – the girl's an impulsive outburst made in response to a sudden situation; the boy's a considered attitude to the future gravely set down in his diary.

The childhood of both children was unbalanced, Victoria being fatherless and Albert motherless; but while Victoria's resilient personality enabled her to recover from the traumatic experiences of her youth, Albert's deprivation left him permanently wounded.

It was not only that his boyhood was deprived of any youthful feminine influence; he also treasured the lovely vision of his lost mother, at first resenting all attempts to take her place. Thinking of his mother, he grew up wistfully chivalrous towards women and horrified by the masculine licentiousness which had driven her to her fate. Thinking of his father and brother, he was terrified of the immorality in womankind to which he attributed his male relatives' downfall. His ineptitude with women, due to his youthful experiences, presented Victoria with a problem as Queen (though not as wife) which she was not entirely successful in solving.

Unlike Princess Victoria's childhood, Prince Albert's was at least outwardly free and happy. He was inseparable from his brother Ernest; he loved his severe, self-indulgent Papa, though given no cause to do so; he was devoted to his tutor, Herr Florschütz, who taught him the meaning of a verb by giving him a pinch; above all he adored his home, the Rosenau, a romantic little *Schloss* outside Coburg, hidden in the green heart of a German forest where in summer he could hear the sound of fountains through the open windows and in autumn the roaring of stags. The room in which he was born seemed part of the forest itself: green wallpaper with a trellis of convolvulus. He was enchanted by the simple pattern of country life: hunting, riding, gardening, arranging an Albert–Ernest museum in which were exhibited stuffed birds and shells and the insects which his cousin Victoria abhorred. He was an excellent shot but could not understand the fanatics who made sport into a business.

At sixteen he was confirmed in the Hall of Giants at Coburg, the vast, pillared chamber where the Coburg heart beat strongest. Here Queen Victoria's father and mother had been married; here Prince Albert was catechized for a solid hour. There was no family tension, no awesome agony such as Princess Victoria endured at her Confirmation; Albert sailed through, pledging himself with noticeable enthusiasm to the Protestant faith.

His visit to England in 1836 was memorable for sight-seeing rather than love-making. Indeed, Ernest went home under the impression that he, not Albert, was Princess Victoria's choice. King Leopold quickly disabused him of this dangerous illusion. Prince Albert, who was a far from sophisticated sixteen, thought his cousin 'extraordinarily self-possessed'. Fortunately he was not told the full purpose of the visit or he might have been even more overwhelmed.

At Brussels and afterwards at Bonn University, where the brothers were next sent to escape the depravity of Berlin, Prince Albert was happy and successful. He became a master of the two most graceful sports, fencing and skating. His good-natured sense of fun came out in a talent for mimicry and practical jokes, all harmless and even popular in an entirely male society.

He studied under professors of international fame, becoming deeply impressed by the nature of scientific law: why should not human beings and governments learn to behave in the same reasonable way? Again, this was totally unlike

Queen Victoria; she never looked for laws in human behaviour, being thrown by events either into surprised ecstasy or equally surprised indignation. She had a shrewd idea, however, of how to deal with them once they had happened.

Queen Victoria's Coronation was the occasion for a rare letter to her from Prince Albert. It contained quite formal congratulations. Later he heard that she wished him to make a tour of Italy with Stockmar, learning the accomplishments required by fashionable Society. As these entailed a gift for flirtatious gossip which Prince Albert did not possess, he looked forward to the tour with apprehension. It meant parting from Ernest and going with Stockmar, not yet by any means the close personal friend he was to become. The worldly little Baron, villain of the Caroline Bauer intrigue and later described by Melbourne as 'very learned in all matters of love',[10] was hardly the person to initiate a hypersensitive youth into these mysteries. The Prince, in fact, informed Florschütz that he did not intend to 'corrode' the inner man by the kind of life which his cousin Victoria desired him to lead.[11]

He felt his work would be cut out in opposing her, for he heard that she was 'incredibly stubborn' and revelled in ceremony, etiquette, trivial formalities, late nights and long lies abed. Saddest of all, she took no pleasure in nature. These were gloomy prospects, concluded poor Albert, and the longer she was left unmarried the more her bad traits would harden.

Prince Albert's information about his cousin, which may also have included criticism of her relations with Melbourne, sent him to England with little hope of success. He was to find the information remarkably inaccurate. Queen Victoria's feelings about Court ceremony were at best ambivalent, her obstinacy was always ready to melt at the touch of love, her boredom with nature was an acquired distaste. 'All gardens are dull,' pronounced Lord M.: 'A garden is a dull thing.'

Stockmar's reports on Prince Albert turned out to be as superficial and misguided as the rumours about Queen Victoria: he 'spared himself', lacked seriousness, and showed not the slightest interest in politics. It was Stockmar's fatal girding at the young Prince which drove him in later life to

163

spare himself far too little. His early boredom with politics was reminiscent of Queen Victoria's recurrent wish to banish them for ever, but between them they were soon to set up an absorbing political partnership: he out of intelligent application and sense of duty, she from natural aptitude and the pleasure of working with him.

Queen Victoria would always remember October 10th, 1839. It opened in the inappropriate way great days sometimes do. She awoke to find that a madman had broken some of her windows at Windsor. This was particularly disagreeable as she and Melbourne were both feeling unwell after eating pork the night before. She went out walking to get rid of her headache.

Suddenly she saw a page running towards her with a letter. It was from King Leopold to say that Albert and Ernest were arriving that very evening. She could hardly believe it but at 7.30 pm she was at the top of the staircase ready to receive the cousins as they drove into the Quadrangle.

Prince Albert had spent September at the peaceful Rosenau, his happy birthplace, fortifying himself against the expected humiliations of Windsor. He set out with a letter of recommendation from King Leopold in his pocket and an ultimatum in his heart. As regards the engagement, Victoria must either make it or break it. He would not wait.

The crossing to Dover was appalling. He sailed in a paddle steamer which was hurled towards the cliffs, white as gravestones, on enormous seas. He was terribly sick and his 'cowardice' attracted unkind attention. He arrived at Windsor Castle without any baggage.

None of these misfortunes could disguise the Prince's triumphant good looks. As the pale young man in dark travelling clothes mounted the stone stairs, the Queen looked down upon an Albert she did not recognize. He had grown tall, he had changed. Her heart suddenly leapt up like a flame for she knew that she was in love. That night she wrote in her Journal: 'It was with some emotion that I beheld Albert – who is *beautiful*.'

Next day when the Prince came to her room with letters

164

from the other German cousins she observed his beauty in detail:

> 'such beautiful blue eyes, an exquisite nose, & a pretty mouth with delicate moustachios & slight but very slight whiskers: a beautiful figure, broad in the shoulders & fine waist.'[12]

Ernest's hollow white cheeks and striking black eyes got no mention in the Queen's Journal.

Never had the afternoon cavalcade been more delicious. They lost their way coming home and returned in the dark with sheet lightning picking out the new, handsome young rider at the Queen's side. That evening they danced and for once it was no pain to sit out the waltzes for she could watch Albert twirling round, holding himself so well 'with that beautiful figure of his'.

After a very late night, she woke with a bad headache, but at once got up and dashed off a note to King Leopold:

> 'Ernest is grown quite handsome; Albert's *beauty* is *most striking*, and he is so amiable and unaffected – in short, very *fascinating* . . .'[13]

As her pen flew over the paper she could hear the brothers playing a Haydn symphony in the room beneath. Albert's charming greyhound, 'Eos', walked round the luncheon table, giving her paw and eating off a fork.

On the third day of the visit Melbourne praised Ernest's brains; Queen Victoria retorted that Albert was far cleverer, though at the moment for obvious reasons under a strain. She herself, she admitted, felt agitated by the whole business. 'Very naturally,' said Lord M., cautiously. Seeing Albert, she continued, had made her feel rather different about marrying. Melbourne gave her another week to make up her mind. But the Queen's heart had galloped ahead of the old man's calculations.

Next day he found her mind made up; he therefore urged her to marry at once rather than wait. They laughed about the awkwardness of telling Albert – these things were usually done the other way round – and frowned over the awkwardness of telling Mama. In the short space of an hour they had planned all the next moves: the marriage in February after Parliament had met and granted the Prince an allowance; all the usual honours such as Field-Marshal and Royal Highness but not a peerage; secrecy for the present but people, including Mama, being allowed to guess by Victoria's marks of affection. Though Melbourne privately thought Prince Albert's character and capabilities inferior to his looks, he nobly supported the Queen's decision to marry him: 'a woman cannot stand alone for long, in whatever situation she is.'[14] There were tears in his eyes and before they parted she took his hand and holding it thanked him for being 'so fatherly'.

That night it was Albert who took the lead in showing affection. He still did not know his fate but as he and the Queen stood in the Corridor saying good night after the informal dancing which Victoria liked so much, he squeezed her hand in a way which she did not fail to notice.

After that handshake the night before, it did not seem so difficult to tell Albert next day. On the morning of Tuesday, October 15th, Queen Victoria watched him charging up the hill after a hunt and at half past twelve she sent for him to the Blue Closet. They both knew what was coming and only a few minutes passed before she asked him to marry her.

'I said to him, that I thought he must be aware *why* I wished them to come here, – and that it would make me *too happy* if he would consent to what I wished (to marry me).[15]

No more words were necessary. All the tensions were broken, the sleepless nights over, the whispering between Lehzen and Albert's valet finished. They fell into each other's arms, kissing again and again while Albert poured out in German his longing to spend his life with her.

Formally and as Queen of England, Victoria had had to propose to her future husband; as she naïvely wrote to her aunt, the Duchess of Gloucester, afterwards, Albert would never have presumed to take the liberty. But guided by her love she swiftly changed round their roles so that almost at once it was she who was thanking her lover, as she 'kissed his dear hand', for the sacrifice he was making in wishing her to be his wife.

For the first dreamlike days the lovers lived only for each other; they sang Albert's compositions, Albert scratched out the mistakes in Victoria's letters – 'he is such a *dear dear* invaluable Treasure!'[16] – they exchanged rings and locks of hair, they held hands tightly while they danced, they flew into each other's arms the moment they were left alone, and as Ernest soon went down with jaundice, this happened more and more frequently. Victoria would drop kisses on Albert's head to his delighted surprise as he sat with her in the Blue Closet or run after him 'to get one more kiss' when he left. It was he, instead of Lehzen, who now took her cold hands and warmed them in his own, and when he took her face in his hands and kissed her lips she wept with happiness and lived in humble ecstasy.

Politics the Prince might not care for but he enjoyed commenting on Queen Victoria's dresses. She was glad to find that he generally approved. When she took him with her to review the troops in Hyde Park on a freezing November day he tenderly settled a fur cape round her shoulders, while shivering himself in a pair of white cazimere pantaloons, with *'nothing under them'*. He enjoyed it notwithstanding. When there was no scratching out to be done in the Blue Closet he would blot the warrants as she signed them, whispering *'Vortrefflichste'* – incomparable one. The fingers that held the royal pen were so small he could hardly believe they were real, for up till now the only hands he had held were Ernest's. As soon as it was finished he would lead her again to the little blue sofa. *'Liebe Kleine,'* he would murmur, kissing her; *'Ich habe dich so lieb, ich kann nicht sagen wie.'* Or standing together by the fire they would ask each other the eternal question, 'Did you expect it?'[17]

Her lover confessed that he didn't expect it to happen so quickly; but he had decided not to wait for three years. That three-year business, she explained, was all the fault of their teasing and pressing her so much; now that she had seen him her only wish was to become his instantly. Whereupon Prince Albert, throwing his English and all to the winds, cried, *'Ich habe dich so unaussprechlich lieb*' and seized her in his arms.

One day when the Prince's visit was almost at an end he asked to see her Journal. She showed him the '*15th* of October' – their engagement day. He read only a little before his own love, made stronger than ever by the poignant account of hers, choked him and there was no more Journal that evening. They played and sang together until it was time for dinner, followed by the last dance Queen Victoria would have 'as an *unmarried girl*'[18] – a fact which grieved her not at all. On the last morning, November 14th, she kissed his cheek, 'fresh & pink like a rose', and then went away to cry and wait for his return.

After he had gone she apologized to Lord M. for being so tiresome and stupid these days. She could think of only one subject. Melbourne gave his stock answer but with fatherly tenderness: 'Very natural.'

It was not long before politics caught up on the lovers. Altogether five major disputes rocked the Palace during the two months between Prince Albert's return to Coburg and the wedding.

King Leopold touched off the first. Two days before Prince Albert left for home he received a strong letter from his uncle urging him to be made a peer: this would get rid of the 'foreignership' of his name. Queen Victoria had already discussed this problem with Melbourne. They were both against the peerage for different reasons. Melbourne thought people would be afraid of the Prince interfering in politics, as a member of the House of Lords. His judgement was at fault, for even without the peerage Prince Albert was accused of meddling and his German title gave a handle to those who wanted to ridicule 'the Coburg lad'. While seeing Melbourne's point, the Queen had her own objection to a peerage. It was not good enough. She had set her heart on her treasure being created King Consort. Melbourne absolutely ruled this out, consoling her with the assurance that Prince Albert would receive the highest precedence without difficulty.

Meanwhile she had to make a Declaration of Marriage on November 23rd to the Council. Eighty-two Privy Counsellors crowded into the chamber at Buckingham Palace.

'Aren't you nervous?' inquired the Duchess of Gloucester.

'Yes,' said the Queen, 'but I did a much more nervous thing a little while ago.'

'What was that?'

'I proposed to Prince Albert.'[19]

She wore Ross's portrait of her lover in a bracelet on her arm. Despite Prince Ernest having brushed his brother's whiskers and 'very slight mustachios' before each sitting, the portrait was not flattering, but she felt it protected her.*

The folding doors were thrown open and the Queen entered, dressed very plainly. Everyone at once noticed the portrait and the trembling of her hands. Her fingers shook so much and the paper was so thin (she complained afterwards to Lord M. about it) that she could hardly read it. For all that, her voice was clear and sweet; once more the cynics were confounded. Greville thought her performance wonderful and Croker, a caustic Tory, admitted that though she was not beautiful, the flush on her cheeks and her clear eyes, soft without being downcast, made her 'as interesting and handsome as any young lady I ever saw'. The young lady herself wrote charmingly to her lover that though it was 'rather an awful moment' (next day she was still shivering with nerves) she felt so happy to do it.

Lord Melbourne had personally composed the Declaration for her. She found it very elegant. Alas, elegance was not enough. He had omitted to make any reference to the religion of the Queen's future husband, since he could not employ the usual formula that she was marrying into 'a Protestant family'. Immediately the country, stirred up by the Press, assumed that Prince Albert belonged to one of the branches of the Coburgs which had, in Melbourne's words, 'collapsed into Catholicism'. To the Queen it seemed monstrous that Prince Albert, who at his Confirmation had so eloquently described the reformed religion as 'the acknowledged truth', should be so wickedly traduced.

The question of Prince Albert's precedence was no better handled by the Queen's advisers. She had decided that 'of

* Melbourne told the Queen that Ross always liked to make his sitters look worse – 'he thinks it's such fun!'

169

course' Albert must rank next in precedence to herself. This meant squaring not only the Tories but also the Royal Dukes. At first her two younger uncles, Cambridge and Sussex, agreed. However, her jealous Uncle Ernest, Duke of Cumberland and now King of Hanover, refused to give precedence to what he called contemptuously 'a paper Royal Highness'. He bullied his brothers into following him and the Tory leaders did likewise. The Queen could not tell which she hated most, 'that old wretch' her uncle or the odious Tories. 'I was quite furious & raged away,' she wrote in her Journal, calling Peel 'a low hypocrite', the Bishop of Exeter 'a fiend', and the Tories as a whole 'infernal scoundrels'. When would the Almighty grant her New Year's prayer? 'From the Tories, good Lord deliver us!' She would never look at the Duke of Wellington again. What was a Queen, anyway, if she had to reverse the laws of nature and put her husband below herself.[20]

'Poor dear Albert, how cruelly are they ill-using that dearest Angel! Monsters! you Tories shall be punished. Revenge, revenge!'[21]

A Bill for Prince Albert's naturalization finally had to go through without any mention of his precedence. Thanks to Greville's constitutional researches, the Queen was later able to declare his precedence by royal prerogative. But not until after her marriage. Many of her tenderest susceptibilities were outraged during the legal process, among them her disinclination to face the possibility of having children. The Tories had wished beloved Albert to take precedence below a hypothetical Prince of Wales.

The Tories' behaviour over Prince Albert's rank was unnecessarily boorish, especially since they had just beaten the Queen on another disputed point – the Prince's allowance; indeed, it was the defeat over the allowance which made both Victoria and Albert set such store by the precedence.

Just as Melbourne took it for granted that the Tories would accept the Prince's precedence and his Protestantism without a murmur, he confidently assumed that they would vote the usual £50,000 a year paid to a Consort. The Government was beaten by 104 votes and Prince Albert's allowance reduced to £30,000. The Queen was frantic. Did this mean that the good, the beautiful, the learned Albert was worth so much less than Queen Anne's Consort, 'stupid old George of Denmark'?

Melbourne found himself for the first time obliged to direct the Queen's attention quite seriously to the state of the country. Up till now he had played down the unemployment and want, the bitterness and rioting which were ushering in the Hungry Forties: violence in Birmingham was 'to be expected'; and the only disgraceful thing about the Chartist riots in Newport was the refusal of the Guards to go and put them down, because their officers would find life in Newport too dull. Now he had to change his tune.

The Queen at once accepted Melbourne's economic and social reasons for being content with the £30,000, though in her heart she felt sure that the opposition was due to party politics and Albert's foreign birth. If she had married George Cambridge, that 'odious boy' with an ugly face and 'schocking' complexion, he would have got the full £50,000.

What made these defeats so much more painful was the fact that yet another battle was raging, this time over Prince Albert's Household. At least poor dear Albert was beaten over grant and rank by Victoria's enemies; over the Household dispute he had to be defeated for his own good by Victoria herself.

Prince Albert wished his Household to conform to his own political and moral standards. On the political front, he wanted a balance between Whigs and Tories. Melbourne at once suspected that being a German and therefore anti-Liberal he would fill his Household with the enemy. Rightly the Prime Minister pointed out to the Queen, who at first hoped to please her lover, that two Royal Households of different political complexions 'would never do'. His solution was to concentrate on Whigs, but Whigs who were 'non-party' because not in Parliament. As a start he offered his own secretary, George Anson, for the key position – the Prince's private secretary.

The suggestion dismayed the Prince. What would become of his political neutrality if he actually shared the Prime

Minister's secretary? That was the only sector of the battle on which the Prince was victorious; he insisted on Anson resigning from Melbourne's staff before joining his own.

Anson's suitability on moral grounds seemed equally doubtful to the Prince. He had heard that Anson was addicted to dancing. Again and again Prince Albert wrote to Queen Victoria entreating her to let him appoint men of good character. Though he did not say so, he was influenced by the violent criticisms of the Queen's entourage since the Flora Hastings and Bedchamber affairs.

The hostile Press called it 'a depraved Court'. Were Melbourne and Lehzen going to make his Household into another 'Paget Club House', as *The Age* called Windsor? Conyngham, married to a Paget, was Lord Chamberlain; his mistress was Housekeeper at Buckingham Palace; the immoral Uxbridge was Lord Steward; his mistress was on the Palace pay-roll, and the sons and daughters of the 'Club' attended Her Majesty personally. The dashing Lord Alfred Paget was excessively disappointed that owing to his parliamentary duties someone else had to travel to Coburg with the Garter for Prince Albert; but Clarence Paget, whom Melbourne described as a 'handy' fellow, turned up to fetch the Prince from Calais and may have employed his handiness in spreading the stories of Albert's cowardice at sea.

To the Prince, an obvious solution to his Household problem was a group of high-minded, non-political Germans in the key posts. He tried to wring Victoria's heart with the tale of his loneliness in a strange land. But Melbourne was at her elbow, never letting her forget that foreigners were disliked in England. It was all very distressing: Prince Albert thought that Queen Victoria had ceased to love him and Queen Victoria found him unreasonable. Adding to their trouble was the irregularity of the mail. Albert was frantic at getting nothing for nine days. Victoria moped for a week until at last the long awaited letter arrived.

The Queen let off her vexation on 'this dear kind old man', Lord Melbourne, partly because Albert was not there and partly because her mounting irritations with her former mentor had come to a head in this collision of love and politics. Melbourne could not resist an 'I told you so'; he had always been against foreigners and especially the Coburg match. Queen Victoria hit back. She would never have stooped to marry a subject, she declared; she did not love Prince Albert because he was a Coburg but because he was lovable; she would have married him anyhow, whatever the consequences.

In for a penny in for a pound and Melbourne now did himself credit by standing up to the Queen and guiding her through a series of minor crises. She fought against the publicity of attending Divine Service before her wedding day and worse still of being married in 'that schocking locale', the Chapel Royal. How much better would be a private room in the Palace from which on grounds of space alone she could exclude every single Tory and all her unwanted relations. Melbourne was adamant: 'it's of great importance that you should get over that dislike of going amongst everybody: mustn't let that be known; it would be very injurious'.[22] When her widowhood brought back this ingrained craving to hide herself away there was no Lord M. to say kindly but firmly that it would never do.

On one subject they were not able to reach agreement – the ethics of love. There was something like a quarrel over Prince Albert's reserve with ladies. Melbourne lightly predicted that he would begin to flirt when he got older but this so angered the Queen that he had to retract. Talking of the Grand Duke of Russia's escapades, the Queen swore that she could never marry a man who had loved another woman.

'Oh! one affair before marriage is nothing,' said Lord M. airily, 'he won't do it afterwards.' The Queen stuck to her point.

'You wouldn't mind if you liked the man,' persisted Lord M.

'Yes, I should.'

'Well, you are not subjected to it,' Melbourne concluded,[23] aware that his beloved Victoria and her Albert stood on the far side of the line drawn between the old morality and the new.

Another disagreement took place over the Queen's bridesmaids. Prince Albert thought no one should be invited who had a mother with an objectionable past. This would have ruled out the daughters of Lady Jersey and Lady Radnor.

Melbourne was dumbfounded. One should take note of character among lowly persons, he said, but it would never do where people were of very high rank. How could there be one law for the high and another for the low? asked the young Queen. She was much less severe than her Consort, however, as she was the first to admit, and in the end her train-bearers were selected according to the rank rather than the morals of their mamas.

A tug-of-war was already going on between Lord Melbourne and Prince Albert for the Queen's soul, though the Prime Minister was too much of a gentleman to pull hard. His leisurely nonchalance compared ill with Albert's youthful zeal. The Queen upbraided Melbourne for not working hard enough – not holding enough Cabinet meetings but dawdling at the play and Holland House: 'I said they ought to set *really* to work.' Queen Victoria's love for Lord M. was tender as ever and she blamed his faults on people who led him astray; she liked to see the sentimental tears in his eyes, whether he was speaking of a long dead gun-dog or herself. All the same, the change in her, which Prince Albert's coming only hastened, was very evident.

It was during an after-dinner word game that the difference between the Prince and the Prime Minister suddenly crystallized. Prince Albert had arranged the jumbled letters of the word 'PLEASURE'. To encourage the players, Queen Victoria told them that it was a very common word. 'But not a very common *thing*,' said the Prince. Melbourne promptly asked, 'Is it truth or honesty?'[24] As Victoria's silvery laugh rang out it was as if bells were ringing out the old era.

The wedding day was fixed for February 10th, 1840 but the course of true love had not yet begun to run smoothly. Just before the Prince left his home for ever he received a letter written unmistakably by the Queen of England. Her Majesty turned down flat his idea of a honeymoon at Windsor lasting longer than two or three days.

'*You forget, my dearest Love, that I am the Sovereign and that business can stop and wait for nothing.*'[25]

Albert was not likely to forget again. Did his wishes count for nothing? Though he did not actually sulk, King Leopold reported that he was setting off for England wan and a little melancholy. On the other side of that dangerous Channel he fully expected to find a hostile nation and a cool Queen.

Sure enough the Channel was again in a perfect fury, tossing the petrified Prince to and fro for five hours and finally drenching the crowds which had assembled to watch him disembark; but the warmth of his welcome at Dover, Canterbury and London belied his fears. As Lord Torrington, one of his escorts, kindly explained, the bad behaviour of Parliament did not reflect the feelings of the nation. By slow stages, to give him a chance to recover from his appalling seasickness, he arrived at the Palace on Saturday, February 8th, still giddy but outwardly beautiful as ever.

The inmates of Buckingham Palace were in no better shape. The Duchess of Kent was nursing two grievances, one old and one new, and would not dine with the Queen. She wanted precedence over the Royal aunts 'just for the day' and she did not want to move into a separate establishment after the marriage. Melbourne dined but had a bad cough.

On February 4th, six days before the wedding, Queen Victoria woke up with an atrocious cold. She felt too wretched to change for dinner and spent a miserable night. Next day she could not eat but dozed fitfully until four o'clock. Rumours spread through the Palace that she had caught the illness which they dreaded for her above all others – measles. Then the cloud lifted. Her natural buoyancy triumphed and she began to feel better. Having dined alone she went downstairs and stayed till half past eleven.

After that things improved. She still had to rest a good deal but at least it wasn't measles. An enchanting letter arrived from the Prince with a book of caricatures. (He had invented two comic characters, *Herr Pamplemus und Herr Zigeuner*.) She was given a new Scotch terrier called Laddie. ('You'll be smothered with dogs,' Lord M. said each time she got another.) Queen Adelaide gave her a necklace and ear-rings of turquoise and pearls and the Royal aunts a diamond bracelet. She was very firm about refusing tickets for the

175

Chapel: there were to be only two Tories – Lord Liverpool, who had saved her from Conroy, and the Duke of Wellington. 'I won't have that old rebel,' she began by declaring, but Lord M. insisted.

On Friday the greyhound Eos arrived with Prince Albert's valet, while dearest Daisy departed for Windsor to see that all was ready for the honeymoon. Next day came the Prince himself. She never forgot her agitation over his arrival: her running down into the equerries' room to watch from their window for his carriage, hearing it at last and rushing to the door to receive him. Then a marvellous peace: 'seeing his *dear dear* face again put me at rest about everything.'[26]

On the Sunday Queen Victoria won a point about not facing the publicity of going to church; she had prayers in the Palace. She had also won a small battle against Mama and Lord M. over having her bridegroom to sleep under her roof before the wedding; the English objection to such a proceeding she dismissed as 'foolish nonsense'. And Prince Albert, with the sweet reasonableness which King Leopold predicted of him, agreed to take Anson as his private secretary. He never regretted it. In the evening the bride and bridegroom spent an hour reading over the Marriage Service and practising with the ring.

At length Queen Victoria was able to write in her Journal:

'Monday, FEBRUARY 10. – the last time I slept alone. Got up at a $\frac{1}{4}$ to 9 – well, & having slept well; & breakfasted at $\frac{1}{2}$ p. 9 . . .'

It was raining and knowing Prince Albert's temperament she sent him a reassuring little note:

'Dearest, – . . . how are you today, and have you slept well? I have rested very well, and feel very comfortable today. What weather! I believe, however, the rain will cease. Send one word when you, my most dearly loved bridegroom, will be ready. Thy everfaithful,

Victoria R.[27]

The Queen drove the short distance from the Palace to the

Chapel Royal, St James's, in a carriage with her mother and the Mistress of the Robes. She wore a white satin dress trimmed with English Honiton lace, a diamond necklace, Prince Albert's present of a sapphire brooch and a wreath of orange-blossom which she afterwards sketched in her Journal. She found her twelve immaculately fresh train-bearers, all in white like village maidens among the gold and jewels, waiting for her at the Chapel, having been securely locked in for ninety minutes. She had made the sketches for their dresses herself. Prince Albert was there, slim and tall in his uniform, Lord M. resplendent in a marvellous new coat which, he said, had been built like a 74-gun ship. He carried the Sword of State as he had done at the Coronation, but nobody said this time that he looked like a butcher. The familiar black skull-cap kept the eccentric head of Uncle Augustus warm. He sobbed throughout the ceremony while the Duke of Cambridge made loud, good-humoured comments. The trumpets sounded and the organ played as the Queen walked up the aisle, unusually pale but without a tear, contrary to the press reports. The singing she did not mention, possibly because the choir of the Chapel Royal always sang 'schockingly'.

In marked contrast to her Coronation, she dwelt more on the meaning of the service than on its splendour:

'The Ceremony . . . ought to make an everlasting impression on every one who promises at the Altar to *keep* what he or she promises.'

She particularly liked the simple way 'in which we were called "Victoria, wilt thou have &c . . ." & "Albert, wilt thou &c . . ." '[28]. Her happiest moment was when Albert put on the ring. The congregation marvelled at her dignity and composure for they could see how the orange-blossom on her head ceased to quiver.

At the end they were all received with loud applause, even Lord M. to his great satisfaction. The Queen kissed her aunt, Queen Adelaide, but only shook hands with her mother, a fact which sharp tongues remarked upon. She returned to the Palace alone with Prince Albert and sat with him 'from 10 m. to 2 till 20 m.p. 2' in her room, before attending an immense wedding breakfast. During that meticulously charted half-hour while they sat together on the sofa, she gave him his wedding ring and he said there must never be a secret which they did not share. 'There never was.'[29] She then changed into a gown of white silk trimmed with swansdown and a bonnet with a brim so deep that the little face inside could hardly be seen.

At about four o'clock they set off for Windsor – 'I & Albert alone, which was SO delightful.' The sun suddenly broke through and a joyful throng of well-wishers on horseback and in gigs galloped along beside them. Charles Greville sniffed because their chariot was neither new nor very smart; but the picture of this happy couple dashing off on their honeymoon with a rumbustious escort disputing every inch of the road is one that fascinates and astonishes a later age.

The Queen was utterly worn out by the experiences of the past week – outbursts of fury, an attack of fever, crowds and excitement, and at last that three hours of swaying rush through the winter evening. Arrived at Windsor she and Albert explored the new suite of rooms together, running like children from one to the other, Albert perhaps a shade anxious to find that Lehzen's apartment was only separated from their own bedroom by the Queen's dressing-room. Then Victoria laid aside her swansdown and returned feeling like a dying swan herself to find Albert playing the piano, wearing his Windsor coat. His embrace revived her for a moment but when she tried to eat a racking headache drove her to the sofa for the remainder of the evening:

'but ill or not, I NEVER NEVER spent such an evening ! ! ! My DEAREST DEAREST DEAR Albert sat on a foot-stool by my side, & his excessive love & affection gave me feelings of heavenly love & happiness, I never could have *hoped* to have felt before ! – really how can I ever be thankful enough to have such a *Husband*!'

CHAPTER XI
THE BLOTTING PAPER
1840

TO BREAKFAST WITH that angelic being, romantically beautiful in Byronic shirt and black velvet jacket, was inexpressible joy. At noon the Queen took her husband's arm and they walked on the Terrace, alone but for Eos, the black greyhound with a silver streak whose name meant 'dawn'.

On the second morning of their Windsor honeymoon, try as they would to work at their two tables in the Queen's room, 'talk kept on breaking out'. The Queen told Lord Melbourne at the end of a week, with wondering enchantment: 'I never could have thought there was such happiness in store for me.' Rather wistfully he agreed that she would find marriage a great comfort: 'You find it already, do you not?'[1]

Back at Buckingham Palace, solitary walks round the garden with the Prince were her great delight. When it grew dark they played duets on two pianos or read aloud: she professed to find Hallam's *Constitutional History* absorbing. State papers claimed her immediate attention but with what a difference; '. . . Albert helped me with the blotting paper when I signed.'[2]

The pleasures of the dance reached their zenith. Like a tiny humming-bird in her blue satin gown from Paris sparkling with jewels, she flew on to the ballroom floor, rapturously gazing round at the new paint, gilding, mirrors and damask. Albert was a 'splendid dancer', and as for herself, everyone agreed that she was the best performer in the room; dignified statesmen, unwillingly submitting to the rigours of Sir Roger de Coverley for an hour on end, could not deny that it was a pleasure to watch her. Her reception by the masses was no less kind. When she and Prince Albert visited their first theatre the huzzas were deafening and she heard one good soul shout, 'Down with the Tories!'

Albert on the dance floor was only equalled by Albert in the riding school. Round and round he dashed with his 'beautiful seat' and beautiful smile each time he passed his wife. At dinner he looked superb in his newest Order, the Bath, and she looked lovely, as he told his brother, in a very low-cut dress with a bunch of roses at her bosom. All the world seemed to smile on them except possibly the Irish, who looked 'cross' while delivering a loyal address. Never mind, said Lord M.; the Irish were all desperate enemies anyway.

Lady Lyttelton was constantly picking up messages of adoration flashed by the Prince to his wife. One day Queen Victoria was sitting for her portrait on a dais; up bounded the Prince, rosy and wind-swept from hunting, and seized her hand 'with the most graceful, smiling bow'. Another time it was at a review; the Prince came past at the head of his regiment and as he gave the salute his eyes spoke to her.

Because the Prince felt lively at Windsor and sleepy in London, the Queen revised her ideas about the royal residences. Windsor under a full moon with a nightingale singing in the old oak and a branch of lilac put into her hand by Albert, was a different place. In the old days she could not have named the oak or any other tree; now she handed on to her ladies the lore of plants and bees, especially queen bees, all learnt from Albert. 'As happy as a queen,' was a phrase which Lady Lyttelton nearly used to Her Majesty but stopped midway. 'Don't correct yourself,' said Victoria; 'a Queen *is* a very happy woman.'[3]

Summer parties in the great London houses were fresh opportunities for romance. After a duty dance with the son of the house and a few words with Lord Melbourne on a sofa, Queen Victoria would waltz once round the ballroom with the Prince 'for appearances' sake' and then follow him into the dark garden softly glowing with coloured lights.

No one could expect coloured lights to shine in every dark patch. The Queen's relations made no attempt to redeem their black record over Prince Albert's precedence.

The Duchess of Cambridge, determined to boost 'the *old* royal family' against the Coburg intruder, ostentatiously remained seated while the Prince's health was drunk at a dinner

180

given by Queen Adelaide. In retaliation Queen Victoria did not invite the Cambridges to her next ball. The Duke of Cambridge got his own back by excusing Albert's precipitate retreat from a City banquet with a jocular reference to his eagerness to return to a 'very fine girl'. The City fathers roared with laughter but Queen Victoria was disgusted. Two years later fate delivered the Cambridges into her hands.

A rumour circulated that young George Cambridge had got his mother's lady-in-waiting, Augusta Somerset, daughter of the Duke of Beaufort, with child. In order to dispel the rumour, the Duchess of Cambridge presented Lady Augusta at a drawing-room, thus obtaining an *imprimatur* of purity. The Queen and Prince were outraged to find that the high reputation of their Court, so laboriously built up, was being abused by parties whose guilt they did not doubt. They sent Lady Augusta Somerset to Coventry. At length Prince Albert was forced to accept the Cambridge family's repeated denials of the scandal, which he did with consummate ungraciousness.* People like Charles Greville uttered cries of horror at the Court's behaviour. Was Lady Flora's ghost to rise again in Lady Augusta? Greville put it down to a combination of Prince Albert's prudery and Queen Victoria's hard-heartedness and love of gossip.

After the death of Lady Flora, the Queen had told Melbourne that she and Lehzen would never listen to gossip again. Lehzen, however, was an incurable gossip, and so was Lord Melbourne; the Queen's Journal is full of titbits from his larder. Her own fondness for gossip to which much of her Journal's liveliness is due, sprang partly from a commendable interest in human beings.†

Greville's accusation of hard-heartedness had been caused by the Lady Flora tragedy and went with charges of harshness

* The Cambridges remained implacably hostile to Prince Albert and a future lady-in-waiting of the Duchess's, Lady Geraldine Somerset, was to enliven her diary with astringent anecdotes about Queen Victoria. See p. 569.

† Nine years later, having listened to a sermon against ill-natured gossip, she wrote in her Journal: 'I feel that this is *not* my inclination, and I am sure I never can bear to hear a person unjustly and unfairly spoken of, and always like to think the best of people.'

over etiquette. Lord Adolphus Fitzclarence, with his 'slouching eyelid and vast pouch-like chops', had it from Anna Maria, Duchess of Bedford (formerly Lady Tavistock), that the Queen was a hard mistress. 'Duchess of Bedford, I have been waiting some time for my shawl,' the Queen was alleged to have said angrily when the Duchess mislaid a wrap.[4] Other impressions emphatically contradict this one. Lady Lyttelton, for instance, was conscious of her own frequent 'bungling' and 'boggling' with the Queen's four wraps, bouquet, bag and opera glasses; Her Majesty remained kindness itself. No harsh words were spoken even at the prorogation of Parliament in 1839 when Lady Lyttelton, having removed the crown from the small, sleek, slippery head, failed to pin the Queen's diadem securely back again. When she poked the diamond pin into the royal head, Her Majesty only gave a 'comical look of entreaty'. There was much merriment afterwards over this supreme boggle. 'Oh, do not mind!' exclaimed Lehzen brightly. 'Do not care *a pin for de pin*!'[5]

Etiquette as a thing in itself Queen Victoria found boring. She insisted on it from a sense of duty. Having thoroughly discussed the whole matter with Melbourne, she had come to the conclusion that though William IV's approachability had made him popular, what the country now wanted was a strict Court and a 'high' attitude in herself.

Did concern for etiquette in fact make her inconsiderate? When the young Mendelssohn visited the Palace, the Queen cheerfully picked up his sheets of music which the wind had scattered; she ran into Lady Lyttelton's room with her feet still wet from a foot-bath to show her a letter from a sick friend; when the children's nurses got separated from their charges on returning from a holiday, she spontaneously fetched and carried for the Governess. The truth is that Queen Victoria was by nature unaffectedly kind.

Prince Albert's so-called prudery is another matter. He was not immune to the impulses of the flesh but was determined never to go in the way of temptation, for his childhood had taught him that sexual indulgence brought domestic disaster. During the first year of his marriage, he and his wife received striking confirmation of this view. Twice his brother Ernest suffered from a fearful visitation, as a result of his excesses in Berlin. The first time, he was staying in Buckingham Palace and his illness damaged the Coburg name with the English nobility, giving support to rumours about Prince Albert's illegitimacy. The Prince urged his brother to concentrate on restoring his health before marrying and risking the birth of 'a sick heir'; meanwhile he continually impressed on Ernest the delights of marriage, once he was fit to seek it. Marriage was the only compensation for the lost pleasures of youth; its bonds could never be too close; the more tightly they were drawn the greater the happiness. Prince Albert illustrated his point from his own marriage: Victoria and he were united in love and ready to make sacrifices for one another.

As the Queen's husband, Prince Albert intended to stand sponsor to the English people in their hour of regeneration. Unfortunately the 'old Adam' seemed to lurk in the old aristocracy, and the Prince lacked the gift for reforming these raffish types with the light touch to which they might have responded. He hovered gloomily over the baptismal font, ejecting from the precincts all those on whom the vows had clearly made no impression. In return he was pronounced a prude.

Neither Queen Victoria nor Prince Albert at first suspected that their relations with one another would present any difficulties. The Prince, when informing his German relatives of his engagement, made some conventional references to the 'storms' and 'thorns' of life which lay ahead but hoped that Victoria's love would prove strong enough to carry him through. Her love proved to be overwhelming. It was her own idea to keep the word 'obey' in the Marriage Service; she delighted to call him her lord and master. How then could there be storms and thorns?

On the day when Prince Albert's father, Duke Ernest, returned to Coburg at the end of February, the Queen saw the first sign of trouble. She met Prince Albert in the hall in floods of tears after he had said goodbye to his papa. He

183

hurried upstairs without speaking to her. She tried to comfort him but he made it clear that she could not understand his grief: she had never known a father and her childhood had been unhappy, whereas he was breaking with a precious past. Then his mood changed. Victoria could make up to him for everything, he burst out in a flood of tenderness. 'God knows how great my wish . . . , is,' she wrote, 'to make this beloved Being happy and contented . . .'[6]

Great as was her wish, she did not yet know how to do it. He was irritable over trifles and every time she flew into one of her rages or sulked over some disagreement – for marriage had not changed her temperament – she would see by his sad, patient look that he was pining for something. She did not know what. Certainly not for women; when she introduced him to her ladies for the first time he found it very tiresome and could not remember which was which. Nor was it for male company. Prince Albert shared to the full the Queen's distaste for the English custom of remaining in the dining-room for port after the ladies had left. He deserted the 'stayers', as Queen Victoria called them, as soon as possible, preferring to sing duets with his wife. When the gentlemen joined them, he would play double chess alone while the Queen talked to her Prime Minister.

In May Prince Albert wrote to his friend Prince William of Löwenstein a sad letter: he was 'the husband, not the master of the house'.[7] Queen Victoria's twenty-first birthday was celebrated soon afterwards and he presented her with a huge bronze inkstand. When would she think of advancing him beyond the blotting-paper stage to wielding the pen?

Prince Ernest made things no better by rhapsodizing from Portugal on Queen Donna Maria's virtues as a wife. She received no one until her King Consort, Ferdinand of Saxe-Coburg, had first seen them and arranged their affairs. Then they were admitted to her presence – but only to kiss her hand.[8] Ernest had no need to cross the t's and dot the i's; with Albert it was painfully the reverse. He was like one of Donna Maria's visitors. Someone else managed his affairs and he could only kiss the Queen.

The Prince's depression strengthened certain rumours

184

started by the Duchess of Bedford that he was not in love. Society preferred to believe that his frustration was caused by failures in his private rather than in his public life.

Why did he not immediately settle the matter with his wife? The ruthlessness with which he later cleaned up the Household and withstood the shameful demands for money from Coburg, seems incompatible with his hesitancy in asserting his own rights. The answer is that Prince Albert's character combined timidity with drive. With the world he could be a masterful innovator; with his wife he was a Hamlet, always awaiting a better moment for doing the deed. They were both strong characters, warm and generous, but whereas Queen Victoria had a secret vein of iron, Prince Albert's hidden streak was of wax. Tenderness, fear of hurting her feelings, an inner quaking all held him back from telling her that he would only enjoy the Blue Closet to the full when he was permitted to enter the Council Chamber.

He also wanted control of Lehzen's keys.

As soon as the Queen's birthday celebrations were over the Prince made a first attempt to seize the nettle. He complained to his wife of not being given her confidence on 'trivial matters' (an oblique reference to Lehzen's sphere) nor any part whatever in politics. Some good came of this protest. The Queen passed on his criticisms to Melbourne, admitting herself to be in the wrong; her excuse was that 'indolence' prevented her from taking up the precious hours with Albert on such matters. Melbourne advised her to alter this. Then he relayed his interview to George Anson, the Prince's private secretary, who was acting with himself and Stockmar to improve the Prince's position.

None of the four liked to hear the Queen pleading 'indolence'.[9] Melbourne suspected that she was really afraid of arguments with Prince Albert. The Prince believed that it was ignorance not indolence from which she suffered: she left politics so entirely to Melbourne that she could not have discussed them even if she had wished.

Queen Victoria's interest in politics had not in fact been growing: she complained to Melbourne that the European question was boring, with which he agreed, and an entry in her Journal for April 3rd, 1840 neatly expressed her feelings at this period: 'I showed Lord M. a box full of Chinese Despatches & asked about reading them.' Amoy, Chusan, Ningpo, Chintu – what did this string of names mean? Lying on her sofa with her feet up, she tried to get her teeth into the dry stuff, now and then sharing a crumb with Albert.

There was also something in Melbourne's view that the Queen dreaded competition with her husband. She had accepted Lehzen's advice to follow the same plan with the Prince as she had adopted in Lehzen's own case. Jealousy on the part of the public, said Lehzen, had been avoided because she held no official position about the Queen. Let Albert do the same; let him be the invisible husband. The Queen was using the public's suspicions of the Prince to conceal from herself her own jealousy.

Was Lehzen in fact at the bottom of the trouble? The Prince, through Anson, put this idea to Melbourne and Stockmar. The Prime Minister, having worked harmoniously with Lehzen during previous crises, did not agree: 'I do not think that the Baroness is the cause of this want of openness, though her name to me is never mentioned by the Queen.' Support for Prince Albert's opinion came from Stockmar. Lehzen, he announced, had strengthened her grip during the last two years and as a consequence Queen Victoria was less confiding, less 'ingenuous' than she used to be. 'The Queen,' said Stockmar darkly, 'is influenced more than she is aware of by the Baroness.'[10] If Prince Albert had dared he might have extruded Baroness Lehzen there and then. She was far too much of a muddler, and even too amiable, to conduct successfully a difficult campaign against a man much cleverer and more beloved than herself. Instead Prince Albert carried on a secret war of attrition against the Baroness which undermined his own happiness more than her power.

Meanwhile nature herself set in motion the events which were ultimately to solve the Prince's problem. Before March was out the husband in the house heard that he was to become a father.

So much for a malicious comment made by Charles Greville

on the royal couple's morning walk on the first day of their honeymoon:

> 'strange that a bridal night should be so short; and I told Lady Palmerston that this was not the way to provide us with a Prince of Wales.'[11]

Among Queen Victoria's charms was a capacity for experiencing a great variety of emotions in any given situation. All the conflicting thoughts, including frank dismay, which come into women's minds at such a time were hers. All of them gave her husband fresh opportunities for capturing the citadel.

On March 21st she felt unwell and cried bitterly; after all, it was only last December that she had described having children as 'the ONLY thing I *dread*.'[12] She and Prince Albert dined alone. A fortnight later she had given up gallops and waltzes and was back at the old quadrilles; but now she had a husband to make the sitting out pleasant. He was her shield against all gloomy thoughts, gloomy events. When old Princess Augusta was dying it was he who attended her last moments, afterwards whisking the Queen away to Claremont lest the funeral should affect her spirits.

The visit to Claremont started a fantastic rumour. The Queen expected to succumb in labour, it was said, and was furnishing Princess Charlotte's bedroom exactly as it had been when she died in it twenty-three years ago. After the last mirror was hung and the last candle lit, Queen Victoria would follow her cousin to the grave.

Not unnaturally the death of Princess Charlotte in childbirth sometimes preyed on Queen Victoria's mind. She understood from her doctors, however, that Princess Charlotte's death had been due to being kept too 'low' from lack of exercise, constant blood-letting and a starvation diet.* The

---

* According to Sir Eardley Holland, 'It seems hardly possible to doubt that Charlotte died of post partum haemorrhage.' (*Journal of Obstetrics & Gynaecology* December 1951.) It was quite untrue that she took no exercise during pregnancy or was starved during her 50-hour labour, as rumour had it. The fault, if any, of the unfortunate accoucheur, Sir Richard Croft (he committed suicide three months after her death), was in not using forceps owing to 'a mistaken system . . . of midwifery'.

Hanoverians, Lord M. always held, needed plenty to eat and drink, especially wine, and the Queen's hearty appetite would now safeguard her health. Prince Albert's task became one of restraining Victoria's exuberant energies even more than of exorcizing her fears. He read to her, sang to her and kept her on her sofa. She gloried in her bounding health, refusing to sit down at levées and drawing-rooms and later battling against the autumn gales. 'I am so strong & active that I brave all that.' She was gratified but not surprised when she heard that the accoucheurs expected a very easy confinement.

Prince Albert would have liked his wife's 'interesting condition' to be formally announced, as was the custom abroad. Melbourne characteristically preferred the news to leak out.

Two pistol shots suddenly swept Queen Victoria on to a new pinnacle of popularity and carried Prince Albert a stage further along his desired path.

At six o'clock on June 10th, 1840 the Queen accompanied by the Prince was setting off for a drive in her low open carriage up Constitution Hill. Suddenly she heard an explosion and at the same time felt Albert's arms flung round her. 'My God! don't be alarmed!' She smiled at his excitement but next moment saw 'a little man on the footpath with his arms folded over his breast, a pistol in each hand . . .'[13] As he aimed at her and fired again she ducked. Then someone on the footpath seized him, her attendants closed in, the crowd shouted 'Kill him! Kill him!' and she sped on up the hill, coolly continuing her drive and at last returning home in the centre of a wildly enthusiastic escort formed by the ladies and gentlemen riding in the Park.

The miscreant turned out to be an undersized, feeble-minded youth of eighteen named Edward Oxford and the man on the footpath who seized him was Mr Millais, whose schoolboy son, John Everett Millais, the future artist, had just raised his cap to Her Majesty. Young Millais dashed to the wall and discovered the bullet holes. A few days later, returning to the spot, he found that with the aid of sticks and umbrellas the bullet holes had considerably multiplied.

Lord Melbourne and Lord Normanby, the Home Secretary, took the crime seriously. 'A little vermin,' exclaimed Lord M. to the Queen; 'quite *la jeune France*', whose wretched hovel was stuffed with the papers of a revolutionary society. Not the least mad, declared Lord Normanby.[14] They were both wrong. After being committed to Newgate gaol for high treason, a crime punishable by death, Oxford was sent to an asylum.*

This was the first of many lunatic attempts on the Queen's life. It set the pattern for her reaction to the others. She always showed courage though fearfully shaken, for the fact that her assailants' grievances were imaginary did not make their weapons any less real. In her heart she never believed that they were too mad to know what they were doing.

Today it is sad to find someone as tender-hearted as Queen Victoria rejoicing at a change in the law several years later which made it possible to charge these miserable half-wits with misdemeanour rather than high treason. Paradoxically, after this change they could be punished (by imprisonment or transportation with flogging) instead of being automatically reprieved from a death sentence. The Queen wanted them punished. She was not vindictive but the influence of her advisers, of her own fear and possibly of her heredity – her father was a notorious flogger – kept her not an inch in advance of her times.

As for her deliverance from Edward Oxford, she took it as a sign that the Almighty destined her for a high purpose. A Thanksgiving Service, however, was thought unwise, since Lord M.'s Radical followers did not care for such gestures and Dissenting ministers were apt to preach violent sermons.

Prince Albert showed her the pistols 'which might have *finished me off*.' Suppose she were finished off like Princess Charlotte? With all possible tact Melbourne approached the young expectant mother.

* Queen Victoria noted in her Journal on September 22nd, 1867 that Oxford had been released after 27 years in a criminal lunatic asylum and allowed to emigrate. He had expressed 'deep grief' at his offence.

' "There is a subject I must mention, which is of great importance, & one of great emergency; perhaps you may anticipate what I mean;" (which I answered I did not), "it is about having a Bill for a Regency." '[15]

She saw the point.

In July it was Prince Albert who despite the raging of Sussex and the regret of Lehzen was appointed Regent by Parliament in case of the Queen's death.

This success was quickly followed by others. In August, Melbourne, after consulting the precedents established by Queen Anne's husband, 'that eternal Prince George of Denmark', discovered that the Prince could ride in the Queen's carriage to Parliament and sit by her side at the Prorogation. She received the good news at luncheon in an official box, turning as red as the box with excitement as she handed Melbourne's letter to her husband. For there had been voices inside the Palace raised against him, including Lehzen's again, and Lord Albemarle's, Master of the Horse. Queen Victoria felt that she read her speech better than ever before because Albert sat beside her.

Her dependence on the Prince even in matters of State was advancing as steadily as her pregnancy. The arrangement of their writing-tables at Windsor, side by side, was introduced into Buckingham Palace when they returned there after the summer. A crisis in the Eastern question, originally caused by the revolt of an Egyptian, Mehemet Ali, against Turkey, and involving Anglo-French rivalries, ensured that more and more dispatches found their way on to Prince Albert's table.

November arrived and with it the event which the Queen, like all expectant mothers, alternately hoped would come off quickly and be indefinitely postponed: 'an event which I cannot say I am quite looking forward to with pleasure.'[16] When a Canon of Windsor asked if he should offer up a special prayer for the Queen in labour, the Prince said, No.

'You pray five times already; it is too much.'

'Can we pray, sir, too much for Her Majesty?'

'Not too *heartily*, but too *often*.'

Palmerston's Eastern policy had this to be said for it; it kept the Queen's mind off the baby. Prince Albert had purposely drawn her into so much political discussion that they agreed the baby, when he came, would have to be called 'Turko-Egypto'. The masculine termination of this name indicated the couple's resolve to produce a son.

A daughter, the Princess Royal, was born three weeks prematurely – 'nothing ready'[17] – to the Queen on November 21st, 1840 at 2 pm, only Prince Albert, Dr Locock and Mrs Lilly the midwife being present.

Their first rush of disappointment was the only blot on an otherwise perfect birth. The large concourse gathered in the next room heard Dr Locock's voice through the open door:

'Oh, Madam, it is a Princess.'

'Never mind,' came the Queen's clipped reply, 'the next will be a Prince.'

After her twelve-hour labour, during which she had 'suffered severely' but not felt 'at all nervous once it began', she found herself with no pain whatever and a good appetite. 'Dearest Albert hardly left me at all & was the greatest comfort and support.' Having swallowed a hasty, late luncheon, he dashed off to represent the Queen for the first time in Council, thus passing another milestone on his journey. The Queen insisted that his name should be inserted into the Liturgy: if the nation would not pay for him at least it should pray for him.

Relations with the little Princess Royal were at first affectionately remote. Twice a day the baby paid her mother a visit, one day carrying on her arm a little bag containing a lock of her own light brown hair. At six weeks old the Queen saw her bathed for the second time and found her 'much improved' despite the funny flannel washing-cap on her head. Until she was christened (Victoria Adelaide Mary Louise) the Queen simply referred to her as 'the Child'. After her christening she became Pussy or Pussette, the Queen discovering with surprise that Pussy was 'quite a little toy for us'.[18] In toyland Pussy remained for many months. The Queen had neither time nor inclination to nurse her and a wet nurse had been obtained appropriately enough from Cowes. Mrs Southey, sister-in-law of the poet, was appointed Superintendent of the Nursery; unfortunately she introduced neither poetry nor efficiency into her kingdom.

There is a belief that Queen Victoria disliked children. This was not the case but until a baby was six months old she certainly considered it 'froglike' and ugly. Nor was she one of those women who positively enjoy the huge, primeval paraphernalia of childbearing. This aspect of wedded life she called 'the shadow-side of marriage' or more often '*die Schattenseite*', since it was an indelicate subject which sounded better in a foreign language. Her first babies were born before anaesthetics were available and though she was profoundly thankful to use chloroform later on she could never see a young girl entering on matrimony without a shuddering thought of the *Schattenseite*. Perhaps submerged memories of the Flora Hastings affair accounted for her almost Jansenist disgust for things of the body, which combined strangely with her healthy Hanoverian nature.

King Leopold was given a characteristically sharp glimpse into his niece's mind on these matters after he had wished her joy of Pussy and of many more babies to follow.

'I think, dearest Uncle, you cannot *really* wish me to be the "mamma d'une *nombreuse* famille", . . . men never think, at least seldom think, what a hard task it is for us women to go through this *very often*.[19]

Scracely had Pussy been christened before the Queen was expecting another baby; 'I wish she could have waited a a little longer,' wrote the Duchess of Kent in her diary.[20] Queen Victoria, for her part, was furious.

Before the Queen had completed her first lying-in, a ludicrous incident occurred which showed that the Palace was yet another sphere in which Albert might profitably get to work.

At half past one in the morning of December 3rd the Queen's monthly nurse, Mrs Lilly, was awakened by the creaking of a door. She called, 'Who's there?' No one answered

192

but the door into the Queen's dressing-room went on slowly opening. Again Mrs Lilly shouted out. Suddenly the door was shut from the inside. Mrs Lilly sprang up, bolted it from her side and sent for Kinnaird, one of the Queen's pages. Lehzen rushed in, long nose quivering, and together they entered the dressing-room. Kinnaird, no hero, looked under the Queen's sofa and hurriedly backed away without a word. The valiant Lehzen, however, pushed the sofa aside and revealed a boy curled up on the floor.

His name was Jones and his perverse passion for the Palace brought him undying fame. The Boy Jones, as he came to be called, turned out to have visited the Palace once before in 1838. On his second visit he was rewarded by hearing the Princess Royal cry. He returned yet again after doing time. In the end they had to send him away to sea where he did well.

'Supposing he had come into the Bedroom – how frightened I should have been,' reflected Queen Victoria after his most famous entry.[21] To the Prince it was a challenge. He itched to reform the Palace but Lehzen still blocked his path and this was hardly the moment to dismiss the heroine of the sofa incident. He hesitated and decided to wait a little longer.

The year ended symbolically with the disappearance of the Queen's closest childhood companion – Dash. He was buried under a marble effigy at Adelaide Cottage.

Here lies

DASH

The favourite spaniel of Her Majesty Queen Victoria
In his 10th year
His attachment was without selfishness
His playfulness without malice
His fidelity without deceit

READER

If you would be beloved and die regretted
Profit by the example of

DASH

'The Child' had much to live up to. At four months old she was put into the arms of Queen Adelaide in the hope that she would show something of Dash's playfulness. 'I am sorry to say,' wrote her disappointed Mama, 'that the Child screamed & was naughty.'

CHAPTER XII

'I AM GOING'

1841–2

NEVER HAD THE Queen prayed so often or so fervently as she did around the beginning of 1841 to be cured of her faults and failings, her wilfulness, her impatience and her temper. At her Churching, at Christmas, on New Year's Eve and when taking the Sacrament in January, she made her customary humble petition for amendment. Never was it more needed, for the year 1841 offered her a chance to redeem the mistakes of 1839 and incidentally an unexampled opportunity for Prince Albert to become master in the house.

More and more frequently Lord Melbourne had to warn the Queen that the revenue was falling. He put it down to the introduction of penny postage, a curious crochet which exposed his lack of flair for economics.

Queen Victoria realized that a falling revenue this time meant a falling government. The Whigs would have been out two years ago but for her savage twenty minutes with Peel. On May 9th, 1841, with Melbourne's knowledge but unknown to the Queen, Prince Albert sent his private secretary, George Anson, to see Peel about the ladies. While Queen Victoria was in the tense, irritable first months of her new pregnancy it seemed better to present her with a *fait accompli*. At all costs a repetition of the 'Bedchamber' scenes which had occurred precisely two years ago, must be avoided: such a catastrophe, all agreed, would mean the end of the Monarchy.

The Prince's courage as well as his kindness in by-passing the Queen were admirable, especially as she might well have expressed resentment when she found out. In fact she felt nothing but gratitude.

Throughout the crisis Queen Victoria herself showed an immense advance in self-control. Though feeling low, exhausted and tormented just as she had been after Lady

195

Flora's death with bad dreams, she came through with nothing worse than a dumb clinging to Melbourne's hand at the last audience and a burst of tears.

Peel proved as human this time as he had seemed harsh before, and if he still could not keep his feet still at the interviews, there was only Anson to see them. He exhibited the Victorian hallmark of genuine feeling – there were tears in his eyes. The party advantage which he would have gained from at long last forcing the Queen to give up her ladies, he chivalrously renounced. Instead it was agreed that the Queen should spontaneously announce three resignations: those of the Duchess of Sutherland, the Duchess of Bedford and Lady Normanby.

Melbourne's Government was beaten in June by one vote – 'very provoking', wrote Queen Victoria. She was eager that even now he should not resign but gamble on a dissolution and a successful general election to follow. She got her way. 'Ministers have a great deal of patience but no resignation,' observed the celebrated wit, Sydney Smith. When, by September, the Whigs were beaten at the polls and all the changes involved in a new Ministry had been smoothly accomplished, Prince Albert could congratulate himself on the success of his bold plan conceived in May.

Of course there were moments of anxiety. Anna Maria, Duchess of Bedford, for instance, showed signs of resisting her 'voluntary' resignation. But it was Melbourne himself who in the end caused the most trouble. Queen Victoria asked him frankly one day whether he minded going.

'Why, nobody *likes* going out but I'm not well, – I am a good deal tired, and it will be a great rest for me.'[1]

Alas, the old man could not rest away from his idol. The daily, hourly intimacy of the last three years had meant more to him than even he himself suspected. At the Queen's urgent request he continued corresponding with her, despite Stockmar's fulminations against so dangerous a practice. When Anson read to Melbourne one day a severe memorandum from the Baron, Melbourne's face began to work: 'God eternally damn it!' he suddenly exploded, leaping from

196

the sofa and striding up and down the room, 'flesh and blood cannot stand this.'[2]

Though most of Melbourne's correspondence with the Queen was innocuous he occasionally gave her advice on controversial matters which Peel would rightly have resented. She had reluctantly agreed, for example, to contribute to the Government's new tax levied on incomes. Melbourne warned her against throwing away her money and her prerogative, according to which she was constitutionally exempt from paying Income Tax. Melbourne's behaviour was unwise. After Prince Albert's death she again found it difficult to sever relations with a favourite Minister and to open them with someone she disliked, such as Gladstone. Her correspondence with Lord Salisbury in the 1880s after his Ministry had fallen was a case of carrying on what Melbourne had begun.

More typical of the shrewd and often generous side of Melbourne's nature was the advice he left to the incoming Prime Minister on handling the Queen. Peel 'should write fully to Her Majesty, and *elementarily*, as Her Majesty always liked to have full knowledge upon everything which was going on.'[3] There was genius in Melbourne's choice of the word *elementarily*, recognizing as it did the unique and awful simplicity of Queen Victoria's requirements. She wanted the whole truth – in one word. Melbourne's advice should have been pinned up for the use of all his successors at No. 10 Downing Street. It might have encouraged Palmerston to be a little fuller and Gladstone a little briefer in their communications.

Best of all Melbourne's services to the Queen was his recommendation to put herself henceforth under Prince Albert's guidance. Apart from the Prince's obvious fitness to be her adviser, it was easier for the old man to hand over his treasure to the husband than to his own rival, Peel. 'The prince understands everything so well,' he said, 'and has a clever able head.' Delighted, Queen Victoria wrote down Melbourne's tribute, adding her own illuminating reflection:

'I am so glad to hear Lord M. say this. Perhaps this may be a good lesson for me . . . I shall never forget what I suffered in 39, though I suffer much now, but it makes all the difference Albert being at my side.'[4]

It took another few months, however, for the 'good lesson' to sink in. The Queen did not as yet realize that the full warmth of Prince Albert's comfort would be felt only when Lehzen had left her side.

While the elections were proceeding the Queen advertised her political bias by visiting great Whig houses such as Woburn, Panshanger and Brocket. Though she thus obstinately smeared herself with the unpopularity of the losing side, the tour had one excellent result. She found that at last she could live without Lehzen. Dearest angelic 'Daisy', whom two years ago she had prayed not to survive, had been already left behind for one day on June 14th when the Prince visited Oxford to receive an honorary degree. 'Feeling a little low,' wrote the Queen in her Journal, plaintively remembering that she and Lehzen had never been parted since she was five. Lehzen wrote to her using as a letterhead the picture of a little golden engine with the words, 'I Am Coming' written underneath it. No little train, however, would bring Lehzen to join them and Prince Albert hoped that before long her motto would have been changed to 'I Am Going'.*

On the Whig tour the parting from Lehzen was much longer. Queen Victoria again had to be content with letters from her favourite, one reminding her to take 5 drops of tincture of rhubarb in a little camomile tea if she felt unwell. Pussy, whose progress in the badly run nursery was not satisfactory, provided Lehzen with a face-saver : she remained behind to look after her.

Prince Albert suspected that half the trouble in the nursery was due to Lehzen's interference. He therefore hinted to Lord Melbourne at the end of August 1841 that he should continue to guide the Queen on private affairs, in order to neutralize Lehzen. Melbourne was too sensible to become

* See *The Prince Consort* by Roger Fulford, p. 62.

198

the Prince's stooge. Now was the moment, he promptly said, to persuade the Queen that Lehzen must go. He, Melbourne, would gladly make this his last act as her Whig Minister, for she would never accept the suggestion from a Tory.

The Prince took another look at the nettle. He pictured the Queen making an 'exciting scene'; besides, the new baby was not far off. Once more his tender heart failed him: 'he must remain on his guard, and patiently abide the result.'[5]

The little Princess Royal was the innocent cause of Lehzen's eventual banishment. In the autumn her health took a turn for the worse. Angry disputes arose. The Queen attributed the trouble to diet, the Prince, secretly, to Lehzen. Sir James Clark put the child on to nothing but ass's milk and chicken broth but still she lost weight. When November came she had fresh troubles to contend with: 'Pussy terrified & not at all pleased with her little brother.'[6] (The birth of the Prince of Wales had taken place on the 9th.) At Christmas the situation was worse. Post-natal depression afflicted the Queen while Lehzen went down with jaundice. According to Albert 'the Yellow Lady' went about spitting venom like a she-dragon.

The climax came in the middle of January 1842. Pussy had again been sick and her parents, on returning from a visit to Claremont, rushed up to the nursery to see her. There on January 16th the 'exciting scene' took place.

Pussy was very white and thin and the anxious young father let fall some criticism or suggestion which prompted the nurse, Mrs Roberts, to reply sharply in kind. For once the Prince could not conceal his resentment. 'That is really malicious,' he muttered to his wife. Immediately Queen Victoria's temper flared up like one of those houses on fire they sometimes watched from the top of the Round Tower. She accused him of wanting to drive her out of the nursery while he as good as murdered their child. Overwhelmed with horror, the Prince controlled himself enough to murmur, 'I must have patience,'[7] and crept quietly downstairs, but later when they were together again his pent-up fury came roaring out. There was a violent quarrel, from which the Queen withdrew in floods of tears while the Prince, still seething with anger, seized a pen and hurled the Queen's accusations back at her:

'Doctor Clark has mismanaged the child and poisoned her with calomel and you have starved her. I shall have nothing more to do with it; take the child away and do as you like and if she dies you will have it on your conscience.'[8]

Racked with sobs and a sick headache, the Queen turned to Stockmar. He must tell Lehzen that there had been 'a little misunderstanding' and that the Queen was too upset to see anyone. Then he must try to pacify Albert. It all seemed like a dreadful dream.[9]

Prince Albert in turn poured out his vexations to the same faithful go-between. What happened yesterday, he wrote, was the result of the whole evil situation in which they were enmeshed.

'Lehzen is a crazy, common, stupid intriguer, obsessed with lust of power, who regards herself as a demi-god, and anyone who refuses to acknowledge her as such, as a criminal.'

Victoria, he continued, had been taught to look upon Lehzen as an oracle to whose training she owed all her good qualities. Their unfortunate experiences at Kensington bound them together.

'I on the other hand regard Victoria as naturally a fine character but warped in many respects by wrong upbring- ing.'

Out of pity and love for Victoria he had borne his own suffer- ings with patience. But he would die fighting rather than see his children and his marriage wrecked by the same person who had harmed her so much as a child and as a young Queen.

'There can be no improvement till Victoria sees Lehzen as she is, and I pray that this come. But it seems like a curse upon our heads that Sir John, Dietz,* and indeed the whole world see the truth; and only the chief person concerned does not realise, it, but regards the object of her infatuation as an angel and the world as suspicious, slanderous, envious . . .'[10]

Next morning it was just as well that Prince Albert went off to open the new Stock Exchange. Lehzen knew nothing of the storm and the Queen did not tell her anything, but the message which she sent to her husband by Stockmar showed that she was still under Lehzen's thumb. She forgave him for his 'thoughtless words' of yesterday and begged him in future not to take trifles seriously nor believe stories but to speak up when he saw anything amiss.[11]

This plea for frankness brought forth another tirade to Stockmar from the Prince. Everything he saw amiss, he said, was caused by Lehzen and as she was the one person Victoria trusted how could he speak up against her without causing another scene?

'Victoria is too hasty and passionate for me to be able often to speak of my difficulties. She will not hear me out but flies into a rage and overwhelms me with reproaches of suspiciousness, want of trust, ambition, envy, &c. &c.'

He felt there were only two alternatives: either to retreat like a schoolboy snubbed by his mother or to match Victoria's violence with an outburst even more terrible. This he had done yesterday. But seeing her afterwards in her misery made the whole operation loathsome.[12]

Stockmar decided that the time had come to grasp the nettle himself. If Prince Albert would not 'speak up', he, Stockmar, would do it for him.

Despite the Queen's piteous entreaties not to be shown a second note from Albert if it was full of 'hard words' which might enrage her again,[13] Stockmar forwarded the Prince's note with a covering one from himself, blandly announcing

* Dietz was a bad imitation of Stockmar. Also hailing from Coburg, he encouraged the Portuguese royal family to behave unconstitutionally.

that tempers were now perfectly cool. His covering letter, marked confidential, was formidable. He would not answer for the future, he declared, if such scenes recurred; nor could he himself remain at Court.[14]

This was a hint that the Queen must choose between Stockmar and Lehzen.

The Queen, appalled by the chasm opening before her, did not wait to digest the arguments in Albert's note. She dashed off a propitiatory reply to Stockmar who, she said, would soon be thinking her as bad as poor Mama.

> 'Albert must tell me what he dislikes, & I will set about to remedy it, but he must also *promise* to listen to & believe me; when (on the contrary) I am in a passion which I trust I am not very often in now, he must not believe the stupid things I say like being miserable I ever married & so forth which come when I am unwell.'

When she reached the subject of Lehzen it was clear that her capitulation was at hand. All she wanted, she wrote, was to give Lehzen a quiet home under her roof, as a reward for past services which even Albert acknowledged; she scarcely discussed anything with Lehzen now. 'A. often thinks I see her, when I don't.' Albert only had to order her not to repeat something '& no human being on earth shall know it'. She then threw in a disarming postscript: 'she can say on her honour that she is not infatuated'.[15]

Next day the Queen wrote again to Stockmar more fully. Albert's note she considered very fair but her two previous points still stood.

1. Lehzen was *not* her confidante, only Stockmar. 'I *never* go to *her* to complain which I fear A. suspects I do; no, never.'

2. As for her own passionate behaviour on being 'spoken to', she feared it was 'irremediable' as yet, but time she hoped would cure her.

> 'There is often an irritability in me which (like Sunday last which began the *whole* misery) makes me say cross & odious things which I don't believe myself & which I

fear hurt A. but which he should not believe, but I will strive to conquer it though I knew *before* I married that this would be a trouble; I therefore wished *not* to marry, as the two years and a half, when I was so completely my own mistress made it difficult for me to control myself & to bend to another's will, but I trust I shall be able to conquer it.'

On the practical issue which brought all this to a head, the Queen now fervently agreed with her husband: the nursery management must be reformed.[16]

The Prince handled Lehzen's departure just as he had handled the departure of the Bedchamber ladies – without at first consulting the Queen. When all was settled he told her on July 25th that Lehzen wished to leave in two months' time for the sake of her health. Victoria was naturally upset though she felt it was 'for our & her best'. As the time approached Lehzen was gently detached. While the Queen and Prince were in Scotland she stayed behind with the children, again sending in her little reports: dogs and babies behaving well, no more biting, and the Princess Royal warned not to pull tails. At the end of September she sent back the keys and began teaching Skerrett, the dresser, to take over some of her work. Pressing the Queen's letters was a tricky business. She advised Skerrett not to get the paper too wet but if it was not quite damp enough to leave it under the letter-press for *four* minutes instead of two – a characteristically confused instruction.[17]

Sir James Clark visited the Baroness on September 27th for the last time and found her covered in the dust of packing. She slipped away early in the morning of the 30th without saying goodbye to Queen Victoria, in order to spare her a scene. Nothing became Lehzen in her service to the Queen like the leaving of it. Queen Victoria was grateful for Lehzen's thoughtfulness but suffered notwithstanding. She dreamt that night that Lehzen had come back to say goodbye and awoke to the sad truth. 'It was very unpleasant.'

The rest of Lehzen's life was no less unselfish. She settled with a sister in Bückeburg and devoted her savings and pension of £800* a year to establishing her brother's children in careers. Photographs of Queen Victoria filled her house but some of her habits became rather more advanced than her pupil would have approved. Eager to the last to know the latest gossip, she enticed local worthies into her sitting-room with a promise of Havana cigars.

Queen Victoria corresponded regularly and saw her occasionally before her death in 1870 at the age of eighty-six. In 1845 they met several times in Gotha and chatted pleasantly enough, the Queen finding her much quieter. In 1858 the Queen and Prince, speeding to see their recently married daughter, passed through Bückeburg in a train while Lehzen stood on the platform waving a handkerchief. After Prince Albert's death Lehzen visited the Queen at Rheinhardsbrunn in 1862. 'Saw my poor old Lehzen . . . she is grown so old. We were both much moved . . .'

The Prince's dislike of Lehzen, as the Queen implied in her letters to Stockmar at the time of the crisis in January 1842, was somewhat obsessional. With his passion for efficiency, he was maddened by what he considered Lehzen's frivolity and incompetence. Why, for instance, had she not immediately informed him when one of the courtiers fell idiotically in love with Her Majesty? The Baroness, used to madmen pursuing the young Queen, saw no reason to do so. There had been the Scotsman who came south at intervals to leer at her on the Terrace, and the Manchester business-man who climbed into the Castle grounds seeking a wife. Lehzen did not care a pin for such things.

In the end Lehzen became in Prince Albert's mind the scapegoat for Queen Victoria. All his dear wife's virtues were her own, all her vices Lehzen's. In particular there was Victoria's resistance to certain plans he cherished for introducing a more literary and scientific atmosphere into the Court; this he traced indirectly to Lehzen's influence.

In 1841 Melbourne had explained to the Prince's private secretary, George Anson, that Queen Victoria suffered from a feeling of inferiority, owing to the failure of Lehzen and

* Over £3,000 today.

Mr Davys to educate her properly. She believed herself un-fitted for conversation with scholars but would not consent to be left out of it; even less would her candid nature allow her to pretend to 'one atom more knowledge' than she possessed.[18] A memorandum written by Anson at the end of that year describes the Queen as 'low' and less and less interested in politics or serious pursuits.

Prince Albert's animosity against Lehzen led him to ex-aggerate Queen Victoria's deficiencies. It was tempting to demolish the teacher by degrading her handiwork and Vic-toria was undoubtedly Lehzen's masterpiece. As Melbourne remarked to Anson in 1841, the world would have considered her accomplished had she been born an ordinary young lady instead of a queen.[19]

Was she really so ill-equipped, even for a queen? Her memory was trained to perfection. Few girls in their early twenties could have equalled not only her experience but her ability to digest and use it. At twenty-two she could appre-ciate most of the books put into her hands, from *Glenarvon*, the romance written by Melbourne's wife, Caroline Lamb, to Arnold's *Sermons*, recommended by Melbourne himself; from Fanny Burney's *Memoirs* to the Life of Sir Robert Walpole. Admittedly Queen Victoria wished there had been a little more of Sir Robert's private and a little less of his public life, but was this so 'warped' at twenty? A severe censorship of her reading material was accepted by her not without protest. Was Dumas' *Les Trois Mousquetaires* really unsuitable? she asked King Leopold wistfully. She had cer-tainly advanced since the days when she found novels too dreadfully interesting and thanked Heaven that she had not developed a taste for them.

Her own style was racy and often took a toss over gram-mar but she had a genius for terse dialogue and could summarize a long argument with undeniable dexterity. After comparing the entries in her Journal with accounts of the same conversations in Greville's diaries and thus establish-ing the Queen's accuracy, fairness and grasp, it might well be concluded that Queen Victoria's upbringing would have fitted her to be a better Clerk of the Council than Greville's to wear a crown.

On one point, however, Melbourne's criticism was fully justified. Queen Victoria certainly felt inferior, a short step to being inferior. Lady Lyttelton noticed that while on country-house visits she was so afraid of getting out of her depth in discussing works of art that she preferred to ignore the pictures and explore the bedrooms. Moreover, her own diffidence and shyness were increased by the awkward manners of learned men. But once she got on terms with scholars, as she did for instance with Macaulay, they found her charming and intelligent. And once the Prince could see his wife without the shadow of Lehzen darkening her, he described her to his brother as 'the most perfect companion a man could wish for.'

In November 1842 Lady Lyttelton noted that the tone of conversation at Court had been raised: there was no gossip, naval and scientific subjects being 'pleasantly' discussed at dinner. Next year Queen Victoria paid a notable tribute to the arts and sciences: she declared that the Tsar of Russia's barbarous character was entirely due to a lack of their softening influence. The Prince took a great pride, shared by the Queen herself, in the success of her re-education.

Faults of character in the Queen concerned him even more than faults of intellect. In particular he feared the violent temper which Lehzen's upbringing had failed to cure. It is true that Lehzen did not inculcate self-control but at least she taught Queen Victoria to recognize her weakness. In a later age, the Queen's childhood would have been held to excuse almost any pathological condition ranging from mild disturbance to delinquency. That Lehzen handed over to the nation a potentially great queen, must be to her credit.

Nevertheless she had to go. It was only after Lehzen's ship, bound for Germany and loaded with the luggage of twenty years, was launched at last, that Queen Victoria entered her own 'safe haven'.

CHAPTER XIII

A SAFE HAVEN
1842–6

THE DAY AFTER Lehzen left, Queen Victoria re-read some of her old diaries. In marrying Prince Albert she had entered what she afterwards described as 'a safe haven'. In this spirit she chose Lehzen's departure as the moment to correct the entry of 1839 in which she had rhapsodized over her 'happiness' with Melbourne.*

'1st October. Wrote & looked over & corrected one of my old journals, which do not *now* awake very pleasant feelings. The life I led then was so artificial & superficial, & yet I thought I was happy. Thank God! I know now what *real* happiness means!'

The end of her 'artificial' life with Melbourne seemed to tie up with the end of her emotional life with Lehzen. The act of rewriting this record was symbolic.

A domestic crusade organized by the Prince was already under way. Many of the evils at Court which he set out to remedy dated from the Queen's Accession. Courtiers had taken advantage of her youth. They would dine at her expense even when not in waiting, while people who had nothing to do with the Palace would order carriages by forging the names of ladies-in-waiting. Sir James Clark was accused of always having a tradesman to recommend and, as the Queen noted, 'a scotchman at that'. The Master of the Household made himself a nuisance by insisting on seeing the Queen about every trivial detail: when asked to buy her a dog he demanded an audience to say that he had done so.

Some of the older ladies were once caught smuggling and the young maids-of-honour needed much managing. They had a fine time in the Queen's service: Lehzen spoilt them, they had comfortable rooms, pianos, sheets like silk, lots of hot tubs and only one serious restriction; they were forbidden

* See above, p. 129.

to walk on the Slopes alone for fear of being assaulted. Miss Lister gave trouble of a different kind: she worried Queen Victoria by sobbing her heart out whenever she came back into waiting. Lord M. advised the Queen to say sharply: 'Come, let's have no more blubbering.'

Money troubles disturbed the Queen soon after her Coronation. The expense of entertaining 'all these Ambassadors & people', as she called her guests, was enormous. She spent £34,000 on pensions and charities alone in 1839 ('God!' ejaculated Lord M. in amazement) and £600 on a box at the opera. During the first three months of 1840 dinners were provided at the Palace for 24,600 persons. Becoming alarmed, she could think of nothing to save on but the Botanical Gardens, Kew. Once, indeed, soon after her victory over Peel in 1839 she had remarked to Melbourne that she seemed to have a good deal of money. 'Don't be deluded by that,' he warned: 'you ought always to have £100,000; £50,000 at least: it's everything; that's the real power.'[1]

The royal residences, despite high expenditure, were abominably run. Service was erratic. Guests wandered about looking in vain for their bedrooms or for the way downstairs. Lord Palmerston might have traded on this well-known feature of Windsor when in 1839, in search of another quarry, he accidentally invaded the bedroom of one of the Queen's ladies, Mrs Brand. By mistake the French Foreign Secretary once burst into the Queen's room while she was dressing. An enormous malachite vase sent as a present to the Queen was left standing in the hall unpacked for days on end – 'schocking'. She was frequently forced to apologize to her Prime Minister for meals being late – 'not my fault'.

Comfort and hygiene were scarcely considered even when alterations were undertaken. The construction of a new lavatory was begun at Buckingham Palace immediately over the Queen's bedroom, the waste being connected to a nearby rainwater pipe which discharged itself on to leads in front of her dressing-room window. Some of the improvements needed in the Windsor kitchens included windows that would shut, oven doors in working order and a pastry board properly planed.[2] Worst of all was the cold. As an unmarried girl the Queen had taken a brash pride in telling shivering Ministers that she did not mind the cold, but now she complained with the rest. On one very icy day she could not get her sitting-room temperature above 55 degrees Fahrenheit. Next morning she lost her voice.

Prince Albert reduced the evil to a simple formula: lack of a single authority in control. His prize example of muddle concerned the laying of a fire. Why was there no heat in the morning-room? Because the fire was laid by the Lord Steward but was lighted by the Lord Chamberlain; until the two could be co-ordinated there would be no fire. The Department of Woods and Forests cleaned the outside and the Lord Chamberlain the inside of the windows. Both sides were never clean at once so that Queen Victoria, whose first pleasure on waking was to observe the state of the weather, often had to depend on guesswork.

Into every corner went the Prince's broom, sweeping out among others a manservant who enjoyed the perquisite of collecting each morning hundreds of candles which had never been lighted. The Prince has therefore gone down to history as a saver of candle-ends. His manoeuvres against the venal and incompetent persons who served Her Majesty required a tact which this zealous young German did not possess. In any case it would have been impossible to dismantle a spoils system without making enemies.

There was a clean sweep in the nursery. Out went Mrs Southey and Lady Charlotte Finch; the Queen and Prince decided to have no more nursery governesses in title only. Queen Victoria 'felt her way' to persuading Lady Lyttelton to take on the job.[3] This estimable Whig lady was old-fashioned in dress and outlook, extremely well read, tolerant and clear-sighted. Though she disapproved of Prince Albert playing chess with Archdeacon Wilberforce on Sundays, she adored him. She had all along agreed with him that Pussy's trouble was being 'over-watched and over-doctored'.[4] From her earliest years she had felt herself destined to be of service, unlike Fanny Burney whom Queen Victoria was astounded to find had once held a post in the Royal Family.

Fancy choosing an authoress to be in *any family* – and as for the Royal Family! 'I think they got off very well,' wrote Queen Victoria severely.[5]

After Lady Lyttelton's installation there was no more friction and it was pure joy for the Queen to visit the nursery. Her only regret was that at Buckingham Palace the nursery wing was 'literally a mile off' so that she could not drop in as often as she wished, to see Albert dragging the children round the room in a basket.[6]

Prince Albert reformed the nursery just in time, for it was soon filled to overflowing. The Prince of Wales's birth on November 9th, 1841, eleven and a half months after his sister, was not as sunny as his nature. Pussy's illness filled the Queen with alarm and she felt 'low', 'depressed', and 'wretched'. In later years she often begged her daughters to space their children, saying that the Prince of Wales's arrival had been bad for her and him. Lady Lyttelton, however, thought that the Queen was fit enough to run right round the Great Park.

She had so many false alarms before her son's birth that Prince Albert seized the opportunity to break with a tiresome tradition. The Archbishop of Canterbury and Lord President of the Council were called when she was so far on in labour that they missed the birth. When the Queen had her next child only the Minister was invited to attend.

There was great gladness over 'the Boy', as Queen Victoria called the Prince of Wales in her Journal. (It was only after the birth of his sister, Princess Alice, that he began to get a name – 'Bertie', while about the same time 'Pussy' disappeared and was replaced by 'Vicky'.) Prince Albert had a brooch of 'our Boy's crest' ready to present to Victoria. Within three weeks Mrs Lilly, the monthly nurse, had the Queen on her feet again and was walking her four steps downstairs before going up, to prevent bad luck. To be speaking of 'the children' seemed to the Queen like a dream.

December came with the present tables, and Christmas trees ordered by Prince Albert from Coburg. Queen Victoria was ecstatic about dearest Albert's innovation. Actually Queen

Charlotte had set up a Christmas tree of yew at Windsor before the beginning of the century, but the country acclaimed the idea as Prince Albert's and enthusiastically followed his lead. At Claremont he made Victoria a snowman twelve feet high, played Blind Man's Buff with the ladies and taught them a delightful new round game, *Nain Jaune*. There was also *Loto*, *Dauphine*, *Maccoo*, *Speculation* and *Vingt-et-Un*, on which a gentleman once won a guinea. *Maccoo*, his brother Ernest's introduction, was too much of a wild gamble to please the Queen.

Prince Albert was the dexterous coachman of the family sledge jingling across the snow with grey ponies and scarlet grooms, the knight of Victoria's ice-chair, the champion skater on Frogmore pond. How she admired the elegant swan's head at the tip of each skate.[7] When he slipped down playing ice-hockey she was amazed at the agility with which he sprang to his feet again. One Christmas a group of Red Indians came to Windsor; they were naked to the waist but, as the Queen said, what with their war-paint, beads and dark skins, 'one does not really notice it'.[8] Christmas entertainments held for Queen Victoria all the happiness in the world.

The Boy was christened Albert Edward in St George's Chapel, Windsor, and for once the contented Queen was filled with peaceful instead of macabre thoughts about her relatives resting below. The best thing about the Boy, she wrote, was that he now had his dear father's name.[9] The children filled up much of their parents' day. The Queen sketched Pussy tearing round the bath-tub trying to get in – a naked cherub beside a huge tank on wheels – and wrote her Journal with Pussy on her lap. Prince Albert played his organ while dancing a baby on each knee.

The peace of 1842 was twice shattered by lunatic attempts on the Queen's life. On May 30th her Journal began with a fine sense of drama: 'We drove out, the 2 Equerries riding quite close up to the carriage on either side, – the reason for which will appear.' She then described how the day before, while driving in the Mall, Albert had noticed 'a little swarthy ill-looking rascal' pointing a pistol which at two paces misfired. The rascal slipped away in the crowd. The Queen felt certain he would try again but she could not endure being 'shut up for days' with the danger hanging over her. This was the reason for the reckless decision to challenge the man to a second attempt. As though nothing had happened and telling none of the Household, the royal couple drove out next afternoon exactly as before except that the Queen thoughtfully left her lady-in-waiting, Lady Portman, behind. 'I must expose the lives of my gentlemen,' she said, 'but I will not those of my ladies.'[10] Sure enough the man fired again, this time at five paces. The Queen heard a slight report and saw him seized. Shuddering at what might have happened, she returned to find Lady Portman, who had sulked at being left behind, covered with blushes.

The man, John Francis, was condemned to death: 'the feeling that he is to be executed is very painful to me,' wrote the Queen. Yet she considered it necessary. When he was reprieved because the pistol was not loaded her reaction was ambivalent. 'I of course am glad' – but more fervently than ever she wanted the law changed.[11]

Francis was reprieved on July 1st. A presentiment that this would serve *pour encourager les autres* prepared the Queen for another attempt two days later, this time by a deformed boy named John William Bean, only four feet tall and with a 'pitiable expression' though 'certainly not a simpleton'.[12] Fortunately Bean's pistol was loaded generously with paper and tobacco and hardly at all with gunpowder.

During the last days of 1842 the Queen and Prince fell again to talking of the two ghosts, Lehzen and Melbourne. What had caused her 'unbounded admiration & affection' for Melbourne? She scarcely knew; she could only suggest it was her having 'very warm feelings' and needing to cling to someone. The Prince was more brusque: 'Albert thinks I worked myself up to what really became at last, quite foolish.'[13] When he went on to reveal his sufferings under Lehzen, she could hardly bear to listen, though it was a relief to discuss everything at last. How she blamed herself for her blindness. Every so often through the happy years that followed Prince

Albert would lift another corner of the veil, finally convincing the Queen that the beginning of his marriage had been a martyrdom borne like a saint. As for Lehzen, her conduct was inexplicable. It was kinder to call her an enigma and leave it at that.

The new year opened calmly. A little cast was made of the Boy's hand to go with his sister's, and the Queen, again pregnant but not this time peevish, placidly went over the baby linen with Lady Lyttelton. Almost nothing new was wanted. On April 25th, 1843 a second daughter arrived, Princess Alice. The Prince was too busy now to spend much time with his wife afterwards; she therefore became bored with lying-in and returned quickly to normal. The christening as usual was the occasion for a family reunion – an event never without its terrors. This time one of the sponsors, the Queen's Uncle Ernest, King of Hanover, deliberately cut the service. After it was all over he landed in England bent, bald, deaf and quite changed, according to the Queen, except for one thing: he spoke 'never a kind word'.[14] He was in fact involved in a bitter dispute with her over the possession of Princess Charlotte's jewels. The Queen claimed them and wore them; the King had a better right to them and lost no chance of saying so. 'I hear the little Queen is loaded with my diamonds,' he once wrote caustically to a friend, 'which made a very fine show.' Princess Charlotte's jewels were at this time the Queen's great standby, for as a young woman her jewel-box was by no means an Aladdin's cave. When one of her bridesmaids, Lady Sarah Villiers, married Prince Esterhazy she received a wedding-present of jewels worth more than anything the Queen possessed.

At the wedding in July of Princess Augusta of Cambridge to the Grand Duke of Mecklenburg-Strelitz, the King of Hanover found another opportunity for displaying spite. The Queen and Prince were barely recovered from an attack of influenza. In this weak state, Prince Albert found himself pushing the King off the altar steps to prevent him from usurping his own place. Soon afterwards the Queen signed the register with the King hovering over her ready to snatch the pen before Prince Albert. Enfeebled as she was and encumbered by her dress and train of brocade, her diadem, diamond fringes and feathers, she nevertheless nipped round the table like lightning, had the register passed across to her, signed and gave the pen to the Prince before the King of Hanover knew what was happening.

The little Princess Royal and Prince of Wales were beginning to have their own squabbles. 'The Children had a tremendous fight in our room, which was really too absurd,' complained the Queen.[15] Next day they had to come downstairs separately though this did not stop Vicky from picking a quarrel with her brother during an overlap of five minutes. 'Fat Alice' or 'Fatima' as the parents fondly called their second daughter, and Prince Alfred ('Affie') who arrived on August 6th, 1844, were no trouble. But the Prince of Wales was almost as backward as the Princess Royal was precocious; he stammered and so she teased him.

These were only trivial annoyances and did not deter the Queen from steadily increasing the time her children spent downstairs. It was nothing to have the baby for an hour and a half during luncheon, as well as the older children. The Queen threw herself into being a good mother. Though conscious of having no great desire nor gift for teaching, she would have felt ashamed not to try to teach her children. So she chose her own strongest subject – history – and read it to Vicky. She gave Vicky religious instruction and heard all her children's prayers, consulting her half-sister, Princess Feodore, as to whether they should kneel or not. Feodore, writing from Lutheran Germany, replied that she simply let her children sit up in bed.

The children's formal education did not yet cause the Queen any anxiety, but one lesson she was determined to teach them: that their dearest Papa was head of the family. Prince Albert sometimes feared that his paternal authority might be impaired by his ambiguous position. Acutely the Queen observed that the solution lay in her own example. If she treated the Prince as her lord and master her children would do the same.

Surveying the four children under four Prince Albert resolved to bring up each one 'for its position': Bertie for King of England, Affie for Duke of Coburg in case Ernest had no heir, baby Alice to carry on some royal line. And the Princess Royal? At Prince Alfred's christening her position was mapped out. The heir to the King of Prussia was invited to be one of Affie's godfathers. He had a son of twelve. Vicky was nearly four. Her position was to be the most interesting of all. She would rule Prussia.

It was after the birth of Queen Victoria's fifth child, Princess Helena, that Prince Albert and Stockmar set her thinking seriously about education.

'A good, moral, religious, but *not bigoted* or narrow-minded education is what I pray for, for my children. But where to find exactly what one wants?'

Princess Helena, born on May 25th, 1846, disgraced herself by crying and sucking her thumb at her christening; but as the Chapel in Buckingham Palace was illuminated for the first time by gas, this christening was no less successful than the others. The gas lamps, noted the Queen resolutely taking an interest in science, were ventilated by Professor Faraday's principle of drawing the noxious fumes down the stems of ormolu candelabra.

The only melancholy event to occur between the departure of Lehzen in 1842 and of Peel in 1846 was the death of Prince Albert's father, at fifty-nine, in 1844. He had been an unmitigated disaster. His licentiousness had broken up Prince Albert's home; he badgered Queen Victoria, through Albert, to settle on him a huge allowance and savaged them both by letter for not calling their eldest son after himself. But death was something different. Albert wept as though he were washing away all Duke Ernest's sins and Victoria cried so much that she could hardly write her Journal. Seven remarkable words finally appeared on the page: 'We shall not see his like again.'[16]

Duke Ernest's death meant that the Prince had to leave the Queen for the first time since her marriage – 'the bare thought of which is terrible to me'. Her life, however, was enriched with his love letters. On the morning he left for

215

Coburg he scribbled a note for her at 6 am. 'Every step takes me further from you – not a cheerful thought.' Later that day came a letter: [17]

> My own darling – I have been here about an hour and regret the lost time which I might have spent with you . . . You will, while I write, be getting ready for luncheon, and you will find a place vacant where I sat yesterday. In your heart, however, I hope my place will not be vacant . . . You are even now half a day nearer to seeing me again; by the time you get this letter, you will be a whole one – thirteen more, and I am again within your arms. —
>
> > Your most devoted
> > Albert.

In these stilted lines some people have seen an expression not of Prince Albert's love for Queen Victoria but of his 'cool pitying devotedness'[18] based on recognition of hers for him. Such an interpretation is contrary to the facts. Within the context of a happy marriage the contrast between, 'I am again within your arms' (the Prince's regular formula)* and 'You will again be in mine', does not represent a different degree of love. His letters, said Queen Victoria, made her *very* happy. And on the day he returned she wrote: 'I had the immense joy of . . . being clasped in his arms.'[19]

At last she had begun to feel, what to her was the acme of desire, safe. The domestic daisy-chain of pleasant, small events was strung out across the peaceful months. In the spring they would play skittles in the Palace garden, coming back to cowslip tea and the family albums; in summer she would take the children into the kitchen garden to gorge themselves with fruit. Her favourite preacher, Samuel Wilberforce, accommodated himself to the scale of her new life. 'We must become perfect,' he said, 'little by little, in small daily tasks.' The Prince sat by the Queen's side as the good Dean preached, nodding appreciatively.

All the Queen's past discontents were melting away. She

* 'I hope tomorrow at half-past six to fall again into your arms,' he wrote in 1851, and in 1858, 'Late Monday evening, I will again lie in your arms.' (R.A. Z297/14, 39.)

was happy everywhere. When the time came to leave Buckingham Palace for one of the other royal residences she felt regret – 'I have been so happy there' – but had to add, 'but *where* am I not happy *now*?'[20]

On returning from a holiday towards the end of 1844 she attempted to sketch her domestic haven:

> 'The children again with us, & such a pleasure & interest! Bertie & Alice are the greatest friends & always playing together. – Later we both read to each other. When I read, I sit on a sofa, in the middle of the room, with a small table before it, on which stand a lamp & candlestick, Albert sitting in a low armchair, on the opposite side of the table with another small table in front of him on which he usually stands his book. Oh! if I could only exactly describe our dear happy life together!'[21]

On New Year's Eve the proud parents tiptoed into the two night-nurseries to see in each a sleeping boy and girl. The Prince heralded 1845 with a hearty, '*prost Neu Jahr!*'

The Queen, though pregnant again, for the first time faced childbirth with a feeling of 'security'. God had been so merciful. She had never lost a baby like Augusta Strelitz, nor fallen ill like the two Russian grand duchesses who both died of consumption within a year of their confinements. She prayed for a continuance of 'my great happiness', looking forward with confidence to 'His protection of us *together*'.

All at Court knew that Prince Albert's spirits suffered from staying too long in London, but the Queen was furious when 'a horrid man from the *Morning Herald*' got into Windsor Castle one day and published an alarmist report on his health. It was for Albert's sake that she gradually trained herself to prefer the country to London.

The family was growing apace but where was the privacy for family life? On Sunday afternoon at Windsor the little Queen would march bravely into a wall of humanity who stood grinning and staring until the last moment, when they slowly backed away. At the Brighton Pavilion the royal couple were mobbed on the Chain Pier, people diving under the brim of the Queen's bonnet and pushing their faces into hers.

The experience confirmed the opinion that the people of Sussex were even worse than those of Kent whom Lord M. considered the worst in England. She never stayed in the Pavilion again. These problems cried out for one solution: a holiday home of their own right away in the country.

As a preliminary, the Queen and Prince had made their first train journey from Windsor to Paddington in 1842. 'Not so fast next time, Mr Conductor,' is alleged to have been Prince Albert's comment on the adventure. The Queen was delighted. She found it much smoother than a carriage and could not understand people's criticism. Smoother it certainly was: the Queen's carriages rocked crazily as they dashed headlong to their destination, for if they slackened speed for an instant a roistering crowd would gather. 'That's right, old girl,' shouted a burly woman one day when the royal nurse reluctantly held up the Prince of Wales to be kissed. Railways brought to an end the Queen's closest physical contact with her subjects. When, seven years later, she came to read Macaulay's *History*, she much appreciated his 'laudation' of modern transport.

That summer she sounded Peel on 'a little trip to Scotland'. Peel agreed but soon afterwards repented owing to rioting in the North. Melbourne, however, urged the Queen to go; a cancellation would make a deplorable impression. It seemed safest to travel by sea. 'How delightful,' wrote the Queen, 'to be quite alone together on board – no Ladies or Gentlemen' – and no Lehzen. There was a cow on board but she was too ill to be used. At Edinburgh her advisers were terrified of attempts on her life. Through the thronged streets her carriage flashed and was gone, to the annoyance of the loyal Scots and the alarm of the Queen. By the end of the visit Scotland had charmed but not yet conquered her. She returned to England feeling that despite all she had seen, Windsor was *unique*.

They next took the sea air at Deal where Wellington lent them Walmer Castle. The rooms were small, the windows rattled like the Iron Duke's musketry, even the Queen shivered in the appalling draughts: 'still, I had formed an affection for it,' she wrote characteristically when it was time to go home.

They travelled on the same Dover Road, stopping at the same inns Prince Albert had stopped at when he came to marry her three years ago; but then he had no 'little wife' – no *Fraüchen* – and children.

A more elaborate burst of fresh air was planned for the late summer of 1843. The Queen and Prince cruised along the south coast – 'the sailor-gypsy life we lead is *very* delightful'[22] – and stayed with the French royal family at Château d'Eu, the first visit to be made by an English monarch since Henry VIII met Francis I on the Field of the Cloth of Gold. She was transported by the gaiety and elegance, but most of all by finding herself at ease 'in a family circle of persons of my own rank, with whom I could be on terms of equality & familiarity'.[23] A call on her Belgian relations concluded this holiday. The novelist Charlotte Brontë saw Queen Victoria passing in the streets of Brussels and was impressed by her laughing face and plain dress. If the governess from Haworth Parsonage said so, it must have been plain indeed. Home again, the Queen felt 'pent up'. Something had been started by her sea trip which must be satisfied. 'During our usual morning walk,' she wrote on October 19th, 1843, 'Albert & I talked of buying a place of our own, which would be so nice; perhaps Norris Castle might be something to think of.'

Something to think of . . . By December their thoughts, guided by Sir Robert Peel, had fastened firmly upon the Isle of Wight and secret plans were afoot to buy Osborne. Thanks to Peel's adroitness, Osborne cost the moderate sum of £26,000.

Meanwhile the royal pair studied others who already had places of their own, such as Peel himself at Drayton Manor and the Duke of Buckingham at Stowe. In the past Victoria had more than once marvelled at the vast possessions of her uncle, King George IV – 'he had such quantities of everything'[24] – but the grandeur of Chatsworth, where the Duke of Devonshire reigned and his gardener Joseph Paxton ruled, took their breath away. Mr Paxton was 'quite a genius', not only laying out the gardens but planning all the buildings including that 'mass of glass', the conservatory.[25] It came flashing back into Prince Albert's mind when he was considering plans for the Great Exhibition.

Just over a year later she paid a more informal visit to the Duke of Wellington at Stratfield Saye. They sat at small tables for luncheon, the Duke himself helping them to huge portions of puddings and tarts all mixed up together. At the end of each evening, having pleased the Queen with some flattering reminiscence of her father, the old Duke would march upstairs in front of Her Majesty carrying her candle.

During this same year, 1845, Queen Victoria met both Gladstone and Disraeli for the first time. The former she invited to Windsor, the latter was a fellow-guest at Stowe. Neither of them, despite the immense part they were to play in her future, won so much as an interested sentence in her Journal. Not so their wives. Mrs Disraeli was picked out for her singularity, Mrs Gladstone for her charm.

By the autumn of 1844 the Queen was already feeling in need of a real break. (People who were always on the look out for madness in the Royal Family, reported that her round of visits was a sign of nervous excitement.)[26] The Emperor Nicholas I of Russia, jealous of her *fêtes champêtres* with King Louis Philippe, had suddenly descended on her un-invited when she was seven months gone with child. She hated seeing him 'in my present condition', and as long as his visit lasted was in a fright lest someone should shoot him. He was not a happy man, she felt, and when at last he took wing in the *Black Eagle* – a sinister tyrant with wild eyes, white eyelashes and a smile more blood-curdling than his frown – she was profoundly relieved.

It was two years since the Queen and Prince had visited Scotland and they now stayed at Blair Atholl. The Queen soon ran out of glowing adjectives. 'I can only say that the scenery is lovely, grand, romantic, & a great peace and wild-ness pervades all, which is sublime.'[27] Many of the patterns for their future life in the Highlands were laid down: Queen Victoria reading aloud from Sir Walter Scott; Prince Albert stalking deer and never losing his temper even when every shot missed; Pussette frightened at Papa saying he would call a roaring stag into the castle; old red-haired Peter Frazer, Lord Glenlyon's head keeper, nursing his master through a serious illness – 'one sees so much of that kind of attachment in the Highlands,' observed the Queen; Albert noting resemblances to Thuringia in every mountain and lake; Victoria saying goodbye to the 'dear, dear *Highlands*' and watching with infinite despondency her life and the countryside steadily becoming flatter and flatter as she travelled south.

Two days after she was back at Windsor, portly King Louis Philippe paid a return visit, heralded by an anxious letter from his wife. Queen Amélie entreated Queen Victoria to see that he did not risk his stomach by overeating nor his neck by horseback riding. It was a delicate assignment, for the King had previously lavished shiploads of imported beer and cheese on his English guests. As before, the main theme, so far as Queen Victoria was concerned, was not politics but human relations. Guizot, the French Foreign Minister, told her that he was amazed to see four pink-cheeked royal babies where four years ago he had seen none. The hospitality, magnificent in the extreme, delighted the country, especially as it was entirely paid for out of the Privy Purse and did not cost them an extra shilling. The phrase '*Entente Cordiale*' was coined.

As soon as the French visitors had departed the Royal Family were rewarded by their first holiday at Osborne, beginning on October 10th, 1844. The Queen found it exactly what she wanted – snug, complete, an excellent place for the children. Sir James Clark came to vet it for the air. They were back in their 'dear little Home' next spring, the Princess Royal in raptures over the shells and Prince Albert over the scope for improvements. They planned to buy up the surrounding estates. 'Our possessions will be immense,' wrote the Queen with mingled awe and complacency.[28] All the remaining grievances of the child who had dropped hints to her aunts when she wanted a little something for herself and of the young woman who had envied George IV's vast possessions, vanished. At last, contemplating the furniture and china in the drawing-room, she could write the magic words, 'all our *very own*.'[29]

Next year she was preparing to say goodbye to the 'dear little Home', for it was soon to be pulled down and replaced by a splendid mansion. As if to set her seal on the new life the Queen did something she had been wanting to do for the past five years. She made her will.

The Queen's fulfilment as a private person was completed during that autumn of 1845. Peel decided that since communications were now so good she and Prince Albert could go abroad together without the inconvenience of declaring a Regency. For the first time in her life she visited Germany and saw the Rosenau, Prince Albert's birthplace. The experience was profoundly emotional.

'If I were not who I am – *this* would have been my real home, but I shall always consider it my *2nd* one.'[30]

A strange feeling gradually developed that she had lived there before, an indication that her rejected Kensington childhood was banished at last. Her diary was a welter of churches, palaces, vineyards, German royalties including the singular King of Bavaria who talked to one with his eyes tight shut; fireworks, a *battue* which she considered a disgusting slaughter rather than sport, welcoming bands, inexpressible fatigue. She loved the peasants in costumes, deploring the native English custom of apeing the upper classes by wearing colourless, limp petticoats. But she was not dissatisfied when she overheard someone say that she looked '*sehr Englisch*'.

It was during these happy years that Queen Victoria's and Prince Albert's favourite portraits of each other were executed. For Albert's twenty-fourth birthday Victoria gave him a head and shoulders of herself by Winterhalter reclining against a velvet cushion. Her long hair is loose, one lock straying romantically over her shoulder; the large eyes are lowered. It is a portrait of 'Fraüchen' in a mood of gentle submission, not of the Queen. Prince Albert was painted for Queen Victoria by Thorburn in a suit of shining armour.

Contrary to the Queen's expectations she found Peel's Ministry an integral part of her safe haven. With her instinct to look on the bright side of people, she was soon remarking that despite his 'pompous' manner he had a good voice. Her first Speech from the Throne she found 'judicious' considering that it was written by a Tory. As Peel gradually unfroze he talked 'very interestingly' about contemporary politics, vividly describing how Cobden attacked him in the Commons, 'twisting his black hair through his fingers'; or telling her that the rising Radical, Mr Roebuck, was a new Robespierre – very dangerous and bold.[31] She admired the refusal of Peel, the cotton-spinner's son, to accept honours, agreeing with Lord Aberdeen that it showed 'a proud humility'.[32] Above all, she was deeply moved by his appreciation of the Prince.

It was due to Peel that from 1842 onwards Prince Albert attended the Ministers' audiences with Her Majesty. In time the Prince was reading dispatches to the Queen instead of her reading extracts to him and when she expressed an opinion to Ministers she spoke of 'we' not 'I'. The man who had sacrificed for his wife's sake the evening game of chess to play *Nain Jaune*, was now moving a real queen.

Prince Albert's artistic interests were recognized by Peel when he appointed him Chairman of the Arts Commission for the rebuilding of Parliament. The Queen noted happily that Albert was always going to or coming from 'his Commission'; her own appreciation of his talents was reserved for the personal presents he designed for her: a group of eight little dogs on chains in kennels, another inkstand with a frosted silver stag, a wreath for her hair of gold leaves, white china orange-blossom and four little green oranges representing the children.

To Peel the Queen always turned for sympathy when struck afresh by the Prince's humiliating constitutional position. At times she almost felt 'it would have been fairer to him for me not to have married him.'[23] The worst moment had been when the King of Prussia gave precedence to a mere Austrian archduke over the husband of the Queen of England. Victoria plainly showed that she was not pleased. The incident was a blot on her first visit to 'dear little Germany' and her unsmiling face attracted adverse comment. She was naïvely surprised to hear afterwards that her manner had given offence. What could she do to improve her manner in the future? Smile, replied the Prince; smile fixedly like a ballerina from start to finish; and he pirouetted on tiptoe, grinning from ear to ear, for the Queen to see how it was done.

Sir Robert agreed with her that something some time *must* be done about Albert: 'oh! if only I could make him King,' she sighed.[34]

In social affairs the Queen rapidly developed interest now that she was guided by Peel and the Prince. Among other things, Peel advised her to placate public opinion by living without ostentation. The Radical Press was fond of contrasting pauperism in the cities with luxury in the Palace. Prince Albert was encouraged to receive two 'respectable' men from Belper who requested him and his wife to wear short trousers and petticoats: this would assist the stocking industry. Considering the difficulty Queen Victoria had with her long skirts in stepping off boats and crossing muddy streets (a Plymouth alderman once laid down his gown for her) it was a pity she could not grant the petition. Shortly afterwards, at the Prince of Wales's christening, all the ladies were required to wear Paisley shawls and English lace.

To assist the unemployed silk weavers of Spitalfields, the Queen and Prince organized a magnificent *bal costumé* at the Palace on May 12th, 1842, going as Queen Philippa and King Edward III. Though the Queen hated 'being troubled about dress', as she told King Leopold, the pages of her Journal glow with water-colour sketches painted by herself: Queen Philippa with slightly curved nose, half-opened lips drooping at the corners, plump arms, tiny hands, a jacket of gold and blue tissue, a cloak of cloth-of-gold and a scarlet velvet petticoat: King Edward is delineated with loving care but inadvertently given a hang-dog look. After the ball they visited Westminster Abbey where Queen Victoria was disappointed to find that Queen Philippa's effigy had not worn as well as the rest.

Despite royal patronage the silk weavers did not recover their prosperity and two years later were taking part in Chartist demonstrations. Outbreaks of fever among them called forth a Commission for Investigating the Sanitary Conditions of the Labouring Classes. In this at least Spitalfields and Windsor joined hands. Though a main drainage system for Windsor was constructed in the 1840s, smells from the

224

old cesspools still made parts of the Castle almost un-inhabitable.

It was in the Queen's nature to help individuals wherever possible but to misunderstand their frantic efforts to help themselves. When she heard that the deaths of two sailors at a Spithead review had driven the wife of one mad, she sent money to both families; she worried about 'the three unfortunate men' in Eddystone lighthouse; she wondered whether a dwarf who acted Napoleon for her on the Palace table was kindly treated.

With the Chartists she felt no sympathy. The workmen, she believed, had been misled by professional agitators and the 'criminals & refuse of London'. But when she actually saw young criminals face to face her heart was wrung. The life of juvenile delinquents in Parkhurst gaol, Isle of Wight, condemned for the first two months to solitary confinement, she found unbearably 'triste & lonely'. Those under twelve, she noted, were removed from their parents for ever as a deterrent to other parents who might train their children in crime. It was touching to find that all these little Oliver Twists had 'a very strongly developed filial feeling'. She asked for a free pardon for 'the most deserving' in each ward.[35]

Queen Victoria was glad to arrange a meeting between Mrs Fry, the great penal reformer, and the King of Prussia. Charles Greville found the King's ambition to meet Mrs Fry, 'odd'.

She supported her husband's successful move to make duelling illegal, although Lord M. had once insisted that to kill a man in a duel was not murder. The horrors of public executions, with distinguished visitors circulating a punch-bowl in the death cell, outraged her a quarter of a century before they were abolished in 1868.

When it came to Lord Ashley's* Ten Hour Bill there was no friendly response from the Queen. This inspired Conservative nobleman wished to limit the hours of workers in mills and factories, many of them children. The Queen duly rehearsed the official argument against his Bill: it would deprive industry of seven weeks' child-power a year, thus

* The great Lord Shaftesbury sat in Parliament as Lord Ashley until 1851, when he succeeded to the earldom.

injuring England's competitive position abroad, and neither manufacturers nor Liberal leaders like Bright and Cobden wanted it. But what upset her most was the fear that this measure must split Peel's Government. Thus one of the greatest reforms of her age, which should have appealed especially to a 'female Sovereign', found no favour in her eyes.

In the middle of 1844 economic affairs caused one of those political upheavals which the Queen so much dreaded. 'Why are the Tories like walnuts? Because they are troublesome to *peel*,' was a conundrum which had been going the rounds since 1842. Now it was not amusing. Distress was still acute, despite several years of buoyant revenue, and cheaper food brought about by the repeal of the duties on commodities like sugar and corn was the insistent demand of the Anti-Corn Law League. Peel, elected to defeat Melbourne's very mild instalment of Free Trade, had become converted by events to the Opposition's creed. In June he proposed to reduce the sugar taxes but was defeated. Only a later vote of confidence saved him from resigning.

Throughout the crisis Queen Victoria had despaired. To lose Sir Robert, so safe, so noble-minded – if anything a bit too much so – was unthinkable. How different from Disraeli who, at the head of the ultra-Tories, was attacking Peel in the unprincipled, disgraceful manner one would expect from a man of such bad, bitter character. The Queen tried to drown her future idol in a sea of furious adjectives. Above all Disraeli was reckless, unsafe. 'Oh! for a little true, *disinterested patriotism*.'

Within a few months the noble-minded Peel was again in danger. This time the Queen's anxieties were focused on Ireland. She longed to go there and it was only the threat issued by the Irish leader, Daniel O'Connell, that she would see 'Repeal' written up wherever she went, that prevented her. O'Connell's movement for repeal of the Union collapsed without bloodshed. Once it was over the Queen threw herself eagerly into Peel's plans for Irish amelioration.

Why should Ireland not be ruled more like Scotland, she asked, with no Lord Lieutenant? Government by troops was

226

dreadful. How cruel of the Irish landlords to evict their peasantry. English tenants were much better treated. Fiercely she defended the Government's decision in 1845 to increase the Maynooth grant (Maynooth was a training college for Roman Catholic clergy): surely it was obvious that in a country so much under clerical influence an educated priesthood would be of great value to England?

The bigoted opposition of Protestants made her blood boil.

'I blush for the form of religion we profess, that it should be so void of all right feeling, & so wanting in Charity.'[36]

She had already sampled what seemed to her the tiresomeness of Presbyterians when they declined to recognize her as head of their Church, declaring themselves governed by Elders. They were worse than the Papists, she felt, who after all had only one Pope. The Puseyites, extreme High Churchmen, she found equally provoking for it was owing to their ritualistic excesses that the rest had become so bigoted.

Her contempt for Mr Gladstone soon eclipsed all other emotions. Though a member of Peel's Government and actually favourable to the Maynooth grant, Gladstone had once written a book attacking the principle of subsidizing Papists. Therefore he now insisted on resigning. The Queen raged at the pedantic ineptitude of a Minister who could shake a Government for the sake of *a book*. Lord Aberdeen, the Foreign Secretary, was reported to have said to Mr Gladstone: 'No one reads your book and those who do, don't understand it.' Her Majesty thought this very good.[37]

Maynooth helped to predispose her against both Gladstone and organized religion. Her naïve spontaneity was offended by the claims of dogma to bend and bind. She recorded drily that Gladstone expressed himself 'cast down' at leaving her service. His speech of resignation she found 'very unintelligible'.[38]

That summer of 1845 the heavens opened and rained away the last of peace and plenty. Peel warned her that a potato famine in Ireland would almost certainly mean a violent clash over the Corn Laws. For a moment he led her to hope that the reports of famine were exaggerated; the peasants might be able to grind their putrid potatoes into meal. By the end of November she learnt that the reports had shown a fearful optimism.

In December, while the Royal Family were peacefully at Osborne, a tornado swept Parliament and the blow fell. Sir Robert Peel announced his resignation to the Queen on the 6th, for neither Lord Stanley nor the Duke of Wellington would support him on Corn Law reform. The Queen could not speak for tears. Good Sir Robert was even safer than Lord M., she wept: the fact that she had taken him so unwillingly and now was so upset to lose him, *proved* his great worth.

Next day she awoke as if to a bad dream. Peel drafted a letter for her to send to Lord John Russell, offering him the Premiership. The prospect of Lord Palmerston instead of Lord Aberdeen as Foreign Secretary was appalling. There would be 'horror' in Paris over the change, she wrote in her Journal, and relations with the French were already none too good. She and the Prince between them, said Lord Aberdeen encouragingly, must keep Palmerston straight. One grain of comfort lay in the fact that Russell's Ministry, if he succeeded in forming one, could only exist with Peel's support.

On December 19th came 'astounding' news. Russell had failed. 'Our excitement & suspense great,' scribbled the Queen. The excitement in Parliament was unparalleled. Next day she was celebrating her miraculous escape. In Disraeli's famous words, Russell handed back with courtesy the poisoned chalice to Sir Robert. Peel promised to 'stand by the Queen'.

With her Prime Minister restored to her, she congratulated herself on the spotless constitutionalism and 'fairness' of her behaviour this time compared with 1839 when she had clung on to Lord M. In this mood she was not prepared to hear Melbourne at a dinner party describing Sir Robert's conversion to Free Trade as 'a damned dishonest act'. After trying without success to dissolve Melbourne's truculence in laughter she said sternly:

'Ld. Melbourne, I must beg you not to say anything more

on this subject now; I shall be very glad to discuss it with you at any other time.'[39]

The old man's pathetic excitement, generated by being once more in the Queen's company, subsided. He fell silent.

Two days later, on December 22nd, the Queen made a diagnosis of Russell's failure. He lacked determination. Instead of saying like the admirable Sir Robert, 'I am the Queen's Minister,' he insisted on consulting fifteen other people. It did not cross her mind that her own opposition to Palmerston as Foreign Secretary had fatally handicapped Russell's first attempt at Cabinet-making.

The Queen and Prince realized that their unexpected reprieve from the Whigs might be short-lived. They supported Peel with intensified ardour. In January 1846 the Queen reported the sinister fact that Peel's speech announcing his programme for repeal of the Corn Laws was cheered by the Opposition while his own Conservative ranks remained silent. More sinister in the eyes of the Conservatives was Prince Albert's appearance in the House of Commons, showing royal bias in favour of Free Trade. Such was the outcry among Protectionists that the Prince was forced to make his first his last appearance at a Parliamentary debate. The Queen was beside herself: it was too bad to be criticized by 'gentlemen who did nothing but hunt all day, drunk Claret or Port Wine in the evening, & never studied or read about any of these questions'.[40] As for Lord Stanley who led the Westminster hunting men in their profligate view-halloo, she agreed with the *Spectator* that he ought to be sent back to Eton.

At the beginning of June, safely delivered of a fifth child, Queen Victoria turned again to the unsatisfactory state of politics. Fortunately her nerves were better after this confinement than ever before: Albert had been with her every moment holding her hand and fanning her. 'I feel quiet & prepared for whatever may come.'

On June 26th the end came. Simultaneously with the passage of Repeal through the House of Lords,* Peel's Minis-

* Wellington had withdrawn his opposition.

229

try was paradoxically defeated in the Commons on a measure for Irish coercion. Coming up from the beach at Osborne Lady Lyttelton noticed that something had happened, try as the Queen would to disguise it. 'Oh! for a woman to have such things to manage & to stand!'

Queen Victoria controlled her feelings. Though she 'hated' the Whigs for their 'indecorous' place-hunting, and felt aggrieved that the crisis had developed when her lying-in was scarcely over, she was now training herself to take politics as they came. From inside her safe haven she looked forward to a time when the defeat of a Prime Minister would cause her scarcely more alarm than the departure of Mrs Lilly, her monthly nurse. Perhaps one day Westminster would run as smoothly as her nursery. Until then, life would continue to offer precious hours of peaceful seclusion.

'Really when one is so happy & Blessed in one's home life, as I am, Politics (provided my Country is safe) must take only a 2nd. place.'[41]

Provided the country is safe ... Queen Victoria had reached the conclusion that she and the Prince could contribute to the safety of the country in two distinct ways, over the heads of whatever governments were in power. In foreign politics, encouraged by Stockmar and Lord Aberdeen, they intended henceforward to assume special responsibilities. In domestic affairs, their happy family life would keep the country morally safe. When Queen Victoria opened the new Royal Exchange in October 1844 her press had been so good that she had called King Leopold's attention to it.

'They say no Sovereign was ever more loved than I am (I am bold enough to say), & this because of our domestic home, the good example it presents.'[42]

Perhaps it was as well that politics no longer came first with her. For whereas her domestic contribution was unassailable (except by 'the fashionables' as she contemptuously called Prince Albert's enemies), her right to control foreign affairs, now in the hands of Lord Palmerston, was soon to be sharply challenged.

CHAPTER XIV

'GREAT EVENTS MAKE ME CALM'
1846–8

As AN UNMARRIED GIRL Queen Victoria had been well aware of Lord Palmerston's darts, both those which charmed and those which hurt. The one-time student of Edinburgh University, nicknamed 'Cupid' for obvious reasons, was a man of fifty-three, still handsome, when Queen Victoria came to the throne. As her Foreign Secretary she found him an agreeable member of 'our pleasant little *cercle*' and at the end of her first three months as Queen wrote: 'I hope & trust I may spend many such *summers* with the *same friends.*'

Palmerston like Melbourne possessed the loud yaffling laugh of the self-confident Whig; he had much better manners than Melbourne, an equally good but more robust temper and a jolly taste in waistcoats and women. With women, as Greville remarked, he was always enterprising and audacious. He had been Secretary-at-War and a Tory from 1809–28 and then as Whig Foreign Secretary in 1830 had set up a throne for Princess Victoria's uncle, King Leopold, in Belgium. In Portugal and Spain he supported her two little royal 'sisters', Maria and Isabella, as constitutional queens. His mixture of Whig and Tory qualities should have made him permanently acceptable to the Queen.

Until she married she knew nothing of her Foreign Secretary's nocturnal wanderings at Windsor. Melbourne kept from her all such irregularities. Her first doubts about him were caused by his marriage in 1840 to Melbourne's widowed sister, Lady Cowper, with whom he had been in love for years. The Queen disapproved all her life of widows remarrying and Lady Cowper is the first recorded object of her criticism. The Queen was fortified in her hostility by the sight of Lady Cowper's daughter by her first marriage, Fanny, a favourite lady-in-waiting, going about with a long face. In vain Lord M. chaffed the Queen, saying that young people were always silly; Queen Victoria felt that Fanny was right.

What should she say if Lady Cowper asked her blessing on the match? Be untruthful or unkind? She placed her dilemma before her Prime Minister. Scruples of this sort never bothered Melbourne. It would be 'very ill natured' not to give it, he said; anyway, 'what does it signify?' A month later the Queen had still not brought herself to write Lady Cowper a letter of congratulation. The battle between fanatical honesty and human kindness was already joined, a battle which reached its famous climax fifty years later when her pen refused to trace one word of regret at the death of Mr Gladstone.

Palmerston's marriage soon seemed to the Queen to have affected his chivalrous manner towards herself. She told Lord M. that somehow she didn't like him as much as she used to. Lord M. burst out laughing at Her Majesty's artlessness.

A few months after the marriage Palmerston was giving the Queen a first demonstration in Egypt of his famous 'gunboat diplomacy'. The impression he made on her then changed little during the years to come, when Europe offered him many chances to repeat the pattern, all of which he seized with gusto. Palmerston's behaviour in 1840, Queen Victoria told Melbourne, was too 'eager'; he was too 'sharp' with people, ridiculing them too much. Why could he not 'ménager' our French rivals in Egypt, instead of sending gunboats and threatening to chuck Mehemet Ali into the Nile? His attitude to the Press, on the other hand, was too friendly: he encouraged them to put in tendentious articles. Lastly he juggled with the dispatches. From Melbourne she extracted the admission that Palmerston delayed sending dispatches which he did not like.

The man in fact was far from 'safe', the quality above all others which Queen Victoria and Prince Albert sought in statesmen. And yet – they could not deny that he was often right. He did the right thing in the wrong way. The question of the 'Spanish marriages' was an example.

On December 28th, 1840, Queen Victoria recorded a discussion between herself, Melbourne and Palmerston as to who should be the future King Consort of Spain. Queen Isabella of Spain was a child of only ten but already Britain and France were planning her nuptials from the point of view of

232

extending their own influence. Prince Leopold of Saxe-Coburg-Kohary, one of the dear young 'Ferdinand' cousins whose high spirits had almost seduced Victoria from her allegiance to Prince Albert just before their engagement, was the British choice. His Coburg brain and sense of duty would forge yet another link between Britain's Royal Family and Europe. His good looks would make him acceptable to Isabella who, though stout and unattractive herself with a bad skin, would need someone outstanding to keep her in order. Unfortunately this ideal match had to be ruled out. The council of three agreed that it would 'enrage' the French, who would find British interference in Spain even more intolerable than in Egypt.

Her feelings towards Palmerston at the time of the Whig Government's fall in 1841 were still ambivalent, chiefly because of his 'rough rude' dispatches. 'We regret it so much,' she wrote on March 26th, 1841, using one of her first married 'we's', 'as Palmerston is such a clever able man.' Melbourne with his usual fatalism assured her that imperiousness was part of Palmerston's nature: it could not be moderated now, particularly after all his successes.

Lord Aberdeen, the incoming Tory Foreign Secretary, proved to be a Minister after the Queen's heart. If ever a man was 'safe', he was. Instead of enraging the French Lord Aberdeen set out to '*ménager*' them, during a second, brief visit by the Queen to Château D'Eu, in 1845. After a delicious breakfast in tents she and Lord Aberdeen found themselves sitting round a small table with Louis Philippe and his Foreign Minister, Monsieur Guizot. There were no rough, rude exchanges but with the utmost suavity a bargain was struck over Spain: England would not push Prince Leopold provided Louis Philippe did not advance one of his own sons.*

At the end of the visit the King leant over the side as the

* Lord Clarendon heard a typically sharp variant to the above account: when the Queen suggested a German Prince for Spain, Louis Philippe 'put down poor Vic rather indelicately', saying that 'naturally she recommended to her sister of Spain what she had taken herself and found had done her good!' (*Life & Letters of Lord Clarendon*, I. 245.)

two yachts were drifting apart and once more confirmed the complicated bargain with Lord Aberdeen: Queen Isabella should be left to make her own choice of a husband from among the Spanish princes, while her younger sister, the very personable Infanta Fernanda, would be dealt with under a separate clause. There was a danger that Fernanda rather than Isabella would become mother to a Spanish heir. Isabella was almost certain to marry her Spanish cousin Francisco, Duke of Cadiz, a despicable character generally supposed to be impotent. Over the calm waters came the voice of the French King carrying the final assurance: if his son Montpensier married Fernanda, as was projected, the wedding would not take place until Queen Isabella had produced an heir.

Russell's Government of 1846 with Palmerston again as Foreign Secretary was scarcely installed before Queen Victoria felt that there were going to be renewed troubles. Her contemplated Irish visit was hanging fire. At first the reports were conflicting. Lord Heytesbury informed her that the material condition of Ireland was excellent and only the moral state very bad, while Lord John Russell took a gloomy view.[1] At the beginning of August he still thought there were arguments for Her Majesty visiting the afflicted island but by the middle of the month he considered the potato famine so shocking that the royal tour must be postponed. Queen Victoria had been anxious to get it over; among other things she did not like her subjects speculating as to whether she *dared* go.[2]

Lord John Russell was described by Charles Greville as a very clever man whose mind was nevertheless 'little'. Curiously enough Greville and the Queen, though wildly disparate characters, often came to similar conclusions about their distinguished contemporaries. There is no doubt that Her Majesty would have subscribed to the essential littleness of Lord John.

To begin with he was small in size, a terrier to Peel's great Dane, impudence to his dignity; so diminutive that when he married the widow of Lord Ribblesdale he was called 'the widow's mite'. Lord Malmesbury one day saw Lord and Lady

John come laughing and chattering together into a thronged assembly; he longed to put them on the chimney-piece like china ornaments to save the poor little things from being trodden under foot. Queen Victoria should have felt at ease with a Prime Minister of her own dimensions; like many tiny women she preferred tall men.

Lord John was a party man and therefore seemed to the Queen 'little', despite the fact that he had introduced the great Reform Bill of 1832. You only had to think of the Russells, to know what it meant to be a Whig. In Lord John she studied her first true specimen. Abroad, Whigs were unmoved by the divinity of kings but were devoted to constitutional governments. At home, Whigs upheld the class structure in their own splendid palaces while intermittently extending the blessings of the Constitution to the lower orders.

The Queen at once sensed an indefinable something missing in Lord John's relations with herself. In appointing her Household, for instance, Lord John consulted his party colleagues unnecessarily instead of keeping it *'entre nous'*. Even Lord Melbourne, she felt, had left rather too much to his colleagues. Peel alone satisfied her ideal of what a Prime Minister should be. He *'kept all* in his own hands'.[3]

Her desire to keep things *'entre nous'* showed itself again in the hopes she built on her new Ambassador in Paris, Lord Normanby. As the brother of Charles Phipps, Prince Albert's private secretary after Anson died, she hoped that Lord Normanby would become 'a family Ambassador'. But the cosy period of *entre nous* and 'family Ambassadors' had in fact passed. Palmerston took action over the Spanish marriages which precipitated an international crisis and a ding-dong battle with the Court.

Without consultation, Palmerston sent off a dispatch to Madrid on July 19th, 1846 listing the possible candidates for Queen Isabella's hand, among them once more the controversial name of Prince Leopold. Isabella was by now sixteen and according to Princess Lieven hungering for a mate: unless they got her married quickly the heir would arrive before the husband. At the mention of Leopold's name, Louis Philippe decided that Palmerston had torn up the Anglo–French bargain. He retaliated instantly by arranging the notorious Spanish marriages: Queen Isabella to the 'impotent' Francisco and Fernanda to his own son, the Duke of Montpensier.

The Queen at first had little anger to spare for Palmerston, whom she credited with behaving temperately and well, after his initial blunder.* Nothing was too bad for the French; '. . . & this is l'entente cordiale!'[4] she exploded. Among other things, Queen Victoria happened to know that Montpensier did not want to be rushed into marrying the Infanta Fernanda, 'in case she did not turn out well', a fear with which the apostle of true love had every sympathy. The whole trans-action indeed seemed to Her Majesty 'quite unworthy of the times we live in'.[5] Such a flouting of natural and diplomatic laws she did not doubt would bring its own punishment.

Sixteen months later the Duke of Montpensier and his bride Fernanda were bewildered refugees at Claremont from a France rocked by revolution. Queen Isabella, on the other hand, having divested herself of the odious husband never-theless became officially *enceinte* at the end of 1849. Queen Victoria wrote:

'It is a very good thing & no one will be inclined to cavil as to who was the *real father* considering her very peculiar & distressing marriage – for which *she* poor young creature is in no wise to blame . . .'[6]

What else could be expected when the whole of Spanish society was riddled with immorality? One of Isabella's cousins had liaisons when she was only fifteen. 'What a state of things & how disgraceful!'

The year 1846 closed with Palmerston showing himself, as the Queen thought, no more adroit in Portugal than he had been in Spain. Her cousins King Ferdinand and Queen Donna Maria were harried by a revolutionary junta but Palmerston would support them only in so far as they might be used to restore constitutional government. Constitutions, she noted

* Many years later she told her private secretary that Palmerston had accused Louis Philippe of stealing the Cabinet key from under her pillow at Château D'Eu and reading the dispatches. No dis-patches, however, were sent to her there.

in 1847, were unsuitable in southern countries. Sometimes she felt that what with her Ministers and these ill-advised, uneducated foreign Sovereigns, she was between the devil and the deep sea. Even her revered mentor, Lord Aberdeen, earned a sharp rebuke in her Journal for so foolishly trusting Louis Philippe over the Spanish marriages.* Nevertheless she and Palmerston still exchanged occasional courtesies. She recorded with pleasure that he considered Winterhalter's latest portrait of herself and her family the best modern painting he had ever seen.†

A feeling of intense pity for suffering humanity swept over Queen Victoria for the first time when she read about the Irish famine. Up till then she had worried over individual cases – gipsies, performing dwarfs or the widows of workmen accidentally flung from the scaffolding while carrying out improvements to her palaces. Now the state of Ireland filled her with that generalized 'social' indignation which is at the root of reform. For once those around her did not minimize the disaster.

> 'Talked of the extreme distress in Ireland & the fear that the Landowners would try & turn the intended employment for the poor into an improvement of their own properties at the public expense.'[7]

The sufferings of the peasants were 'really too terrible to think of' and burials took place to save expense without clergy or coffins – an aspect of their misery which particularly appalled the Queen.

> '. . . & in the midst of all this, the Landlords appropriate the people's corn! after all we have done to supply the needy with food! God alone can bring help, for no human means seem able!'[8]

The Queen did not intend her last entry to be taken too seriously for when it was decided that divine aid should be enlisted through a Day of Fasting, she bitterly derided such an

* Here she was not altogether fair to Aberdeen who thought that no major British interest was at stake.

† See illustration between pages 368 and 369.

'out of date' practice. We boasted of our Blessed Redeemer's atonement for our sins yet always went back to Old Testament superstitions in times of crisis; it was 'presumptious' to attribute the Irish famine to sinfulness. Of course we were all sinful but no more so than last century when the potato plants flourished: indeed the upper classes were less sinful than in those days, while the poor Irish, though no doubt heedless, improvident and violent, could not be directly blamed for the famine.

The idea, in later years, of stopping cholera epidemics, or winning wars by holding national Days of Humiliation, was no more acceptable to the Queen than curing a famine by a fast. This robust attitude set her on the same side as the more advanced among her subjects. It was one of the reasons why she never considered herself a woman of reactionary outlook.

The Queen soon found that the starving Irish were turning to 'human means' for salvation of which she could not approve. What she called the 'insubordination of the poor' began to loom larger in her mind than the 'mismanagement among the higher classes', though in deference to Irish feelings she rationed the Palace bread to one pound per head. Towards the end of 1847 she greeted the murder of yet another Irish landlord with shocked despair. 'Really they are a terrible people.'[9] When the Year of Revolutions dawned the Queen was more preoccupied with Continental eruptions than with Smith O'Brien, 'Young Ireland', and the other demonstrations of that terrible people's feelings, at least when they took place in their own country. She just found time to jot down 'risings in all directions', fires on the hills, bugles calling all night and poor Lady Waterford not allowed even into her garden for fear of being seized as a hostage.

It was not till August 1849 that a royal visit to Ireland was at last considered safe. In view of the continuing distress it was not to be an expensive State tour. She first set foot on Irish soil at Cove,* in order to give the people the 'satisfaction', as she put it, of changing its name to Queenstown. (They had the satisfaction of changing it back again some seventy years

* Now Cobh.

later.) She stuck to the safety of her yacht except for a brief disembarkation at Cork, whence she proceeded by sea to Kingstown, marvelling at the beauty of the women, their rags ('they never mend anything') and their extraordinary manner of expressing loyalty by shrieking. Her warm heart flowed out to these tatterdemalion crowds and only three things in Ireland drew down mild displeasure: the muggy climate, a 'poor little dove' carrying an olive branch which was plumped into her lap, and the two thousand ladies and gentlemen who presented themselves at a levée in Phoenix Park: some were awkward, others ridiculous, all in a dreadful state of perspiration having been packed into a stifling waiting-room – 'not quite pleasant for my *hand*!'[10]

The Queen adored Phoenix Park and if Lord John's scheme for abolishing the Lord Lieutenancy had come off, would have liked to stay there for her proposed biennial visits instead of at the gloomy Castle. Everything that she could do personally to make her Irish visit a success, she did, even to standing up waving her handkerchief on the paddle-box of her yacht and ordering the Royal Standard to be lowered in response to the cheering crowds as she sailed away. Perhaps if she had followed up this visit as Lord John proposed, its good effects might have been more lasting. As it was, 'The idyll had been charming, but it brought no result.'[11] There were too many Irish rebels behind the cheering crowds who wanted to see the Royal Standard not only lowered but rolled up and taken away.

The fourth attempt on Queen Victoria's life was made by a mad Irishman on May 19th, 1849, less than three months before her Irish visit. She was more conscious of the fact that he was Irish than that he was insane. William Hamilton, an unemployed man from Adare, had the sudden idea of frightening the English Queen with a home-made pistol. He tinkered about unsuccessfully with some bits of wood and the spout of a tea-kettle. Finally borrowing his landlady's pistol he achieved his object of terrifying Queen Victoria by firing at her as she drove down Constitution Hill, on her way home from her official Birthday celebrations. Since there was no bullet in the landlady's pistol the authorities transported the Irishman, under Peel's new law, for seven years. Little Princess Helena, aged three, summed up the morals of the situation to her mother's satisfaction: 'Man shot, tried to shoot dear mama, must be punished.'

Queen Victoria reacted more strongly than usual against this renewal of attacks which she had begun to hope were over for ever. A year later, on June 27th, 1850, she was struck violently on the head by a retired lieutenant of the 10th Hussars with the quite too appropriate name of Pate, while visiting her dying Uncle Adolphus at Cambridge House. She had no escort and Prince Albert was riding in the Park with the Princess of Prussia. The Prince of Wales, Princess Alice and Prince Alfred were in the carriage with her; also her lady-in-waiting, Fanny Jocelyn. As the carriage squeezed through the narrow entrance gates the crowd surged round her, pressing the mounted equerry backwards. Her exposed situation, the Queen wrote afterwards, made her think 'more than usually' of an attempt. There was nothing to stop Robert Pate striking her as hard as possible over the eye before he was seized and manhandled by the crowd.

For a moment the Queen was knocked unconscious; Fanny Jocelyn 'roused' her, exclaiming, 'They have got the man' and then burst into tears. The colour rushed into 'poor Bertie's' face and the Queen noted that this was the second time Alice and Affie had seen their mother attacked. She staggered to her feet in the carriage and calmed the people by crying out, 'I am not hurt.' But she was hurt. Only the deep brim of her bonnet saved her from worse than the black eye, severe bruises and headache which she sustained. Too shocked to eat that evening, her medical attendants strangely allowed her to go to the opera. As usual after an attack she was cheered in the streets by all, 'the lowest of the low being *most* indignant'. Her Majesty's arrival at the Royal Opera House interrupted a skating scene; the whole audience rose and cheered for five minutes after which the Italian cast sang 'God Save The Queen'. Lord Hardwicke suggested that her battering was almost worthwhile for the love it elicited afterwards. She could not agree.

'Certainly it is very hard & very horrid, that I, a woman – a defenceless young woman [she was thirty-one and had recently given birth to her seventh child] & surrounded by my children, should be exposed to insults of this kind, & be unable to go out quietly for a drive . . . for a man to strike *any woman* is most brutal, & I, as well as everyone else, think this *far* worse than any attempt to shoot, which, wicked as it is, is at least more comprehensible & more courageous.'[12]

From this last remark it is clear that Queen Victoria did not believe in the insanity of her assailants. As a soldier's daughter she could understand the man with a gun but not the man with a stick. Moreover Pate's cane was the only one of the many weapons brandished against her which did any damage. The whole affair seemed 'unconnected with anything' and therefore particularly frightening; she had often noticed the pale fair-haired young man in the Park, carrying the same cane with which he now belaboured her; his father turned out to have been High Sheriff of Cambridge when Prince Albert was installed there as Vice-Chancellor in 1847. If men of good family could behave thus for no reason at all, what might not the mob do? Looking to the future, of what use was an equerry who got squeezed out of position in the moment of peril? When poor dear Albert was further away even than Hyde Park, the unshakeable bulwark of John Brown on the box was something one could not be sufficiently grateful for.

On the last day of 1847 Prince Albert had an appointment in London, so the Queen spent what seemed a terribly long evening all alone. First she thought over her faults; then her happiness.

'When one is as happy as we are one feels sad at the quick passing of the years, & I always wish Time could stand still for a while.'

But time marched on, into a maelstrom of events she never forgot. Prince Albert returned at 12.30 and wished her as usual his hearty German, '*Prost Neu Jahr*'.

The Year of Revolutions, 1848, had begun.

Halfway through February the Queen heard that the state of France was 'extremely uncomfortable', while Europe as a whole was troubled by too many constitutions and not enough 'social improvement'. On the 24th, stirring news reached her. As usual her Journal heralded events however exciting with a flat reference to the weather. 'A showery morning'. Then came the cloudburst.

'So much, & such extraordinary, incredible things have been happening these days in France, that I hardly know how or what to write.'

Again as usual the Queen made an excellent job of her task and for the next week or so her Journal was a vivid medley of speculation, moralizing and adventure – 'like a novel'. She learnt that the dreadful tocsin in Paris had sounded at midnight on February 23rd and was thought by the poor dear French royal family to be 'only' a local rising. When the King discovered his mistake he promptly abdicated, forbidding the National Guard to fire on the mob. *'J'ai vu assez de sang'*, he moaned over and over again, as his family hurried him across the dark Tuileries gardens, having escaped from the back of the Palace just as the mob rushed the front. Queen Victoria afterwards strongly criticized the old King's collapse and refusal to show fight.

Buckingham Palace throbbed with rumours and the Queen was tortured by suspense. On the 25th she cancelled a dinner engagement, believing that the King had landed at Folkestone. This turned out to be false but meanwhile Palmerston gave her permission to put a steamer at the King's disposal if and when he escaped, though with the warning that she must be careful about harbouring ejected Royalties or the country would not like it. A few days later he generously devised a characteristically clandestine scheme for supplying the destitute French family with £1,000 from secret service funds, disguised as an anonymous gift from 'some wellwisher'. On the 27th some of the 'heart-stricken' French family began to trickle in, but not darling Victoire Nemours nor the Duke of

Montpensier, who had got separated from the rest and were 'God knows where!'

Among the host of children, nurses, physicians and valets there was only one lady's maid and therefore only one Princess who had not lost her jewels – Fernanda, Duchess of Montpensier, of all people. Queen Victoria thought it very strange to be meeting Fernanda for the first time at Buckingham Palace after all that had gone before. Stranger still was the arrival of a letter from Newhaven on March 3rd from the French King beginning 'Madame' instead of 'Ma Soeur', and signed simply and humbly 'Louis Philippe'. The old King had been smuggled across the Channel by a commando-type British Consul at Le Havre who decided to disguise him as his own uncle, 'Mr Smith', for which purpose he was clean shaved, stripped of his wig and equipped with goggles and a cap. Victoire Nemours turned up also, having lost all her clothes to the Paris mob. They were now being worn, remarked the Queen with what sounded like horrified relish, by 'the worst women!'[13]

Prince Albert, looking desperately careworn, organized clothes and other necessities for the travellers, while Queen Victoria tried in vain to dispel her husband's gloom. Things might not be so bad as they seemed.

They became worse. 'It seems as if the whole face of Europe were changing,' wrote the Queen as the revolutionary tornado threatened a great Empire like Austria, kingdoms like Hanover, Bavaria, Naples and Prussia, countless small Duchies like Schleswig, Holstein, Leiningen and even little Coburg and Gotha. Three countries stood firm: Queen Victoria's England, King Leopold's Belgium and the Tsar's monstrous despotism in the East.

While Europe changed its face, Court life went on. Princess Alice and Prince Alfred played merrily with their little cousins; the exiled Princess Clémentine's children sat for their portraits by Ross and the Queen put into quarantine those visitors who had caught bad colds during their flight.

As if to point the contrast between normality at home and chaos abroad, Queen Victoria on March 18th, 1848, produced her sixth child, Princess Louise. The baby, the largest since

Prince Alfred, was a fine child with very white skin but the Queen, no doubt tense with every kind of anxiety, had an unusually bad time. Fortunately Princess Louise was the last royal baby but one to be born without 'aetherial aid', as the Victorians facetiously called the new invention of anaesthetics.

Born into such stirring times, the Queen thought this child would be sure to turn out 'something peculiar'. In fact Princess Louise was a gay sparkling character with plenty of temperament and talent. Some 'peculiarity', however, was shown by her great-aunt, the Duchess of Gloucester, at her christening. The old lady, forgetting where she was, suddenly got up in the middle of the service and knelt at the Queen's feet. 'Imagine our horror!'

On April 3rd the Queen's confinement ended and she breakfasted once again 'in our dear old way with my dear Albert'. Suddenly came news well calculated to spoil Queen Victoria's and Prince Albert's first breakfast together: a gigantic Chartist meeting was planned in London for the 10th – only a week ahead. True, there had already been an attempt on March 6th in Trafalgar Square, but after a contingent of enthusiasts had broken the lamps outside Buckingham Palace, its youthful leader, shouting *Vive la république!* offered to shake hands with the sentry. He was promptly arrested and burst into tears. Afterwards the Queen had felt secure enough to write about 'our little riots here'. The programme for April 10th sounded altogether more ominous.

Frantically worried, the Prince strode out for a calming walk round the Palace gardens, perhaps soon to be invaded by a mob of 'the worst women' who would deal with Victoria's wardrobe as their French sisters had dealt with Victoire's. He returned in somewhat better shape only to find the Queen shivering with nerves and weeping uncontrollably. What would happen to her and the children, she sobbed, and to that little fortnight-old baby?

The Prince forgot his own torments in the business of soothing his distracted wife whose physical weakness entrapped her into recriminations against her best beloved. He was soon able to tell her that her Ministers advised the whole

244

Royal Family to flee to Osborne – of course in a deliberate and orderly manner – two days before the Chartist meeting was to take place. The Queen's tears began to flow less wildly and she managed to gasp out her willingness to accept anything as long as she and Albert were *together*. By the next day, April 4th, her efforts to regain self-command had succeeded so completely that she found herself penning to King Leopold a notable boast.

'. . . I never was calmer & quieter & less nervous. *Great* events make me quiet & calm; it is only trifles that irritate my nerves.'[14]

Like many an honest apologia it was only half true.

For the next few days Prince Albert had to get up earlier than ever – he had taken to rising early and running instead of walking along the royal corridors – and the Queen felt she was not nearly grateful enough for the way he helped her.

News about the Chartist meeting began to pour in. The monster procession to Westminster would be banned. Extra police had been enrolled, among them Prince Louis Napoleon, shortly to become President of France and then Emperor. Great nobles filled their houses with rustic defenders brought up from country estates; Lord Malmesbury had five gamekeepers on guard each armed with a double-barrelled gun. Artillery was posted on the bridges and in other strategic spots including the royal stables. Even if a cannonade were necessary, Buckingham Palace would not be a second Tuileries with Queen Victoria plunging round the lake towards Hyde Park Corner; she would have flitted already. Palmerston, incidentally, used the general pandemonium as an excuse for depriving Her Majesty of the foreign dispatches.

In cold rain the royal party left London on the 8th, Queen Victoria stretched on a couch in the train. Having arrived safely at Osborne her mood characteristically changed. She suddenly felt out of everything. The intense peace 'bewildered' her. Those shady ilexes and primrose paths led away from an experience which, though '*most sad*', had been '*eventful*' and '*ever memorable*'; 'the contrast seems rather

245

trying. Our coming here has made a break which is, at 1st., almost painful to me.'[15]

Good tidings came through on April 10th. Nothing about the Chartist meeting turned out to have been monstrous except its failure. The number of demonstrators who gathered at Kennington Common for the march on the Houses of Parliament – 23,000 instead of half a million – was derisory; a pale and trembling Feargus O'Connor, who was to have led them, shook the hand of the Chief Commissioner of Police with fervent gratitude when informed that no march would be permitted, and with equal thankfulness allowed the police to hail for him and his lieutenants three cabs. In these vehicles petition and petitioners trotted harmlessly to Westminster where the Chartist demands were tamely presented and left to lie on some eternal table, until in the whirligig of history they were dusted down and granted to the Chartists' heirs.

At Buckingham Palace nothing was overturned on the revolutionary Tenth but the royal skittles in the Palace garden.

The Year of Revolutions was one of the few years during this domestically happy period to which the Queen and Prince said goodbye without regret, glad to get out of it with whole skins. The Queen had faced the prospect of her children ending up like Clémentine's or Victoire's. Her prayers for their future took on a new note. 'Let them grow up fit for *whatever station* they may be placed in – *high or low*.'[16] She decreed that Court ladies should appear at her drawing-rooms wearing only British clothes and another huge ball was held which raised £2,800 for the Spitalfields weavers, £1,800 unfortunately going in expenses.*

Queen Victoria's thoughts naturally turned again and again to the subject of revolutions, foreign-type and British-type. There was no disguising that she had been badly shaken by the Chartists. The Prince of Prussia, a temporary refugee in England, saw the Chartists face to face and told her that they were the genuine revolutionary article, 'horrid-looking

---

* A shimmering pale blue dress ordered by the Queen in 1851 and now in the London Museum shows that it was no hardship to wear Spitalfields silks.

people'. The danger haunted her throughout the summer. A rain storm in June brought an invasion of little toads; next day the arrival of forty Chartists was reported at Cowes, said to be making for Osborne. All the men employed by Cubitt, the royal builder, were ordered down from their ladders and labourers called in from the fields. Armed with sticks they awaited the foe. Though the invaders turned out to be only a party of Oddfellows on a Whitsun spree, it gave the police and Royal Family a nasty turn.

Yet the very odiousness of the Chartists impressed the Queen as never before with the devotion of her people as a whole. 'High & low, Lords & Shopkeepers,' she wrote, set an example of firmness and loyalty which would benefit other less favoured countries. '*Our* revolution', as she called the Kennington Common fiasco, was a model revolution. For ever afterwards she felt in her bones – sometimes too confidently – that whatever the little local difficulties, Crown and people would remain faithful to one another.

Revolutions formed the subject of an argument on August 6th, 1848 between Queen Victoria and Lord John Russell. 'I maintain that Revolutions are always bad for the country,' asserted Her Majesty, 'and the cause of untold misery to the people.'

'Obedience to the laws & to the Sovereign, is obedience to a higher Power, divinely instituted for the good of the *people*, not of the Sovereign, who has equally duties & obligations.'

We do not know what thoughts occurred to the pugnacious little Whig as he listened to this Victorian version of the divine right of kings.

CHAPTER XV

THE DEVIL'S SON
1848–50

THEORETICAL ARGUMENTS about revolution between the Queen and her Prime Minister were as nothing to their practical differences over one acute and growing problem – the Foreign Secretary. The uneasy relationship, sometimes inflamed, which had existed between Queen Victoria and Palmerston since he returned to foreign affairs in 1846, came to a head in the Year of Revolutions.

Both Lord Palmerston and Prince Albert explained to her in April 1848 the prickly Schleswig-Holstein question. Their accounts by no means tallied. The Prince earnestly desired that a new, liberal, united Germany, emergent from the revolutionary upheavals, should eventually control the two Duchies, while Palmerston supported Denmark's claim to them. Palmerston was bent on using the revived *entente cordiale* with republican France to free Italy from Austria by a concerted heave, but Prince Albert saw this as tearing to pieces an empire like Victoria's own. The Queen not unnaturally listened to her husband on subjects which after all, as a European himself, he must know more about than Palmerston. Every trick of the Foreign Secretary's, or '*bock*' (blunder) as Albert preferred to call it, was used to frustrate the Court: the delay in sending them drafts until after the dispatches themselves had been mailed; the bland ignoring of alterations agreed upon between them; the sending of a rude dispatch, of course not vetted by the Court, to the Spanish Government in the summer telling them how to behave.

The affronted Spaniards showed that they knew how to behave at least in regard to Palmerston: they sent the British Ambassador packing.

By mid-September the Court, entrenched for the first time at Balmoral, had hatched a plot to banish Palmerston to

Ireland as Lord Lieutenant. The idea had a certain craftiness, for Palmerston, with Irish estates of his own, was not likely to regard the Irish rebels quite so sympathetically as he did those in Europe. In disclosing this plan to Russell the Queen let fall the ominous remark that she might soon be unable 'to put up with Lord Palmerston any longer, which might be very disagreeable and awkward'.

Not only would it be 'awkward', it would also be unconstitutional. The Sovereign had no more right to dismiss her Minister for failure to consult her than the Minister had to treat her with this discourtesy. Constitutionally, both sides were sailing near the wind, Palmerston with unruffled good humour, the Court in a frenzy. Queen Victoria told her doctor that whenever she had to read one of Palmerston's dispatches before dinner, it made her bilious.[1]

Meanwhile in Europe Palmerston continued his rake's progress. His Italian dispatches, the Queen declared when she saw them, were 'unworthy of a gentleman'.[2] In January of the new year, 1849, *The Times* revealed that he had secretly supplied a British contractor with arms out of the Royal Ordnance for Sicilian rebels, thus enabling them to carry on their fight against their local tyrant, King 'Bomba', without openly infringing Britain's neutrality. A typical Palmerstonian *bock*. Queen Victoria was thrown into transports of rage. England *must* apologize to the King. It was too monstrous. 'And *I* have to bear it all.'[3] Russell went so far as to consider bribing Palmerston with an earldom and Garter to remove himself to Ireland – an apotheosis which the Queen strongly opposed – but when Palmerston agreed to apologize, Russell again swung round, begging the Queen to receive her Foreign Secretary at Court. She couldn't bear to treat him with politeness, she burst out – a sentiment which Prince Albert translated into diplomatic language when he wrote up a memorandum for her afterwards: 'she felt it repugnant to her character to show a degree of respect and politeness which she did not feel.'[4]

Who could get him to resign? persisted the Queen desperately. 'Only Lady Palmerston,' replied Russell.[5] They all knew very well that Melbourne's sister, triumphantly conducting the most successful salon in London, would do no such thing.

Nothing but Prince Albert's unceasing help and attentiveness made the Queen's position endurable. After this particular tussle with the Prime Minister, the Prince sat down at his table and drafted for her a complete account of the interview. All she had to do was to change, as she pithily put it, 'the *Queen* and *I*' into '*I* and Albert'.[6]

Even such a combination as '*I* and Albert' was no match for 'Pam', as Palmerston was affectionately called. Next year he was at it again. The notorious Don Pacifico case, described by the Queen as 'a most disagreeable business', was causing her deep anxiety at the beginning of 1850. At first she put down Palmerston's behaviour to 'mere love of mischief'.[7] A Portuguese Jewish merchant, Don David Pacifico, born at Gibraltar and therefore a British subject, had had his house in Athens burnt down by a Greek Orthodox mob. King Otho of Greece and his Government rejected Don Pacifico's immoderate bill for damages and Palmerston intervened on Pacifico's behalf. Eager to thwart Palmerston, France mediated between Greece and Britain but two days after a compromise settlement had been reached in London Palmerston's ever ready gunboats seized all King Otho's ships in the Piraeus and triumphantly vindicated Don Pacifico's claim. Never was a gentleman more misnamed. England stood on the brink of war. France recalled her ambassador and Russia joined in the general howl of hate. Quite coolly, as if nothing had happened, Palmerston gave Queen Victoria the appalling news. 'The levity of the man is really inconceivable!'[8]

As usual the Queen, to cap it all, had just given birth on May 1st to a child, Prince Arthur, her seventh.

The Queen felt it her '*duty to the country*'[9] to celebrate the restoration of her liberty, as she called the end of her lying-in, by radically curtailing Palmerston's. To what dingy office could he be relegated? The Colonial Office? At the beginning of the crisis Russell had suggested Leader of the House of Commons. Too dangerous, said the Court, for he might use it to seize the Premiership. At sixty-five he was too old, replied Lord John. Another perplexing question was who could take his place at the Foreign Office. Russell had wanted his own father-in-law, Lord Minto. Not able enough after Palmerston, retorted the Queen.[10]

In the House of Commons on June 25th, 1850, Lord Palmerston faced his critics. Radicals and Tories, among them Sir Robert Peel making the last speech of his life, challenged the Foreign Secretary to justify the Don Pacifico gunboats. In a 'most brilliant speech of 4 hours & ½ without stopping for one moment even to drink a little water', as the Queen generously recorded in her Journal next day, the Foreign Secretary consummated a triumph of oratory with an appeal to national pride as telling as any in history:

'. . . as the Roman in days of old held himself free from indignity when he could say *Civis Romanus Sum*, so also a British subject, in whatever land he may be, shall feel confident that the watchful eye and the strong arm of England will protect him against injustice and wrong.'

Not without reason Palmerston felt confident that the strong arm of England would protect him also. He won his vote of confidence by a majority of 46 and the Queen was back where she had started, except that her Foreign Secretary's most colossal *bock* of all had made him stronger and more idolized than ever.

The Court was desperate. If Palmerston remained at the Foreign Office they would not have a friend left in Europe; if he were moved Russell might well make him Leader of the House. In an interview with Russell in July, Prince Albert dragged out every weapon from his armoury to prevent such a disaster, including one peculiarly rusty old blunderbuss. How could the Queen take for her most confidential adviser, he asked Russell dramatically, a man 'who as her Secretary of State and while a guest under her roof at Windsor Castle had committed a brutal attack upon one of her ladies? had at night by stealth introduced himself into her apartment, barricaded afterwards the door and would have consummated his fiendish scheme by violence had not the miraculous efforts of his victim and such assistance attracted by her screams saved her?'[11]

Solemnly 'Johnny' Russell shook his head: it was 'very bad'; he would keep the horrid secret; as a matter of fact he had heard of another lady on whom the Foreign Secretary had tried the same thing; no, Palmerston should never get near Her Majesty, he should never be Prime Minister. As for dropping him from the Ministry, that was quite another matter. Until the Prime Minister disagreed with the Foreign Secretary's politics as well as his morals, Palmerston must remain.

When the Court had reached an impasse Stockmar usually helped them out with a masterly analysis. The Don Pacifico affair was no exception. He had completed sometime earlier a two-point memorandum designed to spike Lord Palmerston once and for all on its prongs. In emphatic language it described the minimum which the Sovereign expected of her Foreign Minister: to state distinctly what he intended and not to alter arbitrarily an agreed measure – otherwise she would exercise her constitutional right of dismissing that Minister.

Prince Albert waited for the cheers over Palmerston's Don Pacifico triumph to die down. Then on August 12th he sent Stockmar's document to the Prime Minister, drafted, of course, to look like a letter from Queen Victoria. Lord John showed it privately to Palmerston and on August 15th the Foreign Secretary appeared before Prince Albert. Primed no doubt by his anxious wife and harassed chief, he played his part to perfection. Instead of presenting the usual bland smile he was shaking all over, his eyes filled with tears. The soft-hearted Prince saw a broken man. 'What have I done?' stammered Palmerston. If he had given even the smallest hint of disrespect to Her Majesty he would never again show his face in Society. In regard to future dispatches, Her Majesty's command should be obeyed.[12]

For about three weeks the Foreign Secretary did indeed send her 'informative letters' – 'continually'.

Poor Albert, wrote Queen Victoria, was 'dreadfully fagged' by his gruelling interview. She herself, as with each episode in the titanic struggle, felt physically ill. Pam, on the other hand, wiping away the crocodile tears, retired *pour mieux sauter* next time.

Next time came within a month. General Haynau, an Austrian responsible for putting down Italian and Hungarian nationalists with exceptional brutality, was unwise enough to visit England in September. The indignant Radical Press published a cartoon of General 'Hyaena' flogging a woman. His lank figure, bushy brows, far-flung mustachios and deep-set, carnivorous eyes were thus imprinted in the public mind. When he visited Barclay's Brewery incognito he was at once recognized; one man tried to shave him on the spot, another dropped a bale of straw on his head; having fought his way into the street he was hauled along by his mustachios until, darting into a neighbouring house, he escaped at last filthy and bedraggled by river.

The Queen, horrified at this slur on British hospitality, at first felt sure the culprits must be Hungarian and Polish refugees: 'it is so unlike our people here, who never trouble themselves about foreign concerns.'[13] When she discovered that the Austrian mustachios had been manhandled by British workmen she commented sorrowfully that there were people here as brutal as anywhere. And among the brutes was her own Foreign Secretary who, without consulting her, nullified an official apology to the Austrians by including in it an attack on their illiberal régime.

More angry than ever, the Queen demanded the instant recall of the draft. Palmerston refused, offering to resign; but when a peremptory letter from Lord John Russell crossed his, he caved in and the draft was corrected. This was his usual mode of action, wrote the Queen, 'viz: bullying'; the moral was that Lord John ought always to be '*firm*'.[14] Yet as sometimes happened, she was gradually coming round to Palmerston's view though not to his person. The assault on General Haynau, she was glad to have discovered, was unpremeditated and due in part to his own bad character.

Ten days later, October 29th, 1850, the Queen was immersed in an ecclesiastical crisis which for a brief moment raised her hopes of Palmerston being swept away in the general turmoil.

Pope Pius IX restored the English Hierarchy, appointing Dr Wiseman as Cardinal-Archbishop of Westminster. At first the outraged Queen held that the Pope was behaving as in the days of Henry VIII, while in Cardinal Wiseman's wish that His Holiness should be prayed for 'before me' she saw an 'infringement of my prerogative'.[15] It was not long, however, before the violent reaction of Protestant England brought her as usual to see the errors of both sides. She wished that the Pope had done privately and quietly what he did 'so offensively' in public; there would then have been no trouble.[16] Lord Camoys, a Roman Catholic lord-in-waiting, sat next to her at dinner on Christmas Eve and deplored this 'inopportune' event which made him feel quite uncomfortable in Society. 'Poor man,' sympathized the Queen; 'so sensible.'

Russell, on the other hand, seemed to her every bit as fanatical as the Vatican, with his harping on 'Papal aggression', his dubbing Roman practices 'the mummeries of superstition' and his determination to thwart them with an Ecclesiastical Titles Bill, even at the expense of his own majority and his policy of reconciling Ireland.

What would happen to the new Roman Catholic bishops? the Queen wondered anxiously. Would they be imprisoned? Persecuted? She trembled at the word. 'I cannot bear to hear the violent abuse of the Catholic religion, which is so painful and so cruel towards the many innocent and good Roman Catholics.'

In addition to Lord John's concern over 'Papal aggression' he had pledged himself to a new measure of Franchise Reform. These two ugly customers, as they seemed to the Queen, plunged her into nine days of political crisis, disputes over Reform having brought down the Government and disagreements over 'Papal aggression' preventing a new alignment from taking place. To the Queen's surprise she faced the first days of the crisis almost with exhilaration:

'I thank God that I am keeping so calm & feel that the good of the Country, & *not my* convenience, & my likings or dislikings, – is the only thing to look to. It certainly is a most interesting & exciting time, which we think will be of great use & experience to use personally.'[17]

The Queen innocently supposed that her own exalted mood would instantly create a similar frame of mind among her Ministers resulting in a 'strong Government' of combined Whigs and Peelites. She felt quite sick when both sides failed her; if she could not find a Prime Minister the House of Commons would – and then goodbye to her prerogative. She was sleeping only fairly well now and Prince Albert, between poring over the evening papers, dictating memoranda and interviewing, interviewing, interviewing, was 'done up'. Perhaps a veteran, like the great Duke or Lord Lansdowne, might hit upon an idea for saving the State? The Duke of Wellington presented the Queen with a hard but inescapable solution. Lord John Russell must return to office with the same Whig Government as before and push through a mutilated Ecclesiastical Titles Bill as best he could. And so the excitement was over and at the end of it all no satisfaction whatever – 'not even the charm of novelty'.[18]

With the state of affairs abroad she felt even less satisfaction. The old despots, temporarily dislodged, had dug themselves in again while the Tsar made it his sole mission to put down revolutions – 'in which he includes Constitutional Govt'. As a true disciple of Sir James Clark with his religion of fresh air, she attributed the reactionary spirit in Russia to the 'terribly unhealthy atmosphere' caused by keeping their windows pasted up from September to May.

That autumn, 1851, Palmerston returned to his tricks. The great Hungarian patriot, Kossuth, had failed heroically to free his country from Austrian oppression. He and thousands of Hungarian and Polish refugees fled to Turkey. Russia and Austria demanded their extradition in the autumn of 1849. Palmerston urged the Sultan to refuse and in case there was trouble sent the usual gunboats to the Dardanelles. They were not a threat to Russia, he explained, but a comfort to Turkey – 'like holding a bottle of salts to the nose of a lady who has been frightened'. In 1851 Kossuth visited the land of 'the judicious bottle-holder', as Palmerston called himself. Queen Victoria deprecated the 'stupid Kossuth fever' which immediately broke out among enthusiastic Liberals and Radicals; in Manchester Kossuth's welcome was more tumultuous than that accorded to Her Majesty in person. Kossuth and O'Connell, she felt, were on a par; how could we hold down Ireland and blame Austria for doing the same thing to Hungary? Suddenly she heard to her consternation that the Foreign Minister himself intended to receive Kossuth. Lord John Russell protested. Palmerston rudely replied that he would not be dictated to as to whom he saw in his own house. The Queen informed Russell that if Palmerston persisted she would dismiss him.

This looked like Palmerston's resignation at last. Not a bit of it. As so often when cornered he surrendered. 'Oh! wonders,' wrote the Queen sarcastically on November 1st, 'Lord Palmerston yielded to the general will . . . He lowers himself more and more.' Moreover, by yielding now he would be able to bob up again, as indeed he did a week or so later, when he received a Radical deputation from Finsbury congratulating him on his support for Kossuth, and violently attacking the Tsar Nicholas and the Emperor Francis Joseph. Greville considered this 'courting' of the Radicals the worst thing Palmerston had ever done. Worse was to come and speedily.

A dramatic *coup* in France tempted him to thrust his neck into the noose, as Prince Albert put it. The new 'submarine telegraph' had been working for only eight weeks when it brought the Queen extraordinary tidings. Prince Louis Napoleon, nephew of Napoleon I, who had been elected President of the French Republic soon after King Louis Philippe's exile, proclaimed himself on December 2nd, 1851, Napoleon III, Emperor of France. To Queen Victoria it seemed as if Oliver Cromwell were back on the world's stage. 'How will it end?' She abhorred the *coup d'état* not because she thought France could ever remain a Republic but because she secretly hoped that one of her Orleans relations, discreetly lying low in an English country house, might one day reoccupy the French throne. Her pleasure was therefore

256

great when she learnt from Lord John that the Cabinet had agreed to remain 'entirely passive' towards Napoleon III. No rows; no fraternization. What was her horror when it transpired that the rascally Foreign Secretary had thrown neutrality and passivity to the winds and assured the French Ambassador of his cordial support for the new Emperor. In doing so Palmerston had double-crossed the British Ambassador in Paris, Lord Normanby, who, on informing the French Government that Britain must remain 'entirely passive', was suavely made aware of Lord Palmerston's contrary opinion.

Palmerston's attempt to defend himself lacked his usual dexterity. He protested that his remarks to the French Ambassador had not been made in his official capacity but purely unofficially, a distinction which hard-pressed politicians from time to time fall back upon but which their opponents invariably reject. Palmerston's want of 'decorum and prudence', wrote the Prime Minister to him on December 19th, unfitted him to remain at the Foreign Office.

In the House Russell read out the Queen's famous letter of August 1850. The effect was crushing. How could Pam have lain down under such charges for over a year unless they were true? No one doubted his guilt nor that it was Russell's use of the Queen's letter which had exposed it. 'The moment the House heard that his [Palmerston's] conduct had been ungentlemanly towards his Queen,' she heard, ' – he was lost. He might have been eloquent, he might even have stood on his head! – his case was a lost one.'[19] Greville, his breath taken away by Russell's final audacity, compared the *coup d'état* against Palmerston with that of Napoleon III himself.

Palmerston vowed he would never forgive the Prime Minister's tactics and Lady Palmerston made her salon ring with imprecations against that 'little blackguard'. To the Court Russell's tactics were more than justified: why, we were so much hated abroad through Palmerston's behaviour that the only way for an English traveller to avoid insult was to say, *'Civis Romanus non sum'*[20] –'I'm not English!'

As a sop Palmerston had been offered the ill-fated Lord Lieutenancy of Ireland. A tart reply came back from the indomitable old sinner that since presumably 'decorum and prudence' were required in Ireland also, he could not be guilty of their lack. Served Russell right, said the Queen, for making the offer.[21]

The seals of office still remained to be handed over, a chance for one or other of these spirited antagonists to win the last round. Queen Victoria was tempted by the idea of refusing to receive Lord Palmerston, as George III and William IV had declined to see Ministers when 'in anger', but she was persuaded to invite him to Windsor on December 26th for the ceremony.

Palmerston also was tempted to make a score and succumbed to the temptation. He went home without calling at Windsor at all, having kept Her Majesty waiting for ninety minutes. Though exceedingly cross she was inwardly relieved. A new Foreign Secretary was in any case the very best of Christmas presents. What made it particularly acceptable was that the new man was the Court's friend, Lord Granville, 'a young lordling', as Lady Palmerston sarcastically remarked, who had occasionally 'whispered' a speech about the Board of Trade but mostly 'danced attendance' on Prince Albert. The Court gave themselves up whole-heartedly to the season of rejoicing and goodwill.

The fall of Palmerston brought joy, as the Queen foresaw, to foreign chancelleries and thrones. In Prussia they said:

> 'Hat der Teufel einen Sohn
> Er ist sicher Palmerston.'
> If the devil had a son
> Surely he'd be Palmerston.

Now the devil's son had been driven off and Francis Joseph of Austria, Frederick William of Prussia, Otho of Greece, Bomba of Naples and all the rest of the crowned heads could relax. Prince Albert and King Leopold had long amused themselves by calling Lord Palmerston by a German version of his name – 'Pilgerstein'. Pilger being German for a palmer, no doubt they got a sardonic kick out of visualizing the devil's son disguised as a holy man with staff and scrip. 'Pilgerstein'

– the essential Pilgerstein, inflaming foreign nationalists, establishing constitutional governments, picking quarrels with despots – Pilgerstein was almost done with. For though ten more years of dealing with Lord Palmerston remained to Prince Albert and fourteen to Queen Victoria, they detected the cloven hoof less and less frequently after Lord Palmerston left the Foreign Office.

What kind of devil possessed Pilgerstein, in the Queen's eyes, from which Palmerston was relatively free?

There was a clash in principle between the remedies proposed by Palmerston and the Court for revolutionary Europe. This was the 'neuralgic point'[22] in their relations. It was a question of Sovereigns or Chambers, as the Queen noted in her Journal in 1846. The Prince believed that liberal institutions, where they were desirable, must be left to develop organically without foreign intervention. Palmerston thought that a salvo of dispatches and even cannon balls would hasten their growth.

The clash was intensified by the fact that so many threatened thrones were German and often occupied by German relations of the Queen. Victoria was not only a queen but a cousin. She had a double fellow-feeling with the victims of Pilgerstein's spleen. To an extent which today would be impossible, his behaviour humiliated her personally. Not only did all her fellow Sovereigns lay their complaints at her feet – a situation with which Palmerston brusquely dealt by saying that she must confine her international correspondence to gossip about family affairs – but she herself felt bound to answer to the world for his misdeeds. She did not see that the development of ministerial responsibility gave the Crown its chance to enter an age of innocence. 'And I have to bear it all,' remained a sad refrain, as we shall see, which the Queen had it in her power to drop.

The position of one particular Royal Highness – Prince Albert – carried the clash still further. '*I* & Albert' was all very well as the symbol of a married partnership; but to speak for the Queen was not his constitutional privilege. His only prerogative derived from the human right of a husband to assist the wife who had borne seven children in ten years.

259

As long as Palmerston had the country behind him Prince Albert was a voice crying in the Blue Closet.

The Prince's position introduced one personal note into the quarrel. There were others. 'Cupid's' early amatory exploits did not endear him to a Court which was becoming Puritanical. Nor was his technique with the Queen such as to win her confidence. Lady Palmerston in 1848 sent him some written advice about improving it:

'I am afraid you contradict her notions too boldly. You fancy she will hear reason . . . I should treat what she says more lightly and courteously, and not enter into arguments with her, but lead her on gently, by letting her believe you have both the same opinions in fact and the same wishes, but take sometimes different ways of carrying them out.'

Lady Palmerston was asking her husband to *ménager* the English Court just as the Queen had desired Palmerston to *ménager* foreign monarchs. No doubt relations would have been somewhat better if Palmerston had complied. In a sense, however, his wife's clever analysis was out of date, for Lady Palmerston had married too soon to see the Victoria-and-Albert combination at work from the inside: the Prince's clear, dominant mind could never have been bamboozled along the lines she suggested.

Was it the person or the principles, the man or the measures which really antagonized the Queen? The basic hostility was personal in a sublimated sense. Palmerston's dedication to the liberal cause abroad drove the protesting Court almost into defending Spanish and Portuguese, Austrian and Greek absolutism. Yet Queen Victoria and Prince Albert had set their hearts upon England 'rising above' both revolutionary and despotic Europe and creating a new area of 'reciprocity' and peace. How could reciprocity develop in the blistering atmosphere of Pilgerstein's dispatches? More wounding than his manner, more shocking than his morals was his frustration of the Queen's mission to do good.

One question remains. How was it that the unprecedented clash of Sovereign and Foreign Minister never exploded into irretrievable national disaster? The reason must be that the brinkmanship of the four major actors was deliberately geared to something less than catastrophe. The Prince knew that total war with Pilgerstein would topple the Crown: one must be *grob* (rough) with Pilgerstein, he wrote to King Leopold, but not *pfiffig* (tricky). Palmerston repeatedly allowed his bluff to be called. Lord John Russell kept up the disagreeable job of mediation for over four years, something of an achievement. No doubt Russell's duty was not to act as umpire but to captain his own Cabinet, whose united policy the Queen would then have had to accept. His failure to control his team, particularly Palmerston, gave the Queen an unhealthy interest in Cabinet splits which caused much trouble during the later years of her reign. Palmerston's opponents in the Cabinet were tempted to use her as a joker in the pack while she in turn exploited their discontent. Nevertheless, Lord John's mediation prevented complete disaster.

Finally the Queen herself, despite all, recognized Palmerston's abilities. Without Prince Albert's influence it is even possible that the martial music of '*Civis Romanus sum*' might have piped her in spirit aboard Palmerston's gunboats.

Pilgerstein, as his very name indicates, was in part a figment of the Teutonic imagination, a bold lecherous fiend haunting some dark forest of the brothers Grimm. Pam, the debonair landlord of Broadlands, with its bland acres and smart racing stables, was far removed from Prince Albert's gothic nightmare. When the Queen came to see Palmerston as Home Secretary, through English eyes, the vision if not beatific was much improved.

CHAPTER XVI

'OUR HAPPY HOME LIFE'
1846–51

IMPROVEMENTS IN THE royal residences was one of the subjects to which the Queen could turn when politics became too provoking. Parliament voted £20,000 in August 1846 for alterations to Buckingham Palace, which had long ceased to house either her growing family or stream of guests with any comfort. An appeal to public generosity was always a nervous matter for the Queen. She was relieved to hear that only one 'very ill-conditioned man' had condemned the extensions as extravagant. Among the improvements was the celebrated balcony facing the Mall on which she first appeared at the opening of the Great Exhibition.

A month after the Buckingham Palace vote went through the Royal Family moved into the Pavilion Wing of the new Osborne, a blessing being called down upon their first evening spent there by the singing of a Lutheran hymn. The Queen was afterwards to regret the lost charms of old Osborne – 'the character of that little house is gone' – but accepted the fact that they had outgrown it.[1]

More than once during her lifetime she fled from the pompous and grand to the 'cosy' and snug (two favourite words) only to be forced back again by the exigencies of children, Court and visiting notables into recreating precisely those large-scale surroundings which she had tried to escape. Indomitably she would then begin again planning smaller and smaller Chinese boxes within the all too spacious framework of her overgrown retreat.

The large new Osborne had its compensations. Standing together on the flat Italianate roof the Queen and Prince could now direct the landscaping of their park. The Queen would watch her great ships glide out from Portsmouth and Spithead as she sat on the little sandy beach in a semi-circular beach-hut designed for her by the Prince, with a mosaic floor and domed ceiling of blue, gold and pink. On hot days a loud grating sound would break the stillness of the woods. It was the Queen's bathing-machine running down a sloping pier to the shore. Having donned voluminous bathing apparel by the dim light of two frosted-glass windows high up under its eaves, Her Majesty would step out on to a closely curtained verandah and descending five wooden steps, drop into the sea. It was only after the waves had taken over the concealing duty of the curtains that the machine could be removed.

This exhilarating operation first took place on July 30th, 1847:

'Drove down to the beach with my maid & went into the bathing machine, where I undressed & bathed in the sea (for the first time in my life), a very nice bathing woman attending me. I thought it delightful till I put my head under the water, when I thought I should be stifled.'[2]

In future the Queen sponged her face on shore before her dip and then, head erect, 'plunged about' in the ocean. Three years later she found the bathing customs at Ostend 'amusing and refreshing'. The ladies bathed publicly, their machines being dragged into the sea by women *and* men and their long hair hanging down to dry without even a handkerchief covering it – 'like so many penitents'.[3]

The Royal Avenue, a double line of cedars and ilexes heavy as the mahogany furniture inside Osborne House, led up to the main entrance. The arcaded House Wing, a loggia, terraced gardens and two campaniles –the Clock Tower and Flag Tower – completed the Prince's vision of an Italian villa. Once inside, one could see why the Queen called Osborne her 'little Paradise'. Compared with Windsor or Buckingham Palace the ceilings were low and the rooms so small that for large receptions a marquee had to be erected on the lawn. The Horn Room, dedicated entirely to the antlers which composed every item of its furniture, was as cosy as even the Queen could wish. The Queen's small Audience Room was made smaller by a huge though frolicsome chandelier brought from Germany, its green glass leaves and pink glass convolvulus flowers recalling the wallpaper of the Rosenau bedroom in which Prince Albert had been born. Upstairs each room, bright with chintz and bric-a-brac, had a view to the sea. The Prince's narrow bathroom with its plain, lidded tub and shower, came first in the royal suite. His study followed, austerely utilitarian: a knee-hole desk, a backless stool, a stand for walking-sticks; but dotted about everywhere like luminous white pebbles on a dark shore, small statuettes and busts, among them, on little crimson cushions, the marble hands and feet of his children.

Next came the Queen's sitting-room, its twin writing-tables standing side by side, hers nearest the beech-log fire. Next door, in the centre of her dressing table, stood a folding book-rest at which she would employ herself during the tedious hours of hair-dressing. Her bathroom greatly outshone the Prince's in size and equipment, especially the fathomless bath standing in a curtained alcove. Last came the homely royal bedroom, all chintz and mahogany, a colossal wardrobe extending from wall to wall, its furthest door delicately disguising the entrance to what Queen Victoria used to call the 'little room'. Over the bedhead on the right-hand side hung Prince Albert's watch case. It hangs there today.

Throughout Osborne House the entwined initials V and A still speak of that idyllic Victorian union – everywhere, that is, except over the smoking-room door where there is a single letter A.

Queen Victoria has left in her Journal the picture of an ideal July day at Osborne in 1849: blue sky and sea, breakfast in the summer-house, writing, a sketching lesson, Princess Helena's lesson after luncheon, a ride with Prince Albert, picking strawberries with the children till 8 o'clock, dinner alone with the Prince, walking on the Terrace gazing at the moon and sea with not a leaf stirring.

'How happy we are here! And never do I enjoy myself more, or more peacefully than when I can be so much with my beloved Albert & follow him everywhere!'[4]

At Windsor Prince Albert made improvements both inside and outside: a model farm, kennels with a little stone dog begging on each gable-end and eventually a dairy embellished with stained glass and pillars like the crypt of a church. An extraordinary incident in February 1849 brought about more radical changes in the Castle grounds. A 'gang of harpies', as *The Times* called some impudent visitors to the Slopes, stole a royal sketch-book, copied and published its contents and offered facsimiles of the royal autograph to purchasers. The Queen's privacy became the subject of controversy. Had the public forfeited its right to wander freely about and crowd under Her Majesty's very windows? *The Times*, while defending this right, thundered a warning:

> 'Let the QUEEN of Great Britain be able to sit down to her piano or sketch-book with the same security against intrusion as any other lady in the land.'

The Queen's taste for privacy was sharpened by the discovery of Balmoral. There were two serpents in the Osborne paradise: accessibility and a relaxing climate. Sir James Clark reported the existence of another little paradise far away in the Highlands, situated on dry gravelly soil. The Prince's exhaustion and the Chartists' activities drove the Queen northwards in September 1848 for her first visit to Balmoral.

> 'It is a pretty little Castle in the old scotch style . . . one enters a nice little hall, & a billiard-room & Dining-room. A good broad staircase takes one upstairs & above the Dining-room is our sitting-room . . . a fine large room opening into our bedroom, etc. The Children & Miss Hildyard [the governess] live on the same floor, – the Ladies below & the men upstairs.'[5]

The Queen had bought a print of the 'little Castle' in Aberdeen and made a copy in her Journal of its four picturesque towers, granite walls, slit windows and high-pitched roof. On the very first afternoon she and Prince Albert climbed to the cairn opposite their new home and gazed around at a landscape which at once reminded the Prince of his beloved Thuringia. (When down-to-earth Duke Ernest came to stay he pointed out that the hills round Balmoral bore no resemblance to the towering Thuringian crags; it was just Albert's nostalgic fancy). The Queen drank in peace after turmoil.

They walked across the suspension bridge, unsafe for carriages, to kirk on Sunday. The Queen was impressed by the attentiveness of the peasants but thought the simple service only fairly well conducted. No one wore a kilt. Clearly there was room for improvement and the Royal Family would set an example. 'Bertie & Affie are always in Highland things' – a habit which was later followed by all the Queen's younger children who economically passed on their 'Highland things' to one another irrespective of sex. Their father, too, adopted the national costume though not without tribulation: one evening dinner was late 'owing to Albert's struggles to dress in his kilt'. The Queen chose satin tartan for herself. Life was deliciously informal. They would go on what the Queen called 'a ½ shooting expedition', the family setting out on ponies and Prince Albert breaking away for a short time to stalk deer or shoot ptarmigan while the Queen sketched or chatted with the ghillies. 'I like talking to the people here, they are so simple & straightforward, & I like their curious Highland English.' Grant, the handsome head ghillie, was so 'faithful'; when he and good sturdy Macdonald dragged her pony up the rocky tracks she felt so 'safe'.[6]

One day they made an expedition to the top of misty Lochnagar, the third highest mountain in Scotland and the only one round Balmoral with pointed peaks. Driving back through Ballochbuie, a relic of the old Caledonian pine forest, the Queen was entranced by the forest floor of heather, mosses, juniper, blaeberries and hog myrtle broken with brown streams and pools; as cushiony as a glade in a fairy tale. In the heart of the Ballochbuie they found the Garawalt burn with its foaming waterfall and trembling bridge. Before they reached home, very late, Lord John Russell and Sir James Clark had come out anxiously to meet them.

In the outside world death still struck: Prince Lichnowsky was ambushed and Lord George Bentinck, Peel's enemy, died of apoplexy; on the hills all was peace.

266

'It was wonderful not seeing a single human being, nor hearing a sound, excepting that of the wind, or the call of the blackcock or grouse.'[7]

The Queen, back in London in October, felt 'bewildered' – a favourite word to denote nostalgia, fatigue, nervous irritation and general disorientation. They had travelled by rail, breaking the journey at Crewe, and her fatigue was partly due to the exasperating prejudices of Sabbatarians.

'It being Sunday we had decided to start at 6, in order to arrive in London before the Service, as people are very particular about travelling on a Sunday in England. In my opinion it is overdone. We were therefore called at 5, – rather hard after a long day yesterday.'[8]

They reached Euston at 10.30 am, driving to the Palace without escort, 'to keep everything quite quiet.'

The following autumn, 1849, they were back again at Balmoral soaking themselves in the spirit of the place. The Prince bought a Gaelic dictionary as big as himself; the Queen and her children had lessons in Scottish dancing. 'Beat hop, beat hop, one two three hop', sang out the dancing master; 'a beat before and a beat behind and a beat before and *down* upon it – turn the figure *slightly*; round the arm, *the shoulders* back *nicely* . . .' Lady Augusta Bruce, the Duchess of Kent's lady-in-waiting, imagined the words of encouragement and criticism which the dancing master whispered to Her Majesty: 'Now gently, me deare, try and dance like a lady.'[9]

The Braemar Gathering Queen Victoria considered 'a poor affair' but the cottages of her tenants attracted eager interest. Mrs Grant and Mrs McDougal needed new petticoats. 'For me?' exclaimed the latter in amazement when a smiling little woman popped into her 'placie' and pressed a roll of stuff into her old hand. 'The Lord bless ye.' Charles Greville, staying at Balmoral on official business, was immensely taken by this new version of Her Majesty. 'She is running in and out of the house all day,' he noticed, 'and often goes about

267

alone . . .' There were no sentries on guard, only one police-man to keep off intruders.

Not everyone appreciated so much informality. A Minister-in-Attendance found himself discussing State affairs with Queen Victoria sitting on the edge of his bed; the 'little Castle' had no sitting-room, only bed-sitters for guests. Nothing put out the Queen, not even the perpetual moving of her seat in the billiard-cum-sitting-room, where the ladies could not avoid blocking the way round the table. Indeed she and the Prince wanted to find an even smaller home. About five miles from the Castle were two granite huts or 'shiels' used by ghillies, perched side by side above Loch Muick. Allt-na-Guibhsaich – 'the burn of the fir trees' – became the Queen's favourite and humblest retreat. She had the two huts joined together by a short covered passage and lived in one while her servants inhabited the other, 'the washing & cooking & everything going on in a line with one's own dwelling'. How cosy to have no iron curtain between the workaday world and royalty. Where a path from Allt-na-Guibhsaich met the loch stood a granite jetty and boathouse. In a prodigiously heavy row-boat Queen Victoria and Prince Albert would spend romantic hours fishing for trout until the moon came up over Glen Girnock, when the Prince would help row them home, one of the ghillies piping and the rest bursting into weird shouts whenever the music excited them beyond endurance.

> Ever, as on they bore, more loud
> And louder rang the pibroch proud,

quoted Victoria from her beloved Scott. As they climbed the hill homewards, welcoming lights gleamed through the firs, and they settled down to a peaceful evening of whist.

The Prince now took his sport very seriously; he no longer showed 'angelic good humour' whether he hit or missed and the Queen minded so much about his success that she dared not ask how he had fared. He even submitted to the sports-man's custom of 'frugal' luncheons. The Queen gave him a silver luncheon box for Christmas so that their cold snacks could at least look regal. On the last day of their second holiday in Balmoral she again mentioned in her Journal those Highlanders who had taken most care of her. This time the list included 'young J. Brown'.*

Each year Queen Victoria became a little more Scottish. She learnt to stalk, to eat bannock and dry the Prince of Wales's scarlet socks by her tenants' peat fires and to interpret the Highland characters. 'They are never vulgar, never take liberties, are so intelligent, modest and well bred.'[10] By the time young John Brown, grown older, had began to show quite opposite characteristics it had become a point of honour with the Queen to see nothing but good in Highlanders.

And all the time Mr Landseer was painting away at the Queen disembarking from her boat, the Queen on her pony, the Queen at Prince Albert's side lost in admiration for his skill as a hunter. 'It is quite a new conception,' she wrote of these masterpieces in public relations; 'it will tell a great deal.' She longed for the world to share the miracle of her new life; 'no other queen has ever enjoyed what I am fortunate enough to enjoy.'[11]

These were the nearest to cloudless years in Queen Victoria's life. Anxiety over the Prince's health was only intermittent; the joy of his companionship was interrupted neither by the Queen's friends as in the early days nor by his own later preoccupations. All the fun which Victoria had missed as a child she now had with her children: games of blind man's buff and fox-and-geese; quadrilles with the seven-year-old Prince of Wales as her partner and strolls on summer evenings helping him to catch moths; visits to the Zoo where the hippopotamus was 'as tractable as ever'† but the smell in the large cat house upset Princess Helena; on wet days games of beggar-my-neighbour; *tableaux vivants* and scenes from English or

* Queen Victoria's very first mention of John Brown in her Journal occurred on September 11th, 1849.

† This young hippopotamus had been brought from Alexandria by the Consul-General, Mr Murray, the Queen's former Master of the Household. She admired its sagacity and affection: it screamed for its keeper who had to sleep next to it.

French plays, some so difficult that 'Albert had to make them say their parts over & over again'. After a performance of Racine's *Athalie* (the Princess Royal was eleven and the Prince of Wales ten) the Queen wrote: 'Children though often a source of anxiety and difficulty are a great blessing and cheer & brighten up life.'[12]

When a new baby was born the Queen, like every good mother, would have all the rest of the family into her room that same day. To see 'our tribe' trailing after their father on a walk gave her acute pleasure, and so did the sight of Prince Albert riding with the Princess Royal – 'quite the grande dame' – or with 'his Boy', the Prince of Wales.

Old Lord Liverpool once told the Queen how George III and Queen Charlotte neglected their children's upbringing: 'I never wish to hear any more about these things,' the King had said after a lurid report on his eldest son's doings. The Queen and Prince were deeply shocked by this story, 'which we think speaks volumes for the interest the Parents can have taken in their Children.'[13] Their own unflagging interest would surely bring its reward.

'The Plan', as Queen Victoria called a joint effort by Prince Albert and Stockmar to map out the Prince of Wales's education, was endlessly debated at the beginning of 1847. With the same zeal which the Prince brought to the betterment of fat-stock, retired domestic servants or a Cambridge syllabus, he devoted himself to his son's improvement. Unfortunately Stockmar had injected into the Prince's zeal a fatal dose of anxiety. 'The first truth,' Stockmar had written when the Prince of Wales was only three months old, 'by which the Queen and the Prince ought to be thoroughly permeated is, that their position is a more difficult one than that of any other parents in the kingdom'[14] – some of the worst advice ever given to young parents.

On ice cold, pitch dark January mornings Prince Albert would rise early, light his German student's lamp with its green silk shade and tabulate his son's future. Such industry combined with the young Prince's amiable character at first seemed sufficient guarantees of success. Though a little 'awkward', so that he often did not do himself justice, at five the

270

Queen had found her son 'a very good child & not at all wanting in intellect'. On his sixth birthday she admitted that he was 'more backward' than the Princess Royal, but she could record 'improvement'.

In April 1849 the Prince of Wales entered upon a new phase of 'The Plan'. He was given a suite of his own at Buckingham Palace and a tutor, Henry Birch, young and good-looking, whose kindness belied his name. The new arrangement seemed to the Queen 'highly satisfactory'. Nevertheless rumours began to circulate that the Queen thought the Prince of Wales stupid: 'the hereditary and unfailing antipathy of our Sovereigns to their Heirs Apparent,' wrote Greville in his diary, 'seems thus early to be taking root, and the Q. does not much like the child.'[15]

The Prince of Wales's ninth birthday brought a sense of disappointment. 'There is much good in him,' wrote his mother, 'he has such affectionate feelings, – great truthfulness & great simplicity of character' – but lessons were a complete failure. A week later she was discussing with Lord Granville education and phrenology, Prince Albert having decided to submit Bertie's bumps to the professional inspection of Dr George Combe, with a view to hastening his tardy progress. There were arguments about punishment: the Queen was against 'punishing children with the Bible & making Sunday unbearable', while the chastisement administered by the Prince had not improved his son's scholarship. A new tutor was engaged, Mr Gibbs, after having been interviewed by the Queen and Stockmar in June 1851. What a responsibility it was, finding a tutor. A month later Princess Clémentine of Orleans had to cut short a visit to Buckingham Palace when news arrived from Spain that her boys' tutor had gone off his head.

The Prince of Wales mourned for Mr Birch, heartily disliking his successor. One of Mr Gibbs's first tasks was to break to the Prince the facts of his destiny. He was not so successful as Lehzen had been with Princess Victoria twenty-one years earlier. The Prince, instead of drinking it in and saying 'I will be good', went straight to his Mama for a clarification of the confusion which Gibbs had created in his mind. The Queen's account in her Journal of their subsequent conversation is revealing:

'*February* 12, 1852: Walked out with Bertie . . . He generally lets out to me, when he walks with me, something or other, that is occupying his mind. This time it was how *I* came to the throne, which Mr Gibbs had explained to him before . . . He said that he had always believed Vicky would succeed, but now he knew that in default of *him*, Affie, little Arthur & "another brother, if perhaps we have one", would come before Vicky. I explained to him the different successions . . . He took it all in, very naturally . . .'

The world of the little Prince had clearly been a formidable matriarchy: first came his mother, then his sister. It is probable that Queen Victoria did not at first appreciate her eldest son's feelings of inferiority. The day after the Princess Royal's sixth birthday, for instance, the Queen 'was much touched by Bertie asking me to do his little Sunday lesson with him sometimes', just as she always did it with Vicky. When Bertie's efforts to shine miscarried he got short shrift. 'Mama, is not a pink the female of a carnation?' he asked one day. 'Poor Princey,' said Lady Lyttelton, was howled down. Like many parents, the Queen may have thought her eldest daughter should have been the boy; at any rate her Journal is full of the Princess Royal's prowess at acting masculine parts – 'she made such a fine tall boy' – and when 'poor Princey' at last got a suit of armour for *Athalie*, he was swamped in it.

Notwithstanding these disappointments the Queen was immensely proud of her 'blooming family' and spared herself no effort on their behalf. In the shimmering heat of August 1850 she walked the half-mile down towards the sea at Osborne where garden plots had been laid out for the children, helping them to use their initialled tools: P.o.W., Pss.R., Pss.A., P.A., Pss.H., Pss.L. Prince Arthur had arrived that May so there would soon be another miniature barrow, trolley, spade and fork to keep her busy. Prince Albert's health still caused her some tremors. Even the dry soil of Balmoral did not prevent him from catching a chill every autumn. As for herself, she faced her thirty-first birthday and the turn of the century with 'such perfect health' that it was 'a blessing to us *both*'.

New life was springing up round the Queen; at the same time she studied perhaps more closely than was natural in so young a woman the way in which old or blighted leaves were beginning to fall. The death of the Archbishop of Canterbury in 1846 and of Lord Liverpool in 1851 made her feel 'more & more alone', an unusual sensation for a wife with her mother living, a large family and countless relatives. The explanation lies partly in the Queen's instinct to make the most of death, partly in her attachment to those who had befriended her in youth. Her comparatively rootless childhood drove her into a frenzy of root-growing for the rest of her life. When part of the old precious stock was torn up by death she lived again through the loneliness of her past. Peel's death in 1850 was like losing a father.

Two days after Robert Pate struck the Queen on the head with his cane, Robert Peel was thrown from his horse on Constitution Hill. Sir James Clark as usual reassured the Queen: though Peel was so heavy, full-blooded and gouty, it was 'only a fracture of the collar bone'. Ominous reports, however, arrived from Peel's own doctor on the evening of July 2nd. The Queen could not eat any dinner; she cancelled her visit to the opera. Half an hour after midnight a letter was brought in. Prince Albert tore it open; Sir Robert had 'gone'. Not for the first nor for the last time Queen Victoria addressed the Almighty in a tone of bewildered reproach:

'Oh! God Who alone knowest what is best for us, may Thy will be done, but it does seem mysterious that in these troubled times when *he* could less be spared than any other human being, should be taken from us.'[16]

As Greville once said of another royal observation, it was imperfectly expressed but the meaning was plain. Queen Victoria was not amused by her Creator's inscrutable ways.

By the time of Peel's death, the Queen had come to honour every aspect of his character. His background linked him to

273

the manufacturing classes whom Prince Albert chiefly cultivated and separated him from the 'fashionables' and 'fox-
hunters' who chiefly hunted Albert. As keenly as the Queen
herself Peel promoted the Prince's cause. Above all Peel
represented to Queen Victoria the embodiment of firm leadership and the negation of party politics. A few hours after his
death she wrote in her Journal: 'Belonging to no party, he
stood as the first name in the Hse. of Commons, & his opinion
was invaluable.' At this date the Queen still felt that if a man
had to choose a party he should go for the Liberals. When Sir
Robert's son entered the Liberal Government during the
following year she credited him with a decided advantage
over his father.

'It was poor Sir Robert's misfortune to have been *kept
down* to *old* Tory principles, for which his mind was far
too enlightened.'[17]

Other familiar figures were passing from the scene. William
IV's widow, Queen Adelaide, died in 1849 and her death set
the Queen and Prince talking of a favourite project: to build
for themselves a mausoleum.

In some ways the most poignant of all the deaths during
this period was that of Lord Melbourne on November 24th,
1848, for the Queen's incomparable old friend had been dead
to her long before a succession of fits carried him off. Having
dedicated twelve hours to his memory – 'I thought much &
talked much of him all day' – she referred to him afterwards
rather less than to Peel and in less glowing terms. One fact
is enough to explain this apparent hardness. Queen Victoria
believed that Melbourne, pandering to her supposed wishes,
had allowed her to make the fatal mistake of postponing her
marriage to Prince Albert. About two years before Melbourne
died she and the Prince on a wet, cold day in January
went over for the hundredth time the 'misunderstandings &
harsh words' which had darkened the months before their
marriage.

'Altogether, the state of affairs and the way all went on
from the time of my accession, until my marriage was very

274

unsatisfactory & I cannot bear to think of it. I told Albert that he had really come like an angel of light to save me, & take me out of all my difficulties for I *alone* could not have helped myself. I was young & wilful . . . [criticism of Lehzen follows] Lord Melbourne, whom I clung to . . . did not, from being too good natured, give me a chance of properly extricating myself. But I *might* have done so in the autumn of 38, had I married Albert. Oh! if I *only* had . . . !'[18]

'If I *only* had . . .' The Queen now grudged every hour past and present spent apart from her husband. His absence at meetings in centres like Liverpool or York could only be endured because of the excellent publicity he received. She could ill spare him to lesser gatherings: 'Albert went away after dinner to hear a Lecture on Magnetism,' she wrote in March 1850, 'from which he returned tired & not much edified.'

Anniversaries provided regular opportunities for expressing her deep sense of happiness and love. Her twenty-eighth birthday brought forth a characteristic tumult of emotion. How *very* old she felt, 'but dear Albert's & my love is younger & greater than ever . . .' In blue and white check muslin she listened to the four elder children reciting German verses, and received four different bouquets – lilies, roses, lilac and young oak leaves.

It is unthinkable that with Queen Victoria's temperament there should be no tiffs. During a pheasant shoot in 1849 the Prince ordered Colonel Grey and the Prince of Wales to leave the line and catch a wounded bird, assuring the Queen that no one would shoot in their direction. Next moment Lord Canning shot Grey in the temple and promptly fainted himself. 'I think we should *all* take this little accident as a warning,' wrote Her Majesty reprovingly, 'for no one to leave their places, when shooting is going on.'[19]

In the world of art and culture the Queen under Prince Albert's guidance became a conscientious if not an audacious explorer. Only once did she venture to criticize her husband's handiwork: the new House of Lords, whose decoration Prince

Albert had supervised, had perhaps a little too much brass.* *King John* was her favourite Shakespearean play, partly because Prince Arthur, played by nine-year-old Kate Terry, reminded her of her own son. 'What a man Shakespeare was!' Goethe's *Faust* was a tougher nut. Apart from the painfully clear moral of Gretchen's fate – 'such poor girls who are seduced' – she found herself unable to master it after one performance (it would have been an astonishing feat if she had) and studied the book, carrying it about with her out of doors and learning passages by heart. She came to appreciate what she described in unmistakably Albertian language as its matchless 'beauty of reasoning'.

The Prince's influence with the artisan classes turned her thoughts in their direction. She helped him rehearse his speech to the Society for the Improvement of the Conditions of the Labouring Classes and was gratified that it went over well despite his nervousness. A book he gave her to read entitled *Popular Education*, written by J. & F. Bullock, a tailor and a shoemaker, struck her as an 'extraordinary production' full of deep truths hidden, she would have thought, from all but the highly educated. She sent a copy to Lord Lansdowne, the Home Secretary. Prince Albert became Chancellor of Cambridge University after a contested election in which the Queen proudly recorded that all the cleverest men gave him their votes. Her passion for going about incognito was indulged by a moonlit walk with the Prince along the college 'Backs', a veil over her tiara and a mackintosh over his Orders being considered sufficient to preserve their anonymity.

There was nothing Albert could not do. From the utilization of the Osborne sewage to the design for Winterhalter's portraits, Albert thought of everything. His crowning achievement was the Great Exhibition.

In the frosty darkness of a January morning, 1850, Prince Albert set out from Windsor to preside over the inaugural

* Its refreshment room might have been adorned with Landseer's *Monarch of the Glen* had not the House of Commons declined to vote the purchase money.

meeting of the Commissioners for the Exhibition, 'to take place in 51'. Queen Victoria introduced this tremendous project to her Journal without the expected fanfare, no doubt because it would deprive her of the Prince's company. A few weeks later the publicity given to it kindled the Queen's enthusiasm. 'I *do* feel proud at the thought of what my beloved Albert's great mind has conceived.'[20] The troubles into which the Prince ran almost at once greatly strengthened the Queen's ardour and awakened her fiercely protective feelings. Although the Prince often addressed her in letters as 'Dear Child', their intricate relationship included maternal feelings on her side also.

Prince Albert's lofty conception was for a festival of work and peace housed under domes of glass designed by the creator of Chatsworth conservatory – Joseph Paxton. Here the nations of the world would exhibit their swords beaten into ploughshares – if possible into mechanical ploughshares – by the new industrial processes. All history points, said Prince Albert at the Mansion House, to the unity of mankind. At the Crystal Palace he intended to achieve on a world-wide scale that 'reciprocity' which Palmerston prevented in Europe. 'Paxton vobiscum', giggled the 'fashionables'. At home inspiration would flow from the liberated minds of a thousand independent, self-reliant creators. If Samuel Smiles was the publicist of the mid-Victorian creed of 'self-help', the Prince was its impresario and Joseph Paxton himself, in Professor Asa Briggs's words, its epitome.[21]

At the same time, as President of the Society of Fine Arts, Prince Albert planned to marry art with commerce, praising the simple grandeur of engineering above the richness of architecture. To round off his dream he erected two model artisan dwellings on a plot of land opposite the Crystal Palace, thus beckoning the workers, blessed by a day of toil, home to a model family life.

To work is to pacify and to do both these things is to pray – this was Prince Albert's message to a world barely recovered from the fury of war and revolution. It was his own deepest religion.

Sheer bone-headedness prevented his dream from being

financed by the nation. Undaunted he at once organized private guarantors. They were never called upon for the Exhibition, visited by six million people, made a profit of nearly a quarter of a million pounds. The site chosen, Hyde Park, was fiercely attacked. Joseph Paxton's soaring temple of trade was not only high enough to enclose vast elm trees in full summer leaf, it also spread far enough to obstruct the riders in Rotten Row. No sympathy was wasted on them by the Queen. How dared they endanger the Exhibition 'merely for the sake of the Ride in Hyde Park about which people have suddenly gone quite mad?'[22] Alas, there was no Sir Robert Peel to defend the Commissioners against the dandies, for he had been thrown out riding the day before.

The fact that the Exhibition was an advertisement for Free Trade infuriated the Protectionists. 'Fashionables' and 'fox-hunters' from the shires, led by Colonel Sibthorp, called down curses from Heaven upon this new Babel, including hail to destroy the glass roof. Queen Victoria must have quailed: not so long ago hail had smashed part of the conservatory in Buckingham Palace, creating such devastation that the soldiers had to be summoned to clear it up. Would they need the redcoats in the Crystal Palace?

The experiment in internationalism caused a war on two fronts. At home the foreign exhibitors were denounced as a source of plague, political agitation and crime. England, having resisted cross-Channel revolution for three whole years, was now inviting the vipers into her bosom. Abroad the despots regarded Prince Albert's adopted country, the haven of refugees, as a training ground for regicides, radicals and constitutionalists. On April 2nd, 1851, just a month before the Exhibition was due to open, the British Ambassador in Russia reported to Palmerston that the Tsar had refused passports to the nobility for fear of 'contamination' in London. King Bomba of Naples went further. Not even goods were allowed to be sent for exhibition though how they would be contaminated was harder to see. Not a single crowned head trusted itself under Prince Albert's glass roof; a passport to England was too obviously a passport to eternity. The King of Prussia, influenced by the Russian and Austrian Emperors,

278

asked Prince Albert at the last moment whether it was really safe for the Crown Prince and his family to come. Prince Albert replied bitingly that there was '*no* fear here' but as he could not absolutely guarantee anyone's life he would not invite the Prussians. This, commented the Queen gleefully, 'would cause a great sensation'.[23] The Prussians arrived without further cavil. The Tsar, however, got his own back by forbidding his Ambassador to join with the rest of the Diplomatic Corps in presenting an address to Her Majesty. The whole gesture had to be abandoned. Not a bad thing, thought Palmerston.

Lord John added his quota of trouble. A week before the opening he objected that a salute of guns north of the Serpentine, as proposed, would shatter the crystal dome; the guns must be fired far away in St James's Park. They were fired as proposed; no glass broke.

The birds of the air made their own tiresome contribution. Thousands roosted in the trees under the dome, threatening to do for the Exhibition with their droppings what all the Russian and Austrian malice had failed to do – cover it with contempt. After many remedies had failed – 'Try sparrow-hawks, ma'am,' said the Duke of Wellington.

The Queen showed her fiery loyalty by visiting the Exhibition four months before the opening. She rejoiced in the 'hum of life'. In February she took the children, explaining that the galleries were being tested by a platform made exactly the same size on to which 250 men would charge and spring together. At the beginning of April she took her sons again; the floors were down; she longed to come every day. On the 28th she found the Crystal Palace a fairyland but for the noise of '12–20,000 people' doing last jobs. All day Prince Albert, 'terribly fagged', answered 12–20,000 questions with perfect calm and good temper.

Meanwhile predictions of a gigantic crowd who would charge and spring upon the Queen like the men testing the galleries, caused the Prince to announce that the doors would not open until one o'clock for season-ticket holders, instead of 11 am as first arranged. Her Majesty would have departed before they arrived. There was uproar. *The Times* and

Morning Chronicle blazed away; even Lord Granville, always rosewater to royalty, agreed that feeling was amazingly high. 'The fashionable society in London,' wrote Lord John to Prince Albert, 'might be disregarded, but it would be a pity to alienate the manufacturers and the middle classes.'[24] This shrewd appeal worked. Next day the season-ticket holders' hour of entry was restored to eleven.

On April 30th, a day of showers, Thackeray published nineteen verses of a *May Day Ode* of which this was the first:

> *But yesterday a naked sod,*
> *The dandies sneered from Rotten-row,*
> *And cantered o'er it to and fro;*
> *And see 'tis done!*
> *As though 'twere by a wizard's rod*
> *A blazing arch of lucid glass*
> *Leaps like a fountain from the grass*
> *To meet the sun.*

The sun came out on May 1st, 1851, to meet the Queen, her family, her few bold Royalties and her thousands of exultant season-ticket holders, safely packed into banner-hung galleries or held back by light railings. Dressed in pink and silver, wearing her Garter ribbon and the Koh-i-Noor diamond, a small crown and two feathers on her head, she drove in an open carriage to the Exhibition and then processed up the central aisle, past the flashing fountain to the royal dais, with a blue and gold canopy above her and a vast elm tree behind. One after another the organs burst into music as she passed; in the vast spaces she could hardly hear them. Floods of emotion swept over her: it seemed like her Coronation over again except that the continuous cheering made it 'more touching, for in a church naturally all is silent'. Afterwards she cut out an article from *The Times* likening it to the concourse of all peoples on the Day of Judgement and confessed to having felt more truly devotional than at any Church service. *The Earth is the Lord's and all that therein is.*

Those words, printed at the head of the catalogue, had been chosen by Prince Albert as the Exhibition's motto, though not without the criticism of Lord Ashley (Shaftesbury), President of the Bible Society. He objected to the Prayer Book version being used instead of the Bible version – *The Earth is the Lord's and the fullness thereof.* The Prince stuck to his version and Lord Ashley was soon complaining again: the Bibles on show were badly placed, surrounded by works of art and science. Lord John Russell, sensing Papal aggression, protested at the number of crucifixes. They were balanced by the idols, replied Prince Albert with the patience of a by now rather tart angel.

At the opening of the Exhibition Queen Victoria was particularly touched by the sight of the two ancient warriors, the Duke of Wellington and Lord Anglesey, tottering up the aisle together arm in arm. This and other sights moved her friends, one of them picking out the peculiarly affecting behaviour of the Chinese member of the Diplomatic Corps.

'It was a charming episode, the Chinese commissioner insensibly touched with the solemnity of the scene during the Hallelujah Chorus, taking his way slowly round the margin of the fountain and making a prostration before Her Majesty.'

In fact this oriental charmer was He Sing, a Chinese junk skipper from the Thames who daily showed Londoners over his craft at 1s. a head. He was accidentally but not unwillingly swept along into the procession with the Diplomatic Corps and was afterwards represented by H. C. Selous in the official painting of the Exhibition, complete with black and scarlet cap, blue tunic, gold necklaces and fan.

Queen Victoria visited the Crystal Palace almost daily from its opening until she went to Osborne towards the end of July, getting up early, arriving before 10 am and sytematically working her way through every section. The French courts she found beautiful beyond description, the American machinery 'inventive' but 'not entertaining' (later the 'cotton machines' from Bradford and Oldham won her unstinted applause); only the Prussian and Russian sectors were contemptibly thin. Among individual items she selected for special notice the Indian pearls, the Sheffield bowie knives made exclusively for America, the Chubb locks, the electric telegraph and a machine for making fifty million medals a week.

Particularly desirous was she of sharing her thrilling experience with the humblest of her subjects. John Grant, head ghillie at Balmoral, was brought to London.

> 'It was quite a pleasure to see his honest, weather beaten face again, as quiet, demure, & plain spoken as usual, in spite of all the wonders & novelties around him.'[25]

At Osborne the Queen pored over pictures of the Exhibition in the *Illustrated London News* and feasted on anecdotes relayed by Lord Granville:

> Visitor to Exhibition pointing to a block of alum: 'What's that?'
> Well-informed friend: 'That's a statue of Lot's wife.'

Another visitor was overheard describing a colossal statue of St Michael casting out Satan as 'the Queen and the Pope'. 'The famous Papal Bill', as Queen Victoria sarcastically called the Ecclesiastical Titles Bill, had just passed into law.

The Exhibition closed on October 15th, fittingly, as Queen Victoria felt, for it was the twelfth anniversary of her engagement. Two long-term blessings seemed to flow from it. The visit of the Prussian Royalties which had begun under a cloud ended with the Queen gaining a close new friend in Crown Princess Augusta of Prussia, and the Princess Royal an admirer in her son, Prince Frederick William. Young Fritz, aged twenty-two, though not handsome according to Queen Victoria, had fine blue eyes and was both amiable and liberal-minded. He intended, she noted with approval, to resist the 'old traditionary doctrine' of the Junkers when he joined his regiment at Potsdam. He escorted 'our children' all over the Exhibition and there was no doubt which of 'our children' inspired these attentions. Queen Victoria and Princess Augusta, closeted together in delicious intimacy, discussed their children's future union.

Beyond all other blessings was the vindication of Prince

Albert. In transports of relief and delight the Queen poured out her full heart to King Leopold:

'It was the *happiest, proudest* day in my life, and I can think of nothing else. Albert's dearest name is immortalised with this *great* conception, *his* own, and my *own* dear country *showed* she was *worthy* of it.'[26]

The Queen's perfervid emotions led her to exaggerate the extent of her angel's newly-won popularity; outside the industrial and 'mechanic' classes there were few to admit that Prince Albert himself was the prize exhibit. Her worship of this semi-divine being toppled over into self-abasement. 'We women,' she protested, 'are not *made* for governing.'[27]

Alfred Tennyson, created Poet Laureate six months before the Exhibition opened, dedicated the seventh edition of his poems to the Queen, congratulating her on the countless peoples she had welcomed into her 'halls of glass' as 'friends'. Friendship proved to be far more brittle than the glass halls which sheltered it. Within a few months the Queen and Palmerston were at loggerheads again; within a few years the Crimean War had broken out, Prince Albert's reputation had crashed, and the Queen who thought women were not fit to govern was entertaining the most masterful yet feminine spirit of her age – Florence Nightingale.

The Great Exhibition marked the halfway point in Queen Victoria's married life. The happiest and proudest year of her life also turned out to be the slippery summit of her husband's career and the climax of early Victorian England.

CHAPTER XVII

'EVERY AGE HAS ITS ADVANTAGES'
1852–4

THE QUEEN LOOKED forward to halcyon days with
Lord Granville at the Foreign Office: 'he keeps me regularly
informed of everything,' she wrote happily in her Journal at
the beginning of 1852, 'which Lord Palmerston had long
ceased to do.'[1]

Among the information supplied by Granville was an
ominous detail from France: Napoleon III was restoring
the imperial eagles to the flags and uniforms of the French
army. Queen Victoria wrote it off as 'rather nonsense' but
fears of French aggression soon swept over the country. Lord
Granville, upon his appointment in Palmerston's place, had
received a *douceur* from Napoleon in the form of a magnificent piece of tapestry. It represented 'The Massacre of the
Mamelukes'. Invasion, war and massacre seemed to be in the
air. Lord John Russell proposed to deal with Napoleon's
hordes simply by strengthening the local militia. Palmerston
saw the chance to revenge himself. Nothing short of a national
militia would do, he argued. Parliament agreed with him and
Lord John Russell's Government fell within two months of
Palmerston's own removal. 'I have had my tit-for-tat,' remarked the jocular ex-Foreign Secretary.

To the Queen, though she secretly sympathized with
Palmerston's tough attitude on defence, a change of government with its attendant alarms and excursions always meant
a period of anxiety. How she longed for an end to party confusion and instead of 'this sorry Cabinet', a strong government.

She commanded Lord Derby (formerly Stanley) as Leader
of the Conservatives to form a government, hoping against
hope that he would not succeed – '& yet I am wrong,' she
admitted, for Derby, besides being a constitutional necessity,
might soon be supplanted by a better team, provided he sur-

vived long enough to prove 'his incapacity to rule'.[2] There seemed every possibility that this would occur. 'Do you know what my Government is?' jested Lord Derby. 'It is the Derby Militia, fresh from the plough and going to be disbanded almost directly!' The callow Home Secretary took this joke seriously and created a sensation by announcing that Derby was going to give the vote to every militiaman. Her Majesty must be indulgent to this inept team, said Lord Malmesbury, the new Foreign Secretary: he was always expecting someone to blunder. The Queen privately felt no more confidence in Malmesbury himself than in his colleagues.

The Derby Ministry did indeed prove weak and short-lived. It redeemed itself by a notable advance in Conservative economic policy. Protection was no longer practical politics, confessed Derby to the Queen. At last she saw a prospect of party confusion ending and the two-party system returning, 'without which it is *impossible* to have a strong Govt.'

Lord Derby's advent also gave Prince Albert an opportunity to clarify once and for all the moral standard expected from a Prime Minister, especially in regard to Court appointments.

The Prince had discovered to his consternation that Lord Derby, who belonged to the fast, racing set, proposed to allot the plums at Court to 'the Dandies and Roués of London and the Turf', beginning with 'the wicked Earl', Lord Wilton, as Master of the Horse. Methodically Prince Albert took Derby through the events of the past, demonstrating how immorality at Court injured crowned heads: in 1839 Her Majesty's position had been undermined by scandals: Louis Philippe lost his throne in 1848 because of licentiousness at Court; and so on. Upon the Prime Minister, explained Prince Albert, devolved the Lord Chancellor's former duty of being 'Keeper of the King's Conscience'. Two principles must henceforth guide him in making Court appointments: courtiers must not be on the verge of bankruptcy and their moral characters must bear investigation. Lord Melbourne, continued the Prince, had done great harm to the Court by careless appointments and though he had declared that 'damned morality would undo us all', the Queen found it had 'great advantages'.[3]

Whether or not because of these admonitions, Queen Victoria was soon able to write that Lord Derby '*is* a Prime Minister'; most attentive, fluent and clear. Even Disraeli, the new Chancellor of the Exchequer, awakened the Queen's cautious interest by his 'curious notes' on Parliamentary debates. She copied one or two of them into her Journal. 'They are just like his novels,' she commented; 'highly-coloured . . .'[4] But she was amused. At the beginning of April 1852 she had the satisfaction of amazing 'the world' by inviting Mr and Mrs Disraeli to dinner.

'*She* is very vulgar, not so much in her appearance, as in her way of speaking, & *he* is most singular, – thoroughly Jewish looking, a livid complexion, dark eyes & eyebrows & black ringlets. The expression is disagreeable, but I did not find him so to talk to. He has a very bland manner, & his language is very flowery.'[5]

When Queen Victoria later walked into 'Dizzy's' parlour she had her eyes open.

Something happened in the autumn of this year, 1852, to show the Queen that 'that damned morality' had advantages greater than even Prince Albert suspected. A miser, John Camden Nield, died leaving about £250,000 to his Sovereign who he knew 'would not waste it'. (This was Queen Victoria's own reading of her benefactor's mind.) At first the Queen, taught both by Lehzen and the House of Commons that there was no such thing as easy money, felt sure it was a practical joke. When inquiries revealed that the miser was a genuine eccentric without dependants who though 'brilliant' had lived in indescribable filth, she put up a window to his memory and gratefully accepted the golden handshake from the grave. Stockmar wished him a 'joyful resurrection'.

A few days later death struck again, this time to remove one of the great father-figures in her life. On September 14th, 1852 the Duke of Wellington died at the age of eighty-three, up to the last an arresting figure as he rode between Apsley

House and the Horse Guards in his snowy white trousers and tight blue frockcoat, acknowledging like a king the respectful salutes of passers-by.

No more in soldier fashion will he greet
With lifted hand the gazer in the street.

One of his last services to the Royal family had been to offer Prince Albert the post of Commander-in-Chief before his own retirement – a glittering prize which the Prince nobly rejected on the ground that it would curtail the time available for helping his wife. By way of compensation Wellington said he would start at once to send Prince Albert all the Commander-in-Chief's papers intended eventually for the Queen: 'let it be *done* first,' he told her, '& *then* let the Queen *order* it.' She rightly called it a 'remarkable suggestion'.[6] His last *obiter dictum*, as recorded by the Queen, occurred five months before he died. Her Majesty was investing four shaky old generals with the Order of the Bath. As the last one tottered backwards the deaf hero of Waterloo exclaimed in stentorian tones, 'None of these Generals seem to be able to walk.'

As news of the Duke's death reached the Queen she fled to her writing-table and composed in a vein now becoming familiar a message for King Leopold:

'We shall soon stand sadly alone; Aberdeen is almost the only personal friend of that kind we have left. Melbourne, Peel, Liverpool – & now the Duke – *all* gone!'[7]

In her Journal she wrote, 'He seems to have gone out like a lamp,' and indeed the Crown's most faithful guiding light had left her. Prince Albert insisted on an heraldic State funeral, the last to be held in Britain, and on November 18th, standing on the new balcony of Buckingham Palace from which she had greeted the joyful Exhibition crowds the year before, she wept unrestrainedly as the bands, each playing different dirges chosen by the Prince, announced the approach of the funeral car. The Dead March from *Saul*, with its roll of drums, she found the most harrowing of all.

The culmination of the Prince's artistic directives was the

gigantic bronze funeral car, 21 feet long; an enormous coffin, 6 feet 9 inches long (the Duke was only 5 feet 9 inches), trembled on the top, reduced to insignificance by its monumental surroundings. Queen Victoria saw in the rumbling leviathan, one of whose six wheels stuck in the mud of Pall Mall, a triumph of simplicity, chaste yet gorgeous. Cutting across to St James's, the royal party watched the procession again, this time the Queen being struck by the Duke's 'poor charger' following the mourning coaches, the empty boots of his master hanging, reversed, on either side – 'a touching sight'. She was relieved to hear that the cortège arrived safely at St Paul's where it took an hour to transfer the coffin from the funeral car to the bier. The new Poet Laureate, Alfred Tennyson, celebrated the national hero:

> Bury the Great Duke
> With an empire's lamentation . . .

In the House of Commons Disraeli paid his tribute in a passage cribbed from a eulogy pronounced by the French politician Thiers upon what the Queen called an 'inferior' French marshal.* '*How* could he do such a thing,' she exclaimed in horror.

On December 17th, scarcely a month after the Duke's burial, Lord Derby's Government was defeated by 19 votes. Queen Victoria felt that for the first time in her life she had to face a political crisis without the Duke's advice.

Some weeks earlier, on November 27th, she had discussed with Lord Derby various means of bolstering up his Government seriously weakened as it was by a reverse in the July elections. The obvious solution for a Conservative party which had at last abandoned Protection was to link up with the Peelites. Unfortunately the Peelites would not serve under Sir Robert's tormentor, Disraeli, as Leader of the House. Another possibility, suggested Derby, was to bring in Palmerston as Leader. The Queen automatically refused to plant her old enemy on this stepping-stone to power. 'Why not Gladstone?', she countered. (Gladstone's brilliant debating against Disraeli's budget had in fact been largely responsible for the

* Gouvion St Cyr.

The Duke of Kent,
c. 1818

The Duchess of
Kent, 1829

Princess Victoria as a baby

Princess Victoria, aged 10

Princess Victoria, aged 16, with her spaniel Dash

Queen Victoria receiving news of her accession, June 20th, 1837

Baroness Lehzen

Sir John Conroy, Bt

Baron Stockmar

Lady Flora Hastings

Prince Albert, 1842

Queen Victoria, 1842

Queen Victoria, 1839, painted by Landseer

defeat of the Conservatives.) In her Journal she set out Derby's interesting reply: 'Mr G. was in his opinion quite unfit for it. He possessed none of that decision, boldness, readiness, & clearness so necessary for leading a party . . .'[8]

The Queen sent for Gladstone's chief, Lord Aberdeen, hoping that he would now form a Peelite ministry. To her disappointment Aberdeen suggested a 'Liberal-Conservative Government'. Coalitions, objected the Queen, meant jobbery and a sharing out of spoils. Her real objection, of course, was to the ominous word Liberal which clearly meant Palmerston. The crisis continued to rage right up to Christmas Eve, ruining the royal festivities.

At last after dinner on December 24th she heard that Aberdeen's team was complete: 'an immense relief & pleasure to us.' The fact that Palmerston was Home Secretary and that dear Lord Aberdeen had spoilt Christmas Day itself with an interminable audience, could only diminish not destroy their pleasure. Palmerston, indeed, did not look like being a permanent nuisance. He hobbled into the first Council on two sticks crippled with gout and all his friends, wrote the Queen to King Leopold, thought him breaking up.

Queen Victoria once more let fly in her Journal at the Conservatives: they were 'miserable people', except for Derby himself. The old year had ended very happily after all with a government of all the talents. The royal band ushered in the new year by playing under the Castle windows, 'Now thank we all our God.'

Despite the joyful serenade of New Year's Day, 1853 turned out to be both for the Queen and the country a time of unsettled feelings; of contrariness, criticism and disquiet. The complacent glow of great exhibitionism had faded; the Crystal Palace itself was being transferred bodily to Sydenham; she hailed her twelfth wedding anniversary with joy tempered by '*Wehmuth*' (melancholy):

'I like *not* the speeding fleeting of time, – when one's bright youthful years pass away! But we have with God's

289

mercy many yet before us, & *every* age has its advantages & its blessings!'[9]

Six months later on the eve of Prince Albert's thirty-third birthday the '*Wehmuth*' seemed to have driven out some of the joy:

'My beloved one's last night when 32! As alas! time rolls on, these changes make one pensive . . . at least the feeling is a different one, to when one only seemed to be looking forward!'[10]

It was sad to be looking backward at thirty-three. When the precious wedding anniversary came round again on February 10th, 1853 the Queen was looking forward once more but with some trepidation; she prayed for the safety of 'our 7 children & 8th . . . to appear in 2 months!'

Less than three weeks before the baby was due fire broke out at night in the dining-room of Windsor Castle. The Queen and her ladies, at first huddled in the Green Drawing Room, could see through the Red Drawing Room into the inferno beyond where smoke and flames swirled over a crowd of servants removing furniture, shouting and holloaing above the rush of water and crash of timbers. The Prince flitted in and out reporting progress, soaked to the skin despite his great-coat and goloshes. His reaction was not unexpected: the whole Castle must be 'improved' to prevent such a disaster from happening again. Equally characteristic were Queen Victoria's reflections:

'I was anxious but as generally luckily is the case with me, in moments of great importance & times of trial, I was quite calm & collected, – thankful to be on the spot & to be able to see & know everything.'[11]

This goes far to explain her courage during attempts on her life. When she was in the very centre of the picture knowing what was happening, though in the eye of danger, she could be calm.

The aftermath of the fire may well have upset Prince Albert and caused him to worry more than usual over his wife's approaching confinement. At any rate, he annoyed her by summoning her monthly nurse, Mrs Lilly, as a precautionary measure, 'like warships & soldiers in case of an invasion',[12] long before she felt the event was imminent.

From the birth of Prince Leopold on April 7th, 1853 seems to date a period of some strain in the Queen's family life. While this is important it must not be exaggerated. Her difficulties must always be set against a basic feeling of happiness such as she expressed on her 34th birthday, May 24th, 1853. After grieving for the passage of her youth and wishing 'for Albert's sake' to go back ten years, she continued, '– & yet, every year seems happier. We are still young, & very young to have so large a family!'

A remarkable innovation in midwifery made this birth of exceptional interest to her subjects and less than usually unpleasant for herself. The famous anaesthetist, Dr John Snow of Edinburgh, was invited by Sir James Clark to give Her Majesty chloroform.

Afterwards Sir James, writing to Dr Simpson of Edinburgh, the pioneer of chloroform, described the beneficial results:

'The Queen had chloroform exhibited to her during her last confinement . . . It was not at any time given so strongly as to render the Queen insensible, and an ounce of chloroform was scarcely consumed during the whole time. Her Majesty was greatly pleased with the effect, and she certainly never has had a better recovery.'

Queen Victoria's comment was more lyrical. Dr Snow, she recorded, 'gave that blessed Chloroform & the effect was soothing, quieting & delightful beyond measure.' Dr Simpson's first patient, a doctor's wife in 1847, had been so carried away with enthusiasm that she christened her child, a girl, 'Anaesthesia'.

A battle royal had long raged between those who swore by and those who execrated the new pain killer. The *Book of Genesis* provided ammunition for both sides ('in sorrow thou shalt bring forth children' versus 'the Lord caused a deep sleep to fall upon Adam'), Simpson's opponents further adducing the remarkable argument that a woman's sufferings in labour were responsible for her love for her offspring. The patients themselves, retorted Simpson, would force their doctors to use anaesthetics. It was fitting that the battle royal should be won for Dr Simpson by the Queen herself. The birth of Leopold George Duncan Albert finally canonized 'that blessed Chloroform'. Even the names of the Queen's attendants seemed to share the aura of purity which her royal participation had now given to the subject: Mrs Lilly, Mrs Innocent and, of course, Dr Snow.

In the early days of 1847 Dr Snow had written defensively:

'where the pain is not greater than the patient is willing to bear cheerfully, there is no occasion to use chloroform; but when the patient is anxious to be spared the pain, I can see no valid objection to the use of this agent even in the most favourable cases.'[13]

Queen Victoria was emphatically one of 'the most favourable cases', as she herself constantly boasted. Yet she was not amused at the idea of continuing to 'bear cheerfully' pain which might be eliminated. Dr Simpson's method of elimination was simplicity itself. He merely poured half a teaspoonful of chloroform on to a handkerchief rolled into a funnel and placed the open end over the patient's mouth and nose. The chloroform was replenished after ten minutes.

It might well be claimed that Queen Victoria's greatest gift to her people was a refusal to accept pain in childbirth as woman's divinely appointed destiny.

Queen Victoria's rapid recovery from the birth was not, alas, crowned by an equally thriving infant. At first she thought 'little Leo' was healthy but thinner than the others had been because of a weak digestion. She insisted on getting him a wet nurse from her dear Highlands and when Mrs Macintosh arrived in cap and plaid shawl without a word of English, she felt sure he would improve. A month after his birth he was still ailing, the Queen felt guilty about Mrs Macintosh, and a change of nurse was suggested, no easy matter at such short notice. The Prince of Wales's wet nurse, for instance, Mary Ann Brough, had become morose and 'stupid' and a year after Prince Leopold's birth a horrible tragedy was to haunt the Queen: Mary Ann Brough murdered her own six children. Fortunately a shipwright's wife was found in Cowes to nurse the little Prince. There seemed to be an immediate improvement. The Queen was full of gratitude to Clark, who she believed had detected the cause of the trouble. She had almost given up hope.

Sir James Clark's detective work was not in reality as successful as he and Queen Victoria imagined. Prince Leopold, described by contemporary writers as 'very delicate', in fact suffered from a grave and in those days mysterious condition – haemophilia, or the bleeding disease. This rare malady occurs only in males but can be handed on both through the genes of an affected-male and of a healthy female. A cloud of worry and bewilderment henceforth overhung the Queen caused by her oft-repeated and perfectly correct belief that haemophilia was 'not in our family' – meaning the House of Hanover. Where did it come from?

Since Prince Albert was not affected, Queen Victoria herself must have transmitted the disease. She may have inherited the genes through her mother, the Duchess of Kent, a princess of Saxe-Coburg. This seems unlikely since no instances of haemophilia can be traced on either side of the Duchess's family; on the other hand the records may be faulty or the sufferers may have died, as so many children did in infancy; but the source of the disease is probably to be traced to a spontaneous mutation in the genes which Queen Victoria inherited. Prince Leopold was the only victim in her family and therefore the only male transmitter. Three of her daughters, the Princess Royal, Princess Alice and Princess Beatrice, were transmitters and their marriages spread the disease through the royal houses of Europe.

At the height of the Queen's agonized suspense over her baby's fate an emotional crisis developed. A long memorandum written by Prince Albert to his wife on May 9th, 1853, outlining the cause and cure of these crises, throws a vivid light on their efforts to cope with the stresses of family life.

'Dear Child', began the Prince in his role of father-figure: the scene which took place 'the other evening' over an accidental mistake made by him in sorting their prints, had caused over an hour of hysterics and twenty-four hours of misery. He had been the *occasion* of her sufferings, as so often, but not the *cause*, which was always the same – her habit of 'imprudently heaping up a large store of combustibles'. He was often astonished at the effect on her of a hasty word; 'in your candid way you generally explain later what was the real cause of your complaint'.

The Prince frankly admitted that his treatment of her crises had failed and went on to enumerate the three kinds of treatment open to him. First, he could demonstrate the groundlessness of her charges. This made her seem ridiculous and only increased her distress. Second, he could turn a deaf ear. This she called an insult, demanding a reply to her questions. Third, he might simply say she was too occupied with her own feelings and could avoid her outbreaks if she really tried. 'I know of no 4th. method . . .' If he retired to his room after a quarrel to give her time to recover, she followed him 'to review the dispute and to have it *all out*'. If he tried to forget the scene and get back to normal as quickly as possible, she would accuse him of cold indifference. 'I am told that there are two persons in me, etc. etc.'

The Prince ended on a warmer note. Profound pity for her sufferings overwhelmed him; he would be more patient in future, listen more and instead of wondering how to stop her paroxysms – impossible in any case – he would again beg her not to bottle up the 'combustibles' but bring them out. If she was afraid to speak she must *write*. 'I don't want an answer.'[14]

Poor Albert. The contradictions in his letter (he deprecated the Queen's wish to 'have it *all out*', while advising her not to bottle it up) showed that he was no tactician in the field of feminine emotions. All Victoria wanted was an explosion followed by a good cry, kiss and make up. Albert's advice to write if speech seemed too daunting was really addressed to himself. None of this is incompatible with the most successful of marriages and when the Prince wrote of getting back to 'normal' he meant getting back to their normal state of happiness.

In the same month as this upheaval a Swiss cottage for the children was started at Osborne just behind their garden plots. Albert imported it, prefabricated, from the Continent and very German it is with a wealth of black carved wood, quotations from the psalms and proverbs round the walls and outside staircases, blue and white tiles in the tiny kitchen, small wooden chairs and table in the dining-room, a swinging cradle in the changing-room and little round window panes everywhere which might have come from the witch's house in *Hansel and Gretel*. Prince Albert's idea was to teach his elder children how to do their own cooking and carpentry; Queen Victoria, when she was entertained there by Vicky, Alice, Lenchen and Louise, found in the Swiss Cottage yet another miniature retreat from the too large world.

The corner stone of the large, new, much-turreted and battlemented Balmoral was laid the same year as the Swiss Cottage's modest foundations. Visitors to Balmoral were not always as captivated as the Queen by Prince Albert's interior decorations. 'Tartanitis' was an endemic disease among its wallpapers, carpets, curtains and chair covers. In the opinion of Lord Clarendon, a visiting Minister, the abundant thistles were worse than the plaids: 'they would rejoice the heart of a donkey if they happened to *look like* his favourite repast, which they don't.' A sense of picnicking still hung over Balmoral, for all its new grandeur. One lady-in-waiting who slept in a detached cottage had her breakfast sent over to her in a wheelbarrow. Clarendon summed it up tolerantly as, 'the scramble of rural royalty'.

That autumn of 1853 was the last peaceful holiday at Balmoral for many long months. As usual 'J. Brown' held the pony for mountain rides; as usual the Queen's Ministers sought congenial occupations. Lord Aberdeen danced a reel with Her Majesty 'beautifully dressed in a kilt' and Lord Palmerston, 'who is very old & does not see', played billiards with the Prince. Blind as he was, he could see the war-clouds in the East better than anyone.

'This sad Oriental Question,' as the Queen soon came to call the Russo–Turkish imbroglio, had not greatly troubled her earlier in the year. Who is to have Constantinople when the Ottoman Empire breaks up? she asked calmly while making notes on Turkey in March. As long ago as 1840 she had decided that the Turks were too backward to last. Curiously enough, the argument constantly advanced by Palmerston and the English war party that the Russian forces in Constantinople would constitute an intolerable threat to India, did not yet move her. The Russian Ambassador assured her there was no more danger of the Russian fleet going to Constantinople than of its going to Argyll House, and she particularly liked Lord Aberdeen's attitude of all-may-yet-come-right. Why not? The differences between Russia and Turkey seemed to her so small. Subsequent historians have been inclined to agree with her.

In July 1853 Russia invaded Turkey's 'Danubian Principalities'; dispirited and anxious, the Queen still half hoped that England might not become involved. On October 10th she heard that the British fleet had entered the Black Sea, without her consent having been obtained. Issues of peace and war, she felt, had been left too much in the hands of admirals. She was mistaken. In her absence from London, it was Palmerston who had persuaded old Aberdeen to make this pro-Turkish demonstration. She hurried south, too late. The issues of peace and war might have remained more in her own hands had she consented to return to her capital, as Aberdeen had entreated. The Queen not only lost influence by staying away, she created a dangerous precedent with which Gladstone later had to contend.

On October 23rd a desperate Turkey declared war on Russia. Palmerston at the head of the war party urged immediate support for the Sultan, England's tottering ally, by joint action with France. The 'strong Government' on which the Queen had pinned her hopes, broke into fragments. Her own attitude began to change. She felt herself torn between deep-rooted distrust for Palmerston and incipient alarm at Aberdeen's obstinate faith in negotiations: 'he *still* hopes more from the Emperor of Russia than he is justified in hoping,' she wrote, even before Turkey declared war. But her mind was far from clear. At the beginning of November she believed Palmerston to be in secret correspondence with the vehemently pro-Turkish Lord Stratford de Redcliffe, the Ambassador in Constantinople who was at this time so active with his pen that it was said he would eventually write an autobiography entitled *The Thousand and One Notes*. Of Palmerston's intrigues the Queen said to Aberdeen: '*This* certainly looks like Very Treasonable proceedings.'[15]

By a twist of fate it was herself and Albert, not Palmerston, who were shortly to be accused of treason.

In the midst of this turmoil, 'good Sir J. Paxton', knighted for services to international brotherhood as enshrined in the Crystal Palace, showed her his great new exhibition room for what he called 'the hextinct hanimals'. The Queen was puzzled by these creatures almost as much as by the politicians. 'What beasts they must have been,' she meditated, '& why should they have become extinct?' A few years later Charles Darwin answered her question in his *Origin of Species*.

Mid-November 1853 still found her hoping to keep her country at peace, a policy to which, under Aberdeen's renewed influence, she had swung back. It would be a great advantage, she felt, if the Turks were left alone to be 'well beaten'. A month later (December 15th) she still hoped for a decisive victory of the Russians by land, thus rendering 'the Emperor magnanimous & the Turks amenable to reason'. The country did not agree.

Lord Palmerston, having threatened since December 1st to resign as a protest against further Reform during a time of national emergency, suddenly handed in his resignation on December 16th. As he intended, the whole country read into this manoeuvre a signal that he was prepared to lead it into war – a lead which the majority would have followed. That Palmerston might not only go out but stay out on an issue as unpopular as anti-Reform had been the Queen's fervent prayer. Now that her prayer seemed to have been answered she breathed again. Then, on Christmas Eve – the second one running spoilt by politics – Aberdeen broke to her the disconcerting news that irresistible forces were about to secure Palmerston's return to the Cabinet, among them Mr Gladstone and Lady Palmerston who was 'working herself into a great state of excitement'.[16] Aberdeen's position was in fact too precarious for him to survive without his most popular Minister. Moreover Palmerston's gesture had been rendered superfluous by Russia sinking the Turkish fleet at Sinope three days after he made it. Even Aberdeen could not now resist the drift to war. Palmerston duly returned to office, thus ending what Lord John quizzically called his 'escapade'.

The Queen said goodbye with regret to an old year 'which seemed to have become an old friend' and whose successor might well not be so friendly.

'The year opens gloomily,' the Queen wrote on January 1st, 1854. War was almost inevitable and high prices pressed upon the poor. Nearer home, 'wicked and jealous' opponents of the Government had begun to smear Prince Albert with 'atrocious calumnies'.

It was true that a fit of rare xenophobia had suddenly seized the country. Articles appeared accusing the Prince of having plotted to bring about Palmerston's resignation, of carrying on pro-Russian intrigues through his foreign relatives, and in short of keeping England out of Europe's glorious hostilities.

Queen Victoria had no doubt as to the source of these slanders. Who could it be but Palmerston? In this she was not altogether wrong, for though Palmerston did not inspire the articles he took no early steps to contradict them through the channels which he controlled. 'These horrors,' as the Queen called the attacks, culminated in the mass sales of a scurrilous broadsheet announcing the imprisonment of 'Lovely Albert'. From its ample fertility the following verses are a small selection:

> Last Monday night, all in a fright,
> Al out of bed did tumble.
> The German lad was raving mad,
> How he did groan and grumble!

> *He cried to Vic, I've cut my stick:*
> *To St Petersburg go right slap,*
> *When Vic, 'tis said, jumped out of bed,*
> *And whopped him with her night-cap.*
>
> *You jolly Turk, now go to work*
> *And show the Bear your power.*
> *It is rumoured over Britain's isle*
> *That A— is in the Tower.*

Crowds assembled expecting to see Victoria and Albert coming through the Traitors' Gate. The Prince had no business to attend the Queen's audiences with her Ministers, wrote Lord Maidstone, a member of the 'Paget Club', anonymously, nor to act as her private secretary; indeed he was her Foreign Secretary, Commander-in-Chief and Prime Minister all rolled into one. Beside themselves, the unhappy royal pair took refuge in the thought that war fever had sent the country 'a little mad'.

Eventually the Queen saw no alternative but to ask Parliament, through Lord Aberdeen, publicly to contradict the lies. Aberdeen agreed and in some trepidation she opened this critical Session, prepared for hisses and groans on her way to Westminster and 'similar music' on the way back. The crowd was indeed ugly but things went better in the House than she had dared hope. The 'mad delusions' were exposed both by the Government and Opposition, and next day she was proud and happy to read aloud to Prince Albert all the nice speeches made about him.

Nevertheless the experience was not easily forgotten by the victims. On Prince Albert's mind perhaps the most unfortunate impression was made by one of its side effects. Baron Stockmar sent him a well-meaning screed on January 5th, 1854 analysing under six headings, eight sub-headings and 14 sub-sub-headings the causes of the Court's unpopularity. Having mentioned their hospitality to the exiled Orleans's, he finally laid the blame on a corrupted party system in Britain. Both parties, said Stockmar, were bent on undermining the Crown; the Tories had become 'degenerate bastards' since the Reform Bill and the Whigs (as represented

299

by Palmerston) were sheer Republicans who saw the Monarch as nothing but 'a Mandarin figure'.[17]

Unfortunately this didactic little Merlin went on to reveal to Her Majesty what she really was: someone above the 'temporary head of the Cabinet' – 'a permanent Premier'. The British Constitution knew nothing of this fabulous beast. But when in later years the Queen and Gladstone became locked in controversy she remembered that he was merely 'temporary head of the Cabinet', while she was 'permanent Premier'. True, this was not the first time that Stockmar had woven his constitutional fantasies and laid them at the Prince's feet; but time was running short in which the Prince might discover the mistake.

Both Queen and Prince were not unnaturally in a sensitive state. Righteous indignation which seems to invigorate some people generally made Queen Victoria feel ill. Worse still, the harrowing and complicated situation caused several painful differences between herself and Prince Albert. He refused, for instance, to visit the Orleans family at Claremont until after Parliament had vindicated him, for fear of its being taken as fresh proof that he was scheming against the war party and its ally Napoleon III. 'The attacks on Albert (which are fast disappearing),' observed an angry Queen on January 22nd, 'has the result of making him afraid to do what I should think right.'[18]

The arrival of the fourteenth anniversary of the Queen's wedding day on February 10th, 1854 brought about a complete reversal of her feelings and she repented of her recent independent spirit of criticism. Now her one ambition was to have the Prince publicly recognized as her rightful adviser by making him Prince Consort, if not King Consort. 'Easy,' said Aberdeen, 'but not just now.' She consoled herself by reading over the Marriage Service from which the Archbishop of Canterbury had just suggested expunging the 'coarseness'.

'in which I entirely agree . . . I feel so impressed by the promise I made "to love, cherish, honour, *serve* & *obey*" my Husband. May it ever be duly impressed on my mind, & on that of every woman.'[19]

This mood did not last for long. As the country moved by desultory stages nearer and nearer to war, the Queen saw herself less as a clinging vine and more as the head of her armies in the field. Three days after her Declaration of Dependence on February 10th she was lamenting that 'in these stirring times' she was a woman, – 'though my heart is not in this unsatisfactory war'. Less than a fortnight later (February 25th) her heart was in it, as she showed by a highly characteristic discussion with the Prime Minister, Lord Aberdeen, on the possibility of Palmerston taking his place. Not for a moment would she feel safe with Palmerston, she began; positively she could never take him. Kindly old Aberdeen, humane and mournful, sighed:

'If it comes to being safe, I fear Your Majesty would not be safe with me during war, for I have such a terrible repugnance for it, in all its forms.'

The Queen, alarmed at such sentiments, broke in with her most crushing retort: 'This will never do.' A war now, she insisted, would prevent a worse one later; patching up was dangerous.

'I'm all for patching up, if we can,' said Aberdeen.

'This is unfortunate,' reiterated the Queen.

Three days after this conversation, on February 28th, 1854, Britain made a formal declaration of war against Russia in support of Turkey and in alliance with France.

The Queen had come to reflect, as so often, the opinion of the country. There was a general feeling that the long period of European cold war was over and battle must be joined – no one knew even yet exactly why. It was a kind of bellicose fatalism. Soon it took wing on a jet of euphoria. Exactly a month later, on March 28th, the Crimean War began.

CHAPTER XVIII

THE UNSATISFACTORY WAR
1854–6

THE WAR WHICH Queen Victoria had begun by calling unsatisfactory was 'incredibly popular' with her subjects, as she told King Leopold, and soon absorbed her whole being. The idea of a Day of Humiliation on which her country should repent the sins which had brought it into danger, nauseated her. The Crimean War was all the fault of '*one* man' – the Tsar, while 'our conduct has been throughout actuated by un-selfishness & honesty'.[1] Why not say instead the prayer 'To be used before a Fight at Sea'? The Queen thought it very applicable 'as there is no mention of the sea'. Her idea was rejected.

The least she could do was to rise at 6.30 in the wintry dawn to watch the last battalion of Guards, 'touching & beautiful', march off. A few days later she waved farewell to the Navy at Spithead. 'The man on the topmost mast of the *Duke of Wellington* waved both his arms as we passed by!' How nobly that ardent gesture seemed to stand out against the petty quarrels of her Ministers.

As Britain got deeper into the war the Court came naturally to appreciate Palmerston's policy of using the French Emperor to defeat the Russian. In September 1854 the Prince accepted Napoleon's invitation to visit his camp at St Omer and Queen Victoria faced, with many moans, a parting from Albert which lasted five days. When the glad moment for return arrived Prince Albert positively 'leapt aboard' the Queen's yacht to rejoin her, as an onlooker noticed, full of interesting new sidelights on their mysterious ally. Napoleon was very rheumatic, going to bed at ten so that Prince Albert's evenings were not too long (but his cabin looked 'very blank and desolate' without 'Frauchen'). There was incessant smoking; the Emperor could not understand the Prince not partaking. The French cuisine was good, servants 'respectable-looking', stables fine. The Queen felt much relieved for up till the present she had heard only one good thing of Napoleon – that his wife admired the purity of the English Court.

During Napoleon's exile in England the Queen had never received him. When he set himself upon Louis Philippe's throne King Leopold said it was like finding a snake in one's bed but one dared not move for fear of irritating the creature. In December 1852 the snake had attempted to worm its way into the 'Coburgy' by marrying the Queen's niece, Princess Adelaide of Hohenlohe. Having failed, the reptile thereupon married the fascinating Eugénie de Montijo, daughter of Manuela Kirkpatrick and, some thought, of Lord Palmerston; others thought her father might be Lord Clarendon, until Eugénie's mother explained to the Emperor, her son-in-law, '*Mais, sire, les dates ne correspondent pas.*' In fact her father was the Spanish Count de Montijo.

Soon after Prince Albert's return came a message which the innocent Queen took as a resounding tribute to her beloved. The Emperor declared that he had never met anyone with such profound knowledge as the Prince and who imparted it so freely.

With the autumn began a long period of miserable uncertainty. For a moment at the beginning of October it sounded as if Sebastopol, the great Russian fortress in the Crimea, had fallen. Incredulous yet bursting with excitement the Queen and her three daughters ran up to the cairn and back, where a victory bonfire was to be lit. Five days later came a telegram contradicting the rumour and the Queen was going over and over in imagination the ghastly yet glorious victory of the Alma which had taken place not long before. 'Never in so short a time,' she wrote in language which would now be called Churchillian, 'has so strong a battery, so well defended, been so bravely & gallantly taken.'[2]

Lord Burghersh, just home from the front, did his best to fit the Queen with rose-coloured spectacles: the soldiers '*really* did not seem to mind' their sufferings; the attacks on the medical profession were infamous: 'there was hardly a man who had not at least received water.' A rifleman dying of cholera was commiserated by his friends on only having three more hours to live. 'Don't be in a 'urry,' he protested, 'I'm not going to die in Roosia yet, – if I can only get something 'ot.' Lord Burghersh gave him something 'ot but could not tell Her Majesty of his subsequent fate.[3]

The Queen was not deceived. Lack of authentic information drive her frantic. 'If only one knew the details!' Windsor was shrouded in thick November fog but no thicker than that which hid the Crimea.

When news came she was equally on the rack. Cholera; vermin; the charge of the Light Brigade making her tremble with pride and horror; the Duke of Newcastle (Secretary of War) one moment saying that the soldiers had plenty of flannel shirts, drawers and fur caps, the next moment in tears over their privations. 'What an awful time! I never thought I should have lived to see & feel all this.'[4] Apart from every other frustration the Queen found it difficult to make use of her great standby in times of crisis, her Journal. How could she, so little versed in military matters, understand or describe adequately what had gone so appallingly wrong in the Crimea? The Duke of Cambridge's catastrophe was a case in point. Just when every able-bodied man was desperately needed in the Crimea she was 'very grieved' to hear that George had broken down and gone for a rest to Constantinople.

Fresh from the seat of war, General Bentinck painted an even blacker picture of fever, diarrhoea, endless salt pork and no vegetables or tobacco (in any case the men could not always eat for their unkempt moustaches froze over their mouths), or soap; 'Your Majesty's Army looks very dirty.' He told her that Sebastopol would not fall this year. Worst of all, her troops' great sufferings were 'unnecessary', since the French commissariat worked well and Napoleon's men were quite comfortable. She hung on Bentinck's words but felt he ought to answer Lord Raglan's call for men and go back. A fortnight later he and Lord George Paget decided to return, the latter, she heard, having been cut in the clubs. The Generals, and indeed the upper reaches of Society from whom they were entirely recruited, were in for a rough time. In April of the following year Charles Greville was to report 'a run against the aristocracy'. Queen Victoria had no love for 'the fashionables' but a run against them might lead to dangerous social ferment.

The year 1854 had been a difficult one for both the Queen and the Prince. Beginning with the public clamour against him and the Queen's sharp criticisms of his tendency to give way under it, the first year of war had not brought them closer together. The Queen was filled with atavistic longings to don shining armour. As Mr Hector Bolitho puts it, 'War involved curious, ancient bonds between the Army and their Monarch.' This was the kind of mystique in which the Prince could not participate. It may be that he now regretted his self-sacrificing refusal of the position of Commander-in-Chief which had been offered to him by Wellington in 1850, but with the logical half of his mind he sturdily opposed the regal glamour with which the office was invested. When Lord Hardinge resigned in 1856 and the Queen's cousin, George Duke of Cambridge, was canvassed as his successor, Prince Albert objected that a royal appointment would damage the Crown. Queen Victoria thought otherwise and was jubilant at the Duke's success. The Prince, however, was right, for the Duke's appointment caused her infinite embarrassment in years to come and kept alive the antiquated office of Commander-in-Chief long after it was obsolete.

The Crimean War brought Prince Albert neither exhilaration nor agony comparable to his wife's. For him the donkey work. He slaved at his desk thinking up military improvements and got fiercely criticized for his pains, especially over his idea of a German Foreign Legion. Why German? Why not Red Indian? demanded the insulted troops. Nevertheless he launched the Queen bravely and buoyantly into 1855:

'Everything which disturbed our happiness in 54 shall be forgotten, and we will begin the new year in hope and confidence for the future . . . Your intentions are excellent, and you will have all the help I can give you in carrying them out.'[5]

Parliament had long been on the verge of an explosion and

on January 24th, 1855 the blow fell. Queen Victoria invited John Russell to dine, only to receive from him his resignation. The redoubtable Radical Member for Sheffield, John Arthur Roebuck, nicknamed 'Tear 'em', intended to bring a motion of censure against the Government's conduct of the war and to demand an inquiry. Aberdeen's Cabinet would scarcely sustain this shock and Russell wanted to get out at once.

The Queen was at first 'astounded & indignant' but when the Duke of Newcastle nobly offered to be the scapegoat and give the War Office to Palmerston, she accepted this solution rather than lose all the Whigs from the Cabinet. Such an exodus of the most warlike elements would bring too much comfort to the Tsar. Lord John received a stinging note from the Queen calling him cowardly and unpatriotic, which made him exceedingly angry. As for Lord Palmerston, a curious reference to his future found its way into her Journal. 'I could not confide the Govt. to Ld. Palmerston (though I may yet have to do so.)'[6] The Queen was already half aware that winning the war was even nearer to her heart than defeating Pilgerstein.

Desperate weeks followed, weeks which stretched the Queen's powers to the full but showed that she could take an active, even central part in providing the country with a government.

With the Prince disabled by a feverish chill, Queen Victoria lay awake night after night wondering what would be the result of the Roebuck debate. On January 30th, an infinitely dreary day of east wind from Russia, she heard that the Government had been beaten by 157 votes. It fell, in Gladstone's words, 'with a whack'. Aberdeen resigned. The children were due to act a German play but the Queen felt she 'could hardly quite pull myself round' to watch it.

The next day, in a blizzard, she set off for London and sent for the Conservative leader, Lord Derby. 'It must be Palmerston,' he told her; 'the whole country wants him.' Paradoxically he added that Palmerston's day was past; at seventy-one he was deaf, blind and no good at business. With this the Queen heartily agreed. Disraeli expressed the same opinion to a friend with gusto: Palmerston was 'an old painted pantaloon . . . with false teeth, which would fall out of his mouth when speaking if he did not hesitate so in his talk.'[7] Pam's Radical following called him affectionately 'the Whiskered Wonder'.

Derby was successful in persuading Palmerston to lead the House of Commons on certain conditions, a move which, sanctioned by the Queen in 1853, might have saved Derby's earlier Ministry. Now it was too late. On February 1st Derby gave up. Back at Windsor the Queen battled in her mind with possibilities as she slipped about on the icy paths. She decided to send for Lord Lansdowne, a Whig elder statesman who was after all only four years older than Pilgerstein. Lansdowne arrived at 7.30 pm making them an hour and a half late for dinner and declined on the grounds of age and ill-health. 'Much overpowered' by worries she was off to London again on February 2nd, cheered only by little Arthur's delight in all the driving. At Buckingham Palace, which was like 'an ice cellar', the clouds showed no sign of lifting though the choice of Prime Minister had now definitely narrowed to Russell or Palmerston. The Queen plumped for Russell.

The complexity of choice had been so great that writing it all out in her Journal was an intolerable burden. Henceforth she would confine herself to entering 'the strict necessary'.

Just before bedtime (midnight) Russell said he would attempt to form a government. On February 3rd she saw him twice again. He was in deep waters appealing to *her* to persuade Lord Clarendon to stay at the Foreign Office. She tried, but Clarendon chivalrously refused to 'step over the bodies of his colleagues in order to join the man who had killed them' (Russell). Clarendon advised H.M. to send for Palmerston, promising to serve under him. Lord John came back at six, deeply mortified by a string of refusals. As the Queen set out on February 5th yet again for London 'on our *eternal Govt hunting* errand', a thaw set in. Immense relief. There was no new political freeze. Palmerston would succeed in forming a government, having been at last invited to do so. He had already made amends for past offences and was now too

307

much hemmed in by 'good men' like Clarendon to do further mischief.

An item in Pilgerstein's 'amends' was to comply with the Queen's wish not to have Mr Layard as Under-Secretary for War. Radical, bushy-haired Henry Layard was the far-famed discoverer of Nineveh, and could speak of the theatre of war with aggravating expertise. He had indulged in what the Queen called 'ill-conditioned abuse' of Lord Raglan and Admiral Dundas, the latter being in half a mind to sue him for libel. The Queen was '*not* against his employment' but against it in the War Office.[8]

Thirty years later Queen Victoria made and won a somewhat similar point against Gladstone putting another Radical, Henry Labouchere, into the Cabinet. In each case the Queen's tactics were not to object absolutely but to object to having the man *there*. In each case she got rid of him altogether.

The Queen's dislike for Layard was increased by his social background. His appointment, she was told by the Duke of Cambridge, would make the worst impression on the Army. The Court did not automatically reject those of modest birth, indeed Prince Albert defended his choice of a chemist, Lyon Playfair, to work with him on the Great Exhibition committee; but the Army was another matter. Queen Victoria relied on the aristocratic hierarchy to preserve her own magical balance on the point of the military pyramid.

Another institution in which the Queen felt something of the same personal involvement was the Foreign Office. Curiously enough Palmerston was to plant Layard there in 1861 as Under-Secretary. (He had held the post for eleven days in 1852.) This time the Queen said she would approve only if the alternative were Palmerston's resignation. Otherwise, – 'In the contact with foreign countries we should be represented only by thorough gentlemen.' Palmerston, with the brass of a thorough politician, thanked Her Majesty for 'condescending acquiescence' and appointed Layard forthwith.

To return to 1855, Lord Panmure became War Minister in place of the Duke of Newcastle. Because of his shaggy and uncouth form he was known sometimes as Mars, more often as The Bison. Better a pedigree bison from the Lords than any other political animal from the House of Commons.

The hectic chapter ended with a dinner in the Waterloo Chamber where the Duke of Bedford (Lord John's brother), covered with shame, told the Queen that the only redeeming part in the affair was her own. 'Everyone seems to have confidence in me,' she wrote, 'excepting my poor wretched self, who am so often miserable & desponding.'[9] On leaving the dining-room she brushed past Lord Aberdeen and seizing his hand held it in hers as she wished him goodbye. The poignant moment reminded her of the parting from Lord Melbourne.

An unexpected postscript on Palmerston's Premiership appeared in her Journal after the war was over.

'Albert & I agreed that of all the Prime Ministers we have had, Lord Palmerston is the one who gives the least trouble, & is most amenable to reason & most ready to adopt suggestions. The great danger was foreign affairs, but now that these are conducted by an able, sensible & impartial man, (Lord Clarendon) & that he (Lord Palmerston) is responsible for the *whole*, everything is quite different.'[10]

She gave Palmerston the Order of the Garter. Though she might still describe him to King Leopold as 'the poor old sinner', he had maintained 'the honour & interests of this country'.

Queen Victoria rejoiced to have a strong government at last but she was distinctly uneasy at the way it had come about. Roebuck's Commission, with its threat to democratize the Army, reflected the country's temporary dissatisfaction with time-honoured institutions. When Lord Raglan died of fever in June 1855, she ignored the fact that she had shortly before described him as 'amiable' but 'asleep', and denounced his detractors as vile calumniators. It was some consolation that the Roebuck Report was shelved.

During the course of hostilities Queen Victoria solved the psychological problem caused by her exclusion from the seat of war. At first the knitting-needle and the pen were her substitutes for the sword. Woollen mittens and scarves were posted abroad; letters of condolence no less warm went to the widows of the fallen. 'All these letters,' she recorded with emotion, 'are a relief to me, as I can express all I *feel*.'[11]

Shortly before Christmas 1854 a more intense form of female service came to her notice. She read the reports made by Miss Nightingale from the Crimea itself. Dissatisfaction at her own inadequacy again swept over her. 'I envy her being able to do so much good & look after the noble brave heroes whose behaviour is admirable.'[12] In June 1855 news came that Miss Nightingale, down with fever in Balaclava, was inundated with fruit and flowers from the soldiers whose adoration, thought the Queen, 'amply repaid her noble devoted heart for all! I envy her!'[13]

After the war was over Queen Victoria, in some trepidation, invited the object of her envy into her presence. On September 21st, 1856 Sir James Clark brought over to Balmoral 'the celebrated Florence Nightingale'. Her Majesty had expected something reserved and stiff. She was enchanted to meet a gentle, ladylike person with short hair who must have been very pretty before her Crimean experiences. Even her extreme devotion to the cause of nursing had not bred in her either of the Queen's two pet abominations – exaltation and humbug. Like dearest Albert she believed in 'system'. Three things in her career the Queen found most extraordinary: that a *woman* should travel incognito, that she should refuse all public acclaim and that she should be so forgiving.

A fortnight later Miss Nightingale dined. This time she told Her Majesty stories which put her on her mettle. A certain Corporal Courtney, having had a bullet removed from his eye, took to drink. Miss Nightingale warned him it would kill him. After a royal visit while in Chatham Hospital he had never again touched the bottle. The Queen's influence, said Miss Nightingale, 'will generally keep these poor men straight'.[14] Another drunkard was written off by the Prince as incorrigible. Not so the Queen: 'I *know* he has *now* taken the pledge,' she expostulated, '& I will not give him up.'[15]

Episodes like these were a sacred challenge to the royal touch. If at some future time a poor whisky-sodden Highlander should fail to 'keep straight', it would be better for his comfort and her pride not to admit that such a thing could be.

Her visit to Chatham Hospital in 1855 had stirred powerful feelings: disgust at the cramped rooms, 'not built for the purpose' (an underground ward in another hospital she described as a 'robber's den'); a longing to 'tend' the wounded herself; overwhelming pity for men who could bear pain so much less easily than '*us* women'.[16] After each of her hospital visits she would describe the patients in detail, narrating how she had held a ball of such and such weight and diameter, once lodged in an eye or nose. Her deepest anger was reserved for a hospital where convalescent soldiers ate their meals alongside their dying comrades; a cheerful atmosphere was essential to recovery. Captain Astley of the Scots Fusiliers told a friend he had achieved something better than promotion when Her Majesty asked after his wounds at a levée. The Queen loved this story.

> 'It is very gratifying to feel [that what] one can do easily, gives so much pleasure. It is one of the *few* agreeable privileges of our position & it certainly *repays* us for many disagreeable ones.'[17]

As Dr Johnson had already observed: 'it does a man good to be talked to by his Sovereign.'

Medals were another invaluable device for keeping her literally in touch. She appeared on a dais at the Horse Guards in May 1855 wearing a lilac dress, green mantilla and white bonnet, with Lord Panmure at her elbow and baskets of medals on blue and yellow ribbons between them. Crowds poured into the Green Park, bands played and a stream of noble fellows, some on crutches some in bath-chairs, rattled past to receive the first Crimean awards. So great was her agitation that she could hardly hold the little silver pieces which Lord Panmure, fumbling desperately, passed to her. The precious core of her experience was committed to her Journal:

> 'Many of the Privates smiled, others hardly dared look up – . . . *all* touched my hand, the 1st time that a simple Private has touched the hand of his Sovereign . . . I am

311

proud of it, – proud of this tie which links the lowly brave to his Sovereign.'[18]

The charm also operated in reverse. The Sovereign's hand had touched the soldier's. When she heard that the men refused to give up their medals for engraving in case they did not get back the one she had presented, she was profoundly touched – so much so that Mrs Norton, Melbourne's old friend, afterwards questioned Lord Panmure about Her Majesty's emotion:

Mrs Norton: 'Was the Queen touched?'
Lord Panmure: 'Bless my soul, no! She had a brass railing before her, and no one could touch her.' [This was not true.]
Mrs Norton: 'I mean, was she moved?'
Lord Panmure: 'Moved! She had no occasion to move.'

'Half a crown and a pennyworth of ugly ribbon': [19] out in the Crimea soldierly cynicism about the medals was judiciously mingled with enthusiasm.

Tsar Nicholas died on March 2nd, 1855, his heart broken it was said by the carnage of Inkerman and Balaclava. Characteristically the Queen forgot that she had called him the '*one man*' responsible for the war and remembered only his personal kindness. With one Emperor out of the way it was time to bring the war nearer to an end by encouraging the other.

The Emperor Napoleon III had made various further attempts to improve his relations with Queen Victoria, chiefly through the Cambridges and Duke Ernest, but without success. By February 1855, however, the situation had changed radically: Lord Aberdeen's anti-French influence was removed, it was essential to ease the strains between the English and French armies in the Crimea and an advance was called for by the Queen. The Emperor and Empress were invited to England.

On April 15th, 1855, Queen Victoria went down to the Windsor stables to see the fourteen magnificent horses sent over for Napoleon's forthcoming visit. Afterwards she inspected the State rooms. There was a prodigal supply of dazzling upholstery for the imperial bedroom, with bed-curtains of violet satin topped with feathers and finished off with a golden eagle and the letters L N & E I embroidered on brilliant green. Queen Victoria loved gay colours. On the Empress's toilet table 'my gold set will be put out'.

The imperial pair arrived on a day of contrasts, at once noted by the drama-loving Queen. After a bad start in the Channel, which they crossed in such fearful fog that the British naval escort was not even seen, they received in London a truly magnificent welcome. During the first dinner party at Windsor there was a similar transition in the Queen's mood from extreme agitation at the beginning to delicious friendliness at the end. The Emperor had been a special constable during the Chartist rising in 1848. Did Her Majesty know this? As their acquaintance ripened he revealed that he still remembered exactly where he had stood in the Green Park to watch Her Majesty set off to prorogue her first Parliament. He had paid £40 for the privilege of seeing her again at the opera. More prosaically, she reminded him that they had met in 1848 at a public breakfast in aid of wash-houses in the Fulham Road.

The Empress Eugénie, tall, elegant, with a marvellous complexion, became very talkative when once at her ease, 'which she soon was with me'. Queen Victoria was not at first sure about the Emperor's appearance. He was extremely short, had immensely long waxed moustaches, a head far too big for his body and gait too slow to please the energetic Queen. But there was something delightfully mysterious in his manner which immediately appealed to her. She felt an urge to get to know him. He deferred to her, flattered her, treated her as a beautiful woman. And behind his well-bred ease there was an unmistakable touch of the *outré* which had first attracted her to the Duke of Brunswick when she was sixteen. Napoleon shared her interest in coincidences; he had 'forebodings' and a fanatical belief in his own 'star'; he noticed that the initials of the four royal personages now bedecking the streets of London – N.E.V.A. – formed the word 'Neva', the river on which St Petersburg was situated. This coincidence, however,

313

turned out to be unaccountably pointless for the French and British armies never got beyond the Crimea.

The Queen was charmed to learn that Prince Albert admired Eugénie's *toilette* excessively. She had in fact brought the first crinoline to England – grey with black lace and pink bows, and a wreath of pink chrysanthemums in her auburn hair. Queen Victoria wore white tulle trimmed with Prince Albert's favourite convolvuluses. Brilliant events crowded the short visit: a review in Windsor Park, the bestowal of the Garter upon the Emperor (he put his wrong arm through the ribbon), an ascent of the Round Tower, a ball in St George's Hall, concerts in the Music Room (formerly the Waterloo Chamber but now re-christened in deference to French feelings) where Napoleon enjoyed the conversation but not the music. During one concert the Queen found him in such a '*causant*' mood that she dared to ask if he had really intended to invade England in 1853. '*Mon Dieu!*' gasped the first Napoleon's nephew, '*comment a-t-on pû croire à çela?*' The granddaughter of George III replied that people *had* been able to believe it.[20]

The visit was something of a diplomatic success. The British Cabinet had been exceedingly put out by a recent proposal of the Emperor's to take charge of the Crimean campaign in person. Indeed a major reason for inviting him to England was to extinguish this Napoleonic dream. Queen Victoria knew very well that her army would never take orders from a Bonaparte. Through the Empress Eugénie, Queen Victoria at first tactfully suggested that the Emperor's precious life must not be risked. Afterwards at a council of war between the Emperor and the British Cabinet which the Queen attended, she boldly asked him not to go. He appeared to accept her advice with the face-saving observation that *of course* he could not leave Paris for fear of what his uncle, Prince Jérôme, and his cousin Prince Napoleon might be up to.

This council of war was another highlight in Queen Victoria's experience. She considered it 'one of the *most interesting* things I ever was present at . . .' It made her feel right inside the war.

A week after Napoleon's return home, vowing that all he

314

now wanted was '*de prendre Sebastopol et puis de recevoir Votre Majesté à Paris*', he had a miraculous escape from an assassin's bullet: 'a pistol, thank God!' observed the Queen, 'hardly ever seems to succeed.' The pistol succeeded, however, in finally convincing him that a journey to the Crimea would be unwise.

After he had departed Windsor Castle relapsed into quiet and decorum. Gone were the Gallic screams of laughter as the visiting ladies dressed with all their doors open shouting to one another across the corridors. Queen Victoria indulged in a few moments of introspection. She noticed that she always dreaded 'great events' and then was miserable when they were over. The immense crowds pressing round Napoleon and shouting in Cockney 'Vive le Hemperor!' had made her fear an attempt on his life. Perhaps she herself was now popular enough to have acted as a protection to him? In her anxiety for him she had not once feared for herself. That only proved how right dearest Albert was in telling her that the less she thought about herself the less she would suffer from 'that great & foolish nervousness'.

This is another of those rare glimpses of Prince Albert's incessant campaign to improve his wife's temperament.

A return visit took place during the Paris Exhibition of August 1855. The Queen spent a fortnight at Osborne brooding over her *toilettes* and her children, who had scarlet fever. Just before she was due to start a dramatic message arrived that the Empress was *enceinte* and everyone frantic lest she should over-tax herself: 'they can rely on my not allowing this,' wrote Queen Victoria from the vantage point of her own large experience.

The Royal Family, including the Princess Royal and Prince of Wales, sailed in their new yacht, the *Victoria & Albert*. Crowds of soldiers and citizens met them on the quay at Boulogne, among them a *vivandière* who planted herself exactly opposite their landing place, much to Her Majesty's amusement. The royal party inadvertently caused some annoyance by arriving many hours late in Paris. This was the only real blot on a perfect stay in the city which had not been visited by an English Sovereign since the baby king Henry VI was crowned there in 1431.

Paris the Queen found 'the gayest town imaginable'. All was dazzle: the smokeless brilliant air, the white reflections from the shuttered houses; the white and gold bedroom at St Cloud; the dark skinned Zouave guards; fireworks at the Versailles ball including a set piece of Windsor ('a very pretty attention'); the torchlit scene at Napoleon I's tomb where Queen Victoria made her son kneel down with her while the thunder rolled and the French Generals wept, to say a prayer over the coffin of his great-grandfather's bitterest foe ('strange & wonderful indeed!'); the orange flower picked by the Emperor for her to press; her unflagging smiles and superb curtsies and loud laughter; the transformation of Napoleon's enigmatic melancholy into glowing friendship. The wheel had come full circle as regards the Queen's feelings for this ingratiating parvenu, with whom in 1852 she could 'never for a moment feel safe'. Not only was he irresistible but dependable: 'I should not fear saying anything to him. I felt – I do not know how to express it – safe with him.'[21]

Paris gave Queen Victoria that feeling which was always most precious to her, the feeling of being useful and doing good. She hoped to help Napoleon strengthen his régime by the example of her own constitutional virtues. 'Oh! if our visit might be the beginning of more internal Peace & tranquillity!' At the same time she expected to stabilize his foreign policy: 'I think that it is in our power to keep him in the right course.'

There were a few good natured jokes at the Queen's expense. Victoria was short and stout, Eugénie tall and slender. The Parisians noticed and giggled. Orleanists also noticed that the Empress fussed over trifles, the Queen never; regal composure attended her down to the last detail as when, after bowing to the people at the opera, she resumed her seat without looking behind to see if the chair was there to receive her. Not everyone was bewitched by the *toilettes* over which she had spent so many anxious hours at Osborne, especially her plain straw travelling bonnet which she had not found time to change before her triumphal entry into Paris. General

316

Canrobert laughed at the crude green of her parasol, her massive best bonnet, the white poodle embroidered on her handbag, and the famous dress bursting out all over with geraniums which would have done credit to Paxton's conservatory. If the General could have peeped into Her Majesty's Journal he would have found that she was equally amused by his red face, rolling eyes and copious gesticulations.

So happy was the Queen that she had no difficulty in taking the rough with the smooth. For example, the overpowering heat; the sad discovery that the exquisite French *cuisine* upset Prince Albert's delicate stomach; Prince Napoleon (nicknamed 'the assassin' by Lord Clarendon) saying odious things to his cousin the Emperor with a diabolical smile; Prince Jérôme refusing to be present at any functions because it meant giving Prince Albert precedence; her first sight of the huge Count Bismarck, 'very much a Junker' and even worse, pro-Russian. When she observed how beautiful Paris was Bismarck replied sardonically, 'Even more beautiful than St Petersburg.' Fifteen years later Queen Victoria was to tremble for beautiful Paris, crushed in his fierce embrace.

When the Queen's last evening in Paris arrived she pensively remarked to her Foreign Secretary, 'Isn't it odd, Lord Clarendon, the Emperor remembers every frock he has ever seen me in!'[22] Clarendon later threw out the uncharitable suggestion to Charles Greville that Victoria had fallen for Napoleon simply because he was the first man who ever made love to her: he tickled her vanity without offending her virtue.

Actually Lord Clarendon had begun by suspecting the Queen of a political intrigue. 'What is she hatching?' he murmured to himself.[23] His final, smart, though superficial diagnosis has lent colour to the legend of Prince Albert's deficiencies as a lover. Queen Victoria's private papers expose this dreary libel. As for Napoleon III, he was not the first man to make love to the Queen but he was the first adventurer to flirt with her. Disraeli, on a higher level, was the second. The very transparency of Queen Victoria's affections demanded an occasional diet of colourful speciousness. She enjoyed being mystified. Curiously enough the Duke of

Brunswick whom she admired at sixteen and Disraeli whom she adored at sixty were both linked with Louis Napoleon, whom they befriended as an exile in London. If Prince Albert failed her in any respect it was not through physical coldness but in having a mind too limpid to set fire to her imagination. The opaque splendours of imperialism which meant so much to the Queen were never interpreted to her by Prince Albert. Either she felt them herself instinctively as at certain moments during the Crimean War, or saw them through the glittering, unfathomable eyes of a Napoleon or a Disraeli.

Fortunately a stirring event occurred on September 10th while she was still at Balmoral, to give her something new to think about. Sebastopol fell at last. The premature bonfire still stood on the cairn from the year before. This time it was lit with a will and round the flames whirled what Prince Albert described to his brother as 'a veritable Witch's dance supported by whiskey'. The Queen's patriotic pride was later deeply wounded to hear that Sebastopol had in the end fallen to French arms, while the English attack on the Redan had failed. She could not bear the thought that peace should come before her soldiers also had won a resounding victory. After Christmas 1855, however, she accepted the fact that the French army, now riddled with sickness, would not fight on. She heard in the middle of March 1856 that a not very advantageous peace treaty was being prepared; 'I own that peace rather sticks in my throat, & so it does in that of the whole Nation!' She was right. The heralds who proclaimed the Peace of Paris on March 30th, 1856 were hissed at Temple Bar.

The war seemed to her no less 'unsatisfactory' in its end than it had been in its beginning. Time was to show that her dissatisfaction was warranted but not altogether for the right reasons. She resented her army being defrauded of its triumph. It had in fact triumphed in a way she did not at first realize. The private soldier won a position of respect among the British people as a result of the Crimean war which had never been his before. As for the Russians, though they were punished to her satisfaction by the exclusion of their fleet from the Black Sea, this was repudiated by them in 1870.

With respect to the Queen's own development, the war spurred into activity some 'unsatisfactory' tendencies. Perhaps the best illustration is provided by the chequered story of her relationship with Palmerston. Greville called him 'the man of the people'. As an intensely personal Sovereign she was bound to feel jealousy of a rival. As we shall see, this human frailty afflicted her again more deeply with Gladstone. Again, though Palmerston's uninhibited nationalism and struggle for better peace terms pleased her, she was less quick to accept from him the limitations which must be imposed even on the most vigorous drive for victory. The freedom of debate and the Press in wartime, particularly of *The Times*, were admitted by Palmerston sometimes to injure the country but were 'more than counterbalanced by the great advantages'. Queen Victoria could not see this. She did not actually wish to join an 'Anti-Times League' which some of her subjects proposed, but after the Crimean War was less inclined to take the Palmerstonian view of free speech.

Finally, the Queen's part in extricating the country from the political crisis in the middle of the war, together with her own and her husband's labours in so many other fields, gave a temporary fillip to the power of the Monarchy which was not to endure after the Prince's death. To her, two years of war had proved conclusively how right Stockmar was in seeing a 'permanent Premier' in herself.

The coming of peace did not assuage Queen Victoria's thirst for new, life-giving experiences with the fighting forces. Greville crustily announced: 'She has a military mania on her.' She met hundreds of returning heroes, bearded, sunburnt, knapsacked, in soiled bearskins, 'some strikingly handsome' and all giving her 'a real idea' of what life must have been out there. She yearned to run down and clasp their rough hands. Her first sight of a field day at Aldershot on March 19th, 1856 was seminal. A knoll situated just outside the 'beautiful' new Pavilion built by the Prince offered a vantage ground which she eagerly seized, scrambling up to the top. 'I had never been so completely *in* anything of this kind before – surrounded by the troops, & I thought it *so* exciting.' The climax was reached in a series of great military days at Aldershot. Seated on a horse named Alma, on June 16th, 1856, she wore for the first time a scarlet military tunic with gold braid, brass buttons and a gold and crimson sash, a navy blue skirt piped with white and a round felt hat with a white and scarlet plume, crimson and gold hatband and golden tassels.* Surely even a nurse's uniform could not bring her nearer to her dear troops than this. She addressed them on July 8th in a speech of a hundred words learnt by heart (again for the first time) and on the 30th, in blazing sun, wearing her uniform and sitting Alma she watched the march past of 'the largest force of Britishers assembled in England since the battle of Worcester!' Next day she left the camp, sorry for once to be exchanging the busy world for peaceful Osborne.

The military experience, glittering as it was, did not blind Queen Victoria to sanity and sense. When her ally Victor Emmanuel, King of Sardinia and later of Italy, visited her near the end of 1855 the two Sovereigns compared notes on their regal duties. The burly, eccentric *roué* with eyes so wildly rolling that they looked as if they would drop out and a head carried high like an untamed horse, confessed to Queen Victoria that he did not like 'the business of king',† so if he could not make war he would become a monk. In any case, he told her, another war was inevitable. The English lips were pursed and the blue eyes frosty. Kings must be sure that wars were *just*, she said severely, for they would have to answer for men's lives before God.

One must certainly aim at a just war, agreed Victor Emmanuel, but God will always pardon a mistake.

Queen Victoria, who could not help liking what seemed to her the bizarre relic of a bygone age, replied more gently, 'Not always.'[24]

* Now preserved, small and faded, in the London Museum.
† He was the only constitutional Monarch in the Italian peninsula.

CHAPTER XIX

DINNER À TROIS
1855–9

A GIRL OF ELEVEN joined the Royal Family for their summer holidays at Osborne in 1851. She was Princess Charlotte, only daughter of King Leopold of the Belgians and Queen Louise, the beloved aunt who had died in 1850. The Queen's heart went out to the motherless girl with so much piquant charm, but she was disconcerted to find that she could not treat this girl as a child. Before the visit was over Charlotte, mature and sensitive beyond her years, had established contact with her grown-up cousins. How she would love to have sisters like Vicky and Alice, she told the Queen one day, who commented: 'She is much livelier since she has been at Osborne running and jumping about in the grass'.[1] Rolling in the grass was still the Queen's innocent specific against all ills. Possibly Charlotte's willingness to act the child again in order to give pleasure prevented the Queen from profiting fully from her first encounter with an adolescent.

In contrast to the Queen's uncertain touch with Charlotte was her deft handling of a young woman who had safely passed the adolescent stage. 'You may treat me as a second mama & ask me anything' she told Princess Stephanie of Hohenzollern, who visited Windsor in 1858 on her way to marry King Pedro of Portugal. There was a warm response.

Equally happy on the whole were the Queen's relations with those of her own children who were still some way from their teens. Little Prince Arthur, especially, she longed to keep forever as he was; when he burst into song at luncheon and was told not to sing in company, she accepted his quick rejoinder, 'What's company?' with maternal pride. Perhaps Prince Leopold (born 1853) was an exception to this easier touch. His incorrigibly wilful nature often led to haemorrhages and the Queen despaired. 'Whip him well?' she once suggested to her mother. The Duchess of Kent demurred: the sound of a child crying was too painful. 'Not when you have

321

eight, Mama,' retorted the Queen; 'That wears off. You could not go through that each time one of the eight cried!'[2] Nevertheless she found much to admire in Prince Leopold: he was intelligent, affectionate* and tall.

Though the Queen never considered that her high-spirited children were quite as 'dutiful' as they ought to be, she freely admitted that the two eldest had been much worse than the rest, and she herself less clever with them; everything seemed to come more naturally with the young ones.

The year 1855, when the Princess Royal was fourteen and the Prince of Wales thirteen, turned out to be an emotional one in Queen Victoria's life. She began it with more than usually fervent vows to be a conscientious monarch and a self-controlled mother. Prince Albert's written report on her conduct for the first fortnight of the year was correspondingly encouraging and February brought renewed congratulations from him: Victoria had tackled the last serious political crisis with diligence, endurance and resignation. Unfortunately the Queen had not been so satisfied with her husband under the recent strain as he with her. She complained of his want of sympathy. This was a mere bogy of her own creation, he retaliated, which she must get rid of.

'So be comforted and keep cheerful, and show a *little* confidence in me.'[3]

In March he remarked upon her 'better frame of mind', promising continued help, and halfway through November another note in answer to one from the Queen expressed his satisfaction at her feeling at peace with herself.

'The four weeks of unbroken success in the hard struggle for self-control cannot fail to strengthen your confidence.'

Meanwhile the Queen had taken a long, nervous look at her

* At six he fell in love with Lady Augusta Bruce, his grandmother's lady-in-waiting, and complained that he had seen her running after Lord Elgin. '*Mais c'est son frère,*' explained Leopold's French governess. Leopold was mollified: '*Oh, je ne savais pas cela*'.

322

eldest child and decided that the Princess Royal was – she *must* be – a woman.

There is a story that the Princess Royal had been sharply pulled up by her Mama for trying her hand at a little coquetry the year before. When out on a drive the Princess dropped her handkerchief overboard so that the equerries might have the fun of racing to retrieve it for her. Queen Victoria stopped the carriage, had the steps let down and said curtly to the smirking thirteen-year-old, 'Victoria, go and fetch it yourself.'

At the same time as Queen Victoria ruthlessly suppressed flirtatiousness she excitedly notched up the stages in her daughter's physical growth, sending Princess Augusta of Prussia, Vicky's prospective mother-in-law, a regular progress report. The truth was that conflicting currents of emotion prevented Queen Victoria from viewing her daughter's development with the calm which her husband constantly advocated. Four years earlier Prince Frederick William of Prussia had gallantly piloted the ten-year-old Princess round the Great Exhibition, as we have seen, presenting to her avid intelligence, so much quicker than his own, a spectacle of the nations at work and at peace. One day the young Prince would rule Prussia. Married to the Princess Royal he would save Europe both from Russian reaction and French licence. This was Prince Albert's dream. The Crimean War made the marriage urgent: though France was now England's ally, Prince Albert could put no trust in Napoleon III, and Prussia's obstinate neutrality was a grave shock to his hopes of a Europe under the joint headmastership of Germany and England. On the personal side was a bogy which haunted all royal match-makers: the chosen suitor might be snatched by someone else.

Prince Frederick William arrived for a visit to Balmoral on September 14th, 1855. To the Queen, he was an almost excessively interesting guest.

A becoming moustache had given Fritz a more manly appearance, though at twenty-four he was still the same amiable, unaffected creature he had been at twenty; he shot

323

his stag on the first day, he praised the Princess Royal's artistic talents and held her in animated conversation at dinner. The Queen welcomed these good omens though as usual her feelings were ambivalent. 'The visit makes my heart break, as it *may* and probably *will* decide the fate of our dear eldest child.'[4] Fritz, too, was uncertain. He preferred stalking Vicky to accompanying Prince Albert into the wet heather, but he wished to know her better before deciding. Four days later the pace quickened. He wrote home that Vicky had pressed his hand very hard when they were alone. That night he could not sleep.

After breakfast on September 20th Prince Frederick William was sufficiently recovered from his sleepless night to brave the Queen and Prince alone. There was a nervous pause; then he plunged. Might he have permission to talk of 'belonging to our family?' The Queen, though she had for years been dreaming of this moment, could at first do nothing but squeeze his hand and whisper how happy they would be. It was agreed that since the Queen did not wish her daughter to marry '*till* she was 17', Fritz should not propose until after the Princess's Confirmation the following Easter. A waiting policy, however, was not likely to be carried through by a pair so temperamental as Queen Victoria and Prince Albert, despite the former's passionate disapproval of child marriages. It was she who hardly slept that night for excitement. Would Vicky love Fritz 'as he deserves?' Intoxicated letters to relatives and Ministers were dispatched under seal of secrecy, but the Press splashed the news immediately. By the 25th the royal couple's resolve had melted. When Fritz asked their permission to give the Princess Royal a bracelet it was granted with alacrity: 'We also said, something would have to be told her and that he had better tell her himself!'

For the next four days the Queen fluctuated between irritability and cheerful optimism and on September 29th the four-day drama reached its climax. Perched on sturdy ponies the royal party climbed the heather-covered slopes of Craig-na-Ban, admired the view from the top and prepared to ride across to Glen Girnoch. With pleased anticipation the Queen noticed that Fritz and Vicky were lagging behind. At length they all reached Girnoch School House where the carriage was waiting. As Fritz dismounted he winked at the Queen, 'implying that he had said something to Vicky.'

At home there was a rush for the Queen's room where the whole story tumbled out. Vicky had suspected nothing until the last two days when 'various little things' put it into her head. Did she feel the same about Fritz as he about her? ' "Oh! yes," with an indescribably happy look.' The Queen's burning anxiety was allayed; this was indeed a love match like her own, not that abomination, a loveless arranged marriage. Fritz had picked a sprig of white heather for the Princess on the way up Craig-na-Ban in order to break the ice; on the way down he had declared his love.

Two days later it was time for Prince Frederick William to leave. Mother and daughter had never been closer. The Princess fled to the Queen's room, they both burst into tears and Vicky confessed that she had never been so happy in her life as when Fritz kissed her – though how she could say all this to Mama she didn't know. That evening she and her parents dined alone à trois, three adults bound together by what they still fondly treated as a secret.

When the Princess's fifteenth birthday arrived on November 21st, the Queen leaned over backwards to do justice to her daughter's new status. 'We must look upon her already as a woman,' she noted, '– the child is gone forever!' Forgotten were Vicky's rebellious tears and persistent, childish habits of laughing uproariously, gobbling her food and waddling like a duck. She was a woman.

Queen Victoria's efforts to see her child suddenly as a woman were heroic, generous and misplaced. A month later in writing to Princess Augusta she modified them: though Vicky was 'growing *visibly*' and her health excellent – 'early this year she went through a critical time and did not suffer even the slightest indisposition' – yet she was still half a child and must develop physically and morally before the marriage.[5] In the end, however, the Queen's longing to square the child-marriage with her conscience meant that she pushed her daughter right forward, pretending she was grown up, only to find that two years of this anomalous position were more than a mother's nerves could stand.

The storms did not break at once. On the last day of 1855 Queen Victoria parted regretfully from a year which had been exceptionally happy. In her Journal she enumerated its outstanding events – 'and finally, but not *least* the happy conviction that I have made great progress and am trying energetically to overcome my faults . . . How can I thank my dearest Albert for his unchanging love and wonderful tenderness, quite unchanged during these sixteen years!' But by February 1856 her physician, Sir James Clark, wrote in his diary that he had never seen her so exhausted, nervous and debilitated:

'I feel at times uneasy. Regarding the Queen's mind, unless she is kept quiet and still amused, the time will come when she will be in danger . . . Much depends on the Prince's management . . .'

Clark ended on a more sensible note:

'If I could impress him with what I consider necessary I should almost consider the Queen safe.'[6]

The Princess Royal's promotion by the Queen to womanhood included her dancing henceforth only with princes, 'as I do' and being prepared for Confirmation. 'What she learns from . . . her dear Father,' wrote the Queen, 'makes a far deeper impression than all the rest.' On Maundy Thursday the Princess was confirmed wearing a high morning dress of white glacé silk. Her mother found it most touching, especially 'to *those* who knew she was already an affianced Bride'. There was only one flaw: the 'poor Archbishop' preached a sermon without once mentioning Confirmation. Next day, still pale with emotion, the Princess made her First Communion.

The Princess Royal's Confirmation throws some interesting light on Queen Victoria's religion. As usual the Queen's feelings followed no conventional pattern. She fervently accepted the importance which the Church attached to this

326

Sacrament but lost no opportunity for cutting churchmen down to size. Possibly she was pleased when the Archbishop blundered, certainly she was not surprised. Her belief that her husband could give better religious instruction than the clergy would have appealed to her Nonconformist subjects while her attention to the liturgy would have pleased the High Church. Youthful memories of heartbreak in the Chapel Royal played their part in insuring that Confirmations in the Royal Family would always be impressive if not serene events.

The Queen took it for granted that after Confirmation the Princess would know her own mind. How soon the engagement should become public now became a matter of embittered controversy. The original idea had been to wait until it was necessary to ask Parliament for a dowry. As we have seen, the Press leak upset this plan; what was worse, it embroiled the Prussian and English Courts. *The Times* dismissed Fritz's family as 'a paltry German dynasty' while the Prussians were far from dazzled at this expensive commitment. By January 1856 Queen Victoria herself was having second thoughts.

'I resent bitterly the conduct of the Prussian Court and Government, and do not like the idea now, of *our Child* going to Berlin, more or less the *enemy's den!*'[7]

Nor was the rest of Europe more gratified. Napoleon III, after all the junketings at Windsor and St Cloud, was offended and surprised. With a snort, Bismarck described the Coburgs as the 'stud-farm of Europe'.

The Queen got her way and postponed the official announcement until May 1857. It was agreed with further insulting exchanges culminating in a demand from Berlin to have the Princess married in Germany. Queen Victoria dealt summarily with this outrage in a letter to Lord Clarendon:

'. . . the assumption of its being *too much* for a Prince Royal of Prussia to *come* over to marry *the Princess Royal of Great Britain* IN England is too absurd, to say the least . . . Whatever may be the usual practice of Prussian

327

Princes, it is not *every* day that one marries the eldest daughter of the Queen of England.'[8]

Some months before this climax the Queen had been horrified by a 'heartless' insistence on her daughter having an entirely German court. She decided, however, to have Dr Wegner, Vicky's German physician, sent to England to be vetted. She approved of his freedom from the German habit of coddling and briskly arranged for him to attend as an observer her own coming confinement in spring 1857, 'to see how things are managed here'. Lord Granville added his whimsical advice: the Princess Royal must on no account engage a Russian lady's maid as one had recently been caught eating her mistress's castor oil pomatum for the hair.

The disparity between Queen Victoria's attitude to her husband's and daughter's households brings out an important aspect of her character. In sentiment she was uncompromisingly English. This became particularly evident when her daughter faced motherhood: everything had to be English from nurse to layette; 'rational' upbringing of children began and ended in England while all old wives' tales were Continental. Instinctively she considered Prince Albert lucky to have exchanged a German for a British way of life. Moreover, an uprooted girl who would have to face the 'shadow-side' of marriage – childbearing – without her mother's help, seemed to her more pitiable than an uprooted man.

Queen Victoria shared the mawkish views of her contemporaries about a girl's passage from maidenhood to motherhood. Of her daughter's seventeenth birthday she wrote: 'Our poor dear Vicky's last happy birthday in our circle of Children! It is too sad. Marriage brings trials, sorrows and dangers, as well as joys!'[9] A fortnight later she lamented that in a matter of weeks 'her fate will be sealed'. A glance at the maternal mortality figures for this period, when Joseph Lister was only just beginning the research which was to control septicaemia and initiate gynaecology as we now know it, explains much of the Queen's sadness, but not all.

The courtship was not entirely to her liking. Fritz remained tied to Prussia's 'shameful' politics; he also wanted to have

Vicky entirely to himself, girded at the Queen's strict chaperonage and continually pressed for an earlier marriage. She in turn was bored with having to sit in the next room whenever the young people wished to be alone together, which naturally began to seem far too often. Nevertheless, throughout the long engagement the Queen never forgot one consoling factor. Vicky would re-educate Fritz just as Prince Albert had re-educated Vicky's mother. Because Fritz loved her so much he would listen to her 'liberal English' opinions 'while at the same time she will not play the English Princess, but will (I know) do all she can to conciliate her new country.'[10]

The Princess Royal was in the midst of her first season when the Queen wrote these words. In common with many mothers she began to pay less attention to her own clothes, filling her Journal with minute descriptions of Vicky's pink rose-buds, black velvet bows, cascades of English lace and floral cornucopias. The trousseau, including twenty pairs of goloshes and two drawers full of sponges, occupied the royal ladies after the season was over. More serious preparations were not neglected. In February 1857 Lord Clarendon was instructed to escort the Princess Royal on an incognito visit to the House of Commons, no doubt to see, like Dr Wegner, 'how things are managed here'. She was exhilarated to find Gladstone and Disraeli at their most violent.

Both the Prince and Queen took a personal hand, Prince Albert allotting an hour from six to seven every evening to tuition in subjects ranging from Roman history to what every young girl should know. The latter did not include maternal welfare, for as an unmarried girl Vicky must not discuss such matters with a man, even her father. As soon as she was expecting, however, the Queen advised her to take advantage of her married status to appoint dear Papa her chief medical adviser. Above all her father coached her in her political role. 'A useful alliance,' she wrote to him afterwards from Germany, 'was the real reason for this marriage.' There is no cause for alarm at the bleakness which seems to lie behind this blunt, dispassionate statement; in fact we know from Clarendon that Vicky was in love. It was part of the mystique of royalty in the days of dynastic marriages.

Despite the elements of strain, mother and daughter never lost the habit of frank exchanges, the Princess dilating so vigorously on her love that she completely convinced her mother that the marriage would be a happy one, at least on the domestic side. Queen Victoria was justly proud of possessing her daughter's trust.

While the Queen maintained the bright stream of her married life, turbulent eddies occasionally formed underneath. The trouble was generally touched off by depression due to pregnancy. In the third month of the Queen's ninth and last pregnancy an old grievance flared into a quarrel. Prince Albert's preoccupation with business left her lonely and deprived. His defence, that she had plenty of companionship in eight children, she refused to accept; whereupon he retorted that this was because she scolded and organized them too much. Unconvinced, the Queen let off her feelings in a letter to the Princess Augusta: her elder children were no substitute for her husband, she wrote; she did not find conversation with them easy, she had been accustomed to adults since childhood and could not get used to Vicky being almost grown-up.

Five weeks later the tension in the Queen had increased. They must all turn over a new leaf, admonished Prince Albert in a note to his wife dated November 5th, 1856, though she alone could cure herself. He criticized her for being irritated with Stockmar, and angry with Fritz for preparing to devote his whole life to their child – 'whom you are thankful to be rid of'. Other people, he added, could not bear her physical sufferings (in pregnancy) for her; she ought to take more interest in the outside world.[11]

In the circumstances this letter was harsh. There was a very real sense in which Prince Albert could have borne the Queen's physical sufferings for her: by raising her morale through his presence. Instead, his immersion in affairs was almost total during the day while the blissful dinners and evenings *à deux* which the Queen used to count upon for her support were now shared with the Princess Royal. A year after this particular outburst there is a striking entry in the Queen's Journal:

'We dined with Vicky who generally leaves at 10, and then I have the rare happiness of being alone with my beloved Albert.'[12]

The Prince's exceptional devotion to his eldest child complicated the issue for Queen Victoria. Satisfaction at their mutual love radiated from her conscious self; battened down in the unconscious was a helpless, gnawing jealousy.

Even so, Prince Albert's unkind remark, made in anger, that she wanted to get rid of Vicky, was only fractionally true. Queen Victoria's mental processes were far more complicated than this. Certainly she did not want to share her husband with the Princess Royal, nor for that matter with Stockmar who left England for good in 1857, nor with Professor Faraday who kept Albert so late at a lecture that he only just got to the theatre in time to see 'Barney the Baron'. Such a feeling, though no doubt deplorable, is not uncommon among good wives. As against this possessiveness must be placed the Queen's pride in her husband as head of a large family and her sorrow at its being broken up by marriages or careers. The rootless little girl of Kensington Palace was still capable of making herself heard in Queen Victoria.

How does this apply to the Princess Royal's situation? Having deliberately rushed the engagement through, the Queen was suddenly overwhelmed at the loss of her child. And guilt over the residue of thankfulness she felt at Vicky's departure gave that edge to her sorrow which Prince Albert found so irrational.

It may be doubted whether all the Prince's methods were well suited to stabilizing his wife's emotions. His logical analyses of their relations academically set out under numbered headings, must have made her feel chilled as well as remorseful. Perhaps it would have been better to follow the advice which the old Iron Duke gave to the Duchess of Kent for dealing with her estranged daughter: 'Take her in your arms and kiss her.'

Queen Victoria dismissed 1856 as 'this gloomy year' but in March 1857, a month before Princess Beatrice was born, she still felt disturbed. She entreated the Prince to uphold her authority with the children and not scold her in front of them. Her physical condition, she said pathetically, caused her a deep sense of degradation. This last complaint shows the effect on the Queen of having to deal with the problems of adolescents on top of pregnancy. The two together were beyond her.

The Prince's written reply, after carefully recapitulating her troubles, was kindness itself: 'My love and sympathy are limitless and inexhaustible.' He had been warned by Clark a year ago that 'she felt sure if she had another child she would sink under it'; Clark himself feared more for 'the mind [of the Queen] than the health.'[13]

The arrival, very late, of Princess Beatrice on April 14th, 1857, went far to clear up the Queen's traumas and ushered in what she later called an epoch of progress.* Immediately after the birth she made a vertical ascent from the depths of misery to the peaks of bliss.

'I have felt better and stronger this time than I have ever done before . . . I was amply rewarded and forgot all I had gone through when I heard dearest Albert say "it is a fine child, and a girl"!'[14]

It was worth it, if only to have Albert for a while entirely to herself again.

The prospect of asking Parliament for money always set the Queen in a flutter but the Princess Royal's grant went through with only eighteen dissentients, thanks to Palmerston's adroit consultation of the Opposition. The Queen's target had been an annuity of £10,000 and dowry of £80,000, plus prospective legislation for all the other children except the Prince of Wales – 'All at once and once for all'.[15] She was content with a dowry of £40,000 and £8,000 a year for the Princess alone. She hoped the Radicals would realize they had got a 'bargain' compared with the cost to the country of George III's daughters.

A second hurdle concerned Prince Albert's rank. No Prime Minister had dared to try again since Melbourne's ignomin-

* See p. 355.

ious failure to secure him a royal title in 1840, but by 1857 the old Royal Family who had made such a fuss over his precedence were almost all dead, whereas the new Royal Family were still children. As the Prince wrote to his brother Ernest, 'wicked people' might some day try to give Bertie precedence over his own father. Queen Victoria felt that a move now would be in the nick of time.

Palmerston again rallied to the Queen's aid with a plan to ask Parliament to create Albert Prince Consort *after* the Princess Royal's grant had gone through. Despite the Queen's sensitivity to public feeling on this prickly issue of allowances, the surge towards democracy wiped out much of the good impression which her tact and economy would have made in earlier reigns. Palmerston had to report that Albert could not after all be made Prince Consort by Act of Parliament owing to a legal impediment discovered at the last moment by the industrious Lord Chancellor. Sickened but resolute, the Queen herself by letters patent created him Prince Consort on June 25th, 1857. Prince Albert of Saxe-Coburg disappeared for ever. *The Times* sniffed at his elevation. What did it matter? On his next trip to the Continent he was given precedence immediately after King Leopold.

The Princess Royal's wedding day had been fixed for January 25th, 1858. As was to be expected, the Queen entered upon a new year which promised so much emotional exertion, in a tremulous mood, but she was soon too busy making lists for dinner parties and inspecting the honeymoon suite – all new furniture, a new carpet with orange flowers on a brown ground and Vicky's and Fritz's initials over the bed – to repine. An added comfort was the popular enthusiasm, showing 'how really *sound* and *monarchical* everything is in this country'. Here Queen Victoria's instinct was correct though not her rationalization of it. The Princess's marriage happened to take place exactly in the middle of 'the great mid-Victorian peace'* which began with the Great Exhibition of 1851, received a nasty jolt during the Crimean War and then settled down again until the Second Reform Bill of 1867. Most people

* Asa Briggs, *op. cit.* p. 96.

333

could afford to cheer not only because they were monarchical but because they were prosperous.

Eight days before the ceremony a redoubtable army of Hohenzollern relatives began to descend on Buckingham Palace. The Queen could get along well enough with the older princes but the huge, hideous young ones with their ferocious moustaches and sharp, sarcastic remarks about England set her teeth on edge. Meanwhile a sparkling cascade of dresses and jewels was ready to inundate the small, indomitable figures of the Queen and her daughter – black lace over yellow silk with Indian pearls and a white wreath, white and pink silk with forget-me-nots, satin with an emerald and diamond parure, pale green lace with a violet wreath and black pearls, white tulle sprinkled with pansies, gold-spangled Indian muslin trimmed with blush roses and gold leaves – suddenly the mind is carried back to Princess Victoria's dolls and the myriad gay scraps that fell from Lehzen's scissors.

A mammoth State dinner party scintillated with Royal and Serene Highnesses, Princes and Princesses, Counts and Countesses, Captains *von* and Captains *de*, English Dukes and Duchesses, Marquesses, Earls, Viscounts, Lords, Ladies and Colonels. The Queen of England smothered herself in diamonds and then, with the contrariness which was so much a part of her, decorated her dress and hair with rustic flowers and grass. As the excitement rose the Queen remained calm, though poor Albert 'is quite torn to pieces'. The younger visitors tended to be packed off to the Crystal Palace while the Prince Consort took the older ones shooting. Gradually the Queen began to feel at ease with her new relatives and at the splendid ball for a thousand guests she found herself bursting with happiness. Duke Ernest gallantly told her that she looked too young for Vicky to be a bride.

Prince Frederick William arrived, pale and agitated, on the 23rd; then came 'Poor dear Vicky's last unmarried day!' She was led into the present room where she started and blinked at the glitter of diamonds, opals and emeralds from her parents. She brought her mother a brooch containing her hair. 'I hope to be worthy to be your Child,' she said with a long embrace.

After a vast dinner at which mother and daughter both wore blue, the parents took their child to her room and gave her their blessing. Vicky, wrote the Queen, 'clung to her truly adored father with indescribable tenderness'. Back in her own room the Queen broke down and sobbed: 'After all, it is like taking a poor Lamb to be sacrificed.'[16]

The wedding day dawned, the second most eventful day in the Queen's life. She felt as if she were being married over again, only much more nervous. Just as she had done eighteen years ago, she wrote a note on waking. Marriage, she told her daughter, was a holy and intimate union, meaning even more to women than to men. A 'pretty book' entitled *The Bridal Offering* went with it. While the Queen was dressing the Princess Royal came in and began to put on her wedding gown of white moiré silk trimmed with Honiton lace. Their hair was dressed one after the other. After the Queen had arrayed herself in the lilac and silver beloved of brides' mothers, the bride and her parents were 'daguerrotyped', the Queen trembling so much that the photograph was blurred. Then they went off. On the same spot where the young Victoria had knelt, 'our darling Flower' was kneeling now. The Queen's last fears of breaking down vanished when she saw Vicky's innocent, serious, calm face. Hand in hand the bridal pair walked out to the strains of Mr Mendelssohn's Wedding March, that clever friend of Her Majesty's who had once played for her the Austrian National Anthem with his right hand and *Rule Britannia* in the bass. On the way back to the wedding breakfast Queen Victoria leaned across and invited Princess Augusta of Prussia to call her in future by the intimate '*du*' instead of the formal '*Sie*'. In Buckingham Palace the young couple stepped through 'the celebrated window' on to the balcony above the cheering crowds and afterwards sat at table opposite their respective parents 'but hid by a splendid wedding cake'. When they had departed for Windsor the two mamas settled down for a comforting, confidential gossip.

Depression descended upon Queen Victoria next day. All had been so brilliant, now '*all* was over'.

After what the Queen was pleased to call a 'peaceful Honeymoon' of scarcely four days which included a Garter ceremony and a large dinner party in the Waterloo Gallery, the bride's last day in England, February 2nd, arrived; a dull, thick day of the kind Queen Victoria most hated. In the Audience Room all the children, sobbing loudly, took leave of their sister. Until the grand staircase was reached the Queen managed to keep back her tears; they poured down her cheeks as she led the way to the hall, Prince and Princess Frederick following. She embraced them there and again at the carriage door where the Princess's little figure, wrapped in white velour, hid itself in the cold interior darkness. Then the Queen hurried away upstairs. 'It began to snow just before Vicky left and continued to do so without intermission all day.'

At Gravesend young girls strewed flowers on the snow-covered pier while the Princess and her father said goodbye in what he called 'tears and snowdrift'; then he rushed home to write her the saddest letter of his life: 'I am not of a demonstrative nature and therefore you can hardly know how dear you have been to me . . .'

The Queen awoke next day feeling unwell but like so many desolate parents occupied herself by arranging press-cuttings of the wedding. Very soon 'February 10th' was upon them again, the anniversary of a marriage which seemed happier every year. The Queen wore her wedding veil with tulips in her hair. 'Write daily to Vicky.' At last there was a woman again, a married woman, to whom she could say anything.

The Princess Royal's departure for Germany brought to an end the Queen's vivid but sometimes trying life à trois. Within three weeks she was unashamedly recording her 'great delight' in dining alone with Albert. At the same time the daily letters to her married daughter opened up a new means of self-expression which she seized upon avidly and used without any of the inhibitions she sometimes felt in face of Prince Albert's well-meaning but repressive logic. All her passions, obsessions, contrariness, practicality, immaturity, wisdom and irresistible charm went into this extraordinary correspondence and produced a mêlée of emotions, truceless and

336

lifelong, which only her own eldest child, who happened to be gifted with much the same temperament, could hope to comprehend.

The Queen's first reactions to her daughter as a married woman were insatiable curiosity and an urge to deluge her with advice and where necessary, scoldings. She could not let go. For a cold, Vicky must wash her neck with vinegar; for exercise, as there was no garden, walk on the roof. The Princess's return letters were neither frequent, detailed nor spelt correctly enough to satisfy the Queen: it was wrong to use capital letters for adjectives, as in 'I feel Low . . .'[17] The Queen thirsted for a day-to-day, factual diary, illustrating Vicky's gowns with 'scribbles' and her rooms with a plan. One piece of factual news which vexed the Queen was that the Prussians considered her daughter very small. After all she was taller than the Queen, '& I am *not* a dwarf'.[18]

On social affairs the Queen's advice was eminently sensible and encouraging. She realized the dangers to a young couple of living among a family torn by malice and political faction. One must not give away one's feelings but keep silent and self-controlled. If the Prussian princes continued to annoy the Princess Royal by cracking coarse jokes she must say nothing – very stiffly. Shyness could be 'fought down'.

On the institution of marriage itself the seventeen-year-old bride was inclined to encourage her mother rather than vice versa. Indeed the Princess Royal's ecstasy over the freedom of married compared with single ladies, stung her mother into trotting out once more her familiar hobby-horses. Even the noblest of men were selfish in marriage. But for the fact that the Almighty had ordained things to be thus, who would look without shuddering at the submission of our poor, humiliated sex? The Queen stoutly maintained that there was too much marrying these days. Marriage was a lottery, her own perfect union being little short of a miracle. Next year she rejoiced when Vicky told Alice something of what marriage meant, so that she had a slight, healthy horror of it.[19]

Lugubrious as all this sounds, it represented a genuine attempt to prepare her daughter for what lay in store. Today

337

Queen Victoria would no longer beat against the bars of Victorian sex-relationships, nor see in the Almighty a prison commissioner. The younger generation, indeed, were already beginning to rattle at the gates. Shocked yet envious, Queen Victoria was soon to hear that her daughter discussed all the arrangements for the birth of her first child with her Court Chamberlain, while Princess Mary of Cambridge had actually asked the Prince Consort whether Vicky suffered much from morning sickness – words which Queen Victoria would not have uttered to '*any* gentleman'.

The Queen had devoutly hoped that her daughter would not become pregnant for at least a year. She remembered the agonies of shame she had suffered at her own figure, the black depression which succeeded the births of her first two children. How much better if she and Albert had enjoyed unbounded happiness together for twelve months. In some moods she found herself doubting whether it was ever the right moment to bear a child, 'for it is such a complete violence to all one's feelings of propriety (which God knows receive a shock enough in marriage alone)'.[20] This quotation should provide sufficient answer to those who argue that Queen Victoria, with her erotic Hanoverian inheritance, wore out Prince Albert by sheer greediness. The troubles of this 'female Sovereign' were of a quite different order and were common to perhaps the majority of her female subjects.

The Queen heard in April 1858 that both she herself and her daughter were said to be in what she chose to call an unhappy condition. The rumour was substantiated as far as the Princess Royal was concerned towards the end of May. 'The horrid news' forced the Queen to purge herself with the Princess's help of some deep-rooted prejudices. Babies, she eventually admitted, were nicer than she used to think them, particularly when they had got over 'that terrible frog-like action' one was expected to admire in the bath.[21] Provided lace caps always covered their bald little heads, except for health's sake in the nursery, they could be pretty. All in all, though she could never feel an abstract tenderness for children, they were a great blessing as one grew older. When one was young and happy they got in the way. With her accustomed frankness the Queen recognized that this was a view which few shared, least of all her own daughter.

'What you say of the pride of giving life to an immortal soul is very fine, dear, but I own I cannot enter into that; I think much more of our being like a cow or a dog at such moments; when our poor nature becomes so very animal & unecstatic . . .'[22]

Queen Victoria understood herself well but not completely. The effect of her childhood on these matters she underrated. While realizing that her 'peculiar relationship' with Prince Albert stemmed from her unhappy youth – she called him her father, guide, protector and even mother* – she did not see that the same thing caused her reservations about children. As long as the Prince was alive she did not want to be a mother or even a woman with the full force of her vivid being; only a child, his child.

At the end of May Prince Albert hurried out to his daughter for a few days and the Queen was relieved to find herself bearing his absence better than she had ever done before. The Prince gave her a good report. In August they both visited Berlin and the Queen, who hated to see signs of change in anyone, even an expectant mother, was delighted to discover in the Princess Royal 'quite our *old* Vicky'. Her complicated jealousy of Fritz subsided and she wrote: 'Felt as if she were quite my own again.'

Although Queen Victoria thought so poorly of nature's method of bringing a child into the world her dearest wish was to sit by her daughter's bedside when the time came and receive her first grandchild. When this proved impossible she bewailed the fate which denied to her the right of every mother, however humble – and redoubled the written advice. There must be no abandonment to malaise, no falling off in

* After Prince Albert's death she compared his 'wise Motherly care' of her during pregnancy with the Prince of Wales's habit of taking Princess Alexandra out every night. (R. A. Kronberg Letters, June 8th, 1863.)

fresh air, no losing of one tooth per child. The Princess's lying-in period must last at most six weeks; after that she must forget that anything had ever happened.[23] One parcel among innumerable others from Windsor to Berlin contained two pairs of stays with instructions how to wear them. Vicky should get a larger pair every six or eight weeks, writing date of discard on each pair. 'It is of great use – hereafter.' The Queen's memoranda on the properties of elastic, bone, busk, cushions, lining and gores show her a past-master of the subject and immensely practical.[24]

On one point the Prince criticized his wife's efforts. She was getting more than her fair share of letters from Berlin and exhausting their daughter by writing so much herself. The Queen protested:

'Papa has snubbed me several times on the subject & when one writes in spite of fatigues & trouble, to be told it bores the person to whom you write, it is rather too much!'[25]

A month later Stockmar told Clarendon, who happened to be in Germany, that unless the Queen's 'angry' letters to 'this poor child' ceased, the Princess would become seriously ill. Why did the Prince allow it? asked Clarendon. He was completely cowed, replied Stockmar, and also feared that by thwarting the Queen's will he would bring on 'the hereditary malady'. Stockmar then wrote to the Prince begging him to stop the Queen from 'meddling too much with trivialities' (the Prince's political treatises to his daughter were apparently less tiring) and sent Clarendon home to reinforce his plea.[26]

There is no need to take these and similar revelations too tragically. The Queen had had tiffs with Stockmar in 1853 and 1856; there may have been others. Her 'angry' letters were occasionally peremptory, always affectionate, even apologetic when mentioning her daughter's lapses. (Vicky forgot to send Baby Beatrice a christening present!) Their worst fault was sheer pertinacity, one day bringing four communications from an impatient mama determined to get an answer. As for the Queen's madness, this far-fetched explanation of feminine tantrums had been mooted as long ago as 1839 by Stockmar himself.*

Lord Clarendon duly saw the Prince and extracted from him various complaints about the Queen's severity in making him punish the children. Clarendon then lectured him on bringing up children without punishments (he privately thought the Prince as severe with the Prince of Wales as the Queen was with the Princess Royal). The Prince Consort promised, despite the general panic about upsetting the Queen, to speak to her. His mission succeeded, and next day Clarendon was received most kindly by Her Majesty. She curtailed the correspondence, though sadly, for she looked forward to her daughter's letters as one of the great pleasures in life.

At least from the conclusion of this episode the Queen emerges with credit. It is likely that the Prince also took some of Clarendon's advice to heart for he decided not to punish the Prince of Wales for smoking within reason. (Clarendon had acquired the habit while in the Diplomatic Service and continued lustily in the Foreign Office.) Finally, a new light is thrown on the Prince's strange technique for dealing with the Queen's upsets – his refusals to let her 'have it out', his resort to notes, his periodic reports as if on the condition of a patient. Following him from room to room he saw, through the eyes of Stockmar, not a perfectly sane though angry Victoria, but the mad ghost of George III.

The parting of mother and daughter had brought them really close together for the first time, as both recognized. The Princess wondered anxiously whether her mutinous behaviour as a child had hidden from her mother how much she loved her; the Queen was thankful that her daughter at last understood why she had always disliked the children coming between her and dear Papa. Did not she herself admit that her greatest happiness was to be alone with Fritz? Mother and child agreed that a happy marriage was a foretaste of

* It is significant that Stockmar had diagnosed the Prince of Wales's childish rages in 1853 as George III's madness reappearing in his great-grandson. (Philip Magnus, *King Edward the Seventh*, p. 15.)

heaven. In buoyant mood after the Berlin visit Queen Victoria looked forward to the fun of being a young grandmama. If only she could bear all Vicky's coming sufferings for her . . .[27]

On January 27th, 1859, a son, Prince William, the future Kaiser William II, was born after the kind of terrible labour which Queen Victoria had never experienced.

> 'My precious darling you suffered much more than I ever did, & how I wish I could have lightened them for you!'

It was a breech, the child's left arm being dislocated. For a time both his and his mother's life were despaired of.

The Queen was delighted to be sponsor to a 'William', having playfully warned her daughter that if the baby was a girl and received the kind of 'housemaid's' name likely to burgeon on the Prussian family tree, she would not stand over it. She was not joking when she added that forty-two god-parents were excessive.

CHAPTER XX

LAST YEARS OF MARRIAGE
1855-60

IN THE SAME YEAR that Queen Victoria transformed her eldest daughter with one wave of her sceptre from a child to a woman she gave unusually earnest thought to her eldest son. The thirteen-year-old Prince of Wales was not susceptible to the same magic. He seemed incapable of learning. One evening near the end of March 1855 the Queen escaped with her husband into the garden of Buckingham Palace for a walk: the future of 'our Boys' was under discussion. Prince Alfred (born 1844) presented no problem. His devotion to the Navy had persuaded his parents, contrary to their original intention, to send him to sea. Now the Prince Consort had a new idea – '*Ich habe einen Plan*' – for dealing with the Prince of Wales.

The little Prince's inert mind had been flicked into some liveliness by the Crimean War. He hero-worshipped Napoleon III, saying to him during a *tête-à-tête* drive round Paris, 'I should like to be your son.' Next year it was the outlandish King of Sardinia who dazzled him with a sword which could cut an ox in half at a blow. His first Windsor uniform made him blush with excitement; such things meant as much to him, teased his Mama, as a toy sword to little Arthur.

Prince Albert's plan of March 1855 was therefore to promise his son that if he could pass a general examination he would be allowed to train with the Guards. This innocent bribe might have borne more fruit had not the young Prince's warm affections been severely bruised a year later by the removal of Prince Alfred to Royal Lodge. Queen Victoria accepted the masculine decision that the parting of the brothers was for their own good. Sobbing bitterly, Prince Alfred departed on June 3rd; the Prince of Wales, left behind and feeling 'very low', was allowed to sit with his mother throughout her dinner while she tried to comfort him. Two months later he too was pushed out of the nest. 'Pale & trembling', as the Queen observed, he said goodbye to the family when they set off for Balmoral, doomed to a long period of study and, if he worked well, a walking-tour with the unlovable Mr Gibbs.

The entry in his mother's Journal on his fifteenth birthday was pathetic in its blindness. While praying for divine help in the anxious task of his education she praised his outstanding powers of affection, particularly for Prince Alfred: 'his devotion to Affie is great & very pleasing to see.' Yet she denied herself the pleasure of seeing it. She divided them. The Prince of Wales developed a passion for teasing his younger brothers and sisters which amounted to quarrelsomeness. It is unlikely that a boy with his warm heart would have needed this disagreeable outlet during late adolescence if his youthful affections had not been thwarted.

Most of the blame for this situation must go to the young Prince's father rather than to his mother: as the Queen wrote sorrowfully, sons were no longer one's own after the age of ten. At the beginning of 1857 she took one of her periodic walks with the Prince of Wales and found him as usual 'very amiable & sensible', especially in his wish to travel. Next month, on his parents' seventeenth wedding anniversary, he was photographed together with two of his sisters beside the famous little pony-carriage at Windsor. Queen Victoria holds the reins and the eyes of all are strangely downcast except for the Prince of Wales who risks a sidelong glance. Photography had been invented but not a photographer to pose the Royal Family.

'God bless the dear Boy,' was his mother's prayer when he went abroad, '& may it do him good.'[1] At least it improved his looks, for she found him 'growing so handsome' when he returned in October. Then came a mournful session with his books culminating in an examination at Christmas. Mr Gibbs was a classical scholar of the dry-as-dust variety. His pupil was allowed $2\frac{1}{2}$ hours to answer questions on ancient and modern history. For the whole of his ancient history paper the Prince squeezed out $6\frac{1}{2}$ lines of which the first four ran: 'The war of Tarrentum, it was between Hannibal the Carthaginian General and the Romans, Hannibal was engaged in a war with it, for some time . . .' When it came to English history there was a startling improvement, especially in an essay on

344

the Duke of Wellington. Except that the Duke was said to have 'died peaceably in 1850', the account showed knowledge as well as interest.[2] Yet Mr Gibbs was too obtuse to take the hint and draw out his pupil's mind on the contemporary subjects which stimulated it. And the Prince's mother, despite every contra-indication, continued to pray that he might become like his dear Papa: 'What else better can I wish?'

Six months later the Prince of Wales was again examined, this time by Sir James Stephen.* Stephen was a sledgehammer brought to crack a nut. He found that the examinee's 'power of combination is overtaking the power of extraction with more than usual tardiness'. Next time it is the Prince's spelling which needs attention. He is advised to master the etymologies of all Latin words basic to English and 'scrupulously' to consult a portable English dictionary which should form part of the 'furniture' of his desk. Perhaps the nadir of futility in the Prince of Wales's education was reached when his father took him to see the boys of Westminster School act a Latin play. According to the Queen the play was very improper but of course Bertie 'understood not a word of it'.[3] The boy's sense of inferiority, kept alive by his parents' severity towards him and their admiration for his younger brothers, showed itself in loud interruptions of adult talk, fractious argument and sudden screaming rages.

The Queen consulted Sir James Clark in the summer of 1858 and what almost amounted to a new form of punishment was devised, a most boring diet. Diet sheets were sent to Gibbs at White Lodge which the Queen hoped would improve both the Prince's temper and intellect. There were to be three meals a day, at 9 am, 2 and 7 pm. Breakfast should be a light one: tea, coffee or cocoa, bread and butter; no meat or fish but an egg if desired. Luncheon: meat and vegetables, pudding best avoided, seltzer water to drink. Dinner: as light as possible but a little heavier than luncheon; claret and seltzer water in hot weather, sherry and water in cold; no coffee after dinner but a cup of tea two hours later

---

* Master of Trinity College, Cambridge, father of James Fitz-james Stephen and Leslie Stephen, grandfather of Virginia Woolf and Vanessa Bell.

or better still, seltzer water. The diet was not to be thrown to the winds at Osborne, where during the previous holidays the Queen had noticed far too much eating and drinking and a sick headache from 'imprudence'.

At the end of July 1858 one of the Prince of Wales's equerries, Colonel Robert Lindsay, had the courage to suggest that Gibbs should go. Gibbs left in November when the Prince was seventeen and a new era of freedom was painstakingly worked out. He would begin by having a 'Governor' instead of a tutor – Colonel Robert Bruce, brother of the fascinating Lady Augusta. In future his parents would advise rather than command. The Queen's reaction to these new plans was not sanguine: 'I feel sad at dear Bertie's growing up so fast now,' she wrote on November 9th, 1858, '& it is such a difficult age! I *do* pray God to protect, help & guide him!' There were moments when she positively dreaded the forthcoming emancipation. Suppose Bertie refused to listen even to the mildest advice? She might die next year and then Bertie would become king. He would be fit to rule only if his father did all the work; yet if Albert did the work it would kill him. She writhed in the imaginary dilemma.

Meanwhile strings were attached to the new dispensation – apron-strings. The Prince of Wales was forbidden to leave the house without reporting to his Governor. This last provision anticipated the stringent conditions under which he was also to have short spells at the Universities of Oxford and Cambridge. In vain the Dean of Christ Church, Oxford, Henry George Liddell,* urged that the Prince of Wales should take up residence inside the college walls so as to make friends of his own age. No, replied Prince Albert: his Governor would then be unable to choose the Prince's friends for him. A gloomy, private house became the young prince's lodgings; smoking was restricted, outside lectures banned. His mother confessed to having a horror of Oxford's 'monkish' atmosphere. Her son shared it.

The Queen's unhappiness over the Prince's education was increased by a sense of guilt. She considered him to be a 'caricature' of herself, in that all her faults were exaggerated in

* Father of the Alice who inspired *Alice in Wonderland*.

him, because he did not try to improve. Resistance to learning was so much worse, she held, in a man than a woman.

This was a case where Queen Victoria's self-depreciation damaged her son as well as herself. A kind of honesty verging on masochism inspired her. When the Princess Royal praised her brother's looks the Queen called attention to his small head, his large Coburg nose, receding chin and strange hair style. At the Garter ceremony she thought he looked tolerably well though very short, and Court dress showed up his knock-knees. (At two, when dressed as a peasant in breeches and stockings, he had been praised for his 'good legs'.) As time passed she detected in him a tendency to grow outwards rather than upwards. Above all he was the great-nephew of her 'wicked uncles', an indecorous heredity of which the Prince Consort was petrified. To isolate his son from temptations rather than to strengthen him against them seems to have been the Prince Consort's main concern. A letter had once arrived from Mr Gibbs saying that the Prince of Wales wished to take Holy Communion at Mortlake Church with his equerries. This spontaneous feeling, suggested the tutor, should if possible not be thwarted. The Prince Consort returned a long, earnest letter addressed to his son. Mama and Papa, he explained, took the Sacrament only twice a year to make sure of proper preparation and Bertie should follow this rule. After all, his parents had more experience than he and any division in the family would enable the public to take sides. The Prince Consort concluded, like the good man he was, that if Bertie had 'a real yearning of the heart' he should go to Mortlake. The Prince of Wales did not break the family rule.[4]

Now that the Prince of Wales had less time at home in which to irritate the little ones deliberately and the adults unwittingly, the Queen decided that he was slowly, very slowly improving. Nevertheless she and Prince Albert still had bursts of intense anxiety. Would Bertie be indiscreet in Rome or 'quiz' the 'Yankees'? On his seventeenth birthday the Queen's warring emotions caused a sharp attack of neuralgia; a year later (October 1859) Prince Albert slept very badly before visiting his son at Oxford and returned home to develop a severe gastric attack.

The Queen could not feel that her prayer for the Prince of Wales at his Confirmation – 'May he never feel shame at having broken his vows' – had been altogether answered.[5] His friends at the Curragh camp in Ireland introduced him to what his father had always feared, 'the objectionable life of cavalry officers', which included on this occasion a brief affair with an actress. When this incident afterwards came to light it assumed towering proportions in Queen Victoria's mind partly, as we shall see, because of its effect on her husband's already failing health, partly because it seemed to undermine the three aspects of her family life on which her success as a Queen depended: a moral Court, domestic harmony, and the 'good education of our Children'.[6] On the third point it must be noted that not until just before the Prince of Wales's seventeenth birthday, and in answer to his own puzzled inquiries about the meaning of certain words, did his tutor take the responsibility of explaining to him 'the purpose and the abuse of the union of the sexes'.[7]

Some men have the gift of separating private from public anxieties; women often find it more difficult. Queen Victoria found it impossible. The birth of Princess Beatrice in April 1857 was a case in point. For months past the Queen had felt overwhelmed by her condition. Suddenly in March the Government was defeated by the pacifist John Bright on Palmerston's 'gunboat diplomacy' in China. The Queen was frantic. She implored Prince Albert to make the politicians realize that she was in no fit state to go through a crisis.* The Prince obediently sent this message to Palmerston by Sir James Clark. But rule by pregnancy was disallowed. Palmerston insisted on a general election and came back with the magnificent majority of 79, the largest since the Reform Bill of 1832. The Queen cheered up – 'Bright, Cobden & Layard ALL turned out! – and Palmerston congratulated her in his affable way on the exit of so many 'bores'. Palmerston's grip on European politics now seemed to her indispensable. When the cold weather arrived she deplored his frail appearance.

* See Chapter XIX, p. 331.

What would they do if anything happened to him? Clarendon told Charles Greville about her concern and the two cronies marvelled at this strange woman who three years ago had wished Palmerston dead.

One of Palmerston's first requirements of the Queen was to cement the French alliance. Ever since the dubious end of the Crimean War, Napoleon III's machinations in Europe had been suspect. It was not enough for Eugénie to send Victoria an elegant silk peignoir on the birth of Princess Beatrice: Her Majesty must invite the imperial pair to Osborne. Nothing loth, the Queen received them on August 6th, 1857 and as a start showed them Carisbrooke Castle where an old donkey ceaselessly worked a treadmill. The Prince Consort was later to compare himself to this beast. At Osborne all seemed to go smoothly. Napoleon even found time to gossip about his favourite hobby, the occult, describing to the Queen and Prince a spiritualist named 'Hume'* with whom he was much taken up: 'he told us some certainly extraordinary things'.[8] A week after his departure the Prince, Queen and Duke of Cambridge set out for a cruise, calling at Cherbourg to see the French fortifications.

During the following year (August 1858) the Queen's visit to Cherbourg was repeated in an atmosphere more martial and less friendly. An 'observer' was brought with the English party from the Engineers disguised as a gentleman-in-waiting; Napoleon at once laid bare his identity with a bland smile. No bland smile, certainly not the usual kiss, was forthcoming from Her Majesty for the French Foreign Minister's wife, Madame Walewska; her liaison with the Emperor had become too well known to be overlooked. Napoleon's new arsenal was inspected. Against whom were these weapons to be used? The English Press trumpeted forth that Britannia herself was the target. Napoleon, unusually silent and '*boutonné*' throughout the visit, roused himself to ask if Queen Victoria would not silence her Press. She replied that it was not in her power to do so. Next month as she rode home across the darkening hills, she saw Donati's comet flaring in

* Daniel Dunglass Home. See p. 425.

349

the sky with a star 'distinctly through its tail'. To the country, Donati's comet heralded war.

War had already broken out on the other side of the world.

'If only we had a really good large Army, properly supported by Parlt., not in the miserable way it is at present . . . we could carry everything before us, all over the world!'

The Queen enunciated these Palmerstonian sentiments on April 3rd 1857 a month after the mails had brought the first terrible hint of the Indian Mutiny. By July war was sweeping over India and the horrific accounts sent to the Queen haunted her as the Irish famine had haunted her ten years earlier. She pelted Palmerston with exhortations to act, hinting darkly that she would have flayed him alive had she been sitting on the Opposition benches. He replied skittishly that it was lucky 'for those from whose opinions your Majesty differs that your Majesty is not in the House of Commons . . .' In August the news of bloodshed was even worse; the Queen hoped it was not true. It was true. Her blood ran cold. Palmerston's calculated sang-froid drove her into an agony of exclamation marks. All the Government could do was to decree a Fast Day. As always, the Queen demanded instead a day of intercession – 'However, I was overruled!'

Towards the end of September the British forces began to re-establish control. At once the Queen switched her attention to the peace terms. She insisted that there should be no vindictiveness, no indiscriminate death penalty. On December 14th a 'most dreadful letter' reached her from an Indian officer describing the Cawnpore massacre, and her comment showed the restraint which she liked to think was always her reaction to great catastrophes.

'The horrors of shame & every outrage which women must most dread . . . surpass all belief, & it was a great mercy *all* were *killed*! It shd. never have been made known, for that no good can be done any more, & it can only distract for life the unhappy relations.'

The Queen, like the rest of the country, already realized that the Mutiny was no mere fanatical outburst against the greasing of cartridges with animal fat, as had at first been thought. It was the wholesale rejection of British rule as represented by the East India Company. On November 23rd she noted a universal feeling 'that India shd belong to *me* . . .' Plans were drawn up to transfer India to the Crown, under a Council, and in the new year Queen Victoria, utterly absorbed by the subject, was cosily discussing the future of the Indian Army with Palmerston, Her Majesty being most satisfied with his decision: '*all* . . . to be mine . . .' Two days later, on January 14th, 1858, an event occurred across the Channel which put an end to her congenial Palmerstonian partnership.

Hardly had she reached Buckingham Palace to receive the first batch of guests to the Princess Royal's wedding before the news came of an attempt by an Italian patriot, Orsini, to assassinate the French Emperor and Empress on their way to the opera. At 10 pm Duke Ernest arrived for his niece's wedding hot-foot from the scene of carnage in Paris, where his carriage had been just ahead of the Emperor's. As blood flowed from Napoleon's cheek, spattering Eugénie's dress, she had addressed Ernest 'calmly',[9] having told the police: 'Don't bother about us, such things are our profession. Look after the wounded.'[10] Many bystanders lay wounded and dead. The French police discovered that the bombs had been made in England and Orsini was precisely the type of refugee whom Napoleon during his Windsor visit in 1855 had vainly begged Queen Victoria to expel. This time she was relieved to find Palmerston bowing to the whirlwind of French fury; he brought in a Bill to make conspiracy to murder a felony. At once British national pride burst into flame. The country would not be dictated to by France, Palmerston's Government was defeated in February and he resigned. The Queen found her Government's leave-taking painful: the Bison almost broke down. With foreboding she faced a second Derby Ministry.

Sure enough within a few months the Conservatives had torn up her understanding reached with Palmerston about the Indian Army. Instead of the delectable '*all* . . . to be mine', Derby gave way to what the Queen called the 'bigotry of the older Indian officers' and put the Indian Army appointments under the Council, thus turning her into 'a mere signing machine'.[11] Queen Victoria detested the Council, particularly as it was also to select Indian Civil Servants by examination instead of nomination. Two of her cherished prerogatives were in jeopardy and the whole relation of the India Office to the Crown was 'quite untenable & really too bad'. A head-on collision seemed imminent until a threat of resignation from Lord Derby brought the Queen into line.

One consolation was that she had been able to establish the Crown's human superiority over any bloodless Council. Derby's first draft of a Proclamation to the Indian people seemed to her cold and unfeeling. All the romance she had felt since childhood for brown skins, all the advice she had received from Indian travellers flooded her mind – the iniquity of a 'fire and sword system' of government,[12] the 'immense field for improvement among the natives', the lies about mutilation of women and exaggeration of all kinds, the superior manners of the Indian 'lower orders' compared with ours, the ill-treatment and insulting references to natives as 'niggers'[13] – out it all poured and was translated by royal alchemy into the moving words of a re-written Proclamation.

'. . . Firmly relying ourselves on the truth of Christianity . . . we disclaim alike the right & the desire to impose our convictions on any of our subjects . . . but all shall alike enjoy the equal & impartial protection of the law.'

As she wrote to Lord Derby, it was 'a female sovereign' speaking from the heart to a hundred million Eastern peoples.

At the beginning of 1859 Napoleon III revealed the object of his dockyards and arsenals: they were to be used in a new war of European reconstruction in which Italy should be freed at last from the Austrian yoke.

However bad the Habsburgs' record, Prince Albert could not contemplate the dismemberment of Austria with anything but anguish, for the Austrian court and army were full of Coburg relations. Suddenly the Emperor Francis Joseph decided to strike the first blow by declaring war on Sardinia.

'Too bad,' declared the Queen roundly. Later, however, she was persuaded by her anti-French husband that Austria could not have waited for France to grow stronger: so then it was Napoleon whom she found '*un peu trop fort*'. That neither England nor Prussia should become involved, at any rate against Austria, was the Prince Consort's burning wish and Queen Victoria shared her husband's agitation. European politics sickened her and she fluctuated between reciting the Prince's favourite hymn, *Eine feste Burg ist unser Gott*, and threatening to emigrate with all her children to Australia. Napoleon, according to her information, was intriguing with Palmerston to bring down the neutralist Tory Government and rush England into the war. In June Derby's Government fell on the issue of Reform but fortunately for the Queen's peace of mind the fighting also came to an end with the French victory at Solferino.

Palmerston's return to power after a general election was unwelcome to the Court both for domestic and foreign reasons. In the sense that he was dependent on Radical support, his Government was seen to be no longer the usual Whig-Liberal affair, but the first truly Liberal Government in the country's history. The significance of this new situation did not escape Prince Albert who gave Lord Derby some sharp hints on the reforms necessary in Conservatism to face it. 'We impressed upon him,' wrote the Queen on the day after his resignation (June 1st, 1859), 'the importance of a *really* strong Conservative Party, as a check upon the Liberals & *not* as it had been *now* to a certain extent – competing with the Liberal Party.'

In foreign affairs the Court rightly guessed that Palmerston would continue his pro-Italian, anti-Austrian policy. They therefore made a disastrous attempt to plant the pliant Granville in the Premiership over the heads of Palmerston and Russell. A friend of Granville's leaked this naïve plan to *The Times* and according to the Queen, Lord John's famous sense of dignity forbade him to serve. 'Dreadful personal feelings again!' Palmerston in contrast behaved 'very sensibly' and 'properly' when she perforce invited him to become Prime Minister, with Lord John at the Foreign Office.[14]

On July 12th, 1859, an armistice was signed between France and Austria at Villafranca. 'Truly thankful,' reflected the Queen, 'that we are safely out of it, for we shd have inevitably committed, or tried to commit some great blunder. But it is a great mercy that an end has been put to the bloodshed, & that for the present any further war is averted.' For the next eighteen months her relations with Palmerston and Russell, 'the old Italian Masters' as Prince Albert sarcastically called them, were a series of exhausting ups and downs. Her Ministers' undeviating aim was to secure that full Italian unity which Napoleon III had thrown away at Villafranca. Sometimes the Queen saw Palmerston as being up to his 'old tricks of 1848' again; at other times, especially when Napoleon drew her fire by annexing Savoy and Nice (King Leopold christened him 'Annexander'), Palmerston was 'clear-sighted' and 'reasonable'.

The same ups and downs marked their relations over the Army. An abortive attempt to abolish the Commander-in-Chief was peculiarly obnoxious to the Sovereign. On defence, however, she and Palmerston were as one. He sympathized with every aspect of her interest in the new Volunteer Movement: after an inspection when the noble fellows crowded round Her Majesty so that she put her handkerchief to her nose, Palmerston remarked, 'Ma'am, that is what we call *esprit de corps*.' Mr Gladstone performed the same function in the domestic sphere as Napoleon III in the foreign: his opposition to Palmerston's defence measures, 'strange and excitable' as the Queen found it, won for the Prime Minister her deepest sympathy.

The Queen saw out the old year, 1860, in trepidation. Ever since Napoleon had set the European pot boiling again at the beginning of 1859 the Court correctly diagnosed a revolutionary situation comparable only to 1848. Queen Victoria wrote:

'I felt much moved, so anxious for the future, that no war shd. come, & fear for the state of Europe. My precious husband cheered me & held me in his dear arms saying, "We must have trust, & we have trust that God will protect us".'[15]

It was a poignant scene in view of what lay in store.

The epoch of personal progress which Queen Victoria dated from Princess Beatrice's birth lasted for nearly two years. On the nineteenth anniversary of her marriage she had to record in her private notebook of *Remarks – Conversations – Reflections*, renewed 'moments' of misery caused by 'my foolish sensitiveness & irritability' and 'annoyance to that most perfect of human beings my adored Husband!'

'Again & again have I conquered this susceptibility – have formed the best of resolutions & *again* it returns, but I earnestly pray to God! that this *10th* of February may form another *epoch* in my *life* & that I shall progress, as I did from April 57!'[16]

After a faltering start, another epoch did indeed begin.

Despite parental advice, the Princess Royal quickly had another baby, Princess Charlotte. Her post-natal depression after William's birth had already evoked from Queen Victoria another of her tirades against the relations of the sexes.

'That despising of our poor degraded sex (for what else is it, as we poor creatures are born for Man's pleasure & amusement) . . . is a little in all clever men's natures; dear Papa even is not quite exempt though he would not admit it.'[17]

The extent to which she also fretted and fumed over Princess Alice's future is illustrated by an undated note she received from the Prince Consort round about the beginning of 1860. It is the last frustrated letter he was to send her. There had been a scene, the Queen following her husband from room to room with the plaintive request, 'promise you will *trust* me'. It was not a question of showing 'trust' in her judgement, the Prince replied bitterly, she was a Queen and her wishes were commands to be obeyed; her fault was the old one – 'Your fidgety nature' – which prevented her from calmly assuming that her orders would be carried out but made her enter with 'feverish eagerness into details . . .' The letter continued:

'This is your nature; it is not against Vicky, but is the same with everyone, and has been the cause of much unpleasantness for you.'

The letter ended on a despairing note: 'It is the dearest wish of my heart to save you from these and worse consequences'; but hatred, jealousy and distrust were the only rewards for his pains.

'I look upon this with patience as a test which has to be undergone, but you hurt me desperately and at the same time do not help yourself.'

The Queen must have protested in reply that at least she was improving, for Prince Albert wrote again more cheerfully: 'I willingly testify that things have gone much better during the last 2 years.'[18]

The Prince had clearly been defending his eldest daughter, who had fallen down on her task of assisting the Queen to negotiate with the Hesse-Darmstadt family for a husband for Princess Alice, an approach to Holland having lapsed. The interests of Vicky, who wanted her sister to marry a Prussian, and those of her mother did not coincide, while her father's anxiety over Europe loosened his grip on family affairs. The Prince's lamp was burning low. On January 15th, 1860 he wrote to Stockmar that he was tired and worried to death, to which Stockmar replied that he too was 'very weary of life'. Generally it fell to the buoyant Queen to keep up the spirits of those she loved. But sometimes, as we see from the Prince Consort's notes, a peculiarly vexatious question would throw her into a paroxysm of impatience, and instead of raising the spirits of her adored husband she would plunge him into gloom. Princess Alice's marriage was one of these problems.

The Queen's ideal young man, Prince Louis of Hesse-Darmstadt, arrived for Ascot week and she worked herself into a fever at the thought of doing too much or too little to promote a match she ardently desired. But there were no scenes this time. On June 6th she received a tender note from Prince Albert:

'Dear Child, Thank you for your loving letter. I shall

356

certainly do everything I can to get over your nervousness. It is a great worry to you.'[19]

He implored her to wait patiently and let things take their course but such self-control, she knew, was beyond her power for she could see that the couple were interested in each other. It was decided that Prince Louis should return in six months' time. Prince Louis returned and again she found the suspense unbearable. At last Prince Albert was persuaded to broach the subject with the young suitor. He did so and that day at dinner she noticed Louis' agitation and guessed he was going to propose. Sure enough, he caught Princess Alice alone by the fire after dinner and the Queen's second daughter found herself engaged.

The Queen was ecstatic though later on, as with Prince Frederick William, she thought Prince Louis a 'baby' for being so sentimental over her daughter: in other things he was sensible, intelligent and already 'quite one of the family'; as for looks, she considered this red-faced, weather-beaten young German a perfect answer to her requirements: 'Beauty I don't want, though I shd be glad of it when it was there.' She decided it was there. Above all, Louis was not 'blasé'.[20]

This was a defect from which the Prince of Wales suffered. With his lack of enthusiasm for anything except dress, how could he fall in love? Perhaps Louis' sister would come up to the requisite standards of complexion, figure and intelligence. A good character and education were indispensable, rank and wealth immaterial. As for the Danish beauty, Princess Alexandra, the Prince of Wales's parents did not feel complete confidence in that particular royal house. They kept her name from their son until Uncle Ernest of Saxe-Coburg to their disgust let it out.

Deaths in the Royal Family were becoming so numerous that the Queen began to notice how seldom they were out of mourning. In 1857 the old Duchess of Gloucester died leaving instructions to be buried at Windsor with as much economy as was compatible with the Queen's dignity; she had strongly disapproved of the Duke of Sussex's radicalism which prompted him to choose Kensal Green cemetery – 'they will never take *me*', she told her maid, who passed it on to the sympathetic Queen. A grievous blow was the death of the Queen's first cousin, the lovely Victoire Nemours, after the birth of a baby at 'unhappy Claremont': 'the Prince clasped me in his arms saying how dreadful it would be if he were to lose me!'[21] The Queen attended her Catholic cousin's funeral and expressed a wish after a week to see 'cette triste chambre' again, 'where *all* has remained as she left it. So pathetic'. Revisiting the room a year later she found spread out under a glass case the swathes of her cousin's magnificent hair.

Among the Household servants, 'good Kurt', the Prince's last childhood friend, was gone. Scarcely a loss was 'poor Kinnaird', the craven who had failed to drag out the Boy Jones from under the sofa in 1840. He had been demoted from the nursery to Prince Albert's dressing-room for tippling, and so on, downwards, until he died in 1860 of delirium tremens.

During the years leading up to this date, Queen Victoria's devotion to her husband had become, if possible, more absorbing than ever. So had his work. Though the Queen still called him the most beautiful being on earth, he was in poor condition running to seed, balding and wearing a wig to keep out the cold before breakfast. (Mama, as he wrote to the Princess Royal, did not approve of hot, unhealthy fires.) There were disagreements, there were storms; but more often, day after day of cloudless happiness as in some island of the blest. Even when the mundane veils were necessarily drawn over paradise the Queen was conscious of making steady progress under the Prince's patient tuition.

Baby Beatrice, to whom they owed much of their gaiety, had the grace of a 'little butterfly'; the fact that the butterfly was often 'very hasty' the Queen now took in her stride. 'Baby mustn't have that, it's not good for Baby,' said she one day at luncheon, to which Baby lightly replied as she helped herself, 'But she likes it, my dear'.

Queen Victoria's leisure reading was not unenterprising. She went through Macaulay's *History of England* as the volumes came out, read *Northanger Abbey*, found *Jane Eyre* 'intensely interesting', swallowed the seduction of Hetty in *Adam Bede* with the smallest of gulps – it was 'only a true Picture of what constantly (& vy. naturally) happens' – disliked *Barchester Towers* for having too little romance and too much Mrs Proudie, met Mrs Beecher Stowe at Euston Station and considered her new novel, *Dud, or a Tale of the Dismal Swamp*, quite as good as *Uncle Tom's Cabin*. The southern negro went straight to her heart and as for quadroons – 'they are as white as ourselves!' Scientists did not seem quite so intimidating as of old. She dutifully received at Balmoral in 1859 '4 weighty omnibuses' laden with 'philosophers & savants' from the British Association. Afterwards the Prince commended her efforts that holiday to be 'kind, sociable and unselfish'.

Next autumn Prince Albert arranged for her a treat which appealed a good deal more than the busloads of savants. Thinly disguised as 'Lord & Lady Churchill & Party' (an extra dog-cart accompanied their two shabby vehicles emblazoned with the crown of England) the Queen, Prince, General Grey and Lady Churchill spent two days on an expedition to Glen Feshie, sleeping in a common inn and being convulsed with merriment when John Brown called the Queen 'Your Majesty' by mistake or Grant referred to the Prince as 'his lordship' on purpose. The Queen christened this delectable adventure 'The First Great Expedition'. On the last day at Balmoral she and her ladies made a helter-skelter descent of Craig Nordie, 'Johnny Brown', as she told the Princess Royal, picking up Jane Churchill who had collapsed:

> 'when she thanked him, he said "Your Ladyship is not so heavy as Her Majesty"! which made us laugh very much. I said "Am I grown heavier do you think"? "Well, I think you are", was the plain spoken reply. So I mean to be weighed as I always thought I was light.'[22]

In order to see old Stockmar perhaps for the last time and little Prince William of Prussia for the first time, the Queen and Prince visited Germany in the autumn of 1860. The Prince Consort's last visit to his native land opened sadly. His step-mother 'poor Mama Marie' died of erysipelas. At Coburg the Queen was cheered by seeing her 'darling Grandchild', Prince William of Prussia, at last; he came in holding the hand of Mrs Hobbs, his English nurse, and she admired his sturdy build and white skin. The cold, blue little arm she did not look at too closely; Clark had said it would all come right in the end and her policy was to stop her daughter from worrying. The Princess Royal had not dared to tell even her mother about it until she visited Osborne, alone, in the spring of 1859.

On October 1st the Queen received a message from her husband that he had met with a minor carriage accident. The Prince had in fact jumped from his runaway four-in-hand just before it crashed into a wagon waiting at a level-crossing. The Queen found him lying in bed stiff and shaken with lint compresses on his nose, mouth and chin.

In the days of the horse, accidents were common and the Royal Family and their friends had their full share. That very August the Queen's carriage horses had bolted at Aboyne. Going back over the years, there were comic occasions when Her Majesty's pony-chair was upset on a molehill and her carriage at a meet where she fell on top of Lord Douro, was dragged out backwards and deposited in the mud, much amused. Falls from riding horses were of course frequent: the little Prince of Wales once had a narrow escape on a run-away pony which the Queen managed to hush up. Prince Albert had never taken kindly to accidents. He was thrown while out hunting in 1840, the Queen finding him shaken though only scratched; next winter he fell through the ice at Buckingham Palace; Queen Victoria hauled him out and he ran about indoors, pale with cold and shock. Their State barge was nearly capsized on the Thames in 1843; the Prince turned white as a sheet and it was the Queen who shouted, 'Turn the boat!'

At first the Queen did not realize how near her husband had been to disaster on October 1st, 1860; he seemed to her in high spirits after dinner, 'talking away'. Stockmar, standing by his bed immediately after the crash, had not been deceived. Here lies a man, he said to himself, incapable of fighting a severe illness. On the last day in Coburg Prince Albert went for a walk with his brother Ernest and broke down, sobbing that he would never see his birthplace again. In contrast, the Queen, having contracted a violent chill on the way home, battled through three days of travelling and receptions in huge unheated German rooms without missing more than a few of her engagements.

Fortunately her last Christmas Day with Prince Albert was a glorious one, Windsor at its best. There were twenty-eight degrees of frost, windows frozen over, floods of sunshine, wild games of ice-hockey, Louis and Alice sharing a present table, Mama to luncheon, Leopold and Baby coming down to dessert and the older ones appearing after dinner; Albert telling stories, Albert cracking jokes, Albert swinging Baby in a dinner napkin, Albert, Albert, Albert.

CHAPTER XXI

'HE WAS MY LIFE'
1861

SHORTLY BEFORE Queen Victoria's marriage she had received from Prince Albert a portrait of himself as a child of eight. The face struck her as having been longer, more melancholy and delicate at eight than it was at twenty. At forty-two the Prince was further than ever from the slim contours of youth but his early melancholy and delicacy had returned in force. Rheumatism, catarrh and gastric attacks with fever were his constant foes; a weak stomach, he wrote, would go with him to the grave. The Queen was well aware of this situation: her Journal is sprinkled with references to his looking ill or 'fagged'. During an attack of measles in 1853 he was 'very bad' and five years later there began a steep decline in his general health which she put down to overwork. A particular bugbear was the Horticultural Society. Albert continued to 'busy himself' with its affairs, she wrote bitterly in October 1859, when he was too tired to go out with her for a walk. In 1861 she bluntly told the Princess Royal that dear Papa was often 'very trying – in his hastiness & overlove of business'.[1]

The year 1861 opened without joy. 'A sad blowy night' was the first entry in the Queen's Journal. There followed the news that the mad King of Prussia, Fritz's uncle, was dying at last. An added burden would fall on Prince Albert to guide the new ruler. Then, on January 29th, the first link was forged in the fatal chain which ended in the Prince's death. A railway crash occurred at Wimbledon. 'The only person killed,' wrote the Queen with a hint of reproof to Providence, 'was our valued Dr Baly.' He fell through the broken carriage floor and was run over. William Baly, a brilliant young physician appointed to the Royal Family in 1850, was Clark's successor, that veteran of seventy-three having retired in 1860. The Prince already felt 'the greatest confidence' in Dr Baly and was 'greatly alarmed' by this 'incalculable' loss.

Now Clark had to look round again. Three weeks later he introduced William Jenner, the noted pathologist who had recently distinguished the germs of typhus and typhoid.

Between the loss of one physician and the acquisition of another, Prince Albert suffered tortures from toothache and swollen glands. Nothing would induce him to relax his labours. On the same day, for instance, he attended the Fine Arts Commission and Trinity House winding up with a visit to the farce 'Colleen Bawn'. He 'managed to laugh a good deal', wrote Queen Victoria. Her own spirits were low. Politics she could scarcely bear to discuss in her Journal; she heard too much of them from dearest Albert. The Prince of Wales's future could not be so easily dismissed. To her manifold requirements for his bride was now added a strong character which would not 'knock under'.

On March 16th the Queen's mother died. Early in the month the Duchess had been operated on for an abscess: in the stark language of those days, the Queen wrote in her Journal that 'the surgeon should go to the marrow to see dear Mama's arm'. There was a brief respite; then a message came to the Queen as she sat 'peacefully' at Buckingham Palace marking newspapers that Mama's condition was desperate. The Prince quietly ordered the royal train and they slipped back to Windsor, reaching Frogmore at 8 pm. Prince Albert went in first. When he returned with tears in his eyes the Queen knew what to expect: 'with a trembling heart I went up, sat a long time . . .' The Duchess's repeater in its tortoise-shell case struck the quarters. It was the same clock which Victoria had heard every night of her life at Kensington until as Queen she left her mother's room. With what intricate anguish she listened to its chimes again. The Prince at last persuaded her to go to bed. Twice during the night Augusta Bruce, who was sleeping on the floor, saw the small, white figure of the Queen glide in and out, lamp in hand. In the morning the Duchess died, her hand in her daughter's. Prince Albert burst into loud sobs, gathered up his wife in his arms and carried her out of the room. Then he sent for Princess Alice. 'Comfort Mama.'

Queen Victoria suffered a nervous breakdown after this

363

loss. Normal regret for lost opportunities of showing love was intensified in her a thousand times by painful memories of the past. She was too honest to pretend that her mother had been entirely blameless but while going through the Duchess's private papers – 'almost a sacrilege' – she was overwhelmed to find how much her mother had loved her. Yet there, in her own Journal, stood the damning remark to Melbourne: 'I don't believe Ma. ever really loved me.' 'Two people' (Conroy and Lehzen) she believed were responsible for the tragedy but tragedy it remained.

Remorse alone would not have made the Queen ill. Throughout the last years she had been in the closest touch with her mother either through daily visits or letters. Now she felt abandoned. There was no Mama to gossip about the children, to attend their birthday parties, to add an extra dimension to family life. 'I feel as if we were no longer cared for,' she wrote to King Leopold. The exhausted Prince was unable, indeed unwilling to fill the gap. For the sake of his own health and his wife's happiness it would have been better if he had temporarily withdrawn from the pressure of affairs, but he had lost the power. His speeches, his journeys, his memoranda were a 'treadmill' he dared not defy. Even Baby had picked up the atmosphere: 'I have no time, I must write letters,' she would say if anyone gave her an order.

He insisted on the Queen returning to London to take her mind off Frogmore, though she had no engagements for three weeks and little Leopold was sickening for measles. A great wail went up: how cruel were even the best of men compared with women like dear Mama, all solicitude and tenderness. As for the Horticultural Garden which the Prince opened on June 5th, she could not trust herself to speak of the 'accursed' thing. They had reached one of the familiar deadlocks: Albert urging her to get outside herself, Victoria only capable of doing so under his constant guidance.

Meanwhile, the choice of a bride for the Prince of Wales was finally reduced to Princess Alexandra of Denmark. The Princess Royal arranged that the young couple should meet sightseeing in Speyer Cathedral. How 'fidgety' the Queen felt over this rendezvous may be imagined. Prince Louis' relations were behaving intolerably about providing him with a home for Princess Alice and though the Queen was delighted at the prospect of having the homeless pair with her in England, she loathed the prickly negotiations for their German palace. Even dear Fritz was making trouble? he complained that Louis was allowed to call the Queen 'Mama' and Alice was less strictly chaperoned than Vicky had been. Her Majesty replied that circumstances were different.

Since the Duchess of Kent's death 'everything seemed changed'. Loud noises set Queen Victoria on edge, particularly the Prince of Wales's voice bickering with the children. She shut herself up, nursing her grief. A visit to Ireland in August did nothing to cheer her. She found the climate of Killarney peculiarly oppressive. How sadly the population had dwindled since her first visit fourteen years ago. Prince Albert's birthday on August 26th was celebrated in gloom never before known on that beloved day.

'Alas! so much is different this year, nothing festive; we on a journey & separated from many of our children. I am still in such low spirits . . .'

She prayed as so often now that she would not survive this adored husband who was her all in all.

It is not surprising that the Queen's unremitting grief began to attract attention. The old legend which had been revived in 1858 burst again into vicious activity. The Queen was mad. Or at least, as Clarendon believed, her mind trembled in the balance.* A letter from Vicky warned the Prince Consort of 'monstrous reports' circulating in Germany that Mama was attended by 'all the doctors in Europe'.[1] Prince Albert denied the 'horrid vile rumours'[2] to his brother Ernest and while keeping them from his wife redoubled his efforts to bring her mourning to an end. It was Balmoral and two

* Less than a fortnight after the Duchess of Kent's death, Clarendon was writing to his friend the Duchess of Manchester about the Queen's 'morbid melancholy', and in April he wrote: 'I had some talk with Ferguson [one of the royal accoucheurs] about her & his private opinion about her mind (founded on his attendance upon her years ago when she was in a strange state) is far from satisfactory.' My Dear Duchess, pp. 141, 148.

more Great Expeditions which finally restored the Queen's native capacity for pleasure. On October 22nd the Prince was happy to give her a 'very good certificate' of 'improvement'. He pointed out once again that more outside interests would help her to control her grief: 'controlling your feelings is your great task, you say, in life.'[3]

The Prince Consort's state now began to deteriorate as steadily as his wife's improved. Physician heal thyself; but this second cure was beyond him: 'Prepare to meet thy God' was the text of the last sermon he ever heard at Balmoral. Its picture of the Duchess of Kent in a better world cheered both him and the Queen. Napoleon III would have found it foreboding.

The Prince had taken refuge in a mood of fatalism which Stockmar had always deprecated. Not for the first time he explained to Queen Victoria quite calmly that he did not cling to life as she did; he was happy in his lot but if he were attacked by a severe illness he would let go without a struggle. After his death the Queen ardently commended these words to his official biographer, Sir Theodore Martin, as an example of his saintly submission to God. Nothing would have shocked her more than to learn that later writers would use them to prove that the Prince suffered from a 'death wish' and suffered from it because of her.

Nine months after the death of Dr Baly, a second link in the chain of events leading to the Prince's destruction was forged. At the beginning of November 1861 the Portuguese Royal Family was struck down *en masse* with typhoid. By the 12th Prince Ferdinand and King Pedro were both dead. The King was only twenty-five and like a son to Prince Albert. Like him, he had the Coburg melancholy. His death greatly increased the Prince's depression. 'We did not need this fresh loss,' wrote the Queen, 'in this sad year, this sad winter, already so different to what we have ever known.'

Swiftly another blow struck them on this same sad November 12th – the third link in the chain. A letter arrived from Stockmar breaking the news of the Prince of Wales's amorous escapade at the Curragh Camp, which had leaked out abroad.

Would it ruin his chances of winning Princess Alexandra? The Queen never forgot her husband's woebegone face as he came into her room carrying the letter. He spent the next four days in digesting the news (which was confirmed and expanded by a gossiping courtier, Lord Torrington) before sending his son on November 16th a long, reproachful yet forgiving letter which must have cost him much pain to write. It is likely that the ten days beginning with Pedro's death and Stockmar's bad news coincided with the incubation period of the typhoid germ which killed him – the last link in the chain. Owing to the disease's insidious onset it is impossible to decide exactly when it declared itself but the Prince's doctors believed Friday, November 22nd to be the date.

This black Friday began and ended in a downpour. Prince Albert had been unable to throw off a cold or, since Stockmar's news, to sleep. (Insomnia can also be an early symptom of typhoid.) Nevertheless he inspected the new Staff College at Sandhurst, returning soaked to the skin and shivering with what was considered a fresh chill. Windsor was filling up with guests and there was much talk of how 'good and brave' Baby had been when her ears were pierced for earrings. Albert was good and brave too. He endured a week-end of entertaining and on Monday, still sleepless and now racked with 'rheumatism' (the first typhoid pains) set off for Cambridge, where the Prince of Wales was studying, to thrash out the wretched Curragh incident. Bertie responded to affectionate appeals for frankness and his father arrived home next day with an easier mind but a body aching more wretchedly than ever. In order to prevent embarrassment he had informed his son that Mama did not and must not know of the affair. Had he not died the matter, so far as the Queen was concerned, would have been closed.

Next day the Queen confessed to King Leopold that Albert was irritable and trying. A mixture of fear and faith – fear of even so much as contemplating a serious illness in her beloved and faith in fresh air – led her to spur him on just as she had spurred on her mother. Her role, as she once told the Princess Royal, was always to raise flagging spirits. On

Friday the 29th Prince Albert could neither shoot nor attend luncheon but to please her he walked round in the afternoon while she inspected 200 Eton Volunteers and then watched them eating an 'ample' luncheon in the Orangery – 'a pretty sight'. Poor Albert was not a pretty sight: even the Queen had to admit that he looked terrible. He felt as if icy water were trickling down his spine. Dr Jenner, on the other hand, informed the Queen that he was much better and need no longer have a physician sleeping at the Castle. The psychological treatment was in full swing.

Meanwhile the Queen was suddenly faced with an international crisis, a side effect of the American Civil War then in its eighth month.

The Confederates had dispatched two envoys, Mason and Slidell, with their wives, to plead the Southern cause in England. They sailed in an English vessel, the *Trent*; she was chased by a Federalist, boarded, and her male passengers kidnapped on those high seas which Britannia ruled. The Confederates' documents were saved not by the trident of Britannia but by Mrs Slidell disposing of them inside her crinoline. Palmerston prepared to do another 'Don Pacifico' and Gladstone assured the Queen that the country and Cabinet were at one. Unless there was immediate release of the envoys, our Ambassadors would be recalled from Washington and there would be war. It was fortunate that Prince Albert was 'at one' neither with Palmerston, the country nor, one suspects, the Queen who described the Federalists as 'such ruffians'.[4]

On Sunday morning the Prince looked so wretched that Queen Victoria felt serious concern. 'But still he was well enough on getting up,' she wrote with determined optimism, 'to make a Draft for . . . Ld. Russell in correction of his Draft . . . which Albert did *not* approve.' He had crept to his room at 7 am in his wadded dressing-gown with its crimson velvet collar and lighted his green lamp for the last time, resolved to redraft the terse staccato message of the 'old Italian masters' to the Federal Government, if he died in the attempt. In courteous verbiage he skilfully concealed the bleak outlines of Russell's draft, so that what had seemed a

Queen Victoria with her family, 1846, painted by Winterhalter

Queen Victoria by Loch Muick, painted by Landseer

Lord Melbourne

Lord John Russell

Sir Robert Peel

ord Palmerston

Osborne

Drawn by Queen
Victoria, etched by
Prince Albert

VR del.̲   Dec. 27 1842.   Albert sculp.

The Royal Family
at Osborne

Wedding
photograph of the
Princess Royal
and her parents.
Queen Victoria
wrote in her
journal that she
trembled so much
that the
photograph was
blurred

Buckingham Palace, 1846

Queen Victoria in State Robe
1859, painted by Winterhalt

The Corridor, Windsor Castle

Queen Victoria and the Prince Consort

strident ultimatum was now an invitation to negotiate. Then he left his desk for ever. 'I am so weak,' he groaned as he returned to the Queen at 8, 'I can hardly hold the pen.' He could eat nothing all day; instead he entertained the table with conversation. Then for the third night running he lay awake shivering hour after hour. In the morning the Queen sent immediately for Jenner: 'I was terribly nervous & distressed.' Perhaps the Prince's dry, brown tongue was a little better but in every other respect he seemed utterly forlorn. That day he remained on the sofa upstairs.

On Monday December 2nd Dr Jenner spoke out: though there was still no fever it was likely to develop. Waves of anguish swept over Queen Victoria. The Prince, meanwhile, was given the harrowing details of Pedro's death by two gentlemen just returned from Portugal. It was as well, he muttered to his equerries, who with his valet were all he had for sick-nurses, that he had no fever, for he would never recover from it. The Queen begged him not to say such foolish things. Restless and petulant, he decided to sleep in a small bed at the foot of their large one. So far the Queen had kept the Princess Royal, who at twenty-one was expecting her third confinement, in the dark. Now, in breaking the news, she snatched at a phrase of Jenner's that 'there was no cause for alarm'.[5]

On this same day the Cabinet accepted the Prince's amended draft. After he was dead the Federalists saw that a way had been left open for them to retreat with honour and the *Trent* case, thanks to Albert the Good, passed into peaceful history.

The Prince tossed all night in his small bed; Victoria offered him drinks and listened to the clock striking the hours. Towards morning he went into his own room. She followed him. He knew he was getting a low fever, he moaned, he knew he would die. Tuesday night, December 3rd, was no better. The Prince walked from room to room, the Queen again following him; at 6 she sent for Jenner 'in an agony'. For an hour and a half opiates brought him 'blessed relief'. She swung at once from agony to hope, especially when she noticed that on waking he dressed completely as if for a normal day. The improvement was short-lived; he asked Princess Alice to read aloud but grumbled at the books she chose, which included *Silas Marner*. Bitterly complaining, he took a little raspberry vinegar in seltzer water; he *must* eat, said Jenner, he was starving himself. The physician continued to assure the Queen every day that 'there was no cause for alarm' and every day letters left Windsor carrying to relatives this soothing message.

It is tempting to blame the Prince's doctors for what transpired and posterity has not hesitated to do so. Lord Clarendon, with his gift for the telling phrase, gave a lead. 'They are not fit to attend a sick cat,' he said after the Prince's death.* On the other side it must be remembered that Clark's much-quoted mistake over Lady Flora Hastings had been even more a moral than a medical one. He did not commit himself to a false diagnosis; to please the Queen he jumped to a conclusion with practically no diagnosis at all. He saw the Queen through nine confinements and his belief in fresh air, though a trifle mystical, was justified by the state of the Windsor plumbing. What of his 'psychological' treatment? For it was undoubtedly Clark who took the decision to keep from the Prince, the Queen and therefore the world, the nature and gravity of the case.

Clark knew from of old that Prince Albert worried about himself. Since King Pedro's death his fears had sharpened into an obsession that typhoid in particular would prove fatal. The word 'fever', therefore, must neither be whispered in his hearing nor written in the Queen's face. If Prince Albert saw her looking panicky he would guess all and give up. According to Clark, the calm repetition to the Queen of 'no cause for alarm' was imperative. He remembered, as well he might, her 'fidgets', her 'nerves', her hysterics and recent breakdown. But he disregarded her own saying that 'great events make me calm'. Even without his well-meant deception it is probable that she would have controlled herself in front of the Prince, for his sake. As it was, having endured over three

* Clark's wife was gravely ill at the same time as the Prince, so that the old doctor was torn between Windsor and his own home.

weeks of unavoidable anxiety, she suffered a violent shock at the end.

Clark's determination not to frighten the Prince at whatever cost almost certainly prevented him from being properly nursed. No one was better equipped to treat typhoid than William Jenner, but he had done his great work in hospitals and been with the Royal Family only during the last nine months. He was in no position to challenge the family doctor. One cannot help feeling that if young Dr Baly had been in charge there would have been less of the patient walking about, talking, showing pictures to little Arthur and hearing Baby's French verses between bouts of delirium.

By December 6th the Queen had endured five of the most terrible nights in her life. The Prince could not sleep without ether drops; he coughed and moaned, continually changing his bed. With tears streaming down her cheeks she hovered just outside the bedroom, watching the candles flicker and Dr Jenner's figure huddled near the door. By day the Prince still refused to go to bed; his expression strange and unsmiling, he hardly noticed her but kept asking his doctors, 'How long will it go on?' When Victoria came in at 8 am on the 7th he asked her miserably where his illness had come from.

> 'Over work, as much as worry and annoyance.'
> 'It is too much – you must speak to the ministers.'
> 'It is not that alone; it is your own concerns.'[6]

She had not forgiven the Horticultural Garden.

She was told that at dawn when he heard the birds singing he thought he was back in the Rosenau. This she knew was a bad sign.

> 'I went to my room & cried dreadfully & felt oh! as if my heart must break – oh! such agony as exceeded *all* my grief this year. Oh God! help me to protect him!'

Presently Dr Jenner came and told her that the Prince had gastric or bowel fever – 'the thing they had been watching for all along.' They knew exactly how to treat it: it would take

371

a month, dating from November 22. The Queen sent for Augusta Bruce and wept uncontrollably. 'But God will support me, & I tried to cheer up . . .' Again she was sent to bed in her own room, feeling it 'a terrible trial to be thus separated from him & see him in the hands of *others*, careful & devoted as they are'. In her heart she welcomed the decision for she was ready to drop with fatigue, running in and out of the sick room, 'constantly on my legs', arranging dispatches, going through boxes, doing those countless things which her 'poor Darling' had always done for her. How could she carry on for perhaps another *fortnight* without her guide, her all?

Low fever, slow fever, gastric or bowel fever – they were all contemporary names for the dreaded typhoid. There is something tragic in the way Queen Victoria had inveighed against bad sanitation ever since she was a girl, only to lose her life's happiness from the result of this evil. One of her reasons for buying country estates was to escape the fevers which raged in places like Old Windsor. In 1858, when the Queen and Prince had attempted a short pleasure cruise on the Thames, its malodorous waters drove them back to land within a few minutes. That summer a prolonged wave of heat and drought exposed its banks, rotten with the sewage of an overgrown, undrained city. Because of the stench, Parliament had to rise early.

When the Prince was taken ill one man in every three died of an infectious fever. It was not till 1866 that the passing of the Public Health Act made possible the improvement which began during the 1870s. Deaths from fevers had increased in the overcrowded cities of Britain after 1820.* In 1820 Victoria and Albert were one year old. The Prince Consort was thus born into and lived through a pestilential era; it is not surprising that with his constitution he succumbed.

Next day, December 8th, when Queen Victoria came into the sick-room the Prince did not know her but called out to Löhlein, his valet, '*Wer ist das?*' The Queen, her heart breaking, kissed his forehead and said it was '*Weibchen*', his little wife. Whereupon he recognized her for a moment – '*Das ist

* See G. Kitson Clark, *The Making of Victorian England*, p. 82 and pp. 104–105.

372

recht' – only to drift away again, angrily imagining that she had opened a letter addressed to him containing bad news about the little Prince Leopold. He called continually for General Bruce, the Prince of Wales's Governor. After wandering about the passages, occasionally rattling at a door-handle, he at last decided to settle in the Blue Room – the King's Room where both George IV and William IV had died. Another Sunday had come round. The Prince asked to hear *'einen schönen Choral'*, from a distance. Princess Alice went next door and played *Eine feste Burg ist unser Gott*, his favourite Lutheran hymn. *'Das reicht hin,'* he said at last, that is enough. As the day advanced he became more feverish, one moment slapping his wife's hand, the next clinging to her, stroking her face and calling her *'liebes Fraüchen'*.[7]

Lord Palmerston, who had been staying in the Castle when the Prince Consort fell ill, had become thoroughly alarmed. A week ago he had begun agitating for a second opinion. On December 9th he demanded that the Prince see Dr Watson, a specialist, together with the aged Sir Henry Holland, who, as Physician-in-Ordinary, could not be left out. Terror seized the Queen lest Albert should be frightened; she described herself as 'almost mad with anxiety & despair', adding that she feared her agony had upset Clark and Jenner. Nevertheless she was forced to agree that Watson should see the Prince; but only once, morning and evening, '& *not* be in the way'. Her opposition had some plausibility for the delirious patient now harboured 'the oddest suspicions & fancies against the doctors'. Dr Watson, whom Albert accepted calmly, spoke of 'improvement' and Dr Jenner of 'positive gain'. But the patient's weary lament did not cease: 'if only Stockmar were here . . .' The Queen afterwards persuaded herself that if Stockmar had not brought his visits to an end the Prince would still be alive.[8]

Bulletins were issued on Wednesday, December 11th, for the first time. To the Queen this was an overwhelming sign of doom; she dropped her Journal and did not resume it until December 24th. (To the public the bulletins appeared so mild as to be scarcely interesting.) The Prince's alternations of clarity and incoherence kept her on the rack. He laid his head on her shoulder murmuring, 'It is very comfortable like that, *dear Child*'. But in a moment he was gazing wildly round the room.

'Let us pray to the Almighty!'

'You always do, more than anyone else.'

'But not together.' He seized her hands, putting them between his own.[9]

Finally his anxieties focused on the Princess Royal's health. He turned to Princess Alice. Had she told her sister anything?

'Yes, I told her you are very ill.'

'You did wrong: you should have told her that I am dying. Yes, I am dying.'

In the evening he begged the Queen to come back after dinner and then summoned her from bed. 'I flew over, so happy that he wished to see me.' Dr Brown, however, said he must rest. 'If you don't wish to stay, go,' muttered the Prince, 'but it's the only time you can see me.' Miserably she tried to explain that she must not stay. Perhaps Dr Brown's insistence was due to the fact that an ominous change in the Prince's breathing had been noted. 'Oh, if I had only done as he wished!' she lamented after he was dead.

He could see the Blue Room reflected in a mirror and thought he was back in the nightmarish gloom of Holyrood Palace. She had his pillows lowered so that the mirror and its ghoulish reflections were out of sight. All this time the physicians were placating his restlessness by having him moved from bed to sofa and wheeled from room to room. The Queen would sprinkle his sheets with eau-de-cologne to revive him and follow him with smelling salts. As he passed his favourite picture at the Blue Room door, a Raphael Madonna, he would stop to gaze at it and say, 'It helps me through half the day'.

Thursday was still a day of hope though he lay listless and panting.

At 8 am on Friday, December 13th she found him not asleep but lying with blank, open eyes, his breath coming in shallow gasps. She helped him on to the wheeled sofa. He did not look at the Madonna by the door and in the next room stared fixedly out of the window. The Queen burst into tears. Jenner warned her of congestion of the lungs, adding that his own judgement might be impaired by lack of sleep. After luncheon, when the Blue Room had 'warmed up', the Prince was moved back. Victoria struggled out on to the Terrace. Weeping with anxiety, she returned to hear that there had been a sudden sinking with cold shivers; now he had rallied. Jenner did not tell her that for an hour he had despaired. Princess Alice summoned her brother, the Prince of Wales, from Cambridge but so cautiously that he carried out a dinner engagement, caught the last train and arrived at 3 am full of cheerful conversation. He was aghast at what he found. Augusta Bruce tried to sustain the distraught Queen: 'I prayed & cried as if I should go mad. *Oh!* that I was not then & there crazed! I can't attempt description for he was my life!'

She found the Prince warm and comfortable. '*Gutes Fraüchen*,' he whispered and kissed her. She went to dinner, for the first time unchanged, but could eat nothing. When she came back at nine to say goodnight the doctors would not let her approach.

She was allowed to sit at the foot of the bed with Princess Alice on the floor, while brandy was administered every half-hour and the doctors said he continued to improve. Dr Watson, whom the poor Queen now found 'very kind', explained that it was a crisis, a trial of strength. He had seen infinitely worse cases recover: 'I never despair with fever.'[10]

To describe the Prince Consort's death proved a task for many years beyond Queen Victoria's powers. She tried once on December 24th, 1861 and again on March 27th, 1862; it was not until February 1872 that she at last wrote the date 'Saturday, December 14th' and found the courage to describe from notes scrawled at the time 'this dreadful day'. The struggle between Queen Victoria's emotions and her ruthless, self-imposed duty to her Journal was one of the strangest elements in her sufferings.

After a night of hourly, hopeful messages, she was visited at 6 am by Dr Brown with good news: 'I've no hesitation in saying . . . that I think there is ground to hope the crisis is over.' At seven she came to the Blue Room door, saw the 'sad look of night-watching', the candles burnt down to their sockets, the group of doctors with anxious faces. Then she went in.

'Never can I forget how beautiful my Darling looked lying there with his face lit up by the rising sun, his eyes unusually bright gazing as it were on unseen objects & not taking notice of me.'[11]

At last, after weeks of fever, the Prince's face had recaptured the ethereal lines of youth.

In the course of the bright, calm morning the invalid was wheeled through into the other room. The Queen needed a breath of air. Yes, she might go out for half an hour if she stayed close by. With Princess Alice she went on to the Terrace but the trumpets of a military band playing at a distance were too much for her and she came in crying bitterly. Dr Watson could only say he was not worse. 'We are very much frightened but don't & won't give up hope.'

The Queen noticed that Prince Albert's face had 'a dusky hue'. He spoke of the railway and a journey. They wanted to change his bed but dared not. At 5.30 pm the bed was pushed forward from the wall, ready for the end. He said 'Gutes Fraüchen', as on the day before, kissed her, '& then gave a sort of piteous moan or rather more sigh not of pain but as if he felt that he was leaving me, & laid his head on my shoulder'.[12] His mind wandered; sometimes he spoke in French, worrying over the young Orleans princes who had enlisted in the American forces and might find themselves fighting against England.

Would he see the Prince of Wales? Queen Victoria was afraid it might agitate him but he said he would. His children, except for the baby, came in and kissed his hand. He took no notice. Later he revived and asked for Phipps, his private secretary. Then the Keeper of the Privy Purse and Master of the Household took leave; both broke down but the Queen with heroic self-command remained quietly sitting at his side. Dr Watson motioned her to offer him a sip of brandy. She

376

shook her head. Her hand was the only thing she could not control.

They changed his bed. He got out by himself but could not get back again unaided. The Queen went to lie down next door. Suddenly she heard heavy breathing. She ran in. '*Es ist das kleine Fraüchen*,' she whispered tremulously, leaning over him; he moved his head. She asked for '*ein Kuss*' and he moved his lips. For a moment she rushed out of the Blue Room, throwing herself in anguish to the ground. The brave, faithful Alice called her back, for the end was near.

'Oh, this is death,' cried the Queen, taking his left hand, already cold, and kneeling down. 'I know it. I have seen *this* before.'[13]

Princess Alice knelt on the other side, the Prince of Wales and Princess Helena at the foot, Ernest Leiningen, the doctors and Löhlein nearby, Phipps, Dean Wellesley and General Bruce opposite the Queen, Marie Leiningen and Augusta Bruce in the doorway. Gathered in the Corridor were the gentlemen of the Household, some in their splendid Windsor uniforms, after dining, others in morning clothes.

'Two or three long but perfectly gentle breaths were drawn, the hand clasping mine, & (oh! it turns me sick to write it) *all all* was over . . . I stood up, kissing his dear heavenly forehead & called out in a bitter agonising cry: "Oh! my dear Darling!" & then dropped on my knees in mute, distracted despair, unable to utter a word or shed a tear!'[14]

The time was a quarter to eleven. Phipps lifted her up and he and Prince Leiningen carried her into the Red Room where she lay half-stunned on the sofa. 'We heard her loud sobs as she went off to her solitary room,' wrote Dean Wellesley to his brother.[15] After a short while she was able to see her children, promising to live for them. The Prince of Wales ran into her arms.

'Indeed, Mama, I will be all I can to you.' She kissed him again and again.

377

'I am sure, my dear boy, you will.' Her Household filed past.

'You will not desert me? You will all help me?' They pledged unswerving devotion to her and received in return her pledge of unswerving devotion to duty. Lord Alfred Paget sobbed out that he had been in waiting at her marriage and was in waiting *now*. Then Sir James Clark came for her and led her back into the Blue Room.

> 'Oh! that I can even now write it – & that I did not go out of my mind! – I went in alone with that kind, fatherly old Friend – who so loved us both . . .'

At first she dared not look. Then she took courage and kissed his forehead. As she came out she met the Duchess of Atholl.

'Oh! Duchess, he is dead! He is dead!'

The weeping Duchess and Miss Hildyard, the children's governess, were both taken in by the Queen to kiss the cold hand. Before going to her bedroom she visited the nursery, lifted the baby out of her cot without waking her and held her in her arms.

The worst moments were to come.

'I went to my room & there sat gazing wildly & as hard as a stone on my Maids . . .' They got her to bed. Princess Alice had her own bed moved into the room but the Queen could neither weep nor sleep. The Princess sent for Jenner who gave the Queen a mild opiate. For a little while she closed her eyes, then woke and at last the agonizing, comforting tears poured down. She cried and cried and slept.

It was about midnight. In London men were hastening home across the Park. Among them was Lord Rosslyn, author of many poems and close friend of the Royal Family.

> *I heard a sound by night that chilled my blood*
> *And smote upon each sense;*
> *And as I hurried by I sudden stood*
> *In listening most intense.*

It was the bell of St Paul's Cathedral which Lord Rosslyn heard, tolling for the end of a noble life and a great happiness.

Part Two

CHAPTER XXII

STILL DECEMBER
1861–4

WHEN THE PRINCE CONSORT died a despairing cry broke from the Queen that a whole reign was finished and a new one begun. In a sense she was right. Hitherto the routine business of the Crown had been shared by a man; a conscientious, analytical man whose religion was work and who held that every human being, including his wife, was capable of unlimited improvement if they only tried hard enough. A man of stiff reserve, lacking in flair and deficient in humour, though equipped with self-critical irony and Germanic playfulness; an idealist who believed in all the great mid-nineteenth century syntheses: science and religion, art and industry, capital and labour, self-help and social service. The masses he distrusted but there was nothing in Disraeli's gibe that had the Prince lived he would have given England the benefits of absolute government.

What sort of woman had Prince Albert bequeathed to the nation? Politically she was a natural partisan, cured of Whig bias but not of the instinct to take sides. Her Hanoverian self-will was 'improved' though she was still subject to impatient and hysterical outbursts. She hated any change even when it was for the better, especially changes of government. She approved of social reform when there was no 'excitement' i.e. no imperative demand. She had little opportunity to see for herself the squalor of mid-Victorian Britain. Her advisers accused the reformers of exaggeration or counted on the slums being decently draped in bunting when she visited them. When she drove through a landscape too vast in its obscenity to be concealed, she was deeply shocked. Of the Black Country in 1852 she wrote:

'It is like another world. In the midst of so much wealth, there seems to be nothing but ruin. As far as the eye can reach, one sees nothing but chimneys, flaming furnaces, many deserted but not pulled down, with wretched cottages around them . . .'. Add to this a thick & black atmosphere . . . & you have but a faint impression of the life . . . which a 3rd of a million of my poor subjects are forced to lead. It makes me sad!'[1]

Hustle and bustle got on her nerves even when it meant leaving Windsor for Osborne or Osborne for Balmoral. In the autumn of 1858 she expressed disgust at the change to Scotland only to break her heart again when it was time to leave. Her interest both in Court functions and politics was fitful: she felt a standing temptation long before she was widowed to retreat into a private world. If not flurried, she was zestful and energetic, admiring the same qualities in others. The way little Prince Arthur threw himself into a reel was splendid; the Prince of Wales's habit of lounging around, maddening. 'Idleness is really sinful.' She thought monarchs should be reasonable but 'decided'[2]: as a young woman she had brusquely condemned Hamlet, Prince of Denmark, for 'pottering'.

She was not squeamish if suitably fortified by a protective male. With her first father-figure, Melbourne, she discussed miscarriages, breast-feeding, opening medicines and other mysteries. Under Prince Albert's supervision she could stomach almost anything except Shakespeare's *Merry Wives of Windsor*. After his death she became timid and prudish, though she recommended Mrs Browning's *Aurora Leigh* to the Princess Royal despite its 'dreadful coarseness' – 'poetry I like in all shapes'. With science her reaction was the reverse. 'Clever scientific people are now a positive necessity for me.'[3] Accordingly she learnt that the moon was uninhabited, Jupiter as light as cork and the kangaroo properly possessed of a pouch. Professor Tyndall, the great physicist, once made lightning for her in test tubes.

She was still shy and nervous. In the middle of a short speech she could dry up, forgetting that she held the script. She became selfishly possessive only after the Prince's death. The betrothal of Mary Bulteel to Henry Ponsonby (1861) was received with flawless kindness – 'It gives us great pleasure for both their sakes'[4] – in painful contrast to the howls of rage which greeted Lady Augusta Bruce's engagement to Dean Stanley (1863): 'My dear Lady Augusta, at 41 . . . has most unnecessarily, decided to *marry* (!!) . . . *I* thought she *never* would leave *me*!' Of Victoria Wortley's marriage in the same year she wrote flatly: 'I grudge any change in the Household now.'[5]

In Prince Albert's day duty was duty, whatever the weather: she had launched the *Marlborough* at Spithead in a gale, for 'rain or no rain, it *must* take place'. Above all, he had been slowly teaching her to 'take things as God sent them'.[6] Before the lesson was fully learned the teacher himself was sent for.

It was not until December 16th that the Queen could write a line. Then she scrawled a chaotic note to the Princess Royal:

'God's will be done! A heavenly peace has descended . . . it cannot be possible . . . Oh! God! Oh! God! . . . but I feel I can bear it better today . . . I don't know what I feel . . .'

Two days later the cry was clearer:

'How am I alive after witnessing what I have done? Oh! I who prayed daily that we might die together & I never survive Him! I who felt when in those blessed Arms clasped & held tight in the sacred Hours at night – when the world seemed only to be ourselves that nothing could part us! I felt so vy secure – I always repeated: "And God will protect us!" though trembling always for his safety . . . I never dreamt of the physical possibility of such a calamity – such an awful catastrophe – for me – for All . . .'[7]

Yet apart from occasional paroxysms of weeping, her Household were astonished at her submissiveness. On the Sunday following the Prince's death she wished to take the Duchess of Sutherland into the Blue Room. Her doctors warned her not to kiss the body. Meekly she obeyed, embracing his clothes instead. One more visit later that day; then she decided not to go again lest this last 'sad though lovely image' should be printed too deeply on her mind. The room was meticulously photographed so that it might be cleaned but not changed. She slept with his night-shirt in her arms and a cast of his hand within reach. Over the empty pillow she hung his portrait crowned with a wreath of ever-greens. The borders of her handkerchiefs and writing-paper, already black from her mother, had to be increased to almost an inch. A photograph was ordered of herself and her children grouped around Albert's bust – 'the dear, dear protecting head'. Her Household could not conceive how she would carry on alone; they expected a breakdown and told their friends so. 'The poor Queen, the poor Queen,' they murmured as they passed one another in the silent Corridor.

She had never done a thing without the Prince Consort, not even chosen a bonnet. He had drafted all her letters saying that writing them out in her own hand was burden enough. To him she owed all the private jokes which made official life bearable: jokes about the City father who passed her throne with his wife's cloak on his arm or the provincial worthies who went by at a gallop and then returned for a closer look.

The Queen's initial calm was due partly to numbness, partly to a vow she had taken over the 'sacred remains'. Henceforth every action, every thought would be guided by the commands of her Angel, of which one still rang in her ears: 'Your great task in life is to control your feelings.' The Princess Royal would find her mother 'less unworthy' when they met again.[8] Her initial efforts at restraint were more heroic than wise. 'Crying does me good,' she had written to King Leopold after her mother died. With Princess Beatrice, however, she found some relief, encouraging Baby to climb on her bed every morning and prattle about dear Papa. 'What a pity it is that I was too little to be at your marriage.'

King Leopold lost no time in getting her away from Windsor, despite Princess Alice's disapproval of this up-rooting. 'The parting was a terrible moment,' wrote Lady Augusta Bruce. 'She felt on leaving that all that could be taken

384

from her of him, had been . . ."[9] She moved to Osborne on December 19th. Just before landing at Cowes she requested the support of the Duchess of Atholl, who passed on a vivid impression of the encounter to Mrs Biddulph:

> 'I have not yet recovered [from] the *desolate* look of that young face in Her *Widow's* cap! for somehow the Queen looked like a *child*! – And then her passionate embrace! – I felt – *what* was there that I would not do for her!'[10]

At midnight Duke Ernest staggered in, dripping wet from a wild sea crossing, and the pair mingled their wails with the storm outside.

Sleepless or haunted by terrible dreams, she would resort next day to her little book of *Remarks – Conversations – Reflections*, and under the drawing of a black cross clasped by two despairing arms, utter a brief cry:

> '*What* a dreadful going to bed! *What* a contrast to that tender lover's love! *All Alone! Yet* – The blessings of 22 years *cast* its reflection! –'[11]

Or she would screw herself up to dictate reminiscences of her married life. Having recorded the highlights she turned to the regrets. How she would stay so late over a novel that Albert was asleep when she came to bed; how she interrupted him reading *The Times*: 'Dear Darling – I fear I tried him sadly.' How she wanted to stop him bolting his meals, while still studying – 'Not so fast, there's plenty of time' – and how she kept sending the page to get him out of the dining-room – 'You've been terribly long' – and then pestered him not to hang over the fire. Lastly, all the delightful things she would renounce for ever: she would never make another 'Journey Album' nor play duets – 'poor music – it will *never* be touched again' – nor visit Aldershot, nor wear a *décolleté* dress because he was not there to admire her shoulders – '*Die Frau hat gar hübsche Schultern.*'[12] Her task done she sank into an emotional coma, anxious only to convince the world that the pain was getting worse not better. When the primroses came out at Osborne it was for her '*still* in the month of December'.[13]

Before leaving Windsor the Queen had walked down to Frogmore. There, near her mother's tomb, she chose a spot for the Mausoleum 'for us'. As she pined alone at Osborne, getting back old letters, appointing guardians for her younger children, making her will and working at unintelligible State papers – 'am never in bed before 12' – she felt certain that by the time the Mausoleum was completed she too would be inside it. Until then, 'I will, I *will* do my duty', she would cry aloud, throwing up her window and gazing out on the grey sea.[14]

The Queen intended Prince Albert's Mausoleum to be no '*Sterbezimmer*', no death chamber, but a bright monument to his living glory. Not so the room prepared for Princess Alice's marriage seven months after his death. Here was a *Sterbezimmer* indeed. 'Alice's wedding,' she wrote to the Princess Royal, was 'more like a funeral'. A black trousseau; the Queen wearing her widow's cap – poor Ma's sad cap, as Princess Beatrice called it – hunched in a chair near the altar with her three sons stationed like mutes between her and any peeping Tom; she saw to it that though the ceremony took place in July it was 'still December'.

Overpowering lassitude prevented the Queen from taking proper exercise, talking to more than one person at a time, getting up for breakfast or dining with the family. It did not prevent her from covering the landscape with Albert memorials. Forgotten was the advice once given by Lord Melbourne never to waste her money on memorials. There was one stone to mark where Prince Albert had shot his last stag at Balmoral and another for his last shoot at Windsor; there was the colossal statue in the Horticultural Garden whose neck, she thought, was too thin and shoulders 'not quite right'; there was the Highland statue at Perth with its vast bronze kilt and the pyramid at Craig Lowrigan inscribed with a verse from the *Book of Wisdom*. Most absorbing of all was the great national memorial in Kensington.

In matters of art she desperately needed the help of the departed. How much too easily satisfied she was; it had always been the Prince's role to sharpen her critical faculties. The Albert Memorial, with her Angel holding the catalogue of the

Great Exhibition against his dear knee, was not entirely worthy of its object. The chest was too hollow, the back too round and the left leg drawn up too high; but at any rate – 'It can be seen from a great distance.'

Queen Victoria's feelings about death are generally dismissed as plain morbid. As a young woman, however, her views were healthy. During an argument about burial Melbourne claimed that nothing could be nicer than to be disembowelled and stuffed with spices. Victoria replied firmly, 'I should like to be *burnt* after I died.'[15]

Any youthful mawkishness was primarily romantic. When two young acquaintances lost their husbands, she wrote minute descriptions of the widow's cap and fixed expression broken only by a fleeting smile for the fatherless children. Some years later Lady Jocelyn's husband dropped dead from cholera in Lady Palmerston's drawing-room. Queen Victoria again noted the frozen 'irreparable sorrow' in the widow's face. Essentially a woman of her time, she donned this ritual mask when her own turn came.

Many of her ladies, such as Jane Marchioness of Ely and Lady Caroline Barrington, were widows, one reason of course being that they were free and glad of an occupation. But sentiment entered in. After her bereavement she built up something like a Sacred College of Vestal Widows. They must tend the flame of their sorrow (and of her convenience) for ever. Remarriage was blasphemy.

Frank interest in death-bed scenes was quite normal. Partly because Victorians cared passionately about religion, the moment of passing from this world to the next was not one to be hushed up. Only paupers died in hospital so opportunities for study were plentiful. The young Victoria collected from Queen Adelaide the 'painfully interesting details of the King's last illness'. Today we are interested in sex and the marriage bed has supplanted the death bed in our literature.

A line, of course, had to be drawn somewhere and Queen Victoria drew it at the English Channel. On the Continent all sorts of extravagances were permitted. When the Princess Royal had to stand throughout the interminable death throes of the King of Prussia, Queen Victoria shared her daughter's disgust. In her eyes, the typical German *Sterbezimmer*, embalmed in dust for generations, was the antithesis of the Blue Room, which had its ceiling 'beautifully though simply' redecorated and was embellished with new china, pictures and the Prince's bust between the two beds which had shared his last hours. All mausoleums interested the Queen: she admired King Leopold's ingenuity in adapting Princess Charlotte's summer-house for this purpose: she respected Duke Ernest's delicacy in burying his divorced mother in the family vault at Coburg but not in his father's sarcophagus. Yet *our* Mausoleum at Frogmore was unique precisely because it banished gloom.

Queen Victoria was unable to live up to her ideal. Setting out with the resolve to rescue death from morbidity, she was eventually convicted of it herself. The explanation must be found in her failure to reconcile the claims of public life and private life. Had she fulfilled her State functions adequately, opening Parliament, holding drawing-rooms, driving among her subjects, few would have criticized her for having the Prince Consort's clothes laid out each evening with hot water and a clean towel. Many bereaved Victorians were going almost as far. Lord Brougham's daughter Eleanor died at nineteen and he kept her room untouched all his life. Royal death-chambers were rarely disturbed – except by revolution. Lord Redesdale in 1864 found Tsar Nicholas's bedroom exactly as he had died in it nine years before: brush, comb and shaving tackle ready for use. Lord Redesdale was touched. 'Altogether a pathetic sight!' Similarly when Queen Victoria visited her Uncle Leopold at Laeken Palace in 1852 she found 'dear Louise's room' unaltered. If she had cleared and re-allocated her husband's room she would have considered herself lacking in true love. Even King Edward VII left undisturbed the last tube of tooth-paste used by his dead son, Prince Albert Victor. He is not a byword for morbidity.

Not unnaturally the country hoped that Her Majesty would soon be able to resume her official life. They did not realize how depleted were her resources even before the blow fell.

Thanks to the secrecy surrounding Prince Albert's health, no one guessed the weight of Queen Victoria's anxiety during his last years. She herself had almost forgotten. When Stockmar died in July 1863 her old letters were returned to her and she was surprised to find them so full of alarm, especially over 'his poor dear stomach'.

Courtiers who had to bear the brunt of a house of mourning tended to accuse her doctors of prescribing seclusion purely because Her Majesty ordered them to do so. They suspected that the spirit was weak but the flesh was strong. The public could not imagine any mourning lasting more than three years. Yet there seems reason to believe that the shock to Queen Victoria's system caused the kind of temporary physiological changes which modern drugs can alleviate. It is useful to recall the 'peculiarities' (Sir James Clark's word) of her system.

As a child she had been active, excitable, highly strung, with prominent eyes and great resistance to infection, good teeth, hair and skin and vivid emotions, easily aroused. Most of her life she required a constant supply of fresh, cold air. At seventeen she already recognized this peculiarity in herself, complaining that a hot July was 'quite dreadful for me, *who love cold,* & am always poorly & stupified in hot weather'.[16] As Queen, her passion for low temperatures became a byword and many were the shivering courtiers who longed to modify her partiality for draughts. There were two occasions in her life when severe shock seems to have done it for them. In 1835 the combination of Sir John Conroy and typhoid rendered her for months too weak to walk, her extremities remaining numb and cold despite constant massage. After Prince Albert's death she lost weight yet her legs would hardly carry her; she felt the cold, suffered from neuralgic headaches and became engulfed in a lethargic depression from which all the time she longed to escape.

It is often suggested that the trouble was her time of life. There is no evidence for this theory. When the Prince Consort died she was only forty-two and felt younger; despite her violent attitude towards childbearing, she was hoping for another child. The Princess Royal, indeed, emphasized that

389

much of poor Mama's misery was due to bitter disappointment. The onset of the change could only have increased not caused a neurosis which already had her in its grip.

The first clash between grief and duty occurred when the Queen professed herself unable to receive her Ministers personally; they must communicate through General Grey or Princess Alice. (General Sir Charles Grey, the late Prince's secretary, was now acting in this position for the Queen. It was characteristic of a certain obtuseness, not to say jealousy, in Ministers that the harassed widow had to wait until 1867 before her need for help with government business was recognized and Grey formally appointed private secretary.) Lord Russell* promptly rapped her over the knuckles. She submitted with a good grace, commenting on Lord Palmerston's kindness at a subsequent audience and tactfully ignoring his green gloves and blue studs.

Underneath she was steeling herself against the next thrust. They intended to push her, she believed, always a little further than she could go. This became the growing-point of her neurosis. As the pressures increased so she would brace herself against them, refusing in the end to perform public duties of which she was perfectly capable for fear of being pressed into others beyond her strength. Her early seclusion, at any rate, shows an instinct for self-preservation. She knew and 'they' did not how near she was to a breakdown. Three times during her first visit as a widow to Balmoral she feared that the pressure of incomprehensible business on top of her frantic grief was driving her insane. Considering the Prince's many warnings of what would happen if she lost control, her alarm was understandable.

One of the Queen's first friends to visit her after the Prince's death was Colonel Francis Seymour (afterwards Lord Hertford), in February 1862. He came away with a picture of

'the most desolate and unhappy of God's creatures but one gifted by Him with a strength of mind . . . seldom if ever granted to a woman.'

* Lord John Russell had been created Earl Russell in 1861.

There had been one perilous moment when Queen Victoria, having told Colonel Seymour that the Prince had caught the fever from watching 'old earth' being turned up at the International Exhibition, added that he had been killed by 'that dreadful business at the Curragh . . .' 'Oh, no, Madam,' interposed Colonel Seymour hastily.[17]

Lord Derby also saw the Queen, and Disraeli, who heard about the audience from Derby's son, wrote down some of the Queen's more significant remarks:

'The Queen talked freely of the Prince: he *would* die – he seemed not to care to live. Then she used the words "He died from want of what they call pluck." '[18]

This story rings true. Much the same thought was to strike the Queen during the following year when her son Alfred narrowly escaped death from typhoid: 'like his beloved Father', he had shown 'a great want of stamina, a power of the heart to fight the fever'.[19] Queen Victoria generally interpreted the Prince's failure to fight for life as saintly acceptance of God's will. But she was human, and in certain moods the 'Coburg melancholy' must have seemed a defect, causing the Prince to desert her.

In June 1862 Lord Clarendon, a guest at Windsor, reeled under the full horror of Queen Victoria's nightmare. She was warm and welcoming until the moment when she mentioned an Opposition attack on the Government. Then her manner became strangely excited. Tapping her forehead she reiterated the warning cry, 'My reason, my reason.' Any political crisis would send her mad. He must tell the Leader of the Opposition, Lord Derby, the truth. Clarendon at once obliged and according to this story persuaded the Opposition to hold their fire for that Session.*[20] Persistent rumours that the Queen was insane were foolishly contradicted during the following year by Lord Clarendon to a free-lance journalist named

* A number of writers attribute this incident to 1863. Their error appears to have originated in a confusing phrase on p. 315 of George Villiers's life of Clarendon, *A Vanished Victorian*. ('Another year dawned.') The chapter concludes quite clearly, however, with the words, 'And so 1862 ended . . .' See also *My Dear Duchess*, p. 188.

Mulock, who promptly published Clarendon's letter in April 1863, adding that some people 'in aristocratic circles' were saying the Queen believed her husband to be still alive.[21]

It is sometimes suggested that her advisers made a mistake in allowing Queen Victoria to hide at Osborne for as long as two months after her bereavement; they should have forced her back to Windsor and Buckingham Palace before it was too late. This is to misunderstand the Queen's affliction. She was not an hysteric in search of a sharp slap but someone disabled by a fearful wound.

> *I am going a long way . . .*
> *To the island-valley of Avilion . . .*
> *Where I will heal me of my grievous wound.*

Queen Victoria's Avilion was rarely undisturbed and she repaid her tormentors by spinning out her recovery over twenty long years. Not that she equated the Isle of Avilion with the Isle of Wight. She did not look forward to returning from her seclusion like King Arthur even in the most legendary future. She expected to die within a year.

The next clash quickly followed when the Queen was required to attend a Privy Council. She declined. A solution was found by the new Clerk, who bore the encouraging name of Arthur Helps. Queen Victoria was persuaded to station herself in one room while Helps and three Privy Councillors occupied another, with the door open between; as each item was read out, Helps solemnly replied on her behalf, 'Approved'.

If Queen Victoria had reflected she would have seen that many of dearest Albert's laws were already being broken. Instead of seeking outside interests, she was withdrawing; instead of cultivating the present, she was dedicating herself to the past. He used to chide her for 'looking before and after', building castles in the air or sighing for past delights. Now she was not even building castles. 'It is terrible,' she wrote to the Princess Royal, 'never to look forward to the future but only backwards.'

In other respects, however, she clung tenaciously to Prince

Albert's law. He had mapped out his eldest son's future before he died. In the spring of 1862 the Prince of Wales would make a tour of Palestine followed by marriage, it was hoped, to Princess Alexandra of Denmark.

The Prince's departure was fortunate, for his mother could not look at him without a shudder. At first she shuddered at the 'disgusting details'[22] of his affair at the Curragh. But when the Princess Royal leapt to her brother's defence – dear Mama must try to see his good qualities also – the Queen shifted her ground: her shudder was due to the *result* of the affair. Bertie had broken Papa's heart.[23]

No attitude could have been more unfair nor hurtful to the Queen herself. For despite the slashing attacks she launched at intervals against most of her offspring, at heart she wanted to think the best of 'our children'. At the root of her trouble with the Prince of Wales lay her old obsession about his being a 'caricature' of herself. How could a caricature occupy the throne? Yet she was daily praying for death to take her, when precisely this situation would arise. The Queen's monomania had landed her in a dilemma as pathetic as it was futile.

The Prince of Wales returned from abroad, 'much improved' and bringing Turkish finery for the little ones to dress up in. No more was heard of the Queen's shudders. Only one new sorrow marred their reunion. General Bruce, his Governor, died of a fever contracted on the tour. 'I thought how mysterious this fresh loss was.' To whom could 'the poor boy' now turn for moral support?[24] The Queen bemoaned the lack of suitable counsellors to take his beloved father's place. Fond as she was of Lord Granville and Lord Clarendon, only Mr Gladstone and a few others would understand how she felt about his 'fall'.[25]

As the Prince was nearly twenty-one she appointed a Comptroller instead of a new Governor. He was General Knollys, son of the man to whom her father had commended Madame de St Laurent. Royalty lived in a small world.

Nothing remained but to see her son married. Yet for all her impatience, she would not have him forced into an engagement. 'Alix', she told the Princess Royal, must not dress herself up smartly 'to catch the poor boy' as foolish English girls did; nor must the fact that poor Bertie was 'a regular *mauvais sujet*' be concealed from Alix's family lest 'the poor girl' be trapped into a life of misery.[26] The Princess Royal was accordingly asked to inform Princess Alexandra's mother

> 'that *wicked wretches* had led our poor innocent Boy into a scrape wh had caused his beloved father & myself the deepest pain . . . but that both of us – had forgiven him this (*one*) *sad mistake* . . . & that I was very confident he wld make a steady Husband . . . I looked to his wife as being HIS SALVATION . . .'[27]

In September she visited Coburg and on the way met Princess Alexandra for whose charms she immediately fell.

The Prince was left behind to make his proposal which he afterwards described with an abundance of detail calculated to gladden any mother's heart.

> '. . . She immediately said *yes*. But I told her not to answer too quickly but to consider over it. She said she had long ago. I then asked her if she liked me. She said *yes*. I then kissed her hand and she kissed me . . .'[28]

Between the engagement and marriage the Queen 'got to know' the Princess who emerged triumphant from ten days' grilling at Osborne.* She was 'a jewel dropped from the skies': Lenchen 'adored her', Louise 'kept in her place' without grumbling and Affie would have married her at once if Bertie had turned her down. To the Queen's main requirements for her son's bride – beauty, goodness and education – she had, as we saw, added a character which would not 'knock under'. Whether Princess Alexandra possessed this quality was doubtful but there might be compensations in her soft compliance. The political aspect of this royal marriage presented difficulties.

The Prince Consort had given a simple ruling : there were no political aspects. His ruling was already out of date.

* Four to five weeks had been the Queen's wish but Princess Alexandra's family asked to have her home for her eighteenth birthday on December 1st. General Grey wrote : 'The Queen acceded to the arrangement in the kindest manner, and without a moment's hesitation.' (Grey to Paget, Nov. 8th, 1862, Paget MS, British Museum.)

Trouble between Denmark and Prussia made the marriage anathema to Bismarck who interpreted it as support by Britain for the Danes. Queen Victoria hoped to teach her daughter-in-law political detachment, arranging that she should have no Danish maids lest she held conversations unintelligible to her husband.[29]

On March 5th, 1863 the marriage took place in St George's Chapel, Windsor. Guests were staggered by the magnificence of the ceremony and appalled by the lack of rehearsal. Lord Palmerston and Lady Westminster had to travel back third class on the special train, the latter loaded with half a million pounds' worth of diamonds. Disraeli sat on his wife's lap. Before the ceremony, the Garter Knights, whose robes took the beholders' breath away, rushed forward in a bunch instead of processing up the aisle two by two.

For Baby Beatrice it meant an uncovenanted treat. 'I *never* thought there was *stays* in shops,' she exclaimed as she drove round Windsor with the royal visitors. For little Prince William of Prussia it was a first opportunity to defy the English. He threw his aunt's muff out of the carriage window and the cairngorm from his dirk across the Chapel floor. When his youthful uncles reproved him he sank his baby teeth into their bare knees. His sombre grandmama he addressed familiarly as 'duck'.[30]

The Queen's personal arrangements were flawless. Having reached the Chapel by a specially constructed covered way which led direct into the darkness of Catherine of Aragon's Closet, high above the altar, she stepped forward when the ceremony began, shaking with nerves but able to smile at Princess Beatrice and appreciate the Princess Royal's deep curtsy. It was only when the sound of silver trumpets pierced her as never before that she suddenly felt faint. The wedding breakfast was not graced with her presence; '*I* lunched alone.' After the guests had departed she drove to the Mausoleum '& prayed by that beloved resting-place, feeling soothed & calmed'. As she had observed earlier, 'the gas-light shone softly on the beloved features' and seemed as beautiful to her then as it would now to Mr Betjeman.

It is difficult to defend Queen Victoria's precautions against enjoying the wedding herself or giving pleasure to others. One can sympathize, however, with her desire to frustrate the morbid curiosity aroused by her widowhood. Even a dim retreat like the Closet in St George's was not proof against inquisitive glances. Benjamin Disraeli shamelessly raised his quizzing glass to the Queen; Majesty gave him such a look that he did not try again. Nevertheless, though widows had a right to hide themselves, queens had a duty to be looked at. Which was Disraeli quizzing, widow or queen? When two conflicting mystiques clashed in one temperamental woman there was no easy solution.

The first political problem presented to the widowed Queen concerned Prince Alfred. He was offered the vacant throne of Greece in 1862. Queen Victoria, though flattered, knew it would never do. Prince Albert had marked out his second son from birth to succeed the childless Ernest, Duke of Saxe-Coburg; moreover her Ministers explained that the great powers were pledged not to put up rival kings for Greece. A rumour spread that Lord Derby would go; but no, he preferred Knowsley to the Parthenon. To Queen Victoria's intense indignation Duke Ernest himself, supported by King Leopold, accepted the Greek throne in place of Prince Alfred but insisted on retaining his Coburg dukedom as well. The astute Queen at once saw that Prince Alfred, as caretaker at Coburg, would be made responsible for his uncle's 'sad misgovernment' and his even sadder debts. After a tussle Duke Ernest agreed to stand down in favour of a Dane, Princess Alexandra's brother.

The episode is important as showing Queen Victoria, who at this period piteously described herself to King Leopold as a poor hunted hare or lost child, able to do battle with both her nearest surviving male relatives. Soon after this victory, the Queen heard that Prince Alfred had got into a scrape with a lady at Malta. She took it hard and complained that the Prince of Wales was concealing from her part of the truth. This was 'too bad', since she knew all about his own 'misfortune'.[31] The hunted hare was fast becoming an insistent matriarch.

The contest with Duke Ernest was nothing to the stern political warfare in which the Queen next had to engage. Soon after Prince Albert's death, King William of Prussia, advised by Bismarck, fell foul of his own parliament. In his perplexity he offered to abdicate in favour of his son the Crown Prince. Queen Victoria approved but Fritz and Vicky, with the throne suddenly at their disposal, were distracted by doubts. Meanwhile King William changed his mind and instead created Bismarck his chief Minister. The Crown Prince and Princess thereupon violently opposed Bismarck, becoming so unpopular that they decided to withdraw temporarily from public life. Queen Victoria invited them to England. Albert, she *knew*, would agree. 'They shall come here!' She could hear his voice saying those very words.[32] There is little doubt that Prince Albert would have said the opposite. He would never have left the field to Bismarck. For the Prussian slogan to unite Germany – 'blood and iron' – was about to clang through Europe, incidentally ringing the knell of peace and goodwill in the Queen's family circle.

Bismarck intended that Prussia should eventually challenge Austria's leadership of the German states. He therefore determined to prevent King William from attending a Congress at Frankfurt in a role subservient to Austria. After a titanic struggle, Bismarck at last extracted William's promise not to go. Then he slammed out of the room, wrenching off the door handle as he went.

Queen Victoria, misinterpreting the King's absence from Frankfurt, feared that Prussia was being squeezed out. She forced herself to visit Germany again in 1863 and interviewed both the King of Prussia and Emperor of Austria in the hope of bringing them together. That her interviews accomplished nothing she was candid enough to realize, her most significant recollection being of Bismarck's 'horrid expression'[33] when she happened to run into him afterwards; he deeply resented her interference. On November 15th, 1863 the King of Denmark died. 'What *is* to happen now?' wrote Queen Victoria in her Journal. Bismarck knew.

The Duchies of Schleswig and Holstein, the latter with a massive German population, had not settled down since the

London Protocol of 1852 put them under Danish suzerainty. When the Danish King died and was succeeded by Princess Alexandra's father, Prince Christian of Schleswig-Holstein-Sonderburg-Glucksburg, a cry went up from both the Duchies for self-determination. Three rival princes claimed to rule them. King Christian appealed to the Danish minority while Duke Frederick of Schleswig-Holstein-Augustenburg (Fritz Holstein, married to the Queen's niece, Adelaide Hohenlohe*) disputed with the King of Prussia the allegiance of the German majority. All three candidates obstinately regarded Schleswig-Holstein as a package deal. Whoever had one Duchy had both.

The re-emergence in 1863 of this historical conundrum drew from Palmerston, old and gouty, a memorable epigram. Only three people had ever understood the Schleswig-Holstein question, he said. One was the Prince Consort and he was dead. Another was a German professor and he had gone mad. The third was himself and he had forgotten all about it. What was too complex for Lord Palmerston to remember need not detain us a hundred years later. To the Queen it resolved itself into one poignant question: what would Albert have done?

He had supported the Augustenburg claims in the 'fifties: therefore she began by favouring them. Though sorry for the Danes, she felt the German majority must prevail. When it became clear that Augustenburg was out of the running she gave her support to Prussia; Prussia, which was about to lead her huge ally, the Austrian Empire, against the helpless Danes. For Bismarck had adopted the kind of tactics once recommended to Queen Victoria by Melbourne for dealing with quarrelsome children: 'Let the big "lick" the little and then "lick" both.'

The Queen dreaded a war, partly because it would be fought out at Windsor as well as in Schleswig-Holstein. The family vehemently took sides. Princess Alexandra, expecting her first baby, could think of nothing but poor Papa in Denmark and cried out in her sleep. The country, led by Palmerston and Russell, was traditionally sympathetic towards a small nation like Denmark, besides admiring the

* See page 303.

Wales's brilliant social energy – an agreeable contrast to the Queen's black weepers. The Queen, however, denounced 'those two dreadful old men' for what she considered their mad inconsistency. If they believed in self-determination for the Italians why not for the Holsteiners?

On the other side the Princess Royal bombarded her Mama with furious allegations against England interspersed with savage attacks on Bismarck: 'I could smash the idiots.'[34] At times a coldness developed, the Queen feeling that her daughter's tone to her was 'not quite the thing'. Oh where was Albert to keep this disunited family in their places? Opposed to both the Prince of Wales and Princess Royal were the Augustenburg supporters, including their Aunt Feodore Hohenlohe, who also could be very violent. Queen Victoria finally took Uncle Leopold's advice to forbid any mention of Schleswig-Holstein in her home.

Some indiscreet enthusiasts at Court, notably General Grey, disclosed the Queen's Prussian sympathies. Palmerston rebuked her privately, and Lord Ellenborough in Parliament. She dismissed the first with an acid comment to King Leopold – 'Pilgerstein is gouty' – but the second went deeper. 'The Queen hopes everyone *will* know *how* she resents Lord Ellenborough's conduct,' she wrote, 'and how she despises him!'[35] Everyone did. Nevertheless there were those who thought that Queen Victoria should have taken a leaf out of the Prussian king's book and offered to abdicate when her son attained his majority.

Loyalty towards Prussia led Queen Victoria into worse things than advocating self-determination for Holstein. She supported Russia's brutal suppression of the Polish national rising in 1863. Because it suited Prussia, Queen Victoria found herself straining every nerve to frustrate an attempt by Palmerston and Napoleon III to intervene on the Poles' behalf. 'Don't fear,' she admonished the Princess Royal; 'I have got "the eyes of Argus", in spite of my broken heart.'[36] The eyes of Argus, but for Prince Albert's misconstrued mandate, might have been on worthier objects.

While the Schleswig-Holstein crisis was at its height Princess Alexandra gave birth to a seven-months child, Prince Albert Victor, at Frogmore.* Distress over Denmark's plight was assumed to have brought on the birth and caused the baby's delicacy. This did not make Prussia any more popular. The Queen's comment on the prematurity was characteristic: how touching that this had happened at Frogmore so near the Mausoleum.

'Albert Victor' was a double name much to her liking. She took the opportunity to question her son about his own intentions when he became King – she was, of course, not long for this world – urging him to call himself 'King Albert Edward'. Fortunately this idea went the same way as 'Queen Alexandrina Victoria' in 1837.

The Prussian armies invaded and occupied both Duchies early in 1864. 'God forgive you for it,' wrote Queen Victoria bluntly to her eldest daughter.[37] So catastrophic was the Danes' defeat that Palmerston and Russell feared an attack on Denmark itself. Russell urged the dispatch of British ships to Copenhagen in reply to an Austrian threat to send their fleet. Queen Victoria was horrified. She suffered the 'agonies' of 1859 all over again. 'It is really *too* bad.' Committed to Prince Albert's former watchword of British neutrality, she dinned it into the Prime Minister's irritable ears, until an armistice, signed in April 1864, brought the war to an end without Britain having become involved. Still miscalculating the nature of Prussia's bid for German leadership, Queen Victoria innocently hoped that the victors would now be generous. 'Only make peace,' she wrote to the Princess Royal in July; 'give the Duchies to good Fritz H. [Holstein] & have done with it – & people will be quite satisfied.'[38] Bismarck had other ideas. Prussia and Austria began by sharing the spoils.

Queen Victoria's scuffles with Palmerston and Russell were acclaimed by many, including Lord Granville, as having saved the peace. This is, to say the least, doubtful. The Schleswig-Holstein war was none the less important in the Queen's development. She became more than ever convinced of the

* As it arrived three hours after the Princess had been watching ice-hockey it was said to be 'a n-ice child'.

Sovereign's right to eavesdrop, so to speak, on Cabinet dissensions and to use her knowledge for pushing her own views. When Gladstone challenged this right, she had entrenched herself in precedents.

A happier result of the Schleswig-Holstein affair was to give her confidence in herself. She discovered that she could function without Prince Albert. 'I am glad darling Papa is spared this worry & annoyance,' she wrote to the Princess Royal, 'for he could have done even less than I can.' Lastly she reaffirmed her constitutional duty to accept her Government's decision as final. While privately castigating their anti-Prussianism, she warned the Princess Royal never to quote the Queen's opinions in opposition to her Ministers, 'for THAT beloved Papa never permitted'.[39]

Ever since 1862 Queen Victoria had been fighting on two fronts, against God and man. She could neither show Christian submission nor perform her public functions. At last, in 1864, the spiritual struggle abated. A sense of resignation 'which was so hard for me at first' softened her yearning for the Prince. After a visit to the Mausoleum on June 16th, 1865 she wrote:

'I knelt & prayed by the beloved shrine. Yet thank God! I feel more & more that my beloved one is *everywhere* not only there!'[40]

Meanwhile, the second front, against her subjects, had flared up. Posters appeared in March 1864 outside Buckingham Palace.

'These commanding premises to be let or sold, in consequence of the late occupant's declining business.'

The Times followed with a leg-pull on April Fool's Day:

'Her Majesty's loyal subjects will be very pleased to hear that their Sovereign is about to break her protracted seclusion.'

A similar kite had been flown the year before, announcing that she intended to open Parliament. Promptly she had

401

ordered her doctors to issue a prohibition. This time she decided to beat the Press on their own ground. In the columns of *The Times* an anonymous contradiction was issued whose every dot and dash proclaimed its august authorship. The Queen would fulfil her duty to support Society and encourage trade. 'More than that the Queen *cannot* do . . .' Having made her protest, she succumbed to a bout of neuralgia, Dr Brown advising her to cancel a projected appearance at Court: 'very unfortunate', wrote the Queen, and then, more honestly, 'greatly relieved'. All attempts to force her out of seclusion made her ill and thus drove her back.

Queen Victoria's plunge into journalism dumbfounded her friends but convinced no one, for Sovereign and people were estranged by a genuine misunderstanding. To the Queen, desk-work was enough. If she stuck to her boxes and kept England at peace, what more could she do? Surely they did not want her to ape the showmanship of George IV? Her popularity in the past had depended on 'hard work and domestic purity'.[41] It still did.

The Queen forgot that a monarch must not only work but be seen to work. Or as King Leopold put it: 'the English are very personal; to continue to love people they must see them . . .' Cunningly he fanned her jealousies. Bertie and Alexandra were '*constantly before the public* in EVERY IMAGINABLE SHAPE *and* CHARACTER, and *fill entirely the public mind*'.[42] Princess Alice added her gentler pressure. At last for the first time since Prince Albert's death the Queen drove on June 21st, 1864 in an open carriage. It was just in time, for all the talk abroad was about her forthcoming abdication. How *really* pleased her good people seemed – 'though my poor sad face & garb *must* tell its tale.' Everyone agreed that such enthusiasm never greeted the Waleses.

'Naturally for *them* no one stops, or *runs*, as they always did, & *do* doubly now, for *me*.'[43]

She had attended a flower show, her first public function, three months earlier – significantly, in the 'accursed' Horticultural Garden.

Little by little the Queen was emerging into daylight. But

402

one invincibly gloomy thought remained: that she no longer came first with a single member of her family except perhaps Baby Beatrice and Lenchen. Before 1861 she had been all in all to two precious souls – her mother and her husband. Now her children rightly put their own families first. She often felt '*de trop*' despite their kindness. She had sunk into 'No. 3 or 4 in the real tender love of others'.[44]

This very human feeling was at the bottom of Queen Victoria's insistent denial that her children brought her comfort. In certain moods she admitted that of course their love and solicitude made all the difference. More often she was out to crush any assumption that they could possibly mitigate her overwhelming misery. Indeed she repudiated many well-meant attempts at consolation, as when a clergyman suggested that she must now see herself as the bride of Christ – 'That is what I call twaddle.'[45] Conversely, she was soothed by those who, like the Duchess of Buccleuch, harped on her loss and could not understand 'how I could at all get on, or work or live'.[46] Queen Victoria preferred Job's comforters.

If she could not come first with her family, there were loving hearts below-stairs in which her image reigned supreme. Her wardrobe maid, Annie Macdonald, who had put her to bed, rigid and tearless, on the night that Prince Albert died, was one. John Brown at Balmoral was another. Late in 1864 Queen Victoria brought him south, to become next year her permanent personal attendant. The results were devastating. Her claim to be hard-working was already under fire. Now her domestic purity laid itself open to challenge.

CHAPTER XXIII

BROWN EMINENCE
THE 1860s

QUEEN VICTORIA at last faced a new year in 1865 with the will to live. Remembering her children, her country and Europe she wrote, 'For all this I must try & live on for a while yet!' Fate, as if to mark this step forward, promptly removed two more of her old props, at the same time presenting her with two powerful new ones.

Lord Palmerston died on October 18th, 1865. '. . . I *never* liked him,' she wrote to her moribund uncle, King Leopold, though his death had snapped another link with 'that bright happy past'.[1] A week later she was definitely lamenting Palmerston's loss in a letter to the Princess Royal, citing against him only his 'addiction to earthly vanity' (presumably now cured) and praising his strong will, hard head, knowledge of history, courage and other 'great qualities'.[2]

Within two months, on December 10th, King Leopold himself died. 'Now you are head of all the family,' wrote Princess Alice to her mother.[3] Queen Victoria's matriarchal sense was forthwith affronted by a refusal on the part of the Belgian authorities to grant King Leopold's wish for burial at Windsor. 'All you tell me of the Funeral,' the Queen fumed to the Princess Royal, 'is vy painful & caused by that atrocious Catholic Clergy! Nasty "Beggars" as Brown wld say . . .'[4]

Queen Victoria has begun to quote John Brown. He was indeed a new and formidable influence in her life. But before embarking on Brown's strange story it is necessary to introduce a second person who played a leading part from 1865 onwards.

Henry Ponsonby, one of the Prince Consort's equerries, was thirty-seven when the Queen took him over in 1861. In 1865 he dined with her for the first time, and as a professional soldier enjoyed the discussion about Army reform. How far should education of the soldier be carried? asked the Queen.

It could never be carried too far, he replied enthusiastically. Two months later he himself was carried too far by his exuberant spirits. Invitation cards to a small Court had inadvertently announced that the Queen would receive the 'Corps Diplomatique male *et femelle*'. Gales of laughter swept the equerries' room until a sobering message arrived from Her Majesty: 'It would be as well if Mr Ponsonby was cautioned not to be so funny.'[5]

These two episodes illustrate Ponsonby's impact on Windsor. For thirty years he was to pepper Queen Victoria with Liberal ideas and spice her Court with humour. What the *Greville Memoirs* do for the first half of Queen Victoria's reign the Ponsonby Letters do for the second. They are of exceptional value for the five years (1865–1870) when the Brown scandal flared.

John Conroy was picked out by the Duke of Kent to serve the Duchess. John Brown was picked out by the Prince Consort to serve the Queen. Conroy became known as 'King John'. By the year 1867 it was widely believed that another 'King John' ruled. Three or four years later the scandal was dead. It has never been buried.

At the time of the Prince Consort's death, Brown had been Queen Victoria's 'particular gillie' as she said, for nearly three years, 'combining the offices of groom, footman, page, and *maid*, I might almost say, as he is so handy about cloaks and shawls . . .'[6] In one sense he was less exalted than the chief ghillie, Grant, but he waited at table on expeditions when not too 'bashful', i.e. tipsy, and made the Queen's safety out riding and driving his especial care. Otherwise he was only one among several favourites. It is now often assumed, quite wrongly, that Brown leapt into prominence almost immediately after Prince Albert's death. We are told, for instance, that 'one bright, frosty morning' in early March 1862 the Queen looked down from her window at Osborne. Whom should she see but John Brown leading her favourite pony, Lochnagar. 'The shock must have made her heart turn over . . .' 'Nobody knows who thought of summoning him' from Balmoral.[7]

The reason why 'nobody knows' is because Brown had not been summoned. No one yet considered him the answer to royal melancholia. Brown's first, brief appearance down south was to visit the Second International Exhibition in June 1862 with other ghillies. He returned at once to Scotland. When in August the Queen travelled to Germany she decided to take her pony-chaise with Brown in charge, since the country was hilly and she still felt weak. Not until the autumn of 1863 does Brown's name begin to stand out from her Journal. A series of carriage accidents brought this about. Once the leading horse fell and Brown saved the day by sitting on its head. A few days later Brown rescued her when her coachman drove her into a ditch at night, giving her a black eye and permanently crooked thumb.

John Brown was a rough, handsome, intelligent Scot of thirty-nine with a strong arm, big stick, long legs, curly hair and beard, blue eyes and firm chin. Queen Victoria had a weakness for good chins perhaps because her own sloped and some of her children's, as she frequently lamented, were totally 'wanting'. Brown's brusque manner gave her confidence. His admonishments to keep still while he tucked in her rug or pinned her cape and his habit of addressing her as 'wumman' seemed the plainest guarantee of devotion. 'Hoots, then, wumman,' he was overheard shouting at her one day by a chance tourist, after pricking her chin, 'Can ye no hold yerr head up?' Henry Ponsonby referred to Brown almost fondly as 'the child of nature' and was by no means averse to sharing his salty meditations on the box of Her Majesty's carriage. Indeed Ponsonby's only clashes with Brown were over sport. The child of nature, hopelessly indulged by his Sovereign, had a habit of getting up early and creaming off the game just before a party arrived from the Castle.

At the end of October 1864 the Queen, Dr Jenner and Sir Charles Phipps, Keeper of the Privy Purse, hatched an idea which was to change her life. They decided to bring John Brown to Osborne for the winter. Dr Jenner, she wrote, wished her to keep up her riding and a strange groom would never do. 'Alas! I am weak & nervous, & very dependent on those I am accustomed to.'[8] From Darmstadt Princess Alice sent a message of warm approval. John Brown duly arrived at Osborne in December to lead her pony, Flora.

Scarcely two months passed before the Queen saw further possibilities in 'this good soul'. She wrote in her Journal on February 3rd, 1865:

> 'Have decided that Brown should remain permanently & make himself useful in other ways besides leading my pony as he is so very dependable . . .'

A memorandum of February 4th describes Brown's new status. He is henceforth to be called 'The Queen's Highland Servant', taking orders from none but the Queen herself and attending her both indoors and outdoors. He is to continue as before cleaning her boots, skirts and cloaks unless this proves too much. (By December Brown was relieved of cleaning not only the Queen's boots but also her dogs.) She had already promised Brown a cottage at Balmoral if he married. If he marries now and wants a cottage in the south 'the promise will not be forgotten'.[9]* Nor will she forget his need for holidays. He can always stay on at Balmoral for a day or two after she has departed, if he wishes. His salary is to be £120. At the end of 1866 it was raised to £150, in 1869 to £230 plus £70 for clothes, and soon afterwards to £310. Still looking ahead, we find the Queen in 1872 considering a new title for Brown:

> 'You will see in this the gtest *anxiety* to show *more* & *more what* you are to me & as time goes on this *will* be more & more seen & known. Every one hears me say you are *my friend* & most confidential attendant.'[10]

That November Brown was designated 'Esquire' with a salary of £400. (Six weeks later another rise put him on a level with the Page of the Back Stairs.) A note to 'John Brown Esq.' dated November 17th, 1872 describes these and other privileges as a reward for not having taken '*a single day's holiday*

---

* The Queen gave Brown, though unmarried, a cottage at Balmoral in 1876. His lease contained the usual clause of 'Forfeiture & Irritancy' but she wrote in the margin, 'what does this mean?' (RA Vic. Add. MSS. M54/67).

or been *absent* for *a day* or *a night* from your post . . .' The note was signed 'Your faithful friend, Victoria R.'[11]

Returning to the year 1865, Queen Victoria exulted over Brown's advancement: 'It is a *real* comfort,' she told King Leopold in February, 'for he is devoted to me – so simple, so intelligent, *so unlike* an *ordinary* servant . . .'[12] (On this last point no one would have contradicted her.) To the Princess Royal she wrote on April 5th:

'. . . He comes to my room – after breakfast & luncheon to get his orders – & every thing is always right – he is so quiet, has such an excellent head & memory . . . is besides so devoted, & attached & clever . . . It is an excellent arrangement, & I feel I have here always in the House a good, devoted Soul (like your Grant) – whose only object & interest is my service, & God knows how much I want to be taken care of.'

A week later the Queen expatiated on Brown's moral courage and discretion —

'wh the highest Pce [Prince] might be proud of . . . And in this House where there are so many people, & often so much indiscretion & no Male head now – such a person is invaluable.'[13]

Brown's magic began to work, speeding Queen Victoria's recovery. When in August 1866 the Princess Royal lost a little son, the Queen discussed for her benefit the best kind of comforters in bereavement. A man like Dean Stanley was too cold, '& to me as if he were of no sex'. Jovial, burly Dr Macleod gave great help because of his loving heart (he would read aloud the poetry of Burns while she turned her therapeutic spinning-wheel); so did Dean Wellesley, who was 'tender-hearted' beneath a 'rough exterior'. But there was one who did her more good than all the rest – 'honest Brown'. The Queen then disclosed to her daughter a problem which she had already put to Dean Wellesley. Ought she to reproach herself because her grief for the Prince was becoming less violent? Dean Wellesley had replied that 'a settled mournful resignation' was a more lasting proof of affection than acute grief. If God sometimes threw across our path 'some comforters' who have peculiar powers of sympathy and 'congenial natures' we should not question our reaction to them but consider them providential.[14]

In these words the tender-hearted Dean set the seal of his approval on Queen Victoria's relationship with John Brown. Was it disloyal to feel comforted? The Dean thought not. Neither of them considered for an instant that her feelings for John Brown could be intrinsically wrong. As she made quite clear in her disparaging remarks about Dean Stanley, she needed a man not a machine; but a man to lean on not to marry.

Nevertheless a whisper arose that Queen Victoria had married. In elegant drawing-rooms jokes were made about 'Mrs John Brown' and a scurrilous pamphlet with this title went the rounds. On June 30th, 1866 *Punch* prepared the ground for an attack by publishing *An Imaginary Despatch* from Balmoral in which the Queen lambasted her Ministers for excluding her from public affairs. This piece of heavy sarcasm was followed on July 7th by an imaginary *Court Circular*:

Balmoral, Tuesday.
Mr John Brown walked on the Slopes. He subsequently partook of a haggis. In the evening, Mr John Brown was pleased to listen to a bag-pipe.
Mr John Brown retired early.

A month later *John o'Groats Journal* took up the tale:

London Letter.   11th August.
I suppose all my readers have heard of the great Court favourite John Brown. His dismissal some weeks ago was generally talked about at the time, and I observe that the fact has now found its way into print, coupled with the suggestion of John Brown's probable restoration to power before long. The reason assigned for his dismissal is an inordinate indulgence in whisky . . . Far be it from me to question Mr Brown's powers of suction . . . But Brown's fall has been more commonly ascribed to *Mr Punch* than to any shortcomings of his own.

The paragraph concluded with a reprint of *Punch*'s imaginary *Court Circular*, the whole being copied by the *Elgin Courant*.

The rumours about 'Mrs Brown' crossed the Channel. On October 10th the *Pall Mall Gazette* put in a tiny, waspish paragraph:

'The Hon. Mr Harris, British Minister at Berne, has addressed a complaint to the Swiss Federal Council against the *Lausanne Gazette*, on account of an article in that Journal containing calumnies against Queen Victoria.'

Six weeks later Henry Ponsonby broke the disagreeable news of these calumnies to his brother Arthur:

'We have been rather surprised here by a statement that the Minister at Berne has complained of a libel on the Queen in the *Lausanne Gazette* – a foolish thing to do – and it has brought the matter into notoriety but no further steps are taken as he has apologized. We do not know what the libel is – and I believe the Queen is as ignorant as any of us, but I hope she will not hear it, as I believe it to be a statement that she has married John Brown, and the idea that it could be said she was marrying one of the servants would make her angry and wretched. Brown has always been a favourite with the R. family and has lately been raised to be personal attendant – that is all messages come by him – as he is always dressed as a highlander he is conspicuous and so is talked of. Besides which he certainly is a favourite – but he is only a Servant and nothing more – and what I suppose began as a joke about his constant attendance has been perverted into a libel that the Queen has married him.'[15]

Ponsonby's hopes of the marriage myth evaporating were disappointed, for Queen Victoria's seclusion provided the perfect climate to sustain it. Who could say what was happening in the Scottish hills or on the Island in the Solent? Though her public appearances were steadily increasing, as we shall see in the next chapter, the improvement was never quick enough to overtake fresh criticism. Some of it must have originated from the Palace where Brown and the Queen were innocently blundering into trivial enmities. At the end of 1866 Brown complained that he was worked to death. The Queen passed on his grievances, as she thought tactfully, to the wife of Sir Thomas Biddulph, her Master of the Household:

> 'It is, that my poor Brown has so much to do that it wd be a *gt* relief if – the Equerries receive a *hint* not to be *constantly* sending for him *at all hours* for trifling messages: he is often *so tired* from being so constantly on his legs that, he goes to bed with swollen feet and can't sleep from fatigue! You see he goes out *twice* with me – comes then for orders – then goes with messages to the pages, and lies [ladies]. – & often to the equerries & then comes up with my bag twice . . . he must not be made "a man of all work" – besides it *loses* his position . . . [One of the equerries is] an *extra* fidget, but some of the others do the same & it must be put a stop to . . .'[16]

A climax was reached in 1867. Amid a hail of harsher criticism, one personal letter reached the Queen which is worth quoting as an example of loyal, working-class remonstrance. The writer was a Mrs M. A. Murray.

> 'My dear Queen,
>   I earnestly hope you will excuse a poor subject writing to ask a great favour . . . it is to let your beloved son . . . act as *regent* during the rest of your Life. Not that you have been an indolent Queen a better could not exist and I am so afraid he will not live long enough to be king. You know my dear Queen you will still be Queen Dowager and we will all regonize [*sic*] you just the same . . .'[17]

In June the Queen had agreed to attend a review in Hyde Park. Suddenly she learnt that her Ministers wished to exclude Brown. Fury and indignation possessed her. At the height of the storm the Emperor Maximilian of Mexico was shot dead by a firing squad in Quarétaro. Thankfully the authorities cancelled the review but not before Queen Victoria had made sure that in future Brown's position would be unchallenged. 'The

Queen will not be dictated to,' she informed her equerry, Lord Charles Fitzroy, at the end of an impassioned letter, 'or *made* to *alter* what she has found to answer for her comfort . . .' A month later Lord Charles received another salvo. So the mob would have upset her carriage if she had entered the Park with Brown? '*Mere panic*' –

'. . . the result of *ill-natured* gossip in the higher classes, caused by dissatisfaction at *not forcing* the Queen *out* of her seclusion . . . and probably seizing hold of those wicked and idle lies about poor, good Brown, which appeared in the Scotch provincial papers last year, and which *no one* noticed or *knew* till LONG after, and which probably have been fished up to serve the malevolent purposes of ill-disposed persons.'[18]

Fished up or not, the 'idle lies' were busily multiplying in the pages of *The Tomahawk*, a newcomer in 1867 to the satirical Press.

In May *Tomahawk* began like *Punch* with a skit on a *Court Circular*, making out the Queen's existence to be idle and vapid. This was followed in June by an unsigned cartoon* entitled 'Where is Britannia?' Over an empty throne the robes of State are draped, the crown wobbles tipsily on top, the British lion dozes behind. A short paragraph points out that it is no more exertion for Her Majesty to entertain people of her own rank than ghillies and their families. On August 10th *Tomahawk* reached the zenith of its brief notoriety with a second cartoon which sent up its circulation to nearly 50,000 and the Court's blood pressure to corresponding heights. 'A Brown Study!' shows the crown now reposing under a glass case but the British lion has woken up and is lunging towards a handsome Highlander who, pipe in hand, turns his back on the throne while maintaining that cool, impassive expression which had won him fame on the box of the Queen's carriage. In the same number appeared a burlesque account of the Queen opening the Albert Hall (she had only just laid the foundation stone) sent in, according to *Tomahawk*, by a Highlander with second sight.

* The cartoonist in later numbers signed himself Matt Morgan.

412

Tomahawk collapsed in 1870, weary with well-doing, as the editor put it. Meanwhile it had carried in August 1867 an advertisement for another new journal, *Tinsley's Magazine*, and in October of the following year *Tinsley's* introduced the 'idle lies', hotted up, to a less frivolous readership. In an article on British womanhood an American contributor professed himself deeply shocked to have found Society giggling over a lady – 'Mrs Brown'. Loyal subjects who had never heard of Mrs Brown now read in *Tinsley's* that their Queen had gone mad – Brown was her keeper; had gone spiritualist – Brown was her medium; had gone wrong – Brown was her lover.*

Queen Victoria, naïve and obstinate as ever, kept providing fresh evidence of her infatuation. Brown, for example, complained in 1868 that royal smokers kept him up too late. The Queen, therefore, wrote to her long-suffering equerry, Lord Charles Fitzroy:

> 'Lord Charles would perhaps simply mention to Prince [Christian] *without* giving it as a *direct order* that the Queen felt it *necessary* for the sake of the *servants* . . . that the smoking room should be closed . . . by 12 o'clock – not later.'[19]

In any household, royal or otherwise, the servant whose convenience appears to come before that of the family will not be popular. The Queen's advisers were desperate. No one could move her, not even the Princess Royal nor her intimate friend, the Countess Blücher,† both of whom urged the sacrifice of Brown. Queen Victoria knew in her heart that this storm like others could be ridden out. They had failed to make her, as a young girl, take Conroy, a man she disliked; did they expect her now to get rid of Brown, a man she liked very much?

Gradually the hubbub subsided. John Brown continued to

* The editor, Edmund Yates, added a footnote: 'Without attempting to defend the silly nonsense which was talked on this subject, we think our contributor has taken the matter more *au sérieux* than was intended.'

† English-born daughter of a judge and lady-in-waiting to Queen Augusta of Prussia.

look dignified on the box and speak roughly to the Queen. He once told her sharply to stop complaining about an inconvenient sketching table, 'for I canna mak one for ye'. If he did not like her apparel he would say, 'What's this ye've got on today?' In the Household he was still a disruptive influence. There was the Mayor of Portsmouth row in 1869. While the Mayor was waiting in the equerries' room at Osborne for an answer to a request that Her Majesty should attend a Volunteer review, John Brown burst in. 'The Queen says certainly not!' Biddulph had to cope with the worshipful wrath.

Then there were the Great Pony, Great Factor and Great Knee Rows, all at Balmoral in 1870. The Queen had forbidden her ponies to be used except by competent riders and with Ponsonby's permission. Her chaplain, Canon Duckworth, and the German librarian, Herr Sahl, refused to accept the ban. 'The harmony and comfort of those who are serving the Queen,' expostulated Duckworth to Ponsonby, 'is surely worthwhile with stables full of ponies?' The Queen, however, saw the roles reversed. With the Castle full of courtiers, the comfort of her ponies was worthwhile. Sahl thereupon got the Prince of Wales, who detested Brown, to intercede:

Prince of Wales: 'Sahl said *he* was not allowed a pony while Brown and Löhlein [Prince Albert's valet] rode as much as they liked.'

Ponsonby: 'No, not Löhlein, he wasn't there – as to Brown, I gave him a pony twice by the Queen's orders.'

Prince of Wales: 'Well, he thinks they do and that is just as bad.'[20]

Perhaps it was: nevertheless Brown went on riding while Sahl fumed. Revenge came during the following June. 'Sahl has thawed much the last 2 days,' wrote Ponsonby on the 11th to his wife; 'it is supposed because J.B. is so ill.' A fishing expedition had proved Brown's undoing. He came out in frightful blotches which Fitzroy put down to the bottle.

In October the factor, Dr Robertson, had such a fierce scrap with Brown that he resigned. Ponsonby persuaded 'Bids' (as the Household called Biddulph) to forward Robertson's complaint to the Queen without his resignation. Biddulph did so. 'Directly afterwards,' Ponsonby wrote, 'Eliza [the Queen] saw Robertson, told him he was unnecessarily hurt but that he was quite right to write to her and made J.B. apologize which he did most perfectly and all is love.'

The Great Knee Row began soon after Princess Louise's engagement to the Marquess of Lorne and ended with Brown's alleged marriage to a dresser. Princess Louise sprained her knee out riding on October 15th. There were many at Balmoral already longing to start for the south. The Queen, however, seized the opportunity to prolong her Highland visit: Princess Louise must not travel until she could walk and must see a Scottish doctor – Lister of Edinburgh.* Princess Louise wanted an Englishman and protested that if the journey had been from south to north her mother would have packed her into a carriage forthwith.

'Oh! what a row!' exclaimed Prince Leopold, going into peals of laughter. At dinner a fortnight later Princess Beatrice, the *enfant terrible*, remarked, 'You said, Mama, you'd like to be here at Christmas.' General consternation.[21] Having at last settled on November 23rd for departure the Queen became embroiled in further disputes over a suitable conveyance for the invalid. Brown joined the mutineers and Ponsonby wrote to his wife: 'Brown says he is sick of it and the Queen is irritated about it and I'm exhausted with it.'

It seemed in fact that Brown had already taken secret steps to make his escape. A rumour had reached Ponsonby's wife at Windsor that Brown was married. 'You ask again about the marriage,' wrote Henry to Mary Ponsonby on November 10th, 'but I don't believe it.' However, he added, if Brown was married to anyone it must be Miss Ocklee, one of the dressers, with whom he always danced.† The subject continued under discussion between them until on November 16th Ponsonby wrote:

'Your letter this morning deals principally with the marriage but you don't say who to. I don't see the harm of

---

* Joseph Lister was not in fact a Scot, but was conducting his great researches into antiseptic surgery in Scotland.

† Miss Ocklee married a man from the Steward's department in 1873.

it. I hope he won't go. Here he is we have the best and the worst of him: and now that popular lying is calmed no one thinks much about him. But a new man may be anything and may if he gets the same power not be so harmless – what I do not see is why anyone shd. insist on his going because he is married. He may be very tired of it naturally – again I say who to.'

Unfortunately Mary Ponsonby's answer to her husband's reiterated question must have been delivered by word of mouth for no record of it exists. A laudatory pamphlet, however, published after Brown's death describes him as having married a girl from his native valley. All in all, it is probable that he did once contemplate marriage, possibly as an escape from rows. The Queen's torrential woe may have persuaded him to drop it or perhaps he decided that he was too grand for a dresser. He contributed thirty guineas towards a wedding present for Princess Louise, compared with the Ponsonbys' projected £5.

As a pendant to this curious episode, one more marriage rumour deserves mention. Eleven months before Brown's name was linked with Miss Ocklee's it was said that Queen Victoria intended to marry Fritz Holstein, the disinherited Duke of Augustenburg. The Court believed that her son-in-law, Prince Christian of Schleswig-Holstein, had started the rumour.

One fact emerges from the Ponsonby letters. If it was true that Brown thought of marrying in 1870 he could not have become the Queen's husband in 1866, as the gossips declared. And if he did not marry her before 1870, there is no reason to think that he did so afterwards. By 1871 the Brown crisis was over. Political troubles there were in plenty but Dr Jenner – by then Sir William – actually quoted the John Brown scandal as an example of how smoothly the Queen's arrangements worked once people recognized that she would not alter them. Ponsonby relayed Jenner's arguments to his wife on August 27th, 1871:

'He alluded to the Brown question and said they all tried to press the Queen to send him away . . . Even Uncle C.

416

[Charles Grey] was carried away by the arguments. But the Q. wd. not be coerced, she held her own way and now the thing runs smoothly and we wonder there ever was a row about it. One thing resulted and that was that the Q. knew she had only to make a stand to carry her point.'

That the Queen was neither John Brown's mistress nor his morganatic wife should be clear from a study of her character. Her passionate nature, as we have seen, did not require physical ardours so much as intense, undivided affection producing a sense of safety and comfort. Immorality is a gift wished by tradition upon royal cradles. Queen Victoria's daughter, the Princess Royal, was said to have been the mistress of her Court Chamberlain, Count Seckendorff. Queen Victoria's aunt, Queen Adelaide, was said to have been the mistress of her Court Chamberlain, Lord Howe. John Brown was not even a Court Chamberlain. He was a servant. If Queen Victoria had ever been tempted to marry again, a sense of propriety would have ruled out Brown. It would *never* do. An entry in her Journal dated May 24th, 1871, Brown's heyday, proves that she did not marry again:

'My poor old birthday, my 51st! Alone, alone, as it will ever be! But surely, my dearest one blesses me.'

Four years before her death she made her last will:

'I die in peace with all fully aware of my many faults relying with confidence on the love, mercy and goodness of my Heavenly Father and His Blessed Son & earnestly trusting to be reunited to my beloved Husband, my dearest Mother, my loved Children and 3 dear sons-in-law. – And all who have been very near & dear to me on earth. Also I hope to meet those who have so faithfully & so devotedly served me especially good John Brown and good Annie Macdonald who I trusted would help to lay my remains in my coffin & to see me placed next to my dearly loved Husband in the mausoleum at Frogmore.'[22]

Perhaps it is surprising that two servants got into this exalted company at all. That was the Queen's way. The point is that

John Brown was coupled with the wardrobe maid, no place for a second husband.

One other role besides lover and keeper was cast for Brown – that of the Queen's medium through whom she made contact with Prince Albert. This rumour deserves the closest investigation for today, after a lapse of many years, it has been revived and presented to the world as a circumstantial story.

In 1849, the year after the Fox sisters first brought spirit-rapping from America to England, a boy was born named Robert James Lees. He was psychic. At three he saw a kilted Highlander sitting by his bed. At thirteen or fourteen (1862 or 1863) he is said to have delivered a message from the Prince Consort while 'under control'. James Burns, editor of *The Medium and Daybreak*, put a paragraph in his paper describing the seance and dispatched it to the widowed Queen. She decided to test the boy's *bona fides* by sending two Court officials incognito to the next seance. Lees again went under control, greeted the courtiers by their true titles, gave them the highest Masonic handshake and asked what Queen Victoria wanted. 'She wants a name,' they replied. Young Lees wrote down the secret pet-name with which the Prince Consort always signed letters to his wife, returning it to her in a sealed envelope. Convinced, the Queen summoned Lees, held a seance at Windsor and was put in touch with her husband's spirit. When she suggested appointing the lad her Resident Medium the Prince Consort's spirit intervened: Lees could not be spared but there was a person already in her service through whom the Prince could communicate equally well. Let her send for the ghillie from Balmoral. John Brown was thereupon brought to Windsor and except when too 'bashful' to receive messages from the spirit or any other world, acted as the Queen's medium until he died.

Robert Lees is said to have stood in for Brown on several of these occasions, also being summoned shortly before the Queen's death, when she kissed his hand at parting. Because of the slur attaching to spiritualism, Lees observed the utmost secrecy, corresponding with Queen Victoria only by courier. Nothing of his royal connection (which is said to have included Queen Alexandra) emerged until he died in 1931. Then his daughter, Miss Eva Lees, told the story for the first time to the Press. It has been retold in the course of thirty years to psychical researchers and writers including the present author who heard it from Miss Lees in 1962. By way of tangible evidence, Miss Lees states that in her possession are half-a-dozen envelopes bearing the royal cypher which contained letters from Queen Victoria and other Royalties. Miss Lees also allowed the present writer to see a copy of her father's first and best-known book, *Through the Mists*,* bound in crimson morocco with the royal cypher stamped in gold on the cover – alleged to be a gift from Queen Victoria.

Let it be said at once that no independent source has yet been found to corroborate this remarkable story. It is riddled with difficulties, while the 'tangible evidence' is either nugatory or positively damaging. The envelopes prove nothing since anyone can obtain a reply in an official envelope simply by writing to the Palace. As for the 'gift' copy of *Through the Mists*, the binding is not Victorian. Victorian bindings in the Royal Archives are all in fine-grained calf, not coarse-grained morocco. Nor is the cypher on *Through the Mists* identical with the blocks used by the royal binder: it lacks the diamond point in between each word of the Garter motto. Bindings in the Royal Library bearing the cypher all show this diamond point. The block used for *Through the Mists*, therefore, cannot be one from the Royal Library. Whoever had it bound in morocco and stamped with the royal monogram, it was not Queen Victoria.

The story itself is not viable. *The Medium and Daybreak* did not appear until April 1870 and its forerunner, *The Daybreak*, until 1868. Prince Albert had no secret pet-name, always signing his letters to Queen Victoria either 'Albert' or 'A'. Nor was he a Freemason.† Brown was not sent for from Balmoral

* *Through the Mists* was first published in 1898; its sub-title, *Leaves from the Autobiography of a Soul in Paradise,* with its sequel, *More Leaves* (1909), were perhaps modelled on the Queen's Highland Journals.

† On March 25th, 1874 Queen Victoria wrote to Sir Howard Elphinstone: 'The Queen was rather annoyed at his [Prince Arthur] becoming a Freemason wh his father so very much disliked.'

in 1862 or 1863 but at the end of 1864, by which time Queen Victoria was getting over the worst tortures of bereavement. 'Albert, Albert where art thou?' she had moaned beside his empty bed in 1863.[23] Or again, 'He remains my sole object & ever will – but can't give me a sign of it – & that is so fearful to bear!'[24] Those were the moments when she needed, if ever, to communicate with Albert's spirit through John Brown. But at that date Brown was still only an outdoor servant at Balmoral. Furthermore, whenever the Queen spoke of Prince Albert's spirit she always located it either in the 'dear Mausoleum' or *everywhere* – never in Brown. Queen Victoria's private writings do not suggest that Brown's arrival in the south marked the beginning of occult contacts with her husband, even though Brown could then go in and out of her room until his poor feet ached and was said to do so without knocking. On the contrary, from 1865 the Queen felt increasingly uncertain about what her husband would have thought, wondering distractedly how to apply his principles in a changed world. And from what is known of the Queen's last years, she would have been more likely to arrive for the Opening of Parliament on a tricycle than to kiss a subject's hand.

Since the Robert Lees story is the only detailed account of Queen Victoria's alleged seances, it may be as well to indicate some of Mr Lees' later life and claims. A nonconformist preacher and contributor to the *Manchester Guardian* and *Daily News*, he founded 'The People's League' in Peckham, worked with John Burns, MP, and befriended social outcasts. His daughter claims that he helped Disraeli back to his house after his last outing in the Park, helped Gladstone to write *The Impregnable Rock of Holy Scripture* and through clairvoyance helped the police to detect Fenians*[25] and to identify Jack the Ripper. (The murder of five prostitutes off the Commercial Road at intervals during 1888 shook the whole country, in-

---

* Spotting Fenians seems to have been a favourite occupation of spiritualists. The Queen's private secretary received a humorous note from the Home Secretary in 1867 saying that 'a celebrated Spiritualist in his time' had given two dates – January 15th and March 23rd – for the firing of the Houses of Parliament and the shooting of the Queen at Paddington Station. As they were uncertain which date was which, HM had better avoid Paddington on both.

cluding Queen Victoria. She hoped that every effort would be made to arrest the perpetrator of these 'dreadful murders of unfortunate women of a bad class . . .'[26]) Lees is said to have recognized the Ripper on a bus at Notting Hill, thus enabling the police to trace him to a mad Harley Street doctor with aristocratic connections. Scotland Yard admit nothing of this claim.

The reader must now form his own judgement of the story, remembering that Queen Victoria's lustre, bereavement and reputation for piety acted as a constant magnet to her sympathetic subjects. Many came to the Castle gate, few were admitted. Ponsonby relates the story of a man who arrived at Balmoral saying he had walked from London to ask the Queen to pay for the publication of his religious poems, of which the first was called 'The Pill'. Would Her Majesty accept 'the love and devotion of the spirit encased in the form of William Muller'? Ponsonby sent him off with five shillings for a bed.

Before reaching a final verdict on Queen Victoria and spiritualism in general, it is necessary to cast the net more widely. Apart from *Tinsley's Magazine*, where else did the rumours get into print? As one would expect, in the newborn spiritualist Press. *The Spiritualist Magazine* (1864) contains a paragraph headed: 'Queen Victoria A Spiritualist'. The author begins by wondering whether Her Majesty's spiritualism has brought her comfort. He goes on to quote from *The Northern Whig*, where the Queen's and Prince Consort's readings from a book named *Heaven Our Home* are mentioned by a member of the Household as proof that the Prince was preparing her for contact with the spirit world. The author adds:

'I have been assured by a friend of mine, who has it from a person attached to the Court, that it is generally understood there that Her Majesty holds constant communion with the spirit of Prince Albert.'

Two points emerge: the extraordinary vagueness of the reports which are all second or third hand; and the date of 1864, showing that the rumours had started before John Brown

421

came on the scene. A first-hand report, indeed, from Lord Clarendon dwelt on the widow's eerie behaviour and beliefs: she continually referred to the Prince's opinions as if he were in the next room, and believed that 'his eye is *now* constantly upon Her, that he watches Her & that in fact she never ceases to be in communion with his spirit . . .' But such a feeling is not uncommon in early widowhood, nor is it necessarily connected with spiritualism.[27]

Rumours were probably still current in the 'seventies. A letter dated August 11th, 1873 appeared in *The Examiner* (November 11th, 1876) and was reprinted in *The Medium and Daybreak*, addressed to Queen Victoria by an Anglo-Indian Colonel, Charles Showers. He suggested that his daughter, Mary Showers, should hold a seance for the Queen. Sir Thomas Biddulph would no doubt inform Colonel Showers if Her Majesty was not interested. As no copy of a reply exists in the Royal Archives it seems certain that Queen Victoria declined. (As it happened, the seances of Mary Showers were fraudulent.) By the time serious psychical investigation was under way, towards the end of the century, the rumours about Queen Victoria had died out.

There remains a gold watch, irreverently known as 'Vicky's Ticker' and until the year 1963 exhibited in a glass case by the College of Psychic Science, London. It has since been stolen. Two inscriptions on its back apparently stated that the watch was first presented by Queen Victoria to Miss Georgiana Eagle *for her Meritorious & Extraordinary Clair-voyance produced at Osborn House Isle of Wight July 15th, 1846* and secondly to Mrs Etta Wreidt. The present writer cannot accept it as a genuine relic. The date, 1846, asks us to believe that Queen Victoria was deeply involved in spiritual-ism even before it was first brought to England. Who was 'Georgiana Eagle'? Her name cannot be found either in spirit-ualistic literature or in royal records. The word 'Osborne' is spelt wrongly, without an 'e', a mistake Queen Victoria would never have let pass.

'When Georgiana Eagle, the original recipient, passed on [writes the editor of *Psychic News*, February 9th, 1963],

422

the Queen approached W. T. Stead [later a leading spiritual-ist] and asked him to present the watch to the medium who in his opinion was the most worthy to receive it. After con-sulting Sir William Crookes and Alfred Russell Wallace, Stead presented it to Etta Wreidt, the American who was one of the world's greatest voice mediums . . .'

What was the date of this second presentation? According to legend it was 1883, the year John Brown died, and the watch had been intended for him. The idea that Queen Victoria should then have turned to Stead for advice is absurd. Stead was at the time assistant editor of the *Pall Mall Gazette* (a journal which Queen Victoria did not love) and was soon to shock her with his sensational crusade against vice. Neither Stead's daughter, who wrote his life, nor his present bio-grapher, Professor Joseph Baylen, believe the story.

It may be argued that at any rate some of Queen Victoria's friends and even family became keenly interested in psychical research. That is true and not surprising in an epoch which loved the unseen, which began with Harriet Martineau mes-merizing Charlotte Brontë and culminated in the foundation of the Society for Psychical Research with a membership in-cluding a bishop, dons and a Minister of the Crown. It is, however, surprising that so little is heard about the Queen's spiritualism after the 'sixties, though her daughter, Princess Louise, married into the Argyll family who, as Highlanders, possessed second sight. Her husband, Lord Lorne, had a clair-voyant vision of himself being offered the Governor-General-ship of Canada; her sister-in-law, Lady Archie Campbell, was a spiritualist and, according to Disraeli, looked it. Princess Louise herself became interested, triumphantly informing Ponsonby whenever she heard of genuine cases of second sight. One of the Queen's most trusted friends, Walburga ('Wally') Lady Paget, wrote on the reincarnation of souls in the bodies of animals and corresponded with the novelist 'Ouida' on the horrors of vivisection. Though Queen Victoria also was de-voted to animals and abhorred vivisection, she kept aloof from Wally Paget's fantasies. There is no hint that she believed the dogs which barked and fought under her dining-table until the footman carried them out, contained the souls of Pilgerstein or Dizzy.

It is equally surprising, assuming the rumours to be true, that so many of Queen Victoria's closest advisers were sceptical about spiritualism. The clergyman with whom she was most intimate, Dr Macleod, called 'all the stories of ghosts and . . . spirit rapping . . . *great humbug and nonsense*' (*Good Words* 1862). In the 'seventies, Ponsonby describes how Jenner, the Queen's chief physician, split his sides over an equerry's account of a seance at Lord Balfour's. At a mock Household seance Ponsonby himself, blindfolded, laughed till the tears ran through his newspaper bandage. The Queen's favourite sculptor, Boehm, delighted the Household with his own experiences at a seance where the alleged hand of a spirit touching his knee turned out to be his host's stockinged foot.

There are no references whatever, critical or otherwise, to the Queen and spiritualism either in Ponsonby's letters or those of any of her ladies. Yet Ponsonby's close association with Queen Victoria began, as we have seen, at precisely the same time as Brown's alleged mediumship. Most significant of all is the fact that Queen Victoria wrote countless frank – sometimes almost too frank – letters to her daughter, the Princess Royal, all of which are preserved, without ever mentioning a seance.

What did Queen Victoria believe? In old age she was not superstitious – at least that was the opinion of an intelligent courtier who knew her well, Sir Frederick Ponsonby, son of Sir Henry. In middle age she was perhaps rather more susceptible.

She told the Princess Royal in 1867 that she would never allow one of her children to marry in May, it was so unlucky: look at King Leopold and Princess Charlotte, the Duke and Duchess of Kent, Pedro and Stephanie: they all married in May and death struck. She displayed a normal, human interest in coincidences and was once delighted to vary her usual parlour games with a new invention called the 'willing-game'. 'Magnetism', which had at first irritated her for drawing Prince Albert to scientific lectures, finally caught her imagination. She was convinced that little Prince William's arm could be

424

cured by magnetism, and magnetism seemed to her the explanation for a new craze which London was 'wild' about – table-turning. One spring evening at Osborne in 1853 when the nightingales were singing and all the windows open, she and Prince Albert decided to have a go. The table consented to spin round quite nicely for the royal pair but when Lady Ely applied her hands it fairly rushed along. (This incident may have started a rumour that Lady Ely was psychic.) The gentlemen, however, declined to co-operate. Charles Grey rather irritated Her Majesty by his scepticism. 'Peculiar' was the word used to describe her own sensations; she felt it was some form of magnetism or electricity, not a trick.

Four years later, as already related, Napoleon III intrigued her by spooky stories about 'Mr Hume', the medium.* Here, however, the Queen's initial interest was not followed up. She had evidently never seen the name written for the magician was none other than the celebrated Daniel Dunglass Home (pronounced Hume) who spent much time in England and Scotland during the 'sixties, holding live coals in his fingers and floating in and out of upper windows in the mansions of the great. Lord Dunraven in his *Experiences in Spiritualism with D. D. Home* gives a list of those who attended the seances at Ashley House in 1867, 1868 and 1869; many of the names are aristocratic, none is connected with the Court.

Prince Albert, never strong on dogma, had helped to cultivate an inquiring attitude in the Queen. Randall Davidson, appointed Dean of Windsor shortly before John Brown's death in 1883, tells how she would question him on various Christian doctrines – were they things he *really* believed or just 'pious opinions'? Church-going was another aspect of religion which Prince Albert approached with caution. As early as 1846 he had marked a passage for his young wife from Saint-Simon's advice to Princes: they should show their religion by leading moral lives, not in 'slavishly attending services in Church'. Queen Victoria's church-going was formidable rather than slavish.

One factor in particular made preaching to the widowed Queen a thing of duty but not always a joy. Unable to face

* The prototype of the poet Browning's *Mr Sludge, 'The Medium'*.

the glare of publicity surrounding the royal pew, she often held the service in her own home. This ceremony was something to make the boldest quail; especially when the distance between the minister and the mournful face, with fixed stare and drooping mouth, was only a matter of a few feet. No wonder she found the voices of some preachers 'quite feeble' while others were immoderately loud. Congregation as well as clergy suffered from the ordeal. Ponsonby draws a ludicrous picture of Edward Cardwell, the War Minister, sneaking in late and 'moving about on his knees from one end of the room to the other for 20 minutes trying to find a place'.

In such an atmosphere it was not easy to satisfy the poor widow's spiritual thirst. Yet after the searing events of 1861 – her mother's death followed so closely by her husband's – the thirst was tormenting. Her thoughts turned inevitably towards the most baffling and least defined of Christian doctrines – immortality. Prince Albert was there to help her over the first crisis. He would walk her for hours up and down the Terrace at Windsor discussing the after-life; they read *Heaven Our Home* (a reassuring picture of 'social intercourse' and 'saint-friendship' in Heaven) not through a premonition of his own death but as an explanation of her mother's. It was in this mood of search that the Queen derived such comfort from the famous sermon at Crathie, 'Prepare to meet thy God'! She wrote of it to the Princess Royal: 'I feel now to be so acquainted with death – & to be so much nearer that unseen world.'[28]

She was not near enough. The death of Prince Albert brought her nearer. But it left her, as death paradoxically does, without the only human being who could have made her face it steadily. For one reputed to be unbookish, she turned in 1862 with pathetic eagerness to the help of books. In May she sent the Princess Royal her copy of the book she had found most useful: *New Philosophy* – 'all about the future.' Published anonymously in 1847, its author defended mankind's right, contrary to orthodox teaching, to speculate about the hereafter and predicted that spiritual progress would not come to an end with death: 'each will have to make up where he was wanting.'

The next two books commended by Queen Victoria (in

July) show the trend of her speculations. First came Bishop Butler's famous treatise, *Analogy of Religion*, of which a new edition had just been published in 1859. The Bishop's measured tread – 'First . . . Secondly . . . Thirdly . . . Lastly . . .' – conveyed with unparalleled cogency the message that there is a future life. From this it may be assumed that the Queen had her doubts, and indeed she admitted as much years later to Dean Davidson. 'She asked me,' he wrote, 'if there ever came over me (as over her) waves or *flashes* of doubtfulness whether, after all, it might be all untrue.'[29] The third book dealt with 'psychology', the only subject besides religion on which the Queen said she could fix her mind.

What did she mean by 'psychology'? Not spiritualism as such, or she would have used the word, but possibly the study of psychic phenomena.* A psychic experience which the Queen herself underwent at this date may explain her interest in 'psychology'. She related it to the Princess Royal years afterwards when she also was widowed and feeling suicidal:

'I too wanted once to put an end to my life *here*, but a *Voice* told me for *His* sake – no, "Still Endure".'[30]

This experience, unique in the Queen's life, made an indelible impression. 'Still Endure' became her motto.

Queen Victoria's spiritual advisers quickly saw which way the wind was blowing; or it may be that she only listened to those whose views were compatible with *The New Philosophy*. The Rev. Charles Kingsley suggested that when God thought a good man's career was finished here below He took him to continue *working* at whatever he excelled in, above. 'Oh, surely that is so,' she exclaimed.[31] Dr Caird, the Scottish divine, also agreed that one's life's work continued in the hereafter, and when Dr Norman Macleod died his loss was explained in the same way: he was continuing 'his occupations & capabilities' in a perfected state. Old Mrs Macleod, however, his mother,

---

* It is hard to imagine Queen Victoria studying 'psychology' proper, as expounded by, say, Alexander Bain or Herbert Spencer. Just conceivably Sir Henry Holland, the Prince's doctor, put into her hands his famous *Chapters on Mental Physiology*.

was shocked by such profanity. She still believed in the ortho-dox alternatives of hell or harps. 'My dear mother is very conservative & old fashioned in her views,' explained her second son, the Rev. Donald Macleod, to his more adven-turous Sovereign.[32]

Queen Victoria's imperious need for a clear picture of the hereafter was ministered to by certain members of the laity as well as by books and clergy. Countess Blücher visited Osborne in February 1862 and held long conversations about 'that unseen world' which the Queen remembered gratefully after her death. The poet Tennyson came over from Freshwater to help her, buttoning himself for the occasion into a conven-tional frock-coat; nothing, however, could tame the thunder-ous voice in which he intoned truths about immortality. The Queen found that 'the rough exterior' went, as so often, with a 'great mind'.

Nevertheless, '*flashes* of doubtfulness' still racked her, one outstanding cause being the Almighty's apparent disregard of her reiterated prayer that if Albert were taken she should go too. When other blows fell her desolation was mingled with a sense of grievance. 'It is as if all that was best & greatest were to be taken away,' she wrote in 1862 after the death of her friend Lord Canning; he, however, received a favour denied to his Sovereign: 'Oh! how blessed to follow his wife so soon! He was only 49.'[33]

Suddenly into the terrible void where the winds of loneliness and doubt howled dismally, John Brown planted his reassuring bulk, equipped, it is said, to bring Albert to Victoria if Provi-dence would not take Victoria to Albert.

The time has come when it should be possible to put one's finger on the spark of fire which produced all the smoke – clairvoyance, voice mediums, weird services in the Blue Room, whisky-sodden Brown in a 'trance'.

Taking the Queen's beliefs as a starting-point, they were certainly unorthodox. Too much interest in the hereafter was deprecated by conventional churchmen and praying for the dead was considered rank superstition. Yet according to Sir Henry Ponsonby, the Queen's Roman Catholic subjects believed her peculiar ritual, especially the services in the Blue Room and the annual commemoration of the Prince Consort at the summit of Craig Lourigan, to be her way of praying for the dead. They were not far wrong. Madame Hélène Vavarescu who accompanied the Queen of Roumania to Balmoral as a lady-in-waiting, declared after Queen Victoria's death that she regularly prayed for the dead. This statement is supported by a note in Queen Victoria's Journal after her son-in-law, Prince Henry of Battenberg, had died, to the effect that his widow, Princess Beatrice, was reading *Our Life After Death* by the Rev. Arthur Chambers. From the context it is clear that Queen Victoria knew and approved this book.

No one should be shocked at prayers for the dead, asserted the author, for they were really prayers for the *living*, who were improving themselves in an 'Intermediate-Life' or 'Upper School' between earth and heaven, where you and your 'dear one' would 'talk, love and be together, as in days past'. The idea of Purgatory was true, though Catholics had reared upon it 'a superstructure of rubbish'. Doctrines of hell and the devil, on the other hand, were 'unutterably horrible and revolting'. (Once a preacher asked Princess Louise how her mother had enjoyed his sermon at Crathie on Damnation. 'The Queen does not altogether believe in the Devil,' replied Princess Louise. The preacher sighed: 'Puir body.')[34]

'I was often surprised,' wrote Dean Davidson, 'by the definiteness with which she held her beliefs about the intercourse in the other world of those who have been friends here.'[35] These beliefs were also expressed in her Journal on the day of her half-sister Princess Feodore's death in 1872. After recording that Princess Feodore had been talking just before she died about a beloved child who had recently predeceased her, the Queen continued:

> 'Surely at the approach of death the veil is raised & such pure spirits are allowed to see a glimpse of these dear ones waiting for them!'

Thus, by dint of reading, prayer and congenial conversation Queen Victoria rebuilt her beliefs into a shape so definite that gossips on the fringe of her Court assumed they must be based on personal experience: spiritualism was Society's vivid new interest – why not the Queen's? Among those whose conversation was congenial, John Brown occupied a prominent place. Writing to the Princess Royal in 1865 shortly after Brown arrived in England, the Queen observed that the English peasant had not a grain of poetry whereas the Scotch were full of it. 'One does not require that to lift one up above the heavy Clay wh clogs our Souls!'[36]

If John Brown's soul was replete with Highland poetry it would be strange indeed to find him lacking in another gift equally characteristic of Highlanders. The Queen almost certainly credited him with second sight. On the day that she heard of King Pedro of Portugal's death from typhoid (November 13th, 1861) she recalled to the Princess Royal with awe certain words of John Brown's:

'In speaking & lamenting over our leaving Balmoral, Brown said to me he hoped we should all be well through the winter & return safe, "& above all that you may have no deaths in the family." Well – & then the last day – he spoke of having lost (12 years ago) in 6 weeks time of typhus fever 3 grown up brothers & 1 grown up sister . . . Now not 4 weeks after we left this same fever has entered a royal house nearly allied to us & swept away two & nearly a third . . .'

How much more striking must Brown's premonition have seemed when applied a month later to the death of Prince Albert. Who doubts that Queen Victoria repeated the story to her intimates and they in turn to a wider circle? The following entry occurs in the diary of Lady (Lintorn) Simmons, wife of the Governor of Woolwich. A week after Brown's death her friend the Empress Eugénie was both compassionate about Queen Victoria's loss and 'very entertaining' about Brown's position in her Household: among other things 'the fact that he was a servant, and not a gentleman, ought to have prevented any slander . . . She added more I was not to repeat.' Alas, it is not repeated; but among the stories of Brown's rows and drunkenness there may well have been others about his second sight.

Poetry and premonitions are far from being mediumship but they are enough to build on. A combination of John Brown's *ambience* and the Blue Room should be sufficient to explain away the rumours. There is no evidence that Queen Victoria was a spiritualist. But if the legend should ever be authenticated – contrary to all probability – the fittest comment would surely come from Disraeli's Sheldonian oration (1864) in defence of dogma. The present age, he said, suffered from 'craving credulity': man was a being 'born to believe' and without a creed England would fall to 'the incantations of Canidia and the Corybantian howl'. Dogma, which Prince Albert tended to think a strait jacket, was the life jacket which Queen Victoria needed.

Howls or no howls, John Brown had plenty to offer. Long before Mary Bulteel became Lady Ponsonby she had noticed that both Queen Victoria and Prince Albert were more at ease with servants than courtiers. After the Prince's death Queen Victoria constantly lamented her lack of conversation with people 'of my own rank'. When any new acquaintances of this calibre appeared – the Battenbergs for instance – she gobbled them up. But in default of Battenbergs it seemed safest to plump for Browns.

In the days when domestic servants formed an important community, licensed eccentrics were by no means rare. John Brenton, for example, Lord Malmesbury's family servant, who died in 1861, also cheeked his doting employer. 'I wish I had this lake at Heron Court!' exclaimed the Earl one day when fishing in a Scottish loch. 'I don't,' retorted John Brenton, 'as it would drown your miserable estate and half the country besides'.[37] Lady Airlie describes her faithful Scottish factor, John Black, shaking his head over her estate accounts in the late 'nineties with the remark, 'Wimmin are nae guid for business!'[38] John Brown, John Black and John Brenton, with their 'wimmin' and their 'wumman', had a common ancestry in the Court jester. But Brown's position was peculiar. It was all very well for a private person like Lord Malmesbury to keep a saucy servant. What was sauce to the subject was not mere sauce to the Sovereign. It looked like sinister familiarity.

431

Yet what has been said already about the Queen's morbidity applies also to the Queen's John Brown. No one would have deprecated her cult of the Blue Room if she had been at the same time a bustling public figure. Similarly, she might have been excused John Brown if her drives round London had been more frequent. The people needed to see more of Brown sitting on the box not less. All the Queen's troubles went back to the same source: her seclusion.

The Blue Room

Queen Victoria and
Princess Alice on either
side of the bust of the
Prince Consort, 1862

Balmoral

Queen Victoria with John Brown

Sir Henry Ponsonby

Bust of John Brown
by Edgar Boehm, 1869

William Ewart
Gladstone

The Marquess
of Salisbury

Benjamin
Disraeli,
Earl of
Beaconsfield

The Earl
of Rosebery

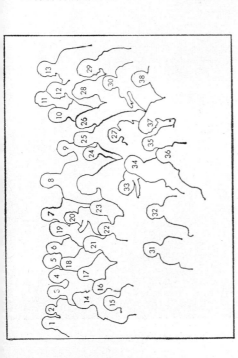

The following are:

1 Prince Louis of Hesse
5 Prince Christian of Schleswig-Holstein
6 Prince Leopold
7 Alfred, Duke of Edinburgh
8 The Prince of Wales
9 The Duke of Clarence
11 The Marquess of Lorne
13 The Duke of Connaught
14 The Crown Prince of Prussia
18 Princess Charlotte of Prussia

19 The Duchess of Edinburgh
21 The Crown Princess of Prussia
25 The Princess of Wales
28 Princess Beatrice
29 Princess Alice of Hesse
36 Princess Elizabeth of Hesse
37 Princess Victoria of Hesse
38 Prince George of Wales

The following are thought to be:

2 Hess baby, ? Mary, born 1874
3 Prince Christian Victor of Schleswig-Holstein
4 Prince William of Prussia
10 Princess Louise
12 Princess Christian
15 Prince Henry of Prussia
16 Princess Sophia of Prussia
17 Princess Victoria of Prussia
20 Princess Marie of Edinburgh
22 Princess Marie-Louise of Schleswig-Holstein
23 Princess Helena-Victoria of Schleswig-Holstein
24 Prince Albert of Schleswig-Holstein
26 Princess Louise of Wales
27 Princess Maude of Wales
30 Princess Alix of Hesse
31 Prince Ernst of Hesse
32 Prince Albert of Schleswig-Holstein
33 Prince Alfred of Edinburgh
34 Princess Victoria of Wales
35 Princess Irene of Hesse

The Royal Mausoleum, Frogmore

CHAPTER XXIV

GRANITE AND ROCK
1865–8

PALMERSTON'S DEATH left Lord Russell, the younger of Queen Victoria's 'two dreadful old men', at the head of affairs. The prospect of a political reshuffle as usual seemed unbearable. She would have to interview a new Prime Minister, for the first time since her marriage, alone, weighing every syllable, recording every word. She had never found Russell sympathetic. Gladstone, she reckoned, would make a prudent but an unpopular Leader of the House – a source of future instability. Worst of all, she would have to leave Balmoral for Windsor several days early: 'Alas, alas,' she wailed to the Princess Royal, ' – I dread it more than words can express.' Once more, reality was less black than imagination painted it. The Russell audience went off splendidly and she felt that Prince Albert's blessing rested upon her labours.[1]

If anyone had had the nerve to cross-question her at this date about her politics, she would have chosen a mixed label much favoured by mid-Victorians. Trollope, the novelist, was an 'advanced Conservative-Liberal'; Arnold, the schoolmaster, believed in 'Liberal Conservatism'; Bagehot, the historian, called himself 'between-size in politics'. In the 'fifties Gladstone was suitably employed in trying to decide whether he was a 'Liberal-Conservative' or a 'Conservative-Liberal'. W. H. Smith stood as a 'Liberal-Conservative' in 1865 and in 1866 the Queen expressed a wish that Russell's Government should be run on 'liberal-conservative principles'. It is important at this stage, when she was on the threshold of new exaltations and animosities, to keep a sense of perspective. Throughout her subsequent battles with Gladstone she retained a maddening habit of asserting that no one was more truly Liberal than she. Two things explain this curious boast.

Queen Victoria had lived almost one third of her life steeped in Whiggery and the Tory Sir Robert Peel was in her opinion a Liberal at heart. Until near the end of the second third she was still breathing Liberal airs. Sir Charles Phipps, General Grey, Lady Caroline Barrington and Sir Henry Ponsonby were all Liberals. When Ponsonby succeeded Grey as the Queen's private secretary, a groan of horror burst from the diehard Duke of Cambridge. How could cousin Victoria place her affairs in the hands of an out-and-out revolutionary? Cousin Victoria contented herself with one warning: it would be as well if Colonel Ponsonby told his wife Mary to be discreet.

Mary Ponsonby soared through the Victorian age untrammelled by any of its inhibitions. From working-class rights to higher education for women, no Radical cause left her cold. Her diminutive size coupled with almost regal dignity reminded people of the Queen and though the two were as unlike as possible in ideas and intellect, they remained close friends.

Two prominent Tories in the Household were not among the Queen's favourites. Sir Thomas Biddulph was too sluggish and Sir John Cowell too much of a 'John Bull' – a prejudiced person with 'unreasonable likes and dislikes'. Sir Arthur Helps whom Queen Victoria chose to edit the Prince Consort's *Speeches* and who corrected the grammar of her own *Highland Journal*, attributed all great English inventions to the 'lower classes' and lost his money trying to work clay found under his estate in accordance with the dignity of labour. Not until Sir William Jenner arrived on the scene did the Queen's physician wield a Conservative influence. The Clark family were Liberals running to Radicalism. Just as Clark found the Tory Jenner for the Queen, so Helps introduced the Tory Sir Theodore Martin. If they could have foreseen her need for Liberals in later life, they might have chosen differently. As it was, she obstinately refused ever to consider herself a Tory. That was to be a part, if a small one, of Gladstone's trouble.

The Queen announced her intention to open Parliament for the first time since her widowhood on February 6th, 1866. So cynical had people become that many thought she would seize the excuse of King Leopold's death to cancel it.

She was approaching, however, a state of mind which Clarendon was to pillory three years later: 'Eliza is roaring well and can do everything she likes and nothing she doesn't.' In 1866 she was up against the eternal problem of her children's annuities. Prince Alfred was about to come of age and Princess Helena to marry a penniless prince, Christian of Schleswig-Holstein. For their sakes the Queen faced a royal function which had always made her nervous and which she now described as a sacrifice, an ordeal, an execution and 'a *Show*', through which the broken-hearted widow was to be 'dragged in *deep mourning*, ALONE *in State* . . .'[2]

Despite a high wind she drove with both carriage windows open so that she could be seen but she refused the State coach, banished the trumpets and by-passed 'that terrible Gallery, with staring people', in the House of Lords. Discarding the crown she adapted the black cap of Mary Queen of Scots. Her long veil and dress were black, her crimson robes were draped over the throne like a discarded skin, while the Lord Chancellor read her speech. Utterly expressionless, she stared in front of her as if she did not hear a word. The Monarch seemed to have abdicated in favour of the Mandarin, but a Mandarin who did not even nod.

Queen Victoria's behaviour, which attracted unfavourable attention, was due to her enormous efforts at self-control. If she had relaxed an iota she would have broken down. On the drive home her reaction was correspondingly violent. Ponsonby glimpsed her talking compulsively with her daughter. In her own words, she felt 'very shaky & much excited'.

This same year she visited a place she had vowed to see 'never again' – Aldershot. There was no pleasure in it, she wrote, without Albert, but to go was right, since Albert would have wished it; therefore 'there *was* satisfaction.' Similarly complex considerations persuaded her to hold one or two 'alarming' breakfasts (garden parties) at Buckingham Palace, where she had to recognize hundreds of people. After so many years' seclusion it was 'very puzzling & bewildering'. An inspection of the Zoo animals was less exacting. She drove in State to the Royal Academy only to find Landseer's famous *Swan attacked by Eagles*, 'not pleasing'. The Highland

Gathering at Braemar, 'a thing we always disliked', she felt just equal to attending. The South Kensington Museum proved wholly delightful, especially its display of china painted by 'ladies or at least women'.

Queen Victoria had never detached herself from her humbler subjects, even in the depths of seclusion. Mrs Lilly, her monthly nurse, lost her husband shortly after the Queen and the two widows met for a good cry. There were visits to hospitals and prisons. After reading *Female Prison Life*, she visited women convicts at Parkhurst; 'only 5 of them in for murder & these not of the worst character as they had killed their illegitimate, newly-born children out of shame.' She supported the abolition of capital punishment for infanticide. Unfortunately some of the prisoners recognized her and 'flopped down on their knees, crying & sobbing for pardon'. Her Majesty escaped up to the nursery where she found the babies well looked after, but *'not* by their own mothers'. A tremendous hubbub was going on inside the 'Refractory cells' which the Lady Superintendent explained: 'Most of the girls, Roman Catholic & Irish, had lately been visited by their priest & were now so unmanageable & excited nothing could be done with them . . .' The Union Workhouse at Old Windsor received a visit from Her Majesty which left her only half satisfied. The poor old couples, though kept clean, were separated. 'Hard on them.'[3]

If the Queen could have been left to potter about on her good works, she would have felt adequate. Her Florence Nightingale cult was far from exhausted. 'More than ever do I long to lead a private life, tending the poor & sick,' she wrote to Augusta of Prussia in 1865.[4] There, she felt, lay her vocation; but she was Queen of England and at this moment a new ferment had begun in the country's political life. It was over thirty years since the first Reform Bill of 1832. The time had come for another advance.

The Reform League was founded in 1865. Manhood suffrage and the ballot were its aims. John Bright, the Radical Member of Parliament, was its most eloquent spokesman. To his persuasions were added those of unemployment, poverty, bank failures, a ruined harvest, cholera and the *rinder pest* or cattle plague. (With the Victorian's enthusiasm for riddles, Ponsonby sent the latest from Balmoral to his wife: why is the rinder pest like a mouse? because the cat'll get it.)

Though not opposed to Reform as such, Queen Victoria detested the disturbances involved. 'This wretched reform,' she wrote in April 1866, was causing another 'dreaded Ministerial Crisis'. Russell, in fact, had reported to Her Majesty acute divisions in his Government over the proposed Bill; there was a good deal of 'earwigging' (flattery) and even more backbiting. Robert Lowe, the waspish albino, led off the Liberal malcontents into what Bright nicknamed the 'Cave of Adullam'. For fear of a crisis the Queen dared not pay her usual May visit to Balmoral, accepting instead the loan of Cliveden – 'within easy reach of my ministers'.* There she thought over the impasse predicted by her Foreign Secretary, Lord Clarendon, if Russell's Reform Bill were beaten. The Conservatives would refuse to take over. 'Lord Derby,' Clarendon explained, 'did not want to be made a fool of a 3rd. time by his Govt. not being able to stand.'[5]

Her old nightmare was upon her – the prospect of no government at all; but now she went into action alone. And a fear unknown to Prince Albert lent wings to her pen. A war between Prussia and Austria for the mastery of Germany was impending. Not the moment for a political crisis in England.

Her first line of action must be to urge Lord Derby '*confidentially*' to prevent Reform from being made into a party question. 'Did this entirely on my own responsibility,' she noted. Old, gouty but astute, Lord Derby replied that he could not support Reform. There was no way out along these lines. So the Queen tried the opposite tactics. She wheeled round upon Russell, pressing him to drop a measure which could not possibly be carried. Russell retorted that he would get it through somehow and anyway his followers would not allow it to be dropped. At the same moment Europe darkened. 'War seems inevitable,' she wrote on June 12th. Two days later

* From the Cliveden Visitors' Book we learn that she took with her 91 persons (including 3 doctors), 10 horses, 12 ponies and 8 carriages.

she left for Balmoral, thankful to get away from it all, 'if only for a short time'.

The Seven Weeks' War between Prussia and Austria had indeed broken out and proved to be one of the century's great watersheds, ending as it did in the rout of Austria at Sadowa. Queen Victoria had striven with tears, prayers and pen to avert a conflict in which her children would be fighting on different sides. At the eleventh hour her niece, Marie Leiningen, put into German for her an astonishing plea for peace to the King of Prussia: 'Beloved Brother, – At this fearful moment I cannot be silent . . . You are deceived . . .' by '*one man* . . .' But the responsibility for war rests on '*you alone* . . .'[6] Princess Louise put the matter more epigrammatically. When the Princess Royal wrote to ask what she should give Lenchen for a wedding present, Princess Louise promptly suggested, 'Bismarck's head on a charger.'

All in vain. The Queen's 'beloved brother' showed her letter to Bismarck and under the monster's eye composed what Queen Victoria called a 'deluded' answer. Lord Clarendon, the Foreign Secretary, had to explain away her intervention as a personal impulse.

War was declared. For a time Princess Alice completely lost touch with her soldier husband. She had just given birth to a third daughter. 'Poor dear Alice,' wrote the Queen in her Journal, '*what* a position for her!'

The respite at Balmoral in June was as short as Queen Victoria expected but too long to please the politicians. Russell's Government was defeated within five days. As it was by only 11 votes she declined to accept his resignation, dispatched a certificate of sickness from Dr Jenner and blocked her ears to the growls from the South. A new retreat for picnics had just been completed at Balmoral – the Gelder Sheil. Standing invitingly beside a trout stream, its carpets were down, furniture in, inkstand on the table. Over the door she had had inscribed in Gaelic: RUID NA BAHN RIGH, the Queen's House.

There, precisely, was the rub. The Queen's House. She could not escape even in the Gelder Sheil. The Princess Royal's little son Siggie died while the Queen was up there and she longed to be with her daughter. Her place was neither in Berlin, comforting Vicky, nor at Balmoral cosseting herself, but at Windsor.

She arrived back on June 26th, saw Russell, contemplated 'the peaceful face' in the Mausoleum and, on return, found a laconic telegram from the Prime Minister:

> ' "Proposition no. 2" (we had agreed upon 2 numbers) which meant resignation! So here we are! but think it is perhaps after all, better so.'[7]

Here we are indeed. Prussia was engaged upon annexing the first instalment of German states which had sided against her in the war with Austria, among them Hanover. Hesse-Darmstadt, Princess Alice's home, had also mobilized against Prussia. The Queen could do little to help except send bandages for Princess Alice's hospitals and give her children asylum. On June 27th, while the little Hesses scampered up and down the Corridor, the Queen held a Council declaring England's neutrality. Just as she finished a violent thunderstorm burst.

One episode diversified the ominous atmosphere. Louis Philippe's widow, Queen Amélie, had just died at Claremont. In the course of turning out the old house, a 'wonderful relic' was discovered and sent to the Queen – Princess Charlotte's hair. 'Such fine, thick long hair,' breathed Victoria; *cela m'a donné de l'émotion* . . . fresh as yesterday, after 49 years!'[8]

Meanwhile Lord Derby was struggling to form his last Ministry. By July 3rd as the Queen lay gasping on her sofa in the appalling heat, sending and receiving messages, she knew that he would succeed. With the Prime Minister in the Lords, Disraeli would be Chancellor and Leader of the House: '. . . all these changes are very trying.' Her hatred of upheavals hid from her the brightness of the future.

The Tories no more than the Liberals could drop Reform. Edmund Beales and other Radicals organized gigantic outdoor meetings at one of which, on July 23rd, the gates of Hyde Park were ill-advisedly closed against them. Her Majesty heard that 'the worst sort of people' had thereupon pulled up the railings and rushed into the Park, trampling flower beds, knocking down lamp standards and setting fire to the gas pipes beneath. Mrs Disraeli, marooned in Curzon Street, in the path of the mob, could not help sympathizing with thwarted democracy.

The Queen was soon urgently commending Reform to the Tories. 'There is a growing feeling for it in the country, amongst all the respectable classes.'[9] Mr Disraeli came to see her and made a fair impression. At any rate he and Lord Derby persuaded her to open in February 1861 the Parliament which was to pass the second Reform Bill. She afterwards regretted having done so. Despite torrential rain she lowered once more the carriage windows to give her 'good people' a clear view. A sea of 'nasty faces' screaming for Reform met her gaze. At such times of agitation, she noted angrily, 'the Sovereign should not be there'.[10] She saw no connection between her seclusion and the nasty faces.

Now the battle in Parliament was joined. She still hoped that Reform would be 'taken out of party politics' but there were too many anti-Reformers on both sides of the House for Disraeli to be able to gratify her. Robert Lowe sailed forth from his Cave of Adullam to attack a Bill which gave power to an illiterate democracy: we must first 'compel our future masters,' he insisted, 'to learn their letters.' Three Ministers resigned, Lord Cranborne (later Lord Salisbury, the future Prime Minister), General Peel and Lord Carnarvon. The Queen succeeded in keeping Peel straight until Cranborne deserted, when Peel followed. Only with Peel would she shake hands when the three came to give up their seals; tears stood in his eyes. Carnarvon also was 'dreadfully distressed' but got no handshake. As for Cranborne, his conduct was unworthy of a gentleman. She took his seals with scarcely a word.

The Reform Bill duly passed its third reading. Queen Victoria's influence on the course of this historic battle for Household Franchise, in which one million new voters were added to the polls, was negligible. Party politics prevented the agreed measure she desired; royal appeals failed to subdue the rebel Tories; Lord Derby's slogan – 'a leap in the dark' – was not her view of a Bill which she regarded as sensible and just. Derby added that it would 'dish the Whigs'. She had as yet no wish to see them dished. She simply wanted both sides to 'buckle to'.[11]

The battle of Reform, however, as interpreted by Disraeli to the Queen, had a profound influence on her own development. She pictured a nation reshaping itself in forms ever more favourable to a benevolent Monarchy, but hostile to Society. A demand from the pleasure-seeking Prince of Wales for sterner measures against 'rebels' among the 'lower orders'[12] coincided with the Queen's annual meditation in the sacred Blue Room. The experience crystallized her thoughts and she passed them on four days later to the Princess Royal. (The Prince had to wait for his answer, couched in much the same language, for over three weeks.)

'A new French Revolution,' she felt, might be impending in England because of the gap between the upper and lower classes. The aristocracy, with a few honourable exceptions, were frivolous, pleasure-seeking, immoral gamblers; the young men ignorant and self-indulgent, the young women 'fast':

> 'The Lower Classes are becoming so well-informed – are so intelligent & earn their bread & riches so deservedly that they cannot & ought not to be kept back – to be abused by the wretched ignorant Highborn beings, who live only to kill time.'

What the upper classes needed was a frightening shock before the 'dreadful crash'.[13]

The Queen's pen often ran away with her. The more she wrote, the more her emotions bubbled out in a Cassandra-like shriek. But now she was drawing on a pool of experience. Who persecuted John Brown? High-born beings. Who condemned her seclusion? High-born beings. Who led her sons astray? High-born beings. Of Disraeli's 'two nations', rich and poor, she was Queen of the poor, the loyal poor who cheered her most, sympathized most with her grief. When she inquired about the appalling problem of vagrancy in London, whom did she find were the vagrants? Not the 'lowest class but criminals, including even clergymen'!! For their own sakes the poor could not all get the vote, but they were all loyal.

441

Memories of the good poor were there to strengthen her intuition – the gipsies of Claremont, the self-educated tailor and shoemaker, the ballast-heavers who christened her husband 'Albert the Good'. Above them was the yeoman army of John Browns; higher still, Samuel Smiles, whose *Lives of the Engineers* she presented to Prince Louis of Hesse; Robert Applegarth whom she appointed to a Royal Commission on Contagious Diseases, the first working man to receive that honour; Edwin Chadwick, the pioneer of sanitation whom she created a Commander of the Bath in 1854 and a Knight thirty years later, 'to distinguish me,' as he said, 'from the great unwashed.'

From her royal eminence all these good people were foreshortened into a single concept – the 'lower classes'. Now they were joined by a new prophet, Benjamin Disraeli. In February 1868 the gout finally disabled Lord Derby and Disraeli became Prime Minister. 'A proud thing,' Queen Victoria wrote to the Princess Royal, 'for a Man "risen from the people" – to have attained!' His father, after all, was not only a Jew, but a 'mere man of letters'.[14]

The Queen's division between lower and upper classes ignored the middle-class – the class *par excellence* of the Victorian era. Disraeli himself was middle-class, not a man risen from the people, as the Queen really knew. During this very period she was studying literary men, among them Carlyle, Froude and Browning, in their natural habitat, namely five o'clock tea at Lady Augusta Stanley's. In 1870 she actually invited Dickens to Buckingham Palace and recorded his view that the division of classes would gradually cease. 'And I earnestly pray it may.'[15]

The truth is that though Queen Victoria was *bourgeoise* enough for the middle-class to claim her as their own, she herself was no more interested in the minutiae of classes than of religious creeds. She distinguished broadly, like the rest of the aristocracy, between those who worked for a living and those who did not. The 'upper classes' did not. They did not need to. If they were good they gave unpaid labour on their estates, in their counties and at Westminster. If bad, they gambled and made love. It was right to marry into money but not to

442

make it. Queen Victoria refused in 1869 to create Lionel de Rothschild a peer as much for deriving his wealth 'solely from money contracts', as for being a Jew. She once remarked to a maid-of-honour who complained of having rheumatism in her legs, that when she came to the throne young ladies did not have legs. A time was approaching when members of the ruling class would not only have legs but salaries. Meanwhile, Queen Victoria stuck to older categories according to which Disraeli was a man of the people.

'Yes, I have climbed to the top of the greasy pole,' said Disraeli with a gay, plebeian flourish.

It is a remarkable fact that Disraeli's and Brown's periods of influence on Queen Victoria almost coincided, Brown over-running Disraeli by two years at each end. Those who would attribute her revival exclusively to one or the other must find room for Brown's 'wumman' and Disraeli's 'faery' inside the same skin at the same time. In their different ways they each helped to supply a need which the Queen herself analysed more than once:

> 'When one's beloved Husband is gone, & one's Children are married – one feels that a friend . . . who can devote him or herself entirely to you is the one thing you do require to help you on – & to sympathize entirely with you. Not that you love your Children less – but you feel as they grow up & marry that you can be of so little use to them, & they to you (especially in the Higher Classes) . . .'[16]

Other factors, of course, contributed to the Queen's recovery. A firmer grasp of politics which, after Prince Albert's spoon-feeding, had seemed incomprehensible, and a better secretarial system. General Grey, as we have seen, was not officially gazetted as private secretary until she had been a widow for six years. Even then Lord Clarendon, her erstwhile favourite, behaved so jealously towards Grey that she opposed (without success) his becoming Foreign Secretary in Gladstone's first Ministry. She might have forgiven him for calling her 'Eliza' or 'the Missus' behind her back, but trouble-makers in her house she could not tolerate.

Queen Victoria's most romantic relationship had begun in the best tradition – with repugnance. 'Mr Disraeli (!) *high office*', she exploded in 1844 when the young Tory dandy asked for and was refused a job under Peel. Disraeli's subsequent attacks on Free Trade were 'dreadfully bitter'; he himself was 'unprincipled, reckless, & not respectable'. By 1849 he was Leader of the Opposition in the House of Commons but for every speech of his which she considered 'most brilliant', another was 'disgraceful'. As Chancellor of the Exchequer in 1852 he was at last able to woo her with his pen. Never had she received such Parliamentary reports. He described speeches as 'elaborate', 'malignant', or 'languid' instead of merely good, bad or indifferent. When he wanted to call a speaker's style elegant, he said it had 'concinnity'. A little dazed, she was nevertheless grateful.

Dizzy was so 'odd'. Odd he remained in her eyes, with his black ringlets and skin like a Dead Sea scroll, until he became Prime Minister at the age of sixty-four. Whenever Mrs Disraeli came with him, she only added to the oddness. 'Mrs Disraeli was very odd.' Nevertheless Queen Victoria had manifested a weakness for the *outré* ever since her girlhood, and given the right circumstances, Dizzy's oddities could turn out to be irresistible. Even his peculiar appearance was unlikely to disturb the niece of King Leopold, who had recently gone to the grave in a rich black wig and wrinkled skin brilliantly rouged. Queen Victoria accepted the many grotesque faces which surrounded her with stoicism, reserving her comments for the handsome ones.

Prince Albert had no taste for the *outré*. He had written off Disraeli as an impostor and his conversion to Free Trade as dishonest. But if the living Albert kept Queen Victoria and Disraeli apart, the dear departed brought them together. No one's condolences pleased her more than Dizzy's. His speech on the Albert Memorial made her weep. While Gladstone delayed its construction by haggling over the cost, Disraeli carried the vote through Parliament. The Irish refused to subscribe to a public memorial and later tried to blow up the Prince's statue in Phoenix Park. She heard that they also had held up the Albert Memorial in Kensington by not carrying out their contract for granite. Gladstone would excuse the Irish. Disraeli reiterated his assurance, given as long ago as January 1861, that she could always rely on the Conservative Party 'as on a rock'. Should she choose Gladstone and the Irish granite or Disraeli and the Conservative rock? When Disraeli struck water from the rock in the form of Tory Democracy – the union of Queen and People – Queen Victoria drank eagerly.

To borrow a phrase of Bagehot's, Disraeli had accelerated 'the march of improvement' not only in the electoral registers but in the Queen's spirits. Yet a price had to be paid. Every step out of seclusion brought the risk of a step away from Albert. She gradually rejected not only the Prince's criticisms of Disraeli but many of his treasured ideals. By the time the Liberals were pushing Army reform the Queen was against it. Duelling, which he had helped to abolish, she now felt was needed to keep chivalry alive:

'There *are* positions which require Duels, I really think & many Gentlemen have said the same.'[17]

Disraeli kissed hands as Prime Minister on February 27th, 1868. Taking the plump little hand in both of his he murmured: 'In loving loyalty and faith.' Her Majesty was touched to see him so humble. She was also amused by his pen-portraits of colleagues. Ward Hunt, for instance, was a giant. 'But he has the sagacity of the elephant, as well as the form.' Disraeli's own sagacity was less cumbersome. He gracefully summed up his future relations with the Sovereign as 'on her part perfect confidence; on his, perfect devotion'. Complimenting her on her great experience which surpassed 'all living princes and most living people', he entreated her not to withhold from him the benefit of her guidance. All great matters he would submit to her; the burden of all trivial affairs should be borne by him alone.[18] In point of fact Disraeli found it more convenient to reverse these chivalrous principles, permitting Her Majesty to settle minor matters and reserving the great decisions for himself.

A display of 'bad taste' marred the formation of Disraeli's first Government. The retiring Lord Chancellor, Lord Chelmsford, literally clung to the Great Seal, afterwards complaining that he had not been given as much notice as a housemaid. Only the sternest possible rebuke, followed by 'a very undignified' tug-of-war, enabled Her Majesty to wrench the Seal from his grasp. 'It really was most disagreeable.'[19]

Disraeli quickly showed himself able to manage the Queen. No head-on collisions but a patient assumption that she would see reason. He persuaded her to repeal the Ecclesiastical Titles Bill: since all titles emanated from her, those assumed by the Catholic Hierarchy were illegal anyway. His reasoning was sophistical, flattering and effective. A warm sensation of national unity under the new dispensation swept over her. Disraeli assured her that a Liberal vote of confidence would prove 'a popgun not an Armstrong gun',[20] and thanked her fervently for redrafting one of his speeches 'in a liberal sense'[21]; Principal Tullogh of St Andrews University preached to her on creeds and classes in a 'liberal Christian spirit'[22]; the new Lord Chancellor, Lord Cairns, showed his liberality by enabling the Court to go abroad while Parliament was still sitting and live 'completely together like a family'.[23]

The Queen chose the Pension Wallace at Lucerne (her courtiers thought she was attracted by its Scottish name), travelling to everyone's amusement as the Countess of Kent. Disraeli wrote of her as 'our dear Peeress' and her daughter Louise mischievously signed herself 'Lady Louise Kent'. Sir Thomas Biddulph remarked to Lady Ely,

'It won't do for you to have Marchioness of Ely on your baggage. You will be greater than her.'

'No, dear, I shall put "Plain Lady Ely" on my boxes.'

John Brown won a battle to occupy the Countess's box-seat while wearing his kilt. His insistence on treating Switzerland as a province of Britain drove everyone mad. 'J.B., of course, asks for everything for the Queen as if he were in Windsor Castle,' wrote Ponsonby, 'and if anything cannot be got, he says it must – and it is.' Jenner, who had never before seen foreign sanitation, rushed about looking for smells. The Queen climbed on glaciers, joked in the 'cheerful little home' and returned to find the skyline of what she called her 'ain dear Heeland home' distinctly flat.

To mark her gratitude for all this happiness she had begun in the springtime to send Disraeli primroses from Osborne. He thanked her in language no less flowery and in return sent her his novels and letters crammed with gossip. For the first time in her life she felt really on the inside, confiding to Lady Augusta Stanley that 'she never before knew *everything*'. Princess Helena, reported Lady Augusta, was even madder about Disraeli than her Mama ('I think he must have spread his butter very thick') but Princess Louise, in the manner of sisters, ridiculed Lenchen's idolatry.[24] On September 19th Disraeli paid his first visit to Balmoral. It rained for five days running. Though the library, where they dined, was as cosy as the Albany, he decided that the place upset him. A different impression was given to Her Majesty; he 'seemed delighted with his visit & made himself most agreeable'.[25]

In November a general election brought the idyll to an end. The 'popgun' (vote of confidence) had defeated Disraeli's Government earlier in the year. He had offered the Queen a choice between his resignation at once or dissolution later. She chose dissolution later, gambling on the chance of Disraeli getting back. Great was Liberal rage, for his constitutional duty was to offer not a choice but advice. Dizzy, however, intended to demonstrate two points : the Sovereign's power to choose – and to choose him.

Despite Disraeli's warnings the Queen hoped for a Tory victory. Though she heard 'a great ringing of bells' on November 17th as polling proceeded, there was less noise from the newly enfranchised voters than she had feared – surely a hopeful sign. Nevertheless the Tories were soundly beaten. As a tribute to her retiring Prime Minister and at his earnest request, she created his wife the Viscountess Beaconsfield and reluctantly yielded herself to Gladstone's political embrace. Her new Prime Minister was already known to the masses by a name singularly unpleasing to their Queen: 'The People's William'. But with the propriety habitual to her, she received him graciously. 'He is completely under the charm,' wrote Granville delightedly to Grey.

William Ewart Gladstone was ten and a half years older than the Queen. At fifty-nine he was a striking figure: tall, upright, with flashing eyes, commanding features and a voice even more remarkable than her own. Beginning as a Tory, he had become a Peelite and finally moved over to the Liberals in 1859. He attended his first Liberal conclave in 1854 and was much shocked at their behaviour. John Russell, however, in telling this story to Queen Victoria, explained that Liberal meetings were 'always like this'.

On paper Gladstone was all set to become a royal favourite. He was clearly in line with Prince Albert, Peel and Aberdeen. The Prince had admired his moral character, choosing his son Willie to accompany the wayward Bertie abroad. Mrs Gladstone had brought four little Gladstones to play at Windsor in 1846 and her sister had married the eldest son of the Queen's beloved Lady Lyttelton. Queen Victoria appreciated Gladstone's virtue. After a dinner at Balmoral a sincere tribute appeared in her Journal:

'He is very agreeable, so quiet & intellectual, with such a knowledge of all subjects, & is such a *good* man . . .'[26]

Perhaps this success was a result of Mrs Gladstone's wifely advice the year before: 'do pet the Queen', she had implored her husband, 'and for once believe you can, you dear old thing.'[27]

There were nevertheless many references in Queen Victoria's past diaries to a different Gladstone, a Gladstone whom she could not trust. Twice he had resigned office for inexplicable reasons. The first time (1845) he told her that he left the Government 'with perfectly unchanged feelings'. Then why resign? Ten years later he did it again, hoping Her Majesty would understand his motive. She did not. 'The good people here are really a little *mad*,' she wrote to King Leopold, applying for the first time to Gladstone and his friends an adjective which she was later to use with angry abandon. Two years after that, in 1857, she was grumbling that the Peelites' consciences always caused trouble. A month later she roundly accused Gladstone of humbug.

To be called a humbug by Queen Victoria was serious.

With her worship of directness, hypocrisy repelled her more than, say, Dizzy's failure to be 'respectable'. Other weaknesses were brought to her notice by Gladstone's Tory ex-colleagues. Lord Derby, for instance, accused him of lacking the temperament for a leader.[28] Sir Charles Wood (afterwards Lord Halifax), a fellow Liberal, repeated this indictment in 1863 and again in 1864 when Gladstone had become the 'People's William'. As Chancellor of the Exchequer in 1864, Gladstone electrified the House and country with a speech assumed to be advocating universal suffrage. Queen Victoria shared the general consternation, describing his act as 'strange' – a word she often used to denote mental derangement. In the same year he refused to sanction improvements in Army sanitation, a subject particularly dear to Queen Victoria's heart. Gladstone's attitude to the Army wounded the Queen where she was most sensitive – in her prerogative.

As ill luck would have it, the main concern of Gladstone's first Ministry was to strike at her prerogative again, this time through the Irish Church. He proposed to disestablish that Protestant Church of Ireland of which the Monarch was head.

During the unspeakable horrors of 'The Great Hunger' (1846–1850) Ireland lost one and a half million people by death and one million by emigration. Those who fled to England brought with them the viruses of deadly fevers. Those who reached America brought, as well as fever, an even more lethal virus – passion for revenge. The Fenians were founded in America to destroy British rule in Ireland.

Gladstone did not admire the Irish. They were an 'unstable' people, he told the Queen in 1866.[29] It was none the less necessary to tranquillize them, for their condition was a 'standing reproach' to Britain abroad. Since the vast majority of Irish were Roman Catholics, a feature of British rule which particularly offended them was their obligation to support the Protestant Church with tithes. By disestablishing this alien Church, Gladstone hoped to bring peace to that distressful island. It was not for nothing that Gladstone, whose hobby was timber-felling, had described the Protestant ascendancy in Ireland during his successful election campaign as 'a tall tree of noxious growth'. He happened to be cutting down a real tree when he received the expected telegram from Windsor. 'Very significant,' he remarked as he plied his axe, adding: 'My mission is to pacify Ireland.'[30]

The Queen had no faith in the brand of pacification preached by this sinewy missionary. 'He thought his measures would do it, which I doubted,' she wrote on December 13th, 1868, 'observing that the tenure of land was of far more importance [than Disestablishment] to the Irish'. When Gladstone sent her a labyrinthine explanation of Disestablishment, she had to ask Theodore Martin to explain the explanation. Not the least of Gladstone's failures with the Queen was his inability to make contact with a mind that was businesslike but not abstract. His dissertations made her feel inferior.

The Queen was no less concerned to pacify Ireland than Gladstone himself. She had several times been the object of imaginary Fenian 'plots', the first alarm having been raised on October 14th, 1867. General Grey rushed in with a report from Manchester that the Fenians were after her. A month earlier Manchester had been the scene of a Fenian *coup*. Five Irishmen had attempted to rescue two Fenian prisoners from a police van and a British policeman had been killed. Now General Grey was determined to surround Balmoral with troops. This looked to the Queen like distrust of her faithful Highlanders and in giving her reluctant consent she commented, 'Too foolish!!'[31] The Lord Lieutenant of Ireland had assured her only the year before that Fenianism was no longer a danger. He did not hold out any early hope, however, of real improvement among this 'peculiar' and 'rather treacherous people'.[32] The Irish lower orders, concluded the Queen, 'had never become reconciled to the English rule, which they hate! So different from the Scotch who are so loyal.'

On November 23rd three of the captured Fenians were hanged. The Queen's feelings about the Manchester Martyrs, as they were called, were mixed. She approved of the severest measures against 'these horrid people' – had not Lord Derby said the Irish were far too much 'cajoled'?[33] – and told her daughter so. 'We shall have to hang some, & it ought to have

450

been done before.'[34] But it was 'dreadful' to have to 'press for such a thing'. A deputation pleading for mercy never reached her. Grey refused to receive them, the townspeople yelled 'to the duckpond!' and they had to be locked into their railway carriage to avoid a lynching. On the day of execution Queen Victoria wrote: 'I prayed for these poor men last night.'[35]

Violence continued. Another rescue attempt resulted in seventy feet of Clerkenwell Prison wall being dynamited and innocent people including children crushed. Then came a telegram from Canada reporting that eighty ruffians were making for the Bristol Channel: they would slide up the south coast, cast anchor one dark night in the Solent, row with muffled oars to the Queen's little beach and next morning, when she was driving in the woods, snatch her out of her pony-chaise from under John Brown's nose. General Grey besought her 'on his knees' to leave Osborne.

The Queen was agitated, sceptical, stubborn. In her heart she suspected that Grey's demonstration was part of a plot, quite as nasty as the Fenian one, to terminate her seclusion. She refused to leave. Grey burst out in fury that in that case he washed his hands of her safety. Royal lightnings followed, but she accepted extra police, outriders, sentries, passes for entering the house, the Guards, and warships off Osborne – 'such a bore'.[36]

Just before Christmas she heard that the eighty mariners were a myth. 'Cannot help thinking that other reports of risings in Britain must be exaggerated.'[37] Much relieved, she lambasted the authorities for their credulity. By next spring (1868) she was thoroughly sceptical about the whole Irish business. Informers were impostors, detectives gullible, Fenians in England dwindling away, Fenians in Ireland or abroad unappeasable. In Australia a Fenian had tried to kill Prince Alfred as a reprisal for the November executions, putting a bullet between his ninth and tenth ribs at a public picnic, where he was about to present a cheque for charity. Fortunately Miss Nightingale had just sent out two trained nurses for the Sydney Infirmary who nursed him back to health. By a pleasant coincidence the Queen had laid the foundation stone of St Thomas's Hospital for Miss Nightingale just before the news of Prince Alfred's convalescence arrived. She felt that people who could shoot her son – someone 'entirely unconnected with politics or the Irish' – were plain wicked. It was in this mood that she derided Gladstone's Bill to disestablish the Irish Church.

The Protestant churchmen with whom Queen Victoria discussed the Bill, affected her in different ways. Dean Wellesley said that good might come of it. The late Archbishop of Canterbury, Dr Longley, had taken a gloomier view and died, the Queen thought, of a broken heart. He was replaced by Archbishop Tait, the first Primate to become her friend. Perhaps it was partly because Mrs Tait, though not of course a widow, had lost five children from fever in one month.

The Queen's Protestant feelings were deeply involved. Prince Albert used to say that the Reformation was left half finished and some day it would have to be completed. Meanwhile, she felt herself 'very much a dissenter, or, even more, Presbyterian'.[38] Not that anything must be done to stir up Protestant agitation. As the Prince had also explained, you could not treat the Catholics in Ireland as 'ordinary dissenters' since they happened to form a large majority of the population. Disestablishment, however, would cause agitation by stirring up 'Ultra-Protestants'. And where would Disestablishment end? Bishop Wilberforce heard it said that Gladstone had gone mad.[39] Both Dr Caird and Dr Macleod prophesied that the Church of Scotland 'would be the next to fall'. She told Granville darkly not to let the impression get about 'that more things were to be disestablished' – such as Irish land.[40]

In face of all these fears she refused to open Parliament and thus seem to approve the Bill, coolly informing the enraged Gladstone that he could say she had a worse headache than usual. When the Princess Royal among others deprecated this backsliding, the Queen tartly summed up her attitude: '. . . I will not appear to have turned quite round.'[41] She forgot that it was the Ministry which had changed, not the Sovereign. In the same breath, however, she remembered her constitutional duty, promising to support her Government 'to the utmost extent'. She was largely, if not to the utmost extent, true to her word.

When Gladstone's Bill reached the Lords, she urged moderation upon the Opposition peers while secretly agreeing with Dean Stanley that they '*must* amend the Irish bill, as much as they can'.[42] Their lordships proceeded to show that they could amend it so drastically as to provoke a constitutional crisis. Whereupon the Queen took fright and all sides ran for compromise. On July 22nd, 1869, she recorded with unspeakable relief: 'Everything is settled!!!' The Irish Church was duly disestablished. When it came to the pinch, she desperately wanted the machinery to work even if she abominated the product.

How did Queen Victoria stand at the end of 1869 *vis-à-vis* the two new forces which were to dominate the second half of her reign – Tory Democracy and Liberalism emergent from Whiggery – each with a leader of genius?

Gladstone was falling behind. Though his last speech on Disestablishment was 'very fine & very *handsome*',[43] her compliments to him were academic rather than heartfelt. Those personal idiosyncrasies of the great man which so exacerbated later struggles already fretted her: she could not find him agreeable, '& he talks so very much'.[44] In vain Dean Wellesley had besought the Prime Minister, as soon as he took office, to respect the Queen's susceptibilities: 'you cannot show too much regard, gentleness, I might even say tenderness towards Her'.[45] She was struck by his strange lack of human understanding, want of foresight and sudden enthusiasms indicating no great grasp of mind; 'but as the Duke of Argyll truly says, Mr Gladstone has a very high character.'

Brutus is an honourable man . . .

Disraeli might not be so 'noble' and earnest nor have such strong convictions, but if anything he was 'even more unselfish' and his ideas were larger.[46]

The duty of expounding Tory Reform to the Queen having fallen to Disraeli, he had inevitably stolen an ideological march on his rival. His 'large ideas' grew larger in her imagination

453

as she mulled them over. In reforming the Constitution he would force Society to reform itself; the working classes would educate their masters. There would be no more misbehaviour on the steps of the Throne, once Society was reformed. Of all Queen Victoria's present anxieties, the greatest was her unreformed family.

CHAPTER XXV

HEAD OF ALL THE FAMILY
1865-9

QUEEN VICTORIA'S forty-seventh birthday (May 24th, 1866) was marked by the restoration of a pious act which had fallen into abeyance. She counted her blessings. They made an interesting short list. Affectionate children and friends; the ability to make others happy and to be of use. Up till now she had performed her matriarchal duties more as a martyr than a mother. When the Prince was alive she had not been able to choose a bonnet alone; five years later she could not trust her family, her Court, her country, Europe itself to choose a children's nurse, a new fashion or a foreign policy without her advice. The remark dropped by Princess Alice at the time of King Leopold's death had gone home. 'Now you are head of all the family'.

A 'royal' visit in 1864 had stimulated her latent energies. The Italian patriot, General Garibaldi, was invited to England and tumultuously fêted by half the aristocracy. From behind the Castle walls Queen Victoria glowered, but the red carpet was unrolled even at Stafford House and her friend the Duchess of Sutherland received Garibaldi like royalty at the top of the stairs.* One reception was attended by the Prince of Wales himself. Queen Victoria castigated her unrepentant son and denounced to the Princess Royal

'. . . the incredible folly & imprudence of your thoughtless eldest brother going to see him without my knowledge!'[1]

She conceded that Garibaldi was 'honest, disinterested & brave'[2]; he was nevertheless a revolutionary who had driven the dear Duchess and the Liberal Party 'half-crazed'. As for

---

* A cork oak (*quercus suber*) was planted by Garibaldi at the Sutherlands' country seat, Cliveden, in 1864 and a hundred years later, though emaciated, it still stands. Immediately in front of it is the bronze statue of the Prince Consort presented by Queen Victoria, complete with kilt, gun and Garter ribbon. The juxtaposition of tree and statue must surely have been kept from her.

the Waleses, this was what happened if she took her eyes off them for an instant. Jealous yet impotent by her own decree, she thanked God when Garibaldi's 'humiliating' visit ended.

Next year she consented to meet the widowed Queen Emma of Hawaii who, though 'a savage' in appearance, was 'peculiarly civilized', discreetly withdrawing after a few minutes. When the President of the United States was assassinated, Queen Victoria needed no urging to send a letter of condolence to his widow. 'Dear Madam, – Though a stranger to you . . .'[3] it began, with a degree of modesty which in anyone else might have seemed artificial. Two years later, when the Government urgently requested her to entertain the Sultan of Turkey, she put up only a token resistance.

Her 'Oriental brother' turned out to have truly splendid eyes and 'ate most things, but (which I was glad to see) never touched wine';[4] his meat was cut up for him. With evident relish she described the return of splendour – the magnificent gold plate out again, everyone in full dress including Brown, Brown's brother Archie and Ross the piper, and the band playing 'the first time these 6 sad years'. The programme concluded with a review at Spithead in lashing rain and a heavy swell. Though constantly obliged to retire below the Sultan managed to receive the Garter on deck, having foolishly let it be known that the Navy was his hobby.

The Prince of Wales and his family kept the Queen's matriarchal feelings in a state of perpetual flux. One day she would expatiate on their charming natures; next, she found the whole family wretched, ill-behaved and selfish. Alix, 'good as she is – is not worth the price we have paid for her – in having such a family connection'![5] A month later word goes forth that Alix must be dearly loved and respected: 'I often think her lot is no easy one; but she is vy fond of B. tho' not blind.'[6] Two years pass and the Princess is going out too much in Society, allowing people to be too familiar with her, coming into her drawing-room knitting, not getting up till eleven so that her poor husband has to breakfast alone. Shortly afterwards no one could be 'dearer & nicer' than Alix: she and the Queen are always driving about together.[7]

Queen Victoria's relations with the Prince of Wales showed a gradual improvement, despite the gloomy prognosis of Sir James Clark at the end of 1865.

> 'No one who knows the character of the Queen and of the Heir apparent can look forward to the future without seeing troubles in that quarter . . .'[8]

Even her over-anxious heart could not fail to recognize his devotion to herself. 'Really dear Bertie is so full of good & amiable qualities,' she wrote to the Princess Royal in 1867, 'that it makes one forget & overlook much that one would wish different.' Nevertheless one did wish much different, indeed, almost his whole way of life. The 'Marlborough House set' who frequented his London home were the fast set. Knitting in public was one of their least offences. Gambling, racing, smoking, associating with Americans and Jews – he had learned all these deplorable habits from Society. She once likened London to Zion before its destruction; her Angel had mourned over its vices as Christ wept over Jerusalem. He could never have lived happily in this wicked world.[9]

Queen Victoria had by now shifted the sin of parricide from her son's shoulders to Society as a whole. As she warmed to him she grew colder towards his circle. Sometimes she felt that Society caused him to neglect her. After they had breakfasted together one day she wrote, 'I am always glad & happy to have him a little with me, & I only wish I could see him oftener.'[10] But she considered him still too indiscreet to share her State duties apart from the ceremonial ones – a division of labour which produced its own embarrassments. When the Queen began holding a few small Courts at Buckingham Palace, no one wanted to be fobbed off with Princess Alexandra's supplementary drawing-rooms at St James's Palace. One day Lord Derby, dining with the Duke of Marlborough, forgot that he was sitting next to the Princess. 'I say, Sydney,' he shouted to the Lord Chamberlain across the table, 'who will you get to go to your skimmed milk affairs at St James's now?'[11]

The Queen longed to receive generous, undiluted confidence from her heir while retaining the right to ration with extreme caution the amount of confidence she gave in return. During the Schleswig-Holstein war, Lord Clarendon was permitted to keep the Prince *au fait* with events without revealing '*anything* of a very *confidential* nature'.[12] Shortly afterwards the Prince asked, through Lord Russell, to see some actual Cabinet dispatches instead of a mere précis written by his mother's secretary. This time the Queen sharply forbade any 'independent communication' between her son and her Government. And for close on thirty years she obstinately kept Prince Albert's golden key to the Foreign Office boxes out of hands which seemed to her both grasping and incapable. She was equally opposed to the Duke of Cambridge taking the Prince to Aldershot in place of his absent Mama, though when she herself took him in 1869 she wrote enthusiastically, 'I am sure no Heir apparent ever was so nice & unpretending as dear Bertie is.' Requests to open a Dublin Exhibition or attend the wedding of his sister-in-law in Russia were granted grudgingly. 'The country, and all of *us* would like to see you a little more stationary . . .'[13]

Even Disraeli's courtly phrases could not persuade her to sanction a scheme for installing the Prince in an Irish holiday residence. 'This would in a certain degree, combine the fulfilment of public duty with pastime,' wrote Disraeli hopefully, 'a combination which befits a princely life.' Queen Victoria, who did not like the sound of 'a princely life', was furious:

'*Any encouragement* of his constant love of running about, and not keeping at home or near the Queen, is *earnestly* and *seriously* to be deprecated.'[14]

She would permit a brief visit as a gesture but never a residence. Nor must he go especially for the Punchestown races, 'which should only come in as an incident.' (Ponsonby believed that the mere sound of the word 'Punchestown' made the Queen shudder.)

In her private opinion, no gesture would do any good to Ireland. The Catholic Irish, even the upper classes, were 'totally unreliable, & utterly untrue .   . grievances they really have none'. Only 'a new infusion of race' would solve

458

the Irish problem.[15] She had in fact been infected by the Prince Consort with vague racial theories which attributed Scottish superiority to a mixture of Scandinavian blood. There was also an element of jealousy. The Highlands of Balmoral might be ousted by the Highlands of Donegal.

The Prince of Wales, twenty-eight in 1869, still had no occupation worth the name. Other young bloods were put into this or that government department to keep them away from the skittles. Queen Victoria could not see that a better way of making her son 'stationary' than tethering him to her widow's streamers, was to plant him in a job. So indelible was the impression left on her by Prince Albert of the Prince of Wales as a 'regular *mauvais sujet*', that she ignored the good advice she herself had often given to other parents. Augusta of Prussia, for instance, had been urged not to guard her Fritz too closely but to give him responsibility. As a parent, however, Queen Victoria was by no means unique in knowing the correct procedure without being able to follow it. Her mistakes seem monstrous because they were committed on the grand scale which royalty creates.

The temptations of Society were no threat to the Princess Royal. Her trouble was being too stiff and brusque. At the Paris Exhibition of 1867, for example, she caused great offence by taking only three old gowns, studying nothing but surgical instruments and sanitation and leaving early. Interminable pages of advice were still dispatched by the Queen with apologies for any criticisms; they were written only out of deep love. Sometimes she was able to congratulate Vicky on a 'great improvement'; but whether Vicky's chart rose or fell, the Queen promised to continue telling the truth, since truthfulness, absence of flattery and 'a tolerable quick and correct appreciation of character' were her only merits.[16]

Gone were the days when the Queen described herself as a bad and the Prince Consort as a good judge of character. Her new claim, if not altogether justified, especially as regards men, at any rate marked the growth of self-confidence.

The Queen's four youngest children brought her more pleasure than pain. Princess Beatrice at eight was still 'Baby' and had no faults save that of behaving occasionally like a child.

'2nd June 1865 – Baby's liveliness & fidgetyness was beyond everything, & she ended by throwing all the milk over herself.'

With Prince Leopold, now struggling through his precarious adolescence, it was a running battle to prevent him from doing too much. The Queen gave him the Garter a year earlier than his brothers because

'he was far more advanced in mind & I wish to give him this encouragement & pleasure, as he has so many privations & disappointments.'[17]

At various times she tried to see a replica of her husband in one or other of her sons. In 'little Leo' she discovered his father's brains. When in 1868 he was 'given back from 'the brink of the grave', she vowed to make him henceforth her chief object in life.

The Prince Consort's character, if not his brains, was reflected in her favourite son, Prince Arthur. She found no blemish in him, as in 'poor Affie'. Quoting (not quite correctly) the famous line which Tennyson had applied to the Prince Consort, she hoped that Arthur, at least, would wear 'the lily of a blameless life',* making sure by her vigilance that the lily did not fade. She instructed the Prince's Governor, Sir Howard Elphinstone, to keep the thermometers in her son's rooms at 60°; to prevent him from going behind the scenes at the theatres and to the Derby with Prince Alfred, from wearing 'frightful *stick-ups*' or a centre parting or putting his hands in his pockets.[18] He must keep a daily journal, like the Queen his dear mother. Ponsonby reported that the devoted Elphinstone was not always pleased by HM's 'crisp incessant' orders.

Princess Louise had developed slowly and at eighteen,

* 'Wearing the white flower of a blameless life.' *Dedication, Idylls of the King,* 1862.

though a sculptress and more talented than her sister, Princess Helena, suffered from feelings of inferiority. Like a good mother, Queen Victoria privately asked the Princess Royal to make Louise godmother to her new baby. It was through Princess Louise that the Queen's singing voice was first heard again at Osborne. She began the new year of 1867 by accompanying her daughter on the piano, 'even trying to sing a little myself'. On Princess Louise's twentieth birthday she paid her a characteristic tribute: 'She is (& who wld some years ago have thought it?) a clever, dear girl . . .'[19]

At twenty-two Princess Louise fell in love with the Duke of Argyll's heir, Lord Lorne, a Liberal Member of Parliament and 'a subject'. Queen Victoria had already prepared her eldest son the year before for a subject as brother-in-law. Louise, she explained to him, was on no account going to marry a certain Prussian Prince suggested by Vicky, nor any other Prussian whatever. What good were 'great foreign alliances' in the modern world? The recent European wars supplied a painful answer. 'Every family feeling was rent asunder and we were powerless.' When beloved Papa advocated them, 'Prussia had not swallowed everything up.'[20]

Never had Queen Victoria admitted so frankly that Prince Albert's world had vanished.

A year later she defended Princess Louise's engagement when the disgruntled Princess Royal criticized it. The Royal Family could not afford to marry penniless foreigners since 'our Children have (alas!) such swarms of children';[21] nor could the Queen afford to entertain large foreign suites, all babbling German at table. Dearest Papa had been able to keep them in order. She could not.

While the Queen championed Lord Lorne to her children, Ponsonby tackled the Tories in the Household. 'No use talking now of this or that Seidlitz Stinkinger,' he said to Lady Biddulph; 'they are out of the question. This is the best Briton. Uphold him – and make the best of him . . .'[22] The country was pleased, apart from the diehards whose violence made the Queen wonder whether Lorne ought not to resign his seat, thus saving her from accusations of Liberal partisanship and removing him from the contamination of London.

The Duke of Argyll put his foot down.

What about precedence? Should Lorne go up or Louise down? Another clash. The Duke did not want any new title for his son; let the Princess be simple 'Lady Lorne' except in her mother's house. The Queen objected: would not Princess Louise gradually lose the H.R.H. altogether? She was unnecessarily alarmed.

What about footmen? 'I don't want an absurd man in a kilt following me everywhere,' said the Princess to Ponsonby, 'and I want to choose the men at once or I shall have some others thrust upon me.'[23]

Amid all these perplexities no one remembered to inform the Waleses that the engagement was to be announced on October 10th. John Brown had to send a messenger over the hills to Dunrobin where they were staying.

'I believe Eliza is a little nervous about the whole thing,' summed up Ponsonby. 'Is not accustomed to the intimacy with a subject.'[24] The Queen soon liked everything about the subject except his voice, though she remained doubtful whether her daughter's Bohemian tendencies would be cured by a husband who wrote poetry.

During these years the affairs of the Queen's three children who came roughly in the middle of the family kept her busy and often caused her anxiety.

There was the question of a husband for Princess Helena. She was determined not to lose yet another daughter abroad and Lenchen was invaluable, having no faults but that touchiness which the Queen attributed to all her children. This meant a son-in-law who would live at Frogmore, where she intended to settle Lenchen for life. The Princess Royal objected. Why should not Lenchen marry a Prussian and help her in Germany? They compromised on a Prince of Oldenburg whom the Queen thought nice, and likely to be nicer when he filled out and got whiskers. She sent the young couple out into the hills, riding 'sadly alone' in front.[25] Unfortunately the rides did not have the desired effect.

With considerable trepidation the Queen finally accepted Prince Christian of Schleswig-Holstein, brother of the Duke of Augustenburg. On one point only was she quite easy; Lenchen would be personally very happy with her upstanding, sensible, not very exciting, bald German who smoked twenty-four cigars a day. Politically the marriage gave her qualms. The Waleses would be annoyed though this could not be helped and Prince Christian's good fortune was only 'a fair return for the poor Augustenburgs';[26] but what about Princess Alice?

Princess Alexandra did indeed turn a trifle 'grand' but the Prince of Wales took it far better than the Queen expected. Princess Alice, however, behaved in a way which she could only characterize as jealous, sly and abominable. When 'Your Parent & Your Sovereign' settled something for a sister's good which did not interfere with your own rights, it was sheer selfishness to object.[27] Remembering that it was Princess Alice above all others who saved the Queen in her hour of desolation, it is sad to have to record a long breach. The business, however, of reconciling the divergent interests of her large family would have been beyond many matriarchs with a calmer temperament than hers. Moreover the year 1866, when Princess Helena's marriage took place, was a peculiarly difficult one.

All were distraught over the Seven Weeks' War between Prussia and Austria, ending, as already noted, with the latter's rout at Sadowa in July.

At the Windsor end, also, problems were multiplying. The Cambridges urged Queen Victoria to give Claremont to the deposed King of Hanover. This she knew would be unpopular in England, besides encouraging Prince Alfred to renew his suit to the blind King's daughter, Frederika. Queen Victoria opposed union with a family afflicted by what she called 'three generations of blindness.'

Peace with Prussia brought no peace with Frogmore. Princess Helena's comparative opulence at Frogmore attracted envious glances from Darmstadt. Many hints were dropped; few taken. The Queen eventually asked the Princess Royal to explain to Alice the exorbitant nature of her requests. With pearls at £30 and £40 apiece, Mama could not give each grandchild two a year; even Louise and Beatrice had not yet had their necklaces completed. She tried to be fair about presents but Sir Thomas Biddulph (Keeper of the Privy Purse) confessed to having 'a horror' of Alice's demands.[28] Princess Alice failed to write on her sister's birthday – an omission little short of a crime – and as a reprisal the Queen refused to invite the Hesses to England during the following year for fear of ruining Lenchen's first months of happy marriage. Moreover on Alice's last two visits, wrote the Queen to the Princess Royal (January 9th, 1867), she had sown 'pernicious' seeds in Louise and, with the connivance of Affie, had 'formed a cabal' to break her seclusion.

A few days later the Queen's natural kindness and good sense re-asserted themselves. She thanked the Princess Royal for acting as peacemaker – 'life is too short to spend it quarrelling' – promised to ask Princess Alice's family for two months in the summer and put down Alice's sharpness to ill-health caused by 'those large Children so quick one after the other . . .'[29] It must be understood, however, that Alice would not try to alter 'the sad way of life' she had worked out for herself. Alice must neither give orders to the servants, nor grumble about rooms and hours and Mama's being read aloud to after dinner (which sent Louis to sleep) and Mama not doing this and that – in short, about everything.

'God knows! if my misfortune had not changed everything all wld be different, – but as my life is made up of work, I must live as I find I best can, to get through that work! . . .'[30]

A remark dropped by the Queen in one of her letters carries the Hesse trouble a stage further and links it with Prince Alfred. The Hesses, she informed the Princess Royal, were consumed with love of Society which did everyone harm, especially Affie, whom it 'ruined', while Alice was so much flattered by the King of Prussia that the simple pleasures of Windsor bored her.

That Princess Alice should be accused of falling for Society shows how far perversity could go. She was no conventional beauty. Her emotions, inflammable as the Queen's, were directed by her sensitive mind to social service and problems of science and philosophy. In connection with her hospital work she studied anatomy and to her mother's protests that anatomy was disgusting, replied that 'where one is surrounded by such as dear Sir James and Dr Jenner, it is perfectly unnecessary and pleasanter *not* to know a great deal'; in her straitened circumstances, however, she could only study and admire the wonderful way human beings were made.[31] Next time there was an argument the Queen changed her ground: if Princess Alice was not too advanced she was old-fashioned. Why did she go on nursing those large children? Princess Alice explained that she saved her babies from being carried off by dysentery.*

Darmstadt and Windsor by no means saw eye to eye. Despite this, the strains would have been negligible but for the Princess's having criticized her mother's seclusion.

Prince Alfred's 'ruin' was another matter.

The Queen had swiftly recovered from Prince Alfred's escapade at Malta. Soon afterwards she was showering him with compliments: 'Dear Affie is a very dear, clever, charming companion – & I think he gets liker & liker to blessed Papa!'[32] Young Princes, however, could not safely remain unmarried in London. For many months the Queen tried to dazzle him with the attractions of a Saxon Princess. His sister Vicky did not approve of the choice. The most Prince Alfred would say in the Princess's favour was that her hands and feet were not large and he had noticed only one bad tooth. By 1866 the Queen was thankful that he had remained unmoved, for despite every precaution the health and moral reports on the Princess proved to have been misleading. 'We must thank God for the escape,' she wrote to the Princess Royal. 'How often do we see clearly that God knows what is for our best – far better than we do ourselves . . '[33]

A recent betrothal in the Royal Family had turned the Queen's thoughts altogether away from blond, northern Royalties. Princess Mary of Cambridge, whom the Queen

* A few years later, Ponsonby wrote of the Russian-born Duchess of Edinburgh: 'The Duchess nurses herself, which somewhat scandalizes prim English ladies'.

loved dearly but referred to as 'poor Mary' because of her vast proportions and prolonged unmarried state, announced her engagement to Prince Teck. Queen Victoria noticed something peculiarly arresting about Prince Teck's appearance. He was handsome, vivacious, and above all *dark*. She recalled how vehemently her beloved husband used to declare, 'We must have some strong dark blood.' Protestant royal families were related again and again. Prince Christian and Prince Teck would both bring fresh blood but oh, if only Prince Christian's mother had been dark.

'I do wish one cld find some more black eyed Pcs or Pcesses for our Children! . . . for that constant fair hair and blue eyes makes the blood so lymphatic.'[34]

Princess Helena and Princess Mary were married within a month of each other and though Prince Teck attracted some ridicule from Society – he would be naturalized under the title of 'Bif-teck' – Queen Victoria evidently thought that 'poor Mary' had chosen well. Meanwhile Prince Alfred must be found 'some dark eyed handsome and amiable Pcess'. The Queen's appeal to the Princess Royal was urgent: 'Can't you find one?'

No dark-eyed beauty was available and Prince Alfred displayed the most difficult side of his difficult character that autumn at Windsor. He was rude to the servants and so reserved with his mother that she suspected him of hiding a guilty secret. In contrast the Prince of Wales was kindness itself and immensely popular with 'the people [servants] here'. Then the atmosphere improved again, Prince Alfred confessing his secret to Princess Helena – he was hopelessly in love with a commoner – and his mother forgiving him. Had not dearest Albert often said that it was no sin to fall in love, only to go in the way of temptation? London must be avoided; 'that Society has done him incredible harm.'[35]

And so the wheel spins round according to changes in the Queen's volatile nature and the chance of some peccadillo having come to her ears. One moment (August 1868) Affie is 'a gt grief' – 'he don't see or feel what is wrong!' – whereas Bertie is 'so anxious to do well – tho' he is sometimes imprudent – but that is all . . .': the next (September 1868), Affie pays 'a very happy visit to Balmoral', reformed – need it be said? – by a strong letter from his Mama.[36]

A hundred minor matters pressed upon the busy matriarch. Often she did not go to bed till one o'clock and the feeling that she could not get up for breakfast was buried with her early widowhood. There were liveries to be chosen for Princess Helena's footmen – a 'slight diversion' from Lord Russell and Reform; fashions to be criticized, especially the hideous tight gowns which prevented ladies from curtseying and sometimes caused them to trip and fall flat; family portraits to be commissioned. When Winterhalter returned to England she consulted the Princess Royal: should she order three half-lengths of Bertie, Alix and the baby or two full-lengths of Bertie and Alix? She could not afford both. Reading material at Balmoral needed checking. At one time there were 26 guide books, 32 *Ladies of the Lake* and 12 *Rob Roys*. The librarian had to send up some new books.

These trivia did not distract her from the claims of the weak and defenceless. Third class passengers must be saved from railway accidents by making a director ride on every train – 'we should soon see a different state of things!'[37] The hazards of life in India distressed her: widows burnt alive and tigers addicted to human flesh, 'women as well as men . . .' Domestic animals came under her especial care: she was afraid dogs were less kindly treated in England than in some other countries. Every impecunious or unhappy relative was her responsibility. Poor Frederika of Hanover, though not the right wife for Affie, must be cherished; Victor Leiningen, her nephew, appointed captain of her yacht. How could Uncle Leopold have allowed Max and Charlotte (now raving mad) to go to Mexico? She had never approved it. The indignant head of the family heard that the murdered Emperor Maximilian's skull, skin and hair had been sold in lots – 'too disgusting & disgraceful! !'

Grandchildren were multiplying. Despite her aversion to natural processes she insisted on being called to the birth of each grandchild, sitting for hours by the pillow, rubbing the arms or gripping the hands of the mother-to-be. Presents and loans poured from Windsor: everything from a bassinet to a little sarcophagus, from a quilt knitted by 'Gangan' as Queen Victoria was called by her grandchildren, to the family christening robe of Honiton lace which scarcely held together. Nothing was wasted. Vicky would like a new hot-dish for baby Charlotte? Then she must kindly return the old one for visiting grandchildren.

In certain moods she deplored the naughtiness of little Victoria and Ella Hesse or Eddy and Georgie of Wales. More often she would nurse a baby granddaughter with croup – 'it seemed to do her good' – and spend hours with one or other of the Wales boys alone in her room. 'One at the time is much the best.' Small girls were allowed in together to help Gangan change her dress. 'Dear little things, I like to see them so at home with me.' With human ambivalence she faced the sudden blank after Christmas: 'It is always sad, when a large family party disperses, but on the other hand, I need a little quiet.'

As the grandchildren grew older she sighed for the memoranda which Albert would assuredly have provided but did her best to supply the want. Let Vicky refrain from pushing little Henry's education:

'nothing is gained by it – & it weakens their brains. We found this, & taught the younger ones all later.'[36]

Let Vicky also beware of arrogance in Willy. There had been an incident at Osborne when he had objected to a back seat in the pony carriage, refusing to speak a word to his attendant. His Grandmama tactfully professed herself 'much amused' at this 'little tinge of pride' in a five-year-old; but ever afterwards she issued periodic warnings.

Always the Queen's thoughts returned to the contrast between the proud and the humble, the high and the low, Society and servants. The names of 'Highborn beings' appeared in the divorce courts; in vain she urged that divorce proceedings should not be reported in the Press. The relations of high-born fathers and sons, Mr Goschen told her, had never been so bad, yet the sons of her gardeners, grooms and ghillies did not give their parents a moment's pain. She maintained an ingenious distinction between what she called 'John Bullism'* and what might be called 'John Brownism'. John Bullism was an arrogant form of bullying prevalent among smart 'slangy' cavalry officers. In the domestic field, John Bullism created class hatred, in the international field, war. Though she did not accuse Palmerston of John Bullism in so many words, it is obvious that this, in her opinion, was the fault of his foreign policy. When he died she confidently expected 'the deplorable tone of bullying' at the Foreign Office to die with him.

More than once the Queen suffered from outbreaks of John Bullism among her sons' equerries. Lieutenant Stirling, for instance, had to be removed from Prince Leopold's Household for having a row with Archie Brown, his valet. Prince Alfred was a bit of a John Bull himself; he never greeted the servants on arrival or departure. Prince Arthur, as yet unscathed by the fiery furnace of army life, must never become a stranger in her home like his brothers. On no account was Lieutenant Stirling to be transferred to his Household: ' "*Manliness*" (falsely called)' might be '*forced* into him.'[39] Fenians or no Fenians, Prince Arthur was not to drop a proposed visit to Canada, for idleness was the bane of princes. Of the two dangers, Society and Fenians, the Queen knew which caused her the gravest fears. At different times she referred to both as 'horrid people' but Society was more horrid.

'John Brownism' stood for all that was fine and noble in human nature: unselfishness, dignified humility, honesty and devotion. If she had any doubts about the relative merits of Brownism and Bullism, John Bright set them at rest. At the end of 1866 a Radical Member of Parliament, Acton Smee Ayrton, attacked her seclusion at a public meeting. John Bright leapt to her defence, proving that despite the abolition of duelling the age of chivalry was not dead:

'. . . I venture to say this, that a woman – be she the Queen of a great realm, or be she the wife of one of your

* See p. 434.

labouring men – who can keep alive in her heart a great sorrow for the lost object of her life and affection is not at all likely to be wanting in a great and generous sympathy for you.'

When Bright entered Gladstone's Government in 1868, the Queen was not in the least put out that his religious principles forbade him to approach her on his knees. This was a form of John Brownism which she could appreciate. Rather was she proud that he consented to appear before her in specially designed knee breeches and kiss her hand, 'which in general, the Quakers never do – '. The qualified homage of the fat, old, white-haired Quaker moved her more than all the ardours of 'Puss' Granville who seized her hand and kissed it twice.

The same year (1868) the Queen brought out her *Leaves from the Journal of Our Life in the Highlands*. The book, illustrated with her own sketches and bound in moss green covers adorned with golden antlers, sold 20,000 copies at once and quickly went through several editions. *Punch* suggested that its chief trait was the tea tray, ignoring through delicacy or oversight the equal prevalence of the whisky bottle. 'We authors, Ma'am,' was the gallant phrase with which Dizzy addressed his Sovereign. Whereas the year before publication Her Majesty had felt it a 'presumption' to sign her name in Sir Walter Scott's journal, Mary Ponsonby now noticed with amusement 'the literary line the Queen has taken up since her book was published'.

Queen Victoria attributed the book's success to its simple narrative, its expression of marital love and the 'friendly footing' on which she lived with her Highlanders. This third point created dismay among some of the Queen's entourage. Lady Augusta Stanley resented the footnotes retailing the life histories of footmen as if they had been gentlemen: it gave the dangerous impression 'that all are on the same footing' – witness the comment in *The Quarterly Review* 'that it is only with *Scottish servants* one could be on such blessed terms!!!!' Lady Augusta choked with indignation. 'These ignorant, stupid remarks,' she wrote, 'are calculated to do great harm to our dear One –.'[40] Elphinstone, on the other hand, wanted a cheap edition of the *Leaves* at once, to clinch the Queen's love affair with the middle classes.

Queen Victoria was no less dogmatic about the book's effect than about the reasons for its popularity. It would reform 'Highborn beings' by showing them the example of a good, simple life at the summit. There is more than a hint that she believed the *Leaves* would in future look after her popularity, rendering a drastic alteration in her way of life superfluous.

The year 1869 marked the end of an epoch. In the course of it Queen Victoria reached her fiftieth birthday. 'Have completed ½ a century now!' She regretted the passing of the 'sixties, hallowed as they were by Prince Albert having lived in them. All her self-confidence and sense of moral purpose would be needed to face the 'seventies, for a new enemy had appeared on the scene. John Bull was to be joined by John Ball, the arrogant cavalry officer by the rank republican.

CHAPTER XXVI

THE ROYALTY QUESTION
1870–4

THE QUEEN AGAIN declined to open Parliament in February 1870. She would catch cold wearing a low-cut dress in her carriage. (Two years later Gladstone suggested clothing herself in ermine up to the neck. She laughed scornfully: the House of Lords was too hot.) In the same month she was punished by the spectacle of a much more painful opening – that of the Mordaunt case.

A member of the dreaded 'fast set', Sir Charles Mordaunt, brought a divorce suit against his wife, as a result of which the Prince of Wales was subpoenaed. Twelve letters from the Prince to Lady Mordaunt (who by now occupied a lunatic asylum) were read in court. So patently innocuous were they as seriously to disappoint the garbage-pickers; nevertheless a whirlwind of condemnation arose. The Lord Chancellor said 'it was as bad as a revolution as affecting [the Prince of] Wales'. In Dublin, the wife of the Lord Lieutenant spoke to Ponsonby about it with as little reticence as if it had been Gladstone's Irish Land Bill. London was black with the smoke of burnt confidential letters.[1]

The Queen unburdened herself to the Princess Royal. She had never doubted Bertie's innocence, she wrote, and his appearance in court did great good, but the whole thing was 'painful & lowering'; the heir should never have got mixed up with 'such people'; she hoped that the trial would teach him a lesson; in future she would constantly remind him of it. As she wrote she worked herself up to one of those wholesale condemnations of family life which, taken out of context, could be wrongly used to prove that she did not like children.

'Believe me, Children are a terrible anxiety & the sorrow they cause is far gter than the pleasure they give. I therefore cannot understand your delight at the constant increase of them!'[2]

In a later letter she continued that whereas it might be sad to have no children at all, the burden of bringing up large upper class families was intolerable. Where children had to support their parents the relationship was fine and natural but when children had no reason to work, 'there is nothing to keep them straight'. The Queen again launched into a piratical raid on the cosy havens of Victorian England:

> 'I am equally shy of marriages & large families . . . better a 1000 times never marry, than marry for marrying's sake, wh I believe the gter number of people do.'

Vicky was wrong in thinking she was not fond of children:

> 'I am – & admire pretty ones – especially Peasant Children immensely but I can't bear their being idolised & made too gt objects of – or having a number of them about me making a gt noise.'[3]

In this mood the old bogy of childbirth was not likely to escape her lash and a week later she trounced Nature and Society with impartial vigour. Childbirth was disgusting and lowering to us poor women:

> 'The animal side of our nature is to me – too dreadful & now – one of the new fashions of our vy elegant society, is to go in perfectly light-coloured dresses – quite tight – without a particle of shawl or Scarf (as I was always accustomed to wear & to see others wear,) – & to dance within a fortnight of the confinement even valsing at 7 months! ! ! ! Where is delicacy of feeling going to!'[4]

The answer is that it was going to the Puritanical limbo where it belonged. Meanwhile three months after this heated exchange the Princess Royal gave birth to yet another baby.

One of the evils resulting from the Mordaunt case was that it interrupted the Queen's slow process of reconciliation with her own nature. Oceanic fears stirred again. Like the row of extinct volcanoes which Disraeli was soon to picture sitting opposite him on the Government front bench, her inhibitions were still capable of causing minor earthquakes 'and ever and anon the dark rumblings of the sea'.

473

Queen Victoria was unfortunate in running into an acute international crisis – the Franco-Prussian War – soon after the Mordaunt case. It brought down upon the Monarchy a fresh load of unpopularity. The Spanish Succession, once again up for auction, seemed likely to go to a Prussian candidate, Prince Leopold of Hohenzollern, but Lord Clarendon, almost with his last breath, warned Queen Victoria that France would resist a German prince with war.

The Queen's natural horror of warfare was to reach its zenith at this date. A glorious day of hard frost and skating at Osborne would merely remind her of what the wounded must be suffering on frozen battlefields. Of the actual war she wrote laconically, 'there has perhaps never been a worse one.'[5]

The campaign, she knew, would again be fought in miniature by a divided Royal Family and she feared that Germany, not yet united, would be beaten by the Napoleonic hosts. Her efforts for peace were as unsuccessful as in 1866, for England, having opted out of European affairs with repeated declarations of neutrality, was no longer an influence. Though Prince Leopold's candidature was withdrawn by his father, the raffish imperialists who surrounded Napoleon III forced him to demand a promise from Germany never again to put up a Spanish claimant.

King William was taking the waters at Ems. He ignored the required promise, merely expressing to the French Ambassador his private approval of the withdrawal, but couched in the most courteous language. Bismarck, by removing all the civilities, was able to change the 'Ems telegram' into a slap in the face for France. Just as Queen Victoria was planning another concerted appeal for peace, a telegram arrived on July 15th to say that war had been declared – by 'these infatuated French'. The Queen made no bones about her Prussian sympathies. The Paris mob screaming '*A Berlin!*' seemed to her a literal expression of French foreign policy. She trembled for her two sons-in-law, Fritz and Louis, and her brother-in-law, Ernest, all in the field.

England's neutrality was proclaimed, promptly followed by reproaches from Queen Victoria's Prussian relatives. As before, she played her delicate role with discretion and sympathy. She would send the Princess Royal linen for the wounded but not under her own name: whatever happened she must not 'swerve from the steep and thorny path' of neutrality nor 'separate herself or allow herself to be separated from her own people'.[6] The Prince of Wales had publicly expressed the hope that Prussia would be beaten. Vicky should not listen to such stories, she urged. But Vicky and all Prussia listened, seething with rage. Meanwhile, the Queen got toothache, Prince Leopold fell ill, Princess Alice was confined, the Italians seized Rome, the Pope was in danger* – and the Prussian armies swept onwards.

Just before dinner on August 6th, the Queen heard 'wonderful news' of Fritz's victory over Marshal Macmahon. Maps were brought into the dining-room, Sahl and Bauer† fell into each other's arms, the Francophils looked glum: 'Could not help thinking of the sad battlefield & all the suffering & misery,' wrote Queen Victoria that night. As the French fell back she exclaimed, 'the poor French always to be driven away', vainly hoping the Prussians would not retain any French territory.

The defeat of Napoleon took place on September 1st, followed by his surrender, the declaration of a Republic and the flight to England of his son, the Prince Imperial. 'Can only get vy late to bed,' sighed the Queen, feverishly rolling bandages and inundated with papers. Two special telegrams arrived on September 9th: the Empress Eugénie had secretly landed at Hastings and the Baroness Lehzen was dead. The Prussians were only forty miles from Paris and in her agitation she forgot to enter her old friend's death in her Journal until three days later. Though Lehzen's mind had given way before the end and her letters for many months had been illegible, the Queen mourned her sincerely, forgave the past and was still writing about her to the Princess Royal several weeks later. 'I owed her much & she adored me!'[7]

* On September 20th the Pope locked himself up in the Vatican, but not before the first Vatican Council had declared what Queen Victoria called, icily, 'this Instability.'

† Fraulein Bauer, German governess, relative of Stockmar.

Beautiful, wicked Paris was besieged and bombarded. 'It is a *great moral*!' wrote the Queen to Gladstone. But before the siege guns opened up she again interceded with King William. The only result was a snarl from Bismarck about 'petticoat' interference. Her position had become an unenviable one by the time an armistice was signed on January 28th, 1871. In Germany she was accused of turning the Princess Royal against her adopted country, in England of having a pro-Prussian bias. She had to warn her daughter that whereas people were formerly 'very German' now they were 'very French'.[8] And what was more they were not very loyal. Vicky must ignore Continental gossip about her mother's unpopularity 'some years ago', – 'I never listen to stories from abroad' – and if she heard any 'stupid rumours' from London about Bertie, Affie or Mama, she must write at once for the truth.[9]

The truth was that Prussian aggression on top of the Mordaunt case and the Queen's seclusion formed a dangerous combination. The news of a republican meeting in October 1870 at which the Court had been derided as 'a pack of Germans', was laughed off by Ponsonby: 'We had better sacrifice Sahl and Bauer.' Next year he was not inclined to be what his mistress had once called 'so funny'.

As far as the Queen was concerned, 1871 was the first, dreadful year in which she stood like one of Landseer's red deer at bay. Ministers, children, servants suddenly seemed to ring her round disclosing unsuspected affiliations with the enemy. In reality, a new campaign against her seclusion had begun, unknown to her, nearly two years earlier.

General Grey had reached the conclusion in 1868 that to approach Her Majesty 'on his knees' as he had done over the Fenian 'plot', was so much waste of time. A more masterful posture was required. Accordingly, in June 1869 he urged Gladstone to counteract the 'strong feeling' against the Queen's seclusion by ordering her in a '*peremptory*' tone to do her duty. It was not in Gladstone's nature to be peremptory towards Royalty. Prodding, however, was well within his compass. He had made it his mission to pacify Ireland. In

1869 he accepted a second mission, to energize the Queen. Along with the Army, Church and other institutions he filed Queen Victoria, under the heading of the 'Royalty question'.

Gladstone found himself perplexed. What was really wrong with Her Majesty's health? Was she nervy, headachy, neuralgic, overworked, as Sir William Jenner invariably reported? General Grey bluntly announced (June 1st, 1869) that her moans 'have simply no effect whatever on me', citing Princess Louise to support his conviction that the royal malingerer was 'wonderfully well'. Though dubious about Jenner, Gladstone was inclined to allow something for the 'weariness' of the Queen's lonely round. By June 7th he had taken three decisions. 'I am desirous,' he wrote to Grey, 'to get at the simple truth with regard to the Queen's health . . .' (Vain hope: for her health, with its mental and physical interactions, was no more simple than Gladstone's intellect.) Secondly, 'will' (i.e. self-will) he thought was probably involved, as it was in so many 'female complaints', and must be eradicated. Thirdly, he would break the spell of Osborne. 'There is no doubt that Osborne during the Session is the great enemy . . .'[10]

Only two small gains were made in the first year of Gladstone's mission to Royalty. The Queen was reluctantly persuaded to leave Osborne a few days early – this 'must NEVER be made a *precedent*', she wrote – and to open Blackfriars Bridge, her only public ceremony of the year. She knew nothing of the Grey-Gladstone correspondence; Grey's moodiness she put down charitably to ill-health, his death taking place in March 1870. She saw as little as possible of him towards the end but afterwards affectionately recalled the old days when he had been 'the life & soul of the Court'.

Ponsonby took over Grey's position, well aware of the pitfalls. Who would speak out to Eliza? That, briefly, was the 'Royalty question' as he saw it. Grey, he knew, had been criticized by Ministers for not doing enough. Yet Grey had gone to the limits of irritating the Queen without exasperating her and his advice was therefore never totally disregarded. Ponsonby likewise resolved not to lose all influence by going too far. Moreover, he soon found that the Queen's Ministers, with the exception of Gladstone and Forster (Minister of Education), were themselves moral cowards. Cardwell, the War Minister, dared not fight this formidable woman. He was in an agony of longing to leave Balmoral but 'Cardwell has succumbed', wrote Ponsonby to his wife, 'and sends to say he is ready to stay as long as he is wanted. All, high and low, dread the chance of a disapproving nod – and yet you tell me that she has no power.'[11]

The Queen was saved from Gladstone's missionary zeal in 1870 by his immersion in political business. Much of his new legislation was distasteful to her but she supported her Prime Minister loyally, never going beyond her constitutional right to warn. She accepted his Land Act as part of the mission to pacify Ireland, concentrating her criticism on its harshness to the landlords. Cardwell's Army reforms she considered 'unwise'. This was not surprising since the Commander-in-Chief, her cousin the Duke of Cambridge, was 'strongly against all'. She was afraid he might resign if the plans for his subordination to the War Office proved too unpalatable. The abolition of Purchase (of commissions), however, had been constantly voted by large majorities and could not now be prevented. Partly for this reason and partly because it was always agreeable to use her prerogative, she signed the Purchase Warrant for Gladstone, by which means the hostile peers were ingeniously compelled to pass his Bill. But she could no more welcome an examination for soldiers than for civil servants. It would cause jobbery and exclude gentlemen.

As a result of the Franco-Prussian War one new Emperor appeared in Europe (the German Emperor William I) and another vanished (Napoleon III); Germany became united and France a Republic. These events had their repercussions in England. Republicanism was in the air and clubs to further it were founded up and down the country. Queen Victoria was deeply concerned by this disloyalty but as usual ignored her own contribution. 'Democratic feeling,' she wrote, 'is caused by the fact that the sins of the upper classes are forgiven while the lower classes are punished.'[12] That made it easy to 'mislead' radical-minded artisans about the Monarch. Why pay nearly forty times as much as a President would cost, said 'wicked people', for a Queen they never saw?

In fact she had promised, health permitting, to open St Thomas's Hospital and the Albert Hall, receiving the congratulations of Gladstone on thus making Monarchy 'visible and palpable to the people'.[13] She had brightened the Opening of Parliament by wearing ermine trimmings and a new crown, and felt she had earned some further kind remarks from Mr Gladstone about Prince Arthur's annuity and Princess Louise's dowry. (Enemies suggested that she opened Parliament only when she had to come with her February 'begging-bowl'.) Gladstone had promised 'to see whether something better could not be devised' than these piecemeal applications for money. Meanwhile he offered her the consoling thought that the present system, undignified as it was, gave the Sovereign 'more power over the Royal Family'.[14] He did not add that it also gave the people more power over the Sovereign.

Princess Louise was married to the Marquess of Lorne on March 21st, 1871 at Windsor with the maximum of visible and palpable pomp. The Queen covered her black satin dress with gleaming jet, wore rubies as well as diamonds and led the procession up the nave. She did her duty by the heir, allowing him to attend an Investiture. She did her duty by the poor, helping to quash a proposed Match Tax which would bear hardly upon them – '*vy wrong* – & most unpolitic at the present moment'.[15] Mr Lowe assured her there was no fear of French republicanism in England though democracy had brought in 'the reign of stupidity, vulgarity and ignorance'.[16]

Yet still the growls went on. News of her abounding energies may have leaked from Balmoral in June, undermining the official reason – ill-health – for her seclusion. (She had climbed up Craig Gowan the steep way for the first time in ten years.) At any rate, violent Radical attacks on Prince Arthur's annuity resulted in 54 votes being cast against it.

Without comment she recorded the ominous figure. It was August 1st, the beginning of a black month.

On the 4th she woke to find that she had been 'painfully stung' on the right elbow. Four days later, with the 'sting' getting worse and other symptoms developing, she received a letter from Gladstone asking her in her 'wisdom' to postpone her departure from Osborne to Balmoral until the House of Commons had been prorogued, a fortnight later than usual. The Queen's wisdom prompted her to send back an evasive telegram: '. . . What I can do I will but no more.'[17] Gladstone answered that the House required some return on Prince Arthur's money. (It was Ponsonby's opinion that 'Gladdy' should have made the Queen promise to postpone her departure *before* Prince Arthur's vote. Now it was too late.)

The battle for Balmoral was joined. Auxiliary troops were called up: Jenner by the Queen; the Lord Chancellor, Helps, Granville and the Princess Royal by Gladstone. Vicky composed a splendid letter signed by the whole family lamenting that 'our adored Mama and our Sovereign' seemed unconscious of the dangers to the Monarchy 'which are daily spreading'.[18] Queen Victoria put her case: the more she gave the more she was asked; she had '*not prorogued* Parlt *in person* since the year: 52. That would *next* be asked!!' (It was.) After lashing out with mingled threats and jeers, she found relief in a final burst of rhetoric:

'What killed her beloved Husband? Overwork & worry – what killed Lord Clarendon? The same . . . & the Queen, a woman, no longer young is supposed to be proof against all . . . She must solemnly repeat that unless her Ministers *support* her & state the whole truth she *cannot* go on & must give her heavy burden up to younger hands. Perhaps then those discontented people may regret that they broke her down when she might still have been of use.'[19]

She hoped that the incompetence of those younger hands would enable her to blackmail the Government into accepting her terms.

On the 14th she was suddenly smitten by an acute sore

throat and could no longer take meals with the family. Gladstone chose this day to describe the situation to Ponsonby as the most deplorable he had ever known: the 'woes of fancy' could do as much real harm as 'the most fearful dispensations of Providence'. Even Sir Thomas Biddulph did not believe her. When she wrote, 'The Queen is feeling extremely unwell', they all heard the old cry of 'Wolf!'

She said goodbye to the Princess Royal on August 15th, preparatory to her departure for Balmoral. For once the melancholy ritual of parting did not move her. 'I feel almost too ill for any other feeling.' On the same day Ponsonby decided to warn Gladstone that she suspected him of wishing to keep her at Osborne for personal political reasons, as a prop to his Government. Deeply wounded, Gladstone summed up the Queen's behaviour as his most 'sickening' experience in forty years of public life.

> '*Worse* things may be imagined but smaller and meaner causes for the decay of Thrones cannot be conceived. It is like the worm which bores the bark of a noble oak tree and so breaks the channel of its life.'[20]

When Gladstone wrote again on September 6th there was a marked change in his tone. He was 'extremely concerned' to hear of Her Majesty's 'suffering state'.

The illness turned out to be serious. A *précis* of Queen Victoria's Journal (in italics), interspersed with other comments, brings out the poignancy of her situation.

August 17th. *Travelling to Balmoral with sore throat & very painful arm.*

Ponsonby noted how 'knocked up' she looked, clutching his arm as she got into the carriage at Ballater.

August 18th. *Sleeping during day – 'very unusual' – reading 'Misunderstood.'*

August 20th. *Suffering tortures until 'something seemed to give way in the throat & the choking sensation with violent spasms ceased'.*

481

Jenner put an anonymous paragraph into *The Lancet* to the effect that HM could never go to London or do more than she was doing already. Ponsonby regarded it as most injudicious: 'destroys all hope and will lead I think to some steps being taken about her': the 'abdicationists' would ask why they should wait any longer. Jenner defended his paragraph next day on the ground that hundreds of people had said to him, 'Tell us the truth.' If that was the truth, observed Ponsonby, people would insist on what 'Gladdy' called 'an alteration in our form of Government'. He wrote to his wife: 'The Queen is really better now.'

August 22nd. '*Never felt so ill since typhoid at Ramsgate in 35.*'

Next day Ponsonby again reported the Queen much better: 'Here away . . . from all her children she feels herself comfortable.' Jenner told him the abscess in the arm was subsiding. Two days later, according to Ponsonby, the Queen was full of the articles in the Scottish press denouncing suggestions that she should hand over Buckingham Palace to the Prince of Wales. 'Her *faithful* and *ever-sympathising* Scotch subjects have stood up to defend her,' she crowed, '– when not *one other* paper would dare to do it in *England*!!' Jenner reported confidentially that the Queen had another abscess in her arm and 'he dont clearly know what it is'.

On August 26th a discussion took place between Biddulph and Ponsonby about the Queen's right to reject any Minister sent to her by the House of Commons. 'The Sovereign has this Prerogative,' said Ponsonby, 'but not the Queen.' She had forfeited it by not living in London. What guidance did she get in making her decisions? None, except from her private secretary, immured like herself and relying on newspapers. Biddulph 'differed at first but gave way by degrees'. This was the beginning of a 'hot argument' between Jenner and Ponsonby. 'Whoever wanted to go to London,' began Jenner, 'except the frivolous habitués of Society?' Even Granville did not think it important (Ponsonby's comment afterwards: 'a whopper') while 'hundreds' had told Jenner how much they admired the Queen for living in retirement. Ministers pestered her with telegrams after she had fallen seriously ill, 'and by Heaven if she had died I would have borne testimony they had killed her!' If she had been a man they would never have dared to treat her so.

Ponsonby: 'No, they would simply have turned him off the throne.'

Jenner: 'Colonel Ponsonby! You must know, at any rate *I* know that there is not a woman in the kingdom who does so much work as the Queen.'

Ponsonby: 'Wait until the next time she asks for money; the middle and lower classes think she is hoarding.'

Jenner: 'Nonsense! I know hundreds of middle-class people who have the highest respect for her. There *will* be a difficulty about money no doubt, but that is the advancing Democracy of the age.'[21]

Jenner then challenged Ponsonby to name any men of weight who criticized her. 'The Lord Chancellor and Speaker.' 'Men of Society,' bellowed Jenner, dismissing them both.

On the following day he attacked Ponsonby's view that the Queen's absence from London prevented her from seeing the Foreign Ministers. 'And a good thing too! A parcel of rubbishy old people trying to make something to do.'

August 29th. *Everything tried; 'arm will not respond to treatment.'*

Jenner told Ponsonby that at one moment he thought the Queen might have only twenty-four hours to live. Lady Churchill longed to say, 'Then why didn't you immediately send for her children?' 'Good heavens,' exclaimed Biddulph when he heard this, 'that would have killed her at once!'

The condition of the Queen's arm was still critical.

September 1st. *Bad night. Bad arm. Rheumatism now in leg.*

September 2nd. *Sleeping in tent; 'unsuccessful attempt at luncheon . . . everyone so kind & good to me'.*

September 3rd. *Jenner wanted to send for distinguished surgeon, Professor Lister. Reluctantly agreed.*

483

September 4th. *Bad night despite soothing draught.* '*Crawled out with difficulty to the tent, supported by Brown who is most attentive.*' Lister lanced abscess in arm.

September 5th. *Could hardly turn over in bed. Terribly long dressing, preceded by use of Lister's 'great invention', a carbolic spray 'to destroy all organic germs'.*

There was no good news in answer to Gladstone's kind inquiries of September 6th and the rest of the month was a tale of 'spasms', 'flying rheumatic pains', gout in the hand, knee, side, foot ankle, shoulder and back to the right arm. Owing to the Queen's serious state, the Prince of Wales wrote that 'Vicky's celebrated letter' of August should not be sent until the following January or February 'if at all'.[22] With each 'new outburst' the Queen became more exhausted: her irritability increased, together with her remorse. 'Am in despair.' The gouty foot prevented her from walking a step and she found the helplessness 'dreadful'. John Brown had to lift her from couch to bed, as the maids were not 'strong enough for my weight'.[23]

September, indeed, proved to be another altogether black month. A typical 'John Brown row' with the Duke of Edinburgh (Prince Alfred) broke out. No one could unravel this tangle of petty grievances – the Duke ostentatiously shaking hands with everyone on arrival at Balmoral except Brown, a message from the Duke to the Queen not delivered because Grant declined to give it through Brown, the fiddlers ordered by the Duke to stop playing and countermanded by Brown. Queen Victoria decreed a thorough sifting of the dispute. The Duke was therefore persuaded to see Brown with Ponsonby as a witness. 'If I see a man on board my ship on any subject,' said HRH, 'it is always in the presence of an officer.' 'This is not a ship,' stormed the Queen when his remark reached her, '& I won't have naval discipline introduced here.'

Meanwhile the Princess Royal became involved. Her daughter, Princess Charlotte, was with the Queen when Brown entered the room one day.

'Say how de do to Brown, my dear.'

'How de do.'

'Now go and shake hands.'

'No, that I won't. Mama says I ought not to be too familiar with servants.'

Ponsonby reported 'no end of a row with Vicky' about her children's upbringing.[24]

'In re Brown v Alfred', as the Queen's harassed secretary called it, there was at last better news. Brown made a handsome apology. But when Grant's name cropped up Ponsonby interposed hastily, 'I think His Royal Highness seems satisfied.' 'I am satisfied too,' said the incorrigible Brown before Ponsonby could get him out of the room.

Things were no happier with Jenner. As the Queen's doctor, he was fiercely slated for not telling Ministers the truth. 'But how can I?' said Jenner pathetically to the Minister-in-Attendance, Lord Halifax. 'Isn't it better to say the Queen can't do so and so because of her health – which is to a certain extent true – than to say she won't?' After talking to Jenner, Halifax would tap his forehead, calling the Queen's obstinacy and nervousness 'small evidences of insanity'. He hoped they wouldn't increase, 'and as we know she has always been much the same in these matters there is no reason to expect they will'.[25]

The Queen's ladies rejected Jenner's diagnosis, pitching into him for his gloomy medical reports. 'But what can poor Jenner do?' wrote Ponsonby. 'If he makes it too light the Queen washes his head. If he makes it out too heavy the women here wash his head. Actually he prefers the latter.' In response to Jenner's efforts *The Times* on September 18th printed an apology for its attacks on the Queen. It had taken six weeks of illness, said Ponsonby, and 'a vast amount of bodily suffering to convince people she was not shamming'.

At that moment a copy of a pamphlet purporting to be written by 'Solomon Temple, Builder' but actually the work of a Liberal MP, George Otto Trevelyan, reached Balmoral. *What Does She Do With It?* asked the writer – 'It' being the £385,000 voted annually for the Civil List, Nield's (supposed)

'£500,000' legacy, the Prince Consort's (supposed) '£100,000' legacy and other inheritances. 'Solomon' answered that she hoarded it to the extent of £200,000 a year.

The Queen's advisers quaked. Newspapers with a working-class circulation such as the *Bee-Hive* (trade unions and co-operatives) and *Universe* (Catholic) had already raised this subject, the former asking why 'the gee-gaws of the Court' could not be 'thinned' and the latter, having touched upon the Mordaunt case, suggesting sarcastically that Her Majesty lived in seclusion because she could not afford to drive about London in a new bonnet. There was nothing the working-classes disliked more than a mean Monarch. Ponsonby thought of asking a reliable reviewer to refute the most flagrant of 'Solomon's' lies, such as those about Nield's and the Prince's legacies* and the Queen's savings. On the other hand it might blow over. He remembered a pamphlet in 1875 attacking Household salaries, in which the name of Mary Bulteel had occurred – how his heart had thumped – but no one remembered it now.

That the Queen was hoarding, Princess Alice refused to believe but she begged Ponsonby to make her mother read hostile as well as friendly newspapers; Ponsonby, however, did not believe in shock tactics; in any case Jenner would forbid them. A week or two later Jenner told him that the Queen's seclusion was due to 'nervousness'. Even her high colour after dinner, which made people think her well, was really nerves. 'But these nerves are a species of madness, and against them it is hopeless to contend.'[26]

Jenner had evidently been coached in the royal temperament before Clark handed over to him ten years earlier. Unfortunately Jenner saw no reason afterwards to question the Stockmar–Clark analysis and tackle his patient's 'nerves' – a crusade which might have resulted in his own dismissal. His sole responsibility, he insisted, was to maintain Her Majesty's physical health.

Halifax, impressed like Ponsonby with the Queen's pathetic

* Nield had left the Queen about £250,000, while the Prince Consort's death, according to Ponsonby, had involved her in financial loss, not gain.

loneliness to which he attributed much of the trouble, sighed for some 'good woman' to attend her – an old nurse, or governess or lady – whom she really liked and through whom Ministers might exert influence. None of the Queen's children, he thought, had their mother's own tact and 'management', as witness the way she had stopped the Duke of Cambridge 'making a fool of himself' over Army reform. The Princess Royal was useless, having quarrelled about not being accommodated at Buckingham Palace. 'Alice might do good though he doubted it.' No one would go to the Prince of Wales for advice. 'Edinburgh was distrusted.' The rest did not count.[27]

Towards the end of September, though still stiff and 'achy' the Queen was well enough to receive Gladstone and to discuss the creation of a new 'Faithful Service Medal' for those who had helped her through her illness. Ponsonby hoped the award would be limited to Brown and Löhlein. It may have been during researches into Löhlein's record of service, first to Prince Albert and then to the Queen, that a story was unearthed about his being the Prince's half-brother, natural son of the Duke of Coburg. Ponsonby had always been impressed by Löhlein's physical resemblance to his master.

The Queen had lost two stone in weight and when she emerged again all were startled by the change in her manner and appearance. This may partly account for Gladstone's impression that during his audience she exerted her 'repellent power'[28] against him. The Queen was probably more ailing than angry. Gladstone confessed to Ponsonby that her retirement, more than any other political matter, now gave him 'blue devils'. He violently disagreed with Jenner's latest ukase that she was to be shown no articles which might excite her. 'How can one drag the Monarch's chair from the fire . . . if the Doctor forbids you to touch the chair?'[29] Jenner, he felt sure, had also inspired a calamitous remark about her seclusion made by Disraeli at the Harvest Festival of his Buckinghamshire home, Hughenden. The Queen, said Disraeli, was 'physically and morally' incapacitated from pageantry.

The Rev. Norman Macleod felt bound to retort in public that during all the years he had served the Queen he had never seen 'the remotest trace of mental or moral weakness'. Did Disraeli mean that the Queen was crazy? asked the *Telegraph* indignantly. *Reynolds Newspaper* understood that she would abdicate.

Her convalescence dragged on. It was not till November 5th that she was able to go to kirk again, Brown helping her up the steep steps. Next day Sir Charles Dilke, a Radical Member of Parliament, delivered a momentous attack at Newcastle on Queen Victoria's dereliction of duty, inciting his audience to depose her and set up a Republic – 'let it come'. Apparently in militant mood, she commanded the Government to repudiate Dilke forthwith; Lady Ely, however, painted a different picture of her 'crying a lot and being regularly unhappy . . .'[30]

While the royal hive was still buzzing over Dilke's vicious kick, a telegram arrived from Sandringham on November 21st saying that the Prince of Wales had a feverish attack. Next day the Queen heard it was 'mild' typhoid; news followed of a high temperature and delirium. Obsessed with '10 years ago', she drove to the Mausoleum and then, on November 29th, hastened to her son's bedside.

At Sandringham the utmost discomfort reigned. The house was so overcrowded that Queen Victoria had to make invidious decisions about which relatives to invite; no windows were opened in the intense cold and the Duke of Cambridge discovered a typhoid-bearing smell; Ponsonby thought it was mere fug but it turned out to be a gas leak. The anxious groups waiting for news divided themselves into 'improvementors' and 'depressors'. Party spirit ran high. The depressors upstairs denounced Prince Alfred and Prince Arthur, castigating 'those fools below who talk as if he were fit to go out shooting tomorrow'.[31] The Queen was a depressor: 'somehow I always look for bad news & have not much confidence.'[32] Superstitious dread swept the house as the fatal December 14th, tenth anniversary of the Prince Consort's death, approached, Henry Ponsonby alone maintaining that according to the theory of chances the Prince of Wales was less likely to die on the same day as his father than on any other.

The Queen watched her son from behind a screen, not daring to leave the house for more than half an hour each day. On December 12th she went to bed 'with the horrid feeling I may be called up'. Princess Alexandra once crawled into the bedroom on all fours lest the patient should catch sight of her. The Prince of Wales, however, in contrast to his father was attended by professional nurses and his ravings revealed a robust temperament. His pillows went flying about the room as he laughed and sang, one of them felling the Princess. 'That's right, old Gull,' he roared to his doctor in high good humour – 'one more teaspoonful.' At moments he thought he had succeeded to the throne, proposing reforms in the Household which made his attendants' hair stand on end.

On the 13th, the crisis was at hand. Queen Victoria was allowed to sit without a screen by his bed. 'In those heart-rending moments I hardly knew how to pray aright, only asking God if possible to spare me my Beloved Child.' Who can doubt that in the ten years which had passed since her first agony she had learnt to pray aright? According to Lady Augusta Stanley, she showed her finest qualities 'by being taken out of herself – taken out of Doctors and maladies (I mean her own) and nerves and fighting off what Her own righteous conscience tells her would be right'.[33] Lady Augusta was one who did not think the Queen mad, but self-indulgent and neurotic, because of a guilty conscience.

On December 14th the Prince took a turn for the better. 'Dear Bertie had been on the very *verge* of the grave,' wrote the Queen after a talk with Dr Gull; '. . . hardly anyone had been known to recover who had been *so* ill as he was'![34] Mysteriously, God worked the miracle this time. Next day, when only the nurse was with him,* she was allowed to go in. He smiled, kissed her hand 'in his old way' and said, ' "Oh! dear Mama I am so glad to see you. Have you been here all this time?" . . . I was so thankful & comforted.'[35] His

---

* When Prince Arthur had smallpox in 1867 a night nurse was reluctantly obtained and forced to sit outside his bedroom.

recovery from a serious relapse only increased her thankfulness. She was sorry to part with the circle of doctors and nurses, 'with whom I had become so acquainted'. Queen Victoria, whose longing for homely intimacy was insatiable, never guessed that she struck terror into many members of her own family. One day Ponsonby encountered a party of Royalties dashing for cover with shrill cries of 'the Queen! the Queen!' Next moment the short, sad figure hobbled into Sandringham House.[36]

A letter of thanks to her people for their sympathy was the way Queen Victoria naturally chose to express her overflowing feelings. The Government, however, insisted on a public Thanksgiving Service at St Paul's. She conveyed her dislike of 'public religious displays', which were apt to degenerate into *merely a show*', at the same time demanding an open carriage 'to enable the *people* (for *whom this is*)' to see properly.[37]

Her enjoyment of the actual event (February 27th, 1872) was unclouded save by the 'dingy' interior of the Cathedral.[38] The deafening cheers at Temple Bar where she dramatically raised her son's hand and kissed it were music in her ears, and John Brown, sitting on the box 'in his vy fullest & vy handsome full dress', gladdened her eyes. Next day old Lady William Russell, cousin of Lady Flora Hastings, who had refused to set foot inside the Palace since that disastrous affair, received a visit in her home from Queen Victoria. The two ladies were 'most amicable'.[39]

The day after this pilgrimage, a sixth 'attempt' was made on the Queen's life – at any rate, a weak-minded youth named Arthur O'Connor pointed an unloaded pistol at his Sovereign with the idea of frightening her into releasing the Fenian prisoners. Prince Arthur tried to jump over the carriage to reach him but was too slow; John Brown seized him and was afterwards rewarded by the shaken Queen – 'I was trembling vy much and a sort of shiver ran through me'[40] – with public thanks, a gold medal and £25 annuity. The Prince of Wales, greatly disgusted, complained that Prince Arthur had behaved just as gallantly and had received nothing but a gold pin. When the Queen heard that O'Connor's sentence was only one year's imprisonment she implored Gladstone to have him transported, not as a heavier punishment but to prevent him from trying again next year. O'Connor amiably agreed to go voluntarily abroad, provided the Home Secretary chose a healthy climate.

Next month the persistent Dilke urged the Commons to delve thoroughly into Her Majesty's expenditure. He was howled down. Typhoid fever, which had just failed to dispatch her son, destroyed Dilke's campaign and dealt republicanism a crippling blow.

Politics had taken a back seat in the Queen's mind during recent anxious months. When she thought of them it was more likely to be in connection with France than England. Revolutions alarmed her more than education, though there were signs that she felt social amelioration was going too far. She quoted Mr Stansfeld, a Liberal Minister, on the London poor being rendered 'too dependent' by social help.[41] Sir William Jenner went further, believing that high mortality among the workers' children was not a bad thing: it kept the strain hardy.[42]

Rather to Gladstone's annoyance the Queen decided to 'run over to Baden-Baden' during the Easter recess of 1872 to see her dying half-sister, Princess Feodore. She found time for a little sightseeing, including the 'terrible thrill' of an iron Virgin who clasped her heretical victims in arms full of knives, and the equally terrible thrill of the local gambling dens full of 'the worst characters of both sexes in Europe'. Not long after her return home she was greatly put out by a fresh crusade of Gladstone's. Having failed to reform the Queen's way of life, he now brought down from Mount Sinai what he termed a 'Plan of Life' for her son. If the worm was in the oak he would at least save the sapling.

The Prime Minister had arrived at Balmoral in September 1871 with a solution to the problem of the Prince of Wales. He must be put to work – on art, science and philanthropy. The Queen did not hear of these proposals. Those who did thought little of them. Ponsonby and Knollys, the Prince's private secretary, agreed that he possessed neither his father's talent for art and science nor his mother's for philanthropy. When Knollys went on to suggest, however, that he should instead be shown dispatches, Ponsonby demurred. The Ministers would not trust his discretion, the Queen would be jealous and – a last item which he did not reveal to Knollys – the Queen herself was not seeing enough dispatches to make real work for her son, even if they were all sent. Princess Alice, having discussed the subject with Gladstone, had spoken also to Ponsonby. Her mother, she said, saw no point in planning for the Prince of Wales.

'She thinks the Monarchy will last her time and it is no use thinking what will come after if the principal person himself does not, and so she lets the torrent come on. To keep up her dynasty, to keep up her family, such as parents do for their children, doesn't seem to trouble her mind. But no one can suggest what should be done and we must sit quietly and let the approaching calamity crush us without an effort.'[43]

Fortunately the Prince's miraculous escape from death had deeply impressed both him and his mother with the need to turn over a new leaf. She rejoiced in the regenerate tears with which he greeted the sight of his little wheelbarrow at the Swiss Cottage, fondly hoping that he had returned to an age of innocence.

By May 1872 this halcyon interlude with her heir had passed. When she hinted that he was again going about too much, 'What can I do,' was the exasperated reply, 'if you go about so little?' Ponsonby summed up this scene as 'a little unpleasantness'. A big unpleasantness arrived two months later when Gladstone saw Ponsonby, rejected a Court proposal that the Prince should go on the India Board which he derided as a 'puddling little employment', and propounded a new solution – that the Prince should join the mission field in Ireland. Long periods of residence there would pacify the people and occupy the Prince.

This time the unpleasantness was between Queen Victoria and her Prime Minister, for her son was as strong as she against going to Ireland. They both believed that the Plan of

492

Life was a ruse to shore up Gladstone's own crumbling policies. To his interminable memoranda on the subject she replied with increasing exasperation.

The case of 'Regina v Gladstone' lasted for well over a year, counting Gladstone's missions to activate the Queen and occupy the Prince as part of the same 'Royalty question'. Gladstone recognized the effect of his failure: the prolonged correspondence had made the Queen ' "shut up" (so to speak)' towards him. Ponsonby noticed another sinister result.

> 'Ministers are getting rapidly reconciled to keeping her well away and in point of fact enjoy the outward appearance of having all the power in their own hands.'[44]

Next year (1873) his point was proved by the War Minister, Cardwell, offering his personal congratulations to the troops instead of speaking on behalf of the Queen. Victoria was furious but her secretary took the opportunity to remark that this was what would happen if Ministers never saw her.

The last year of Gladstone's first and greatest Ministry did not impinge unduly on the Queen though an early crisis developed. Disraeli defeated him by three votes in March 1873 on an Irish University Bill. 'Good Mr G.,' she wrote sarcastically to the Princess Royal, 'is not judicious & this "Mission" to redeem Ireland wh has signally failed – has been the cause of his defeat.'[45] Disraeli then refused to form a Government himself. He intended to keep the humiliated Liberals in the stocks, throwing abuse at them for a few more months. Gladstone admitted to Ponsonby that the artful dodger's sly manoeuvre 'has thrown me back'. It was designed eventually to throw him out. Disraeli pleased the Queen by expatiating on the 'fine state' of the Conservatives and touched her by saying that since his wife's death the year before he went to 'a homeless home, alone, every night'.[46] She knew what he meant. To Gladstone she felt no gratitude when he reluctantly agreed to withdraw his resignation, tersely informing her daughter that his behaviour had been tactless, tiresome and obstinate – 'doing himself no good'.

Ponsonby complained in April that Osborne was 'enveloped

in Tory density' – generated by the ladies. Peel had been right in wishing to change them.

'I must say the Queen says as little as possible but one can't help seeing she is impressed by being told that Goschen knows nothing of naval matters . . . his whole object is petty economy – or that Cardwell does not care for the Army . . . or that Lowe sends orders to the British Museum to use half sheets [of paper].'[47]

Nevertheless there was one success that summer. Gladstone held Queen Victoria to her promise to entertain the Shah of Persia. As a result she enjoyed a magnificent farrago of pomp and nonsense. Rumours of three wives discreetly dumped in Europe preceded the Shah's arrival but other charmers were said to be in his suite. Gladstone, scandalized, threatened to withdraw Government hospitality. The Queen found this 'Oriental brother' unexpectedly punctual, dignified and improvable. Never forgetful of her vocation to do good, she lectured him (through Lord Granville) on prison reform. Great was her satisfaction when she heard that he had publicly kissed her photograph at Windsor railway station. In response to his display of blazing gems she wore her Koh-i-noor diamond. Not all the incidents of the Shah's visit were revealed to her – the roasted lambs devoured under the table, the tripods burning little holes in the carpets – but she heard without amusement of his watching a boxing match in her Palace garden.

To Queen Victoria, by far the most overwhelming event of 1873 was the engagement of Prince Alfred, Duke of Edinburgh, to the Tsar of Russia's only daughter, Marie. She displayed unusual tetchiness. When everyone else was congratulating him, she expressed nothing but surprise. 'The murder is out' was how she announced the betrothal to the Princess Royal.[48] A complicated *histoire* lay behind this ungraciousness.

Prince Alfred, after the marital frustrations which have already been described* had finally in 1869 set his heart upon the young Russian Princess. His suit, however, failed to

* See pp. 463 and 465–7.

494

prosper either with the Russians or his mother, who had by now changed her mind about Frederika of Hanover and favoured Affie's earlier choice. In 1872 the affair therefore lapsed. To Queen Victoria's dismay, in January 1873 she heard that negotiations had been reopened. The reason, according to unsubstantiated rumours picked up by the British Ambassador, was because Marie had compromised herself with Prince Golitsyn, if not others, and her family were ready to see her settled. The Queen, no less ready to 'avert' the match by applying her customary family and diplomatic pressures, could not believe that Marie really loved her son. A marriage into the Greek church would mean priests constantly running in and out of the Edinburghs' home, Clarence House. Above all, Russia was 'unfriendly' to England and the Romanovs were personally 'false' and arrogant. Was it likely that a princess with 'half Oriental Russian notions' of self-indulgence would make the kind of unaffected, hard-working partner she always desired for her children? Several months of further Russian shilly-shallying deeply mortified her while Prince Alfred's determination not to feel humiliated filled her with disgust.

A week after the engagement her phobia of the Russians reached a new peak. The Tsar flatly refused to present Marie at Balmoral before the wedding for the Queen's habitual inspection of a future daughter-in-law. In private he gave vent to abuse: 'Silly old fool.'[49] The Tsarina, in an effort to soothe, only made matters worse by telegraphing Queen Victoria to meet her instead at Cologne. How could 'a Sovereign & a lady' be ready in three days 'to run after her?' demanded the Queen of the Princess Royal.[50] To Lord Granville she fumed about 'Asiatic ideas of their Rank'. When Princess Alice unwisely pressed for the visit to Cologne, partly on the ground that the Tsarina felt the heat more than dear Mama, Queen Victoria's indignation with her second daughter knew no bounds:

'You have *entirely* taken the Russian side, & I do *not* think, dear Child, that *you* should tell *me* who have been nearly 20 *years longer* on the throne than the Emperor of

495

Russia & am the Doyenne of Sovereigns & who am a *Reigning* Sovereign which the Empress is *not*, – *what I ought to do. I* think *I* know *that*. The proposal received on *Wednesday* for me to be *at Cologne* . . . tomorrow, was one of the *coolest* things *I* ever heard . . . How could I who am not like any little Princess ready to run to the slightest call of the *mighty Russians* – have been *able in 24 hours* to be *ready* to travel! I *Own every one* was shocked.'[51]

All this accumulated anger was afterwards largely dispelled by Marie's warm spontaneity. As long as she quickly learnt English ways – 'good not fast' – she would be a 'treasure'.[52]

A private treasure, be it understood, not a political one. For the Edinburgh marriage, despite much international speculation, was never one of those 'great foreign alliances' which Queen Victoria had already abandoned by 1870.* In the words of Professor Merritt Abrash, it was at most 'an apolitical dynastic curiosity'.

One nagging doubt haunted Queen Victoria: would 'poor Affie' make a good husband? Rather tactlessly she urged him just before his marriage to drop all former habits and give his whole heart to Marie. Not surprisingly there was no answer. She summed up Lady Augusta Stanley's account of the glittering fairy-tale wedding in St Petersburg (January 1874) in three words: 'What a day.'

One genuine tribute to Gladstone burst from Queen Victoria during his last year of office: ill as he was, he 'struggled' to the House of Commons to speak in favour of Prince Alfred's marriage settlement. Another subject on which they fervently agreed was that of womankind. Their respective problems over sex, different as they were, united them in abhorrence of Women's Rights. Queen Victoria exerted herself to keep women out of the professions, especially 'the *Medical Line*', enlisting Gladstone's aid in 1870. Sir William Jenner, she said, would 'tell him what an *awful* idea this is – of allowing *young girls* & young men to enter the dissecting room together . . .' The training of

* See p. 461.

female doctors, agreed Gladstone, was a 'repulsive subject'.[53]

The idea of Votes for Women excited Queen Victoria slightly less, for unlike the dissecting room it did not necessitate their studying 'things wh cld not be named before them . . .' Indeed her chronic rage at the exploitation of 'us poor women' by insatiable husbands (her own brand of feminism) sometimes made her appreciate jokes against men. She was delighted when Lord Dufferin revealed to her the grounds on which a deputation of women had demanded the vote: 'Men were seldom fit for the work'.

Gladstone's Ministry continued to run downhill throughout 1873 until it fell early in 1874. Queen Victoria took an uncharitable view of his fall.

> 'I cannot help thinking, as many do, that the proposal to remove the Income Tax was a bait, to catch the electors, in which he has signally failed.'[54]

She sweetened his last audience, however, with a reference to his loyalty to the Crown, and he left once more 'quite under the charm'.[55]

On February 10th, 1874, the anniversary of her wedding day, she recorded Disraeli's arrival at the head of a 'healthy' Conservative majority – the first since Peel. Disraeli, tottering and wheezing in the east winds, nevertheless came to her like a second bridegroom.

CHAPTER XXVII

THE FAERY QUEEN
1874-8

QUEEN VICTORIA, though far from vain, gave much thought to her official portraits. It was important that each new impression should be the appropriate one. The Viennese painter, von Angeli, who was engaged upon her portrait in 1875, several times inquired anxiously whether she was not looking 'too earnest'. No, replied Her Majesty firmly: it was right that her expression should be 'serious' since 'it represents the Queen'. A copy with a softer expression could be executed later for the children.[1]

Her sons might not have recognized the softer version. 'They are in terror of the Queen,' wrote Ponsonby, lamenting that they dared not discuss their grievances face to face. The Queen also favoured go-betweens. An outburst of temper – her old enemy – must be avoided at all costs. Nevertheless, indirect communication was a mistake, for the go-between was too often Brown.

The graph of 'Brown rows' climbed steeply between 1871 and 1874. Two courtiers, Biddulph and Fitzroy, threatened to resign after misunderstandings with Brown; the Prince of Wales refused to stay at Abergeldie because of shooting regulations to protect Brown's sport. Ghillies' balls were fruitful causes of scandal. On one occasion Lord Cowley while performing the Perpetual Jig was tripped by a groom and fell flat, amid loud laughter. 'Even J.B. saw that this was unseemly,' reported Ponsonby, 'and ordered the music to stop.' A visiting Lord Chancellor protested about Brown's rough ball-room manner with the Queen. 'What a coarse animal that Brown is!'[2]

Every member of the Queen's family caused her anxiety during these years. The expense of visits was still at the bottom of quarrels. Not all the faults were hers. Ponsonby considered that the Princess Royal went beyond a daughter's rights in proposing herself and a huge suite at any time without consulting her mother's convenience. For several weeks in 1874 Queen Victoria broke off all communication with her eldest daughter after acrimonious exchanges on this subject.

Prince Alfred also was to blame: according to his private secretary, Sir John Cowell, his concern with money amounted to a disease; no mother could be expected to lend her married son a house (Buckingham Palace), pay for lighting and heating (as she did) and £50 a day for his very *recherché* food as well. Nevertheless disputes over hospitality brought Queen Victoria an unfair reputation abroad for stinginess. Her real fault was the old, morbid refusal to do the entertaining herself. 'My head is still on my shoulders,' boasted Disraeli after persuading Her Majesty to come south two days early in honour of Prince Alfred's Russian 'in-laws'.

The Queen's earlier, happy relations with Prince Leopold were now wretchedly bedevilled by a series of terrifying hacmorrhages. Not unnaturally her passionate concern was to shelter him from accidents but she became hopelessly over-protective. Prince Leopold's brothers and sisters made plots to liberate him. A pet scheme of the Prince of Wales's was for Leopold to command a corps of Balmoral Volunteers. The Queen rightly considered this unsuitable, since Prince Leopold suffered from a chronically affected knee; nor had she any wish for her peace to be disturbed by constant bugling round the house. There was much heart-burning before the project was dropped.

Princess Beatrice also suffered from over-protection – against marriage. Her mother felt that she could not get on without this last sweet-tempered, submissive 'Benjamina'. The Household was therefore forbidden to mention the word 'wedding', dancing-partners were limited to brothers and at meals the Princess dared not discuss any subject beyond the weather without an imploring look at her mother. The Queen's behaviour was a gloomy example of the selfishness to which, under stress, she could descend.

The raffish company kept by her son and heir, together with his financial difficulties, never ceased to appal. To add to her troubles, memoirs and biographies were beginning to unlock the secrets of her own era. Ernest Stockmar shocked

her in 1872 by writing a life of his father in which he pictured
the old Baron moving at ease among British State secrets.
The *Greville Memoirs*, edited by Henry Reeve, burst upon
Balmoral two years later. To do the Queen justice she began
by enjoying Greville's masterpiece: though 'very exaggerated'
it was nevertheless 'full of truth'.[3] Closer inspection convinced
her that revelations about kings, even those long deceased,
might have dangerous repercussions.

Anti-monarchical feeling was by no means extinct, as she
discovered during the following year when a collision in the
Solent involving her yacht, the *Alberta*, caused three deaths
by drowning. 'Take care the people are saved!' the Queen
had screamed, rushing forward until stopped by Ponsonby.
The Portsmouth mob hissed the *Alberta*'s captain, her
nephew Ernest Leiningen, and a court case kept feelings for
months at boiling point; the 'horrid foreman' of the jury was
said to be a Communist. She wrote in exasperation to the
Princess Royal:

> 'I assure you I wish I cld avoid ever going on the Sea
> again wh, as we happen to be an Island & Osborne is on
> one, is impossible.'[4]

As usual Jenner forecast (incorrectly) a nervous breakdown.

Meanwhile Balmoral read nothing but Greville. Disraeli
called the book a social outrage perpetuated by a man consumed with vanity: 'I have never witnessed the disease in
so violent a form,' he told Lady Ely, 'yet I have read Cicero
and I know Lord Lytton.' The Duke of Richmond, utterly
absorbed, found the book monstrous. Lord John Manners
tore himself away for a moment to remark: 'It is like Judas
writing the lives of the Apostles.' Ponsonby was fascinated
by the parallels between 'then' and 'now': there was the same
minute interest in servants' lives; George IV was very ingenious about turning conversation from any subject he did
not like – 'Exactly what the Queen does'; Greville spoke of
the dullness of his Court – 'What would he think of this –
even rows are almost watched for.'[5]

The Queen, to whom the book now appeared dreadful,
scandalous and abominable, particularly resented Reeve's

excuse for publication: that she would shine the brighter against her uncle's blackness. Shine at the expense of 'Uncle King'? He had always been so kind to her personally.

Amid much literary disturbance there was one compensating success. Theodore Martin's deferential *Life of the Prince Consort*, Volume I, came out after Greville. Martin had been inspired, supplied with material, even fought for by the Queen. In defending her wisdom in publishing the truth, however intimate, against her children's advice, she incidentally provided Stockmar, Reeve and Greville with their own defence: 'in these days people will write & will know...'

The Queen could still amuse people when she wished. There was the dinner when she described how her mother had once carried a fork out of the dining-room in mistake for her fan; and another when she told Ponsonby with roars of laughter how shocked poor Sir Thomas Biddulph had been by the dreadful design for the Ashanti medals: 'Roman soldiers with nothing – nothing at all – but helmets on!' But she did not often wish to amuse.

Disraeli during his five years in opposition had kept in touch with Queen Victoria at a distance. He had written assiduously during her illness of 1871 and defended her in speeches in 1872 and 1873. All these things made their mark and when she saw a copy of his election manifesto she turned her back on Ponsonby for venturing to criticize it.

What attracted her about this mediocre document was the promise it held out of a more active foreign policy. Disraeli's election victory of 1874 was a post-dated reward for the votes he had bestowed on thousands of heads of households in 1867 who were not unwilling to see Britain once more throwing her weight about, much as they themselves lorded it over their own families. Queen Victoria shared their feelings. The mood was not yet jingoism and certainly not aggression. She rejected the Princess Royal's congratulations on the annexation of Fiji: 'I have such a horror (unlike what is felt by many in Germany now) of the love of acquisition & conquest'.[6] The two words which expressed her ideal best were 'high tone'.

She wished her Ministers to maintain a 'high tone' towards foreigners – a blend of the high horse and high principles. 'High tone' could permeate Society also, in which case it meant caring deeply about moral issues instead of carrying tolerance to the point of indifference. A letter to Gladstone in 1883 illustrates the parallel she drew between political and domestic life. Why had he not exacted proper reparation from the French for arresting a British missionary?

> 'What she fears is, a growing tendency to swallow insults . . . & of not taking them up in that high tone wh they used formerly to be, & wh is so much the case in private transactions nowadays . . . since duelling (a thing in itself not to be defended but wh still kept up a high tone) – has ceased . . .'[7]

Duelling and Don Pacifico had gone out together.

Posterity might consider Gladstone the very high priest of 'high tone' and Disraeli its feeblest exponent. Queen Victoria reversed this judgement. In Gladstone's internationalism she missed that appeal to national arrogance which was among its essential features.

Disraeli treated his friend Lady Bradford to an idyllic version of his first visit as Premier to Osborne in August 1874. 'The Faery', as it amused him to call the plump, graceful little being who now dominated his burlesque imagination, greeted him so warmly that he half expected to be kissed. 'She was wreathed with smiles and, as she tattled, glided about the room like a bird.'[8] He was offered a privilege not accorded to a Prime Minister since Lord M.: he was asked to sit down. Disraeli deemed it judicious to decline on this first occasion.

Those who watched the tropical growth of this bizarre friendship were apt to see in it nothing beyond masculine guile and feminine infatuation – one of the stock man–woman relationships of Victorian mythology. Disraeli's confession at the end of his life to Matthew Arnold – 'You have heard me called a flatterer, and it is true. Everyone likes flattery and when you come to royalty, you should lay it on with a trowel'[9] – might suggest that they were right. Disraeli, however, like many highly-strung people in positions of great power, genuinely needed the support of women, and Queen Victoria occupied as real a place in his affections as any of his other female friends. Indeed they all had something in common. As the Russian Ambassador once remarked, Dizzy's ladies were '*toutes grand' mères*'.[10] The majority were also widows. Both Disraeli and the Queen venerated that deity of Victorian England – the bereaved spouse. Like the Queen, Disraeli mourned extravagantly. He wrote to Lady Bradford after his wife's death:

'It is strange that I always used to think that the Queen, persisting in these emblems of woe, indulged in a morbid sentiment; and yet it has become my lot, and seemingly an irresistible one.'[11]

Whenever he thought of diminishing the heavy black borders round his letters he remembered, like Queen Victoria, that there was no one alive now to whom he was all in all.

When Disraeli said: 'I am fortunate in serving a female sovereign,' he was quite genuine. True, he made use of this susceptible woman as he could not have used a man, to boost his imperial policies, but no King–Emperor could have fired his oriental imagination like a Queen–Empress.

Queen Victoria never entirely departed from her early view that Mr Disraeli was just like his novels; but whereas his exotic compliments to Parliamentary colleagues merely amused, those to herself amused and ravished. Snowdrops from Osborne he called 'a Faery gift' from Queen Titania herself; primroses were a sign that 'your Majesty's sceptre has touched the enchanted isle'. Who would not find it more agreeable to be called the Faery Queen than the Missus, or even Eliza? Ponsonby wrote to his wife:

'He has got the length of her foot exactly, and knows how to be sympathetic. You and I know that his sympathy is expressed while his tongue is in his cheek – but are not her woes told in the same manner?'[12]

In a talk with Lord Rosebery she showed herself alive to

Dizzy's methods: 'He had a way when we differed . . . of saying "Dear Madam" so persuasively, and putting his head on one side.'[13]

The Queen had the measure of her Prime Minister's foot also, and together they savoured the delicious fictions of their relationship with as much gusto as they brought to the facts. Under the stress of asthma, gout and a tiff with the Faery, Disraeli could write with perfect simplicity and truth: 'I love the Queen – perhaps the only person in this world left to me that I do love . . .'[14]

In comparing Gladstone and Disraeli Queen Victoria had ascribed Disraeli's superiority to greater unselfishness and larger ideas. Nearer to her true feelings was Disraeli's own pronouncement: 'Gladstone treats the Queen like a public department; I treat her like a woman.'

She was not the only woman to find Gladstone unattractive. 'Mr Gladstone may be a marvel of erudition,' said Lady Rosebery, 'but he will never understand a man, still less a woman.'[15] Emily Eden, the writer and traveller, complained that Gladstone did not converse, he harangued. His 'parvenu-ism' put her off and he lacked humour. 'If he were soaked in boiling water and rinsed till he was twisted into a rope, I do not suppose a drop of fun would ooze out.' Fun did not ooze from Disraeli either but even in his last years, between bouts of silence when a veil fell over his face, he would shoot small, pungent darts into the conversation. Despite a weakness for romping the Queen appreciated wit. Mary Ponsonby was another woman who shrank from Gladstone's 'terrible earnestness'. She preferred Gladdy's politics but Dizzy's table-talk.

Behind Gladstone's unprepossessing façade the Queen thought she detected ideas to match. At the beginning of the new Ministry she created two opportunities for exposing Gladstone's insubordination and establishing Disraeli's compliance.

Early in 1874 the Queen took her revenge on all those who in her opinion were undermining the Anglican Church.

From behind the scenes she drove through a Public Worship Bill, introduced by Archbishop Tait, to purge it of Romish practices. After the Bill's passage she hoped there would be no more 'bowings and scrapings' and above all *confession*. Disraeli considered this unwise piece of legislation to be the hardest nut he ever had to crack. To her it brought a satisfying sense of personal power and ministerial obedience.

Her Protestant militancy dated from an earlier experience. The declaration in 1870 of Papal Infallibility followed by Bismarck's campaign against the Catholic Church fired her with longing to show that in Britain also there was a Defender of the Faith. What could be better than to give a lead in Protestant solidarity by taking the Scottish Sacrament at Crathie Kirk? First attracted towards this step by the sight of old crofters tramping to kirk through the snow in 1870, she finally took it on November 3rd, 1873.

As usual with all her most profound needs she felt that merely captious objections were raised. The Archbishop of Canterbury, backed by Gladstone, criticized her proposal as repugnant to loyal churchmen, while others read into it an attack on Prince Alfred's Greek marriage or put it down to the influence of two Presbyterians at Court, Lady Erroll and John Brown. All agreed that it must be kept very dark.

Ponsonby was more sympathetic.

'What she does is not prompted by a deep design . . . she really does like the kirk and its Scotch entourage and she felt a comfort in taking the communion at Crathie simply for its own sake. Increased possibly by a dislike to the ritualists but this was only an accidental cause.'[16]

Ponsonby was several times pressed to take the Scottish Sacrament with the Queen and at last consented, having no theological objections but finding it, unlike the Queen, 'cold and cheerless'.

New storms arose. Prince Leopold fell ill in the course of violent opposition; the Free Kirk accused Crathie of stealing its membership, for only the gardener and the carpenter at Balmoral maintained their allegiance to the Free Kirk against the Queen's pressure. (When Guy Fawkes Day, 1878, arrived, she suddenly headed her Journal with the bellicose words, 'Remember, remember the 5th of November, gunpowder treason, and Plot'.)

In this perfervid atmosphere the Public Worship Bill came to birth. Disraeli's famous boast to Lord Esher about his handling of the Faery – 'I never deny; I never contradict; I sometimes forget' – was not substantiated. The Queen would not let him forget. Her hair stood on end at some of Dean Stanley's stories: how, for instance, a bishop visiting a High Church was so distracted by the ritual that he accidentally spilt some altar wine, whereupon the three attending clergy fell flat down and licked it up. Worse still, Lord Ripon apostasized to Rome. Queen Victoria was horrified that one so lately a Minister could have done such a thing, 'without anyone having suspected it!'[17]

Gladstone's behaviour over the Bill greatly increased her hostility to him. Having appeared to defend Romanism by attacking the Bill, he then published an *Expostulation* against the Catholic claims. This seemed sheer perversity. Not for the first time she quoted Palmerston's remark that Gladstone's changes of principle were 'dangerous'. John Brown, who was thought to echo her opinions, told Ponsonby that Gladstone was a 'Roman'. So did Jenner. 'Ripon was a friend of Gladstone's,' Jenner announced, 'and that is enough.' Disraeli airily supposed that Ripon's conversion to Rome would cause a landslide among the Liberal leaders – 'Ah! yes,' he smiled to Ponsonby, 'they will all go sooner or later.'[18]

It is possible that Queen Victoria toyed with the idea that Gladstone was a secret Papist. She may also have suspected him for a moment of being a secret libertine. He had long performed rescue work among prostitutes which was just now beginning to interest his enemies and worry his friends. On his part, it represented a conscious expression of practical Christianity and probably also an unconscious sublimation of his vigorous sexual instincts. His family believed that when foul rumours reached the Queen's ears Disraeli did not contradict them.

'High tone' seemed everywhere in jeopardy and Queen Victoria saw a chance to bring it back.

506

Empress of India: what new title could be better calculated to raise Queen and country on high? Like the Public Worship Bill, the idea of a Royal Titles Bill had long been in Queen Victoria's mind. Indeed, it went back to the transfer of India in 1858 to the Crown. Suddenly her latent longings were given a jolt by the King of Prussia becoming an Emperor and tactlessly showing that he considered his son grander than hers. In high indignation Her Majesty eventually summoned Ponsonby in January 1873.

'I am an Empress & in common conversation am sometimes called Empress of India. Why have I never officially assumed this title? I feel I ought to do so & wish to have preliminary enquiries made.'[19]

She felt as a Pope might feel in promulgating a dogma already believed by the faithful. But when Ponsonby made the inquiries they fell on stony Liberal ground.

Prince Alfred's connection by marriage with the world's haughtiest Imperial Highnesses also provoked argument over precedence. A letter from the Tsar required his daughter Marie to be called Imperial, not Royal, 'as in all civilized countries'. Queen Victoria, when questioned, said she didn't care whether Imperial was used or not provided Royal came first. This touch of crispness did not end the matter. There were still Marie's Duchess-ships. Which took precedence, Duchess of Edinburgh or Grand Duchess? Queen Victoria felt handicapped in the battle of protocol by not being an Empress herself. Her private secretary, less helpful than usual, quoted Dr Johnson to his wife: 'Who comes first, a louse or a flea?'

Politics as well as precedence were involved in the Titles Bill. The Duke of Cambridge warned Queen Victoria that Britain would soon be fighting Russia for mastery of the East. What better way of crying 'Hands off India' than by declaring her Imperial title? Her oriental brothers, the Shah and Sultan, were particularly encouraging.

Meanwhile, the Prince of Wales successfully bounced his mother into giving him permission to tour India. She had not time effectively to deploy her instinctive objections to his

507

going anywhere, before he was gone. Health, expense, precedence and the list of his companions which included the 'fast set' led by Lord Aylesford, were all hastily raised and dismissed. Disraeli himself got 'the list' passed by promising to caution Lord Carrington and Lord Charles Beresford against 'larks'.[20]

Lord Aylesford, the soul of good nature, was famous for a parlour trick consisting of crawling about on all fours while his friends banged away at the only prominent part of him visible. While the Prince was abroad the notorious Aylesford divorce scandal broke. Lord Randolph Churchill tried to protect his brother Lord Blandford (who planned to elope with Lady Aylesford), by involving the Prince in something like a second Mordaunt case. At one point the enraged Prince challenged Lord Randolph to a duel, because the latter had brought pressure upon the Princess of Wales. Queen Victoria exerted herself to assist her son, though she tartly refused to boycott the Churchill family, as he wished. Their improving relationship was not in the long run affected. Duelling, after all, she had always secretly equated with 'high tone'.

The Prince's success in India impressed her: his tiger and elephant shoots, his sabbatarian rectitude and his speeches. He returned in triumph in May 1876, his ship stuffed with presents for dear Mama, of which the best was a copy of her own *Leaves* translated into Hindustani with covers of inlaid marble. She gave a family dinner in his honour where 'everybody was pleased & pleasant, a great & rare thing, in such a large family party'[21] and informed him that the Royal Titles Bill had got through.

Its extremely rough passage through Parliament had appalled her, for Disraeli did not tell the Faery Queen that nobody wanted a Faery Empress. Ponsonby wrote:

'I really think that if matters are fairly and properly put before her she sees them. It is that terrible plan of telling her she is right, not explaining the real issue, and letting it burst upon her afterwards.'

Sir Stafford Northcote, a Cabinet Minister, brought her

news of a Radical who could get up no feeling against the Bill after agitating for three weeks – 'the people were all in favour of it!!'[22] Though quite untrue, this myth seemed to be confirmed when she opened a new wing of the London Hospital. Amid touching inscriptions like 'Welcome Victoria the friend of the afflicted', she was entranced to see in huge letters, 'Welcome, Queen and Empress'.

Her friends finally persuaded her that opposition to the Bill was caused by 'misunderstandings'. Disraeli must explain that she would only be Imperial in connection with India and that she had not forced the Bill on him. Both assignments he carried out as well as circumstances permitted. For in fact the Bill was a triumph of what Gladstone called 'female will' and the female took the Bill's limitations lightly. According to Ponsonby:

'The Queen is now quite the Empress of India . . . wants to have a troop of Sikh cavalry over. Bids says it will never do.'[23]

On May Day 1876 Victoria was declared Queen-Empress. She signed a New Year card to Disraeli 'V.R. & I.' – *Victoria Regina et Imperatrix*. Disraeli no doubt smiled indulgently; when Mrs Disraeli had become a Viscountess in her own right she had signed herself to him 'Your own devoted Beaconsfield'. On January 1st, 1877 the little Queen-Empress, every inch of her weighed down with opulent gems, was toasted under her new name. Prince Arthur proposed 'The Empress of India' and all the guests except Lord Beaconsfield drank in silence, much to the relief of Ponsonby, whose wife had vowed to say 'The Queen' if she said anything. 'Your Imperial Majesty!' cried Beaconsfield, thereby giving an impression to some of those present that he had proposed the toast. After dinner he asked the Queen whether the Indian jewels she was wearing were all she possessed. 'Oh, no,' she replied, 'I'll send for the rest,' and three portmanteaux were brought in. Another of the guests, Lord George Hamilton, thought the tribute of Empire glittering on her small person would have suited a big dark woman better.

On St Valentine's day their Imperial Highnesses, Fritz and

509

Vicky, received a medal each 'in remembrance of the Empress of India'. There was no danger that her title would be forgotten. Queen Victoria ended by signing herself 'V.R. & I.' here there and everywhere instead of reserving it, in the words of an angry critic, W. S. Blunt, 'for communications east of Suez'.

The successes which the Queen had scored inspired her to further efforts. But for her, a Vivisection Bill for the humane control of research on animals would not have seen the light of day. Disraeli informed Ponsonby that the arguments against vivisection were not worth listening to, 'but the Queen insisted . . .'[24] Five years later (1881) she was prodding Gladstone on the same 'dreadful subject'. Her belief in the special vocation of a 'female sovereign' kept her compassion aflame. All this activity was building up to a major explosion of her energies throughout the decade 1875–85, the most political of her life.

In 1875 the Queen happened to be studying Theodore Martin's new volume of the Prince Consort's *Life*, dealing with the Crimean War, just as the Eastern question flared up again. In consequence she found herself much better up in the history of the Middle East than her advisers.

Inevitably the new 'crises' as she called them, seemed a continuation of the old. Had the world learnt its lesson? Disraeli was cast for the role of Palmerston, Russia was still the enemy, Turkey the ally; if she could find a Radical to denounce any truckling to Russia, so much the better. She found old Arthur John Roebuck and triumphantly summoned him to Osborne where they agreed that the present Liberals would make Palmerston turn in his grave.[25] The same frustration was to torture her in 1877 and 1878 as in 1855 : 'Oh, if the Queen were a man,' she wrote to Disraeli, 'she would like to go & give those Russians . . . such a beating!'[26] On November 5th, 1877 she headed her Journal 'Inkerman Day'.

Two new features in the situation she had not bargained for. The Bulgarian peasants rose against their Turkish masters and Gladstone rose from a bed of sickness to de-

510

nounce the atrocities perpetrated against them by the Turks. There was no role for which Queen Victoria could cast Gladstone's demonic apparition except Satan.

News of the peasants' revolt in 1875 turned the attention of Europe to reforming its Sick Man – Turkey. Disraeli, however, made it his first business to snatch a plum from the dying tree. With the help of the Rothschilds whose financial expertise Queen Victoria had once disparaged, he bought 177,000 Suez Canal shares out of a total of 400,000 from a bankrupt Turkish vassal, the Khedive of Egypt. It cost the country £4 million and, as the Queen truly remarked, 'may have far-reaching consequences'. Disraeli's announcement of his triumph shows what he meant by treating the Queen as a woman. 'It is just settled,' he wrote on November 25th, 'you have it, Madam.'[27] Gladstone would never have thought of depositing anything as a personal gift at the Faery Queen's feet. Next day in a letter to Theodore Martin Queen Victoria re-emphasized the differences she had already noticed between Disraeli and Gladstone. Disraeli had *very lofty views* of England's destiny. His mind was so much 'greater' and 'quicker' than that of Mr Gladstone.[28]

Yet not quick enough, as it proved, to distinguish between authentic news of a monstrous crime and 'coffee-house babble' – Disraeli's phrase for the Bulgarian atrocities. Mr Gladstone, on the contrary, was to demonstrate a physical and mental quickness almost inconceivable in an old gentleman approaching seventy who had retired that year from his party's leadership.

Queen Victoria hoped that her Government would organize a European solution to the Eastern question. Disraeli preferred to act alone. He dispatched the fleet to Besika Bay and by this unilateral action prevented the possibility of an international conference. The Queen was not impressed. She dreaded having to fight alone for the delinquent Turks though she had what Ponsonby called 'a professional feeling' for the Sultan, who was a Knight of the Garter. Unfortunately he was also insane. The Queen was shocked to hear that after being supplanted by his nephew at the end of May

511

1876, he had committed suicide with the scissors used to trim his beard. 'Scissors?' exclaimed Hermann Sahl, her German librarian, 'that implies a woman at the bottom of it!' The Household agreed that though the Sultan's harem, 'like our regiments', was below its full establishment there had been enough disgruntled wives on the books to effect their purpose. The new Sultan turned out to be a dipsomaniac whose mother, the Sultana, had once slapped the Empress Eugénie *'sur l'estomac'* for appearing on her son's arm.[29] Within three months he too was deposed and replaced by his brother, Abdul the Damned.

That summer Queen Victoria heard with profound horror about the 'Bashi-Bazouks' – savage bands of Turkish irregulars who had murdered 12,000 Bulgarian Christians. The very name Bashi-Bazouk, like 'Gauleiter' in a later age, suggested unspeakable cruelties. The Queen described them in her Journal as 'horribly cruel mutilators, with narrow faces, pointed beards, no uniform & knives stuck about in their belts'. It was therefore disturbing to her that Disraeli continued to refer to the 'Bulgarian atrocities' in inverted commas, as if they were a Liberal invention.

Meanwhile on August 11th, 1876 Disraeli, satisfied that Gladstone would never again lead the Commons, considered it safe to take a peerage. The first boxes which arrived for the Queen signed 'Beaconsfield' contained confirmation of the Bulgarian atrocities.

The Government's sceptical sang-froid disintegrated, a Liberal flood of moral indignation broke loose and every conscience in the country, from Gladstone's High Church precision instrument to Shaftesbury's Evangelical pickaxe and the indefatigable road-drill of the *Daily News*, got to work on the Government's façade. On September 6th Gladstone issued his famous pamphlet, *The Bulgarian Horrors and the Question of the East*. The finest invective of the century, it sold a thousand times faster than any royal *Leaves* and swept the masses into monster rallies at Blackheath, St James's Hall, Piccadilly, and elsewhere.

'Let the Turks now carry off their abuses in the only

512

From *The Blot on the Queen's Head.* A lampoon inspired by her assumption of the title, Empress of India

Little Ben took off his dress coat, assumed an Aryan artistic air, and set to work with a big paint-brush on the new sign-board.—p. 29
Front.

From *John Brown's Legs* 1884

MOVING THE ROYAL THUMB.

Victoria R.I., 1875, painted by Joachim von Angeli

Four Generations: Queen Victoria, Prince Edward of York, the Princess of Wales and the Duchess of York

A unique family group of Queen Victoria smiling broadly, with Princess Beatrice (Princess Henry of Battenberg), Princess Victoria of Hesse (Princess Louis of Battenberg) and Princess Alice (mother of the present Duke of Edinburgh)

The Golden Jubilee official photograph, 1887

Queen Victoria and the Munshi with Sir Arthur Bigge

The Diamond Jubilee, 1897

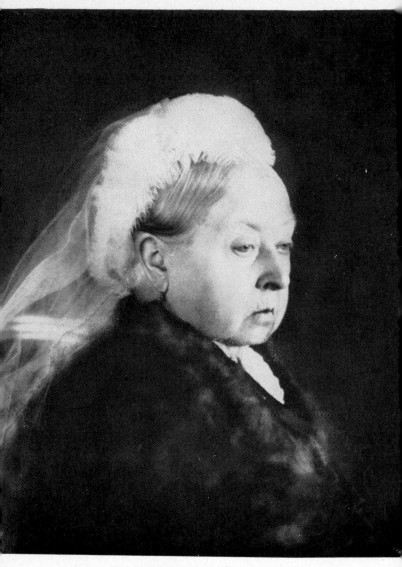
Queen Victoria in old age

possible manner, namely by carrying off themselves. Their Zaptiehs and their Mindirs, their Bimbashis and their Yuzbachis, their Kaimakams and their Pashas, one and all, bag and baggage, shall, I hope, clear out from the province they have desolated and profaned . . . '

The Queen's dilemma had been excruciating. 'She don't like the Turks,' wrote Ponsonby towards the end of August, ' – hates them more because of their atrocities', and wants the Government to 'speak out at once'. But she could not bear to blame Beaconsfield. His levity last June, she argued, 'was not his fault but that of his Cabinet who disagreed with him'. Ponsonby drily suggested that Beaconsfield should now correct what Disraeli had said.[30]

It took her a month of anxiety and rheumatism to find the way out. By the end of September her rheumatism had gone and so had Turkish responsibility for the Bashi-Bazouks – on to the shoulders of the Russians. She wrote to Beaconsfield:

'Hearing as we *do* all the undercurrents and knowing as we do that Russia *instigated* this insurrection, which *caused* the cruelty of the Turks . . . the world *ought* to know that on *their* shoulders and *not* on *ours* rest the *blood* of the murdered Bulgarians!'[31]

The final step was easy. Who had instigated the Russians? None other than that 'disgraceful . . . mischief-maker', that 'fire-brand', that 'half madman', Gladstone. *His* meetings and pamphlets, his furies and frenzies, his St James's Halls and Blackheaths had inflamed the Russians. Let *him* clear out, to Hawarden Castle, bag and baggage.

As the Queen worked her way round to this astonishing position she added constantly to the list of guilty men. The Minister at Constantinople was to blame for misinforming the Government; Prince Alfred for taking the side of his Russian father-in-law and daring to quote Gladstone's pamphlet; the Duke of Argyll (always 'so impulsive', as she wrote angrily in her Journal) for providing semi-royal lustre on anti-Turkish platforms; Ponsonby for stubbornly defending the Liberal crusade.

A stream of anti-Gladstone propaganda directed upon the Queen by the Prince of Wales, among others, inevitably damaged the Liberals in her Household. After the shouting was over Ponsonby found himself still suspect. At the death in 1878 of Sir Thomas Biddulph, Keeper of the Privy Purse, the Prince wished Montagu Corry, Lord Beaconsfield's private secretary, to supplant Ponsonby in his key position, leaving the latter with only the Privy Purse. Queen Victoria actually considered Monty Corry but finally rejected him as a 'man of pleasure'.[32]

Ponsonby felt sure that it was really Beaconsfield who had poisoned the Queen against him. In his own fall from favour he could trace the growth of Beaconsfield's ascendancy, which in turn kept pace with the titanic struggle for the soul of the country going on outside the Palace.

'Upon my word, I verily believe that Gladstone thinks Dizzy himself had a hand in those outrages upon women and children,' said Delane of *The Times* to Lord Redesdale one day.[33] Queen Victoria felt precisely the same about Gladstone.

Her pen worked incessantly to prevent a Russian attack upon Turkey and when Russia declared war in April 1877 she felt as if the Tsar's challenge had been thrown down, not to the Sultan, but to herself. Beaconsfield ruthlessly exploited this tendency in his Sovereign to see political events as a personal struggle. While at the end of 1876 Ponsonby reckoned that she was not 'unreasonably anti-Russian', by the time Beaconsfield had done with her she was rabid.

To show her support for Beaconsfield she volunteered to open Parliament in February 1877 and stoically bore 'the long trying pause' till the Members of the Commons 'came along with a great rush'. For the same reason she ostentatiously lunched with the Prime Minister in his home at Hughenden, a public demonstration of friendship not shown since she had visited Melbourne at Brocket in 1841. Beaconsfield's comparison between 'our' policy and Gladstone's was diligently quoted in her Journal. Ours was 'the Imperial policy of England', Gladstone's 'the policy of crusade' – mere 'sentimental eccentricity'.[34]

Dean Stanley was secretly telegraphed for, 'to correct' Ponsonby's 'opposition proclivities'. Ponsonby's hurt feelings were relieved in a series of long letters to Mary who, herself a suspect, reacted with characteristic vigour, threatening to 'put on a mysterious look as if I were in hourly communication with the opposition'.

> May 23rd, 1877: '. . . What I think is a mistake is that Beaconsfield, should bully everyone for speaking out his mind . . . he must see that the Queen originally was not pro Turk – and there is a lurking doubt in her mind still when she talks – but he has skillfully described the situation as a struggle for mastery between England and Russia and that the point at issue is who shall be the first, the Queen or the Czar . . .'

> May 28th: '. . . He has hushed me – and made me silent – implying a silent approval!'

> November 18th: '. . . [The Queen] evidently distrusts me . . . and shows me only parts of her discussions with Beaconsfield . . . what I might be hurt about, would be that she employs Lady Ely to write to Monty Corry . . . Corry answers as if from himself but clearly in the Beaconsfield sense . . .'

In Biddulph's words, Beaconsfield was 'humbugging' both with Lady Ely and the Queen while the private secretary was being by-passed.

Even Beaconsfield's policy soon did not seem dynamic enough to the impassioned Queen. Though lip service was still paid to peace, 'I am sure you wld not wish Gt Britain to eat humble pie to those deceitful cruel Russians?' she demanded fiercely of the Princess Royal in June.[35] The Russian atrocities had put 'the so called Bulgarian atrocities' into the shade. By July she felt almost too strongly to write. A returned traveller assured her that the Turks sincerely believed in God, 'whilst the so called Christians of the Principalities are the most superstituous horrible creatures possible.'[36] Bandages – tokens of her highest regard – were sent to the Turks and requests for subscriptions to the maids-of-honour. Miss Stopford and Miss Lascelles told Ponsonby they would prefer to assist Russia. 'Say you have already devoted all your spare cash to your fellow subjects in India,' Ponsonby advised them. When the Russians were unexpectedly held up before Plevna the Cabinet saw it as a breathing space but the Queen as a breathless opportunity for checkmating their next advance. Occupy Gallipoli – send the fleet to Constantinople – join the Turks in the field – join the Austrians – only let the Government decide what to do and do it.

Yet even in this tornado of emotion she did not altogether lose her head. When the Princess Royal excitedly suggested that Britain should annex Egypt, Queen Victoria replied crushingly: [37]

> 'Why shd we make such a wanton aggression . . .? It is not our custom to annexe countries (as it is in some others) unless we are obliged & forced to do so – as in the case of the Transvaal Republic.'

Forced, that is, by the cruelty of the Boers to the natives.

To her disgust she realized that Beaconsfield was having trouble with two 'deplorable' colleagues. The Foreign Secretary, Lord Derby, and the Colonial Secretary, Lord Carnarvon, were for 'peace at all price,' while Beaconsfield longed to take the highest possible tone with Russia – or so he made her believe. Not for an instant did she suspect that he was playing on her bellicosity to push his Cabinet forward while trading on their reluctance in order to hold her back. It is sometimes a help to steer between Scylla and Charybdis. With feverish excitement she bent herself to the task of disembarrassing Beaconsfield both of his hesitations and his colleagues.

'Be bold!' *'Pray act* quickly!' In August Colonel Wellesley, British Military Attaché, was sent to the Tsar with a secret warning from the Queen and Beaconsfield not to advance or Britain would fight. This time it was the Foreign Secretary who was being by-passed. Horrified, Ponsonby saw Queen Victoria.

'Why not tell Lord Derby?'

'How can we? He tells Lady Derby – and she tells all to Schouvaloff.'*

Ponsonby admitted this was 'a tremendous fix'.[38] In the event it was less of a fix than a farce, for the diplomatic bag containing the Tsar's reply mysteriously disappeared. 'It is a miserable thing to be a constitutional Queen,' Victoria lamented to her daughter, '& to be unable to do what is right!'[39]

Beaconsfield's parched frame shuddered under incessant doses of royal tonic, unpalatable as strychnine. 'The Faery writes every day and telegraphs every hour,' he moaned faintly to Lady Bradford.[40] Queen Victoria felt no compunction. 'Supported by me,' she exulted to the Princess Royal (December 26th, 1877), Beaconsfield had seized the reins and defeated Derby:

'we are now ready to act – in the right sense. Ld. Beaconsfield will not loosen the reins again & I work vy hard in writing to him & cyphering almost daily – sometimes.'

Ld. Beaconsfield will not loosen the reins again . . . It was more of a threat than a prediction and indeed the Queen had not reached this point without threats of resignation spiralling across the political Sahara from every quarter, including the Throne. In April 1877 she menaced Beaconsfield with the joint abdication of Queen and Country: if Russia were allowed to occupy Egypt, Britain would 'abdicate' as a Great Power 'to which she will never submit, and another must wear the crown'[41] – the thorny crown. Five times between April 1877 and February 1878 did she threaten to abdicate, rather than see the country 'kiss the feet of the great barbarians . . .'[42] The resignations of Derby, Carnarvon and even Salisbury were on and off the cards and Beaconsfield once had to play the resignation card himself. Queen Victoria personally tackled 'that absurd (though in some respects clever) little Ld. Carnarvon' in January 1878, describing her dramatic interview to the Princess Royal:

'I pitched into him with a vehemence & indignation –
* The Russian Ambassador in London.

517

who was at any rate inspired by the British Lion – & he remained shrinking but still craven hearted! – wishing to say to the world we cld not act!!! oh! that Englishmen were now what they were!! but we shall yet assert our rights – our position – & "Britains never will be Slaves" – will yet be our Motto. I own I never spoke with such vehemence as I did last night.'[43]

Carnarvon crept out looking like 'a naughty schoolboy',[44] sent in his resignation – and then retracted. 'That *wretched* little "*Twitters*"!' wrote Prince Leopold to his mother of Carnarvon, 'to have caused you so much annoyance.'[45]

The Queen felt 'half distracted' by the 'low tone' of the country, by incessant appeals from the Sultan and an avalanche of business which made writing her Journal an agony. Even the installation of a telephone did not please. The demonstrator, 'a Professor Bell', was very pompous and the sounds of a bugle and organ 'rather faint'.[46]

Jingoism came to birth. Mr Gladstone was soon to be hooted in the streets and the windows of his house broken while the mob chanted their new hymn:

> *We don't want to fight but by Jingo if we do,*
> *We've got the ships, we've got the men, we've*
> *got the money too.*

Meanwhile the ships were ordered to Constantinople on January 23rd by the new First Lord of the Admiralty, Mr W. H. Smith of station bookstall fame, whose appointment had been celebrated by the Radical MP, Wilfrid Lawson:

> *A paper fleet they say is ours*
> *If what we hear is true.*
> *Let's hope the fleets of other powers*
> *Are stationary too.*

Carnarvon and Derby were both expected to resign: 'Great news, feel so relieved', wrote the Queen, only to find on the 26th that the ships had been stopped and Derby's resignation withdrawn. Beaconsfield, in breaking to his Faery the horrible news, abandoned the formal third person. 'I answer

518

you as you kindly addressed me,' replied Queen Victoria emotionally, 'and as I hope you will do, whenever it is easier,' signing herself 'Yours aff'ly, V.R.I.'[47] In her Journal she wrote: 'It is a terrible time.' Two days later there was an earth tremor; she felt her chair rocking under her.

The torture was not to last much longer. At the beginning of March 1878 Russia forced upon Turkey the secret Treaty of San Stefano, which was suspected of threatening British interests. The Queen, together with a vociferous section of the country, demanded warlike action: Derby and Carnarvon must go. The reserves were called out and Derby and Carnarvon went of their own accord.

The Russian Ambassador described the partnership of Queen Victoria and Beaconsfield as 'this conspiracy of a half-mad woman' with a 'political clown.'[48] Schouvaloff was mistaken. The 'clown' was in control, the woman though agitated was quite sane, and there was no conspiracy. In fact Queen Victoria, for all her frantic activity, did not materially change the course of events. At times she was Beaconsfield's fulcrum; never his partner.

Lord Salisbury, who succeeded Derby, proved in Queen Victoria's words 'up to the occasion' – an occasion which after all did not necessitate war on 'the Dizzy brink'. A conference was agreed upon in Berlin under the chairmanship of Bismarck. 'Now we know that England *has* a policy . . .' wrote the Princess Royal on April 5th jubilantly. 'How much easier you must feel.' The Queen did indeed. That she had asked for a war and been given a congress was forgotten. She got up an impromptu dance and for the first time in eighteen years waltzed again. 'Arthur dances like his beloved father. The Band played admirably.'[49]

The Congress of Berlin met in June. It was hard to say which of the old men in charge seemed in worse shape – Gortchakoff withered by age, Disraeli racked by disease and Bismarck flatulent with overeating. Between them, however, they achieved a solution for Europe which was not finally dismantled until 1918. Disraeli represented the result as a surrender by the Emperor of Russia to the Empress of India.

Queen Victoria was shrewd enough to feel reservations. It was all 'vy triumphant', she wrote to the Princess Royal, but she regretted 'that Russia had got anything'.[50] On the other hand, the Liberals would have done far worse. Two 'very bad Members' actually proposed that all treaties should be submitted to Parliament before being ratified. 'Even Mr Gladstone spoke most strongly against so monstrous an idea.'[51]

Every detail of the Congress enthralled the Queen, from the 'ceremonious and costumish' opening to Bismarck's last dramatic *tête-à-tête* with Beaconsfield, the former drinking oceans of champagne and stout, the latter fraternally choking himself with cigars. Most of all she enjoyed the account of Bismarck's family dinner given in Beaconsfield's honour. The Iron Chancellor poured a stream of indelicate stories into his guest's ear, while Beaconsfield fixed his mind steadfastly on *'her'*. Put not your trust in princes, was Bismarck's advice: his health had been broken by the German Emperor's 'horrible conduct'. Beaconsfield retorted that he 'served one who was the soul of candour and justice, and whom all her Ministers loved.' As Mr A. J. P. Taylor suggests, this was probably not the only remark he made about the Faery.

On July 16th the Prime Minister drove into Downing Street in an open carriage. Ponsonby handed him a bouquet. 'From the Queen!' he shouted above the din to the man who had brought back 'Peace with Honour'. The exhausted, masklike face seemed incapable of response but the hat was touched, a word spoken to the crowd and a line written to Queen Victoria. 'Well, we have done it,' said he to Ponsonby, laying down the pen. 'And I trust it will be approved – the work, the trouble, the deep great anxiety, the incessant interviews knocked me up at last.'[52]

Bismarck hailed the old Jew as the hero of the hour – *'Der alte Jude, das ist der Mann'* – and at Osborne Queen Victoria was a rapt listener to Beaconsfield's reminiscences: 'Bismarck, Madam, was enchanted to hear Your Majesty had ordered the occupation of Cyprus. "That is progress." His idea of progress is the acquisition of fresh countries!' They both laughed.

Bismarck's relatives, male and female, showered one another with kisses: 'Madam, I was embarrassed.'

Lady Salisbury had arrived with her whole family including 'the infant at the breast'.

When the Prime Minister and Foreign Secretary were afterwards given the Garter, Dizzy produced another sally: 'To become K.G. with a Cecil is something for a Disraeli!'

Wilfrid Lawson parodied Beaconsfield's slogan, 'Peace with Honour', as 'Peace with Honours' and Wilfrid Blunt as 'Peace with Plunder'. No amount of sarcasm could have shaken the Queen's allegiance. Indeed, she had renounced all truck with the Liberals. 'The harm they have done their Country is irreparable & I can never forget it.'[53] Her dislike of Gladstone had taken on a new, unpleasing dimension. His family's commercial background was subtly invoked to explain his politics. 'Sordid gain' was the sole inspiration of his fiery crusade. The 'so called, but not real, Liberals,' she wrote, 'wld make England a mere Cotton spinning Country.'[54]

Others no doubt encouraged the idea of Gladstone's banausic soul. Lord Dufferin, for instance, told Ponsonby that Gladstone, though honest and able, was 'essentially a middle class man' whose manner of phrasing speeches offended the Queen even more than their substance. And Disraeli wrote to Lord Derby that whatever Gladstone did, whether it was preaching, praying, speechifying or scribbling, he was 'never a gentleman'.

The supremo himself, who had recently been photographed at Osborne with a delicate hand on an emaciated knee, one wire-thin curl writhing on his forehead and a look of such sublime and sprightly cynicism upon his face as to make it appear almost youthful, wanted one of two things. To go to bed for a week or, like the young Victoria, to lie on the summer grass.

CHAPTER XXVIII

'*I HAD NO ALTERNATIVE*'
1878-80

'MY AUSPICIOUS SISTER of sublime nature to whose wishes events correspond' – thus exquisitely did the Shah of Persia address a business letter to Queen Victoria in 1874. From then onwards events did indeed begin to behave more as they ought.

The Queen's health at sixty was much better than it had been at fifty. 'My nerves' no longer dominate the pages of her journal. She was delighted to find herself executing reels with her grandsons Prince Eddy and Prince George. A rumour in the Press of her suicide in 1874 provoked the indignant retort that she was 'quite well'. Even her letter-writing marathon of 1876–8 had no ill effects, apart from momentary sensations that her 'poor head' was going to burst. She was, in fact, working with more zest than ever before in her life. Yet Ponsonby complained that Dizzy's letters contained so much love and so little politics that she had every excuse for prolonging her seclusion indefinitely.

Sickness, when it came, was endured, as in her youth, stoically. She caught a feverish cold, for example, towards the end of November 1879 soon after the sad and almost simultaneous deaths of 'old Grant' the ghillie and 'old Sharp' the collie. Due on the 28th to entertain the Russian Ambassador and feeling 'wretched & shivery', she consulted her physician.

> 'The doctor did not wish me to go to dinner, but I had no alternative, as I knew people would say I had only stayed away to avoid Ct. Schouwaloff. So I went. – Got through dinner but unable to eat, feeling stupid & shaky.'

Next day she held a Council – 'could hardly get through' – and the day after developed a violent cough and temperature. But it was not till December 1st that she put off anything important (an Investiture). Duty was again paramount. 'I had no alternative.'

Another pointer to emotional changes can be found by comparing the entries in her Journal at times like the New Year, when she tended to be introspective. For a period after her husband's death she felt that the first day of January no longer seemed to be a 'new chapter'. Towards the end of the 'sixties she was still immersed in self but with an impetus to 'fight on'. By the end of the 'seventies the wheel had come full circle. On December 31st, 1879 she sat quietly writing, her thoughts not at first upon herself but on those families bereaved in the Ashanti war; when she did turn to her own record it was with sorrow for her failings rather than for her misfortunes. 'I wish I felt I had got the better of many weaknesses & faults!' Here speaks the old Victoria, once more strong enough to risk contemplation of her sins.

Hers was a character needing a basis of serenity from which to set out on the road of self-improvement. Similarly, she had to feel happy with a Minister before she could resolve a dispute by admitting she might be mistaken. Disraeli's success with her was not in showing that he was right but in showing that he was her friend.

It was inevitable that the new woman now emerging should be a different creature from the one who had gone into seclusion in 1861. In the interval much of the Prince Consort's laborious legacy had been forgotten. Apart from penitential pilgrimages to the Horticultural Garden, she now carried on his cultural crusades with frank boredom. A visit in 1873 to an international exhibition was typical: while waiting unwillingly for a demonstration of how to cook an omelette she had to listen to 'a rather tiresome lecture'.

Some of Prince Albert's taboos were lifted, if only on special occasions. Smoking was one of them. In the 'fifties it was considered out of the question for the Queen, a woman, so much as to touch with her lips an oriental pipe of friendship on board an Egyptian ship at Southampton. Protocol demanded that the twelve-year-old Prince of Wales should take a ceremonial puff on his Mama's behalf.

Twenty years later Queen Victoria, Princess Beatrice and Horatia Stopford were blithely smoking cigarettes on a picnic at Balmoral to keep the midges away.[1]

The attitude to gentlemen smoking indoors, however, was scarcely relaxed. When two of her sons appeared before her hurriedly one evening to offer their condolences on some disaster, they apologized profusely for wearing smoking-jackets. She noted the apology in her Journal. Occasionally Her Majesty was the victim of a mild leg-pull: as when someone informed her that certain ladies were in the habit of joining the gentlemen for a smoke in their dressing-gowns with their hair down.

Nor did she diminish her efforts to save weaker brethren from stumbling in other directions. When Mr W. H. Smith became a Cabinet Minister she asked him, as the 'son of the great bookseller', to stop those 'bad society papers' from going into people's homes. Hastily Mr Smith explained that though still 'very interested' in the business he no longer belonged to it.

Political impartiality, as taught by Melbourne and preached by the Prince, was the most serious casualty of the Queen's renaissance. She convinced herself, however, that circumstances, not she, had changed: the Liberals had become socialistic while the Conservatives were now the sole repositories of 'true Liberalism'. In her defence it must be emphasized that few of her Ministers tried to re-educate their Sovereign in political neutrality. Party warfare had grown fiercer with the coming of democracy and Ministers themselves felt less inclined than Melbourne had been to give opponents their due. Gladstone, who had once been a Conservative and always admired them, probably stood alone in trying to be fair to his enemies. Disraeli's early flirtation with Radicalism simply enabled him to defame its exponents more effectively.

The temptation to spoil Her Majesty was almost irresistible. Many Liberal Ministers actually condoled with her on the intolerable behaviour of their own side. Earl Russell, for instance, when visiting her in April 1869, became 'quite overcome' in speaking of 'my many trials and difficulties' (with Gladstone!) and said 'he felt very much for me'.[2] Goschen and Forster were always running down their leader while Lord Halifax, another Liberal, told the Queen that Army reform had been 'very badly managed' by his colleagues.

An unnatural striving after intellectuality, painstakingly nurtured in her by Prince Albert, had also passed peacefully away. Novels and biographies such as Disraeli's *Coningsby* and *Endymion* or Mrs Gaskell's *Life of Charlotte Brontë* were read but there was no more constitutional law. The kind of title which now features prominently in her reading list is *Aunt Margaret's Troubles* or *The Unkind Word*. Who can blame her? It was restful to be herself again. Moreover, a monarch who ventures far into the literary world is likely to be overwhelmed with strange offerings. When Queen Victoria told the Reverend Charles Dodgson, author of *Alice in Wonderland*, how much she liked his tale and looked forward to another, he forthwith sent her his *Syllabus of Plane Algebraical Geometry*. The problems of 'Aunt Margaret' were at least intelligible.

Left to herself the Queen's judgements on art became a matter of hit or miss. Landseer's early works, particularly his sketches, she rightly valued above his later productions; George Richmond's new style of portraiture – 'green flesh & blue lips & Chinese sorts of leaves as a background!!' – repelled her.[3] She refused to be painted by Watts or Millais quite apart from the fact that she understood the latter had seduced his future wife while painting her. Indian art she found beautiful except when it descended to 'rather tasteless' imitations of Europe.[4] Her 'misses' were most apparent in the frenzied bijouterie of her private apartments. Queen Victoria never pretended to elegance in her sitting-room; her aim was to make it 'cheerful' and 'cosy' or, when it got a new carpet, 'very gay'. But if a total absence of empty spaces on walls, floors, tables, chests and desks can create the charm of an over-stuffed cottage garden, it possessed charm as well. The crowd of miniatures, medals, photographs, lithographs, engravings, water colours, bronzes, marbles, plaster-casts, embroideries, woolwork, beadwork, pressed flowers and a hundred other knick-knacks kept it vibrating with the chirpy folk-music of humanity.

The Queen's attitude to social progress had also acquired an incalculable element. Round about the year of Disraeli's Reform Bill she reached the apex of her enthusiasm for national education. Ten years later education had become mixed up in her mind with a supposed threat to morals.

A long letter to the Princess Royal on June 17th, 1878, sets forth the Queen's views. The date is significant, for a fortnight earlier the German Emperor had been shot at and wounded by a Socialist who also happened to be a Doctor of Philosophy. 'So much for philosophy!' exclaimed the Queen when Lord Salisbury's telegram announcing the assassin's qualifications reached her.[5] This attempt confirmed her feeling that rationalism, science and Bismarck's attacks on religion had all gone too far. Since nowhere else is Queen Victoria's view so fully and forcefully set out, this letter must be briefly summarized:

The mere abstract idea of goodness will not help people to lead good lives, only belief in God.

Clergy may have taught absurd and monstrous doctrines such as that of Hell, but they should be improved, not ridiculed. Disbelief in God leads to lack of reverence for those in authority, including parents.

Belief is more important than knowledge. 'Shake this in the masses & you shake the foundations of everything. An Empire without religion is like a house built upon sand.'

Education can be overdone, making people selfish. According to Principal Tulloch, head of the Scottish School Board, the working-classes are becoming discontented with 'the simple & necessary occupations in life'[6] (notably with domestic service).

Next January another visitor warned the Queen about 'over-education' but, unlike Principal Tulloch, thought it would 'die out'. Principal Tulloch gave it another hammering on June 1st, 1879. By over-educating the lower classes, he de-

526

clared, politicians could not turn them into 'superior people' – except very rarely. 'It was a fatal error, as it kept back the clever ones, & placed all on the same level.' The Queen, nodding gloomily, no doubt felt how lucky Samuel Smiles had been to come into the world before the Education Act of 1870 could hold him back.

A gathering of social scientists, redolent of the Albertian era, were shown round the grounds of Balmoral in the 'seventies. Henry Ponsonby, instructed to keep them out of the house at all costs, approved of the embargo: 'I seldom saw a slummier lot . . .'[7]

The Queen no longer tried to admire famous people if she did not like them. The African explorer Stanley she found 'a determined ugly little Man – with a strong American twang'. She wrote to King Leopold II warning him against Stanley's harshness to the natives: far from opposing slavery, he kept female slaves for himself. An American Presidential family fared not much better. Mrs Grant, though 'civil & complimentary in her funny American way', spoilt her son, 'a very ill-mannered young Yankee', speaking of him as 'our pet'.[8] According to Lord Dufferin, 'our pet' paled beside the 'Yankee yahoos' of the past. One of them, he told the Queen at dinner, had said to his English hostess:

'How old are you? How long have you been married? I should like to see your nuptial bed.'

The Queen burst out laughing but raised her napkin to protect Princess Beatrice and the maids-of-honour who sat on the other side of the table.[9]

The Queen no longer tried to keep the pleasant things of life exactly as they had been in the past. At first she had been hardly able to reorganize even the children's museum at the Swiss cottage, though Prince Albert himself had planned to do so. By 1869 she was glad to abandon the old royal railway coach, hallowed by the Prince's occupation, for a new smart one with all compartments communicating at last: no more steep clambering down on to the line for ladies-in-waiting, necks and legs exposed to every kind of risk and indelicacy, to reach the Queen. During the previous year she had built for herself the first house since her marriage in which the Prince had never lived – the Glasallt Sheil – a small (fifteen-roomed) villa planted on smooth turf at the far end of Loch Muick. There is no escaping the fact that Queen Victoria's most precious retreat was henceforth one of her own creation. The single bed with its plain peacock blue head board, on which is still fastened her green watch-case, has no room for the sacred portrait wreathed in *immortelles*.

The Queen actually preferred her sitting-room at the Glasallt to the one designed for her at Balmoral by Prince Albert. 'Felt quite lost in my big sitting-room after the snug little one at the Glasallt,' is a typical comment on return. Queen Victoria's Household could not fathom what drove her into this solitude where, by shutting a baize door in the little passage, she could exclude even the sounds of her ghillies' carousals; but Ponsonby noted that she always returned from her humble retreat remarkably improved in health and spirits.

Some of her best holidays were now in southern countries abroad where she and the Prince had never been together, her initial qualms at 'doing anything new without Albert' having been stifled in the pious thought that he would 'rejoice in seeing me take an interest in all I see'. She had not forgotten his homilies on her need to get out of herself. By 1877 she could exult in an achievement of her own which the Prince had always thought impossible: the 'noble forest' of Ballochbuie was at last added to the Balmoral estate, rescued from the 'ruthless' and 'lamentable' depredations of its former owners.

Queen Victoria now recognized in herself a certain toughness of character and capacity to handle human situations which her beloved one had lacked. There was her conviction, already noticed, that he could never have faced up to the realities of the new Prussia. As the years passed, she added to the list of 'inevitable' changes which she had accepted philosophically but which the Prince would have opposed, thereby only injuring himself: disestablishment of the Irish Church, Army reform and 'the style of life of Bertie & Affie'. In some ways Papa, she told Vicky in 1872, could have helped her; in others his difficulties with his sons would have been even greater than hers.

A few years later the Princess Royal received from the Queen one of her last *cris de coeur* delivered in the old manner:

> 'The vy large family with their increasing families & interests, is an immense difficulty & I must add – burthen to me! Without a Husband and father the labour of satisfying all (wh is impossible—), & of being just & fair & kind – & yet keeping often quiet wh is what I require so much – is quite fearful! you will some day encounter this, tho' never like me; for you will not be the Sovereign—'[10]

Stripped of its lachrymose atmosphere, this was a not unfair account of the far-reaching demands made upon a woman who in theory disapproved of female sovereignty, female careers, fashionable society and, in certain moods, marriage and motherhood as well – demands which she now in fact met with increasing success.

Queen Victoria was growing fonder of the Prince of Wales. Whereas she had written in 1870, 'no one looks up to him, though all like him', her approval three years later was unqualified: 'he is loved by all above & below . . .'[11] The Prince of Wales's geniality towards those 'below' endeared him to his mother even more than his patent devotion to herself. For the Queen's tenderness towards servants was one of the things in her life which never changed. An obstinately drunken ghillie was dismissed in the 'seventies but the event was so rare that the Household discussed it with bated breath.

In the middle of 1875 Prince Leopold was the subject of a new, good resolution. Having recovered from a long illness, he hoped at last to live as other young men. Queen Victoria began by muttering angrily about 'undutifulness' and 'base ingratitude' to God, herself and his doctors'.[12] Then, on July 1st, a new note is struck:

> '. . . if I show gt indifference to his movements excepting when my authority must be obeyed, I don't think his

love of opposition (a family defect) will be roused & he
will learn what he owes to me.'

However ungraciously phrased, this was a reasonable parental line: not to interfere except on essentials.

That perfect concord should immediately result was not
to be expected. On May 19th, 1878, Prince Leopold perpetrated a crime which in his mother's eyes placed 'the whole
authority of the Sovereign & Throne' in jeopardy: he
expressed an 'intense aversion' to Balmoral and refused to
go there. Loudly she appealed to the Princess Royal to rally
the rest of the family, particularly the Prince of Wales,
against the rebel. Bertie would never tolerate such conduct
from *his* children and she hoped he would refrain from inviting Leopold to Epsom or Ascot. Then Leopold would not
be able to 'think he has carried the day & put me down,
& will go to Bertie's House & amuse himself as he likes!' In
London he must stay upstairs at Buckingham Palace in his
own rooms, 'where he cannot so easily get in & out'.

Two days later the storm was subsiding: 'I will leave him
alone & take no notice of him for some time' – unless he got
into mischief. Alas, he did so, all too soon. She heard on the
26th that having obtained permission to spend three or four
days in Paris, he intended to stay a fortnight. 'It is too
abominable'; he would of course fall ill. But she had soon
simmered down again. Hot indignation would not affect
Prince Leopold, she decided, but only 'persuasion' and an
appeal to his feelings.[13]

The Queen's acceptance of Prince Arthur's engagement in
1878 to Princess Louise Margaret, daughter of estranged
parents, Prince Frederick Charles and Princess Marianne of
Prussia, is a further example of improved family relations.
At first she could not understand him falling so quickly for
this child of a broken home; she was not even attractive. 'I
had to give way of course,' she wrote in her Journal, 'but it
was a great shock.'[14] Arthur was so 'good' that there was
really no reason for him to marry at all. And why did he not
give her time to show him 'alternatives'? This said, the
Queen completely relented, praising 'Louischen' for her

profile* and Arthur for rescuing a girl who was desperately unhappy at home. As for showing him 'alternatives', she had seen too many ill-assorted marriages to be a match-maker.

Later that year an example of what she meant occurred on the Continent. 'How too monstrous & disgusting,' she wrote to the Princess Royal, 'is the idea of this poor young Waldeck girl marrying that drunken horrid King – who is 41 yrs older than her!! I think abroad people consider it a perfect crime if a Pcess is not married to someone!!'[15]

Perhaps the brightest sign of all was a concession to new social customs. The 'modern' habit of engaged couples going about alone together had always scandalized Queen Victoria, ever since Fritz had tried in vain to see a little more of his Vicky, unchaperoned. When her granddaughter, Princess Charlotte of Prussia, became engaged in 1877 she at once warned the Princess Royal against this pernicious habit:

> 'I think there is a gt want of propriety & delicacy as well as of dutifulness in at once treating your Bridegroom as tho' (except in one point) – he were your Husband.'

Engaged couples, she went on, thought nothing of being stared and laughed at as they drove, walked and visited together. 'In short young people are getting vy American, I fear in their Lives & ways.'[16] On the other hand, once the pair were married the Queen had now come to believe in non-intervention:

> 'A young *Menage* (tho' one feels so much at 1st the wish to help & direct) – ought to be left a good deal to itself.'[17]

When in June 1878 the blameless Prince Arthur drove down to Frogmore alone with his fiancée the Queen, though 'a little surprised', took the monumental decision to say nothing. After all, Louischen's visit was almost over.[18]

Between the Queen and her eldest daughter the understanding deepened each year. The Princess Royal's difficulties

---

* Disraeli, who met her at the Berlin Congress, wrote almost lyrically about her lovely eyes and complexion, fine brow and 'singularly beautiful hands'. (*Hughenden Papers*, B/XIX/C/28. June 17th, 1878.)

with Prince William were instrumental in bringing mother and daughter together and in making the Queen see her own children in a rosier light. His behaviour caused increasing anxiety. 'Why does Willy always sign himself "William Prince of Prussia"?' the Queen asked her daughter – 'his father never does.'[19] In fact she knew very well it was Willy's pride, fostered by Bismarck and his grandparents. Prussian arrogance had taught him to listen with approval to their insulting remarks about his English mother.* How fortunate she herself had been compared with Vicky:

> 'excepting Affie, who is vy wanting in attention & consideration, & Leopd occasionally, I have not had to suffer in the way you speak of. Bertie & dear Arthur are always most attentive . . . Do you think any of my Children wld be friends with or tolerate anyone who has spoken of me with insult?'[20]

On May 21st, 1878, the Queen described in another letter to her daughter the change which she had felt in her bones for some time:

> 'the older you grow – the older your Children grow, the more our feelings will be in harmony.'

Unknown to the writer, a tragic event was about to set its seal on the new family unity.

For several years now the friends of Princess Alice, the Queen's second daughter, had been watching her frail figure with apprehension. She lost a little son, 'Frittie', a haemophiliac, in 1876 and a year later the Duke of Hesse-Darmstadt died leaving his son Louis to succeed and Princess Alice, as the new Grand Duchess, to exhaust herself with the chaotic affairs of their inheritance. The Queen sent the whole family to Eastbourne in the summer of 1878 at her own expense, and her Journals make frequent references to poor Alice looking so 'ill & drawn'.

---

* When suffering from a violent nose-bleed as a boy, Willy was said to have forbidden his attendants to staunch the flow, announcing his wish to part with every drop of his English blood.

On November 8th one of those important messages (like that of Baroness Lehzen's death) arrived which the Queen in the excitement of war and politics forgot to note at once in her diary.

'10th Nov. 1878. – omitted saying 2 days ago I got a telegram from Alice saying dear Victoria had diphtheria, with high fever, & that she was very anxious.'

On the 12th another daughter, 'Alicky', went down; then in quick succession May (the baby), Irene, 'Ernie' (the only son), Duke Louis and 'Ella'. All the cases were severe and the Queen was soon dreading every telegram. Princess May died on the 16th and on the 22nd Prince Ernest fancied himself dying. His mother, in her longing to comfort him, gave him what Beaconsfield later described as 'the kiss of death'. Three days afterwards he was out of danger but on December 8th the fearful news reached the Queen that 'darling Alice' had caught it. 'Oh! it surely cannot be true! she will never have the strength to get through it.'

Next day the Queen sent Jenner to Darmstadt and repaired instinctively to the sad Blue Room where she and Princess Alice had watched together seventeen years ago. After a broken night on the 13th she woke to a date which seemed to have some strange power over her happiness. '14th Dec. – this terrible day come round again!' There was no news so she went as always on the anniversary of Prince Albert's death to the Blue Room and prayed. On her way to breakfast she met Brown with two 'bad' telegrams from Duke Louis and Jenner; a third announced the Grand Duchess's death at 7.30 that morning. The heartbroken Queen was not one to overlook the dramatic element in this tragedy. That the child who had supported her should be 'called back' to the father she had tended on this of all days seemed to her 'almost incredible & most mysterious!'[21]

To her biographer it is almost equally incredible to find the helpless woman of not so many years ago now voluntarily shouldering the task of breaking the dreadful news to each member of her family. First she told Princess Beatrice, then Prince Leopold who threw himself into her arms; then the

Prince of Wales who came out pale and haggard in his dressing-gown to say, 'It is the good who are always taken'; then the Princess of Wales who sobbed, 'I wish I had died instead of her'.[22] Next day, feeling pathetically deprived, – 'I was so proud of my 9!' – but comforted by the therapeutic business of commissioning a statue of mother and child for the Mausoleum, she paid a significant tribute in her Journal to Princess Alice's 'talent, initiative & energy' combined with a character 'so friendly to those in the house, always simple, never proud or haughty'. This was the kind of woman Queen Victoria truly admired: one with spirit who was also kind to the servants. 'High tone' without 'John Bullism.'

Death was at last beginning to lose its sting and mourning its poisonous enchantment. Queen Victoria had already taken a timid look at the family vault in St George's Chapel and been surprised to find it so 'roomy & airy'; to be standing by her father's coffin – 'his only child' – deeply moved her.[23] In June 1878 she forced herself for the first time to attend a funeral there, that of the exiled King of Hanover. 'I feel this will be a gt trial, but *still* one, that *must* be gone through.' She had no alternative.

There was no attempt to make the death of Princess Alice an excuse for spoiling the Connaught wedding. Queen Victoria wore a long white veil, a court train for the first time since 1861 and the Koh-i-Noor diamond. Nothing marred the occasion except the incorrigible bad temper of the bride's father, Prince Frederick Charles, who informed Queen Victoria that he had hoped his previous visit to England would be his last. The presence of Mr Gladstone was not allowed to cast a blight: the Gladstones were not invited. The Queen would have preferred an earlier date for the wedding but the German Emperor insisted on waiting until Lent was over; she did not know why. 'A marriage is no amusement but a solemn act,' she wrote to the Princess Royal, adding with a sardonic flash, '& generally a sad one.'[24]

At Berlin, family relations were stormy as ever and Queen Victoria tried to mitigate Prince William's rudeness and want of tact. Vicky must bear with her mother-in-law, she wrote, who 'responds vy keenly to affection', while Willy might improve if he got a kind wife. Prince William decided to marry Princess Victoria ('Dona') of Augustenburg, daughter of Adelaide Hohenlohe and of the Duke whom his grandfather had deposed. The Emperor was furious but Queen Victoria felt it was 'a sort of atonement'.

Queen Victoria's sixtieth birthday occurred on May 24th, 1879, twelve days after she became a great-grandmother – 'Quite an event'. Her own anniversary produced a somewhat tremulous response:

'My poor old 60th birthday. I feel that I am getting old, & that these last months, & the loss of my beloved child have aged, & shaken the elasticity out of me.'

She prayed once more for improvement 'in every way'.

Improvement in one way, at any rate, had come. It was only a pity that the Queen's increased patience with her children seemed to go with a more peremptory spirit towards those of her Ministers with whom she disagreed. Gladstone was to find that the elasticity had by no means been shaken out of her.

One political act of Lord Beaconsfield's and one only really pleased Mr Gladstone. This was the appointment of Lord Lorne to be Governor-General of Canada at the end of 1878. With considerable hesitancy Queen Victoria had given permission for 'poor dear Loosy' (Princess Louise) to go so far from home – 'but it is better always to live for something I suppose', she wrote doubtfully to the Princess Royal. Everything else that the Prime Minister had done Gladstone criticized and in these criticisms the Queen felt herself to be included. Was not Beaconsfield's militancy inspired by her? The results of Beaconsfield's African and Far Eastern policy – the Zulu, Ashanti and Afghan wars – seemed to her the necessary concomitants of holding enviable possessions.

'If *we are* to *maintain* our position as a *first-rate* Power . . . we must, with our Indian Empire and large Colonies, be *Prepared* for *attacks* and *wars, somewhere* or *other*, CONTINUALLY.'[25]

535

Before the first Afghan war broke out in 1878 people constantly asked the Liberal Ponsonby, 'Why don't you advise the Queen?' – against war. His answer was always the same: 'One can do so once – but she takes care you shan't press unwelcome advice upon her'. In any case, he felt that there was no real danger of the Queen running into a peace party.

He was wrong. In little over a year Gladstone had whipped up more than a peace party – a peace passion – in his Midlothian constituency and throughout the North, anointing the suffering Afghans with language as superb as any he had summoned to excoriate the Bashi-Bazouks: 'Remember the rights of the savage, as we call him,' he thundered at Dalkeith on November 26th, 1879:

> 'Remember that the happiness of his humble home, remember that the sanctity of life in the hill villages of Afghanistan, among the winter snows, is as inviolable in the eye of Almighty God as can be your own.'

Every word of Gladstone's Midlothian oratory, every act in the stage management of his heroic campaigns seemed to search out the Queen's tenderest spots and jab them. 'Mr Gladstone is going about Scotland, like an American stumping orator, making most violent speeches,' she wrote in her Journal on December 2nd, 1879. British annexations of territory which even Bismarck had lauded as 'progress', Gladstone stigmatized as 'false phantoms of glory'. Gladstone demanded a Chancellor of the Exchequer who would save the candle ends and a Prime Minister with a gospel of honest work, thus prostituting the creed of dearest Albert in order to belabour dear Lord Beaconsfield. The 'Empress of India' came in for specific abuse: Gladstone denounced the title as 'theatrical bombast and folly'.

Equally intolerable was Gladstone's objurgation to 'remember the rights of the savage'. Standing up for dark skins had always been the Queen's prerogative. The Zulu War of 1879 left her with a burning wish to have as allies instead of enemies these 'singularly honest', 'brave', 'merry', 'cleanly' warriors who did not smoke but carried snuff-boxes neatly in their ears. This, despite the fact that the son of her beloved friend, the widowed Empress Eugénie, had been stabbed to death by Zulu spears. The Zulus, she was delighted to hear, had behaved 'mercifully', severing two arteries so that the young Prince Imperial died without suffering, and sewing up the cuts in his patrol jacket; they destroyed nothing but his watch and that was only 'to see what was inside'. How different from Captain Carey, the Prince's personal ADC, who ignominiously fled.

> 'It showed a gt want of chivalry . . . which everyone owes, not only to a Prince, but to any superior, friend, or indeed fellow creature . . .'[26]

'What nerve! What muscle! What energy!' wrote Beaconsfield in ecstasy after an audience with the Queen at Windsor on November 26th, 1879. On that very same date Mr Gladstone, at the Dalkeith Corn Exchange, Midlothian, was rousing the masses with equal energy, muscle and nerve. It was only a matter of time before these 'two ironclads', as Ponsonby called them, would be again in collision.

At the end of February 1880 the Prime Minister took a snap decision to go to the polls in April. Queen Victoria had opened Parliament in person on February 5th, resplendent in a new State coach topped by a crown, lavishly gilt and furnished with so much glass that the people could see her from every angle. Lord Beaconsfield, ignoring the ill-omened fact that he was too weak to carry the Sword of State in the procession, banked on the fervour created by a State Opening enhanced by two remarkable by-election successes, to bring him victory. An immediate dissolution was announced on March 8th. The country gasped; the Queen spiritedly looked forward to the Tories coming back 'stronger than ever'.

Who could have foretold that Gladstone would at once set forth on a second Midlothian procession which made her gilded coach rumbling down the Mall look like Cinderella's pumpkin? Again the monster crowds surged round the 'People's William'; again the bonfires blazed and the fireworks banged; again Lord Rosebery, Scotland's greatest magnifico, acted as Gladstone's host. Was the Sword of State too heavy for Lord Beaconsfield? The Grand Old Man swung an axe in Lord Rosebery's park and having levelled the Tory Party to the ground, scanned the splendid election news and wrote in his diary: 'It seemed as if the arm of the Lord had bared itself for work . . .'[27]

If Gladstone confused himself with the Almighty, Queen Victoria had reason to suspect that he also confused himself with the Sovereign. What did he mean by appealing beyond the aristocracy, beyond the landed interest, beyond the Established Church, beyond all wealth and rank to '*the nation* itself'? The right to speak directly to the people over the heads of faction had always been her own prerogative. Nothing could explain such colossal, such imperial arrogance but the presumption that Gladstone had gone mad.

Insane, insulting, arrogant, un-British – she might call Gladstone all these things but he did not yet seem dangerous. The fact was that he had resigned the Liberal leadership to Lord Granville, with Lord Hartington in charge of the party in the Commons. It never entered the Queen's head that Gladstone might become dangerous in the sense of becoming Prime Minister again.[28] Ponsonby, for instance, noticed that he infuriated her without really weighing on her mind. 'She considers him out of the range of practical politics.' Moreover, she had reinsured herself against his becoming dangerous by letting her Court know that she 'never *could*' take Gladstone, Lowe or Dilke as 'a *Minister*' again – Gladstone for Primo was not even mentioned. As early as September 21st, 1879, she had written in this sense to Lady Ely, adding that Ponsonby had so many Whig friends 'he might easily *get* these things *known*'. Ponsonby wrote to his wife in November: 'Everyone knows she will not have G. as Minister'. But as the Liberal successes piled up during the following April it became obvious, in the blunt words of Prince Arthur, that the Liberals were 'mad about' Gladstone and none but he could head a new Government. Gladstone shared this view: if God called him back it was not to play second fiddle to two colleagues like Granville and Hartington whose very nicknames proved their remoteness from Mount Sinai – 'Puss' and 'Harty Tarty'.

Meanwhile the Queen, undeterred by the crisis, pursued her intention of visiting Darmstadt for the Confirmation of her motherless granddaughters, the Princesses Victoria and Ella of Hesse. Here, on April 1st, 1880, she was pleased to find Princess Alice's room exactly as she had left it. According to principle, Queen Victoria shared in the Lutheran Sacrament. Scarcely was this 'never to be forgotten day' safely over and she had moved on to Baden-Baden before Lord Beaconsfield telegraphed the stunning news of electoral defeat. 'This is a terrible telegram,' scribbled the Queen to Ponsonby; and in her Journal for April 3rd: 'The govt. Majority which has never failed them for 6 years has vanished'. So great was her shock and mortification that her courtiers congratulated themselves on having her tucked away at Baden-Baden where the first bitterness might break its edge on them. Again and again they heard that she was losing in Beaconsfield the only Minister since Melbourne who had become her 'friend'. As for Gladstone – 'she will sooner *abdicate* than send for or have any *communication* with *that half-mad fire-brand* who wd soon ruin everything & be a Dictator.'[29] Gradually her courtiers' genuine sympathy soothed her. Ponsonby wrote:

'She spoke so well, so much to the point and listened so patiently that I was very much taken with the belief that she is determined to carry out the constitutional principles most conscientiously. . . . But when preyed upon by other influences I cannot of course say what they may do.'[30]

The 'preying' soon began. A leading Conservative, Sir Michael Hicks Beach, arrived at Baden-Baden. He rarely touched on politics to Ponsonby but at the bare mention of Gladstone's name 'Beach broke into furious abuse. It is extraordinary what bitterness they show towards him (Gladstone),' reflected Ponsonby, 'and it is this of course which has so exasperated the Queen against him.'[31] The Queen herself described Beach's review of the situation as 'calm & impartial'.

In an extremity her natural instinct was now to try diplomacy; not to put her foot down as in the Bedchamber Plot, but to tell the world that she intended to put her foot down — and then see what happened. From Baden-Baden she had telegraphed to Beaconsfield her wish to have it 'known (*unofficially of course*)' that she would send for Hartington, and Ponsonby was ordered to play the diplomatic role of Stockmar in 1841 when the latter agreed to 'smoothen the way for Sir R. Peel's coming into office'.[32] Ponsonby saw at once that he was not intended to 'smoothen' the way for Gladstone but for Hartington or Granville. Ponsonby declined. 'How can I flirt with the Liberal chiefs except by letter,' he wrote to Mary, ' – wh. wd. never do.' The Queen again pulled out all the familiar stops: she would fall ill, she would abdicate. Still Ponsonby refused. After explaining that Stockmar had been able to mediate because he daily met persons of both parties, Ponsonby added: 'Sir Henry Ponsonby has not been much in London of late years.' Afterwards he deleted this barbed sentence, mildly advising the Queen to wait for Lord Beaconsfield's advice.[33]

Nevertheless, threats of abdication began to alarm even the hardened private secretary. He remembered Gladdy once saying that 'this threat was the grtest. power the sovereign possessed – nothing cd. stand against it, for the position of a Minister who forced it on wd. be untenable'. Ponsonby also foresaw the 'ruin' to the Queen which would follow such a 'terrible victory'. He fervently prayed that her dire 'mutterings' would not go beyond the private secretary's room.[34]

Meanwhile the Queen thrashed out with him the pros and cons of Granville and Hartington. She was not enthusiastic about either of them. Granville's refusal to support her Imperial title had earned him an indelible black mark and Afghanistan would not be safe in his hands. That left Harty Tarty. His long-standing liaison with the surpassingly beautiful Duchess of Manchester* was well known to Society and to the Queen. She feared this influence, just as she feared his 'too friendly' relationship with the Marlborough House set; moreover he was not 'a hard worker'. But she would

* He married her in 1892.

540

take him if Beaconsfield so advised. The name of Gladstone Ponsonby dared not utter – 'otherwise my advice would be for her to send for Glad . . .'

At last on April 15th the Queen left Baden-Baden. Three days later Beaconsfield gave what seemed to her the right advice: 'irrespective of any personal feelings I might have,' to send for Hartington.[35] Hartington was sent for – and gave the wrong answer. Neither he nor Granville, he feared, would succeed without Gladstone, while Gladstone would decline a subordinate position. In that case, replied the Queen, she must mention 'one great difficulty': she could not give Gladstone her confidence.[36] This was like a bride at the altar raising just one objection to the marriage – she could not take that particular husband. Hartington agreed with her that Gladstone should never have returned to public life after resigning from the Party leadership as he did, and promised to find out whether he would not accept second place. Might he also acquaint Gladstone with Her Majesty's opinion of him?

'I replied that he might, for I would say the same to Mr Gladstone himself, if I saw him.'[37]

Hartington returned on the 23rd with a grim account of his mission. He had 'thought it best *not* to tell him *what* I had said, for no one knew what the effect would be . . .' but had simply asked whether Gladstone would enter a Hartington Government, to which the answer was, No; she must therefore send for Gladstone, but on no account 'begin by saying that I had no confidence whatever in him, as one did not know how such a man as he would take it . . .'[38] Again the Queen probed the wound which Gladstone had inflicted on Hartington by his Messianic return to the leadership. When she expressed a doubt whether Gladstone would add 'stability' to any Government, Hartington 'merely smiled' but upon her adding that it was 'very unfair on him', agreed that 'it was certainly not generous'. Queen Victoria was not likely to miss this rift in the Liberal lute. She 'entirely absolved' Hartington of cowardice despite Beaconsfield's subsequent declaration that he had abandoned a woman in her hour of need.

Lord Granville at his own request saw the Queen next. 'Sadly fluttered', Puss nevertheless remembered to kiss the royal hand '*à deux reprises*', as if taking two helpings of a choice dish, and while expressing the fear that he had forfeited her confidence, hoped to regain it. Inexorably the Queen offered him in return nothing but the bare unpalatable truth: 'I replied he certainly had done so, but that I should be very glad if he could regain it.'[39]

In some trepidation Ponsonby afterwards visited the two delinquents in their room, wondering what sort of shape he would find them in. He had observed their nervousness before the audience and Hartington's relief when he was informed that Queen Victoria wished him to see Prince Leopold first. 'Oh! I am shy of the Queen,' he had exclaimed, '– but I don't care for Leopold.'

Inside the room all was sunshine. Hartington with a triumphant 'Ha! Ha!' threw himself into a chair, while Granville, kissing his hand to Ponsonby and smiling like a ballet dancer receiving applause, purred, 'No difficulty at all – all smooth!'[40]

Queen Victoria, seated squarely at her desk, dismissed the double audience in her Journal as 'a trying ordeal'. Then she prepared herself to face Mr Gladstone at 6.30 that evening. She had no alternative. Even the Prince of Wales now told her so. But while Hartington relaxed she braced herself. Like the war-horse in the *Book of Job*, she saith among the trumpets, Ha, Ha, and smelleth the battle afar off.

CHAPTER XXIX

AMONG THE TRUMPETS
1880–3

GLADSTONE'S AUDIENCE was brief, quiet and tense as the moment between the lightning flash and the thunder. He noted afterwards that the Queen had been 'natural under effort'. A contemporary sketch of him kissing her hand suggests that the effort was greater than the naturalness. A look of detached disgust is depicted upon the royal features, as if the hand which suffered such indignity could no longer be her own.

She did not ask Gladstone why he had won. Beaconsfield had already declared that like Napoleon he had been 'beaten by the elements' – six bad harvests running. The Queen wondered how people could be so perverse as to expect a change of government to change the weather. Sir Stafford Northcote listed hard times, love of change, lazy candidates, Gladstone 'getting hold of the common people' and the Ballot which tempted them to promise one way and vote another – 'a very bad thing'. The Queen summed up the Conservative defeat as 'over-confidence'. In future they promised to spend money and organize like the Liberals (a reference to their famous 'Caucus'). She hoped this would be a lesson, 'so that such a thing should not occur again.'[1]

She did not mention the catastrophic rout of a British force by Cetschwayo, the Zulu king, in the burning gullies of Isandhlwana (1879); nevertheless this fearful blow to British arms played a part in turning the masses temporarily against Beaconsfield's exhibitionist imperialism.

Since Queen Victoria admitted no connection between Beaconsfield's policy and the Conservative defeat, she did not hesitate to spend most of the few minutes allotted to Gladstone in telling him that the foreign policy he had just pulverized at the polls must on no account be changed. Never had an incoming Prime Minister received a stranger mandate. Gladstone, however, pleased the Queen by the meekness with which he accepted her ukase. She relied on Lord Hartington to keep him meek. Beaconsfield had told her that Hartington was 'in his heart a Conservative'.

Disunity, she knew, was the Liberal Party's fatal weakness. One wing relied on rich, blue-blooded Whigs like Princess Louise's father-in-law, the Duke of Argyll; the other wing included Radicals, Socialists, Republicans, Irish, atheists and immoral exponents of other 'horrid things' – a dark reference by the Queen to the fact that Charles Bradlaugh, Radical MP for Northampton, stood for 'anticonception' (as it was then called) besides being anti-God. Bradlaugh's provocative refusal to take the Oath, followed by Parliament's vengeful opposition to his 'affirming' instead, launched the Ministry upon waves of acrimony from which it never recovered. So nauseating did this aspect of Radicalism seem to the Queen that when Lord Spencer came to dinner looking unwell she attributed his indisposition to Bradlaugh. The appearance of this ogre, as depicted by Prince Leopold, was just what she expected: 'horrid & repulsive'.

In the Queen's opinion nothing held the two wings together but sheer office-seeking. She hoped their leader would soon collapse. During Gladstone's first audience he told her 'he should not be able to go on for long' and she remarked how 'ill & haggard' he looked. She repeated this comment three times in the next fortnight. Apart from one occasion when he was 'amiable' and another 'in good spirits' the Queen's subsequent reports on Gladstone's health right up to his fall in 1885 scarcely varied: he was always 'looking ill'. It was a transparent case of wishful thinking. Once when she drew Ponsonby's attention to Gladstone's stricken appearance, her secretary noted that he had never seen the Grand Old Man looking better. Gladstone himself confided to Lord Granville that he felt better at the end of the stormy 1881 Session than after any other he could remember.

The enemy which was to defeat the GOM was not old age but a new age of violent protest against the old ways. Besides Bradlaugh, there was Parnell with his Irish Home Rulers and Lord Randolph Churchill with his Fourth Party of Conservative hatchet men whom Dizzy appropriately called his Bashi-Bazouks. Joseph Chamberlain, the Radical, helped to stir the pot.

Comforting rumours reached the Queen that Gladstone's first Cabinet appointmens had infuriated the Radicals. With Lord Granville as Foreign Secretary and Lord Hartington at the India Office, they accused him of forming 'a Tory Government'; why did he not include 'some of them'? The Queen heard with delight that Gladstone would not listen and meant to fight it out.[2]

Gladstone failed to fight it out and 'some of them', to put it mildly, got into his Cabinet. Old John Bright she could tolerate but Joseph Chamberlain, the steely screw-maker who had risen to the top in Birmingham, cast a Jacobinical glare over the Board of Trade. On the Government front bench he looked to Beaconsfield like a 'cheesemonger'. To others less prejudiced he looked surprisingly dandified, with his eye-glass and orchid. As a youth of sixteen Chamberlain had sat on a very different bench, a cobbler's, learning his ancestral trade. Cobblers were notorious Radicals. Another Radical was Mr Mundella who, according to Dizzy, resembled 'an old goat on Mount Haemus'; but in Sheffield the old goat owned a stocking factory where he collected statistics on the lives of the poor, to confound Dizzy's successors.

In May Queen Victoria was writing of Gladstone with all the old venom: 'To me "the people's William" is a most disagreeable person half crazy.'[3] In June Granville was threatened with her secret weapon – abdication:

'A Constitutional Sovereign *at best* has a *most difficult* task, and it *may* become *almost* an *impossible one*, IF things are allowed to go on as they have done of late years.'[4]

By September she was boasting to Beaconsfield: 'I *never* write except on formal *official* matters to the Prime Minister!'[5]

Nevertheless, life under the Liberal Government was not

at first so bad as the Queen sometimes liked to make out. Her health was good. She commissioned a new portrait by von Angeli: 'It better be done before I get too hideous to behold – but people say I look now much better than I did some years ago.'[6]

As early as April 1880 she had reconciled herself to seeing Sir Charles Dilke, the Republican bogy-man, in a ministerial post. She heard that he had 'drunk in the honeyed words of royalty' at Marlborough House, writing down his name in the book and inquiring about the date of the next levée. Ponsonby hinted that it would be politic to accept him. 'The Queen did not disagree – but said she supposed he would only be suggested for a small place at first.'[7] Dilke was given the Under-Secretaryship for Foreign Affairs after the Queen had extracted from him a written repudiation of his Republican views. When Dilke was finally let into the Cabinet (December 1882) Queen Victoria reckoned him a sound imperialist. An opinion-forming book of the 'eighties, Seeley's *Expansion of England*, which she read on the recommendation of the Princess Royal, was Dilke's gospel.

By no means all the Liberal reforms provoked her. A bill in 1880 to allow Dissenters to bury their dead in parish graveyards won her warm approval. The only provision she disliked was one permitting Anglican clergymen to conduct a shortened service over criminal members of their own communion. How could she be sure that among the many clerical bigots there would not be some who declared it a crime to stay away from church?

The Queen strongly supported the Deceased Wife's Sister Bill of 1883 by which, among other blessings, eligible Protestant princes would not be lost to match-makers through premature widowerhood. The Bill passed the Commons to her joy – 'because it will give such a slap to the bigots' – but the bishops threw it out. Fortunately a royal plan which the Bill was to have facilitated also collapsed. The widowed Duke Louis of Hesse and Princess Beatrice, his deceased wife's sister, showed no mutual interest and both gave their hearts elsewhere.

A 'sporting line' was developed by the Queen during a

spring honeymoon with her Liberal peers. In May 1880 she discussed the Derby runners of Lords Hartington and Westminster as if she were on Epsom Downs, urging her courtiers to get up a sweepstake. Two tickets were taken by Her Majesty and others by the Princesses.

While gambling light-heartedly on Whig horses she took no chances with Tory opinions. She kept in the closest touch. Ponsonby was invited through Lady Ely to correspond secretly with Lord Rowton, Beaconsfield's faithful Monty Corry who had been ennobled in the Dissolution Honours. (Gladstone compared it to Caligula making a consul of his horse.) When Ponsonby peremptorily refused, Rowton was advised by the Queen to keep in touch through 'Leopold or Capt. Edwards (an equerry) or Miss Stopford – all QUITE SAFE.'[8] Trouble over Cyprus tempted the Queen to find out from Lord Salisbury his view of Gladstone's proposals. Would Ponsonby inquire? Again her private secretary considered it unfair to invite the Opposition to criticize a Government measure. 'She agreed to what I said,' wrote Ponsonby, ' – but as she agreed easily I can't help thinking she is trying some other channel.'[9]

She was in fact exchanging letters with Beaconsfield himself. The aged statesman realized, however, that what his beloved Sovereign chiefly required was soothing affection. On one occasion only did his gift for phrase-making lead him into unconstitutional paths.

Apparently Lord Hartington, foolishly hoping to avoid trouble, had omitted to show the Queen in advance her Speech for opening the Session of 1881. It contained the controversial decision to evacuate Kandahar in Afghanistan. A scene of unexampled bitterness took place in the Council Chamber at Osborne, which left the Queen 'shaken' and her Ministers on the point of resignation. She refused to approve the Kandahar paragraph; they refused to submit the Speech to her without it. The fifteen-stone Home Secretary, Sir William Harcourt, was already in a bad temper having been fetched from Cowes with three colleagues squeezed into a small, one-horse bathing-carriage. Eventually Her Majesty agreed to reserve the expression of her

547

disapproval for a memorandum to Gladstone. 'I spoke to no one,' she recorded in her Journal, 'and the Ministers nearly tumbled over each other going out.'[10] Harcourt, however, had left behind a dart which stuck quivering in the Queen's *amour propre*: 'the Speech of the Sovereign,' he announced, 'is only the Speech of the Ministers.' The Mandarin must nod but not argue.

This made no sense to Queen Victoria. Why had they ever made her read the Speech herself if Harcourt was right? Prince Leopold must ask Lord Beaconsfield for his opinion. The old oracle produced a remarkable verdict. The principle of Sir William Harcourt, he declared, was not known to the British Constitution. 'It is only a piece of Parliamentary gossip.'[11]

Thus the pillar of the Constitution – ministerial responsibility – and the crime of the century – the Bulgarian atrocities – were dismissed by Beaconsfield as 'Parliamentary gossip' and 'coffee-house babble' respectively. But before the great magician could palm any more political facts, death played the vanishing trick on him.

Lord Beaconsfield died on April 19th, 1881, choked by the grime of London borne on unrelenting east winds. 'I only live for climate,' he had written to Mrs Goschen a month before, 'and never get it.' Lord Rowton performed the last act of a perfect secretary by giving to the world his master's 'last words'; 'I had rather live but I am not afraid to die.' Raising himself as if to address the Commons, he fell forward and was dead. Other 'last words' have been attributed to the weary old man who sometimes found his energetic Faery a little too much for him. Would he like a royal visit? 'No, it is better not. She'd only ask me to take a message to Albert.'

After he was dead a huge memorial tablet arrived over his pew at Hughenden Church, 'placed by his grateful Sovereign and Friend, Victoria R.I.' – to the scandalized amazement of the country. She had already sent him a message in primroses which posterity has sometimes tried to ridicule. 'His Favourite Flower' was written by the Queen on the card she attached to a primrose wreath for Beaconsfield's grave. The streak of pinchbeck make-believe in this famous affair has already been noted: indeed, a romance between a Queen and a Prime Minister could hardly exist without it. Dizzy's primroses were part of this midsummer night's dream. In letters to the Queen he himself picked out the primrose;* between two personages of such grandeur it formed a piquant bond, with just that touch of paradox he appreciated most.

To the Queen it meant more. The primrose convinced her that her own contrasting passions for style and naturalness, etiquette and informality, Versailles and the Glasallt Sheil were present also in her favourite Minister. His glamour had never been in doubt; what she came to value more and more as they both grew older were the signs of a rare simplicity. As if to justify her faith, he chose to be buried quietly at Hughenden by the side of his wife instead of in Westminster Abbey, which would have been his for the asking. The Queen understood at once and exulted. He had always 'hated display', she told her sceptical eldest daughter.

Gladstone, on the other hand, was dumbfounded by the choice of Hughenden. He felt it could only represent the Artful Dodger's last trick. Though his tribute to Beaconsfield in Parliament impressed the Queen so deeply that she invited him to sit down during his next audience, Gladstone himself confessed in the privacy of his diary that the very thought of composing it had brought on diarrhoea. To him, Dizzy was more than a bad influence on the Queen; he was corrupting the people. 'Dizzy is of course looking for the weak side of the English people', Gladstone once wrote, 'on which he has thriven so long.'[12] In 1882 Gladstone told a friend that his two worst experiences had been the Bradlaugh affair and eulogizing Beaconsfield.

Queen Victoria sustained the loss of her friend with fortitude. This was the more surprising since Lord Salisbury, his eventual successor as Conservative leader, gave her none

* For example: 'of all flowers, the one that retains its beauty longest, sweet primrose . . .' and 'He likes the primroses so much better for being wild . . .'

of that fervid personal devotion which had been Beaconsfield's great gift and was indeed the breath of life to her in all relationships. Salisbury's attitude towards the Throne, in fact, had certain resemblances to Gladstone's. He reserved the imaginative warmth of his heart for the institution while directing the courteous light of his reason upon the occupant. Until Lord Salisbury actually took over, she constantly told Ponsonby and Lord Rowton with great heat that she intended to have her trusted friend, Sir Stafford Northcote, for the next leader. During the critical years 1876 and 1877 Salisbury had shown signs of sympathizing with Derby and Carnarvon. Moreover, he did not conceal his dislike for her Highland home – its customs, climate, scenery, all. Yet the Queen gave up Northcote without a struggle. The fight, after all, was against Gladstone.

How much did Queen Victoria owe to Disraeli? Her good spirits, certainly, without which no one can do a good job. A renewed conviction also that she had a vocation: that her letters, her telegrams, her jobations, her tirades were the things which prevented statesmen from pursuing 'downward' policies. Did Disraeli carry the good work too far, giving the Queen-Empress an inflated sense of her importance? Lord Derby thought so, and so of course did Gladstone. Referring to her as Dizzy's 'pupil' he wrote bitingly in 1880: 'He has over-educated the said pupil a little.'[13] On the whole, however, they exaggerated the harm she could do as much as Disraeli exaggerated her right to do it. The royal prerogative was a failing force and the Queen too sensible to insist on it in practice, despite her paper protestations.

Nothing but a grand, even exaggerated conception of her vocation could have roused her from lethargy. One side of her never liked politics. To make her exert herself in this uncongenial sphere, brilliant colours and bold designs were necessary. It was easier to be a Queen-Empress with the world to save than a constitutional Monarch who was required only to sign and drive. Without Disraeli the Queen might have gone down to the grave an unpopular recluse, carrying with her a discredited British Monarchy. In 1871 Princess Alice thought this was pretty sure to happen; her

550

talented daughter, Princess Victoria of Hesse (afterwards Battenberg), squarely faced the possibility that princes and princesses everywhere were doomed, and a good thing too.[14] The majority of them were. But in Britain Disraeli's audacious magic, though not of a kind to transform a neurotic widow into an unimpeachable, sober figurehead, lifted the Monarchy out of the trough which was its greatest danger. Dizzy's Faery was a stage on the way to Queen Victoria's apotheosis.

Beaconsfield died and the withdrawal from Kandahar took place. The Queen was ultimately brought to view it in a somewhat less lurid light; not because Gladstone convinced her reason but because a soldier who had seen a lifetime of service in India, Sir Neville Chamberlain, made an appeal to her heart:

'never let anyone persuade you to make such a fatal mistake as to keep Kandahar – a hateful useless abominable hole which it is dishonourable to stay at one instant longer than we can – I implore you to come away.'[15]

Queen Victoria was deeply moved by words which depicted the operation as her personal responsibility.

She might have swallowed Kandahar completely had it not been followed by further retreats, rumoured and real. Theodore Martin alarmed her with the report (false) that Cyprus was to be abandoned. A statement that Gladstone would fulfil his election promise to give independence to the Transvaal was the painful truth – painful because the Transvaal Boers had just wiped out a British force at the battle of Majuba Hill.

Queen Victoria disapproved of withdrawals: she held that they always led to hasty, improvised returns at enormous cost. To make peace immediately after a defeat like Majuba, before honour had been 'retrieved', was especially short-sighted: 'I fear future difficulties are being laid up there.'[16] Above all, she loathed the idea of handing over African natives to the Boers – 'a most merciless and cruel neighbour, and in fact oppressor', just like the southern slave-owners in *Uncle Tom's Cabin*.[17] In the light of after events who is to say that Gladstone had all the right on his side?

The Cabinet received a mock mourning card:

> In Memory of
> Honour
> Wife of John Bull
> Who died in the Transvaal
> And was buried at Kandahar.
> Her End was peace.

Apart from defeats and withdrawals, the Army was in for another dose of reform and the Queen for another dose of her cousin the Duke of Cambridge. As always, she began by hoping that things would not be too bad. Changes in equipment which reduced the need for cleaning she highly approved, khaki she found very ugly as a colour but did not swear like the Duke of Cambridge to reject it totally; keeping 'red, red, red' for Court, parade and active service. Uniform, however, was a minor matter. Throughout 1881 a ding-dong battle raged between the Duke on one side and on the other the War Minister, H. C. E. Childers, and the Quartermaster-General, Sir Garnet Wolseley, over linked battalions, short service, the abolition of flogging and the elevation of Wolseley himself to the peerage.

In the Queen's eyes this last move threatened her prerogative, for it would make the Army into a 'political department'. Ever since the revolutions of 1848 when King Louis Philippe had not dared call upon his soldiers for help, it had been a fixed principle with Queen Victoria to maintain her emotional relationship with the Army. She felt personally responsible for each one of her soldiers, counting on absolute loyalty in return. Bumptious Sir Garnet, with his waxed moustaches, must never come between them, particularly after speaking so rudely about sweeping away 'the boulders of prejudice in the pathway of reform'. The biggest 'boulder' was clearly her stout, slow-witted cousin, 'poor George'.

Queen Victoria habitually referred to the Duke of Cambridge as 'poor George' owing to his gifts for making bad situations worse. Complaints about soldiers' deaths from heat stroke, for instance, with which Queen Victoria sympathized, were taken by the Duke as personal insults. For months he went round asking all and sundry whether to resign or not. Queen Victoria would not hear of such 'stuff' and characteristically wished the Duke to have it out with Wolseley, say frankly why he disliked him and find a basis for agreement. Only one aspect of the quarrel really got her on the raw: people who ought to know better like Ponsonby, Prince Leopold and Wolseley himself kept saying that the reforms would have been welcomed by the Prince Consort. The problem of fitting the dead Prince's views into a changed world was, as she had discovered long ago, a most delicate one. Crude attempts to drag him in she regarded as emotional blackmail.

Meanwhile the Wolseley row was bringing Gladstone to Ponsonby's private room to predict once more the fall of the Monarchy:

'My day is drawing to a close and when a man gets worn out he gets gloomy. Formerly I saw no reason why monarchy should not have gone on here for hundreds of years, but I confess that the way in which the monarch has been brought to the front in political and foreign affairs by the late Government has shaken my confidence . . .'[18]

On and on Gladstone went, agitated and mournful, while the object of his concern pushed herself forward still further.

Not one of her present Ministers, she decided, matched up to his responsibilities. Granville's reports on foreign affairs showed a lack of concentration: sometimes they even left out an important 'not'. She heard that he wrote them with his wife and children in the same room; it was 'domestic but not business like'.[19] Besides, they merely told her what everyone knew already. She asked, through Ponsonby, for details of Cabinet meetings. With unusual curtness Granville replied that this was the Prime Minister's business, at which she exclaimed in disgust that Granville would never burn his fingers for anyone.

553

Gladstone's memoranda lacked Granville's pithiness and were equally secretive. More than ever she missed Dizzy's revealing epigrams. There had been his letter, for example, breaking the news of the Carnarvon split in 1877: Dizzy only had to write, 'Carnarvon coughed', and she knew all. Though Gladstone told her nothing about Cabinet disputes, she knew from other sources that he could not control his colleagues. Nor could he keep the heady House of Commons, lavishly laced with Irish Home Rulers, in order. Her fiercest indignation during the first three years of this Government was roused by the sight of English administrators dithering in Ireland and Irish politicans rampaging at Westminster.

Granville, in an early attempt to please and reassure, had told the Queen that the new Parliament was like bread sauce – a very few Radical peppercorns to flavour a great deal of bread. He had forgotten Charles Stewart Parnell, the black-haired, white-faced young leader of the Irish party in the British Parliament, and his sixty Nationalists.

Queen Victoria was not unaware of what a bad harvest meant in England:

'not a blade of grass, the potatoes destroyed, the turnips gone wrong, the oats fit for nothing, no food for the cattle, & no means of selling them!'[20]

She wrote thus one summer after driving through her blighted fields at Osborne. What the same thing meant to her Irish subjects in terms of starvation, arrears, evictions and agrarian outrage including the maiming of landlords' cattle, the shooting of landlords' agents and the murder of the landlord himself, she did not divine. There is a snatch of satirical dialogue in Anthony Trollope's novel, *The Eustace Diamonds* (1872) in which Lizzie Eustace, a naïve English girl, questions her lover about his Irish estates:

'What is the name of your place in Ireland?'
'There is no house, you know.'
'But there was one . . . ?'
'The town-land where the house used to be is called

Killagent. The old demesne is Killaud.'
'What pretty names!'

The Queen was far from naïve but her advisers on Ireland, beginning with Melbourne and including the Anglo-Irish Ponsonby, had left her in a state of ignorance as total in its way as that of Lizzie Eustace herself. On November 7th, 1880, for instance, she received from W. E. Forster, the Irish Secretary, an account of Ireland based on police reports. It confirmed her chronic suspicion that the Irish people were more sinning than sinned against. 'In few Counties is there real distress,' she read, 'but in few no crime'; the Land League, founded by Parnell to fight rack-renting, was the cause of all the mischief, while the only remedy was force. The Queen agreed with the men on the spot.

A month later, with the papers full of fresh murders, the Colonial Secretary, Lord Kimberley, told her that Mr Gladstone 'did not quite realize' the hatred of Ireland for England and her wish to separate.[21] Again the Queen agreed. For this exactly fitted with what she had always heard in the past: that the Irish were 'impossible' and it was no use trying to satisfy them.

Gladstone, on the contrary, brought in a Compensation for Disturbance Bill to mitigate the hardships of evicted farmers and did not renew the Peace Preservation Act. These two measures, known more bluntly through months of furious controversy as the 'Land Bill' and 'Coercion' respectively, represented the fundamental division between government by the carrot and the stick. The London season would have to close down, prophesied Beaconsfield gloomily, if the Anglo-Irish landlords got no rents. Queen Victoria, who cared little for the season but everything for law and order, passionately desired Coercion first and a Land Bill afterwards. Gladstone and the Radicals were pledged to a Land Bill first; after that carrot they fondly believed the stick would be unnecessary.

Unfortunately, Gladstone's carrot did not satisfy the have-nots while it scandalized the big property owners in his party. One month after the Government had taken office the fiery little Duke of Argyll (a Cabinet Minister) revealed to Queen Victoria that the Cabinet were divided on Coercion, he himself demanding its renewal. On July 7th, 1880 the Land Bill passed its second reading; three days later Lord Lansdowne resigned from the Government. He was considered a good landlord himself and resented this reflection on the ability of his class to put their house in order. His resignation shook the Cabinet but delighted the Queen. The Princess Royal was informed that others were longing to resign also but she was letting the Government 'work out their own ill-gotten power', as she knew that over Ireland they would be 'checked'.[22] Sure enough, the House of Lords 'checked' Gladstone by throwing out the Land Bill.

'Tremendous!' The jubilant Queen fervently hoped that Gladstone would now have to drop 'this dreadful Bill' and defy the 'monstrous land league' or resign. Instead Gladstone tried to convince her that opposition to the Bill was exaggerated and due to its being badly drafted. Queen Victoria was too much of a woman to believe that people went to war for drafts. Later a second reason for not dropping the Bill was brought to her notice: Chamberlain and Bright would resign. When Mr Goschen (another Cabinet Minister) later said to her, 'I should have let them go & the Cabinet would have been none the worse without them,'[23] she could congratulate herself on having already given that advice to Lord Hartington: '*Don't yield* to SATISFY Messrs Bright and Chamberlain; *let* them *go* . . .'[24] Forster was urged to threaten resignation and for good measure she threw in her abdication:

'she *cannot* and will not be the Queen of a *democratic monarchy*; and those who have spoken and agitated . . . in a very radical sense must look for *another monarch*; and she doubts if they will find one.'[25]

Amid all these dissensions, the Irish set about making government at Westminster impossible. It was the next best thing to having their own government in Dublin. With every form of 'brutish' obstruction, as Gladstone called it, from filibustering to uproar, the oppressed tortured their oppressors. The Grand Old Man was humiliated by the very people whom he had made it his mission to pacify. The savages were chewing up the missionary.

During the autumn of 1880 Parnell convulsed English rule in Ireland by the invention of the 'Boycott'. His Irish-American mother had nurtured in him a violent hatred of England while his upbringing among the Protestant landowners of Wicklow gave him a feeling of ascendancy over all mankind. He combined magnetism with aloofness in a unique degree. Lord Erne's agent, Captain Boycott, had been spontaneously outlawed by his whole community for evicting tenants; he could not even get a shirt washed or a letter delivered. His punishment was now methodically applied by order of the Land League to all subsequent evictors. 'Boycotting' threw John Bull into such a passion that the Government retaliated at last with the stick. The Irish organizers of the Land League were arrested in December, their trial opening on the 28th. The Queen heaved a sigh of relief. 'I felt at peace with all,' she wrote on New Year's Eve, '& prayed for peace & strength, to meet the coming unseen trials & difficulties . . .'

One of the unseen difficulties was the Dublin jury's refusal to convict the prisoners. There was nothing for it but a Coercion Bill. After an orgy of obstruction culminating in a Parliamentary sitting of over forty-one hours, the Speaker took the law into his own hands. On February 2nd, 1881 he put the question. 'At last he has shown courage!' exclaimed the Queen. Next day she was 'amazingly startled' to learn that all the Irish Members had been expelled – 'Alas! only for the night' – amid scenes of wild pandemonium. As long as the Irish debates continued she had them all read aloud to her, braving the Nationalists' language which she still found 'most monstrous' despite the printed reports having been cleansed of the worst enormities.

In this month of 'unseen trials', the Queen got rheumatism, Prince Leopold fell ill and two days after the Coercion Bill was carried under the 'closure' system (February 26th, 1881) she read the news of Majuba. Fenian dynamiters renewed their activities and next month, on March 13th, she heard that Nihilists had assassinated the Tsar. 'It gave me a thrill of ineffable horror.' Queen Victoria put it down to the unpopularity caused by his marrying his mistress; he ought to have done it, she felt, but kept it secret. Nihilists, Fenians, Land Leaguers – they were all alike. 'Firm' measures were the only solution. She also advocated restriction of the sale of dynamite, which was so easy to make: just a cupful of nitrate acid and sand mixed with glycerine and you could blow up anything.

Far from instituting such measures Gladstone reintroduced a Land Bill. The Duke of Argyll promptly resigned. To Gladstone this was a fearful loss on top of Lansdowne's defection, casting grave doubts on his treasured belief that the best of the aristocracy were with him. Whigs and Radicals must go together like faith and works; Gladstone was temperamentally unwilling to save or be saved through Radicals alone. The resignation of Argyll dealt Queen Victoria also a severe blow for in him she lost her last *independent and true friend*' (i.e. source of secret information) within the Cabinet. The Duke of Bedford next threatened to make his wife resign as Mistress of the Robes but was persuaded not to act unless the new Land Laws were applied to England – and 'when that occurs,' wrote Granville to the Queen, 'I shall request leave to join the Duchess.' A year later, however, the Duke removed his wife, the affronted Queen describing him as 'disloyal & uncivil'.[26]

More and more Queen Victoria listened to Gladstone's Whig critics. Gladstone himself could no longer ignore the change. 'She is as ever perfect in her courtesy,' he recorded in his diary for July 16th, 1881, 'but . . . she holds me now at arm's length.' Four months later he felt himself 'outside an iron ring', with no desire to 'break it through'. Ponsonby had noticed in June 1881 that when Lady Ely read aloud the speeches of Chamberlain the Queen listened 'with sniffs', whereas the right-wing Mr Goschen made cautious progress at Balmoral. Ponsonby wrote:

'The Queen has taken the correct measure of Goschen's foot. She is very clever at this appreciation. She sees how

558

anxious he is to please her where he can agree with her –
but how he is utterly silent not giving her the chance of
argument where he is doubtful.'[27]

The Land Bill was not a part of Gladstone's programme
which the Queen and Goschen criticized, for a measure of
reform was by now inevitable. In accordance with past
practice, the Queen exerted pressure on the Lords not to
oppose it and Salisbury had to apologize for so misinterpreting Her Majesty's wishes as to meditate a constitutional crisis.
On August 22nd, 1881 the greatest Land Act of the nineteenth century reached the Statute Book, too late. As an experiment in Land Courts it increased the excitement in Ireland
while, as a compromise mangled by the Peers, it disgusted the
Land League. Parnell went for both it and Gladstone in an
inflammatory speech at Leeds; Gladstone made an equally
flaming reply and on October 13th, 1881 Parnell and two of
his lieutenants were clapped into Dublin's Kilmainham gaol.
'Parnell's arrest a great thing,' telegraphed Queen Victoria to
Gladstone from the peace of the Glasallt Sheil. Thirteen days
later, on October 26th, Queen Victoria's reign reached exactly
the same length as that of Queen Elizabeth I – 16,199 days –
and like her ancestress, she thought prison the best place for
public enemies. She was able to bring a year of horrors to a
close on a 'cheerful note' by singing Gilbert and Sullivan's
Patience with her ladies.

Parnell's incarceration produced untimely results. At first
he boasted that 'Captain Moonlight' would carry on his
work, but he soon found that the 'Moonlighters', freed from
his discipline, were plunging Ireland into chaos. Parnell
therefore negotiated his release from Kilmainham through
two unusual go-betweens, Captain O'Shea, an ambitious
Nationalist MP whose wife was his mistress, and Joseph
Chamberlain, President of the Board of Trade. The Irish
Secretary, Forster, resigned: the so-called 'Kilmainham
Treaty' had been arrived at over his head and he accused
the Government of buying Irish support for Radical measures at the price of Parnell's freedom.

Gladstone might well have conducted the 'Treaty', a

perfectly sensible operation, more cleverly. Fate punished his clumsiness with unparalleled ferocity. Lord Frederick Cavendish, adored husband of Gladstone's niece, Lucy Lyttelton, was sent to Dublin on May 4th, 1882 to replace Forster. On the 6th the Queen returned from a State opening of London's Victoria Park to hear that in Dublin's Phoenix Park Lord Frederick Cavendish and his Under-Secretary, Frederick Burke, had been knifed to death.

Queen Victoria had already denounced the release of Parnell as 'Gladstone's most fatal move'.[28] The appalling double murder made her feel more Cassandra-like than ever. 'Surely his eyes must be opened now,' She wondered whether she would be able to sleep that night or whether she would have nightmares. 'Fortunately the dreadful event did not haunt me.'*[29]

Gladstone's broken appearance could not but be pitied; the Queen noted, however, that he 'is still always excusing the Irish.'[30] Her feelings were soon as violent as ever against him and his Government. Gladstone, already bruised by Ireland, faced an adversary whose self-confidence was constantly increasing.

On March 2nd, 1882 a seventh 'attempt' on the Queen's life provoked an outburst of shocked loyalty. 'It is worth being shot at – to see how much one is loved.'[31] Roderick McLean, an imbecile, fired at the Queen's carriage as it stood outside Windsor station. The Queen did not realize the shot was 'meant for me' until Brown, his face working with alarm but his voice controlled so as not to frighten her, opened the carriage door. 'That man fired at Your Majesty's carriage.' The limelight, however, was for once deflected from Brown by two Eton boys who rushed forward and belaboured the assassin with their umbrellas. McLean was arrested and three days later the Queen received 900 Eton boys in the Quadrangle, addressing 'the 2' personally. So elated was she that

* Queen Victoria recorded four events in her Journal which gave her nightmares: the death of Lady Flora Hastings, the death of Prince Albert, the *Mistletoe* accident and a grisly episode when poachers stole the embalmed body of Lord Crawford and held it to ransom.

no nervous reaction set in until some weeks afterwards. Gladstone kindly pointed out that whereas foreign assassins had political motives, in England they were all madmen.

The increase of Fenian outrages during 1882-3 made her nervous of driving about London, so much so that Harcourt offered to drive with her. As Ponsonby remarked, the sight of the elephantine Home Secretary alongside the tiny Sovereign would have been 'most interesting'. But Queen Victoria had a sense of humour. 'Good gracious, no!' she exclaimed.

Family affairs, both grave and gay, tightened the people's bonds with their Queen. There was the recent death of Princess Alice, followed by that of young Prince Waldemar of Prussia from the dreaded haemophilia. Prince Leopold unexpectedly focused public loyalty by becoming the hero of an event even more irresistible than a royal funeral – a royal marriage.

The ailing Prince's ambition to get married had met with the same frustrations as all his other attempts to lead a normal life. The Queen could not believe that anyone suitable would have him: besides, how could she do without his unofficial liaison work between herself and the Conservatives? When at last a possible bride was discovered poor Prince Leopold's hopes were blighted by a 'sacred' embargo placed by the lady's father, the late Duke of Augustenburg, on his daughter marrying him. Since this embargo had been unearthed by Prince Christian, the Royal Family became wretchedly embroiled. 'Christian owes everything on Earth to me,' wrote the Queen reproachfully; perhaps Vicky would 'frighten him a bit.'[32]

Thanks to the Queen's efforts the tide soon turned for Prince Leopold. She created him Duke of Albany, with the proviso that he should continue to be called Prince Leopold 'in my house', for 'I always say no one can be a Prince, but anyone can be a duke'.[33] And she found him a wife. 'It suddenly struck me,' she wrote to the Princess Royal, that he should 'go & look at Princess Helen of Waldeck,' adding defensively, 'It was entirely my own idea,'[34] for the Princess Royal as usual criticized a German princess not selected by herself.

It was also an entirely successful idea. The young Duchess of Albany turned out to be 'quite a personage'; she insisted on conducting all arguments with her mother-in-law face to face. This innovation Queen Victoria did not at first like; eventually it contributed to the great respect in which she held Prince Leopold's wife. Another of Helen's merits was that she liked 'to go among the people'. Queen Victoria always dreaded lest her treasured English tradition of visiting the poor should be broken by intermarriage with stiff Germans. On the wedding day, April 27th, 1882, she wore over a black dress her white wedding lace and veil for the first time since 1840. Ten months later, to her joy and amazement, she was presented with yet another granddaughter. 'I can scarcely believe that dear Leopold has got a child.' She had to be carried in to see the young parents, having missed a step and badly strained her leg.

'He was lying on the sofa, she on another and when I came as a 3rd helpless creature, it had quite a ludicrous effect.'[35]

Ludicrous was a word the Queen could now use in her Journal without loss of dignity, for she was within sight of public deification. Her drum-major habitually referred to the day of her Accession as Ascension Day and the St James's Gazette had just discovered that, beginning with the year 1839 and adding 11 each time to her age, her age and length of reign were the same, with figures reversed: year 1839 age 20 reign 02, year 1861 age 42 reign 24, year 1883 age 64 reign 46, etc. The royal mystique grew apace.

Meanwhile the Gladstone legend received additions of a very different kind. One evening at Windsor during July 1881 the Duchess of Somerset and Lady Salisbury fell to abusing his ambition, selfishness and 'devotion to low women'. The Duchess did not hesitate to name names and Lady Salisbury added that he told fearful lies. Ponsonby resisted the temptation to retort, 'So does Salisbury.'[36]

A story about the Queen and Gladstone was going the rounds. How Miss Lambart, a sprightly maid-of-honour who made toffee-cakes for the Queen, threw apple peel over her shoulder in the hope that it would form a P for Portland and was twice reproved for wearing make-up, had danced before the Queen and asked for Gladstone's head on a charger. Though the Queen indignantly denied that Miss Lambart had ever danced for her, a time was not far off when the grand old head would be welcome.

About the same date a woman friend told Gladstone that Princess Christian had told her that the Queen hated him. He was deeply incensed and the Queen, to whom this piece of mischief-making was reported by the Princess Royal, angrily deplored the indiscretions and exaggerations of her Court. Bad relations between Downing Street and Windsor were matched by bad news from Africa.

'18th June, 1882 – Waterloo Day – let us never forget the glorious memories of this day.' The Queen sounded this martial note in her Journal after hearing that Arabi Pasha, the Egyptian Foreign Minister, had revolted against the Khedive's authority. Britain's efforts to suppress Arabi were hampered by the hesitation of her partner in Egypt, republican France, to put down a popular leader. 'Egypt is VITAL to us,' the Queen dashed off to Ponsonby, – for the passage to India. By July 1st there was still no improvement:

'Already 6 months of the year passed! How terribly time flies! and in what awful times we live! Ireland no better . . . Egypt in a dreadful state, – the Sultan unmanageable and the other Powers behaving very ill ! ! God help & guide me! – a very fine day.'

Then Gladstone unexpectedly decided that military operations against Arabi would be a holy war. Instead of sending the Salvation Army* against him, as the St James's Gazette ironically predicted, he ordered the fleet to bombard Alexandria. Anger and exaltation met in an explosion of passions which rocked the whole country. 'Gladstone?' shrieked W. S. Blunt in his diary, 'Great God, is there no vengeance for this pitiful man of blood, who has not even the courage to

* The Salvation Army had been formally constituted under that name by its evangelistic founder, 'General' William Booth, in 1880.

563

be at the same time a man of iron?' John Bright sent in his resignation – 'The old leaven of the Non-conformist will break out,' said Gladstone acidly to Ponsonby – but the Queen quivered with pride at her Navy's firmness. Next day the Duke of Connaught was pronounced fit for active service; he left at the head of the Guards to take part, on September 3rd, 1882, in Arabi's defeat at the battle of Tel-el-Kebir. A bonfire roared on Craig Gowan, as after Sebastopol, and for a time all was joy; black was black and white was white, just as the Queen liked things to be. Her son distinguished himself; the Khedive proved to be a non-smoker with only one wife, while Arabi and the Sultan were scoundrels, bribing a tobacconist to poison the Khedive; 'poor George' joined in praising his old enemy, Sir Garnet Wolseley, who had commanded in Egypt; she herself got on splendidly with the returned hero when he visited Balmoral.

Wolseley declared that Arabi ought to be hanged. This opinion was supported by the Queen, and, as she heard, by the unanimous votes of Eton. She marvelled at the vigour of the Eton boys compared with the vacillation of her Ministers. Gladstone, having told her that Arabi was guilty of 'duoduplicity' and must die, later allowed Wilfrid Blunt to put up money for an English Counsel to defend him. The duo-deceiver thus escaped the Khedive's vengeance and was merely banished to Ceylon. When the Foreign Office requested Queen Victoria to congratulate the Khedive on his magnanimity in order 'to give him courage to face his womankind, who are frantic', an equally frantic woman at Windsor telegraphed her refusal. Let the British Government send their own messages. 'The "womankind" show a right feeling in being "frantic".'[37]

A letter of congratulation on the victory of Tel-el-Kebir from Gladstone to the Queen gave less than satisfaction. He failed to say one word about the Duke of Connaught's part. She made up for Gladstone's omission by personally receiving the victorious troops on November 17th with her son taking pride of place. 'He looked so like his beloved father I felt quite overcome.' Next to the Duke she praised the 'brilliant contingent' of Indians. Sir Garnet's admirers were much annoyed.

The rest of the year was a whirl of social duties and celebrations: a State dinner, State opening of the new Law Courts, where she recognized the great Florence Nightingale sitting near the dais in order to see *her*; endless decorating of war heroes and visits to hospitals. Netley Hospital seemed comfortable except for a shortage of armchairs.

'I gave the Egyptian medal to a number of them [wounded], it was very touching to bend over the beds of these brave, noble, uncomplaining men, & pin the medals on their shirts. Took good care to prick no one.'[38]

Haslar Hospital was less satisfactory: there were no nurses and an air of severity.

Everything was so like the dear past, so interesting, from the Indians' magnificent turbans over which she struggled to push their decorations, down to the peculiar appearance of Colonel Home who had commanded the Blues in Egypt though 'slightly off his head'. (Contrariwise, Sir Havelock Allan went out to Egypt to prove he was not mad and asked Sir Garnet for a certificate of sanity.) When December 14th came round and found her busier than ever, she could scarcely believe that she had once longed to die. On Boxing Day the Christmas tree was lit for the last time and stripped of its presents as of old, her little granddaughters drawing lots for the fairy doll at the top.

'How much has happened during this year. I have to thank God for very much, & only wish I was more worthy of His great mercies & goodness to me.'

Among the mercies had been a Government reshuffle in December. The raising of Dilke and Derby to the Cabinet was more than counterbalanced by Lord Hartington's appointment as Minister of War. At least, the Queen had thought so. But when she congratulated Hartington on his important new responsibilities he replied that there would not be much for him to do: 'I think everything has been done; & the Army should rest now.'[39] Less than ever could she rest.

CHAPTER XXX

THE BITTER CRY
1883–4

DURING THE FIRST months of 1883 the Queen began
to hope that her Prime Minister was in for a period of rest
even longer than the British Army's. Temporarily broken by
insomnia, Gladstone went abroad in January and Harcourt
told her that if he returned at Easter it would be only to
resign. The Queen gathered that Harcourt for one would not
be sorry. He was busy rounding up the Phoenix Park mur-
derers whose identity had been betrayed by an informer;
whatever 'delusions' Gladstone might cherish, Harcourt
assured Queen Victoria that Ireland would have to be governed
under a Crimes Act for the next twenty years.[1]

Hartington and Goschen also expressed nervousness at the
prospect of Gladstone's return: though a genius, the Government was doing 'wonderfully well' without him. When the
Prime Minister finally reappeared Harcourt reported that he
looked as if he couldn't do much work. The Queen agreed.
Had not Gladstone at a drawing-room failed to hear what she
said to him? 'The Diplomatic Corps are numerous today,'
she had said. The Siamese suite happened to be passing and
Gladstone replied, 'Yes, they are very ugly.'[2]

The ever-present hope of his retirement brought a crumb
of comfort to the Queen during a sudden wave of misfortune
which now smote her.

The Queen's fall downstairs at Windsor on March 17th,
1883 started up a succession of painful rheumatic attacks.
After a week spent on a sofa she was carried by John Brown
and a footman into her little pony-chair 'which I used to use
long ago'. With Jenner's help she tried to walk but failed.
Next day was Easter Sunday. A sad entry in her Journal
greeted this festival. 'Had not a good night. Vexed that Brown
could not attend me, not being at all well, with a swollen face,
which it is feared is erysipelas.' He had caught a chill combing
the grounds for Fenians. Bad days and nights followed, Brown

getting worse and the Queen no better. He was nursed in the Clarence Tower by Sir William Jenner and Dr Reid, the Queen's most valued new physician whose father, to add to the gloom, suddenly died on the 27th. 'He is greatly upset but said he would rather not leave me just now.' On the 29th Prince Leopold told her that John Brown had died.

The Queen was crushed. Just at the crisis of her own pain she had lost not only an excellent servant but a real friend. 'He became my best & truest friend, – as I was his,' she informed the minister at Crathie. For the second time she would have to reorganize her whole way of life.[3] She sent for Brown's brothers and herself broke to them the dreadful news. It was like 'one of those shocks in 61', she wrote to the sympathetic Ponsonby; she had not been able to walk before Brown's death, now she could not even stand. Lord Rowton, whose master had always treated 'Mr Brown' with studied respect,* called on the Queen personally to condole; so did Tennyson, much to Ponsonby's alarm who feared an official elegy. The Prime Minister paid a tribute to 'Mr J. Brown' and the Queen filled half a column of the *Court Circular* with his praises. All the tributes were collected in a special scrapbook. The sculptor, Edgar Boehm, was engaged. A statue rose at Balmoral which Lady Erroll, a strict Calvinist who abhorred graven images, likened to Nebuchadnezzar's image of the idol Bel. Tennyson wrote a singularly gawky inscription:

> *Friend more than servant, loyal, truthful, brave:*
> *Self less than duty even to the grave.*

He also found some lines from Byron for a granite seat dedicated to Brown at Osborne.

As the weeks passed the Queen's spirits began to recover, but the double burden of her own pain and Brown's loss would suddenly plunge her in the middle of lively conversation back into gloom. On June 28th she wrote, 'I walked just

* A letter to Brown written on 10 Downing Street paper by Lord Beaconsfield in 1880, thanking him for a 'Leviathan' of a scotch salmon, ends: 'I hope, some day, you may throw a fly into the humble waters of Hughenden.' (Royal Archives. Victorian Additional MS C3.47.) Dizzy once caught a 4½ pound trout in his charming stream which he sent to the Queen.

a little but my attempts were very unsuccessful. How I miss my good Brown's strong arm to help me along.' It was not till July 13th that she could get in and out of her carriage at Balmoral without a 'platform'. She remembered that the Duke of Orleans had been killed by falling out of his carriage exactly forty-one years ago; to that tragedy she attributed all France's troubles. *She* must not fall. August found her arranging her testamentary papers and reading a little book by Dr Hutton called *The Mystery of Pain* – 'which makes one think a great deal'. A masseuse, Madame Charlotte Nautet (known to the Court as 'the Rubber'), came from Aix-les-Bains and 'kneaded & worked backwards & forwards' every limb, muscle and joint, leaving the Queen rolled up in flannel for fifteen minutes: 'it made me very late & feel tired.'[4] The Rubber also forbade her to picnic on wet grass. Dr Reid was delighted though no one, not even the Rubber, could stop her from driving in an open carriage in a drizzle. A host of remedies poured in from well-wishers, including a tricycle recommended by a Mrs Cash whose *bona fides* the great John Ruskin himself would vouch for. At the end of the year she was still very lame and very sad.

About a month after Brown's death Ponsonby got wind of a royal plan which caused him some misgivings. With the assistance of Brown's private diaries, Sir Theodore Martin had been requested by Her Majesty to write Brown's life. News leaked into *The World* that Martin had refused on the excuse of his wife's ill health. Ponsonby suspected that a Miss Macgregor, who was hovering about Osborne, had been given the commission instead. The last thing he wanted was to know anything about it. 'I can't conceive what can be said in such a history,' he wrote in November. All too soon he was to find out.

Queen Victoria had been working on a further instalment of her *Leaves** throughout 1883 and it was published on

---

* She had already printed an intermediate volume of wonderfully fresh 'leaves' in 1880, 'for strictly private circulation', consisting of extracts from her Journal during the two State visits in 1855. (*Leaves from a Journal*, edited by Raymond Mortimer.)

February 12th, 1884, under the title of *More Leaves from a Journal of Our Life in the Highlands*.

Everyone was kind about the Queen's book except, as before, the Queen's family. According to the old Duchess of Cambridge's lady-in-waiting, Lady Geraldine Somerset, the Prince of Wales felt 'indignant' and 'disgusted' while the Duchess herself exclaimed, 'Such bad vulgar English! So miserably futile & trivial! So dull and uninteresting!'[5]

Max Beerbohm found it by no means 'dull and uninteresting' when he set about embellishing his copy in 1919 with a mock inscription in the Queen's hand, friendly parodies and caricatures. 'For Mr Beerbohm', appeared on a fly-leaf, '– the never-sufficiently-to-be-studied writer whom Albert looks down on affectionately, I am sure – From his Sovereign Victoria R.I. Balmoral, 1898.' An imaginary review from the *Spectator* ran: 'Not a book to have lying about on the drawing-room table, nor one to place indiscriminately in the hands of young men and maidens . . . Will be engrossing to those of maturer years –'

Queen Victoria swiftly demolished the Prince of Wales's written complaint that his name had not once been mentioned: it occurred five times. She annihilated with equal dispatch the Princess Royal's criticisms: having reigned forty-five years she knew what her people liked and what was good for them; her *Leaves* had done good in 1868 and *More Leaves* would do more good now; publication of the truth caused 'false biographies & Lives (endless ones have been published of me)' to 'fall into the background & vanish altogether'. Queen Victoria then turned her thoughts temporarily from biography to the more amenable problems of her family portraits at Windsor. She had bought pictures of the Duchess of Connaught's parents, Prince Frederick Charles of Prussia and his 'ill-used wife'; on second thoughts she had tried to cancel the picture of Frederick Charles but having failed to do so, remarked with unfailing resourcefulness: 'never mind, it is a fine picture & I need not hang them up together.'[6]

Ponsonby had received an advance copy of *More Leaves* as a New Year present. On February 23rd another parcel arrived for him.

It contained a manuscript with a covering note from the Queen announcing that she was engaged upon the enclosed 'little memoir' of John Brown. Owing to constant interruptions she needed some help in completing it; she had started at 1849, and had reached 1865, Miss Macgregor 'striking out all unnecessary repetitions'. Her object was to show by her gratitude and friendship that Brown was a 'gt deal more' than a devoted servant. Its circulation would at first be private.[7]

Cautiously Ponsonby wrote back that Her Majesty would be right to get help from the Bishop of Ripon and Dr Cameron Lees of Edinburgh who knew about 'authorship'.[8] Next day there was another note: 'Sir Henry has not said if he liked the extracts . . .'[9]

Ponsonby was in a quandary. Far from 'liking' the extracts he thought them calamitous. So did Dr Lees. Neither dared tell the Queen.

It was not till the 28th that Ponsonby drafted a lengthy reply, making two main points: the memoir was 'invested with a degree of interest which must be felt by all who knew Brown' but Sir Henry made bold to doubt whether 'this record of Your Majesty's innermost and most sacred feelings' should be published to the world; passages would be misunderstood and unfavourably criticized by strangers, causing the Queen pain.[10]

Sir Henry got two answers, both on March 2nd:

'– She thanks him *very much*. She wishes him to remember that this very full account is *not* intended for publication but *for private* circulation . . .'[11]

A second note asked for the memoir back to show to Lord Rowton, 'who takes a gt interest in it'.[12] In returning it, Ponsonby thanked 'Your Majesty most sincerely for receiving so graciously the remarks he made in all sincerity but with much anxiety as to whether he was justified.' He still felt there were things in it which 'people in general might convert into other meanings and take up in a spirit which was not intended'.[13]

570

Lord Rowton read the memoir and an undated memorandum by Ponsonby followed:

'Saw Rowton. He suggested delay in any form – proposed that the diary as it stood should be printed – by one confidential man. This would take six months and then H.M. would see how impossible it was to issue it. H.P.'[14]

Rowton's stratagem must have failed for the next thing we know is that the Dean of Windsor, Randall Davidson, has gone into action. The opinion of his colleague, Dr Lees, had convinced him that publication of the memoir would be 'most undesirable'. He therefore seized the opportunity on March 6th, while thanking the Queen for a presentation copy of *More Leaves*, to hint that yet more leaves would be a mistake. Queen Victoria expressed haughty surprise at this view and announced her intention to proceed with publication. The intrepid Dean then wrote again with more vigour, the Queen ordered him, through Lady Ely, to withdraw and apologize for the pain he had caused and the Dean, having apologized in writing for the pain only, offered to resign.

There was a long, terrible silence. Offended Majesty retired for a fortnight into a deep thunder-cloud and Davidson ceased to exist – another preached on Sunday from his pulpit. Suddenly, a few days later, he was sent for. A smiling goddess received him 'more friendly than ever'. The memoir was never mentioned again. As the Dean realized, Queen Victoria never bore a grudge, actually preferring those people who, from the highest motives, 'occasionally incurred her wrath'.[15]

Sir Henry has left a summary of the affair which is surely a masterpiece of under-statement from a master of discretion:

'The Queen asked me to help in the publication of Brown's Memoirs. I suggested postponement. The Dean backed me up. The Queen did not say much. Rowton was consulted and Lees of Edinburgh. H.P. 1884.'[16]

Dr Lees heard later in the spring that John Brown's memoir had been 'postponed'; according to Sir Henry's biographer, Arthur Ponsonby, it was destroyed.

There the matter might have ended had not a legend sprung

up fifty years later that Ponsonby's bonfire was not the simple act of common sense which it seemed. It was said and is still repeated that he had burned the records of Brown's spiritualist seances with Queen Victoria. The obvious sequel to this story made its appearance thirty years later still: namely, that these interesting skeletons were not cremated by Ponsonby after all but are still lying closely guarded in some royal cupboard. According to *Psychic News*, Lionel Logue, the distinguished speech therapist who cured the stammer of King George VI, told Hannen Swaffer and Lilian Bailey, well-known spiritualists, that the King told him he had read one of Brown's diaries describing seances.

Though Mr Logue shared their spiritualist beliefs, his private papers contain no confirmation of this story and it is not in fact credited by Mr Logue's family.

The ghost of Brown the Highlander, with his second sight or double sight or both, will probably continue to haunt Windsor Castle much as Herne the Hunter haunted it in medieval times. There is no evidence whatever of the kind acceptable to historians that Brown's diaries are extant; nor that, if they were, they would describe the spirit visitations of Prince Albert to Queen Victoria from 'behind the veil'.

Though the Queen's script has gone the way of Brown's diaries, some fragments remain of the kind which she might have included in the memoir if she had ever finished it. These fragments alone are enough to make it crystal clear why Davidson, without for a moment believing in an immoral relationship between the Queen and Brown, nevertheless risked his whole career to prevent publication. A few greetings cards have survived, some garish, some charming in lacy frames, all addressed by Queen Victoria to John Brown.

On January 1st, 1877, for example, Brown received the following verses printed beneath the picture of a dashing little parlour-maid:

> *I send my serving maiden*
> *With New Year letter laden,*
> *Its words will prove*
> *My faith and love*

> *To you my heart's best treasure,*
> *Then smile on her and smile on me*
> *And let your answer loving be,*
> *And give me pleasure.*

In the Queen's handwriting was written:

> 'To my best friend J.B.
> From his best friend. V.R.I.'

Next year the Queen chose a Scottish card:

> *A Guid New Year.*
> *Yon heather Theekit Hames were blythe*
> *When Winter Nights were lang,*
> *Wi' spinning wheels and jonkin lads*
> *An' ilka lassies sang.*

On the back of the card was written:

> A happy New Year to my kind friend
> from his true & devoted one.
> V.R.I. Osborne, January 1st, 1878.

Christmas 1878 seems to have been the occasion for one of those dramatic 'have-it-out' scenes, followed by a reconciliation, which Queen Victoria so much enjoyed, for on January 1st, 1879 she chose the following illuminated verse:

> *Forgive & Ye shall be Forgiven.*
> St Luke. vi.37.

She added in her own hand:

> 'From a devoted grateful friend.'[17]

As a postscript to these astonishing but also artless and innocent effusions, the reader should consider an extract from a letter of Queen Victoria's announcing John Brown's death to her grandson Prince George of York. The tone is scarcely less ardent. The Queen had nothing to hide.

'... I have lost my *dearest best* friend who no-one in *this World* can *ever* replace ... *never forget* your poor sorrowing old Grandmama's *best & truest friend* ...'[18]

573

No doubt the Queen's advisers were right at the time to stop publication but today it can only be regretted that the *Life of John Brown* is lost to history. As the Queen herself always insisted, true biography drives out false.*

Deprived of the comfort of writing Brown's memoir, Queen Victoria contented herself with having dedicated her own *More Leaves* to him, after inserting a paragraph about him at the end. Even this mild expression of her feelings had worried a Court determined to have no revival of the old scandals. When the Queen consulted the Duchess of Roxburgh, her Mistress of the Robes, about the wording of the paragraph, the Duchess hinted that any mention of Brown's death in a book which ended at Tel-el-Kebir would be an anachronism. The Duchess reported back to Ponsonby that Her Majesty had 'shut her up' with the laconic remark that only the *wording* was under discussion.[19]

Brown's later years at Court had passed without undue commotion. This was something of a miracle considering his addiction to the bottle. As a Scot living in the raw Highlands he thought nothing of it and it was due to his cheerful frankness that the world now knows how Queen Victoria liked her tea. One day a maid-of-honour was told by Brown that she could have two hours off as the Queen was going out.

'To tea, I suppose?'

'Well, no, she don't much like tea – we tak oot biscuits & sperruts.'

As a girl the Queen had disliked tea, in middle age she considered it unhealthy, and made out of doors with tepid water it must have been disgusting (Prince Albert possessed a patent stove for boiling water which often did not work). The Queen once congratulated John Brown on the best cup she had ever drunk.

* Mr Tisdall describes the photostat of an alleged note from Queen Victoria to John Brown, written in more extreme language than any of the above, which mysteriously came into and vanished from his possession, and so cannot now be evaluated. (*Queen Victoria's Private Life*, by E. E. P. Tisdall, pp. 96–9.)

'Well, it should be, Ma'am, I put a grand nip o' whisky in it.'

Brown was by no means the only Highlander to succumb: even the telegraphist at Balmoral had to be superannuated for 'illness'. When Brown himself was 'unwell' the Queen asked no questions.

His 'strong arm' was always in evidence. Times without number he saved the Queen from horses with staggers, runaway horses, horses driven by drunken coachmen into the ditch. His speed in seizing the pistols of madmen put her equerries to shame. The Empress Eugénie, who had sent a large wreath to his funeral, told her friend Lady Simmons* how much the Queen depended on him for protection: while she worked in her tent in the garden, 'for four or five hours at a time, he would be on the watch with his dogs to answer her little bell . . . and see that she was not molested'.[20] Tourists and reporters got short shrift. 'Oh! by God I gave them a bit of my mind,' he boasted at Glencoe, after driving off some journalists. A tourist sketching at Balmoral was ordered to 'stop scribblin' and whusslin'.'

Brown's official duties ranged far and wide, from receiving doctors' reports on the health of royal employees and undertakers' reports on their funerals, to dealing with the mud at Cowes Harbour and collecting donations from the Household for a monument to Lord Beaconsfield. With admirable calm he accepted Miss Pitt's curt refusal to contribute a penny. For all his prestige and power he never tried to interfere in politics but when questioned his judgement was often sound. 'I asked J.B. today,' wrote Ponsonby to his wife in February 1878, 'if he wanted war and he exclaimed most vehemently – damn no I beg yr. pardon – but I think it would be awful – dreadful deal of fighting and at the end no one would be better and a' would be worse for it.'

Brown was somewhat quarrelsome, keeping up a running feud with Kanné, the Queen's courtier, Grant and the other ghillies; but when his 'objurgations', as Ponsonby called them, were silenced by death, the courtiers had their work cut out to prevent all the Highlanders from going direct to the Queen

* See p. 430.

with every petty problem; unlike Gladstone, Brown kept his subordinates in order. He was even known to have silenced Gladstone himself with the words, 'You've said enough.'

His worst fault was getting between the Queen and her children. Princess Alice, though aware of his merits as 'an honest and really faithful servant', denounced his freedom to discuss anything he liked with the Queen while her children were restricted to subjects which would not excite her. With the Prince of Wales Brown was particularly offensive and the Queen, it must be admitted, devoid of her usual tact. She once told the Princess of Wales who had just given a ball at Abergeldie that she was sorry it had not been a success – Brown had told her so.[21]

Brown was the arbiter on all day-to-day arrangements. One September at Balmoral there was a dispute as to the date agreed upon for a visit to Inverary. Ponsonby said the 21st, the Queen said the 20th. Brown was sent for, confirmed the 21st and the private secretary was believed.

He was not above jobbery, as when he tried to get a friend into the canteen at Netley Hospital; and he was a regular 'John Blunt', as H. L. Williams, author of *Boys of the Bible*, wrote in a eulogistic penny pamphlet after his death. He once terminated a discussion as to how many courtiers could share the Queen's pew at Crathie without overcrowding her when she took the Sacrament, by shouting, 'She had better have a place all to herself and have done with this hombogging.' He horrified a director of the Great Western Railway by summoning the little Waleses into the royal compartment with the cry, 'The Queen wants the boys in the carriage.' 'He calls them boys!' exclaimed the top-hatted gentleman rolling his eyes up to heaven.[22]

Perhaps Brown's oddest disservice to the Queen personally was in preventing her from getting the most out of holidays abroad. Loathing the language, sights and smells himself, he forced her to maintain a strict Balmoral régime in Baveno, Mentone or Cannes. The royal party rarely set out early and Brown, imagining Fenians everywhere, refused to stop during the drive lest a crowd should collect. His own Highland garb always made sure that it did. With folded arms and lowered eyes he sat doggedly between the Queen and the view, so that she saw nothing. At Baveno the Italian sunshine pleased him less than ever for he went down with a violent attack of erysipelas. But even abroad there were good moments. In Coburg one day the German guard emerged as the Queen was starting on her drive and after presenting arms began to drum furiously.

'Oh! I wish they would turn in,' she groaned.

Up strode Brown to the astonished officer and silenced the drumming with a peremptory, 'Nix boom boom.'

Ponsonby, who knew the best and worst of Brown, summed up his influence fairly on May 26th, 1883, after escorting the Queen in a low state to Crathie churchyard:

'Wreathes from Princesses, Empresses & Ladies in Waiting are lying on Brown's grave. He was the only person who could fight and make the Queen do what she did not wish. He did not always succeed nor was his advice always the best. But I believe he was honest and with all his want of education – his roughness – his prejudices and other faults he was undoubtedly a most excellent servant to her.'

John Brown was in fact well on the way to sharing his Sovereign's canonization. The holders, labels and string attached to the wreaths on his grave were all carried away as relics, while coaches and carriages plying between Ballater and Braemar made a regular stop of ten minutes at Crathie to give passengers a chance to see the handsome tombstone. In the summer a hundred pilgrims visited it a day. 'You ought to charge them a shilling a head,' said Lord Bridport to the minister's wife. In 1884 Gladstone himself asked to be shown the shrine.

Brown's fame travelled to countries where his bare knees and kilt had never been seen. The year after his death a satirical paperback was published in New York: *John Brown's Legs or Leaves from a Journal in the Lowlands*. The author, 'Kenward Philp', dedicated his work 'To the Memory of those extraordinary Legs, poor bruised and scratched darlings . . .' Queen Victoria's *Leaves* and *More Leaves* (just out) were parodied.

'We make it a point to have breakfast every morning of our lives . . . Brown pushed me (in a hand-carriage) up quite a hill and then ran me down again. He did this several times and we enjoyed it very much. . . . He then put me in a boat on the lake and rocked me for about half an hour. It was very exhilarating.'

Brown tends the Queen's thumb, sprained in a carriage accident, and when he develops a wart on his own thumb the Queen, accompanied by a battalion of forty-two Highlanders, marches round to his cottage to support him with a fine old whisky. He pours stout into the soup tureen, is thrashed by 'Bertie' and is jealous of Beaconsfield whom he calls 'that d——d Sheeny'. To the Queen's fury he declares himself a Gladstonian: 'I'm a Leeberal in politics, I want ye tae understan' – there, noo.' His rages reduce her to tears, he is constantly giving notice, he enters her room without knocking, sits in her arm-chair, escorts her to her bedchamber, swears. He also refers to her as 'Her *Mad*-jestie'. Can she endure it any longer? Suddenly a letter arrives from New York saying that O'Donovan Rossa, the Fenian leader, is after him. The Legs scamper away from 'Windsoral' for ever.

It is perhaps significant that from this rich farrago only one ingredient is missing – spiritualism. The rumours of twenty years earlier concerning the royal medium were already dead before Brown himself passed over.

'I cannot cease lamenting,' wrote Queen Victoria in her Journal on March 27th, 1884, the first anniversary of John Brown's death. That same day a telegram arrived from Cannes where Prince Leopold was holidaying while his wife waited for her second baby, to say that he had hurt his knee. Next day came the news that he had died from a haemorrhage of the brain. The Queen's stiff, aching limbs were still being massaged by the Rubber and incessant alarming telegrams from Egypt made her head swim. Now to all this was added a new and terrible heartache. Though Prince Leopold's faults had never escaped her, in her agony after his death she called him 'the dearest of my dear sons'.

578

Prince Leopold had spirit, intellect, considerable book-learning and a vivid interest in politics. If he were not soon created a Royal Duke, he once exclaimed impatiently, he would stand for a Parliamentary Borough. 'In which interest?' asked his equerry. 'Extreme Radical!'[23] His political advice to his mother, however, was of an equally extreme Conservatism and for this reason it was perhaps not wholly regrettable that she had one go-between the less after 1884. The young man who had never been permitted to wear even a Volunteer's uniform was given a military funeral. It was his last wish and one which he mournfully expected to be denied. Like his brothers, uniform was his passion. Abroad, where uniforms were everything, he could only say he was a Brother of the Trinity. This created a strange impression.*

The Queen's immediate reaction to death was, as ever, clear-sighted and true:

'For dear Leopold himself we could not repine . . . there was such a restless longing for what he cld not have; this seemed to increase rather than lessen.'[24]

But insight, however clear, could not lift the shadow and it may have been the sorrow of these years which helped to turn Queen Victoria's thoughts to the distress of the poor – now again at a dreadful peak. She made a determined effort to find out what was really going on in the slums of London and among the unemployed. Stories about 'General' William Booth and his Salvation Army had awakened cautious interest at Court, so much so that when W. T. Stead was arrested in 1885 for publishing his *Maiden Tribute of Modern Babylon* – an 'obscene' exposure of the white slave traffic in the pages of the *Pall Mall Gazette* – Mrs Booth ventured to ask Queen Victoria to intervene on Stead's behalf and also on that of her son William Bramwell Booth, who was indicted with him. Stead and the *Pall Mall*, however, were more than Her Majesty could stomach. She drafted a harsh telegram to Mrs Booth (afterwards softened by Ponsonby) pointing out that

* The same story is told of Lord Salisbury and Sir Winston Churchill.

Stead's case was still *sub judice* and she could not interfere. As her Journal shows, her real objection was to public revelations about immorality, between which and sensation-mongering she saw no difference. 'There have been horrible things published & talked about of late, under the plea of virtue & humanity, which has & will do fearful harm.'

In justice to Queen Victoria it should be remembered that a more experienced sociologist than herself found *The Maiden Tribute* 'shallow & sensational'. This was Beatrice Potter, later Mrs Sidney Webb, the mother of the Fabians. Three months later Mrs Fawcett, widow of the blind Postmaster-General, wrote to the Queen asking her to mitigate Stead's sentence of hard labour. Ponsonby was allowed to get in touch with the Home Secretary on Stead's behalf, only to find that he had already been made a 'first class' prisoner. Meanwhile the Queen was glad when the Criminal Law Amendment Act of 1885 became law.

The Bitter Cry of Outcast London, an inquiry into the slums by a group of Nonconformist missionaries, had stirred her more deeply. She put questions to Gladstone about the homes of the poor. If improvements had indeed been made (as she was constantly being told) we surely need not despair of making more? The Prime Minister replied by dilating yet again on past improvements without showing much enthusiasm for future experiment. (The same thing was to happen later when Queen Victoria suggested public works to mitigate unemployment. Gladstone again stalled. His old-fashioned Liberalism in home affairs had not caught up with the needs of the 'eighties.)

Far from satisfied, the Queen repeated her questions to others. Sir Richard Cross, a leading Tory, told her that the *Cry* was somewhat exaggerated.* The Liberal Home Secretary, Sir William Harcourt, produced the complacent view that the London poor were no worse off now than formerly. The Queen even turned to Sir Charles Dilke who, though a

* Charles Booth, 1840–1916, the Liverpool shipowner turned sociologist, brought out the first of a series of epoch-making statistical surveys in 1889, *Life and Labour of the People in London*, which proved that the *Cry* had not been exaggerated.

Radical, was also an expert on housing. The Rev. Harry Jones, who had worked in the East End, was summoned to tell her whether the poor had been irrevocably turned against the upper classes by their misery. The answer was No, despite their lives being utterly dismal. At Balmoral the Rev. Storey inveighed against the practice of landlords letting their grouse moors to parvenus who cared nothing for the starving crofters. Queen Victoria expected her clergy to champion the oppressed and had recently warned the Princess Royal against a fashionable preacher, the Rev. Thomas Teignmouth Shore, who boasted of 'never having had to do with the poor'.[25]

The culmination of her hopes was a Royal Commission on Housing set up in February 1884, on which the Prince of Wales served – at least until other calls grew too insistent. She also remembered that in periods of scarcity the Palace set a good example. At the time of the Corn Law agitation she had cut down on bread; now she banned mutton. Letters of thanks poured in. The ban was lifted two or three weeks later to the relief of the Household, especially Lord Sydney who greatly missed his *côtelettes à l'agneau aux points d'asperge*.

Gladstone's coolness over housing was more than matched throughout 1883 by Her Majesty's icy displeasure at his positive interests. Church appointments caused minor irritations: Gladstone argued that High Churchmen made the hardest workers; the Queen insisted as always on Broad Churchmen with large-minded ideas, like Deans Stanley and Wellesley who had lived and died 'finding something to respect in every creed & in every person'. Friction was hot on the subject of Radical oratory. Joseph Chamberlain fired his Brummagem-manufactured explosives into nobility and Crown alike, to the immense exhilaration of Midland audiences: the peers he compared to the lilies of the field, 'who toil not neither do they spin', while as for royalty, he told a delirious company assembled to honour John Bright that though Royalties were not present, 'nobody missed them'. Repeated angry demands by the Queen to stop this kind of Radical propaganda found Gladstone in a weak position. He had to defend a reasonable amount of ministerial freedom while privately agreeing with the Queen that Chamberlain had overstepped it.

The chronic dispute about Cabinet secrets was becoming ever more rancorous. The Queen persisted in her assertion that past Prime Ministers had revealed to her the details of Cabinet conflict. This was certainly true of Melbourne, Peel and Disraeli. Palmerston and Russell were two black sheep but when they did vouchsafe information it was not confined to generalities. Gladstone, on the other hand, considered the Queen's claims 'intolerable', 'ill-judged', 'inadmissible' and her Court 'oriental' and 'Byzantine' due entirely to Disraeli's encouragement. He had burst out over a year before to Lord Rosebery – 'The Queen alone is enough to kill anyone.'

In the autumn of 1883 the exhausted and exasperated Prime Minister decided to escape for a few days on a trip round the British Isles as guest of the wealthy shipowner, Sir Donald Currie. The public were amused by this 'Currie's tour', in contrast with those of Thos Cook & Son who had recently conveyed Wolseley's army to Egypt.

> *The Grand Old Man his place has booked*
> *And off to sea has hurried*
> *Plain travellers are only "cooked"*
> *But G.O.M. is "curried".*

The Queen followed Gladstone's tour without a smile. For he suddenly decided to accompany his fellow passengers (among them Harcourt and Tennyson) on a surprise visit to Norway and Copenhagen, without Her Majesty's permission. He was entertained by a galaxy of reigning princes, including the Kings and Queens of Denmark and Greece and the Emperor and Empress of Russia. Toasts were drunk, guns fired. Queen Victoria fired back.

Lord Granville received the first salvo on September 18th:

'The Prime Minister – and especially one *not* gifted with prudence in speech – is not a person who can go about *where* he likes with impunity. At *this moment* too, when our relations with France are *not* of the best [over Egypt]

582

. . . and his presence at Copenhagen may be productive of much evil and certainly lead to misconstruction.'[26]

The People's William was bad enough; the Emperor's William was more than Queen Victoria could stand.

That Gladstone's royal visit had really occurred on the spur of the moment (as was in fact the case) she soon ceased to believe. Though she assured Gladstone on September 20th that she gave him 'full credit for not having reflected',[27] a fortnight later she was confiding to the Princess Royal her secret conviction that Gladstone knew the Emperor of Russia was at Copenhagen before the pilot told him – he went deliberately because he 'trusts Russia, hates Austria & don't like Germany. Republican France & Italy are all he cares for!!'[28]

Gladstone found the Queen's letter of the 20th 'for the first time – somewhat unmannerly', for it included a hint that he had taken a press reporter on board. Nevertheless he wrote an abject reply, excusing himself on grounds which must have seemed to the Queen exceptionally ill-chosen:

'Increasing weariness of mind under public cares for which he considers himself less and less fitted, may have blunted the faculty of anticipation, with which he was never very largely endowed.'[29]

Then why did he not retire? The answer that in fact he intended to do so, came sooner than she dared hope.

On Gladstone's seventy-fourth birthday (December 29th, 1883), his private secretary, Edward Hamilton, wrote in his diary:

'Is this to be his last birthday spent in office? Who can tell? The odds are, I think, that it will be the last . . .'[30]

Gladstone arrived at Osborne at the beginning of February 1884, full of good resolutions for the future. After the longest audience he could remember (one hour and a quarter) and an agreeable discussion about the last man to wear a pig-tail, the Queen and Gladstone maintaining that it was Lord Westmorland and Ponsonby arguing for his wife's grandfather, Lord Grey, who cut off his pigtail at the passing of the 1832 Reform Bill, Gladstone brought up the subject of retirement. The Queen's private secretary was informed with much heat and emphasis that only the Bulgarian atrocities had 'dragged' him out of his privacy and 'forced' him back into the front rank ten years ago.

'I regretted it but I couldn't help it. I could not keep silence and I did not.'

After next year he would for ever hold his peace. 'My business will cease,' he declared, in the summer of 1885 when Parliament would be dissolved. Nothing would induce him to go through another general election.[31]

Neither the Queen nor Ponsonby took this with the scepticism which long experience of the Grand Old Man should have taught.

CHAPTER XXXI

GORDON AND THE TUP-TUPPING
1884-5

ONE DAY EARLY in March 1885, George Trevelyan, Chancellor of the Duchy of Lancaster, presented himself at Windsor for the 'pricking' of the new sheriffs. As the Queen dug the point of her steel 'bodkin' into one of the top three names, she remarked how well the Duchy's revenue was doing. 'I think it's the only thing that does well in the country,' laughed the Chancellor ruefully.[1] Queen Victoria did not disagree. She had just come through a testing year.

Arabi's defeat in 1882 brought no peace to Egypt. The revolt moved southwards into the Sudan and found a new leader in a fakir calling himself the Mahdi, the Expected One. As soon as Queen Victoria realized what was afoot, letters and telegrams began again to descend upon the Government, urging them to crush this false prophet without delay. But Gladstone wanted no more African adventures and Hartington was for giving the Army a rest. Throughout the following year the country was divided between those like the Queen who wished to keep British troops in Egypt and the mass of Liberals clamouring for evacuation, not to mention Lord Randolph Churchill, calling upon Gladstone in the name of Tory Democracy to get out of Egypt 'bag and baggage'. Queen Victoria could understand neither the Duke of Marlborough's 'strange' troublesome son nor Britain's 'strange' Prime Minister.

Stranger things were happening in the Sudan. Ten thousand Egyptian soldiers under Hicks Pasha had been slaughtered and the Expected One was at the frontiers of Egypt. Gladstone's Cabinet announced on December 3rd, 1883 that they must abandon the Sudan, rescuing only the garrisons scattered over the country with Khartoum as their centre.

Though appalled by this humiliation Queen Victoria at once concentrated on the rescue operation. Her prayer for the New Year was brief and breathless: to be spared further sorrows and given strength for her arduous duties. Chief among them was her duty to goad the Government.

'2nd January. – They do nothing but delay, & then at the 11*th* hour are forced to act.'

'8th January. – The news from the Soudan are very bad, but the Ministry do not seem to see it. Telegraph & write to them continually.'

'11th January. – The govt. does nothing!'

Suddenly, a week later, the Government did something. While Gladstone was laid up with a chill, a Cabinet presided over by Hartington took the momentous decision to send out General Gordon.

The Gordon story, a tragedy of obstinate logic-chopping on one side and perverse heroism on the other, is unique in British imperialism. No villain was at work; everyone behaved at some point rather badly. Nor did things go wrong because of accidents; common sense could have foreseen all. But temperatures at Westminster were too high for common sense to operate; it was as hot as in Egypt. With three prophets involved – Gladstone, Gordon and the Mahdi – what else could be expected? Queen Victoria, in her role of Cassandra, made a fourth.

Gordon's instructions seemed explicit enough: to report on the situation in the Sudan with a view to evacuation. Nothing whatever was said about reoccupying the territory; nevertheless vague references to performing 'such other duties' as Sir Evelyn Baring, the Controller of Egypt, might require, made the orders less explicit than they sounded. Besides, Gordon did not listen very intently to human sounds. 'We are pianos,' he wrote to his sister; 'events play on us.' He was a mystic and a fatalist.

Charles George Gordon was just fifty-one; the wrong man for the Sudan but one after the Queen's heart. He had earned the nickname of 'Chinese' Gordon from victories, not evacuations, in the Far East. Her cousin King Leopold II of Belgium had just chosen him as the right sort of genius to let loose on the Congo but Gordon was persuaded to drop this prior

586

engagement. Like Napoleon III he had blue, magnetic eyes and 'destiny' seemed to him, as to Napoleon and Disraeli, more important than human will. He carried a cane into battle like a later man of destiny in Africa, Cecil Rhodes, and called it his 'wand of victory'. Gordon's Bible was the most important thing in his life but he was not interested in church-going. His contempt for Society – '*dinner* parties and miseries' – equalled the Queen's.

Gladstone was the first to have doubts about the wisdom of giving this valiant eccentric, decorated with the Yellow Jacket of a Mandarin, the British, French and Turkish medals of the Crimean War, the Order of the Bath and the Khedive's Order of the Medjidieh First Class, the dreary job of winding up British rule in the Sudan. Press and public, however, hailed his appointment as a rare inspiration. The Jingoes took it for granted that Gordon would not stick pedantically to his orders. Queen Victoria's only fear was lest he had been sent 'too late'.

Gordon took a hero's departure from London on January 18th, 1884. Khartoum welcomed him on February 18th as their Expected One and kissed his feet. Four days earlier the Queen had received his sister at Windsor – 'very anxious about him, but great confidence in his will to be preserved.' On that same day she discovered from Foreign Office telegrams that Gordon thought reinforcements would 'help him'.[2]

Help him to do what? Smash the Mahdi? The Government desired him to do one thing only – evacuate the Sudan. They were convinced he could do this without any further help. When Gordon next demanded that a notorious slave-trader, Zebehr, should be set up in opposition to the Mahdi, the Cabinet shuddered. False prophets were multiplying under Gordon's mesmeric glance (the idea of Zebehr had come to him in a mystical flash) and the public would never swallow a slaver. But Sir Evelyn Baring backed Gordon and the Queen backed Baring. 'IF this is refused,' she exploded to Ponsonby, 'the Queen will *hold* the govt. responsible for any sort of misfortune which *will* happen.'[3] In her anxiety she went to the Blue Room almost every day.

Again exactly a month passed and on March 18 the Mahdi

closed in. Khartoum was besieged.

Four days later Prince Leopold died.

Everyone knew that 'poor Gen. Gordon,' as she now called him, was in greater danger than the garrisons he had been sent to save; everyone, except the Government. They still believed that sheer cussedness prevented him from returning to Cairo. Next month Gladstone was hissed in London and on May 19th he suddenly told the Queen that an expedition might after all have to be sent from England to Gordon's relief.

The Queen felt 'low'. Egypt itself was to be evacuated in five years' time to please the French. A serious, despondent note pervades her Journal and the kind of minor troubles for which she generally found space were excluded: a dog falling ill or a stableman absconding. ('How dreadful! – & his predecessor drowned himself.') After listening to 'a very fine sermon' she opened her heart to her friend Dr Lees of Edinburgh, who had recently advised against the memoir of Brown. Her own life was irreparably saddened, she told him; to give others pleasure was the only pleasure left for her. Then she returned from Balmoral to give pleasure, for once, to Mr Gladstone.

Queen Victoria was about to make her last eruption into politics which was both on the grand scale and entirely beneficial in its results. For a short time it even took her mind off Gordon. Sir Henry Ponsonby also reached the zenith of his usefulness, manoeuvring the Queen's go-betweens instead of being short-circuited by them.

A great increase in the Franchise, extending the vote from the Boroughs to the Counties, had been promised by the Liberals in 1880. Now, four years later, Gladstone passed his Reform Bill through the Commons. Lord Salisbury refused to accept it unless a 'Seats Bill' was also introduced, redistributing the Parliamentary constituencies so as to save his party from being swamped by new voters. Gladstone stuck by Reform first, Redistribution afterwards. The Lords therefore threw out the Reform Bill on July 9th, 1884.

This gave the Radicals their chance. To the Queen's horror

a virulent campaign against the House of Lords swept the country. 'Peers versus People,' they chanted joyfully; 'Ancient Monuments,' 'Interesting Ruins,' 'End them or Mend them.'

Queen Victoria was not afraid of reforming the Franchise. She did fear a burst of reform applied to the House of Lords, for who could tell where it would stop? As she was to write fiercely to Gladstone towards the end of that tempestuous month:

> 'The Monarchy would be utterly untenable were there *no balance* of power left, *no restraining power*! The Queen will yield to no one in TRUE LIBERAL FEELING, but not to destructive [sic], and she calls upon Mr Gladstone to *restrain, as he can*, some of his wild colleagues and followers.'[4]

She was too experienced, however, to imagine that simply by silencing the wild men she would dissolve the obstinacy of the tough men. Bearded Lord Salisbury, with his knitted brows, half-closed eyes, domed forehead and slight, unexpected tilt to his firm Victorian nose, must also be made to see reason. Her vocation to do good was suddenly crystallized. By throwing herself between the two Houses she would save the Crown.

Ponsonby and Rowton were mobilized.

Lord Rowton was sent to tell Lord Salisbury that he must on no account attack the *principle* of Reform, but the reply came that Salisbury 'while fully appreciating my kindness, sees no possible mode of an agreement'.[5] The tough man stood pat. And the wild men continued to create 'violent & disgraceful scenes'.

There was hope, however, in other quarters. Gladstone, whose tone the Queen had hitherto not liked, now gratefully agreed to leave the next stage 'in what Mr Gladstone calls my skilled & experienced hands' – a dizzy compliment from the GOM. Then she heard from the Prince of Wales that Churchill regarded Lord Salisbury's attitude as 'dangerous to party and Constitution'. The Ponsonby dove returned to the Windsor ark from frequent excursions to town with reports that junior Tories were for compromise, while moderates were terrified of being obliterated by the extremists.

Patiently the Queen worked upon the moderates. A couple of 'ancient monuments', the Dukes of Argyll and Richmond, were pressed into service to soften Gladstone and Salisbury respectively. The Queen's tame moderate, Mr Goschen, was informed of Her Majesty's idea for a 'union of Moderates' in the House of Lords. He agreed with alacrity, suggesting that this 'third party' should be led by Argyll.[6] Yet summer passed into autumn and Salisbury was still 'impulsive', Gladstone 'imprudent'.[7]

When the campaigning season opened Gladstone carried the message of Reform to his 'foolish adorers' in Scotland. Ponsonby's attention was called by an angry Sovereign on September 16th to Gladstone's

> '*constant* speeches ... without which the country *would not* be *excited*. . . . The Queen is *utterly* disgusted with his *stump* oratory – so unworthy of his position – almost under her very nose.'[8]

He had made a stop at Ballater. Ponsonby was instructed to inform the Prime Minister that his habit of putting his head out of the carriage window and orating at every station was 'absurd'. The discreet private secretary translated Her Majesty's blunt language into a hope that 'Mr Gladstone would not exhaust himself' with these repeated speeches.[9] The patriarch replied that he had no wish to speak but had to acknowledge the crowds. Queen Victoria, convinced that the crowds were whipped up, asked why Gladstone did not stop his 'Court Circulars' in the Press. Far from stopping them Gladstone, in his extraordinary ignorance of human nature, sent her a press cutting which began: 'The Prime Minister has arrived at Midlothian after a triumphal procession which recalls the glories of his great campaign.' Lady Ely returned it to Ponsonby with a covering note: 'Her Majesty says she has not read it, as she did not like the commencement.'[10]

Nevertheless she worked harder than ever to bring together the imprudent object and the impulsive force. She welcomed a proposal of Lord Carnarvon's for a Committee of Independents and when Salisbury crossly objected that Carnarvon should not have 'troubled' her, she retorted that it was not Carnarvon's advice she wanted but his views. At the same time she again called upon the Government to disavow Chamberlain.

> 'He approves of the *disgraceful* riot at Birmingham! If a Cabinet Minister makes use of such language . . . he ought *not* to *remain* in the *Cabinet*.'[11]

Liberal hirelings had invaded a Tory rally at Aston Park, Birmingham, captured the fireworks, let off an effigy of Sir Stafford Northcote upside down and brought the meeting to a fiery close.

Gradually under the Queen's insistent eye a scheme for joint consultation took shape. Hartington met Hicks Beach, since Argyll had advised her to keep Salisbury and Gladstone apart for the present, 'as both were hot!' (Granville predicted that if they met there would be a dog-fight and 'two tails, but no Redistribution Bill, would be left'.) Back and forth travelled Ponsonby, urbane and resourceful. The Hartington–Beach talks broke down but Gladstone agreed to meet Salisbury 'if I should deem it expedient'. They duly met. Meanwhile on November 17th he presented a compromise to both Houses which the Queen, deeply impressed, had already recommended urgently to the Tories. It was well received. Next day she tasted the first sweets of success in the form of a letter from her Foreign Secretary:

> 'If Lord Granville may venture to say so, your Majesty must feel rather proud of the powerful influence which your Majesty has brought to bear . . .' – 'which I certainly am, or rather, more than thankful . . .'[12]

On the 21st she told the Princess Royal that both sides attributed the happy result to her efforts – a welcome reward for all the 'dreadful worry, work & bewhildering [sic] proposals & failures wh for the last 6 weeks almost drove me wild'.

The obvious compromise was reached. A Reform Bill passed through the Lords while an agreed Redistribution Bill simultaneously came before the Commons. The relief brought

591

a 'devilish twinkle' to Gladstone's eye and left him 'splitting and chuckling'[13] – though not quite so devilishly as Parnell who calculated that after the next election he would control over 80 Home Rulers at Westminster.

Not everyone was satisfied. The Queen heard that Lord John Manners, an extreme Tory, had 'raised his eyes in silent horror' when Salisbury announced the compromise to the Carlton Club. Gladstone told her that some of his people objected to the new method of party leaders settling everything in secret: it was a bad precedent. 'A good precedent,' maintained the Queen stoutly, 'to avert serious dangers so much desired by Radicals & Republicans.'[14]

There seems little doubt that Queen Victoria looked upon this 'precedent' as a new way of dishing the Radicals. If she could not create a third party of moderates she would establish instead an informal coalition of party leaders under the supervision of the Crown. The teeth of democracy would thus be gently and painlessly drawn.

Gladstone's reaction to Queen Victoria's schemes is significant. He began by impatiently declining to argue with 'her Infallibility' and ended with an almost gushing letter of thanks. Queen Victoria telegraphed a characteristic reply: 'To be able to be of use is all I care to live for now.' A year later Gladstone was still so taken with the new convention that he offered Salisbury his support over the next great political problem – Ireland.

Lord Salisbury had never really liked the bi-partisanship of 1884. While Gladstone was 'splitting and chuckling' the Queen noticed that Salisbury, to whom she gave an audience on November 27th, looked depressed and 'evidently not exactly pleased' at the peaceful solution:

'I think we could have made a good fight,' said he regretfully.

'But at what a price!' retorted the Queen.[15]

The Reform Bill was the last great problem which Queen Victoria and Gladstone worked out in harmony. A few weeks later the issue of the Sudan, now fast approaching a decision, opened a new and terrible chasm between them.

Queen Victoria had a gift for beginning a New Year on a prophetic note. 'Life is very sad,' she wrote on January 1st, 1885, 'I will not look forward!' Next day came a message from General Gordon to Wolseley which filled her with foreboding. 'Bring plenty of troops if you can ... we want you to come quickly.' The Queen wrote, almost as if all were already over, 'poor, poor Gordon, whom the govt. would not listen to!' Poor, poor Queen, whom they would not listen to either. As early as February 9th, 1884, she had written to Gladstone: 'The Queen trembles for Gen. Gordon's safety. If anything befalls *him*, the result will be awful.'

Three weeks after Gordon's message she had a fierce brush with Lord Hartington, the War Minister. Without going through the War Office she had personally congratulated Wolseley on a military victory at Abu Klea. This procedure had landed her in trouble before, notably over messages to Sir Bartle Frere and Lord Chelmsford in 1880, and Hartington complained to Ponsonby of his 'false position' in relaying to Wolseley a royal message which had already been received. The Queen's reply to Ponsonby was a tirade on the subject of her prerogative and Lord Hartington's presumption:

' – The Queen always *has* telegraphed direct to her Generals, and *always will* do so, as they value *that* and *don't* care near so much for a mere official message. But she generally sent an official one too, and somehow or other she forgot ... But she thinks Lord Hartington's letter *very officious* and *impertinent in tone*. The Queen *has* the *right* to telegraph congratulations and enquiries *to any* one, and won't stand dictation. She *won*'t be a *machine* ...'[16]

Gladstone had delayed sending a force to relieve Khartoum until the last possible moment. He held that since Gordon had no right to be in danger, danger did not exist; moreover, the Mahdi's followers (unlike Arabi's) were 'rightly struggling to be free' and so an expedition would be wrong. 'He can persuade most people of most things,' said the disillusioned Forster, 'and above all he can persuade himself of almost anything.' Queen Victoria always believed that he called 'black white and wrong right', to suit himself.

At last in September 1884 when Gordon had been besieged for nearly six months Gladstone was forced by public opinion to call black black and send Wolseley to Egypt, but it was October before the relief force started up the Nile. On the 24th Gordon wrote in his Khartoum Diary:

'If they do not come before 30th November the game is up, and Rule Britannia.'

Food was almost gone. Day and night he swept the desert from the palace roof with his old telescope, picked up for £5, but it showed him no rescuers. Then on November 12th he heard the sound of drumming.

'This is our *first* encounter with the Mahdi's personal troops. One tumbles at 3 am into a troubled sleep; a drum beats – tup! tup! tup! comes into a dream ... The next query is, where is this tup tupping going on. A hope arises it will die away. No, it goes on, and increases in intensity.'[17]

On that same day Gladstone wrote urgently to the Queen of 'the approaching crisis' but he was thinking of Parliament where the tup-tupping of Lord John Manners was getting very tiresome. One hoped it would die away.

Gordon's last entry was made on the 'fatal' December 14th:

'Now Mark THIS, if the expedition ... does not come in ten days, The Town May Fall, and I have done my best for the honour of our country. Good bye. C. G. Gordon ...'

The first of ten thousand rescuers arrived before Khartoum on January 28th, 1885. They were just too late. Two days earlier the Mahdi's soldiers had burst into the palace and speared Gordon to death.

Queen Victoria had written a year ago that 'the result will be awful' and she made sure that it was. Mary Ponsonby was startled on February 5th by a black figure suddenly appearing at Osborne Cottage and saying in a sepulchral voice, 'Gordon is dead!' The Ponsonby family were convulsed with horror but Cassandra still had a duty to do. She telegraphed identical messages to Gladstone, Granville and Hartington *en clair*:

'These news from Khartoum are frightful, and to think

594

that all this might have been prevented and many precious lives saved by earlier action is too frightful.'[18]

Gladstone was handed this open rebuke by the station-master at Carnforth on his way back to London. Holding himself blameless, his indignation was colossal and he wondered whether he ought to resign.

Unforgivable as the Queen's action was, it was prompted by the intensity of her suffering, which in turn was due to her romantic view of the Sovereign's responsibility. Owing to 'the old Sinner', she wrote to the Princess Royal, we were just too late 'as we always are – & it is I who have as the Head of the Nation to bear the humiliation.'[19] It was particularly in facing Continental Royalties, many of them seething with envy and malice, that Queen Victoria felt personally abased by Gordon's disaster. Far from being a nodding Mandarin she saw herself as a scapegoat for the sins of the Government. Moreover, the Government might well escape punishment by resigning whereas she, for all her threats, could never really abdicate. Hence three telegrams sent *en clair*.

As so often, the Queen's pangs reflected those of her people. Gordon had been the idol of the young Army officers and they nicknamed the Grand Old Man the Grand Old Spider. On the music-halls he became the MOG – murderer of Gordon. Gladstone did nothing to make amends. He appeared thoughtlessly at the theatre while the whole country was mourning and the nearest he could get to a tribute in Parliament was the cold phrase, 'the lamented Gordon'. Queen Victoria was sickened. 'Mr Gladstone in his speech never alluded at all to poor General Gordon's tragic death!'[20] It is usual to say that the tragedy affected her so deeply as to make her ill. Some substance is given to this tradition by a sentence written to Ponsonby on September 17th, 1885 and published in her collected *Letters*: 'It is this that has made the Queen *ill*.' This is not the whole truth.

The truth is that she caught 'a very troublesome cough' from her grandchildren, as she recorded in her (unpublished) Journal on the 10th, and it turned to one of her feverish attacks with neuralgia in the bad arm. Sir William Jenner, however, who attended her, was always on the look-out for a nervous breakdown and in this case he might even have welcomed one, for his hatred of Gladstone was obsessive. He probably encouraged the Queen to believe that Gladstone alone had sent up her temperature.

For a few weeks it seemed that public clamour would force the Government into reconquering the Sudan. Queen Victoria implored them to take Baring's advice and make Wolseley its Governor-General without loss of time. 'Remember the example of Gordon!'[21] Not content with this injudicious jab, she sent a secret letter to Lady Wolseley of the 'frighten-them-a-bit' type she often used against her family.

'. . . I do think that your husband should hold *strong* language to them, and *even* THREATEN to resign if he does *not* receive strong support . . . I tell *you* this; but it *must never* appear, or Lord Wolseley *ever let out* the *hint* I give *you*. But I really think they *must be frightened* . . .'[22]

Wolseley was later approached in the same clandestine manner. It was no good. 'How I have written & cyphered & spoken & warned – & all in vain!'[23] For the sudden threat of a third Afghan War frightened the Government a great deal more than any rebellious spark which Lady Wolseley might strike from her husband. The Government cancelled Wolseley's second expedition into the Sudan and concentrated on forcing the Russians to come to terms. The Queen's expostulations were no less agonized because they took a familiar form: '*she* cannot resign if matters go ill . . .' 'We are becoming the laughing-stock of the world!'[24]

She was wrong. Bismarck had indeed been laughing up his sleeve but it was at the prospect of the Russians and British destroying each other while he quietly assumed the mastery of Europe. His laughter abruptly ceased when agreement was reached in Afghanistan and in the Sudan the Mahdi, the Expected One, unexpectedly died.

Gladstone's conduct of foreign affairs, though it avoided war, did not strengthen his hold over the Cabinet. The Queen noted on May 6th, 1885 that Hartington, his War Minister, was 'rather amusing' about Britain's friendlessness. Rather amusing, one presumes, at Gladstone's expense. At the same time Hartington told her about a new Coercion Bill for Ireland. Though Gladstone was 'so reserved and writes such unsatisfactory letters', she soon realized that his Cabinet was acutely divided on this Bill. The two leading Radicals, Dilke and Chamberlain, insisted on modified forms of Home Rule before any new Coercion Bill. A vote was taken on May 9th. All the commoners except one (Hartington) voted for a start in Irish self-government; all the Peers except one (Granville) voted against. Gladstone marched out of the room saying, 'Within six years, if it please God to spare their lives, they will be repenting in sackcloth and ashes.'[25] Chamberlain and Dilke resigned, though they agreed to postpone the official break.

With the Cabinet in so shaky a condition Gladstone was no longer able to keep his secrets from the Queen. On May 23rd he wrote her a full account of the split on Irish policy. Among other things he admitted that Local Government for Ireland was the brain child of 'two markedly Radical Ministers'; nevertheless it was 'in the highest sense Conservative'.[26] This oddly phrased statement must have seemed to the Queen a typical example of Gladstone calling black white. (He had once spoken of making war on Arabi 'on the principle of peace'.) In her Journal she described the letter as 'very interesting' and a few days later showed it to one of Gladstone's Whig colleagues, Lord Carlingford. Sure enough the letter contained things which Lord C. would 'never be a party to.'[27]

Before the Liberal split could go further a Budget proposal to increase the taxes on beer and spirits was defeated by a combination of Tories and Irish Nationalists in a snap division on June 9th. The beaten Ministers thankfully escaped from the tumult which broke out in the House and later presented their resignations.

Queen Victoria's last exchange with Gladstone was sharp. Unfortunately the crisis had caught her at Balmoral and neither of them would travel to meet the other. She jeered at his wish to remain in London to evacuate his house, while solemnly declaring herself unable to move without several days' warning to the railways. (Since Lord Rosebery was in the habit of ordering special trains at a moment's notice, the Queen's excuse could only be justified by her secret fear of railway accidents.) Besides, as 'a lady nearer 70 than 60' she was 'quite unable to rush about as a younger person and a man could do'.[28] The man in question being nearer 80 than 70, he was hardly in a better position to rush about than she.

'Have felt terribly worried & alone, but God did not desert me. Sir H. Ponsonby has been indefatigable.' Everything was settled on June 24th, thanks to this unbeatable combination. When the retiring Government came to give up their seals they were radiant. Ponsonby asked Lord Derby, the Colonial Secretary, whether he expected to be back soon. 'What does it matter?' cut in Hartington hilariously. 'It is a family arrangement at the Colonial Office. They divide the pay between them.' (Frederick Stanley, a Conservative, succeeded his Liberal elder brother as Colonial Secretary.)

The Queen shook hands with Hartington and Granville but not with Gladstone. Humbly he asked if he might kiss her hand. She gave him her fingers but there was no forgiveness. Wolseley had just sent her a large white donkey from Egypt where white donkeys were royal, yet her writ no longer ran in the Sudan. Wolseley followed up his donkey with a visit to Osborne on July 15th. In speaking of 'poor heroic Gordon' he burst into tears. It was a consolation for her to possess Gordon's Khartoum Diary, presented by his sister. She kept it in the Corridor at Windsor just outside her private apartments, where the attention of passing guests could be easily directed to such entries as, 'I hate her Majesty's government...'

The political tup-tupping was quickly followed by a crisis in the Queen's domestic life.

The Princess Beatrice's painful shyness had not improved with the years and she still 'lifted her shoulder against her neighbour' at dinner. Ponsonby, however, who watched her faithfully piloting the Queen round foreign resorts found himself admiring as well as pitying her. If only a strong, handsome man would turn up and sweep her off her feet; but what chance was there of that?

The chance came in April 1884 at the marriage of Princess Beatrice's young niece, Victoria of Hesse, to Prince Louis of Battenberg, cousin of the bride. The wedding was the occasion of many alarms and anxieties. Prince Leopold had died suddenly only a month before and when Queen Victoria arrived at Darmstadt, sad but ready to be cheered, she was faced instead with most unwelcome news of more nuptials. At first no one dared tell her. Lady Ely, in a terrible state of nerves, was finally persuaded to do her duty and Queen Victoria learnt that the widowed Grand Duke Louis, father of the bride, had been 'entrapped' by a 'depraved' and 'scheming' woman of Russian origin, named Alexandrine.[29] (Her name was in fact Kolémine and she was charming.)

Chaos reigned at the Grand Ducal palace: everybody thought up wild solutions, from Queen Victoria who suggested that the Grand Duke's wedding day should be adjourned indefinitely, to the English governess who decided that the Tsar must order the Kalomine back to Russia. 'But if she won't go?' asked Ponsonby. 'Ah! but she must!'

In the end, the Grand Duke, having gone to the altar immediately after his daughter, was persuaded to terminate the misalliance by divorce. As the Prince of Wales said, 'We are a very strong family when we all agree.'[30]

Meanwhile, a second ill-starred love affair was occupying the Queen's mind. Her granddaughter, Princess Victoria of Prussia ('Moretta' or 'young Vicky'), had fallen in love with another Battenberg, Prince Alexander of Bulgaria ('Sandro'), a young man no less clever, tall and handsome than his three brothers.* Unfortunately for young Vicky, her Sandro had quarrelled with the Tsar. Bismarck, determined not to upset Russia, violently opposed the marriage, dragging with him the Princess's grandparents, father, and brother, Prince William, the future Kaiser. On the lovers' side in this 'Romeo and Juliet' affair were only the Princess's mother, the Princess Royal, and English grandmother, Queen Victoria. But these

* The four Battenberg Princes were Ludwig (Louis), Alexander (Sandro), Henry (Liko) and Francis Joseph (Franzjos).

two were a formidable alliance. During the house-party for the Darmstadt wedding, Fritz was packed off to shoot caper-cailzie so that the billing and cooing of Sandro and young Vicky should not be disturbed.

With all this going on Queen Victoria may have missed the signs of yet another Battenberg romance. Her description of Princess Victoria's wedding mentions only such harmless facts as that all four Battenberg brothers were present, that she admired Sandro's Bulgarian servant, that a photograph was taken of 'four generations' – herself, Vicky, Vicky's daughter Charlotte and Charlotte's baby daughter Victoria – that she watched the Rhine sadly by moonlight and returned home to find twenty-three official boxes awaiting her attention.

It was therefore with something like panic that she heard from Princess Beatrice of her wish to marry Prince Henry of Battenberg. For months the Queen refused even to discuss the idea, telling herself that it was nothing but an aberration which would never have happened if Princess Beatrice had not lost her dear brother Leopold. In time, however, she realized the strain of this situation on her daughter's health. Prince Henry came to England and having promised to make his future home with the Queen so as not to deprive her of Princess Beatrice's services, received her consent. The engagement was announced on December 30th, 1884. Four days later Ponsonby reported: 'She [the Queen] is beaming and proud of him.'

On January 7th she wrote to the Princess Royal:

'The marriage is immensely popular here & the joy unbounded that she, sweet Child, remains with poor, old shattered me!'

(If by 'here' she meant the Court, this was true. In the country another German marriage was severely criticized.) She expressed surprise at her own complete serenity, after the 'horror' and 'most violent dislike' of 'my precious Baby marrying at all'; it was all due to Liko himself having won her heart by his modesty and consideration.

'There [is] no kissing etc (wh Beatrice dislikes) wh used

to try me so with dear Fritz. But the Wedding Day is the gt trial – & I hope & pray there may be no results! That wld aggravate every thing & besides make me terribly anxious.'[31]

The wedding day (July 23rd, 1885) brought nothing worse than some tears when the Queen sat alone in her room after the couple had driven off, stopping her ears to keep out the sounds of the band. 'I think that going away horrid – as though it was a punishment or a necessary execution . . .' Otherwise she was enchanted by the atmosphere of this 'village wedding' at Whippingham.[32] As for the 'results', Princess Beatrice's four children brought their grandmother great happiness, though they were rather unmanageable: constant moving around with 'Gangan' prevented their nurses from teaching them to be seen and not heard.

This second Battenberg union brought to a head a quarrel with Queen Victoria's German relations which had broken out over the Hesse–Darmstadt match. The four Battenbergs were minor princelings on the father's side. His morganatic marriage to a mere countess deprived his sons of their Hessian rank but they were magnanimously granted the title of Battenberg without an HRH. With her advanced ideas on royalty and rank, Princess Victoria of Hesse was thought to have fallen in love with Louis Battenberg (an officer in the British Navy) precisely because he was not a 'real prince'. Whatever her inspiration, she brought down upon herself and her husband a rain of insults. In Russia Prince Louis had found himself given the precedence of a Lieutenant in the Royal Navy and placed at table below Captain Fawkes of the yacht Osborne. The Hessian Parliament refused to vote him any money. Queen Victoria as usual came to the rescue.

'Of course, those who care only for great matches, will not like it,' the Queen had written to the Princess Royal about the Darmstadt marriage, 'but great matches do not make happiness.'[33] When Princess Beatrice also chose great happiness in preference to a great match, the Germany of the Almanac de Gotha registered the most unmannerly disgust. Queen Victoria had conferred upon Prince Henry an HRH for use in England. Several of her German kinsmen refused to employ this title when answering her invitations to his wedding. Her blood boiled. How dared they say that Liko was not '*geblüt*', not pure bred. Their language was 'a little like abt animals', she wrote furiously to the Princess Royal. 'Don't mind my saying this.'[34]

During the following weeks she complained that Prince William, his wife and brother, Prince Henry, were all being unkind to Liko and Beatrice. Willy needed a good 'skelping', as the Scotch said. As for Dona, 'a poor little insignificant pcess raised entirely by your kindness, I have no words.' But she found plenty. Quoting Lord Granville she continued: 'If the Queen of England thinks a person good enough for her daughter what have other people got to say?'[35] Her sharpest retort, aimed at her once respected friend the Empress Augusta, had come just after the engagement. Augusta's own daughter had married the son of 'a vy bad woman' and an inquiry into all princely families would reveal many black spots. Moreover – and now she was on a favourite theme – if there were no fresh blood, the royal race would degenerate 'morally & physically'.[36] A few weeks before the marriage she recommended the Princess Royal, when she became Empress, to sweep away all these absurd German prejudices about '*Nachgeborene*' – younger sons. As her anger blazed it lit up painful scenes from the past. 'I do not forget how rude they were to Papa . . . & how bitterly I resented it.'[37] 'Court Battenbergism', as Queen Victoria's championship of this family was called, did not interfere with her vigilance in other directions. There was always 'tup-tupping' on the periphery of the huge family: scandals in Coburg, Teck debts, the Brunswick fortune, Hanover exiles. Queen Victoria corresponded tirelessly about them all. Opportunities to display her increased tact with her children were not wanting. As early as 1881 the magazine *Truth* had drawn attention to Princess Louise's absence from her husband's side in Canada. The Princess had suffered an appalling sleigh accident the year before, when she was dragged by the hair for several minutes and lost one ear. To this shock the Queen attributed an aversion to her husband which had to be accepted as a sad but inescapable fact; they must try to live on friendly terms under the same roof, but the Princess could not be 'forced' to do so. 'That is all we can do,' she wrote to the Princess Royal in September 1884. Short of allowing a formal separation, the Queen in fact did everything in her power to ease the pressure on her daughter while 'feeling very much for' Lord Lorne.[38] Nevertheless, the necessity of continually seeing the Duke of Argyll (Lord Lorne's father) over the Franchise crisis produced one of those situations in which the strain of being both Queen and mother was at its greatest.

The Connaughts and Albanys were subject to jealousies: would Vicky, in return for her Mama's help over young Vicky and Sandro, say a word to Louischen about being kind to Helen?

And Princess Christian, whose nerves were in a bad state after childbirth, while she could not be blamed for her condition must be helped and encouraged to cure herself.

The Queen's anxious temperament often led her to worry unduly over the kind of problems which face all families. But though, like many women, she could not overlook the failings of her children she was able to focus on the virtues of her grandchildren. Young Prince Albert Victor of Wales was perhaps 'languid' from growing so fast but such a good boy that he would never go astray; little Daisy Connaught's roaring disobedience was forgiven because she was so 'funny'.

Not a few of the third and even fourth generation were assisted into the world by their indefatigable grandmother. True, the Queen's children sometimes arranged that 'dear Mama' was not told in time. But when her granddaughter, Princess Victoria of Battenberg, arrived at Windsor for the birth of her first baby on February 25th, 1885, the Queen took complete command. Despite Gladstone, Gordon and all the rest, she sat beside her motherless granddaughter from seven in the morning till the child was born at five. The accoucheur, Dr Duncan, wondered how she could do it.

The circumstances of the birth seemed to Queen Victoria 'strange & affecting'. For the child, a daughter, was born in the same bed as her mother, and the Queen held Princess Victoria's hand and rubbed her arms just as she had ministered to the baby's grandmother, Princess Alice, twenty-two years ago. The baby was christened Alice and became the mother of Prince Philip, Duke of Edinburgh. Queen Victoria would have found it even more 'strange & affecting' had she known that he was to marry her great-great-grand-daughter, Queen Elizabeth II.

CHAPTER XXXII

HOME RULE
1885-6

THE QUEEN'S AUTUMN manoeuvres started off with an alarming bang. News reached her on September 19th, 1885 of a popular rising in the Balkans which had placed Prince Alexander Battenberg at the head of an enlarged Bulgaria – an eminence from which she correctly guessed that the Tsar would have him removed as soon as possible. Her breathless interest in the British general election, due in December, was mainly focused on finding a Foreign Secretary favourable to her beloved Sandro.

A situation of the wildest improbability had arisen at home. Political parties seemed to be standing on their heads. Parnell, after a secret interview with the Conservative Lord Carnarvon in a shuttered Mayfair house, ordered every Irishman to vote against Gladstone. Gladstone's decision not to fight another election was again revoked; but instead of bidding for Irish support during the last weeks of Salisbury's Government, he bewildered his followers by leaving Salisbury to set the pace on Ireland and Chamberlain to make the running on the home front.

Chamberlain fulfilled this congenial task partly by denouncing his Whig colleagues (Lord Hartington was a 'Rip Van Winkle') and partly by campaigning on an 'Unauthorized Programme'. Not all the reforms of this Radical document were unauthorized by Gladstone, but he had little sympathy with its revolutionary tone. Among its demands were 'Three acres and a cow' for every agricultural worker. This dazzling slogan (originally a Tory jibe) penetrated the royal Household, causing Herr Sahl to remark as the immense cavalcade of Queen Victoria's grandchildren embarked for Osborne, that every royal baby had 'three nurses and a cow'. Hartington and Chamberlain were united only in opposing any separatist measure of Home Rule. The Queen admonished Gladstone to make no speeches, to dissociate himself from

'visionaries' and to realize that *liberalism is not Socialism* &
that *progress* does *not* mean *Revolution*.'[1]

She did not as yet build great hopes on these divisions in
the Liberal ranks. Having decided that the Conservatives
would lose the election, she began to look ahead for a pro-
Sandro Foreign Secretary among the Liberals. Granville had
already been written off as 'weak & sweet as rose water';[2]
Kimberley was hated in foreign courts; Derby could never
make up his mind. 'She asked me what I thought of Spencer,'
wrote Sir Henry to Lady Ponsonby on October 20th, 1885.

> '. . . I suggested Rosebery. This she jumped at. However,
> these are questions for the coming Prime Minister more
> than us. She puts Dilke out of the question altogether.'

Sir Charles Dilke was involved in a divorce case of the kind
which was to arouse all Queen Victoria's instinctive hatred of
the predatory Victorian male:

> 'This poor young Woman,* whom he has ruined & whom
> he seduced, under the most atrocious circumstances is
> driven out of the pale of Society.'[3]

When the election results were complete it appeared that
after all Salisbury could carry on his Government provided the
Irish Nationalists supported him; 'but of course neither the
Govt or opposition can count upon these,' as the Queen truly
observed. While he made his attempt her thoughts turned
once more to a 'middle party' under Goschen. Goschen, however, let her know that he would not join the Tories; though
if Gladstone went in for Home Rule he would 'at once
separate himself from him and hope that others will'.[4]

On December 17th, 1885, the Press, inspired by interviews
with Gladstone's son, Herbert (the 'Hawarden Kite'), carried
sensational headlines that Gladstone indeed meant to 'go in
for Home Rule'.

A long-drawn crisis ensued. For several weeks unstable
political groups formed and dissolved, Chamberlain and
Labouchere meeting Lord Randolph Churchill, Foster denouncing Home Rule with his dying breath, Campbell-

* Virginia Crawford, wife of Donald Crawford, a Liberal MP.

Bannerman (Liberal) publicly suggesting an agreed Irish solution, Gladstone secretly offering, through Arthur Balfour (Conservative), to support a Conservative initiative. No one was more active than the Queen. She laid siege to Mr Goschen through four different go-betweens: Jenner, Salisbury, Lady Ely and Mrs Goschen. When Goschen finally received a letter from the Queen herself he read that all patriotic Liberals must form a coalition to save 'our dear great country' from falling into 'the reckless hands of Mr Gladstone'; a Queen, 'well on in years ... ought not to appeal in vain to British gentlemen, who have known and served her long!'[5]

Having taken off a few days at Christmas to arrange the affairs of a new Dogs' Home, she returned to the political battle in the new year, promising to open Parliament in person if it would be 'of any real use' to the Conservatives and unless there were fog or storm. Accordingly on January 21st, 1886, Prince Albert Victor and Princess Beatrice shared the duty of helping the lame old lady up and down the crimson carpeted steps. She never opened Parliament again. Nor were her efforts after all 'of any real use', for Lord Carnarvon, the Viceroy of Ireland, had already fatally weakened the Government by resigning over Coercion. He was the first person ever to tell Queen Victoria the unflattering truth about Ireland. There was 'no loyalty to the Queen personally,' he reported, but 'a determination to arrange their own affairs, & something would have to be done.'[6]

The Liberal Party were able to do something, at any rate. With the support of Parnell they turned out the Conservative Government.

This coup of January 26th, 1886, proved to be a blow with a paper truncheon. It had been achieved only by a vote on agriculture, not on Ireland, and even so the Liberals were far from unanimous. The Queen was entitled to feel, as she wrote to Lord Salisbury the following day, that only 'a Combination of Moderate & Patriotic men of both sides could last as a Govt.' This cannot excuse her method of working for one.

She refused at first to accept Salisbury's resignation, then tried Goschen again and was only persuaded by the combined efforts of Goschen, Ponsonby and Salisbury himself to send for Gladstone. When Ponsonby warned her that the Liberals were sharply criticizing the delay, she answered defiantly:

'The Queen does not the least care but rather wishes it shd. be known that she has the grtest possible disinclination to take this half crazy & really in many ways ridiculous old man . . .'[7]

Ponsonby tracked down Gladstone on January 29th, going to bed. He was pathetically touched that Her Majesty had summoned him by word of mouth in deference to his age. (Actually she had done so in the hope that at the last minute she might avoid sending for him at all.) As in 1880, he was peremptorily confronted with Her Majesty's terms: foreign policy must not be changed and she would not have Granville for Foreign Minister. 'This is most painful,' exclaimed Gladstone, piteously clasping his hands: 'I know the general feeling; it is most unjust towards my best colleague; but I cannot say the Queen's views come unexpectedly upon me.'[8] What might have come upon him unexpectedly was the fact that the Queen's terms had been drawn up in collusion with Salisbury.

Lord Salisbury, as she blandly noted in a memorandum of January 28th, had suggested whom she should accept and whom reject, ending with the lordly remark that Rosebery 'would do very well' for Foreign Secretary, 'though he was inexperienced'. The day before Rosebery kissed hands, Salisbery further advised her to coach him in statesmanship: Rosebery should 'bring as little as possible before the Cabinet', arranging everything with Gladstone and herself. 'Nothing was ever settled satisfactorily in the Cabinet.'[9] The Queen duly followed Salisbury's instructions. She was also encouraged by Salisbury to consult Goschen, an active politician, on the false analogy of her consultations with Wellington and Lansdowne, two retired elder statesmen, in the past. Goschen himself pointed out the fallacy.

The Queen and Salisbury officially parted on February 8th with great anguish on her side and an exchange of gifts – his portrait by Watts for her; an enamelled photograph, a bronze bust and the offer of a dukedom (declined on grounds of expense) for him – but such parting gifts were scarcely necessary in view of their close and continuous contact throughout Gladstone's Ministry. Only one or two examples of this practice need be mentioned here; the rest as they occur.

On February 19th Queen Victoria gave Salisbury a lively account of Gladstone's failure to enlist a complete royal Household: the Mistress of the Robes would have to remain in abeyance as no Liberal duchess would accept! (In a letter to the Prince of Wales she described Granville's efforts to foist on her first a duchess who had fits and then a mere marchioness.) A Bedchamber crisis could not thwart Gladstone as it had Peel; nevertheless, resignations from the Household could and did harass Gladstone throughout the battle for Home Rule. 'A constant *sputtering* of resignations,' as he himself said, 'would be almost ludicrous.'[10] If the Queen did not actually encourage the sputtering (she often found it harassed her as much as him) she openly spoke of it as 'patriotic'.

In March and April the Queen sent Salisbury copies of letters from Liberal Ministers and various reports on the prospects of a Liberal breakaway. From May 7th onwards, when the struggle over Home Rule was rising to its climax, she forwarded to Salisbury copies of all Gladstone's important letters to herself, carefully instructing him to send them back.* Her own replies to Gladstone were often included. This stepping up in the correspondence was perhaps due to Lord Salisbury having told Rowton that he was completely in the dark as to Gladstone's intentions. Through the Queen's secret activities Lord Salisbury was henceforth kept thoroughly informed, without risking the kind of inter-party consultations which Gladstone still desired but which Salisbury instinctively disliked.

A letter from the Queen to Salisbury on May 20th shows signs of understandable exhaustion: 'She is very tired ... Pray excuse this very badly written letter. The Queen has

---

* Some extracts from this batch of letters are published in the *Letters of Queen Victoria*, edited by G. E. Buckle, III. 1. 119–24.

609

much to write.'[11] Nothing in her constitutional position required her to tire herself by writing to Lord Salisbury at all, rather the reverse; but the success of her intervention over the Reform Bill had gone to her head. Keeping the various leaders in touch through the Crown seemed the order of the day, and when Salisbury made use of her new taste for political action, she was too much inflamed by hatred of Home Rule to see that bi-partisanship had changed into bias.

The unconstitutional nature of this correspondence should not blind anyone to the innocuousness of its results. Salisbury's patent duty was to lay down his pen after the first letter, having referred the Queen sternly to her new Prime Minister. He did the next best thing: gave her temperate advice. Nor did Queen Victoria's machinations hasten Gladstone's defeat by one hour. It was brought about, as we shall see, by Joseph Chamberlain, a member of Gladstone's own Cabinet.

The Queen observed Gladstone closely during his first audience at Osborne on February 1st. He came in looking very pale; 'there was a momentary pause, and he sighed deeply.' She thought that much of his previous radicalism had evaporated but all the intense earnestness was there, as of old; indeed, he seemed to have acquired an almost fanatical belief that he was 'sacrificing himself for Ireland'. He did not stay for luncheon but left by the next boat, 'dreadfully agitated and nervous'.[12]

Lord Hartington had declined to enter a Cabinet pledged to any kind of Home Rule and the Queen counted on him to form a coalition with Salisbury, carrying into it his 'Liberal Unionist' friends. She reported to Salisbury that she had seen Hartington's written refusal to join Gladstone's Government 'which was *very firm & uncompromising*'.[13] Among those who did agree to serve in Gladstone's Cabinet were one or two bright spots. Rosebery, she told the Princess Royal, 'is our way of thinking' and his connection with the Rothschilds* 'is also a security'.[14] She prided herself on keeping Dilke out

* Rosebery had married an heiress, Hannah, daughter of Baron Meyer de Rothschild, in 1878.

altogether; on keeping Ripon out of the India Office because of alleged weakness, and Childers out of the War Office, which would have enraged 'the Army' (ie the Duke of Cambridge); and on appointing instead Campbell-Bannerman, 'a good strong Scotchman'. A place for Childers was found at the Home Office where he almost at once had to deal with a riot in Trafalgar Square. The rioters were not the 'deserving unemployed', the Queen hastened to explain to her daughter, but 'horrid thieves & a few Socialists'.[15]

She had let John Morley and Chamberlain into the Cabinet on Salisbury's advice to prevent them from becoming martyrs; in any case Morley as a Free Thinker, 'in fact a Jacobin', would scarcely make a popular Secretary of State for Catholic Ireland. Queen Victoria shared the universal English delusion that Ireland was ruled entirely by priests. Chamberlain she had called Gladstone's 'evil genius'; she did not yet know that the feelings of the terrible Radical towards his leader had undergone a change.

In the summer of 1885 Chamberlain's efforts to satisfy Ireland with local, self-governing councils had earned him the violent hostility of Parnell's extremist followers. If Chamberlain visited Ireland they threatened to duck him in a horse-pond or bog hole. From that moment Chamberlain was through with Parnell. When in February 1886 Chamberlain temporarily subscribed to Gladstone's Irish policy – vaguely defined as an 'examination' of Home Rule – it was in the private belief that he might soon be looking for a bog hole in which to dump it.

Gladstone cared little what Chamberlain believed. He told Harcourt that he would go forward with Home Rule if need be without Hartington or Chamberlain, '– without anybody!'[16]

The new Ministers met on February 15th. For the next four weeks Chamberlain was left to kick his heels in deep suspicion and discontent while the aged wizard worked furiously to complete his 'examination'. There was no need for the Queen to urge Gladstone to hurry, though she did so. In the incredibly short space of just over a month Gladstone had ready his first Home Rule Bill. It contained a vast land scheme to buy out the landlords, a draft for political self-government and no coercion. Parnell accepted it. Rather tactlessly, Gladstone pointed out to the Queen that the astounding speed, scale and intricacy of his Bill made even Peel's famous Corn Law reform look pretty small. The Queen was more startled by Rosebery's news that Chamberlain and Trevelyan would resign. Trevelyan she knew disliked the Irish Nationalists for he had recently told her that he would prefer not to meet any of them 'alone in a wood'; but a fierce Radical like Chamberlain – 'how could it be?'[17]

The decisive Cabinet meeting took place on March 26th, 1886. Chamberlain came determined to be conciliatory. He asked Gladstone whether, among other things, under his Bill the Irish Members of Parliament would no longer sit at Westminster where they could at least be controlled? Without any attempt to persuade, Gladstone answered, 'Yes'.

'Then I resign.' Chamberlain and Trevelyan walked out.

Let them go, thought Gladstone, convinced that he could do without them.

On the same day that the Liberal Party broke in two, Queen Victoria was busy with Goschen thinking out a name for the alliance which in her imagination had already won the next election. For its members to stand as Liberal or Tory 'would never do'. She suggested 'Loyalists' or 'Constitutionalists'. Since Salisbury would not serve under Hartington if Chamberlain joined the alliance, she made the neat proposal that Chamberlain should be permitted to unite with Hartington only for the purpose of opposing Home Rule – 'in which he – Goschen agreed.'[18] Her ideas were submitted to Salisbury the following week and received a cautious assent. As for Gladstone's scheme to buy out the landlords, costly as it was and harmful to England, she felt sure it would not satisfy the Irish.

Notwithstanding Queen Victoria's scepticism the Nationalists cheered loudly when Gladstone introduced his Bill to Parliament on April 8th, 1886, in a speech that lasted three hours and twenty minutes. Such phenomenal vigour at his age caused universal wonder. Even Gladstone himself was surprised that his voice had behaved so well. Mrs Gladstone cherished him more tenderly than ever; it was said that rather than disturb him while he was sleeping, she would tie knots in his night-shirt to remind her of things to tell him next morning; sometimes on waking he found himself literally tied up in knots.

Next day Chamberlain opened the attack on the Bill.

For two months the battle raged. Ponsonby feared that the Queen's excessive eagerness to promote a coalition against Home Rule would defeat its own object. Nevertheless he, and sometimes his wife, kept her in touch with each move in the unity campaign. A huge meeting was held at the Opera House on April 15th where Lord Fife, Lord Salisbury, Lord Hartington and Mr Goschen thundered from the same platform. Lady Ponsonby drove to the meeting in a royal carriage (which she was warned not to park too near the doors) and immediately it was over, telegraphed from the Haymarket a glowing account to her husband for the Queen. The telegram reached Windsor at dawn in time to be placed on the royal breakfast table.* The Queen was in transports. Two days later she sent Salisbury a secret call to organize many more meetings like the one which had gone off so 'admirably' at the Opera House. When she was told that the Liberal Party had fought the Conservatives too recently to make a formal alliance at present, she wrote again denouncing the Liberals for their 'narrow, timid, unpatriotic objections'. This was followed on May 5th by a broad hint to Salisbury that he himself was keeping too quiet. The Queen wanted more and more oratory and doubtless would not have stuck even at the 'stump' variety in such a cause.

For her part, she had done her best to sustain the image of an expanding Empire by opening the Indian and Colonial Exhibition in person on May 4th. In two respects only did she fall short of Lord Rosebery's hopes. Her romantic-minded

* This unsigned telegram was tentatively attributed to Lord Rowton by the editor of Queen Victoria's *Letters*, III. L. 105. One phrase in the telegram, 'Lord Fife tiresome', could hardly have fallen from Rowton's sycophantic pen. Lord Fife was soon to marry the Prince of Wales's daughter, Princess Louise.

Foreign Secretary had begged her to invest this imperial occasion with all conceivable pomp. 'With all the pomp you like,' she replied, 'as long as I don't have to wear a low dress.'[19] Nor would she break the rule of widowhood and wear a crown out of doors. In vain Rosebery urged that great Empires were symbolized by crowns not bonnets. Bonnet it must be. Queen Victoria's instinct to mother her dark-skinned children rather than to dazzle them was a true one.

Meanwhile Gladstone was considering whether by redrafting the Bill he might not satisfy Chamberlain and heal the split. The Queen feared any compromise. 'The [new] proposals are incomprehensible,' she wrote angrily to Salisbury on May 9th enclosing as usual Gladstone's letter, and in her Journal: 'What a peculiar idea! trimming & balancing will please no one ...' She was right, in that it did not please Chamberlain. On the same date Salisbury received a note saying that any message for the Queen while she was in Liverpool on the 12th opening an International Exhibition should be sent 'under cover' to Lady Ely at Fischer's Hotel, Bond Street. Before leaving for Liverpool the Queen dashed off yet another letter to Salisbury (May 10th) frantically warning him against Gladstone's latest expedient:

'There is one *vital point* wh she hopes Lord Salisbury, Lord Hartington & Mr Goschen will *fully consider* & wh must *not* be *tolerated*. It is the Withdrawal of the Bill, for Mr Gladstone to bring it forward again next year ... Pray advise me how to protest agst such a fearful danger & *possibility* & consult *together* HOW this contingency can be stopped.'

'Pray advise me' – a strange thing for the Sovereign to say to the Leader of the Opposition.

The Queen returned from 'a never-to-be-forgotten' success in Liverpool to find political excitement rising and Gladstone for the first time mentioning the possibility of defeat. The interminable debate was expected to end in a week. Queen Victoria had never doubted that the Bill would be killed, and she now privately invited Salisbury to concert with her a plan for making sure that the killing would be followed by a change of government. Salisbury sent under cover of Lady Ely a detailed answer to the Queen's main question: if Gladstone asked for a dissolution should she grant his request?

After two pages of political analysis Salisbury changed from black to red ink and approached the problem in relation to the burning question of Her Majesty's health. Assuming that she left as usual for Balmoral, a change of government without a dissolution would involve the 'novel' situation of all her Ministers being dispersed either on board railway trains or in the wilds of Aberdeenshire. Salisbury summed up for a dissolution: it would certainly seem more fair, probably result in the return of a Conservative government and cause no interruption to Her Majesty's summer holiday.[20]

Queen Victoria replied at length. She too favoured a dissolution, but if Gladstone did not ask for one she would not break her holiday to come south again so soon:

'She had *not* been abroad – she has not had any holiday as other people can & has exerted herself more than she has for the last 24 years!'

It might be 'novel' as Lord Salisbury said, for the new Ministers to kiss hands at Balmoral '– but in these days of *telegrams, telephones & changes* – it cd easily be arranged – if it *came* to the *worst*.'[21]

In her state of nervous tension all unwelcome news assumed immense proportions. She heard that huge baits were being offered to Hartington. Would he stand firm? Gladstone's motives, which she had respected at the beginning of the month, were now vehemently impugned, for he had stooped to use that horrible man Labouchere to try to catch Mr Chamberlain . . .' Instead of leaving Gladstone to be defeated, 'busybodies' were still trying to get him to withdraw the Bill. Goschen, with whom she conversed for $5\frac{1}{2}$ hours, was much discouraged by 'the stupid short-sighted clinging to a Leader!'[22]

She was still waiting impatiently at Windsor. On May 20th, having decided not to stay beyond the 27th whatever happened, she wrote again to the Leader of the Opposition to make sure that she understood his wishes:

'The Queen relies on Lord Salisbury telling her *if* after all he wishes her to refuse Mr Gladstone if he asks for a Dissolution ... she has *now decided* to *go* on Wednesday to Scotland for she does require it very much & will not be kept here as a Slave of the H. of C. – & the GOM.'[23]

Just before she left, a monster petition against Home Rule signed by 20,000 women of Ulster arrived at Windsor. It went twice round the Corridor. As for the men of Ulster, Lord Randolph Churchill incited them with his notorious slogan: 'Ulster will fight and Ulster will be right.' Queen Victoria was shocked, though when Gladstone compared Churchill to Smith O'Brien and the revolutionaries of 1848, she was more shocked still.

An 'excellent telegram' from Ponsonby reached her on the 31st at Balmoral. Chamberlain and 44 of his Radical followers had decided to vote against the Second Reading after a dramatic meeting in Committee Room 15. Goschen sent her a jubilant message from the House. 'This ensures its defeat.'

At last the supreme moment came. Gladstone spoke with all the inspiration of his genius and his cause. His closing words are still remembered:

'Ireland stands at your bar, expectant, hopeful, almost suppliant ... think, I beseech you, think well, think wisely, think, not for the moment, but for the years that are to come.'

The division was taken at 1.15 AM on June 8th, 1886. A combination of Conservatives, Whigs and Radicals defeated the Bill by thirty votes. Thirty was an appropriate number in the circumstances, for the embittered Irish were soon to feel that the Radical who they believed had betrayed them was a regular Judas. 'There goes the man who killed Home Rule,' said Parnell as Chamberlain went through the 'no' lobby.

After a disturbed night the Queen awoke to hear the glad news. 'Cannot help feeling relieved, and think it is best for the interests of the country.'[24] The restrained note in her rejoicing was perhaps due to a twinge of conscience. She knew well and had often pointed out to her foreign relatives that it was her constitutional duty to support the government of the day. For five months in 1886 she had done the opposite.

Gladstone asked for a dissolution and the Queen granted it on condition that it took place at once. She offered him an earldom. He declined: even so, it seemed impossible that this white-faced, haggard old man, with a voice that often gave him trouble and eyesight, like her own, beginning to fail, should ever lead the Commons again.

Twice the Queen advised Lord Salisbury to be '*very conciliatory*' as well as firm towards Ireland during his election campaign. Then she resigned herself to a month of anxious waiting for the results. Her Journal began again to deal with subjects other than Home Rule; on June 14th, for instance, she had leisure to be shocked by the news of a royal suicide. The mad King Ludwig II of Bavaria who had once talked to her with his eyes tightly shut, was discovered drowned with his doctor in Lake Starnberg. The Queen telegraphed for 'details' and, as the head of the world's most efficient Court, commented brusquely, 'surely the whole thing must have been very badly managed.'[25]

The elections showed that the temporary revolt against Beaconsfield's imperialism was over. Europe had begun in earnest its race for Africa during Gladstone's second Ministry. Bismarck's colonial acquisitions together with Majuba and Gordon's death convinced the teeming populations of English and Scottish towns that they needed a strong Tory government to obtain for Britain her share of the loot. 'Primrose Day' had been inaugurated on April 19th, 1886, Disraeli's birthday, to fan imperialist ardour. At Osborne everyone was ordered to wear a primrose, even the Liberal Lady Ampthill (though with a little encouragement from Ponsonby she threw it away). Voluntarily to let Ireland go did not fit in with the country's rapacious mood.

Lord Randolph Churchill helped to annihilate Home Rule by calling it the dream of 'an old man in a hurry'. When the votes were counted Gladstone and Parnell between them controlled 276 seats and Salisbury, Hartington and Chamberlain

394. To the faithful, such a blow at the GOM seemed incredible.

'The elections are beyond man's understanding,' said a visitor to Mrs Gladstone at Hawarden; 'the course of events can only be guided by the One above.'

'Oh! yes – and if you wait he'll be down to tea in five minutes.'

The Queen was sorry to hear that her ally Mr Goschen had been beaten in Edinburgh – 'my dear Scotch behave like fools'[26] – but Dilke's loss of his Chelsea seat was 'a great thing'. The intemperate letters of condolence which Gladstone launched from Hawarden to his defeated followers – 'monstrous, wicked, socialistic letters' – deepened her horror of the GOM.

'For long I stood up for his Motives, but now they are clearly actuated by Vanity, ambition & malice & shew signs of madness.'[27]

The Cambridge circle believed that Gladstone was 'quite mad and always had a keeper in attendance'.[28]

Gladstone tendered his resignation on July 20th, 1886, and the Queen accepted it briefly. He was pale and she nervous during their final meeting on the 30th, but as Ireland was not mentioned at all it went off amicably. Gladstone's diary recorded that the Queen had become 'seriously warped' since 1874, while hers made no reference, as in 1874, to his loyalty to the Crown. Sir Henry Ponsonby received instead of the Queen the full force of Gladstonian eloquence on the subject of Home Rule, so that it was with difficulty that he got the old man off in time to catch his boat. On August 3rd the Liberal Cabinet came to give up their seals. The Queen thought they looked ashamed of themselves.

The Tories came an hour later, among them Lord Randolph Churchill, whose appointment as Chancellor of the Exchequer had been greeted by Queen Victoria with an exclamation mark. He was known to stand for rigid economy which she feared he might apply to royal grants. The question of claiming grants for all her grandchildren on marriage had exercised both the late Governments. In the end she was advised to be content with allowances for the Prince of Wales's children only.

Lord Randolph's passion for economy produced one of the only two upheavals during the remainder of that year. He resigned on the Service Estimates in what the Queen called 'a very improper manner'. He was dining with Her Majesty on December 21st, confidently explaining the Government's plans for the forthcoming Session. He then went up to bed. Queen Victoria described to her eldest daughter what happened next:

> 'That vy night in my House, on Windsor paper he deliberately wrote his resignation & sent it to Ld Salisbury, who did not consider it (I believe) as final & wrote to him again upon wh he sends a final resignation wh Ld Salisbury recd at his Ball on Wednesday night at 1!'[29]

The Windsor paper was clearly an outrage and the resignation 'unpatriotic' because it might well bring down the Government and let Gladstone in again. She recommended the immediate appointment of Goschen as Chancellor in Churchill's place. Churchill had not expected Salisbury to take even his second note as 'final'. Ruefully he confessed to the flaw in his strategy: 'I forgot Goschen.'

The tempestuous career of Prince Alexander of Bulgaria provided Queen Victoria with her dominant interest between August and December 1886. The Bulgarians' vigour in repulsing a Russian-inspired invasion during the previous autumn had redoubled her faith in the brilliant future of 'dear brave Sandro'. But on August 22nd, 1886, she received the devastating news that Sandro had been taken prisoner the day before and deposed. The Queen guessed at once who had perpetrated the crime. 'It is these Russian fiends,' she telegraphed to Salisbury. Throughout the international crisis, which lasted for just over a fortnight, she relieved her feelings in a hail of execrations and exhortations.

> 'Russian fiends ... the stepping-stone to getting Constantinople ... intriguing right & left ... a slap in *our*

face ... checkmated and duped ... sickening treachery ... Russia *must* be unmasked ... *Russian villainy* ... not one minute must be lost ... we must stand by him ... Russia must not triumph ... the Paul-like Tsar*[30] ...'

The Battenberg brothers stood together, Francis Joseph sharing the kidnapped Prince's fantastic journey down the Danube, Louis going to meet them at Lemberg where they were released and Liko encouraging his mother-in-law's efforts to rouse Europe. No one else raised a finger. Prince Alexander got as far as returning to Sofia at the beginning of September but after a narrow escape from being murdered in the Cathedral, he abdicated. The Bulgarians secured Prince Ferdinand of Coburg in his place. Despite the Coburg name and the fact that Ferdinand was a son of Queen Victoria's youthful playmate, dear merry 'Gusti' who had been sent by King Leopold in 1839 to pave the way for Albert,† she dismissed him as reactionary, sickly, effeminate and a fop. Though clever he would not last in Sofia a year. Not for the first time she had allowed her overwhelming emotions to affect her judgement. 'Foxy Ferdy' lasted until 1918.

At least the Queen did not allow herself to ignore the repercussions on Prince Alexander's romance. Within a week of the kidnapping she was tactfully suggesting to the Princess Royal, 'young Vicky's' mother, that 'an engagement without hope would not be quite right towards Sandro'. Britain's impotence to intervene on Prince Sandro's behalf she put down to Gladstone's 'dreadful Govt from 80 to 85 wh lost us all our power ...'[31]

On November 23rd a joyful event took place, the birth of Princess Beatrice's first child. 'Was off & on with dear Beatrice during the night.' The Queen received her baby grandson wrapped in flannel from the monthly nurse at 5 o'clock in the morning. 'Your Majesty must have him first.' Exhausted, she returned to her room to find the moon still shining brightly;

---

* The Tsar Paul I was said to have been insane. He was assassinated in 1801, while planning to invade India in alliance with Napoleon I.

† See p. 157.

half an hour later there was 'a splendid sunrise'.[32]

On December 8th the exiled Prince Alexander arrived in England and was received by the Queen at Windsor with a welcome which had only once been rivalled, and that was when she had greeted Prince Albert on the same staircase forty-seven years ago. Sandro was handsomer than ever, though crushed and sad; gentle, calm, dispassionate and so wise. He still hoped to marry 'young Vicky' some day. Princess Louise told her mother on the sacred December 14th that she too had fallen under the Battenberg spell: 'I don't know what it is, Sandro reminds me of Papa.' Fervently the Queen agreed. It was his 'wonderfully handsome' appearance, his dignity, modesty and that complete absence of bitterness which had been so characteristic of Albert. 'I think he may stand next to beloved Papa . . .'[33]

If these months were not exactly the 'splendid sunrise' of little Prince 'Drino's' birthday, at least there was a glow in the sky. The Queen spent the last day of the old year in thankfulness for Princess Beatrice's safe delivery and hoped that 'all present anxieties be dispelled'. Ponsonby on the same day was already absorbed in official preparations for Queen Victoria's approaching Jubilee. What should he and Mary give her? She would like 'a made thing' better than 'an old thing'. Ponsonby was right. The Queen, far from moving along a traditional road, was about to break new ground.

CHAPTER XXXIII

THE JUBILEE BONNET
1887–91

A STATE TRIUMPH and a family tragedy absorbed Queen Victoria during 1887. She left politics in Lord Salisbury's 'experienced hands', to borrow Gladstone's gracious phrase once applied to herself.

Home Rule was still the issue and the Irish Nationalists, forced to remain at Westminster, buffeted the Mother of Parliaments throughout Jubilee Year. 'Shameful' were the scenes in the Chamber according to the Queen's Journal, and 'shameful' the Plan of Campaign initiated in Ireland to fight a new era of the big stick. Otherwise her expletives were reserved, as we shall see, for Germans rather than Irishmen. She let pass without undue excitement the publication by *The Times* in 1887 of an alleged facsimile letter from Parnell condoning the Phoenix Park murders; and when a journalist, Richard Pigott, eventually confessed to having forged it and then committed suicide, thus vindicating Parnell, the Queen was chiefly concerned lest the drama should help the Liberals to reunite. Lord Hartington must prevent his followers from 'drifting over to the GOM, to keep whom out once for all, seems the one gt object of all the wise & moderate Statesmen'.

Over the Cabinet reconstruction after Lord Randolph Churchill's resignation the Queen gave Salisbury little trouble. She refused to have Lord Cross moved but agreed sadly that another old friend, Lord Iddesleigh, must be superseded at the Foreign Office. When he fell dead outside the Prime Minister's door she recorded her displeasure at the callous way it had been done. The tragedy stirred in Lord Salisbury a rare tumult of emotion: 'Politics is a cursed profession!'

The prospect of the Jubilee seemed to the Queen hardly more inviting than politics to Lord Salisbury. How could she welcome an orgy of 'hustle & bustle'? It was due to the Prince of Wales that her imagination was first stirred. His New Year present to her was a Jubilee inkstand: a crown formed the lid while on the inside the royal face gazed benignly into a pool of ink – 'very pretty & useful'. Jubilee apart, it was a gay New Year thanks to the Battenbergs, who organized an impromptu dance, old Sahl turning the barrel-organ and Lady Ely hopping about like a two-year-old.

February opened with an unpleasant surprise from Germany. Two grandchildren, Prince Henry of Prussia and Princess Irene of Hesse, who were doubly related, became engaged; if there had to be a double relationship it would have been better for William to have married Ella.* Ella's strength of character would have been excellent for 'Master Willy'; Dona merely made him 'a submissive blind wife, wh I cannot call "excellent" '.[1]

The Queen's rheumatism was so painful that she resumed her massage and the backache from which she suffered during a drawing-room may explain her acid comment on March 3rd: not 'many goodlooking people'. There were shortly to be some lucky people, however, at drawing-rooms: the Queen insisted on modifying the Prince Consort's strict Court regulations, in order that 'poor ladies' who were the innocent parties in divorce cases might share her Jubilee. Before the end of Jubilee Year she had even asked Lord Salisbury if innocent foreign divorcees might also be excluded from the ban. Her Prime Minister advised against: 'It is on account of the risk of admitting American women of light character ...'[2] Two days after the first drawing-room she was horrified to find that she had fallen asleep in her chair after tea – 'a very rare thing for me'.[3]

It was no good feeling exhausted so early in the year. Rehearsals had to begin. Remissions of sentences in honour of the Jubilee had to be signed. She remitted all but one – for cruelty to animals, 'one of the worst traits in human nature'.[4] All over the Empire prisoners were released in her honour. A grateful ex-convict from Agra sent her a vast acrostic in Hindustani and English of which this was one verse:

* 'Ella' was Princess Elizabeth of Hesse with whom Prince William had fallen hopelessly in love. She married the Grand Duke Serge of Russia.

Her Majesty's name is Victoria, Good God!
The Indian word for Victoria is Fath
And it happens that my district is called Fathpur.
This coincidence is marvellously auspicious.

Countless telegrams from the East had to be read:

Empress of Hindoostan, Head of all Kings and Rulers, and King of all Kings, who is one in a Hundred, is Her Majesty Queen Victoria.

At Mithi in Sind the authorities celebrated by opening 'The Queen Victoria Jubilee Burial and Burning Ground'. From Madras a poem in Sanskrit welcomed railways and steamers as 'celestial messengers' from the Queen–Empress. In Mandalay, Jubilee robes of saffron were presented to distinguished Buddhist monks. In Singapore, extra rice was given to hospital patients including, by the Queen-Empress's command, lepers; the Colony wished her a reign of ten thousand years.

Jubilee medals had to be dispatched and Jubilee coins examined; endless lists of visitors had to be made. If the Prince of Wales had not been 'very kind & helpful' she could not have got through. As it was, she had practically lost her voice by the time she laid the foundation stone on March 23rd of the new Law Courts in Birmingham. Afterwards Joseph Chamberlain informed Ponsonby that his people had not received their money's worth. Why was the Household Cavalry absent from the procession? Simplicity was all right in a Republic, explained the ex-Republican leader, but a Sovereign must bring splendour. On future provincial occasions the Queen brought her Household Cavalry.

A holiday in Cannes and Aix took her mind off the Jubilee for a few weeks. At Aix she made a conquest of the Chartreuse monks, among them an English-born monk of twenty-three: 'I am proud to be a subject of your Majesty,' he managed to enunciate with difficulty, kneeling and kissing her hand. Lady Ely whispered hoarsely that he had been immured against his will. The Queen's highly Protestant entourage put leading questions to the Fathers which they answered with bland smiles.

'Is it true that you have a monk here,' asked Dr Reid, 'who was a Russian General and murdered three wives?'

'I can't say about the murders, but as he has never married he can't have murdered his wives.'[5]

The *curé* of Aix later congratulated the Queen on the visit: '*Votre Majesté est une Reine avec des vertus austères.*' The Queen had to smile.[6]

'We wish you were our Sovereign,' cried the French peasants, offering her flowers.

She was back at Windsor by the end of April. Urgent problems now had to be settled. What should be done, for instance, with the surplus from the Women's Jubilee gift of £75,000? (Part of it was already earmarked for yet another statue of the Prince Consort.) Jenner suggested supporting emigration, where the Queen could assist people personally; Ponsonby wanted a Committee of advice graced by Miss Nightingale and Mrs Fawcett, to shield the Queen. He himself hoped they would help nursing. The Queen's Jubilee Nursing Institute was duly founded, though not without some scratching and screeching between the great Whig and Tory ladies involved.

A few disagreeable experiences remained to be undergone before the great day. There was the business of bringing Prince Arthur home from India. She noted bitterly that a private soldier could get leave whereas the Queen's son needed a special Bill. When she opened the People's Palace in the East End of London on May 14th the gala effect was 'damped' by sporadic outbreaks of 'a horrid noise', as she told Lord Salisbury, '(*quite* new to the Queen's ears) "booing" she believes it is called.'[7] They explained that it was only Socialists '& the worst Irish'.

Worse than the worst Irish was the behaviour of the German Court to her daughter. The Crown Prince Frederick William had been sick for several months with a throat infection – cancer, asserted his enemies. On May 19th a cypher telegram arrived from the Princess Royal. After a frantic hunt for the key it was revealed that the German doctors wished to perform a tracheotomy but were in favour of first consulting the English surgeon, Dr Morrell Mackenzie. Desperately the Princess Royal implored her mother to send out this great specialist who would surely save Fritz from the terrible operation. Queen Victoria immediately questioned her own doctors; that Mackenzie was clever they agreed, but he was grasping; the profession disliked him. She sent him to her daughter with this warning.

Meanwhile, the dying Crown Prince had decided to make his daughter happy by sanctioning her engagement to Sandro. The Empress Augusta thereupon threatened to have both her and her mother disinherited. Queen Victoria choked with rage:

'*Very private* – I cannot find words to express my horror & indignation at the wicked old & young´ ——'s ——'s conduct abt poor dear Moretta . . .'[8]

She vowed she would stop this outrageous treatment of 'a Princess of Grt Britain & Ireland'; in any case, she had a small sum invested in Germany which she would gladly give to her persecuted granddaughter. Thank Heaven Dr Mackenzie had overthrown the diagnosis of cancer and dear Fritz was coming to England for the Jubilee after all. Here he would be treated for hundreds of guineas instead of thousands.

'BUCKINGHAM PALACE 20th June.
The day has come and I am alone, though surrounded by many dear children . . . 50 years today since I came to the Throne! God has mercifully sustained me through many great trials and sorrows.'[9]

She had awakened at Windsor to a brilliant morning, exultingly hailed by her subjects as 'Queen's weather', though it was devoid of that snap and sparkle which she liked. Breakfast was under the trees at Frogmore; there was nowhere private to sit out of doors at the Castle. After breakfast she drove through festive crowds down the short, steep hill to Windsor station and from Paddington through the Park to Buckingham Palace. There she found a magnificent present from Sanders, the orchid growers: a bouquet of cattleyas and odontoglossums four feet high, the letters VRI being formed by scarlet epidendrums. Assembled for luncheon in her honour were a host of Royalties no less exotic. In the evening she sat among over fifty Royal and Serene Highnesses with the King of Denmark on her right, the King of Greece on her left and the King of the Belgians opposite. She described it simply as 'a large family dinner'; the gold plate, she admitted, looked splendid. 'At length, feeling very tired, I slipped away.'

Next day, June 21st, the Thanksgiving Service took place in Westminster Abbey. Everything reminded her of 1851 and the Great Exhibition. Now it was a greater exhibition, an imperial one, though her arrangements were a characteristic mixture of magnificence and simplicity. She turned down the glass coach flat, but had six of the famous creams to draw her open landau with an escort of Indian cavalry. Then came the males of her great family*: three sons, five sons-in-law and nine grandsons. Cheers were loudest for the voiceless Crown Prince, a golden bearded Charlemagne clothed in white and silver with the German eagle on his helmet. Queen Victoria agreed with her people that dear Fritz outshone all the rest.

She had obstinately refused as usual to wear the crown and robes of State. When in desperation her children sent in the Princess of Wales to make her change her mind, this favourite daughter-in-law came out precipitately: 'I never was so snubbed.' What did it matter if Lord Halifax had said people wanted 'gilding for their money', or if Mr Chamberlain thought a Sovereign should be grand, or Lord Rosebery that the Empire should be ruled by a sceptre not a bonnet? Or even that the Cambridges' coachman 'deplored' her driving to the Abbey 'with a *bonnet on*'†? Bonnet it should still be. A very special bonnet, however. It gleamed with springy white lace and diamonds. All the ladies were bonneted also accord-

* A court case concerning family trusts in 1961 established that on April 25th, 1944 Queen Victoria had 194 known living descendants.

† Ben Cooper, until fairly recently the gamekeeper at Cliveden, remembered Queen Victoria frequently driving over alone from Windsor and taking tea with the housekeeper on the terrace. She came, he recalled, in a one-horse carriage wearing a bonnet 'that couldn't have cost 5s.'

ing to printed instructions: 'Ladies in ... Bonnets and Long High Dresses without Mantel.' Slowly she proceeded up the Abbey to the strains of a Handel march. At the altar she was able to look round, picking out the Royalties, Household, Members of Parliament. A merciful Providence prevented her from recognizing Gladstone, 'though he was there'.

'I sat *alone* (oh! without my beloved husband, for whom this would have been such a proud day!)'; but the congregation gave thanks to the music of her husband's *Te Deum* and the choir sang his anthem, *Gotha*. When the Princesses came up to kiss the Queen's hand and receive their mother's embrace, it was the Prince's favourite child whom she clasped longest.

Back to the Palace where there were still Jubilee brooches and pins to distribute to her daughters and sons. (Later in the year, the Duke of Cambridge got a pencil case in the shape of a Field-Marshal's baton.) Luncheon began at four, followed by a march past of blue-jackets which she watched from a balcony and present-giving in the ballroom. 'I felt quite exhausted ... & ready to faint, so I got into my rolling chair and was rolled back to my room.' More telegrams to open, the children to kiss good night, another dinner-party – still the great day was not over.

Her old dresser, Skerrett, who had ordered her Coronation robes forty-nine years ago, was now ninety-four, so another dresser had to produce the sparkling Jubilee dinner-dress, embroidered with silver roses, thistles and shamrocks. After dinner the Indian Princes and Corps Diplomatique swam past her in a shimmering mist: 'I was half dead with fatigue ...' Again she 'slipped away', this time for good. At 10 o'clock rockets began to shoot up from over six hundred hills. Her attendants rolled her into the Chinese Room to watch the fireworks, but the golden tide was breaking out of sight, so that she had an excuse to leave. The roar of London kept her awake for a little and then lulled her to sleep.

Forty-nine years ago she had returned from her Coronation ready, not to faint, but to give her spaniel, Dash, his bath. Yet Thomas Carlyle, the biographer of strong men like Cromwell and Frederick the Great, had failed to perceive the vein of

628

iron in Victoria's character. She was like a tiny canary, he said, gazing in terror at a thunderstorm. Queen Victoria was sometimes like a thunderstorm, never a canary. As she drove to her Coronation she had seemed too young even to choose a bonnet.

Since that day she had chosen a husband; husbands for her daughters and wives for her sons; ministers, prelates, an imperial creed, a religion, a way of life; and as her sign-manual she had chosen a bonnet.

Next day was dedicated to the rising generation. First the poor, in Hyde Park. There were tents, six military bands and a bun, milk and Jubilee mug for 30,000 schoolchildren. As a huge balloon rose from the grass a little girl cried out, 'Look! there's Queen Victoria going up to Heaven!' Then the rich, in the Quadrangle at Windsor. Hundreds of Etonians sang their school song and when she said in her clear, musical voice, 'I thank you very much,' the applause was deafening.

Another Jubilee dream of her own was fulfilled on June 23rd. The Queen found herself the excited possessor of two Indian servants.

Abdul Karim was twenty-four, slim and clever; Mahomet, fat and smiling. Abdul's father, the Queen understood, practised as a doctor in Agra. Abdul studied incessantly. The Queen bubbled with enthusiasm. She engaged an English tutor for him who was disgusted to find that his pupil was not a prince but a servant. Abdul Karim soon turned the tables on this small-minded pedagogue by acquiring a much grander pupil of his own – the Queen. She wrote in her Journal on August 3rd:

'I am learning a few words of Hindustani to speak to my servants. It is a great interest to me for both the language and the people, I have naturally never come into real contact with before.'

Indian curries, cooked for her by Abdul, expanded the contact in a delightful way.

In the golden haze of the Jubilee, Abdul Karim stirred

once more that same royal imagination which had magnified the virtues of John Brown. Queen Victoria could not keep a good servant down and her Golden Jubilee, for all its glory, had to answer for some curious aberrations both on the personal and the national front. The Queen's instinct to draw dark-skinned peoples into her fold, banishing racial prejudice by royal example, was no mean one. Nor were the horizons towards which the nation strained altogether ignoble. Nevertheless, the Jubilee insinuated into her confidence an inferior person, while it increased the nation's dizzy infatuation with an inferior dream, the dream of Colonial Empire.

By the time Queen Victoria reached Osborne on July 19th she had a month of hot, hard work to her credit. There had been drives, receptions, the Garden Party (at which she and Gladstone played a grim game of hide-and-seek), and a review in Hyde Park of 28,000 Volunteers in a dark heat-fog through which she could just discern two sons, the Duke of Cambridge and two Tecks; back to Windsor for dinner, 'very tired'. She laid the foundation stone of the Imperial Institute – 'The heat was quite terrific & I felt dissolved' – then on to the Albert Hall where the RSPCA and Battersea Dogs' Home were celebrating. She was asked to present 14 prizes but alas, in 'terrible confusion', only one prize could be found. To Windsor again, 'too exhausted to do anything but rest on the sofa'. Aldershot. Wolseley had advocated a 'monster' review to boost the Empire. Home through billowing dust. A garden party at Hatfield, the home of Lord Salisbury. A memorial stone for the women's statue of the Prince Consort laid on Smith's Lawn. More addresses, more presents. Lord Rowton gave a miniature of Queen Elizabeth saying it was one great Queen to 'the other one'. She marvelled at the flow of presents. When she and Albert married they had not received a single one from 'the country'. Now this torrent.

At Osborne it all began again. There was the Spithead Review; 20,000 officers and men, 26 armoured ships, 9 unarmoured, 43 torpedo vessels, 38 gunboats, 12 troopships, 1 frigate, 6 training brigs. 'I was very tired.' An elaborate farewell to the Indian Princes. 'I don't know why they take up the Indians so much,' muttered Ponsonby.

Heat had become an obsession. Even on cool evenings a huge block of ice squatted in the centre of the Queen's dinnertable, radiating chill. Still she must smile and drive. 'Good Sovereign – no Change required', ran the loyal inscriptions at Cowes, 'Fifty runs not Out,' 'Better lo'ed ye canna be.'

She reached Balmoral at last to give her mind to the other side, the dark side of this 'never-to-be-forgotten year'.

The German Crown Prince left England in good spirits believing that Dr Mackenzie had cured him – without an operation. All he needed was a peaceful convalescence. He and his wife went to San Remo but there was no peace. From Berlin came angry demands that the Princess Royal should bring her husband back. The old Emperor was failing. Willy dashed to San Remo and made an appalling scene. On no account must Fritz return, wrote Queen Victoria: 'The more failing the Emperor becomes the more Fritz must make sure of getting well.'[10]

Meanwhile she was sifting poisonous rumours left behind after her daughter's Jubilee visit. Count Radolinski, one of Bismarck's spies, had drawn Ponsonby into the garden whispering that Seckendorff, the Princess's Court Chamberlain, was her lover: 'He goes everywhere with her – he is complete master.' By preventing her husband's operation, it was believed, she had made sure of keeping him alive just long enough to become Emperor; after which he could fade away leaving her with an imperial dowry – and Seckendorff.[11]

Queen Victoria had long realized the dangers of her daughter's dependence on a court official, however innocent. Why did she take Seckendorff up Lochnagar? she once asked Ponsonby; 'I never take my gentlemen with me.' Now her only thought was to comfort her deeply wronged child. When the Crown Prince begged her to knight Dr Mackenzie she did so. It is sometimes suggested that she was reckless to honour a man involved in bitter controversy. The charge is unjust. She did not trust Mackenzie, but not to knight him would have been a cruel way of telling her son-in-law that he was going to die. The disease itself told him this soon enough.

Cancer was again diagnosed in November, this time with Sir Morrell's agreement.

With more than usual regret the Queen parted from the old year. On October 24th Prince Henry of Battenberg had put into her arms 'a little Jubilee grandchild'. The baby, a girl, was christened Victoria Eugénie Julia Ena* in Crathie Kirk, to the sound of madrigals sung by the Aberdeen choir accompanied on a harmonium. Queen Victoria chose this service for its simplicity, though she did not hesitate to import godparents into a rubric which made no provision for them. She saw the New Year in, alone at her desk:

'never, never can I forget this brilliant year, so full of marvellous kindness, loyalty, & devotion of so many millions, which really I could hardly have expected.'

She could hardly have expected such varied well-wishers: 'We the Postmen of Kensington . . .', employees of the West African Telegraph Company, the Metropolitan Opera House of New York, 5,000 Bristolian Salvation Army 'soldiers', Ragged Schools, the crew of a Norwegian brig, the editor of a Japanese woman's magazine who congratulated Her Majesty on 'awakening even in these distant parts the ambition to become empress over self'.

In such glorious retrospect, it seemed almost laughable that someone should have thought it necessary to issue a broad-sheet† rebutting the old charge that the Monarchy was too expensive. By setting the Crown Revenues (which Queen Victoria had surrendered at her Accession) against the total cost of the Monarchy, the writer argued that the country had to pay no more than £173,000 a year for all this splendour.

Yet it was only a year ago that there had been a disagreeable outburst of Republicanism. At a Liberal Parliamentary dinner over 100 diners had failed to stand up for the loyal toast; in one corner of the room there was even hissing. Press criticism of the Queen's seclusion had erupted again. *The Times* demanded that she 'show herself to the present generation which knows her not'. The *Telegraph* declared that there

---

* She became Queen Victoria Eugénie of Spain.
† No. 1 of *The Banner Empire Leaflets*.

were better things for a Sovereign to do than to preserve her health. 'We are well aware that the seclusion of the Queen is not an idle seclusion' – but that was not good enough. 'There has been no Court for many years,' wrote the *St James's Gazette*.

After all this she had hardly expected such a Jubilee. First she had been warned and then 'petted', to use Dean Wellesley's word. The mixture worked. When the Jubilee was over she did not return to the old seclusion.

Queen Victoria found 1888 a strange number to write. 'Never can it be written again!' she announced, as if other, less strange years, had a habit of recurring.

She had feared for the Jubilee – 'And *all* was the most perfect success.' Would the fears for 1888 vanish too? 'Thank God and touch wood,' she wrote to the Crown Prince for the New Year, 'you are so much better . . .' [12]

Within a few weeks he was much worse. In February the dreaded tracheotomy had to be performed. A month later to the day (March 9th) the old Emperor died and the new Emperor Frederick, mortally ill, arrived in ice-bound Berlin to begin his reign of 99 days. Queen Victoria was convulsed with emotion:

'My OWN dear *Empress Victoria* it does seem an impossible dream, may God bless her! You know *how* little I care for rank or Titles – but I cannot *deny* that *after all* that has been done & said, I am *thankful* & *proud* that dear Fritz & you shd have come to the Throne.' [13]

How close they were now: the one Empress–Queen, the other Queen–Empress, and both Victorias.

On March 16th Queen Victoria held a funeral service for the late Emperor at Windsor. Mr Oscar Wilde arrived from the *Telegraph* to report it. Much annoyed at this intrusion, she nevertheless allowed him to see the Chapel. According to Ponsonby, 'he was most affected.'

Again there was news of strife in Berlin. She advised her daughter to 'send William & his odious ungrateful Wife, to travel & find his level'. His brother, Prince Henry, should go to sea.[14] Then she set out on her own travels, to Florence.

Memories of Prince Albert and a sharp breeze off the Alps made Florence a delight. She passed the Casa Gherini where he had lived in '38 and listened to the organ in the Badia which he had played. Crowds rushed after her mistaking her Indian servants for princes. Why did Vicky suggest that she did not like art? She liked it as much as anyone, only she had a lame leg and less time. The Empress Frederick later made amends by conceding that dear Mama did not *need* to learn about art, as her collections were ready made, whereas others had to assemble their own.[15] Before leaving Florence the Queen announced her resolve to visit the dying Emperor Frederick at Charlottenburg on the way home.

This plan was received with universal protests. The Bismarck family raised a fictitious howl: if the Queen of England was coming to push her granddaughter's marriage with Prince Alexander of Battenberg, Bismarck would resign: it would embroil Germany with Russia; besides, his son Herbert wanted to marry Princess Victoria himself. Even Lord Salisbury begged her at least to take a Minister with her. She brushed them all aside. It was not a political visit and in any case she had already advised the Empress Frederick by cypher telegram against pursuing Prince Alexander, who she knew had fallen in love with a singer. It was infuriating that the Emperor of Austria should want to meet her on the way to Berlin, thus increasing the false impression that her mission was political. She met Francis Joseph but kept the discussion off politics.

The formidable old lady reached Berlin on April 22nd. She agreed to give Bismarck an interview. Historians have not been able to decide which charmed the other most, the Iron Chancellor or the Iron Queen. Bismarck retired from the interview mopping his brow: 'That was a woman! one could do business with her!' (Afterwards he adopted a more patronizing tone: 'Grandmama behaved quite sensibly at Charlottenburg.') Bismarck's admirers claim that he 'bewitched' Queen Victoria into dropping her granddaughter's engagement. It is true that she afterwards confessed to being surprised that the horrid monster was so amiable and gentle, but as no witchcraft was required to make her see the objections to the marriage, the celebrated encounter was shadow-boxing. Bismarck later told his biographer that he had expected 'the old Queen' to descend in 1885 with 'the parson in her travelling bag and the bridegroom in her trunk'. She had not done so. He expected her in 1888 to be similarly equipped. Again he was wrong. Politics apart, he did not understand Queen Victoria's ambivalence about match-making.

She kissed the dying Emperor goodbye, accepting from him a bunch of forget-me-nots, made Prince William promise to behave better and returned home. Her bold visit caught the public imagination, though some newspapers expressed doubts. 'If I can be of any further use,' she wrote to her daughter, 'only tell me, & I wd even run over, papers & all . . .'[16] Mackenzie had informed her that the Emperor could not last three months. How mysterious and cruel, that the best should always be taken. We must trust that they were working elsewhere – 'though it is often, vy often even, *dreadfully difficult* & hard!'[17] She let a few weeks pass before again urging her daughter to break the doomed engagement. At last it was done.

Multifarious remedies poured into the Emperor's sick chamber from a sympathetic world: a bag of live worms from America, whisky and oatmeal from Scotland, ground oyster shells from England, carbolic acid from France. On June 15th, 1888, the Emperor Frederick died. Queen Victoria wired to her grandson, the Kaiser William II: 'I am broken-hearted . . . Help and do all you can for your poor dear Mother . . . Grandmama V.R.I.'

For the rest of this year and far into the next the Queen devoted herself to mitigating her daughter's purgatory. She reminded her of Tennyson's *In Memoriam*, Queen Constance's speech in *King John*, the building of a mausoleum. They would all contribute to the expense as Vicky had done with the Albert Chapel. She confessed, however, that her own feelings about mausoleums had changed: as time went on you felt that your dear ones were not bound to the place 'where their cast off garment lay', but were '*everywhere* near you'. Then there were the Empress Frederick's children: they would be a comfort, as the Queen's had been – 'tho' at *that time* there *was bitterness*'. But it was no comfort to read 'nasty' newspapers. 'It only irritates & does no *good* . . . I never did or do! or I cd not go on & do my duty.'[18]

Whatever consolations the Empress might find, Queen Victoria never for an instant doubted that her child's calamity was far greater than her own.

'Darling, darling unhappy child . . . You are far more sorely tried than me. I had not the agony of seeing another fill the place of my Angel Husband, wh I always felt I *never* cd have borne!'

'Another', in the shape of the Kaiser William II, was filling Fritz's place in a manner which drove the Queen to despair. 'Still Endure', must be Vicky's motto as it had been and was her own; but she had no words strong enough for the '2 wicked Bs [Bismarcks] & their unworthy pupil'. She was 'too furious, too too indignant, too savage . . .'[19] Sometimes she wondered whether William's head was 'quite right', he did such extraordinary things.[20] He had declined to meet his uncle, the Prince of Wales, at the court of the Emperor Francis Joseph in Vienna, because of some ill-advised conversation between the Prince and Herbert Bismarck at his father's funeral. The Vienna incident was never forgotten in England, and for a long time the Queen found it hard to forgive her grandson's airs. Speaking for herself and the Prince of Wales she wrote to Lord Salisbury on October 15:

'We have always been very intimate with our grandson and nephew and to pretend that he is to be treated *in private* as well as in public as "his Imperial Majesty" is *perfect madness*! . . . . *If* he has *such* notions, he better *never* come *here*.'[21]

Two publications that autumn did not improve the Empress Frederick's position. One was her husband's war diary, whose unauthorized appearance almost landed the editor in gaol. The other was an attack by Sir Morrell Mackenzie on his German colleagues in a book entitled *Frederick the Noble*.

That was the only noble thing about it. The Queen 'trembled'. If only it had not mentioned Dr Bergmann's drunkenness. She felt bound to tell her daughter that she could not possibly present Sir Morrell with another Order while feeling ran so high.[22] He was even said in Germany to be a Jew called Moritz Markovicz. Dr Reid sided with the German doctors. He stuck into his own copy the official condemnation of Mackenzie's book by the Royal College of Physicians.

The Empress Frederick's troubles seemed to the Queen an unanswerable reason for offering her a winter retreat in England. When Lord Salisbury and the Prince of Wales objected to such an awkward visitor the Queen flew at them: were they frightened of William and the Bismarcks? The Empress stayed with her mother till February 1889, after which the Queen reluctantly consented to a summer visit from the Kaiser. He telegraphed his unbounded joy at being allowed to enter that 'dear old home at Osborne'.

It was thought judicious to allow him to enter it in the uniform of a British Admiral, an honour which he acknowledged with ebullient charm. 'Fancy wearing the same uniform as St Vincent and Nelson; it is enough to make one quite giddy.'[23]

That the Kaiser had brought sunshine into the dear old home she could not afterwards deny. How right the Battenbergs had been to persuade her not to go away during his visit. The tenderness she had always felt for Prince Albert's first grandchild reasserted itself. She forgot her promise to the Empress Frederick not to address a word to 'those horrid people', Willy's suite, or only just 'Good Mng'. The chief of the suite turned out to be both 'pleasing' and 'straightforward'.[24]

A few days after the Kaiser left Osborne there was another departure which the Queen regretted a great deal more: Abdul Karim, sobbing bitterly, went on leave to India.

There had been a critical time during the previous year when Abdul wished to give notice. Waiting at table, he complained, was beneath him; at home in Agra he was a clerk, a Munshi, not a menial. (This was technically true, for he had

been a vernacular clerk in Agra gaol at ten rupees a month.)
No one was quicker than the Queen to appreciate a situation
where human dignity seemed to be involved. Abdul was
created the Queen's Munshi in 1889 and like the young
Prince Albert, rapidly graduated from blotting the Queen's
letters to assisting her in their composition. Petitions from
India, for instance, which she saw required 'merely a civil
refusal' she handed over to him. His position was 'confidential'
she told Ponsonby, and must be 'kept up';[25] she had had to
scold one of the Indian servants for refusing to carry the
Munshi's messages.[26] His going on leave again in 1890, she
wrote to the Empress Frederick, was very inconvenient, since
besides giving Hindustani lessons and holding 'instructive'
conversations, he looked after 'all my boxes'. That year the
Munshi was painted by von Angeli against a background of
gold.

Meanwhile over the golden background two shadows crept.
The Court, who were at first delighted to see Indians putting
the noses of Highlanders out of joint, now realized that King
Stork had supplanted King Log. At the Braemar games in
September the Duke of Connaught spotted the Munshi's
turban among the gentry and angrily reported it to Ponsonby.
The wily secretary, employing a technique which had proved
successful in Brown's day, suggested that HRH should tell
the Queen himself. 'This entirely shut him up.'[27] When it
came to lifting the colour bar in the billiard room or passages,
the Household were not so easily reduced. The most they
could be persuaded to say was, like the Queen to the Kaiser's
suite, 'Good Mng'. Sir Fleetwood Edwards, an equerry, failed
to give Abdul his title of Munshi and seated him at theatrical
performances among the dressers. After Abdul had made a
scene and stalked out, Ponsonby promised the Queen that
such things should not recur.

At the same time Abdul involved the Queen directly in a
skirmish with the Viceroy of India, Lord Lansdowne. She
requested the Viceroy to obtain a grant of land for the Munshi
in Agra and a place for him and his father at the forthcoming
Durbar on November 24th, 1890. Rather sharply the Viceroy
replied that though he had accommodated Abdul between

his own staff and the 'distinguished visitors', Abdul's father was barred through earning less than 3,000 rupees a year; moreover there was jealousy among Indians over the land grant.[28]

Opposition only increased the Queen's fervour. It was strictly forbidden at Court to call Indians 'black men' and Lord Salisbury once had to apologize for using the term.[29] She tried in vain to save the Indian ringleader from hanging after a massacre of whites in 1891: 'That harsh crushing policy will not do now.'[30] She pegged away at Hindustani, for Abdul was 'a vy strict Master', as well as 'a *perfect* Gentleman'; she was soon able to greet Maharanees in their native tongue and hear in return that if English ladies would only do likewise there would be no more massacres.

Her preachers paid regard to her feeling for Mohammedanism, informing her that non-Christians could have the spirit of Christ in them. The Munshi instructed her in sociology as well as religion and language. Prompted by him, she urged the wife of an Indian Governor not to tamper unnecessarily with the seclusion of widows nor to over-educate their menfolk to the point of being able to read 'objectionable European literature'.[31]

Her preoccupation with her Indian Empire was demonstrated by the building of a 'Durbar Room' at Osborne for large receptions. The decoration was entrusted to Rudyard Kipling's father, keeper of the museum at Lahore. Its dazzling white, fretted plasterwork enchanted her and she found no fault with the paintings which Mr Kipling revealed had been executed by an artist in a high fever. Her Household hoped that he would do better when his temperature had fallen.

What the Queen called 'treats', including professional theatricals, became plentiful after the Jubilee. She saw Henry Irving, Ellen Terry, John Hare – 'a gentleman as so many are nowadays' – and the D'Oyly Carte Company. Towards the end of 1890 her Court were rehearsing under her supervision *Little Toddlekins*: 'Beatrice & Louise are excellent but Sir Henry Ponsonby did not know his part.' Next year George Grossmith sent her into fits of laughter with an item entitled *How the Ladies of the Future will make Love*. Downey, the Windsor photographer, tried to photograph the theatricals with a flash light. Nothing showed on the plate but the stage carpenter's nose. A gramophone was brought to Balmoral by Mr Morse and after the Household had recorded whistles and German jokes, Her Majesty spoke a few words. Mr Morse was warned not to tour the country playing them.

She fought as hard in the 'nineties to establish the robustness of her health as in the 'sixties she had emphasized her 'nerves'. From 1889 onwards her sight began to fail: indignantly she wrote that there had never been such murky weather at Windsor, necessitating candles on the luncheon table. She often felt too sleepy 'of an evening' to finish her Journal and a severe attack of sciatica, with many sleepless nights, increased this tendency. Her wrist was badly strained by a fall at the Mausoleum; this did not prevent her from keeping an engagement at Aldershot the same day. While at Grasse in 1891 *The Times* reported a royal cold; as soon as it was better she announced that she had never had one. A rumour from New York that she was dangerously ill made her savage; Ponsonby put it down to wicked stock-jobbers hoping to profit from a subsequent rise. Of a villa at Biarritz owned by an Englishman she wrote in 1889:

'I should not have cared for it, for not only does one not see the town, but not a single habitation, & when one is in a foreign country one likes to see some life about one.'[32]

In the same year, the death of her venerable aunt, the Duchess of Cambridge, brought home to her the fact that henceforth she must 'see life' from an increasingly lonely eminence. 'Ah! me,' she sighed when they gave her the news. 'There is the last one gone who had the right to call me Victoria.'[33]

Having renounced matchmaking, Queen Victoria was inexorably drawn into a fresh round on behalf of her grandchildren. This new generation of swarming Victorias and Louises sometimes stirred in her a curious jealousy. 'Little Louise' of Wales, for instance, made a charming picture when she married the Earl of Fife – 'but not like my own Brides'.[34]

Princess Victoria of Prussia presented the saddest problem. Sandro, in laying down his crown of thorns (as the Queen habitually described an abdication), had transferred the thorns to Princess Victoria. In 1889 the Queen heard that Sandro was engaged to his Austrian singer; she at once invited 'young Vicky' to be her companion while Princess Beatrice was abroad. The Queen helped to wipe away many bitter tears, while Princess Victoria's letters home shed some sharp light on Grandmama's habits. English royal nurseries were incomparably sweet and clean; the robes of Grandmama's Indian attendants were incomparably white; but Grandmama at night, on the royal train, was an incomparable fidget. Princess Victoria never stopped opening and shutting the window, a duty she was not the first to find wearisome. When Prince Leopold was alive he had been in charge of the train window on the journey to Osborne. One year the railway company put on a new carriage with a window that would not open. The Queen was outraged but Prince Leopold rejoiced.

With mingled relief and trepidation the Queen learnt in 1890 that 'young Vicky' was to console herself with a German princeling: 'there is nothing so horrid as a daughter's engagement & marriage,' she wrote to the Empress Frederick. 'One never knows how it will turn out . . .'[35] It turned out badly.

Another engagement, that of her granddaughter Princess Marie Louise of Schleswig-Holstein to Prince Aribert of Anhalt, also caused her doubts. This time the Kaiser was the matchmaker. The Queen hoped he would not begin poaching on her territory. This marriage was later dissolved.

There was no end to the advice needed. One day it was for chloroform in childbirth; another, for better handwriting and spelling. Then there was an unfilial youth: 'Be a little lenient,' the Queen advised his mother, young people were often merely thoughtless rather than unkind. There was a young wife who was not expecting: it was fortunate not to be tormented with children too young, but – well, the girl *must* see a doctor.

Little Sophie of Prussia would surely be no problem for she was marrying into the Greek family, a charming one.

Next moment Princess Sophie, too, was in trouble. She decided to enter the Greek Church, an act of which her grandmother could not but approve, provided it was sincere. The Kaiser, however, threatened to banish his sister. Disgusted by such bigotry, the Queen wrote to him 'calmly but strongly'; when he replied 'in a fit of anger' she simply ignored him. 'I shall always be happy to do my best to set Wm right,' she told his mother.[36] On one point only she sympathized with him: why did Sophie have to announce her conversion with so much publicity? 'We Protestants never require it.'[37]

The marriage prospects of the Wales Princes also occupied the Queen. Prince Albert Victor had fallen in love with his dazzlingly beautiful cousin, Princess Alix ('Alicky') of Hesse. She would not have him. 'She shows gt strength of character,' wrote Queen Victoria to the Empress Frederick in 1889; 'all her family and all of us wish it, and she refuses the gtest position there is.'[38]

At the beginning of 1891 a disaster befell the Prince of Wales. What Queen Victoria described as 'this dreadful "Card Scandal" ' broke at Tranby Croft, a country house where the Prince and some friends were playing baccarat. One of the guests, 'this horrid Sir Wm Cumming', cheated. He was exposed and forced to promise never again to play cards for money. In return his fellow guests, including the Prince of Wales, pledged themselves to secrecy. Someone broke his word, the 'Baccarat Case' leaked into the papers, Cumming brought a court action and the Prince of Wales for the second time was subpoenaed as a witness.

Here indeed was the material for regal explosions, and if Sir William Jenner had not already retired he would doubtless have prepared for a nervous breakdown. Queen Victoria abhorred gambling for high stakes and once refused when staying on the Riviera to accept a bouquet from Monte Carlo. Now she had to listen to the Churches accusing her son of corrupting the middle classes, for the owner of Tranby Croft had made his money, wholesomely it was assumed, in shipping. The Prince's reputation plunged again to the depths it had reached during the Mordaunt case. In Germany a cartoonist devised for him the new motto, *'Ich Deal'*. Yet the Baccarat

Case left Queen Victoria relatively calm. 'It is a sad thing as Bertie is dragged into it,' she wrote to the Empress Frederick on February 18th, 1891, '– but people think good will come of it & that it will be a shock to Society & to gambling lies [Ladies], etc.'

Autumn came and the Queen had regained her confidence in the future. Buckingham Palace was still standing and Tranby Croft, lost in the mists of Yorkshire, was forgotten. The Prince of Wales stayed with her at Balmoral where they both enjoyed the feeling of old times. Prince Albert Victor had got over another disappointment and was now engaged. After Princess Alix, this susceptible young man had given part of his heart to Lady Sybil St Clair Erskine and the rest, with the Queen's approval, to Princess Hélène of Orleans. Since no amount of confabulation could get over the fact that Princess Hélène, a Roman Catholic, would not be allowed to change her religion, Lord Salisbury convinced the Queen that the affair must lapse. She wrote in June 1891 that though 'some people wish for May Teck,' they must 'let him alone for the present'.[39]

The holiday season at Balmoral presented the next opportunity. Queen Victoria invited Princess May to stay and suddenly her cautious approval broke into ecstasy: May was nice, quiet, cheerful, sensible, good-mannered, very fond of Germany, very cosmopolitan and grown very pretty. The Prince thought the same. They became engaged during a ball at Luton Hoo, to the 'satisfaction' of both Queen and nation. Queen Victoria rightly interpreted the public rejoicing as a reaffirmation of loyalty to 'me & mine'. No doubt there were a few disappointed faces but the Queen was emphatic that Princess May had no rival:

'I must say that I think it is far preferable than ein kleines deutsches Prinzesschen, with no knowledge of anything beyond small German Courts ... It would never do here for Eddy.'[40]

Queen Victoria's sturdy belief in the value of 'shocks' was put to a severe test at the end of the year. A fresh 'shock to

Society', which might have proved fatal to the Prince of Wales, was only prevented by Lord Salisbury's skill from bursting into the open through the quaking upper crust. A week of diplomacy, closeted with the Queen, enabled Salisbury to bury the Lady Brooke–Lady Charles Beresford scandal sixty years deep – until its seismic force was spent. Gladstone, incidentally, showed his incredible naïvety over worldly affairs by suggesting that this was the moment for Queen Victoria to abdicate and her son to reign.

Politics seemed to be following the improved domestic trend. The Queen felt, to be sure, that Salisbury's Government was mean over money and he did not always approve of her candidates for bishoprics: there was a fierce tussle over Dean Davidson which the Queen lost.

She was more successful when Parliament, through the Hartington Report, made yet another attempt to get rid of 'poor George' as Commander-in-Chief and was again thwarted. Shortly afterwards she heard that two battalions of the Guards had mutinied, having been corrupted by some 'horrid Socialists'. What could one expect when even Tories and Unionists signed these disgraceful Reports? Sadly she watched the troopship *Tamar* steam down the Solent bearing the mutineers to Bermuda for a year's penance.

She confessed herself 'startled' in 1890 to hear that Salisbury was giving Germany Heligoland in exchange for Zanzibar and wrote censoriously:

'Giving up what one has is always a bad thing.'[41]

Nevertheless, she could not get on without Lord Salisbury and it seemed that she would not have to.

The Liberal Party appeared to be weaker than ever, since the Irish Nationalists had broken in two over Parnell. Captain O'Shea had at last brought a divorce suit against his wife, naming Parnell as co-respondent. The suit was undefended, Parnell married Kitty O'Shea and the Nonconformist conscience promptly dissociated Liberalism from a party led by an adulterer. The Queen watched from a distance, occasionally giving vent to a 'dreadful!' or a 'horrid!' Up and down Ireland Parnell fought with tragic desperation to maintain his position. His fiery spark was suddenly extinguished on October 6th, 1891, a few hours after the Queen's 'good excellent' Mr W. H. Smith had also passed away. She was suitably impressed by reading the accounts of two such different funerals on the same day – 'what a contrast!'

To her immense satisfaction, Arthur Balfour became Leader of the House in place of W. H. Smith, afterwards conducting a successful campaign in Scotland, where Gladstone was feeble. 'A great thing, for it will take the sails out of the abominable old G. Man' (sic).[42] She ignored Lord Rowton's warning that the Tories expected to be beaten at next year's elections. In any case she would not send for Gladstone. Ponsonby let her have her say: 'No object in beginning the troubles now.'[43]

But for the fourth time in the reign, 'the abominable old G. Man', with or without the sails taken out of him, prepared to run in under the Queen's guns.

CHAPTER XXXIV

'STILL ENDURE'

1892–5

QUEEN VICTORIA began the new year with her accustomed survey of last year's profit and loss. On the credit side were the safe birth of another son to Princess Beatrice, Prince George's recovery from typhoid, her own good health, peace at home and abroad and Prince Albert Victor's engagement to Princess May. The wedding was fixed for February 27th.

After a festive Twelfth Night a telegram arrived on January 9th from Sandringham saying that Eddy had caught influenza but was going on 'all right'. The Queen took illness seriously: she had recently engaged a combined nurse and masseuse from the London Hospital to live permanently at Windsor Castle and look after herself and the Household. Nevertheless the Prince's condition did not seem to warrant the cancellation of eight tableaux planned for that day, concluding with 'Empire' in which the sturdy, blonde Princess Beatrice impersonated a Maharanee. 'We were much pleased.' Next day the Queen was startled to hear that Prince Albert Victor had developed pneumonia and on the 13th (a date always associated with her first suspicion that the Prince Consort might die) the report was 'as bad as possible'. She longed to 'fly' to Sandringham but was afraid of being in the way. When morning broke Princess Christian brought a telegram from the Prince of Wales: 'Our darling Eddy has been taken from us . . .' It was the 14th of the month. 'Poor, poor parents: poor May,' the Queen lamented, 'to have her whole bright future to be merely a dream! poor me, in my old age, to see this young promising life cut short!'[1]

In mid-February she heard that her little granddaughter, Princess Patricia of Connaught, had pneumonia. 'I felt I could hardly bear more sorrows.' The child recovered. More sorrow, however, had to be endured. Her son-in-law Louis, Grand Duke of Hesse, died on March 13; 'it is too dreadful to have to lose him too ! . . . Again so near that terrible number fourteen!'[2] She held a service for him at Windsor and for the second time that year listened to the organ playing *Now the labourer's task is o'er*. So many labourers had finished their tasks but one labourer still had to struggle on. 'Still Endure.'

It was fortunate that the Queen's spring holiday abroad supervened at this point. She left England in a state of nervous depression but once at Hyères her spirits rose – no one to see whom she did not choose, no jarring sounds except the naval guns at Toulon, nothing to inspect except the lovely woods. One morning Ponsonby caught sight of her limping smartly along with Lady Churchill, while the white donkey and bath-chair followed. Even from this paradise, however, sublunary matters could not be altogether excluded. The Riviera was a centre of gossip and *The Times* correspondent made himself very tiresome in the corridors of the Hotel Costabelle.

'It is assumed that Prince George and Princess May will of course marry, as they are always together.' Ponsonby put on a stern expression.

'Oh yes, I know you can't say anything but we know the Prince of Wales is all for it and the Queen dead against it.'

'That's not true,' snapped Ponsonby before he could stop himself. He decided to explain that HM had not yet expressed any opinion.

'Oh, no of course not – much too soon – but we more than suspect . . .'[3]

Another day the Queen broached with Ponsonby a subject which was often in her thoughts in these times of change – the constitutional rights of sovereigns. The King of Greece had just dismissed his Ministers for 'leading the country to Bankruptcy'. Queen Victoria defended his right to do so. 'But whether it is wise to exercise this right,' she added, 'must depend on circumstances.' Amid the babel of monarchist propaganda on the Riviera a few Liberal voices were heard: George Childers went about wearing a primrose because it was the Queen's favourite flower which he hoped to rescue from becoming a Conservative emblem. Only one Liberal enclave was completely out of bounds. The Souspréfet of

Hyères wanted to show her a beautiful garden belonging to a *'Sénateur anglais'*. Ponsonby cautiously asked the name.

'Sir Charles Dilke.' Hastily the private secretary excused himself.

'It is getting late and we must hurry home before it is dark.'

Over thirty years later, a local fisherman told Mr Laurens van der Post that he remembered as a boy watching with amazement a strange woman land on the rocky, off-shore islet where he and his family lived in caves. She shared their *bouillabaisse*, this unknown woman, out of the big pot . . . The old fisherman drank to her memory: her wonderful bearing, her sea-blue eyes, her stupendous purple bonnet. *'La Reine Victoire!'*

At length the golden holiday ended. Queen Victoria spent a week in Darmstadt teaching the young Grand Duke Ernest how to govern and reached Windsor at the beginning of May to find that Lord Salisbury wanted a dissolution in June. He and Chamberlain would actually have preferred October but the rest of the Cabinet could not keep their supporters working any longer. Parliament was accordingly dissolved. While the election campaign proceeded the Queen was again pre-occupied with family affairs.

At the beginning of June the engagement was suddenly announced of Prince Alfred's daughter Marie ('Missy') of Edinburgh to the heir to the Roumanian throne. An acute family disturbance resulted. Prince George of Wales, now twenty-seven and the Queen's eventual heir, had hoped to marry his cousin Marie himself; his grandmother had felt sure that 'Missy will have him'.[4] In fact she would not, preferring to remain a 'beloved chum'. Much provoked, the Prince of Wales abruptly terminated his son's suit, to the surprise and annoyance of his brother, Prince Alfred. Such a situation in the old days would have thrown Queen Victoria into a violent state of excitement. Privately, she was not at all taken with the idea of Roumania, which seemed to her 'very insecure' and the society 'dreadful'; as the wedding would not be a Protestant one it would have to take place at Coburg 'or very quietly here'. Nevertheless she controlled her own feelings, begging the Empress Frederick to 'soften Bertie, for family quarrels are so bad', and assuring him herself that his brother had had 'no other wish than for the much grander match'.[5] She mollified Prince Alfred by inviting the King of Roumania to Windsor.

On May 26th, the birthday of Princess May of Teck, Queen Victoria wrote significantly in her Journal, 'may she yet be happy'. It was followed a few weeks later by the entry: 'George came to have a little talk with me.' There is no doubt what the little talk was about. The royal line must go on and it could not be denied that Prince George possessed qualities conspicuously lacking in his brother. Particularly as boys, she had written about them in ways reminiscent of the young Princes Ernest and Albert of Saxe-Coburg. Both Ernest and Albert had been clever and beautiful, 'especially Albert'; both her Wales grandsons were good dancers and riders, 'especially Georgie'. After the Edinburgh débâcle her admiration for the rejected suitor was boundless.

'I think dear Georgie so nice, sensible & truly right-minded, & so anxious to improve himself.'[6]

On the great battleground of self-improvement it was wonderful to find at last a future heir to the Throne standing squarely at her side.

Some minor domestic shocks remained to be endured before the Queen could settle down again to politics. Her granddaughter Princess Margaret ('Mossy'), youngest child of the Empress Frederick, got engaged. The Queen was upset. Remembering the tireless devotion of Princess Beatrice, she felt that Mossy ought not have left her widowed mother so soon.* 'I agree with the Mohammedans,' she told the Empress, 'that duty towards ones Parents – goes before every other but that is not taught as part of religion in Europe.'[7] The Munshi had not stood at Her Majesty's elbow for five years in vain.

Two more of her Prussian grandchildren, Prince Henry and Princess Sophie, got into hot water at the end of June by declining their grandmother's third invitation to Windsor,

* Notwithstanding her grandmother's views, Princess Margaret married Prince Charles of Hesse in January 1893.

to show her Sophie's fiancé, Prince Tino of Greece. Yet Princess Sophie had already been shown to the Tsar. 'I shall not ask them again,' she informed their mother curtly.[8] Jealousy of Russia was always one of Queen Victoria's tormenting passions.

'The poor but really wicked old G.O.M. has made two dreadful Speeches,' the Queen wrote to her eldest daughter on July 6th, 1892. The election campaign was drawing to a close and the first results beginning to come in. Not unprepared for a Home Rule majority, the actual figure of 45 did not surprise her. What shocked and horrified was that a mere majority, of whatever size, should be the deciding factor in a matter so important as the country's future.

'These are trying moments & seems to me a defect in our much famed Constitution, to have to part with an admirable Govt like Ld Salisbury's for no question of any importance, or any particular reason, merely on account of the number of votes.'[9]

Stockmar's old pupil did not find the workings of democracy easy to understand. In the *Court Circular* she actually announced Lord Salisbury's resignation 'with regret', to the consternation of Gladstone's followers. Her annoyance with the Liberals did not prevent her from giving the Conservatives a larruping, as she had done in 1880. If they had all put their backs into it like their opponents, she told Balfour and Cross, they would not have been beaten. 'Elections need much harder work than formerly,' agreed Balfour dolefully.[10]

For the third time in twelve years her burning vow not to send for Gladstone was extinguished by the necessities of 'the much famed Constitution'. She confided her anxieties to her friends. The Marquess of Lansdowne was told how much she dreaded entrusting the Empire 'to the shaking hand of an old, wild incomprehensible man of eighty-two and a half', her only consolation being that 'the country is sound and it cannot last'.[11] Gladstone's strength was indeed insufficient to lead the House at night as well as during the daytime, so that Harcourt had to take over half his burden – 'a greater light to rule the day and a lesser light to rule the night' as Mr Darling, MP, remarked. Lord Cromer (Sir E. Baring) was warned by the Queen to expect 'fresh dark Gladstonian days'.

Gladstone's appearance at his first audience (August 15th) only confirmed the Queen's fears. They were both leaning upon sticks:

'You and I, Mr Gladstone, are lamer than we used to be!'[12] After this human start she relapsed into cold distaste.

'I thought him greatly altered & changed, not only much aged, walking rather bent, with a stick, but altogether; his face shrunk, deadly pale, with a weird look in his eye, a feeble expression about the mouth, & the voice altered.'[13]

Not long before this distressing encounter the Queen had noted that the wife of the Vicar of Whippingham, Mrs Prothero, had 'a strange anxious look in her eyes'. She went mad, standing at the vicarage door 'in a *hat*' to receive Her Majesty. 'She was taken away.'[14]

The only hope of similarly disposing of Mr Gladstone was to let him try and fail. At the moment, however, 'the really wicked G.O.M.'[15] (Queen Victoria soon dropped the 'poor') instead of being taken away, seemed likely to bring with him into the Cabinet which Salisbury had swept clean, another devil immeasurably worse than himself. This was her old enemy Henry Labouchere, or 'Labby', as everyone called him. His newspaper, *Truth*, was dreaded at Court for its needling of royalty.

She left Gladstone in no doubt that she would refuse Labouchere except on two conditions: that he severed his connection with *Truth* and occupied a non-Cabinet post where there would be no personal contact with herself. According to her own record, she made this latter stipulation on grounds of morality rather than politics. It was said that Mrs Labouchere, whom the Queen would be required to receive as a Cabinet Minister's wife, had lived with Labouchere before marriage.

Ponsonby returned to Windsor after delivering this ultimatum and the Queen reported drily that Gladstone had seemed 'strangely ignorant'[16] of Labouchere's moral character. In fact, Gladstone cultivated a kind of holy cunning which prevented him from attending to gossip. He is said to have once killed a discussion about the relationship of Parnell and Mrs O'Shea with the words, 'I did not know they were related.'

Truth was a small goldmine which the Court understood Labouchere could not afford to abandon. He spurned the Queen's conditions and proceeded to harry her unmercifully in his newspaper. His excessive violence helped to swing opinion back to the Queen, whose attitude had provoked much criticism.

The Labouchere affair led to a grass-roots discussion between the Queen and Ponsonby about her constitutional rights. In a letter to Lady Ponsonby on September 4th Ponsonby summed up his Sovereign's attitude with which, incidentally, he himself agreed :

'It was a pouring wet day yesterday so the Queen talked over the constitution with me at some length – Labby says she is acting unconstitutionally in objecting to him. She says it does not matter what he says. But as a fact his name was not submitted so the question does not arise – yet if she had objected she had a perfect right to do so – and she has a perfect right according to the constitution to dismiss Gladstone which means dismissing his ministers. But she thinks that when once appointed she cannot dismiss any one minister serving under the Prime Minister. Of course the discussion was 'academic' as to dismiss a ministry would be impossible as long as they have a Majority in Parliament. But it would not be unconstitutional.'

Mary Ponsonby argued back that a Minister should not be barred because of his private character – a view which finally converted her husband but not the Queen.

Queen Victoria's victory over Labouchere did not help her to appreciate Gladstone or his Government any more highly. The Foreign Secretary, Lord Rosebery, was the most acceptable. Rosebery took an early opportunity to right what most Ministers considered an ancient wrong: he presented the

Prince of Wales with his father's golden key. Queen Victoria had rightly judged her son to be indiscreet. Nevertheless, in the past she had tended to get the worst of both worlds: Ministers who disobeyed her by feeding Cabinet secrets to the Prince behind her back, and an ill-equipped heir.

When the Liberals arrived at Osborne for their first Council on August 18th the Queen gave a horrified gasp: 'A motley crew to behold.' Sir William Harcourt (whom she described elsewhere as having grown 'rather awful looking now, like an elephant') assured her how anxious they all were to please her. 'I merely bowed.' The bulk of the 'crew' had to be sworn in together and instead of rising afterwards to kiss her hand they all crawled forward on their knees. This struck her as ludicrous rather than loyal.

The Empress Frederick and Ponsonby tried to ease the tensions by emphasizing Gladstone's importance as a bulwark against the democrats. No good would come of personal contacts with him, replied the Queen to her daughter impatiently on August 20th:

'He listens to no one & won't bear any contradiction or discussion. He is really half crazy, half silly & it is better not to provoke discussion.'

The story of a dramatic encounter between the Prime Minister and an angry heifer in September has all the beauty of a political allegory. The cow, surrounded by twenty-six hostile men, suddenly evaded her enemies, dashed into Hawarden Park, charged Mr Gladstone and threw him to the ground. He escaped only by lying absolutely still and shamming dead. Sometimes the roles were reversed and Queen Victoria would make her escape from Gladstone's thundering hoofs by fixing upon him a mute, deathly stare.

In November the Queen wrote to the Empress Frederick that Gladstone had become prosy and very deaf. He had to sit excessively close to his shrinking Sovereign in order to hear even her pellucid tones. In any case there was nothing to talk about. Ireland, Uganda and all great imperial questions were 'impossible' so they talked about what she called 'other things': generally the ill-health of mutual friends. With her natural forthrightness she loathed the atmosphere of constraint, though it was at least partly of her own making.

'It is really a farce & a form merely seeing a Prime Minister with whom one is on such terms.'[17]

An appeal to the Almighty in Crathie Kirk by wee Dr Macgregor to 'send down His wisdom on the Queen's Meenisters who sorely needed it', created joyful havoc in the royal pew. Queen Victoria went purple with suppressed laughter and her lady-in-waiting, Lady Antrim, could not resist a half-audible Amen.

The plaintive language with which Queen Victoria chose to begin her Journal on May 24th, 1883 – 'My poor old birthday, my seventy-fourth' – was a familiar formula, nothing more. In reality she felt distinctly pleased with her recent record, as she proved by her very next words: 'I wish now it was instead sixty-fourth.' Besides the satisfaction of seeing Egypt strongly garrisoned and expecting to see Home Rule beaten, she observed that all branches of her family were moving harmoniously forward along the lines she had chosen for them.

First and foremost came the engagement on May 3rd of Prince George, now Duke of York, and Princess May of of Teck. 'The Country are delighted,'* only 'poor dear Alex', the bereaved mother of Prince Albert Victor, was 'very tried' by the rejoicings but 'knows it must be' – an attitude which to Queen Victoria seemed impeccable. The wedding took place on July 6th, 1893, in overpowering heat and a bath of tears, most of them cheerful ones. The Queen enjoyed every minute of it, except possibly the one when Gladstone sat down in her tent. 'Does he think perhaps this is a public tent!!' she exclaimed to her cousin Augusta, Grand Duchess of Mecklenburg-Strelitz.[18] By a happy little muddle in the

* The usual lunatic charges brought against royalty on such occasions were not wanting: W. T. Stead's *Pall Mall Gazette* published a letter accusing the Queen of encouraging bigamy since the Duke of York was already married with two children in Malta. The Prince of Wales, Prince Christian, Prince Albert Victor and the Prince Imperial had all previously been accused of similar offences.

arrangements, Queen Victoria's carriage reached the Chapel too early, so that for once she was able to watch all the processions arriving. At the same time, her age and infirmity allowed her to opt out of anything she did not fancy. Instead of joining the large family dinner party at Marlborough House, she had a quiet dinner and gossip *à deux* with Augusta. For the first time she met the young Tsarevitch ('Nicky') and he too pleased her greatly by not looking at all like a Russian but 'very like Georgie'.

She had by no means given up hope of bringing her grandson, the Kaiser, and his mother together again. Sometimes she would show her understanding of the Empress Frederick's problems by sharing a little joke at William's expense. She told her daughter, for instance, that she had received a birthday present from him, 'as usual very funnily inscribed';

'May God preserve our revered belovedest Colleague for the benefit of Europe, its nations and their Peace . . .'

The Queen concluded slyly, 'I think the colleague will amuse you.'[19] Another time she would give her daughter friendly advice: the best way to gain influence over William was by kindness and by cautioning him on particular subjects, rather than issuing general warnings.

Unfortunately she herself had to take up William on a tiresome issue. He had invited himself to England for the fourth year running and had been told that he must stay this time on board his yacht, since there was no room for him at Osborne House; the British Ambassador in Berlin was instructed to 'hint that these regular annual visits are not quite desirable.' The Emperor was not one to take hints. Not only did he arrive, but having won the Queen's Cup at Cowes Regatta, kept the Queen waiting for dinner next day. Her Journal spoke volumes: 'Only got up to my room late, & felt very tired.'

That August when the Queen was going into ecstasies over 'the dear young *ménage*' of the Yorks, the scandalous old *ménage* of her brother-in-law, Duke Ernest II of Saxe-Coburg, at last came to an end. The Queen's final judgement on the departed sinner adroitly killed two wicked old birds with one

655

stone. In one respect, she told her daughter, he was like Gladstone, for 'he persuaded himself that things were right which were wrong.'[20]

Gladstone's second attempt to pass a Home Rule Bill for Ireland seemed to Queen Victoria a case in point. The right course was surely to introduce 'gradual self-government'; it could only be wrong to rouse the kind of storms which rocked Parliament during this summer of 1893. A climax was reached on July 27th when an attempt by Chamberlain to liken Gladstone to King Herod was violently interrupted by Irish shrieks of 'Judas! Judas!' Fisticuffs broke out on the floor of the chamber and hissing in the gallery; despair swept over Gladstone at what he called 'a black day'. Nevertheless it ended satisfactorily for him with a majority of 30 for the preamble of his Bill.

Queen Victoria had not been idle on the other side. While Gladstone was busy dismembering the Empire, she supported its growth by opening the Imperial Institute in person. She read her answer to the loyal address without spectacles, 'which I was rather proud of.'

The annihilation of Home Rule for ever, so far as Queen Victoria was concerned, came in September 1893. The Bill passed its third reading in the early morning of the 2nd, by the slender majority of 34; the Queen heard that it would have been even less if many Liberals had not relied on the House of Lords killing the Bill. They did not rely in vain. An almost indecent vote of 419 to 41 against the Bill showed what these 'ancient monuments' could do and dare, when not in fear of demolition. But 'the Mob' also, as Queen Victoria noted, cheered Lord Salisbury after the debate and sang 'Rule Britannia'. Indeed the country as a whole was no longer on the side of small nations; if people had to choose between Home Rule and Rule Britannia they would choose Britannia.

Gladstone's days were numbered, for a crisis over national defence was beginning to open a fatal rift between him and his Cabinet colleagues. Ever since 1884, when W. T. Stead turned from white slaves to bluejackets, exposing the weakness of the Navy in the *Pall Mall Gazette*, alarm had been growing. While Germany was eagerly preparing for a great maritime triumph – the opening of the Kiel Canal in June 1895 – Britain in June 1893 suffered a sensational naval disaster. Admiral Tryon made an error in turning his flagship, HMS *Victoria*, collided with HMS *Camperdown* and sank to the bottom of the Mediterranean taking with him more than half of the *Victoria*'s officers and men. 'Too awful!' wrote the Queen: 'Too dreadful to contemplate!' She immediately cancelled a Court ball, sent one of her famous letters of condolence to Lady Tryon ('forgive my intrusion on your terrible grief'), made some remarks in her Journal about the unwieldiness of 'these ironclads' and found a crumb of comfort in the nobility of Tryon's last words: 'It was all my fault.' But she could not forget two grim facts: Britain was yet another ship short, and Gladstone refused to replace it. It also appeared that even 'poor Adml Tryon' suffered from 'one small failing, and that was that he never thought he was wrong'.[21]

Criticism of Gladstone's attitude towards proposals for a more powerful navy became widespread during the autumn and winter. In vain the Queen sent him a strong message to be read out at an emergency Cabinet meeting; Gladstone took to his bed. In vain the Opposition tried to initiate a general discussion on the country's naval strength; Gladstone said it was not their business. He became what Rosebery mildly described to the Queen as 'irritable', a state which included suddenly turning his back on his Chancellor, Sir William Harcourt, at a Cabinet meeting and maintaining this posture for the rest of Harcourt's speech. The word 'mad' was freely bandied to and fro. Gladstone thought the Admiralty was 'mad! mad! mad!' and Rosebery recalled Palmerston's prophecy (a favourite of the Queen's) that Gladstone would die in a madhouse.

On December 29th, 1893, the GOM, still in the saddle but only just, reached the impressive age of eighty-four. The Queen could hardly endure to enter a new year in the hands of 'a deluded old fanatic'.

For two months of the new year, but no longer, Queen

Victoria was required to remain in those 'deluded' hands. Lord Acton, who met Gladstone in Biarritz during January 1894 recharging his batteries, found him 'loud, unreasoning ... wild, governed by resentment'. He was never 'able to see any argument but his own'. It might have been Queen Victoria speaking. When, at the beginning of February, the amazing old fighter felt sufficiently restored to spring on his Cabinet a proposal for a snap election on the issue of the House of Lords, one of them called him 'preposterous', another 'absolutely insane' and all put their names to a decisive telegram: 'Your suggestion is impossible.' Gladstone, still at Biarritz, looked southwards towards Gibraltar, compared himself to the Rock and dismissed his colleagues as criminals. Everyone knew he must resign but having arrived back in Downing Street he kept the Cabinet for another fortnight in suspense.

Characteristically, Gladstone broke to the Queen his intention of resigning by stages, cloaking his first intimations that some news was on the way in so much mystery that the Queen was bewildered and alarmed. Was the abominable old G. man still contemplating a last mad assault on the Lords? Would he demand an election? It was not till February 27th that his vague hints took positive shape: on grounds of increasing deafness and blindness, he wrote, a decision had been reached to tender his resignation at the end of the Session. Queen Victoria politely accepted the official reason though she knew very well that the cause was not physical but political. He had been sunk by the Navy; or rather, by Britannia herself, whose estimates for ruling the waves at a greatly increased cost he persisted in regarding as 'mad and drunk'.

On the 28th the old man hobbled in for what the Queen took to be his last real audience. She asked him to sit down. They gazed at each other, neither seeing very clearly. He had served her four times in the highest office and had sat in Parliament for over sixty-one years, five years longer than she had sat on the throne. She brought herself to say that she was sorry – 'for the cause of his resignation'. Gladstone did not miss the innuendo. A conversation, lame as the Queen herself, soon petered out. Her rheumatic leg indeed was giving her continuous pain and there was no temptation to prolong the interview. To Gladstone, however, desperately waiting for a sign of emotion, she seemed heartlessly cheerful.

On March 1st he at last informed the Cabinet of his decision to retire. The tears which his Sovereign had failed to shed were more than made up for by 'that blubbering Cabinet' – Gladstone's later caustic description of what at the time he called 'a really moving scene'. Lord Kimberley was the first to attempt a valedictory address; sobs choked him. Gladstone was about to respond when a muffled voice cried out, 'Stop!' It was Sir William Harcourt, who proceeded to draw from one pocket his handkerchief and from another a manuscript, yellow with age and heavily scored with corrections. Gladstone listened to the pompous phrases, the gulping and spluttering, with distaste. When Harcourt had finished he replied briefly without emotion. Then he drove to the House of Commons and addressed it for the last time. His speech was a battle cry against the Lords and many of the members failed to realize that it was a leave-taking.

Next day, March 2nd, Queen Victoria invited the Gladstones to dine with her at Windsor and stay the night. On the following morning, a Saturday, she saw Mrs Gladstone after breakfast. 'She was very much upset, poor thing,' wrote the Queen afterwards, and poured out, between sobs, an assurance that her husband 'whatever his errors' had always been devoted to the Queen.

> 'She repeated this twice & begged me to allow her to tell him that I believed it which I did; for I am convinced it is the case, though at times his actions might have made it difficult to believe. She spoke of former days & how long he had known me & dear Albert. I kissed her when she left.'[22]

That same afternoon Gladstone solemnly entered upon the last lap of his devious road to retirement. He wrote out a formal resignation, placed it in a dispatch box and carried it to the Queen. This should have been the moment for a grand finale. Unfortunately the Queen dealt with him as casually as he himself had dealt with his blubbering colleagues. They had another desultory conversation which, in Gladstone's words, was 'neither here nor there'. He then kissed her hand and left. She had neither asked his advice about a successor nor offered him a word of thanks.

It is improbable that even if the Queen had realized that this particular Sunday was 'Resignation Day', she would have marked the occasion in a manner to satisfy Gladstone. Through his own fault she did not realize.

The inability of Queen Victoria and Gladstone to converse together seriously and naturally during their later years was a prominent aspect of their unhappy relationship. Curiously enough, both longed to break the boring circle of small talk and each accused the other in their respective diaries of obstinately clinging to trivialities. On the Queen's side, the habit had begun as an attempt to avoid losing her temper; it developed into a hopeless feeling that Gladstone never listened, so why talk? She once told Archbishop Benson that all her efforts to keep Gladstone *au fait* with Continental opinion was received with the same frigid comment: 'Is that so? Really?'[23]

After he had gone the Queen opened the box and read his formal resignation. Surprised to find yet another elaborate statement so late in the day, she nevertheless sat down at once and drafted what seemed to her an appropriate reply. After going over the old ground for the very last time – his age, his eyes and his 'arduous labours', now happily concluded – and wishing him a peaceful future with his excellent wife, she brought her letter somewhat abruptly to an end: 'The Queen would gladly have conferred a peerage on Mr Gladstone, but she knows that he would not accept it.'[24]

To Gladstone, the letter was an insult. It confirmed his bitter suspicion that he meant nothing to her. Their separation reminded him of a day sixty-three years ago when he parted without a pang at the end of a Sicilian holiday from his mule:

'I had been on the back of the beast for many scores of hours. It had done me no wrong. It had rendered me much valuable service. But ... I could not get up the smallest shred of feeling for the brute. I could neither love nor like it.'[25]

Queen Victoria would certainly have taken a fonder farewell of the mule than she took of her Prime Minister, for the mule was a dumb animal.

Gladstone's terrible discovery had a traumatic effect on his waking and sleeping hours for the rest of his life. Lover-like, he pursued Queen Victoria vainly at garden parties and he dreamt more than once that she invited him to breakfast alone with her at ten o'clock. As she always breakfasted at nine-thirty and only with her family, the dream-favour was clearly of the rarest kind.* The nature of Gladstone's trouble was further emphasized by his telling his sons that her unkindness was due to foul stories about his work for prostitutes. If she really believed them, he added, it was surprising that she should have treated him so well. To the end he described their relations as 'something of a mystery'.[26]

Was Gladstone's theory correct?

It is true that Queen Victoria's feelings about prostitution were strong and sometimes unbalanced. While pitying pro-foundly 'the poor girls' and detesting their seducers, she was inclined to regard all unorthodox forms of rescue work as exhibitionism or worse. The Salvation Army, for instance, made several appeals for support from the Privy Purse which were not granted and she sometimes thought that their 'Halle-lujah lassies' were no better than they ought to be. Gladstone's activities among the 'fallen' were of course known to her. There was a time also when his innocent delight in notorious beauties of a different class got him talked about at Court. In September 1884, for instance, Ponsonby wrote to his wife:

'... Mrs Gladstone had told the Queen all sorts of stories about [Lady Lonsdale] before she went to Mar – where she found much of what she had heard was untrue. The fact is that Mrs G. had a roughish time of it there with "William" who immediately was captivated by Ly. Lonsdale & cld. not tear himself away from her and Ly. Dalhousie.'[27]

* The fact that Victorian garden parties used to be called 'break-fasts' may also have affected the dreamer.

These 'Lonsdale rows', as they were called, involved the Waleses but not, directly, the Queen, though she made inquiries through Lady Ely.

Taken altogether, Gladstone's interest in women of whatever class was not the cause for Queen Victoria's dislike. Perhaps she had paid undue attention to the rumours about street walkers when they first reached her;* but that was twenty years earlier. In her countless diatribes against him she never mentioned his personal morals. Indeed, she continued to refer to him as a 'good' man while expostulating at his 'wicked' ways. The word 'good' in the Queen's vocabulary always included sexual virtue.

Gladstone's famous analogy of the Sicilian mule further illustrates both his brilliance and his blindness. To compare himself to a mule was a stroke of genius for his mulish obstinacy undoubtedly caused enormous offence; but to suggest that she felt he had done 'much valuable service' and 'no wrong', like his Sicilian mule, was a sad fantasy. Far from entertaining no feelings whatsoever, 'not the smallest shred' for the brute, she disliked him intensely.

Biographers of both Gladstone and Queen Victoria have always found it necessary to decide whether the dislike was political or temperamental. Much can be made of their fierce political divisions over the whole gamut of Liberal reform and the converse fact that where the Queen might be said to have taken a 'modern' line, Gladstone tended to be old-fashioned, orthodox or reactionary. She thought that education should be practical rather than scholastic: he was a passionate classicist and a devoted son of Oxford. She welcomed new ideas in religion and freedom to speculate; he was a devout High Churchman. She thought public money should be used directly to help the poor; he saw in such proposals the end of honest finance.

Today, with the increasing publication of private papers, it is more usual to throw the emphasis on incompatibility of temperament. The case of Rosebery shows that Queen Victoria could greatly like someone with whom on occasions she disagreed greatly, and she fell for Lord Bryce's fascinating per-

* See p. 506.

sonality despite his belief in Home Rule and vigorous opposition to the sanctity of deer forests.

Her favourite characters were either witty, romantic and mysterious or safe, simple, sensible and brisk. A preacher who finished his sermon in nineteen minutes, a conjurer who did his tricks in ten, won her applause. Gladstone was grotesquely long-winded and his tricks were interminable. There was a joke in the Queen's Household that when he went over to Rome he would pour forth such eloquence in the confessional, proving his sins to be whiter than snow if looked at correctly, that the priest would abdicate. Lord Salisbury once told her that no one could understand how Gladstone listened to a sermon without 'rising to reply'.[28] He was complex, audacious, sometimes fanatical and like all visionaries, inclined to take himself too seriously. He never entertained the Queen with wit though very occasionally he amused her by describing misadventures, as when he once got lost in a fog.

His manner towards her combined exaggerated deference with a want of gallantry. More than once she compared his 'cold loyalty' with the 'warm devotion' of others. The imbalance between deference and warmth was exactly reversed in John Brown, and though productive of storms it seemed to the emotional Queen a fault on the right side.

Queen Victoria was profoundly jealous of Gladstone. Jealous in a way that only women already in positions of power are jealous of men. Mr Frank Hardie has shown that the 'People's William' could not also be the 'Queen's William'.[29] It would be even truer if put another way. The 'People's William' competed with the 'People's Victoria'. Deeside as well as Midlothian acknowledged his sway. Portraits of the GOM adorned cottage walls which ought to have been dedicated solely to VRI. When he visited Kirkwall in 1884 the Liberals in the town proclaimed a whole holiday and all the shops shut.* Pointedly she dubbed his campaigns 'Royal Progresses', his press reports 'Court Circulars'.

Their first deliberate approaches to the masses had occurred

* All but one and that was the only Tory in Kirkwall. When the Gladstones landed they did their shopping in the one place they found open.

at the same time – in the early 'sixties. As a newcomer to the Liberal Party, Gladstone turned for invigoration to the people; the Queen, in her desolate widowhood, found comfort in the same direction. Thus two rival giants were both trying to draw strength from the same earth. In 1864 the scrupulous Gladstone was already searching his conscience over his phenomenal success with mass audiences. 'God knows, I have not courted them,' he wrote in his diary. 'Somewhat troubled by dreams of halls, and lines of people and great assemblies.' The interpretation of these dreams would have presented no problem to the Queen. They were like Joseph's dreams of the lines of sheaves and the great assembly of the sun, moon and stars bowing down before him. Jealousy clearly entered into the Queen's specific disputes with Gladstone. As his influence over the country grew, he seemed to curtail hers. Constitution, Army, Church, Ireland, Europe, Africa – wherever she looked, he had done his best to diminish her prerogative and power. He would neither listen to what she told him nor tell her what her Ministers were saying. When one of them declined to pass on information withheld by Gladstone, she remarked bitterly that his first 'allegiance' should have been to the Sovereign.

It has been argued with great cogency by Sir Philip Magnus that from Gladstone's most dismal failure – his relations with the Queen – sprang his most enduring success.

'He cut a new pattern of constitutional monarchy which, rejected by Queen Victoria, was triumphantly followed by all her successors ... It transformed the Crown politically into a rubber stamp, but it enhanced to an incalculable degree the force of its moral and emotional appeal.'[30]

No woman cares to consider herself a rubber stamp, however great her moral appeal, and the Queen loudly proclaimed her intention to abdicate rather than become one. Nevertheless, it was always her pride to be a constitutional monarch, in contrast to most of her royal colleagues on the Continent, though she frequently misinterpreted that role. Another than Gladstone, say Rosebery if he had stayed the course, could have eased her gently into the new pattern. With Gladstone she felt that every inch of ground must be jealously guarded against the encroachments of a usurper.

After Gladstone's retirement the Liberal succession was expeditiously decided by the Queen without consulting Gladstone. She chose Lord Rosebery. His rival, Harcourt, she neither liked nor trusted, and the feelers she put out through Ponsonby convinced her she was right to pass him over. Owing to a mistake, however, the unfortunate Harcourt was brought into the presence but promptly dismissed with perfect composure by gracious Majesty. Five years later Rosebery asked her if this legendary accident had really occurred. 'Yes, that was terrible,' she replied laughing heartily. 'No one knows to this day how it happened – no one can explain it . . .'[31]

Rosebery's neurotic ambivalence about accepting office was known to the Queen and she expressed herself 'immensely delighted' at the result. He was something of a kindred spirit, suffering from 'nerves' and chronic shyness like herself. When as a widower he broke his morbid seclusion to become Foreign Secretary again she promised to help, assuring him that work would do him good. In imperial affairs he shared the Queen–Empress's 'large ideas'. A final reason for making her choice swiftly and choosing Rosebery was that she had planned to go abroad almost at once for her indispensable spring holiday and another wedding of grandchildren. It was therefore necessary to find someone who would carry on the Gladstone Government without a break.

This ruled out the dissolution and election which she had often secretly discussed with Salisbury, and which he now might well be expecting. In case Salisbury felt let down, she sent him an explanatory message which concluded sententiously with the words, 'It must be remembered that the present Government have still a majority in the House of Commons.'[32] Lord Salisbury was doubtless amused, for Gladstone had also had a majority the year before, when Her Majesty had suggested dissolving him, Home Rule and Parliament together.

Three days before her departure she received a rude shock. A glance at the draft of her Speech with which Rosebery intended to open the new Session disclosed his intention to complete the disestablishment of the Welsh and Scottish Churches, just as if Gladstone were still there. Rosebery had told her that they were not going to revive Home Rule – 'Oh, no, there has been enough of that last year!'[33] – and she had jumped to the conclusion that he would likewise drop all other obnoxious items in Gladstone's programme. After an exchange of aggrieved letters in which the Queen expressed herself 'horrified' and Rosebery unutterably 'distressed', a remarkable compromise was reached. Instead of promising 'Bills for the Disestablishment', the Government proposed 'Measures dealing with the Ecclesiastical Establishment'. Her lifelong refusal to accept the constitutional fact that 'the Queen's Speech is the speech of her Ministers', constantly exposed her to the horns of a dilemma more ludicrous even than those of Gladstone's cow. Either she had to be unconstitutional in rejecting the Speech, or untruthful in approving it.

Having arrived in Florence, she began to wonder anxiously whether, after all, her holiday might not seem to the public ill-timed. She asked Ponsonby to put something in the papers but he strongly advised against making any excuses, writing to his wife:

'It looks as if she was out of her mind. "Excellent health but requires rest for 4 weeks".'[34]

He added that her mind, far from being unhinged, was 'very keen and decided on all things'. Her Journal was filled with fierce criticism of Rosebery for having gone as far as Gladstone, 'without Gladstone's conviction'. She even regretted, if only for a week or two, that she had not left Rosebery as Foreign Minister and 'had a combination Cabinet'. This wild idea, as Ponsonby truly observed, 'never would have done'.

By the middle of April Florence had soothed away her irascibility and she could endure to read Rosebery's unanswerable plea that a House of Lords which went to sleep during a Conservative administration but roused itself to veto every Liberal measure, must be reformed. She finally agreed that the Lords ought to be 'reconstructed' but not in response to agitation. Nor as a result of Rosebery's sallies. She ordered

666

him in June to 'take a more serious tone and be, if she may say so, less jocular, which is hardly befitting a Prime Minister'.[35]

When agitation showed signs of becoming violent in the autumn she was again tempted to dissolve Parliament, particularly as Lord Salisbury, in answer to her *Very Private* question, 'is the Unionist party fit for a dissolution *now*?', replied 'Yes.' Fortunately the Queen took the advice of a Liberal Unionist, Sir Henry James, that the time for the Crown to intervene had 'not yet come'.[36] With this the sagacious Salisbury then concurred.

Meanwhile Queen Victoria had moved from Florence for another Darmstadt wedding on April 19th. Three months earlier she had received an exciting telegram from Prince Alfred, now Duke of Coburg, since his Uncle Ernest had died without heir: 'Your and my great wish has been fulfilled this evening. Ducky has accepted Ernie of Hesse's proposal . . .'* She hastened to inform her eldest daughter that this intermarriage of close relations did not, as might appear, contravene her own theories: from Ernie's point of view, since all Affie's girls were so strong, 'the same blood only adds to the strength & if you try to avoid it you will marry some unhealthy little Pcess wh wld just cause what you wish to avoid.' The Queen concluded her rejoicing over this and another family engagement with her usual reservation: 'Although I am not a matchmaker or delight in marriages.'[37]

The Darmstadt ceremony was impressively performed – 'But I like ours so much better,' the Queen could not help observing. Hardly had she finished breakfast next morning before she was 'thunderstruck' to hear that her loveliest granddaughter, Princess Alix of Hesse, had at last accepted the Tsarevitch Nicholas. It was in fact the Kaiser, Queen Victoria's rival matchmaker, who had persuaded his cousin to swallow her scruples about joining the Russian Church and marry the man she loved. The Tsar of Russia died suddenly in October, so that Princess Alix became an Empress as well

* 'Ducky' was the Queen's granddaughter, Princess Victoria Melita of Coburg, 'Ernie' her Hessian grandson.

as a wife in the space of three weeks. The Queen was not altogether happy about this most splendid of her grand-children's matches. She noted that 'the position is an anxiety' and, as if with prescience, wrote on the eve of her grand-daughter's Coronation: 'Alicky's fate will be sealed tomorrow morning.'[38] A quarter of a century later the Russian Revolution ground her into the dust.

An event which brought almost universal joy occurred on June 26th, 1894 – the birth of a son to the Duke and Duchess of York.* Queen Victoria's relief was tempered by a touch of impatience at the public excitement generated by this achievement. After one newspaper had suggested it was the crowning glory of her reign, she wrote to the Empress Frederick:

> 'It is a great pleasure & satisfaction, but not such a marvel, for if Alicky had not refused Eddy in '89 – I might have had a gt-gd Child 4 years ago already. As it is, however, it seems that it has never happened in this Country that there shld be three direct Heirs as well as the Sovereign alive.'[39]

As the second generation of the Royal Family married and multiplied, the older generation of the Queen's Household began to die off. Lady Ely and Sir John Cowell† had both gone, the quest for Cowell's successor causing Ponsonby some concern. Little Aleck Yorke was 'not good in shape for a Master of the Household', nor could a young man be put 'over the head of a lot of old patapouffes as we all are ... here'. Moreover, it must be someone who would accept the Queen's habit of sending all her messages by women. Lord Edward Clinton eventually agreed to give it a trial. Soon he was warming to a programme of radical reforms. 'Don't do too much,' warned Ponsonby, 'which will make people cross & appeal to the Queen.' 'No,' replied Clinton, 'I want to talk to HM and get her to recommend these reforms.'[40]

Two months later the Queen was recommending to Ponsonby a reform in his handwriting. She pointed out that ever since Lord Palmerston's day it had been the rule to write a

* Afterwards King Edward VIII, now Duke of Windsor.
† See p. 434.

'good round distinct hand' but recently Ponsonby had taken to sending drafts in very small handwriting and very pale ink. Lord Rosebery was an even worse offender.

> 'The Queen (whose eyesight has become very faulty, & has not yet got glasses to suit) can hardly read them *at all*.'[41]

There was an element of comedy in this poignant appeal. Dashed off in pale mauve chalk which shows through the paper, blurring what is written on the other side, Queen Victoria's note is a thousand times more illegible than anything Ponsonby ever wrote.

Nevertheless, the Queen was not mistaken in detecting a deterioration in her secretary's script and a listlessness in his manner. A sentence from his last letter to his wife, written from Balmoral on October 1st, 1894, has a prophetic ring:

> 'I must make some coup d'état to get away . . .'

Three months later, the *coup d'état* arrived.

Queen Victoria had heralded the new year with a desperate prayer for the preservation of her remaining friends: 'I have lost so many in 94 . . .' On January 7th, 1895 Sir Henry Ponsonby suffered a severe stroke. The Queen was deeply distressed. In the following November he died. 'Too, too sad!' The inevitable hymn, *Now the labourer's task is o'er*, struck her as being 'particularly applicable' to 'dear Sir Henry'. Within days she was commemorating him with the inevitable bust.

While Ponsonby lay paralysed at Osborne, the last Liberal Government of Queen Victoria's reign battered itself to death. Most of its social legislation was withdrawn by the Government itself or sent up to the House of Lords for painless killing. Liberals complacently called this 'filling up the cup' of their Lordships' guilt, preparatory to reforming or abolishing them. A Bill for the payment of Members of Parliament won a majority in the Commons but only of eighteen. 'Where is the money to come from?' demanded Queen Victoria.

Equally obnoxious to her were the Government's two successes. Harcourt's epoch-making introduction of death duties she rightly regarded as a 'revolution', inciting Rosebery to emasculate them even at the eleventh hour. Gloomily Rosebery replied that as a peer he had no voice in the country's finance. A decision to shift 'poor George' at long last from the post of Commander-in-Chief found the Queen between two fires. Her cousin's mulish attempt to hang on until he got a pension caused her annoyance; but a realization that neither Liberals nor Tories would fill up the vacancy with another Royal Duke (Prince Arthur) provoked her far more.

'Poor George's' end was instantaneously followed by that of the Government which had beaten him: on June 21st, 1895 the Government triumphantly announced the Duke's resignation; a few hours later they were blown sky-high in a snap division on the War Office's supply of cordite. The Government at once resigned. It had been the most uncomfortable Cabinet in British history. Rosebery was not on speaking terms with Harcourt and also had to endure his old enemy, insomnia – a greater agony to rule the day and a lesser agony to rule the night. To the Queen he confided that 'quite dreadful' scenes had regularly disgraced the Cabinet. 'His only regret was to leave me.'[42] None of the Cabinet was sorry to resign.

Queen Victoria, however, with her talent for the *volte face* which makes her such a fascinating character, would gladly have kept them longer. The change of Government, she wrote on July 1st to the Empress Frederick, was 'not such a source of satisfaction as it might have been for I am losing some people who cannot be replaced.' She then listed Lord Spencer, Mr Campbell-Bannerman ('a good & pleasant man'), Mr Fowler (another 'good man'), Lord Herschell, the Lord Chancellor ('full of anecdote & passionately fond of music') and several of her Liberal lords-in-waiting, especially Lord Acton. On first meeting Acton she had been amazed to find that someone 'so light in hand & agreeable on all topics' could be 'a learned scientist'. He was 'such a gt ornament' that she would have tried to keep him on but for the many Tories who were already after his place.

670

She concluded her list of sad losses with this unique admission:

> 'And personally I am vy fond of Ld Rosebery & prefer him (not his Politics) to Ld S. – he is so much attached to me personally.'[43]

She admired Salisbury because he was supremely adult; Rosebery, even at his worst, was in her eyes that far more fetching character, a prodigal son.

It looks as though, with the passing of Gladstone, Queen Victoria might have settled down happily with moderate Liberal Ministers. But the opportunity, if there really was one, had come too late. The general election of 1895 resulted in a huge majority for the Tories. 'If only the Lords are prudent,' she wrote, 'it ought to last a long time.'[44]

It outlasted Queen Victoria.

CHAPTER XXXV

THE LABOURER'S TASK
1892–1900

QUEEN VICTORIA'S Indian attendant, Abdul Karim the Munshi, was responsible for her positively last clash with Ministers of the Crown. Her wisdom may have been questionable but it is impossible not to marvel at the old lady who, partly as a protest against prejudice, challenged two Viceroys, two Prime Ministers, two Secretaries of State, many other officials and most of her Court.

Unlike John Brown, the Munshi did not make history. Most of our information on this astonishing affair has hitherto depended upon the sprightly *Recollections* of Frederick ('Fritz') Ponsonby, Sir Henry Ponsonby's second son.* As an old man's memories, they have inevitably telescoped certain events.

The Munshi, always a pusher, climbed steadily. Cottages were built for him; his wife, nephew and 'aunts' were brought from India and every time Mrs Abdul Karim fell ill, Dr Reid reported that a different tongue was put out for him to examine. The Munshi also interested the Queen in a clever young Mohammedan friend of his, Rafiuddin Ahmed. Sir Henry was ordered to introduce the Munshi to the Lord Chancellor in 1892 with a view to assisting Ahmed's career; three years later we find Ahmed reading for the bar at Gray's Inn. Suspicion and jealousy, especially among the Munshi's Indian fellow servants, kept pace with his advance. A note to Sir Henry from the Queen, for instance, in 1892 complained that the Munshi had been fobbed off with a hired carriage instead of being given one from the royal stables. The Court believed him to be a low-class impostor, supplying Afghanistan, through Ahmed, with State secrets extracted from Her Majesty's boxes.

At length the news of yet another promotion for the Munshi

* *Recollections of Three Reigns* by Sir Frederick Ponsonby, Lord Sysonby, edited by Colin Welch (1951).

in 1894 inspired four of the younger courtiers, led by Colonel Bigge (assistant secretary) and Dr Reid, to act. Abdul was to be formally designated the Queen's 'Indian Secretary' with an office, clerks under him and the appropriate title of 'Hafiz'; all early photographs which showed him waiting at table were to be destroyed. The dauntless four sent a report to the Queen, purposely obtained from India, casting doubt on Abdul's social origins. Shocked and offended, she dashed off a hasty defence of her favourite to Sir Henry, following it up on April 10th with a powerful counter-attack:

'... to make out that the poor good Munshi is so *low* is really *outrageous* & in a country like England quite out of place ... She has known 2 Archbishops who were sons respectively of a Butcher & a Grocer ... Abdul's father saw good & honourable service as a Dr & he [Abdul] feels cut to the heart at being thus spoken of. It probably comes from some low jealous Indians or Anglo–Indians ... The Queen is so sorry for the poor Munshi's sensitive feelings.'[1]

Queen Victoria's attitude to racialism has only recently begun to be appreciated.* It is still not realized that her crusade was part of a deeper, private revolt against discrimination of all kinds, including class. Twenty years earlier she had restated her rules for Court appointments in an outspoken letter to Sir Thomas Biddulph. While not absolutely forbidding the selection of noblemen's sons, she insisted on equal opportunities for the sons of 'faithful old servants' of the Sovereign:

'That division of classes is the *one thing* which is most dangerous & reprehensible, never intended by the law of nature & wh the Queen is always labouring to alter ... The present Archbishop of York's Father was a butcher, & so on.'[2]

It was a pity that the Radical members of Queen Victoria's later Parliaments could not hear her dilating on that butcher in a manner worthy of John Ball himself.

* See for instance Mary Lutyens' *Lady Lytton's Court Diary*, pp. 38 *et seq.*

Sir Henry duly recorded in a memorandum dated June 11th, 1894 that the Munshi was now 'Hafiz'. Rumbles over his social status did not diminish. 'Might the Queen ask Sir Henry,' she wrote on August 19th, 'kindly not to ask Dr Reid anything abt the Munshi's affairs & people ... as he has not always been very nice; though he has abt illness.'[3] In order to settle the matter she instructed Sir Henry's son Fritz, then serving on the staff of the Viceroy but about to join the Court as an equerry, to visit the Munshi's father, Doctor Waziruddin, at Agra and report on his condition.

Fritz Ponsonby presented himself to the Queen in December with the incredible news that 'Doctor' Waziruddin was 'only the apothecary at the jail'. She flatly rejected his story – he must have seen the wrong man – and sent young Ponsonby to Coventry.[4] He promptly joined the ranks of Abdul's implacable foes. In the midst of this crisis came Sir Henry's stroke on January 7th, 1895. His place was filled by Sir Fleetwood Edwards as Keeper of the Privy Purse and as private secretary, the vigorous Colonel Bigge.

This able young soldier had been selected for the Court by Queen Victoria herself in recognition of services to the ill-fated Prince Imperial. No scion of a ducal house, Arthur Bigge was just the type of 'faithful servant' for whom the Queen was always on the look-out. To brains he added character, popularity, years of training under Sir Henry and a singing voice which could move Her Majesty to tears with a fine rendering of *The Lost Chord*.

Queen Victoria's first words to Sir Henry's successors on their formal appointment in May 1895 were significant:

'The Queen is sure that they will follow in his footsteps, and be as kind to all of all ranks, as he always was.'[5]

There were no signs at present, however, that Sir Henry's kindness (or rather, grudging tolerance) towards 'these Injuns', as he called the Munshi and his colleagues, would be practised by the new generation.

Throughout the next two years there was a running battle between Queen Victoria and her advisers, the Queen determined to 'keep up' the Munshi and the rest to pull him down.

Edwards won a victory in refusing to take tea with him and Dr Reid in declining to show his father round the London hospitals. The Queen retaliated by having a seat reserved for him next to the lady-in-waiting at the tableaux. 'I have now got to think it lucky that the Munshi's sweeper does not dine with us,' wrote Fritz Ponsonby to the Viceroy. The Queen's greatest triumph was in squeezing a high honour for the Munshi out of Lord Rosebery and Sir Henry Fowler – the CIE – after having failed to make the Viceroy acknowledge a sentimental Christmas card ('*a wish of my heart be yours today*') sent to him by her protégé. The Governors of Bombay and Madras had returned similar cards to sender. Fritz Ponsonby, however, failed to persuade Lord Elgin to use the affair of the Christmas cards as an excuse for personally denouncing the Munshi to the Queen.[6]

The truth was that successive Ministers, Liberal and Conservative alike, found the Munshi a 'bore' rather than a danger. They assumed that Rafiuddin Ahmed passed on 'the most extraordinary stories ... from English palaces to the Kabul Court [Afghanistan]'; they knew that the Munshi bought plots of Government land 'at his own price'; they understood that the Queen showed their letters to him and they must therefore write 'accordingly'; they were even willing to have him watched though not 'shadowed'; but nothing would induce them to get mixed up in what Lord George Hamilton, Indian Secretary in Lord Salisbury's Ministry, called 'the Court's mud pies'.[7] On February 21st, 1896, Hamilton wrote to Lord Elgin:

'I do not think that the Munshi is as dangerous as some suppose. Salisbury concurs in that view; he is a stupid man, & on that account he may become a tool in the hands of other abler men.'[8]

As for prevailing upon the Queen to get rid of him – it was no use, said Hamilton, arguing with an old person about a servant. In fact Hamilton had given Queen Victoria the impression by 1895 that he was perfectly happy about the Munshi.

Meanwhile the Queen and the Munshi pursued their joint

campaign. Abdul got his picture into the French press as *Le Munchy* – the man of *'grandes capacités et beaucoup d'integrité'* who took his promenades *'dans un riche landau'* apart from the Household, as a sign of respect. The Queen, having reminded the Empress Frederick that the Munshi ranked as a 'gentleman' in her suite, asked her to show him round her 'charming house' at Kronberg; he ate no meat, only a little milk and fruit – 'I hope I am not troublesome?'[9] Her family considered her very troublesome indeed.

In the autumn of 1895 she was busy recommending to Lord Salisbury a plan to revolutionize diplomacy. Why not a Moslem 'attached to the Embassy at Constantinople', she suggested, naming none other than Rafiuddin Ahmed for the post. She felt that he would know better than anyone how to placate Moslem opinion in India while curbing the Turk. Europe was again shuddering under the horrors of Turkish mis-rule, Gladstone surged out of retirement for the last time to denounce the 'Armenian atrocities' and Queen Victoria yet again denounced 'the impolitic half-mad attitude of Mr Gladstone'. Personal letters from herself to the Sultan containing firm but friendly remonstrances seemed to her the sane course. Lord Salisbury checked both her impulses.

It may have been naïve of Queen Victoria to suppose that Mr Rafiuddin Ahmed would succeed where Mr Gladstone had failed. At least she was open to new ideas not generally associated with palaces nor indeed with the Victorian age. Lord Salisbury parried the suggestion: Mr Ahmed certainly had the ability but had he the fitness? With unanswerable logic the Queen made Lord Salisbury find out for himself by interviewing Ahmed on October 23rd; the wily Prime Minister, however, kept the discussion to pious platitudes about religious toleration. The Queen would not let go. Over a year later Lord Salisbury was protesting that he would gladly employ Ahmed but for the prejudice against him 'in Your Majesty's services', which did not exist 'in other governments dealing with races of different origins'.[10]

It was in the spring of 1897 that the whole affair finally exploded. On Queen Victoria's spring visit abroad she proposed to take Abdul with her, which meant that he would have to eat with the Household. At this they 'put their feet down', deputing Harriet Phipps, the Queen's personal secretary, to deliver an ultimatum – no Munshi or no Household. The Queen flew into one of her now rare rages, sweeping everything off the top of her desk on to the floor. In the end Lord Salisbury himself had to be summoned and ingeniously persuaded her that the French were too 'odd' to understand the Munshi's position and might be rude. Abdul, therefore, did not join the huge royal caravanserai on its semi-public progress to Cimiez. But he turned up soon afterwards, as Princess May wrote to Prince George, 'to the despair of the poor gentlemen'[11] and what's more invited Rafiuddin Ahmed to come too. This descent of a political suspect upon the royal residence, without so much as a by-your-leave, gave Arthur Bigge and Fritz Ponsonby their chance. At forty-eight hours' notice Rafiuddin Ahmed, protesting loudly to the Munshi who had been forced to act as go-between, was sent packing, and confidential requests were flashed in cypher all over India for fresh information on the Munshi's birth, parentage, history, 'wife or wives'.

Nothing fresh was forthcoming except that his father, Sheikh Mohammed Waziruddin, Hospital Assistant at 60 rupees a month, was 'respectable and trustworthy'. In desperation Fritz Ponsonby wrote on April 27th to the Viceroy's private secretary for any hostile cuttings about the Munshi from Hindu or European papers which might open the Queen's eyes. The Court, he added, had done their best —

'But it is no use, for the Queen says that it is "race prejudice" & that we are all jealous of the poor Munshi (!) She has found one or two people who would say anything to please her, to back her up . . .'[12]

Three days later the Secretary of State, Lord George Hamilton, was writing to the Viceroy about what he called this 'Court commotion'. While admitting that the Munshi's friend, Rafiuddin Ahmed, was probably 'a disreputable fellow', he refused to initiate 'any fishing inquiry' into the Munshi himself, against whom there was no evidence; 'whatever may be the outcome of this little storm,' he continued, 'I am sure the influence of the Munshi will hereafter be on the decline.' [13]

He was right. When the Court returned from Cimiez, Hamilton wrote again to the Viceroy describing an interview with Bigge. The concerted pressure of 'old Indian officers in her Court', added to that of Bigge himself, had persuaded her to put the Munshi more into his 'proper place'. Hamilton reiterated his decision to 'sit still' and not interfere.

It looks as if Queen Victoria had been defeated in the final round. But a remarkable postscript to Hamilton's letter suggests that if she gave way it was not out of necessity but tact:

'PS. I think you can write with perfect freedom on general matters to the Queen. So far as I know nothing we say or write to Her is communicated to the Munshi. He may of course get hold of papers, but I doubt if he does. Where care has to be exercised is in opinions [of] individuals.'

What is to be the verdict on Queen Victoria's last exotic friendship? From the political angle, the case against the Munshi was void, while according to the Queen, Rafiuddin Ahmed was no longer regarded as a 'security risk' by the autumn of 1897. Extraordinary woman that she was, she had reopened her crusade with a barrage of letters to Lord Salisbury the moment she was released from the Diamond Jubilee celebrations. First she cleared the Munshi of spying and herself of indiscretion:

'With reference to the subject on which Lord Salisbury has been so kind & just – the Queen would just wish to assert that *no* political papers of any kind are ever in the Munshi's hands, *even* in her presence. He only helps her to read words which she cannot read or merely ordinary submissions on warrants for signature. He does not read English fluently enough to be able to read anything of importance . . .' [14]

Then she turned to Rafiuddin Ahmed. Having reluctantly promised Lord Salisbury not to allow Ahmed into her houses or palaces uninvited, since he was 'a journalist & a meddler', [15] at the end of July 1897 she was again urging the Prime

Minister to employ Ahmed – this time in getting information from Mohammedans which would be useful to the Government. 'People have often been employed to gather information whose characters are not unimpeachable.' She added loyally that Ahmed had been recommended by the great Professor Jowett of Balliol College, Oxford, especially to Arthur Godley, now the Permanent Under-Secretary at the India Office. The Queen concluded:

'She fears we did act wrongly in treating him as a suspected person of which we had no proofs . . .'[16]

In August she was badgering Lord Salisbury to express regret to Ahmed for his expulsion from Cimiez and to explain that it had been entirely due to his being a journalist – 'otherwise he had done nothing to displease or offend the Queen . . .'. By September she was 'much relieved' to hear from Lord Salisbury that the suspicions against Rafiuddin Ahmed had been 'unjust', while the editor of the *Nineteenth Century* (for which Ahmed wrote) testified that he was 'much too honourable' to give information.[17]

Throughout 1898 Queen Victoria was labouring away for Abdul and Ahmed as zestfully as ever. She wished to give the latter a Jubilee medal – thousands got them including 'clergymen, *actors*, artists' – but Salisbury advised her to wait.[18] She also insisted that the 'disgraceful affair' of last year* should not prevent Ahmed from being asked to '*one* Court Ball': he had gone in 1894 and 1895 *and* to the Duke of York's wedding; his present exclusion would be looked upon in the Moslem world as a political reprisal for the Sultan's Armenian atrocities.[19] The Munshi's social position continued to concern her: 'It is *not* a high one & it is *not* in *England* that *one* should speak of *that* . . .' After reverting to her favourite butcher who sired an Archbishop she brought 'this long yarn' to an end by quoting the late Sir William Jenner: 'if the Queen chose to raise a chimney sweep they had no right to say a word'.[20]

When the Aga Khan visited Windsor she saw to it that he

* Ahmed's expulsion from Cimiez.

had the benefit of a conversation with the Munshi, and it was only due to a gentleman from the India Office 'poisoning' his mind in the train returning to London that he failed to invite Abdul to meet him again. How dared the India Office say her Munshi was not a gentleman, stormed the Queen, when the Gaekwar of Baroda was raised to a prince from a goatherd?[21] Lord Curzon, the new Viceroy, was warned by her not to believe stories about the Munshi and Lord Hopetoun was exhorted to set a good example at Windsor by being kind to him.[22] At the end of the year she was exhilarated to hear that Lord Curzon favoured the building of a Mohammedan College; she promised to subscribe, 'even if it should mean giving something to a Hindoo College – but they do not need help as they have plenty'.[23]

The Queen's worst fault was in allowing the Munshi to bias her in favour of Mohammedans: during a period of increasingly serious Hindu–Moslem riots, this was dangerous. She was also indefensibly violent about her Court during the 1897 crisis, contrasting their 'shameful' behaviour with Salisbury's 'kind good advice'. She seems to have recognized afterwards the weight of their responsibility for her personal contacts. '*All* is quiet & satisfactory now,' she wrote to Lord Salisbury on December 27th, 1898, '– excepting that the injured individual cannot get over it'. It was upon the 'redtapist' India Office and a 'jealous' Parsee MP that she ultimately laid the blame for what had happened.

The wind of change which she had hoped to see blowing through the Foreign Office and India Office was quietly allowed to drop after her death. A bonfire of the Munshi's papers was made by order of King Edward VII at Frogmore Cottage, one of the Munshi's homes. Solemnly watching the flames stood Abdul himself, his nephew, Queen Alexandra representing the King and Princess Beatrice representing Abdul's late protectress. He lived on at Karim Lodge, Agra, until his death in 1909, when King Edward ordered a second holocaust of papers. Lord Minto, the Viceroy, begged that old Mrs Karim might be allowed to keep a few letters in Queen Victoria's handwriting. 'It will do good.'[24] Permission was granted.

A fantastic event took place in Africa at the close of 1895 which heralded the cataclysms of the next century. Under the command of Dr Jameson, Administrator of Rhodesia, a few hundred mounted police made a midnight dash into the Transvaal to raise a revolution against President Kruger. The 'Jameson Raid' was brought to an ignominious end by the Boers who surrounded the raiders on January 4th, 1896. From captured papers a British conspiracy was uncovered to reoccupy the Transvaal, involving Cecil Rhodes and his South Africa Company and to some extent *The Times*, the Colonial Office and the Secretary of State, Joseph Chamberlain, himself.

The Raid led directly to the Boer War – the first struggle against a white enemy which Queen Victoria's soldiers had waged since the Crimean War nearly half a century ago. Like the cataracts which were steadily darkening her sight, events in Africa spread a shadow over her last years.

At the time of the Raid, the Queen's thoughts were not on Southern Africa. Early in December 1895 Prince Henry of Battenberg, the indispensable support of her old age, had joined the Ashanti expedition. It was with 'astonishment and concern' that she had learnt of Prince Henry's intention: 'I told him it would never do.' Her experience of fevers convinced her that Liko would not survive the climate. Princess Beatrice, however, got the ban lifted. The truth was that the high-spirited Prince found the eternal round of Windsor, Osborne and Balmoral stifling. Even hunting was strictly rationed by his nervous and doting mother-in-law. Moreover, the faith she openly put in his judgement contrasted with her qualified confidence in the Prince of Wales, thus creating jealousies.

On December 7th Princess Beatrice returned in tears from Aldershot station where she had seen off her husband to the strains of *Auld Lang Syne* played by a military band.

The first day of the new year, 1896, opened sombrely. The wet morning made Queen Victoria feel 'low', thinking of those she had lost in the past twelve months. Suddenly came the message of the Jameson Raid. 'Everywhere difficulties seem to arise,' groaned the Queen. One of the difficulties hardest to bear was the Kaiser's exultant telegram congratulating President Kruger, who was still supposed to acknowledge the Queen's suzerainty, on the preservation of his 'independence'. This loaded word produced a howl of rage from millions of British throats, hitherto choked by shame. The Prince of Wales wanted to know 'what business the Emperor has to send any message at all'? He only hoped William would not appear at Cowes this year. (The Kaiser had distinguished himself the year before by picking a quarrel with Salisbury, again keeping the Queen waiting for dinner, audibly referring to his uncle as 'the old popinjay' and going home early in a huff.)

The Queen agreed that she must administer a rebuke to William, though not the 'good snub' her son suggested. 'For those sharp, cutting answers and remarks only irritate and do harm.' In her Journal she noted with satisfaction, 'Sent off my letter to William in which I gave him a piece of my mind as to his dreadful telegram,' later informing his mother that the anger against him would 'last for some little time'.[25] The 'little time' dragged on through a series of Anglo–German rivalries until it encompassed the rest of her reign and beyond.

It was not till 1899 that the Kaiser's huge white yacht, *Hohenzollern*, was invited once more to the Solent. A dispute with Lord Salisbury over Samoa prevented the visit. Queen Victoria heard that William was 'vy cross – declared Ld Salisbury to be his enemy & that he won't come to England while he is P.Minister.' She commented drily: 'I think he will have to wait a long time.'[26] Three weeks later the Kaiser gave her his own version of the facts: Lord Salisbury had treated Germany in 'the most unhappy way' over Samoa – 'a stupid island which is a hairpin to England compared to the thousands of square miles she is annexing right and left unopposed every year'.[27] The hairpin seems to have pricked the conscience of the Queen. She had already observed, apropos of China, that she 'could not quite understand why nobody was to have anything anywhere but ourselves'.[28] Accordingly, she invited the Kaiser to Windsor for the autumn. This visit, the last, was an unexpected success, Willy being 'sensible & kind' and Dona 'not at all stiff'.[29]

Meanwhile on that January 8th, 1896 the Queen confessed to her daughter that there was as yet no knowledge of what had prompted the Raid. Dr Jameson, an 'excellent & able man', had won much sympathy. 'The Boers are horrid people, cruel & over-bearing.'

As usual, she accurately reflected her people's feelings. The subsequent rumours of Government complicity in the Raid scarcely touched her. This was to be expected since her adviser throughout was the chief suspect, Joseph Chamberlain, whom she found 'sensible' and 'prudent'; she already liked Cecil Rhodes personally and the Duke of Fife, married to her granddaughter, Princess Louise of Wales, was President of Rhodes's South Africa Company. Why should she be suspicious? The Committee of Enquiry into the Raid, with its disastrous evasions, passed over her head. She was too busy with her Diamond Jubilee to attend to it. Mercifully, perhaps, she was thus enabled to face the Boer War – last and most inglorious of the major events of her great reign in the certainty that England was right.

Nine days after the news of the Raid, Princess Beatrice brought in a telegram to say that Prince Henry had 'slight' fever. A cloud of anxiety hung over Osborne for a week. At last, on January 18th, mother and daughter heard to their unspeakable relief that he had 'improved' sufficiently to leave for Madeira; but on the 22nd her Journal began with the melancholy words, 'This has been such an awful day that it is almost impossible to describe it.' While she was dressing there had been a knock on her door. A white-faced Prince Arthur came in. ' "Poor Liko is dead!" Can I write it . . . He was our help, the bright sunshine of our home.' It seemed as if the dreadful years of Prince Albert's and Prince Leopold's death had come back. Princess Louise, unhappy in her marriage, exacerbated the situation by treating the tragedy as peculiarly her own and wounding Princess Beatrice deeply, according to the Duchess of Teck, 'by calmly announcing, that *she* (Louise) was Liko's *confidante* & Beatrice, nothing to him . . .'.[30] The Queen's maternal task was not an easy one.

She noticed how much more patiently this youngest child bore her tragedy than she herself had done. Nevertheless, it was a relief to the Court ladies when Princess Beatrice left Osborne in February to recuperate at Cimiez; the Queen, they hoped, would shake off her misery. But the Victorian instinct to dramatize 'last moments' gave the Queen little chance. Relatives, friends and doctors fed her with morbid details of Liko's end. It was a relief to the Queen herself when the Colonial Secretary, Mr Chamberlain, came to see her after tea on March 4th and talked 'very interestingly' about the Transvaal.

He told her a secret which she hid in the recesses of her Journal. 'He [Chamberlain] had seen Dr Jameson, but without anyone knowing.'[31] Even to her Journal she did not confide what Chamberlain and Jameson, who was awaiting his trial in London, discussed. Probably she was not told. For the murky background to the Raid was not the kind of subject with which one burdened a sad old lady of nearly seventy-seven.*

The Court moved from Windsor to Osborne, from Osborne to Balmoral; but the light had gone out of the house. The Journal speaks of an awful blank, stillness everywhere, weather 'very dreary, as dreary as our hearts', Hindustani lessons not going well. Throughout the summer her political comments are noticeably less vivid than during the previous year. 'Saw Ld Salisbury under the trees & talked to him about everything,' is a typically lifeless entry.[32]

Lord Wolseley struck from her a spark of the old fire when he came in May to discuss the Sudan. An expedition had at last been sanctioned to the territories abandoned twelve years ago by Gladstone. Wolseley feared that Egyptian fellaheen troops would not fight very well for Her Majesty. 'I remarked we *must* not be defeated . . .'[33] Because of the Sudanese campaign, though indirectly, the autumnal gloom suddenly lifted. It occurred to Lord Salisbury that the Queen might invite the

---

* It looks as if Chamberlain was making sure that Jameson said nothing during his trial to implicate the Government in the Raid – in which case Queen Victoria has inadvertently let a cat out of the bag. See *Jameson's Raid* by Elizabeth Pakenham, pp. 116–20.

young Tsar and Tsarina to Balmoral and persuade them to sweeten the rest of Europe towards British exertions in the Sudan.

Politically, the Tsar's visit was a failure. Nicholas had several talks with Queen Victoria but remained non-committal, afterwards telling his mother that he had not enjoyed himself. Emotionally, the visit heralded a new wave of happiness. The Queen heard on September 20th that Kitchener had captured his objective on the Nile, Dongola. Two days later the imperial party reached Balmoral. 'It seemed quite like a dream,' sighed the Queen in ecstasies, 'having dear Alicky & Nicky here.' Church bells rang, pipes played, Alicky looked charming in white serge, mountains of luggage perfumed the passages with sweet Russian leather and every bush and ditch concealed a detective. The family aspect of the visit pleased the Queen immensely. Two-year-old Prince 'David' of York came in every day at the end of luncheon to amuse his great-grandmother with an impromptu turn. 'Get up, Gangan,' he would cry shrilly, trying to heave her out of her chair; then, to the handsome bearded Indian at her side: 'Man pull it.' One day the Tsarina showed her jewels to her grandmother; not only were they gorgeous but 'all her own property'.[34] On the last morning a family photograph was taken on the terrace 'by the new cinematograph process'.

Queen Victoria had awoken on September 23rd, 1896 to an avalanche of congratulatory messages. 'Today is the day on which I have reigned longer, by a day, than any English sovereign.'[35] Her grandfather, George III, had hitherto held the palm but for many of his long years the record had been an unhappy one – the King mad and the Regent bad – whereas the old Queen seemed to be increasing in sense and virtue with every year she reigned.

The labourer's task was still not o'er. On January 1st, 1897 Queen Victoria prayed as usual to be of use to her country. The country decided that she could be put to the highest possible use by a spectacular celebration of her Diamond Jubilee.

Sixty years a Queen! It was a thought to evoke the quintessence of loyalty – imperial glory radiating from a little 'Lady Ruler' (as Alfred Harmsworth, founder of modern popular journalism, delicately called her) touched with many sorrows and the magic of old age. The Golden Jubilee, as we have seen, had inflamed the people's imagination with imperial dreams. Ten years later those dreams were recognized to be national policy. The Colonial Minister, Joseph Chamberlain, was the first to think of turning the Diamond Jubilee into a festival of Colonial Premiers rather than Crowned Heads. Queen Victoria adopted the imperial idea with alacrity. Apart from its intrinsic appeal, it would have been more than she could bear at her age to cram Buckingham Palace and Windsor yet again with kings, emperors and their suites. As it was, the problems of fitting mere princes into the Jubilee processions were bad enough. 'Was again occupied with Lenchen in this troublesome precedence,' she wrote in her Journal on June 4th; 'we always kept forgetting someone, which was maddening.' One emperor in particular would have been entirely unacceptable. The Kaiser was so unpopular, 'so fearfully & senselessly violent'[36] over a quarrel which had broken out between Greece and Turkey, that she could not possibly have paraded him in the London streets. 'Sir A. Bigge may tell the Pce of Wales,' she wrote to her private secretary on January 30th, 1897, 'that there is *not* the slightest fear of the Queen's giving way about the Emperor William's coming here, in June. It would *never* do . . .'[37]

She was characteristically torn between a desire for minimal celebrations and the wish to respond worthily to her people's devotion. She begged Lord Salisbury to keep the Honours List 'as low as possible', perturbed by the 'quantity' which he proposed. Questions poured in. Would she review Windsor Fire Brigade? Drive past the National United Temperance Demonstration in Hyde Park? Accept a bicycle, ribbon and watch from the Mayor of Coventry? Might Quintin Hogg put in for a photograph? What to call the celebration provoked considerable controversy. The name 'Diamond Jubilee' was already in use when the Home Secretary suggested that Her Majesty would prefer the 'Queen's Commemoration', the 'Queen's Year' or even the 'Jubilissimee'. Bigge thought that the last suggestion would not catch on, and anyway Her Majesty already 'fancied' the popular name. To clinch the matter he sent her a note asking if he might inform the Home Office that it was to be the 'Diamond Jubilee'. Scrawled across his note in faint blue chalk came the terse reply: 'Appd V R I'.

The Queen restricted official celebrations on the great day to a procession through London, pausing at the steps of St Paul's for the briefest of services. The length and heat of a Thanksgiving Service at Westminster Abbey, as in 1887, would have been exhausting, while to get inside St Paul's, she explained, was impossible owing to the steps and her lameness. 'No!' gasped Augusta Strelitz, when she heard of the plan, '. . . after 60 years Reign, to thank God in the Street!!!'[38] Fortunately a suggestion to take the eight creams out of the shafts at the door and drag her bodily into the Cathedral, carriage and all, was dropped. One well-wisher suggested that a puppet queen should ride in the carriage to save Her Majesty fatigue.

When the time came, Queen Victoria rose to the occasion on the same surge of emotion that carried her subjects to a climax of loyalty. She travelled from Balmoral to Windsor on June 16th, sorrowfully leaving behind for the first time in thirty-one years her beloved wardrobe maid, Annie Macdonald, who was dying. Sunday June 20th was the actual anniversary of her Accession. Prince Albert's *Te Deum* was sung once again at a family Thanksgiving in St George's Chapel, followed by a special Jubilee prayer and Bishop How's Jubilee hymn set to music by Sir Arthur Sullivan.

> *Thou hast been mindful of Thine own,*
> *And lo! we come confessing –*
> *'Tis Thou hast dower'd our queenly throne*
> *With sixty years of blessing.*

(A first attempt at a Jubilee hymn had been made by the Poet Laureate, Alfred Austin: Sullivan rejected it as unworthy of his music.) Jubilee services were held at eleven o'clock in every church, chapel and synagogue throughout the land. After the long string of royal carriages had departed for

London, the Queen and her eldest daughter slipped down to the Mausoleum for even more congenial devotions.

On the 21st she went to Paddington by royal train magnificently refurbished. The outside, as admiring journalists reported, was painted 'rich chocolate brown, highly polished, with white panels on the upper portion and handsome mahogany beading round the plate-glass windows'. The interior was of satinwood and cream silk upholstery, the couches being finished with green and white cord and lace. From the engine flew the Royal Standard and all the directors were aboard.

The national Press poured out articles, most of them with the same proud title: 'The Queen's Long Reign'. *The Times*, however, kept its head and published a piece on 'The World's Longest Reigns' showing that King Feridoon of Persia had put Queen Victoria into the shade by occupying the Peacock Throne for 500 years. Cardinal Vaughan, on the other hand, issued an unequivocally jubilant pastoral letter: 'How great has been the religious progress during these sixty years!'

Queen Victoria made her historic progress through London on June 22nd, 1897 in brilliant sunshine. As if to put a seal on the legend of 'Queen's Weather', the sun came out from a dull sky as the first guns in Hyde Park announced that she had left the Palace, having previously touched an electric button which telegraphed her Jubilee Message round the Empire:

'From my heart I thank my beloved people. May God bless them!'

Queen Victoria's account of her reception by London was by no means exaggerated.

'No one ever, I believe, has met with such an ovation as was given to me, passing through those six miles of streets ... the crowds were quite indescribable, and their enthusiasm truly marvellous and deeply touching. The cheering was quite deafening, and every face seemed to be filled with real joy.'[39]

London's sense of its own greatness, as the metropolis of a far-flung Empire, vied with a poignantly personal affection for the venerable figure who was both a living and a symbolic mother. 'Our Hearts Thy Throne', declared a triumphal arch at Paddington; the Bank of England declaimed: 'She Wrought Her People Lasting Good'. 'Go it, old girl!' called an ecstatic voice from the crowd as she appeared on the Palace balcony in her wheeled chair.

Londoners had spent a quarter of a million on street decorations, mingling thousands of tiny gas jets, which had been a novelty when their Queen was young, with electric light bulbs which were still an experimental marvel of the new age. In Whitehall, a £25,000 stand illustrated the material progress of the longest reign. It was equipped with the ladies' rooms and lavatories which at her Coronation had been sadly wanting and with the telephones which had not yet been invented.

The Queen had sent message after message to the Home Office to make sure that no accident occurred on the loaded roofs and balconies of small houses south of the Thames. Her natural nervousness was increased by recent memories of a disaster at the Tsar's Coronation when 3,000 Russians were trampled to death, and of a fire at a charity bazaar in Paris where 200 aristocrats were incinerated. Nothing went wrong. Gradually she relaxed in her carriage beneath the parasol of black Chantilly lace presented by the Father of the House of Commons; tears of happiness filled her eyes and sometimes rolled down her cheeks, whereupon the Princess of Wales would lean forward and gently press her hand.

Immediately in front of her rode the Commander-in-Chief, Lord Wolseley, the man who had succeeded in ousting 'poor George', while the gorgeous procession was led by Captain Ames of the 2nd Life Guards, the tallest man, at six feet eight inches, in the British Army. Alone among the gilded representatives of foreign powers, the occupant of the United States carriage wore ordinary black evening dress and hat. President McKinley's official greeting began in the same democratic spirit: 'Great and good friend ...' A cinematograph picture was taken at the steps of St Paul's. Though 'very wonderful', the Queen considered the result 'a little hazy & too rapid'. It was a kind description of what looked like a blizzard. When all was over the beacons on the hills were lighted, some by electric switches. This time there were 2,500 of them, nearly four times as many as at her Golden Jubilee. Likewise the mountain of orchids on her dining-table stood eight feet high instead of four and was packed with sixty thousand blossoms in every possible variety from all over her Empire.

Jubilee summer blazed and cheered itself to a standstill. For the first time in her life she was pelted with confetti as she drove through Windsor on June 24th after a long thundery day. Smiling gaily, she swung her little parasol from side to side to ward off this strange manifestation of joy. A reception of bishops attending the Lambeth Conference appealed no more to her now than it would have done sixty years earlier, as she made clear to a shocked Lady Lytton:

'A very ugly party. I do not like bishops.'
'Oh, but your dear Majesty likes *some* bishops . . .'
'Yes, I like the man but *not* the bishop.'[40]

Soldiers, ships, fire brigades and public schoolboys were all reviewed. At a march past of Volunteers from thirty public schools, Her Majesty felt that Eton and Harrow were 'perhaps' the best. It was 'very thrilling' to hear the frantic cheers from the throats of 4,000 'young fellows' though sad that owing to the heat 40 of them had to be laid out under the trees. On a Jubilee mug 'a few' of the Queen's 'Notable Achievements in Peace and War' were listed – from 'Railways 1837' to 'Imperial Institute 1897'; from 'Afghan War 1839' to 'Capture of Benin 1897' – while beneath a triple portrait of Her Majesty draped in laurels and supported by the Bible was inscribed the remarkable line:

The Centre of a World's Desire.

Nevertheless, it was not entirely bombast. She was incomparably the best Queen the world had got and more than one foreign nation, still struggling under a rule of tyranny, self-indulgence or fatuity, wished she were theirs.

As the Imperial troops marched past in the Royal Procession of June 22nd a *Daily Mail* journalist was moved to philosophize:

690

'. . . And you began to understand, as never before, what the Empire amounts to . . . we send out a boy here and a boy there, and the boy takes hold of the savages . . . and teaches them to march and shoot . . . and believe in him, and die for him and the Queen. A plain, stupid, uninspired people, they call us, and yet we are doing this with every kind of savage man there is.'

Mr Gladstone, in a spirit more consciously cynical, hoped that Queen Victoria would celebrate her Diamond Jubilee by abdicating.

When Princess Mary of Teck died on October 10th, 1897 Queen Victoria heard that this beloved, slapdash cousin had left no will. Such breezy defiance of convention drove the Queen in the opposite direction, particularly as she discovered that the undertakers had not performed the embalming properly. ('A stern telegram from Balmoral'[41] soon put this right.) She drew up a memorandum, dated October 25th, giving the most meticulous instructions for her own funeral. There was to be as little pomp as possible, draperies of white and gold, no black cloth in the Mausoleum or anywhere else; no dead march from *Saul*. As head of the Army, she decreed a military funeral with a gun carriage covered in flowers and eight horses – 'not black ones'. The Munshi and her German secretaries were to have places in the procession.[42]

Two months after this good work was accomplished she heard that the old lady who used to keep the shop at Balmoral had died. It is said that on Queen Victoria's last visit, as she hobbled out of the cottage she murmured sadly, 'Poor old soul.' The dying woman compassionately watched the Queen's receding figure and turning to her husband whispered, 'Puir auld creetur.'

Not long after her return from the spring visit to Cimiez the Queen heard of another death. 'Poor Mr Gladstone' had passed away on May 19th, 1898. They had last met in the South of France the year before when she had been persuaded by Princess Louise to invite him to her hotel room after tea and had shaken hands with him for the first time. The need to be courteous, even complimentary to him in death caused her a good deal more effort. Harriet Phipps asked if she were not going to write to Mrs Gladstone? Queen Victoria liked Mrs Gladstone and had sent her many kind messages while her husband yet breathed. But – 'No, I did not like the man. How can I say I am sorry when I am not?' Eventually she found a way of thanking Mrs Gladstone honestly, if temperately, for her husband's personal loyalty:

'I shall always gratefully remember how anxious he always was to help and serve me and mine in all that concerned my personal comfort and welfare ... as well as that of my family ... believe me, ever yours affectionately, V.R.I.'[43]

In her Journal she had felt bound to state once again what amounted to her reason for disliking him:

'... He had a wonderful power of speaking and carrying the masses with him.'[44]

Jealousy was not dead. The 'People's Victoria' could never forgive the 'People's William'.

No expression of royal regret appeared in the *Court Circular*. Further remonstrances provoked an even sharper reaction from the Queen. 'I am sorry for Mrs Gladstone; as for him, I never liked him, and I will say nothing about him.' It was left to the Prince of Wales to find a solution. On the day of the funeral another, warmer message was drafted for Mrs Gladstone, to be sent to the papers. But when Queen Victoria heard that the Prince had been among the pall-bearers and had kissed Mrs Gladstone's hand, she relapsed into bitterness. A letter to the Empress Frederick expressed her final judgement:

'I cannot say that I think he was "a great Englishman". He was a clever man, full of talent, but he never tried to keep up the honour and prestige of Gt Britain. He gave away the Transvaal & he abandoned Gordon, he destroyed the Irish church & tried to separate England from Ireland & he set class against class. The harm he did cannot be easily undone.'[45]

Then she recollected herself. 'But he was a good & vy religious man.'

Queen Victoria, in this sorry episode, stands convicted of putting a narrow regard for truth before charity. It must not be forgotten, however, that Gladstone himself, a professional politician, found his stomach literally turning at the prospect of praising Disraeli. In many ways nature had intended her for something more spontaneous than politics, and when political duty clashed with long-cherished prejudice, she allowed her mutinous feelings to become vindictive. The last sentence quoted from the letter to her daughter shows that charity did in the end prevail.

Between Gladstone's death and burial came Queen Victoria's seventy-ninth birthday. She wrote in her Journal that despite all she still felt fresh and even young. Then, on December 4th, a new shadow fell.

'Was greatly upset by being told something about the state of health of one of my dear children, but will say no more now, & trust any real trouble may yet be arrested.'[46]

Behind the tremulous phrases lay the news that the Empress Frederick probably had cancer of the spine. Death was still the most pertinacious of the Queen's foes.

She had long known that her second son, Prince Alfred, Duke of Coburg, was suffering from some mysterious malady. Early in February 1899 consumption carried off 'young Alfred', his only son, and heir to the beloved Duchy. He was buried on February 10th, the 59th anniversary of the Queen's wedding day which, as she recorded plaintively, 'still casts a reflected light of former days, & it grieves me that the funeral of the poor dear Boy should just take place today.' The compulsive power of anniversaries had not declined. When the Duke of York's second son had elected to arrive on 'Mausoleum Day', 1895, as the Royal Family called December 14th, Prince George had broken the glad news to his grandmother with trepidation. Though not denying the strange ineptitude, she had saved the day by deciding that 'it may be a blessing for the dear little boy, and may be looked upon as a gift from

God!' The baby became King George VI, father of Queen Elizabeth II.[47]

The death of 'young Alfred' brought no blessings. Disputes with the Coburgers about the next heir presumptive involved almost all the Queen's family, stretching her powers of mediation to the full. At length her grandson 'Charlie' Albany was accepted, removed from Eton and sent to Germany to imbibe new ideas. He succeeded to the Duchy in 1900 and lived to embrace National Socialism.

Queen Victoria returned from what was to be her last visit abroad (Cimiez) at the beginning of May 1899. 'I shall mind returning to the sunless north,' she wrote in her Journal. 'But I am so grateful for all I have enjoyed here.' On her eightieth birthday she was 'deeply touched' by the countless messages of affection and 'beautiful presents'. Appropriately enough, many were antiques – a miniature of King George III, another of Prince Charles Edward and a morsel from the hammer-beam roof of Westminster Hall, built by William Rufus in 1099. Though Queen Victoria did not go back 800 years she seemed equally historic.

Her friends commented on her rosy cheeks and good spirits; in August she sported a new, fashionable hat which her maids were furious to see described in the illustrated papers as a 'bonnet'. The old familiar symbol died hard. The Queen laughed at their indignation and also at a kind stranger's suggestion that she should tether a balloon to her jacket in order to take the weight off her legs.

A new portrait painted from imagination by Benjamin Constant and presented to her this year, shows the person she would have liked to be in her decline. Instead of the resolute old lady of reality, concealing her anxieties beneath a stiff upper and drawn-down lower lip, Constant pictured a pale, shimmering figure from the world of poetry and romance. This unreal vision won Queen Victoria's instant approval, apart from the colour of the Garter ribbon, which was too pale.*

* She promptly sent him a pattern of the ribbon; poor Constant, on opening the box, thought at first that he had been presented with the Order.

There was to be no renaissance of a Faery Queen. Scarcely had Coburg been settled before the sky over Africa turned a fierce red.

The Boer War broke out on October 11th, 1899. Queen Victoria saw it as a struggle to avoid national humiliation and as an expression of 'high tone'. She had by no means become a warmonger; a clash with the French the year before, at Fashoda on the Nile, had prompted her to write of the 'awful responsibility to God and man it would be were we to go to war';[48] she felt scruples, as already noted, about a policy of grab. Lord Kitchener's destruction of Mahdism at the battle of Omdurman in September 1898 seemed to her an example of righteous warfare; we were returning to a land which had belonged to us and for which Gordon had died – 'surely he is avenged'. The Queen's imperial philosophy, in fact, involved neither give nor take, but a simple assertion of 'what I have I hold'. Britain had held the Transvaal up to the disaster of Majuba Hill in 1881. Britain must hold it again.

For the first few weeks of the war the Queen busied herself in wishing God speed to departing troops – 'quite a lump in my throat' – and looking after the interests of the weak. Lord Salisbury was urged to prevent war taxation from falling on the working classes and Lord Wolseley to arrange a comfortable voyage for the horses – both in vain; but a year-long battle to get commissions for Army bandmasters was won. By the end of October, however, events had moved too fast and unfavourably for the Queen to draw pleasure from her small works of mercy. Crack British armies were besieged in Ladysmith, Kimberley and Mafeking; that the disaster to Sir George White's column had been caused by stampeding mules rather than by the General himself, afforded her but a crumb of comfort. The entries in her Journal are short and depressed. 'No news today only lists of casualties.'

When news did arrive it was always of more reverses. There were no ghillies' balls at Balmoral, no games at Braemar. Reginald Brett (Lord Esher) was amazed to see her turn pale on receiving a telegram at dinner. Opening telegrams about the war, she explained, made her ill. By a strange fatality,

Mausoleum Day fell in 'Black Week'. Three Generals were defeated in a row: Gatacre on December 10th, Methuen on the 11th and Sir Redvers Buller at Colenso on the 15th. The Queen's blindness had caused her on one of these candle-lit black mornings to mis-read defeat as victory. She arrived, a radiant figure, for breakfast only to learn the truth from Princess Beatrice. After a moment's silence she said: 'Now perhaps they will take my advice, and send out Lord Roberts and Lord Kitchener, as I urged them to do from the first.' The panicky advice of Sir Redvers to abandon Ladysmith seemed to her 'too awful to contemplate' but she was equally dumbfounded by the Government's clumsiness in superseding 'Sir Reverse', as he was now called, by Roberts and Kitchener without telling Lord Wolseley first. The Duke of Connaught wanted to rush out and the Prince of Wales to withdraw his patronage from the Paris Exhibition because of scurrilous attacks on the Queen. Black Week was finally engulfed in fogs of such density that carriages had to be guided by footmen down the Long Walk.

Queen Victoria's personal feelings were ruthlessly suppressed as soon as she became aware of the crisis in national morale. This surely was the climax of her vocation to 'be of use'. When Mr Balfour visited Windsor Castle during Black Week he was given a stiffener:

'Please understand that there is no one depressed in this house; we are not interested in the possibilities of defeat; they do not exist.'[49]

She was flying about reviewing troops and visiting hospitals as if she were young again. Parcels of knitting were dispatched to her 'dear brave soldiers' and when it transpired that the dear brave officer-class had got them all, she ordered 100,000 tins of chocolate for the men. One of the tins, she afterwards heard, had stopped a bullet, while another had compensated for the wound it could not avert. 'I would rather lose a limb than not get that!' declared a legless hero to whom she offered a tin.[50]

As early as October she had visited Bristol for the first time since her 'Royal Progress' of 1830, meeting an old soldier whose father had sounded the charge at Waterloo. The Queen's own thoughts continually went back to the Crimea. There must be no Day of Humiliation to repent of this war, which ought to be stopped at once if it were unjust; indeed, no praying 'by order' at all; and no official inquiry into military mistakes until after victory. The War Office would then need radically reforming. One thing she could not understand: the prejudice which prevented coloured troops, especially her loyal Indians, from serving alongside the white soldiers in Africa. Lord Salisbury, whom she exhorted to 'put his foot down', regretfully replied that if he did so he would bring down the Government also.[51]

In February 1900 the tide turned. Ladysmith was relieved on the 28th. Queen Victoria repaired at once to the Mausoleum. A week later she made two triumphal drives through London, at which her welcome outshone in spontaneity both the Jubilees. No police, no soldiers. Lord Esher spoke of 'a domestic nation on a gigantic scale'. Ever since Black Week her Journal had been a model of vigorous courage – no complaints, no self pity. Now, with the spring, came the moment for her last sacrifice. French press attacks on Britain had increased and it was decided that she must not risk a holiday in Cimiez, though the journey to Italy might possibly be undertaken. On March 7th she informed the Empress Frederick that even this was not to be. Vicky would be startled to hear that despite her pining for 'the sunny flowery south', she was going next month to visit Ireland.

'It is entirely my own idea as was also my giving up going abroad – and it will give gt pleasure, & do good.'[52]

A slight exaggeration of the extent to which it was the old lady's 'own idea' may be forgiven. Her choice of Ireland filled everybody with relief and awe. Lord Rosebery wrote especially to congratulate her on the grand renunciation. The police hoped her courage would not be rewarded by an attempt on her life.

And so, for just over three weeks (4th to 26th April) Queen Victoria visited a part of her dominions which she had not set foot in for thirty-nine years. Gratitude to the gallantry of

Irish soldiers in South Africa had chiefly influenced her decision; she was suddenly consumed with longing to be loved by Ireland. In furtherance of her desire, she decreed the wearing of shamrock by Irish soldiers on St Patrick's Day and created a new regiment of Irish Guards. Even so, there were few flags in the back streets of Dublin where she did not drive, and these few caused scuffles. The Dublin Council voted to present an Address provided it did not mention loyalty to the Crown. Copies of *The United Irishman* were seized before she landed, Home Rule meetings broken up and Dubliners arrested for tearing down decorations and smashing shop windows adorned with Union Jacks. The French newspaper *Charivari* published a cartoon of British bayonets forcing the cheers from Irish throats:

'Attention! Une, deux, trois:
Hip! Hip! Hip! Hurrah!'

It was too late for the Queen to learn from these things; better that in old age she should hear only the cheers of the loyalists, which were 'almost screams', just as she remembered them in 1843 only a thousand times louder; better that she should not hear the 'bagpipe drone' of booing, twice detected by her young equerry, Fritz Ponsonby, beneath the applause. Characteristically she threw herself headlong into a mission to pacify Ireland along her own lines, meeting the Cardinal, criticizing Dublin Castle for being so 'gloomy looking' and even pushing the cause of Catholic education:

'I regretted that the proposal for a Roman Catholic University had not been agreed to in Parlt . . . Ld Salisbury said that many of their supporters in the Hse of Commons were much against it, which I could not understand.'[53]

Her own heart had been melted by 'this warm hearted sympathetic people', who burst into 'God Save The Queen' every time they caught sight of her, a small, rotund, black figure drawn by a white donkey round and round the grounds of Viceregal Lodge.

Five days before her eighty-first birthday Mafeking was liberated. Queen Victoria happened to be visiting Wellington

College and was hailed on a streamer as 'Queen of Mafeking'; people were 'quite mad with delight', she recorded in her Journal and the goings-on in London 'indescribable'. The word 'mafficking' was coined to describe them. Even in the sober purlieus of the London County Council attendance at evening classes on the night of May 19th, 1900 dropped spectacularly.

She held the last of her many birthday celebrations on May 24th, 1900 with mixed feelings:

> 'Again my old birthday returns, my 81st! God has been very merciful and supported me, but my trials and anxieties have been manifold and I feel tired and upset by all I have gone through this winter and spring.'

Six extra men had to be rushed to Balmoral to help with the torrent of nearly four thousand congratulatory telegrams.

In Calcutta the Queen's horoscope for the coming twelve months was drawn with more loyalty than insight. 'Her Majesty will enjoy good health in this year,' it is predicted. A 'great reformation' of the Cabinet would take place in March 1901. 'After which, harmony and peace will reign all over her dominion.'

It seemed impossible that this living symbol of an era and an Empire should not be eternal.

CHAPTER XXXVI

'MOTHER'S COME HOME'
1900-1

QUEEN VICTORIA'S advisers would gladly have seen a transfer of burdens to her heir. Of recent months she had only once got out of her chair alone, and that was to pin a medal on a hospital patient: otherwise it was always, 'Man pull it.' Having accepted glasses for reading in 1877, it was not till 1899 that she consented to put on the unsightly things in public.* The film over her eyes was treated with belladonna. Her repeated demands for larger, darker handwriting had given rise to many experiments. Fritz Ponsonby tried ink as black as boot polish and Arthur Bigge constructed a small copper oven in which script half an inch high could be dried without blotting. She attempted as long as possible to read communications about confidential matters herself – witness an agonized cry to Lord Salisbury on December 27th, 1898 regarding the Munshi: 'Pray write with as black ink as you can on these *private* questions.' State papers, memoranda and newspapers were all read to her by Princess Beatrice. 'Hideous mistakes,' says Fritz Ponsonby, constantly occurred. Yet her advisers dared not expostulate. Her mind was still clear. Indeed, her prayer for the new century was in the course of being granted: to be spared 'yet a short while' with all her faculties and just a little of her eyesight to serve her family and country.

The Queen's summer holiday in Scotland was marred by persistence of fatigue and indigestion. As if to defy her troubles she went at once on returning south to visit the victims of a railway accident, among them '2 poor Indian gentlemen'. By the beginning of July her busy life was in full swing again: visits from the Duchess of Coburg, the

---

* Sir Harold Nicolson remembers as a boy running 'beside the carriage of an old lady, crouched deep among the cushions of her barouche, of an old Queen Empress whose eyes were cross and tired behind her silver spectacles. . . .' *Comments* 1944–8, p. 214.

Connaughts, Mr Chamberlain, the Khedive and Mrs Victoria Randle, her black goddaughter; the usual reckless outing in a thunderstorm with the hail pouring into her lap and the horses on the point of bolting; visits to a newborn great-grandchild; a Council; a piece of her mind to the Duke of Devonshire for not keeping *The Times* 'straight' on the war; endless study of casualty lists; the bestowal of nine Knight-hoods, among them 'no interesting people'. It sounded as if Her Majesty were quite herself again. There was only one concession to increasing insomnia: 'I now rest daily for a short while after luncheon, which is thought good for me but loses time.'[1]

She put down the slowness of her recovery to two new misfortunes. The 'Boxer' outbreak in China against foreigners left her 'horror-struck'; the 'cruel treatment' of her grand-daughter, Princess Marie Louise of Schleswig-Holstein ('Louie'), by her husband, Prince Aribert of Anhalt, roused her to indignant action. 'Poor Louie', rudely summoned from Canada to face divorce proceedings in Germany, was promptly rescued by a telegram to the Governor-General from her grandmother. 'Tell my granddaughter to come home to me. V.R.'[2] The calamitous marriage was annulled in December.

Osborne might have set the Queen up again, for her symp-toms were still only insomnia and slight aphasia. On July 25th she had her little York great-grandchildren up for breakfast and tea: 'Feel on the whole better today.' At that moment a killing blow fell.

A telegram announced that 'poor dear Affie's state of health' was despaired of: he had an incurable disease of the throat – 'alas! one can only too well guess at its nature!' Within a week he was dead. 'Oh, God! my poor darling Affie gone too . . . It is hard at eighty-one!' The Queen, suffering from shock, felt that 'they' should not have kept the truth from her as long as they did. A few days before the King of Italy had been assassinated. And all the while 'desperate winds' swept the Solent, wrecking even 'the poor old swimming bath'. 'It is a horrible year, nothing but sadness & horrors of one kind & another.'[3]

The duplication of sorrows, so constant a pattern in Queen

701

Victoria's life, pursued her to the end, for her soldier grandson, Prince Christian Victor of Schleswig-Holstein, died in October at Pretoria of enteric fever. Shaken to the core, she could not sleep and an unconquerable disgust for food prevented her from taking anything but arrowroot and milk. All through this 'horrible year', moreover, she had been without the comfort of a visit from the Empress Frederick who was desperately sick at Kronberg.

'It was wretchedly gloomy & dark', she wrote in her Journal on November 6th. In this weather and mood she left Balmoral for the last time. At Windsor her insomnia and general wretchedness increased until she was, in the words of her grandson Prince George, 'very seedy'. It is therefore all the more astonishing to find her again immersed in business. Lord Salisbury had defeated a divided Liberal Party at the 'Khaki Election' and there were many Cabinet and other changes to discuss. Among them was the resignation of her old friend George Goschen. She had replied to his first intimation of retirement, given two months earlier (September 19th), with a characteristic reflection:

'Mr Goschen will be a most serious public loss ... the Queen, however, feels that he is fully justified in wishing for rest. She wishes she could have the same, even for the shortest period; for she does need it, and feels the constant want of it, at eighty-one – very trying and fatiguing.'[4]

Could courage and perversity go further?

The Queen struggled into December. 'Did not feel well,' she wrote on the 9th, 'though they say I am getting better.' There was a kindly conspiracy to blame her blindness on the weather – 'No one ever remembered such cloudy days' – and to conceal from her the effect of the Boer War on her popularity abroad. German attacks, they told her, were due to jealousy, French to a few agitators, Austrian to the middle classes and Russian to Heaven knows what. The old Queen was not deceived.

She insisted on attending the Irish Industries Exhibition at Windsor, her last public function, and on December 18th said goodbye to Windsor, as it turned out, for ever.

The magic of Osborne now failed her. She fell into an erratic, unaccustomed routine which irritated her enormously. She would go to bed exhausted at 10 PM. Draughts of chloral and Benger's food would then prove insufficient to send her to sleep. After hours of tossing she would fall into a drugged slumber not awaking until noon. The whole morning would thus have been 'wasted'. Her afternoon drive would be spoilt by a fresh access of overwhelming sleepiness, her evenings by the inexorable task of signing papers and dictating her letters and Journal. For the past year or so her ladies had succeeded in keeping her awake in her carriage by constantly rearranging her mantles. Now her drowsiness was invincible. On Christmas Eve she went into the Durbar Room for the Christmas tree. There was no sparkle, the candles seemed dim. 'I felt very melancholy as I see so very badly.' On Christmas Day it was gradually broken to her that her last intimate friend of nearly fifty years, Lady Churchill, had died from heart failure in the night. 'Beloved Jane' was carried to the mainland on the night of the 28th in a fearful tempest. Queen Victoria lay shivering in agony lest the ship should founder.

The 'horrible year' blew itself out in a wail of wind and rain. For the first time the Queen allowed a new year to crawl in without a good resolution. 'Another year begun & I am feeling so weak and unwell that I enter upon it sadly.' But Lord Salisbury received his New Year card as usual, a pathetically appropriate one – 'The Old Year dies; God beckons those we love' – signed with a quavering hieroglyph which stood for the once proud VRI. Nor would she admit to her stricken daughter, the Empress Frederick, that she had given up. In her last letter (January 6th) she hoped soon to 'improve'.

The monotonous procession of nights and days dragged on. A morning like spring on January 11th tempted her out early, a return to normal which greatly pleased her. Next day a dense fog blotted out the Island as if to herald what was coming. The following day was January 13th, as the Queen in other circumstances would have noted with melancholy interest, for her Journal came to an end. On January 14th – the fatal fourteenth – there was a blank for the first time in sixty-nine years. Lord Roberts, to whom she had given the Garter, was the last soldier and Joseph Chamberlain the last Minister to be received. Her inveterate foe, Wilfrid Blunt, afterwards surmised that the unsatisfactory news from South Africa conveyed in these audiences had killed her. She was put into her pony-chaise as usual on January 15th, her widowed daughter-in-law, Marie of Coburg, sitting beside her ready to take advantage of any break in the clouds. None came and they did not send her out again. Indeed, Sir James Reid decided to inform Fritz Ponsonby officially next day that the Queen was ill. Notwithstanding her condition she issued her last order on this day, a characteristic one: that her Ambassador in Berlin should respectfully decline an honour from the Kaiser.

On the 17th there was difficulty with speech and mental confusion. A heart specialist was summoned and on the 18th her children; the Duke of Connaught happened to be staying in Berlin so that the Kaiser heard the news and included himself in the invitation. The Prince of Wales arrived on Saturday the 19th and the first bulletin went out. 'The Queen has not lately been in her usual health,' it began, going on to describe the 'great strain upon her powers' during the past year. Meanwhile the Queen had rallied and the Prince returned to London. That night Randall Davidson, now Bishop of Winchester, crossed to the Island; outside a storm raged and below decks a team of home-coming footballers shouted and sang. All through the Sunday Queen Victoria lay still and alone in her room, seeming to maintain her strength. At midnight she began to sink and Davidson was sent for. In the small hours she rallied again and next morning, 'Am I better at all?' she asked her doctor.

'Yes.'

'Then may I have Turi?'

They brought her little Pomeranian dog and he lay, unwillingly, for a short while on the dying woman's bed.

As the day wore on consciousness ebbed and flowed. 'Nothing else but the Queen's illness is spoken or thought of,' reported *The Times* foreign correspondents: in Vienna 'keenest anxiety', in Brussels 'painful suspense', abstentions *en masse* in Athens from the Parnassus ball; a chivalrous wish from President Kruger for 'prompt recovery'. On January 22nd *The Time*s still hoped that her 'extraordinary fund of vitality' might yet pull her through.

At Osborne House the Kaiser waited, tactfully out of sight, and the Prince of Wales returned to his mother's room. She opened her arms whispering her last word, 'Bertie'. He buried his face and wept. Davidson went to her bedside once or twice: 'She lay very quietly looking white and thin.'[5] The Vicar of Whippingham was also in attendance, having been called in earlier by the Queen herself lest he should feel hurt. Before luncheon was over Davidson and the vicar were urgently sent for. She was much weaker. The family were assembled, including the Kaiser whose dignified sorrow earned the admiration even of his cousins. He only wanted to see Grandmama before she died, he told them, but if that was impossible he would quite understand. He won his place at the deathbed.

At intervals the two clergymen prayed aloud. No response came from the figure on the bed until Davidson happened to recite the last verse of her favourite hymn, Newman's *Lead Kindly Light*. Then he noticed that she was listening.

And with the morn those angel faces smile
Which we have loved long since and lost a while.

She had waited forty years for the 'morn' and now at last it was coming.

As the frosty darkness began to fall about four o'clock another bulletin was issued: 'The Queen is slowly sinking.' Her doctor assisted by the Kaiser supported her on her pillow, one on each side. Not until she died two and a half hours later did the Kaiser withdraw his arm; nor could he ease the strain by changing sides with Reid, for his left arm was withered. His Grandmama deserved every sacrifice.

Around the bed stood her children and grandchildren. As she drifted further and further from them they took to calling out their names, as if to bring her back. It is doubtful whether

Queen Victoria would have appreciated this piteous drama. Writing to condole with her eldest daughter on the death of Princess Charles of Prussia, she had once spoken her mind about conventional family deathbeds:

'I think it very dreadful that everyone was there. That I shall insist is never the case if I am dying. It is awful!'[6]

As the end drew near the appealing voices fell silent. 'Then came a great change of look,' Davidson noticed, 'and complete calmness.' She died just after half past six.

Immediately the house was surrounded by police to prevent the news from spreading before the Prime Minister had been informed. Ten minutes later a message was read to the crowd at the gate:

'Her Majesty the Queen breathed her last at 6.30 PM, surrounded by her children and grandchildren.'

Pandemonium broke loose. A yelling stampede of journalists on bicycles hurtled down the hill to Cowes to be first with the telephones, bawling as they went, 'Queen dead!' 'Queen dead!' The famous 'hush' which had always surrounded 'The Widow at Windsor' was shattered at a blow. A new age had begun.

Queen Victoria's funeral has become part of the English saga, for people saw in her passing the end of their own way of life. A sense of desolation was mingled with sudden alarm, for while she lived England's power had seemed to be steadily increasing under the protective shadow of her formidable bonnet. Now 'all, all is passed', and who could tell what lay in store? One phrase was on many lips – God help us.

'Oh! Dearest George,' wrote the Queen's first cousin, Augusta of Strelitz, to the Duke of Cambridge, 'what a calamity! ... anxiety terrible as to what poor England will have to go through now! God have mercy on us all!'[7] Princess May lamented in similar vein: 'The thought of England without the Queen is dreadful even to think of. God help us all!'[8] The Times declared that people felt they had lost not only a Sovereign whom they had almost come to 'worship', but 'a personal benefactress'. 'She was our Mother,' wrote Marie Corelli the popular novelist.

On the day in 1900 when Queen Victoria had arrived for her ceremonial drives through London, a policeman pointed to the Royal Standard floating above Buckingham Palace. 'Mother's come 'ome,' he said to a bystander among the watching crowds. Nine months later the same crowds, all in black, realized with bewildered grief that their Mother had indeed come home.

The Queen always drew a sharp distinction between personal mourning, of which she approved, and a black funeral. Having once seen the local hearse at Balmoral, complete with plumed horses, she never allowed it to appear again. Her resolve to dissociate death from darkness was strengthened by a conversation with Tennyson in 1873 when she showed him over the Mausoleum:

> 'I observed that it was light & bright wh he thought a gt point & went on to say that he wished funerals cd be in white!'[9]

An account of funeral rites at St Peter's, Rome, impressed her deeply: music, brilliant uniforms and cloth of gold had banished the gloom 'so much seen with us'.[10] Tennyson's coffin was covered by a white pall embroidered with the last stanza of *Crossing the Bar*, the church being lined with Balaclava heroes. Her own funeral, like Prince Leopold's and Prince Henry's, should be military and like Tennyson's, white.

Faithfully her minute instructions were carried out. As Ponsonby once said, there was nothing the Queen liked more than arranging a funeral. Undertakers having been expressly forbidden, the Kaiser measured her for her coffin and would have lifted her in had not the Prince of Wales and Prince Arthur fiercely asserted that this was the right of her sons. With amazement Prince Arthur found that his awe-inspiring mother had dwindled to a featherweight. Her little silver crucifix from above her bed was put into her hands; spring flowers were sprinkled on her white dress; her lace wedding-veil covered her face and her white widow's cap her hair. For ten days she lay in State at Osborne House, the crimson velvet

707

of her robes and the diamonds of her Imperial Crown, placed upon the coffin, matching the brilliance of the four Grenadiers who stood on guard. At the Kaiser's suggestion a Union Jack was hung in the room, which he afterwards begged as a memento. Bishop Davidson noted that the services which he extemporized were 'calm and bright'.

After all the darkness and storm, it was 'a midsummer day transplanted into winter' on February 1st, when the coffin, covered with a white and golden pall embroidered with a cross and the Royal Arms, was carried to the smallest of the royal yachts, *Alberta*, placed on a crimson dais and transported between many miles of warships to the mainland. The minute guns which Queen Victoria had always hated saluted her from each ship. As she approached the Gosport shore, where a black throng awaited her, the setting sun picked out the *Alberta* in red and gold. Next morning Lady Lytton travelled on a special train, blinds drawn, with the coffin to Victoria station. People knelt in the fields as the train sped by. Black hangings were banished from the London streets and purple cashmere with white satin bows used instead; the ominous drum-roll of Handel's 'Funeral March' was replaced, according to instructions, by Chopin, Beethoven and Highland laments. The Royal Standard, 'thrown partially over the pall' as the Queen had commanded, blazed upon the summit of the gun-carriage which bore her to Paddington Station.

The crowds at Windsor lining the long route expected to see the Royal Artillery drawing the gun-carriage home. But after waiting in the icy cold one of the horses shied and snapped the traces. There was a moment of panic. Dared they continue the procession or must the Queen be hurried up the short cut to the Castle? 'I would wish just to say that as a gun carriage is very rough jolting & noisy,' she had written in her will, 'one ought to be properly arranged . . .'[11] In the emergency Prince Louis of Battenberg ordered a guard of sailors, using the royal train's communication cord, to drag the gun-carriage the long way round. There was a salute of 81 guns, one for each year of her life, in the Long Walk. After a short service in St George's – the most that Queen Victoria could endure in that uncongenial place – she lay until February 4th in the Albert Memorial Chapel. Then the family alone took her to the 'dear Mausoleum'. There under its Victorian *cinquecento* domes shining with gold and mosaics she joined her husband at last.

> Lay her beneath the shade
> Of Windsor's Royal towers
> Where in sad widowed hours
> Her tomb she made.

Just over thirty-six years ago she had gone down to the Mausoleum to see the sarcophagus unpacked. 'It gave me a strange feeling to contemplate what is to be *our* resting place. Oh! could I but be there soon!'[12] Strong faith rather than 'strange' feelings inspired the Latin words which she put over the doors:

> *Vale desideratissime.* Farewell most beloved. Here at length I shall rest with thee, with thee in Christ I shall rise again.

The anthem for the service had been written by Tennyson for her grandson, Prince Albert Victor, and contained a great shout of 'Onward'. Her hymn was cheerful:

> Life's dream is past,
> All its sin, its sadness.
> Brightly at last,
> Dawns a day of gladness.

Today the two white marble statues executed by Marochetti in 1862 lie side by side upon the sarcophagus of Aberdeen granite. Queen Victoria had seen to it that every detail of the Prince's dress was correct, down to the straps which held the ends of his trousers tidily over his boots – straps which in later years she was sad to note young men left undone. Not a millimetre too much or too little composed his marble features, for she was accustomed to assist her sculptors by giving them accurate measurements. As for her own statue, it had been inadvertently locked up in a cavity of the Castle walls awaiting the day of resurrection, and was with difficulty located by the Office of Works. When her statue finally reached the Mausoleum it appeared that Prince Albert's face gazed almost straight ahead into eternity while Queen Victoria's, as if still alive, was inclined gently towards him.

After the funeral was over and the family had streamed out on to the winter grass dotted with snowdrops, sleet began to fall. Inside the Mausoleum the gas lamps were left burning quietly. The sleet soon changed to snow and the doors of the Mausoleum closed softly upon a white world. The Queen had had her white funeral.

'People are too kind,' Queen Victoria wrote to Theodore Martin when discussing the kind reception accorded to her *Leaves* from the Highland Journal. 'What has she done to be so loved & liked?'[13]

The immediate answer to her question presented no problem. She was loved for her simplicity, her domesticity, her interest in the lowliest of her retainers and her confiding nature in sharing the intimate details of her happiness with thousands of her subjects. There was also the humility which led her to ask the question at all, a humility rooted in a lifetime of self-criticism. 'The Dean is far too kind in his estimate of the Queen,' she once wrote to Dean Wellesley. 'He thinks her *so* much better than she is.'[14] 'How I wish I could have done more,' was her first thought on one of the many anniversaries of her Accession.

Gladstone named two other high qualities which in his eyes went far to neutralize her faults: good manners and love of truth. Her love of truth was a plain fact but her good manners were a more subtle ingredient of her character. Fundamentally, they were an expression of her resolve to be a constitutional Queen. So far as duty dictated she would treat all her Ministers, of whatever party, with the same gracious respect. Duty, however, did not urge her beyond a certain point. If a moment came when the welfare of the country seemed to be threatened by the policies of a party, she believed it to be her duty to sacrifice even good manners to the higher cause. Hence Gladstone in the 'eighties began to find her 'somewhat unmannerly'.

No one today would argue that among her gifts was strict

constitutionalism. Mr Kingsley Martin, indeed, states bluntly that 'Queen Victoria was never a constitutional monarch'.[15] It is doubtful whether she read Bagehot's celebrated definition of the Sovereign's rights – to be consulted, to encourage and to warn. Had this doctrine been quoted against her she would have asked what was the use of a right to be heard if it was not also a right to be heeded? She would have stared glassily and claimed the right to oppose.

Well-disposed critics like Sir Philip Magnus have had to fall back on the existence of 'a wide and dubious border land' which remained open to the Sovereign's initiative throughout the nineteenth century, in order to excuse some of Queen Victoria's forays. Her successors wisely withdrew even from this zone, which has since been claimed for democracy.

According to Lord Esher, Queen Victoria herself looked upon royal power as 'her appanage by the gift of God.' As such it was inalienable. Hallam's *Constitution* she found 'too Republican' in deriving the Sovereign's rights from the people alone. Against all the evidence, she held that the royal prerogative had been preserved intact throughout her sixty glorious years. Nevertheless she made one concession to facts: monarchs, she said, would be wise in these unsettled times not to enforce their full rights. Unable to grasp the changing Constitution intellectually, she nevertheless played it by ear.

At the root of her trouble was failure to understand the party system.* For this she could be excused, for in the course of her long reign it had changed radically. Until her later years party allegiance was so variable that party strength could rarely be reckoned in firm figures. Of all her Prime Ministers, only Russell and Salisbury were unequivocally party men. Melbourne was manifestly a Tory calling himself a Liberal; Peel split the Tories with Liberal support; Aberdeen applied Pope's line to himself:

The Tories call him Whig, the Whigs a Tory.

* The two-party system was 'not fully understood even by young Queen Victoria' (W. Ivor Jennings, *The British Constitution*, p. 63). Nor by old Queen Victoria.

711

Derby, a Tory Prime Minister, had been born a Whig; Palmerston was a Tory Minister before he became a Liberal; Gladstone changed sides from Tory to Liberal; Disraeli started as a Radical; Rosebery, a Liberal Prime Minister, confessed that he ought to have been a Conservative.

Inflexible party loyalty such as Gladstone's aroused shocked Queen Victoria. 'The Conservatives are never so pertinaciously factious,' she wrote to her Liberal eldest daughter in 1878. Her close contact with ambassadors only confirmed her prejudice. 'Party rules everything,' said Lord Cowley; 'Party really goes much too far,' echoed the Queen. Through the Prince Consort and Lord Melbourne she learned the first half of her political lesson – that the Crown is above party. She never learned the other half – that in a democracy the only protection for the individual lies in unlimited choice of representatives. Queen Victoria would have curtailed that choice by resorting whenever possible to coalitions. Her agile but illogical mind confused loose party affiliations with the elevated neutrality enjoined upon herself.

In crusading against party spirit (which in effect meant crusading against the Left) she scarcely dented the increasingly tough party apparatus of both sides, while seriously compromising the neutrality of the Throne. It is therefore at first sight surprising to find so many people, including the French newspaper *Le Temps*, selecting her constitutionalism for special praise. (*Le Temps* called her 'the ideal constitutional Sovereign'.) This paradox need not be explained away. Queen Victoria's extraordinary character was honeycombed with contradictions. She was not just inconsistent in the sense of believing one thing and doing another. In the very depths of her being were lodged contrary qualities which might have caused another personality to split into fragments. In her, it meant that there was something for everyone; that courtiers who might otherwise have revolted against tedium or petty tyranny were fascinated to serve her for twenty, thirty and forty years. Though unconstitutional in action she was constitutional in temperament. You only had to look at her contours to see that she was no rangy Russian autocrat but a comfortable Britannia with the required genius for com-

712

promise. On occasion she might flout the will of her people, constitutionally expressed at the polls, yet in some inexplicable way the General Will – that most elusive of political concepts – was expressed in her person. 'Her prejudices and her convictions,' writes Mr Kingsley Martin, 'were so exactly those dominant in her age that she seemed to embody its very nature within herself.' Lord Salisbury, in his eulogy after her death, picked out her interpretative genius:

> 'I have always felt that when I knew what the Queen thought, I knew pretty certainly what views her subjects would take, and especially the middle class of her subjects.'

In a Queen, this was the best substitute for meticulous constitutionalism and her people knew it. They were not amused by Labouchere's suggestion in 1890 that Buckingham Palace should be converted into a home for fallen women.

It is difficult to convey the richness of her contradictions. She was both brave and nervous. So greatly did she fear the sea that though born a good sailor she became a very bad one; the Empress Eugénie had to assure her that 'Queens are not drowned'. She was afraid of sports, from ice hockey to hunting. When her son-in-law, Prince Christian, lost his eye in a gun accident she wrote: 'my dislike to & fear of shooting will only increase.' She was so terrified of railway accidents that she never used expresses, even for the sake of dining-cars, or travelled at more than 50 miles an hour. Even so, her engine driver was killed in 1898 by standing up when going under a bridge. She once had the train stopped at Wigan, sending Brown with a message for the superintendent which emerged as: 'The Queen says the carriage was shaking like the devil.'

She was intensely loyal to old places and old ways, yet she would never buy a villa abroad for fear of being tied down to one place. She loved change. In the same way she appreciated new amenities. Though she said that 'negotiating by telegraph is a dreadful business', she made full use of it and the Princess of Wales complained that the telephone between Balmoral and Abergeldie never stopped ringing. She was reported to have fallen for the tricycle in 1881 and even to have

713

gone for a spin. Electric light was one of the few inventions she did not praise; it either hurt her eyes or was not bright enough.

In human relations she was both unselfish and inconsiderate, tactful and blunt, sympathetic and hard, patient and fidgety, direct and devious, irresistibly charming and bristling with 'repellent power'. While receiving her at a library the librarian seized the opportunity to make an introduction:

'Your Majesty, this is my daughter.'
'I came to see the library.'

Majesty swept on.

She was generous with money, often having to be restrained by the Keeper of the Privy Purse; but when Princess Beatrice's family were moved into a more commodious wing at Balmoral while the Queen happened to be away, they were ignominiously bundled back again as soon as the extravagance was detected. She could be both hysterical and composed, reckless and discreet, overpoweringly regal and naïvely modest. When told that Cecil Rhodes was a woman hater, 'Oh! I don't think that can be so,' she replied, 'he was so very civil to me.' Rhodes gallantly assured her that he could not hate a sex to which the Queen herself belonged. She attended a bazaar at Balmoral in 1894, humbly recording in her Journal that several of the plaited baskets she had made with her own hands were unsold and had to be auctioned at the end.

She was stiff and clinging, incurably shy and superbly poised, every ounce a bourgeoise and every inch a queen. Some of these contrasts seem to sprout more paradoxes the further they are investigated. In the handling of her children she practised what she preached even less than the average parent. She strongly deprecated back-biting among her children though capable of critical remarks herself. One daughter would be laughed at for supposing that tight lacing made her slim; another for wanting to commission a statuette of herself without having the requisite figure. The classical example of Queen Victoria's tactlessness is related by her own grand-daughter, Princess Marie Louise of Schleswig-Holstein. The Queen telegraphed to the Princess's parents who were abroad:

714

'Children very well but poor little Louise very ugly.'[16] Yet she never forfeited her family's affection. As her friend Augusta Stanley said: 'She is so innocent and lovable with it all.' (Augusta regularly referred to Queen Victoria as 'the Blessed One'.) The occasional growl from Henry Ponsonby that she was a 'despot' need not be taken too seriously. He was hardly the man to have served a despot for over thirty years.

On the whole her children held their own. Indeed, a visiting sculptress once observed that some people considered their upbringing 'too free and easy'; the sculptress herself overheard a brisk exchange when an unclaimed handkerchief was picked up in her room:

'Yours, Mama.'
'Oh, no.'
'Must be – it has VR on it.'[17]

Prince Leopold in particular never hesitated to answer back. An argument like the following, recorded by Ponsonby, was not infrequent at the Queen's dinner table:

Queen (to Prince Leopold): 'I heard your musical box playing most clearly this afternoon even as far off as your room.'
Prince Leopold: 'Impossible, for my musical box never plays.'
Queen: 'But I know it was your musical box – there was that drum in it I recognized.'
Prince Leopold: 'That shows it wasn't my musical box, there is no drum in it.'[18]

Queen Victoria was not the exemplary mother her contemporaries felt bound to call her in deference to the legend of her supernaturally perfect family life.* Her failures, however, will not seem extraordinary to most parents even in 'these civilized times' – to borrow one of her phrases. Certain special difficulties of her own – rejection of her physical

* There is the story of the Victorian matron who remarked to her friend as the curtain fell on Sarah Bernhardt's highly coloured performance in the role of Cleopatra, 'How different, how very different from the home life of our own dear Queen.'

nature and an over-riding impulsion towards father-figures – exacerbated her maternal problems. Nevertheless she loved children: in her later years she is remembered as hardly moving without a child in tow and the spectacle of six children and seven dogs romping together on the lawn seemed to her idyllic. She felt 'dreadful' when the nursery was 'broken up' in 1865 and delighted to open it again for her grandchildren: 'I love to hear the little feet & merry voices above.' Unlike many of her contemporaries she did not confine the little feet to 'above'.

For one who justly boasted of an 'open nature', who rarely bore a grudge and liked to 'have things out', she was devious to a degree. Her passion for go-betweens was complicated by an equally strong compulsion to keep everything in her own hands. Not a curtain could rise on a tableau, not a round of applause begin without Queen Victoria first ringing her little golden bell, clapping, or tapping her fan. She appointed even her grooms and ushers, interviewed every housekeeper herself, chose nannies for her grandchildren and would not let Princess Christian select a lady-in-waiting for her own establishment whom she, the Queen, did not know.

Contrary urges to control all yet face nothing occasionally brought Queen Victoria to a full stop. Never has a ruler threatened more often to abdicate, to leave for Australia or generally to opt out of everything. Her routine retirements to the Continent, Balmoral and Osborne were abdication-substitutes; but the tight hold she kept on her Court during these retreats shows that she could never really let go.

Those who heard about life at Balmoral coined an ugly word for it – 'balmorality'. Balmorality implied cold stuffiness, simplicity jellied in convention, all pleasure meretricious, all privations purely tiresome. Queen Victora had countless fires put out in bedrooms and sitting-rooms during the rigours of June, kept old gentlemen with gout standing for hours after dinner, forbade loud talk or laughter, gave 'toko' to her courtiers if they went for a walk before she herself had gone out, held ghillies' balls in all weathers, so that rain would dash under the tent flaps and Lady Ely become positively maudlin after an extra nip to keep out the cold. When suffering from an overdose of balmorality, Jenner confided to Ponsonby

> 'how bad it was mentally and physically to be here [Balmoral] long . . . he found himself excited about small things which when he got away he didn't care a damn for – and he asked himself was it worth while.'[19]

Worst of all the Queen herself would eventually react against the monotony of her Highland life, envy her children 'junketing' in London and make 'rows' out of sheer boredom.

One cannot read through her private Journals, with their frequent regrets at having to leave Windsor for Balmoral 'in a burst of spring' or Osborne at the height of summer, without asking why no one saved her from herself. Bishop Davidson, distressed to find that whenever she received him in Prince Albert's dressing-room before dinner a footman would bring in hot water and a clean towel for the ghost of the dear departed, deplored the lack of any one 'on the appropriate terms with her for friendly remonstrance or even raillery of a kindly sort.'[20] What she needed was that well-known Victorian character, a candid female friend. 'She lived all her life subject to the guidance of wise men,' wrote *The Times* in her obituary notice. This was only half true. As a widow, her headstrong will would have been more truly 'subject' to wise women and what Ponsonby called 'hen talk'. Even among men, she got on best with those who possessed a touch of the feminine – Prince Albert, Disraeli, Granville, Rosebery. Where was the female friend?

The ultimate blame for Queen Victoria's isolation on what Tennyson called her 'terrible height' rested with her interpretation of royalty. Some profound, princely impulse prevented her from being intimate with the ladies who occupied the intermediate zone between the royal stratosphere and earthbound servants. It is significant that when her cap was accidentally twitched off in front of Court ladies at a drawing-room she described it as a 'dreadful misadventure'; when she was rescued from an overturned carriage by her Highland servant, Frankie Clark, she was more than a little amused: 'Would you believe it,' she told her granddaughter Princess

Marie Louise; 'all my petticoats came undone!'

She was the first to recognize her dilemma. Once when the Empress Frederick complained of loneliness Queen Victoria confessed that she too could talk to 'very few' of her ladies. Her solution was to entrench herself in her family. She advised Vicky to do likewise:

> 'In our position which is so totally different from other people's one ought not to be left alone, without a Child or a near Relation.'[21]

The trouble was that children had not the authority to guide her, while the Ladies Ely and Churchill were too easily bullied. Someone like Florence Nightingale, whom the Queen greatly admired, was needed to keep her Sovereign 'straight', much as the Queen expected Ministers to keep *The Times* 'straight'. And if the 'kindly raillery' advocated by Bishop Davidson produced a tart 'We are not amused', the lady of the lamp would not so much as flicker.

Balmorality in its narrower sense meant little more than the awkwardness of a spoilt old lady. Certainly the stiffness of her Court etiquette increased with age, though she mellowed in other directions. Towards Catholics, Jews and even Sabbatarians, for instance, she relaxed her vigilance: compare her comment on a contemplative order of nuns at Carisbrooke in 1869 – 'What a dreary existence, & to our ideas a useless one' – with her gratitude twenty-six years later to the Franciscans of Cimiez who promised to pray for her always. The victim of anti-semitic persecution in France, Colonel Dreyfus, she described as 'this poor martyr'. Two Wesleyan bandsmen who had been dismissed from her band for refusing to practise on Sundays were reinstated by her orders, and all Sunday practising was cancelled.

Balmorality became a dangerous charge when her enemies declared that it was not a quirk but a vice – one-tenth morality and nine-tenths ballyhoo. Ample ammunition was furnished by such a story as that of Sir James Reid, the Queen's physician, and the Hon. Susan Baring, a maid-of-honour. They became engaged in 1899, to the Queen's astonished disgust, who unburdened herself to the Empress Frederick. How could a

Baring accept him? It was a great misalliance for her, though he had money of his own.

'If I had been younger I wld have let him go rather – but at my age it wld be hazardous & disagreeable & so he remains living in my House wherever we are!! and she quite consents to it. But it is too tiresome & I can't conceal my annoyance. I have never said a word to her yet.'[22]

That it was Reid's class which upset her is suggested by her reaction in 1895 to the marriage of another maid-of-honour, Ina McNiell, to the Duke of Argyll, Princess Louise's father-in-law; the union was warmly approved, 'though I much regret losing her.' Lady Lytton relates that Sir James Reid, famed for his sense of humour, finally made peace with outraged Majesty by promising never to commit the offence again.

No less reprehensible was her refusal to give the Fritz Ponsonbys the usual grace-and-favour house after she had finally, though still reluctantly, consented to their marriage.

Against such aberrations can be set shining examples of humanity and broadmindedness. When a young Strelitz princess was found to have been seduced by a footman the Queen's sympathies were entirely with the girl, who she decided had been drugged. She wrote indignantly to the Empress Frederick: 'the *family* have forbidden that poor unhappy girl's name ever being mentioned *in* the family ... I think it too wicked'; and later: 'It is too awful & shameful & almost sinful to send the poor Baby away.'[23] Some years earlier her heart had gone out to Countess Valeri Hohenthal who, on principle, refused to marry her lover, the Hungarian Count Üxküll, though they lived together and produced four children.* Queen Victoria described this unorthodox union as '$\frac{1}{2}$ crazy but holy', comparing it favourably with loveless matches contracted out of expediency.[24]

* Valerie Hohenthal, a younger sister of Walburga Paget, broke with her family in 1869 and died in 1878, her 'husband' having predeceased her, raving mad. She apparently got her theories from her mother who had fallen in love with the philosophical revolutionary, Lassalle.

Prejudiced and prudish,* tolerant and romantic; still the contradictions mount up and could be multiplied. She despised the Tsar's and Kaiser's itch to wear British uniforms and her dentist's attempts to win from Lady Ely a baronetcy 'at the point of his forceps'. At the same time she took her position as 'the fountain of honour' most seriously, striving to keep the flow to the purest trickle. When Lord George Sanger paraded his celebrated circus round the Quadrangle, she greeted him drily with the question, 'You call yourself Lord George Sanger, I hear?' The 'Lord' bowed assent. 'Very amusing.'

The argument over her intellectual ability has never been settled. Dilke credited her with 'great ability' and Balfour enjoyed the company of one so intelligent and well-informed. 'Let us have the Queen's opinion,' Lord Clarendon used to say. 'It is always worth hearing even if you do not agree with it.' Others have intemperately derided her as a stupid, indolent woman. It is true that she lacked spontaneous intellectual curiosity. Without that gift, neither her immense industry nor taste for intelligent discussion could greatly extend her mental range. Within these limits her mind was alert and her understanding well above the average. No one has ever emerged from old letters more alive; no one without talent could have produced her Journal. From having been a safety valve it became a burden. Her success in keeping it going to the end, in case she or others needed it for the record, shows both ability and a high sense of historical and political duty.

Despite Queen Victoria's contradictory qualities she faces history all of a piece. She is immediately knowable though few agree about what is to be known. Even her appearance has left impressions as divergent as Mr Pope-Hennessy's – 'an amiable field mouse' – and Mr V. S. Pritchett's – 'a mixture of national landlady and actress'. Her Continental 'in-laws' found her sombre, civil and terrifying; her middle-

* Canon J. N. B. Woodroffe once took as his text for a sermon to the Queen at Nice, St Paul's 'I have a sting of the flesh', explaining that it simply meant eye-strain caused by malaria. She was so pleased that she presented him with a gold pen. It was also at Nice that she received the lurid queen of actresses, Sarah Bernhardt.

aged eldest son, when late for dinner, perspired behind a pillar at the prospect of facing her; her grandchildren fondly remembered her 'looking so dear' in white cap, black bombazine dress filled in with white *lisse* at sleeves and neck, black silk stockings with white soles, and on her face a shy, benign smile.*

It is sad that Queen Victoria's most fetching physical traits had to be seen or heard to be believed. The last chances to hear her silver voice disappeared when she requested the Emperor of Abyssinia to destroy a gramophone record she had given him and declined to send one to the Chicago Fair. Her radiant smiles, except for one or two photographs, are irretrievably lost. We can take it from Sir Edmund Gosse that she had 'a genius of movement'; to Gustav Freytag it appeared as something between a glide and a goose-step, for he described it as 'a march-like gait'. All agreed that her matchless dignity triumphed over her diminutive size and indeed gained from it.

Many of her peculiarities should be treated as common to the period. Her sentimentality, for instance, was equalled by Mrs Gladstone's: while Queen Victoria was 'Fraüchen', Mrs Gladstone signed herself 'Wifie'. Over animals, the Queen was less sentimental than Canon Wilberforce, who buried his late father's horse next to the churchyard. Her hypochondria must be seen against the general expectation of life – or rather, of death. Miss Nightingale's health became delicate thirty years before she died at ninety. Cardinal Newman treated his life as virtually ended when he finished his *Apologia* at sixty-three; he reached eighty-nine. Lord Rosebery envisaged 'a complete breakdown of health' followed by death at fifty-five; he lived to be eighty-two.

Every Victorian woman going into labour was said to have been 'taken ill'.

Her sense of humour was not so elementary as is often suggested. Lord Granville once observed that wit was wasted on the Royal Family since nothing made them laugh like hearing one had shut one's finger in the door. This quip has

* The last of these curious little dresses is preserved in the London Museum.

been overworked. It is true that Prince Albert's jokes were simple.* True also that Queen Victoria laughed immoderately when Napoleon III spilt coffee on his cocked hat, when Lord Kinnoul tumbled head over heels down a slope, and when the Duke of Argyll dropped the crown and then brought it into the Robing Room squashed 'like a pudding that had *sat down*'. She could also appreciate the subtler humours of Court or clerical life. She once told the Rector of Whippingham about a conversation between herself and Bishop Wilberforce, of whose High Church beliefs she disapproved.

Bishop Wilberforce: 'It was Your Majesty's fault that Manning went over to Rome.'
Queen Victoria: 'Why?'
Bishop Wilberforce: 'Oh! If Your Majesty had made him a Bishop he wouldn't have gone.'

The Queen longed to answer: 'Then if I had not made you a Bishop, *you* would have gone to Rome.'

Her concern for social welfare was greater than is usually admitted. Though not so superlatively charitable as her cousin Princess Mary of Teck, she could never have perpetrated a remark like Sarah Spencer's (Lady Lyttelton) when the latter heard that a cargo boat had been wrecked off Cowes: 'My indifference about colliers is prodigious. Now if it had been a wrecked warship . . .' The cynicism of her Whig Ministers about the working classes glanced off her. When the young Prince Albert asked what peasants were called in England, Melbourne suggested, 'Common people – common fellows – labouring men'; 'Clods!' said Palmerston. A man of Dean Stanley's distinction could describe himself as totally uninterested in factories. Not so the Queen. She rightly said that her heart 'always feels so intensely for the sorrows & anxieties of others'. In her letters of condolence to widows of all sorts she showed such solicitude about how they were left that the

* There was one about a stout, prim lady at Coburg who came down to dinner in a white dress; a short-sighted gentleman took her for a porcelain stove and turning his back on her parted his coat-tails to warm himself.

Keeper of the Privy Purse feared some of them would expect her to support them for life.

It was in her feelings for the East and coloured peoples generally that she showed herself most in advance of her times. After a long talk in 1883 with 'a real female doctor', Mrs Scharlieb ('nice & intelligent' but 'quite unconnected with any missionaries'), she threw herself into plans for saving 'quantities' of Indian women from death in childbirth. In 1900 she gave five Kaiser-i-Hind medals to women doctors, having followed closely the work for medical schools, and was delighted to hear that many Indians had successfully completed their training in the Munshi's home town, Agra. In 1898 she complained that there were not enough Indians in the Birthday Honours.

The mission of Britain, according to her view, was 'to protect the poor natives and advance civilization'. This was not a disguise for white exploitation; to the Queen it meant hospitals and home truths. When 'Saintly' Bishop Patteson was murdered by Melanesians in 1871, she later noted in her Journal that the 'poor natives' had been so often killed and kidnapped that they thought every white man their enemy; when rumours reached her that Kitchener had desecrated the Mahdi's head by keeping it on his desk (the Victorians were liable to make anything into an inkstand) she wrote to insist on decent burial. So great was her passion for India that soon after her Golden Jubilee she conceived the wild idea of a visit, writing to the Duchess of Connaught:

'I wish (*quite seriously*) I cd take the children out to you!! If Vicky was not coming to me in November I *WD* make the effort!! I have *such* a gt longing sometime to go to India ... You may think me crazy for saying this – but I can assure you I have been thinking of it – vy much of late.'[25]

'If they only knew me as I am!' said Queen Victoria, overwhelmed by her people's devotion during her last years. Enough is known of her today to see her as she was. The extended view will modify but not obliterate the impression of greatness she left with the country and the world. The debate about whether she possessed power, influence or only prestige is by now a somewhat sterile one; she correctly described herself as at any rate no 'mere puppet' in the formation of governments.[26] Her prestige was phenomenal. Old women believed that her royal touch would cure their ills; gentlemen, mortally sick on the Riviera, rallied after she visited them; fathers brought her their young children saying that it would be *une bénédiction*' merely to have seen her; a Negress of seventy-six who had saved up for fifty years, 'walked' from the United States in order to speak to her for a few minutes; the fat spokeswoman for the fish-wives of Nice kissed her on both cheeks; Sir William Jenner treated her as omnipotent:

Jenner: 'Is the Queen going to Inverary?'
Lady Churchill: 'It depends on the Duke being able to receive her.'
Jenner: 'Receive her! Why she has only to say she wishes to go and he *must* receive her.'
Lady Churchill: 'You talk as if she was Queen Elizabeth.'[27]

Queen Victoria and Bismarck were the only people who ever frightened Lord Rosebery. Dr Reid slept 'none', according to the factor, the night before his first audience with the Queen; an Albert medallist looked more terrified at his investiture than when he faced death in a storm. 'He always said he wished to die for you,' exclaimed the widow of a soldier. 'I could die for her!' said the Canadian Adjutant of the last troops she reviewed.

What was the chemistry which transformed a highly-strung, only partially integrated woman into the reality of Queen Victoria? – 'little mysterious Victoria', as Henry James called her, who melts her critics from Lytton Strachey downwards and causes her biographers to part from her with regret. 'Essentially, the simple Sir Theodore* and the serpentine Lytton S.,' wrote Max Beerbohm, 'are at one about her'.

* Sir Theodore Martin published a eulogy of Victoria 'the great and good' in 1909 which Philip Guedalla picked up for 6*d*. twenty years later. He presented it to his friend Max Beerbohm as an example of how things change.

Bishop Davidson plumped for common sense as the supreme 'welder' of all her qualities. Undoubtedly common sense extricated her from many tight corners and saved her advisers from making fools of themselves,* but it takes more than common sense to create a legend. And legend she was. Even her seclusion in the end added another, impalpable dimension to what the New York *Evening Post* called her 'mythic glory', making her all the more revered for being so seldom seen.

I will be good. The words, as spoken by the child of eleven, were little more than a stiff, doll-like gesture; they became the guiding thread in Queen Victoria's life. At her most absurd, at her most impossible, she still had the will to be good. This was her secret. In this she represented the Victorian age.

> *I am whatever you do; I am your vow to be*
> *Good ...*

It has been suggested that her remoteness from the adventurous, inquiring mind of a Tyndall or a Huxley placed her among the Edwardians rather than the great Victorians. Though stimulating, this view ignores the essence of the Victorian age – belief in and striving after improvement – which was also the very fibre of Queen Victoria's being. To some of her contemporaries improvement merely meant more material wealth. 'We may not be more moral, more imaginative, nor better educated than our ancestors,' ran a sentence from the catalogue of the 1862 International Exhibition, 'but we have more steam, gas, railways, and power-looms, while there are more of us, and we have more money to spend.' This neat declaration of faith in the affluent Victorian society would not have satisfied Her Majesty, for she hoped that morals, like everything else, had improved during her reign; not that she blamed her royal predecessors for their bad example – 'for in those days even the best people were

---

* Sir John Cowell wrote her a long letter protesting that the Protestant Church would be in danger if a Mr Courtenay were allowed to call himself 'Rev. & Hon.' Cowell's letter came back marked: 'It is a matter of perfect indifference to the Queen what he is called.'

excessively coarse'. As early as the 'forties she had remarked to Lord Melbourne that modern women had more accomplishments, men drank less and dogs behaved better towards the furniture than in the past. That dedicated pessimist replied firmly that he could see no improvement.

Many of her contemporaries saw improvement in terms of Reform. This, to Queen Victoria, sounded too revolutionary unless interpreted by someone she trusted like Disraeli. But simple improvement – yes, that was something which she could worship. Improvement was safe; even the most immutable things like the dear Blue Room could be improved by interior decoration, and self-improvement could brighten up the human interior in exactly the same way.

The injunction to improve was universal. 'In after years,' she once wrote, 'God would not distinguish between the good life of a Crowned head or a peasant.' She would be judged along with the humblest of her people – the poor heedless Irish, the innocent Africans, the faithful Indians, the old Highland women hidden away in dark cupboard-beds, or the London mob. The most that she and any of them could hope to say was that they had tried to be good.

REFERENCE NOTES

LIST OF ABBREVIATIONS

RA. The Royal Archives, Windsor Castle.

Vic.Add.MSS. Victorian Additional Manuscripts, Royal Archives.

Journal. Queen Victoria's Journal, preserved in the Royal Archives.

Girlhood. The Girlhood of Queen Victoria, A Selection from Her Majesty's Diaries between the years 1832 and 1840, edited by Viscount Esher (2 volumes, John Murray Ltd, 1912).

Letters. The Letters of Queen Victoria, A Selection from Her Majesty's Correspondence, First Series, 1837–61, edited by A. C. Benson and Viscount Esher (3 volumes, John Murray Ltd, 1907). Second Series, 1862–85, edited by G. E. Buckle (3 volumes, John Murray Ltd, 1926). Third Series, 1886–1901, edited by G. E. Buckle (3 volumes, John Murray Ltd, 1930).

Kronberg Letters. The Letters of Queen Victoria to her eldest daughter, the Princess Royal (Crown Princess Frederick William of Prussia and afterwards Empress Frederick of Germany), who died at Kronberg in 1901, R.A. Vic. Add.MSS, U32.

Dearest Child. Dearest Child, Letters between Queen Victoria and the Princess Royal, 1858–61, a selection from the Kronberg Archives, edited by Roger Fulford (Evans Brothers Ltd, 1964).

Empress Frederick. Letters of the Empress Frederick, edited by Sir Frederick Ponsonby (Macmillan & Co. Ltd, 1928).

English Empress. The English Empress, A Study in the Relations between Queen Victoria and Her Eldest Daughter, Empress Frederick of Germany, by Egon Caesar Conte Corti, with an Introduction by Wolfgang Prince of Hesse (Cassell & Co. Ltd, 1957).

Further Letters. Further Letters of Queen Victoria, from

the Archives of the House of Brandenburg–Prussia, edited by Hector Bolitho (Thornton Butterworth Ltd, 1938).

Greville. The Greville Memoirs, 1817–60, edited by Henry Reeve (8 volumes, Longmans, Green & Co. Ltd, 1875–87); by Lytton Strachey and Roger Fulford (8 volumes, Macmillan & Co. Ltd, 1938); and by Roger Fulford (1 volume, B. T. Batsford Ltd, 1963).

Disraeli. The Life of Benjamin Disraeli, Earl of Beaconsfield, by W. F. Monypenny and G. E. Buckle (6 volumes, John Murray Ltd, 1910–20).

Ponsonby Letters. The Letters of Sir Henry Ponsonby to his wife (unless otherwise stated), 1865–95.

PART ONE

CHAPTER I

Born to Succeed 1815–19

1 Knollys Papers, Duke of Kent to General Knollys, September 22nd, 1815.
2 RA Geo. 46652, Duke of Kent to Mademoiselle de St Laurent, November 23rd, 1790.
3 RA M2/25, Princess Leiningen to Duke of Kent, January 25th, 1818.
4 Knollys Papers, Duke of Kent to General Knollys, April 22nd, 1819.
5 RA M2/39, Duke of Kent to Princess Leiningen, April 23rd, 1818.
6 RA M2/68, memorandum, 1818.
7 RA M2/73, Duke of Kent to Princess Leningen, December 31st, 1818.
8 Kronberg Letters, July 25th, 1891.

CHAPTER II

'I Will be Good' 1819–30

1 RA M4/26, Duchess of Kent to Earl Grey, January 28th, 1831; Sir Sidney Lee, *Queen Victoria* (1902) I.12.
2 Journal, May 16th, 1838.
3 RA M4/26, Duchess of Kent to Earl Grey, January 28th, 1831.
4 RA Y203/79, Baroness Lehzen to Queen Victoria, September 6th, 1867.
5 *Letters,* I.I.14, 'Memoir of Queen Victoria's Early Years.'
6 *Greville,* May 29th, 1829.
7 Frances Low, *Queen Victoria's Dolls* (1894).
8 RA M5/60, 'The Education of Princess Victoria', January 1st, 1835.
9 RA M5/3a, Dean of Chester (George Davys) to Duchess of Kent, 1830.

10 RA M5/3, Dean of Chester to Duchess of Kent, March 2nd, 1830.
11 RA Y203/81, Baroness Lehzen to Queen Victoria, December 2nd, 1867.

CHAPTER III

Royal Progress 1830-4

1 RA M5/7, Duchess of Kent to Bishops of London and Lincoln, March 1st, 1830; *Letters* I.i.21-2.
2 RA M5/9, Duchess of Kent to the Bishops of London and Lincoln, March 13th, 1830.
3 RA Z485/6, 'Sir John Conroy 1878-79', Mrs Henry Conroy's memorandum, September 1878.
4 RA Z485/6, Queen Victoria's marginal notes on the above.
5 RA Z485/6, Queen Victoria's marginal notes.
6 RA M4/19, Princess Sophia to Sir John Conroy, October 14th, 1830.
7 *Greville,* September 8th, 1831.
8 RA M5/84, Duchess of Kent to Princess Victoria, September 2nd, 1835.
9 Journal, July 29th, 1833; *Girlhood,* I.83.
10 Journal, November 4th, 1834; *Girlhood,* I.102.
11 Journal, January 21st, 1838; *Girlhood,* I.260.
12 Journal, March 4th, 1837.
13 Journal, September 25th, 1835.
14 Journal, January 8th, 1837.
15 Journal, January 19th, 1837.
16 Journal November 3rd, 1836.
17 Journal, May 29th, 1834.

CHAPTER IV

'She Must be Coerced' 1835-7

1 *Girlhood* I.109, January 21st, 1835 and I.116, May 24th, 1835.
2 RA M5/78, Duchess of Kent to Princess Victoria, July 30th, 1835.
3 Journal, September 25th, 1835.
4 *Letters* I.i.141, Princess Victoria to Prince Leopold of Saxe-Coburg, February 16th, 1828.
5 Journal, October 4th, 1835.
6 RA Y79/64537, King Leopold of the Belgians to Queen Victoria, February 16th, 1846.
7 Journal, January 25th, 1836.
8 Journal, February 26th, 1838.
9 *Letters* I.i.61, King Leopold to Princess Victoria, May 13th, 1836.
10 *Girlhood* I.157, May 18th, 1836.
11 *Girlhood* I.159, May 21st, 1836 and I.160, June 10th, 1836.
12 Journal, June 10th, 1836.
13 *Letters* I.i.162, Princess Victoria to King Leopold, June 7th, 1836.
14 *Greville,* September 21st, 1836.
15 Journal, September 21st, 1836.
16 Journal, February 8th, 1837.
17 Journal, April 8th, 1837.
18 Journal, May 5th, 1837.
19 RA M7/67, Prince Charles Leiningen's memorandum dictated to Prince Albert's German librarian, 1840.

20 RA M7/67, Prince Charles Leiningen's memorandum.

21 RA Z482, 'The Duchess of Kent's Situation', Sir John Conroy's memorandum, 1837.

22 *Greville*, February 11th, 1837.

23 Journal, May 19th, 1837.

24 RA M7/14 and 20, 'The Accession'.

25 RA M7/15, Baroness Lehzen's memorandum.

26 Journal, April 29th, 1838.

27 Journal, September 5th, 1838.

28 RA M7/38, Baroness Lehzen's memorandum.

29 RA M7/15, Baroness Lehzen's memorandum.

30 Journal, May 24th, 1837; *Girlhood* I.190.

31 *Letters* I.i.87, King Leopold to Princess Victoria, May 25th, 1837.

32 RA M7/52, Duchess of Kent to Princess Victoria, [13] June 1837.

33 RA Vic. Add. MSS, A11, Lord Liverpool's memorandum, June 17th, 1837.

34 RA Vic. Add. MSS, A11, Lord Liverpool's memorandum.

35 Journal, June 15th, 1837; *Girlhood* I.194.

36 RA M7/67, Prince Charles Leiningen's memorandum, 1840.

37 *Greville*, June 18th, 1837.

38 RA Z294, Duchess of Kent's Diary, June 20th, 1837.

CHAPTER V

Little Victory 1837

1 Journal, June 20th, 1837; *Letters* I.i.98.

2 Journal, November 12th, 1847.

3 *Greville*, July 30th, 1837.

4 Journal, June 20th, 1837; *Letters* I.i.98.

5 RA M7/68, 'The Accession', Baron Stockmar to Queen Victoria, October 28th, 1837.

6 RA M7/68, op. cit., Baron Stockmar to Queen Victoria, October 28th, 1837.

7 RA M7/68, Duchess of Kent to Queen Victoria, [20] June, 1837.

8 Journal, September 5th, 1836.

9 Journal, April 29th, 1838.

10 Journal, November 1st, 1837; *Girlhood* I.231.

11 Journal, August 1st, 1838.

12 *Greville*, September 12th, 1838.

CHAPTER VI

The Wonderful Year 1837–8

1 Journal, March 23rd, 1838.

2 *Greville*, July 30th, 1837.

3 RA Z482, Duchess of Kent to Queen Victoria, February 1838.

4 RA Z482, Duchess of Kent to Queen Victoria, November 6th, 1837.

5 RA Z482, Duchess of Kent to Queen Victoria, November 6th, 1837.

6 Journal, November 16th, 1837.

7 Journal, December 12th, 1837.

8 Journal, June 24th, 1837; *Girlhood* I.203 and 206.

9 Journal, February 15th, 1838.

10 Mrs J. S. Haldane's Papers, Miss Haldane, 1837.

11 Journal, January 28th, 1838.
12 Journal, January 30th, 1838.
13 Journal, February 4th, 1838.
14 Journal, February 9th and 26th, 1838.
15 Journal, January 17th, 1838.
16 Journal, June 27th, 1838.
17 Journal, June 24th, 1838.
18 Journal, June 28th, 1838; *Girlhood* I.357; *Letters* I.i.154.
19 Journal, June 28th, 1838; *Girlhood* I.360.
20 Journal, July 6th, 1838.
21 *Greville*, June 27th, 1838.

CHAPTER VII

Disenchantment 1838–9

1 Journal, March 10th, 1838.
2 Journal, April 24th, 1838.
3 Dormer Creston, *The Youthful Queen Victoria* (1952), p. 308.
4 Journal, March 22nd, April 12th, May 28th, 1838.
5 Journal, August 1st, 1838.
6 Journal, August 1st, 1838.
7 *Letters* I.i.126, King Leopold to Queen Victoria, December 26th, 1837.
8 Journal, February 27th, 1838.
9 *Letters* I.i.192, King Leopold to Queen Victoria, April 19th, 1839.
10 *Letters* I.i.193, Queen Victoria to King Leopold, April 30th, 1839.
11 *Letters* I.i.221, King Leopold to Queen Victoria, May 17th, 1839.
12 Journal, December 13th, 1838.
13 Journal, November 4th, 1838.
14 Journal, January 4th and 9th, 1839.

15 Journal, September 19th, 1838.
16 Journal, October 17th, 1838.
17 *Greville*, March 11th, 1838.
18 Journal, October 29th, 1838.
19 Journal, December 15th, 1838.

CHAPTER VIII

'Mama's Amiable Lady' 1839

1 Journal, September 18th, 1838.
2 Journal, February 7th, 1838.
3 Journal, April 18th, 1838.
4 Journal, February 2nd, 1839.
5 Journal, January 18th, 1839.
6 Journal, January 21st, 1839.
7 Stratfield Saye MSS, Lady Tavistock to Lord Hastings, March 15th, 1839.
8 Journal, February 2nd, 1839.
9 Journal, February 2nd, 1839.
10 Journal, February 21st, 1839.
11 Journal, September 19th, 1839.
12 RA Z486, 'The Case of Lady Flora Hastings', Queen Victoria to the Duchess of Kent, undated.
13 RA Vic. Add. MSS, U62, 'Dr Allen's Journal', March 17th, 1839.
14 Journal, March 22nd, 1839.
15 Journal, April 5th, 1839.
16 Journal, April 16th, 1839.
17 Journal, April 21st, 1839.
18 Journal, April 18th, 1839.
19 Journal, April 18th, 1839; *Girlhood* II.154.

CHAPTER IX

Ladies of the Bedchamber 1839

1 Journal, April 26th, 1839.
2 Journal, May 7th, 1839.
3 Journal, May 7th, 1839.
4 Journal, May 8th, 1839.

5 *Girlhood* II.167, Queen Victoria to Lord Melbourne, May 8th, 1839.

6 *Girlhood*, II.166; *Letters* I.i.200, Queen Victoria to Lord Melbourne, May 8th, 1839.

7 Journal, May 9th, 1839; *Letters* I.i.208, Queen Victoria's Journal.

8 *Girlhood* II.168, Queen Victoria to Lord Melbourne, May 9th, 1839.

9 Journal, May 9th, 1839; *Letters* I.i.208, Queen Victoria's Journal.

10 *Greville*, August 15th, 1839.

11 Journal, May 9th, 1839; *Letters* I.i.209, Queen Victoria's Journal.

12 *Letters* I.i.205, Queen Victoria to Lord Melbourne, May 9th, 1839.

13 *Letters* I.i.206, Queen Victoria to Lord Melbourne, May 9th, 1839.

14 Journal, May 9th, 1839.

15 Journal, May 11th, 1839.

16 Journal, May 10th, 1839; *Girlhood* II.175.

17 Journal, May 16th, 1839.

18 F. P. G. Guizot, *Sir Robert Peel* (1857), p. 81.

19 Stratfield Saye MSS, Duke of Wellington to Lord Tavistock, May 10th, 1839.

20 RA L17/58, Sir Arthur Bigge, October 30th, 1897.

21 Journal, May 19th, 1839.

22 Journal, May 27th, 1839; *Girlhood* II.188.

23 Journal, May 29th, 1839; *Girlhood* II.191.

24 Roxburgh Club, *Wellington Correspondence*, Duke of Wellington to Sir John Conroy, July 6th, 1839.

25 RA Z484, 'Sir John Conroy's Claims 1844–54', Duchess of Kent to Sir George Couper, February 16th, 1850.

26 RA Z484, op. cit., Duchess of Kent to Queen Victoria and Queen Victoria to Duchess of Kent, March 2nd, 1854.

27 Journal, December 14th, 1838.

28 David Cecil, *Lord M.* (1954), p. 304.

29 Journal, December 10th, 1837.

30 RA Y86/66728, King Leopold to Queen Victoria, February 16th, 1864.

31 Roxburgh Club, *Wellington Correspondence*, the Duke's memorandum, June 3rd, 1839.

32 Journal, June 4th, 1839.

33 Journal, June 13th, 1839.

34 Journal, June 9th, 1839.

35 Journal, June 16th, 1839.

36 Journal, June 14th, 1839.

37 Journal, June 17th, 1839.

38 Journal, June 19th and 26th, 1839.

39 Journal, June 26th, 1839.

40 Journal, June 27th, 1839.

41 Journal, July 5th, 1839.

42 British Museum MS; R. B. Martin, *Enter Rumour* (1962), p. 64.

43 Journal, July 10th and September 22nd, 1839.

44 Journal, August 10th, 1839.

45 Journal, October 9th, 1839.

CHAPTER X

'My Beloved Albert' 1839–40

1 Journal, July 15th, 1839; *Girlhood* II.215; *Letters* I.i.224.

2 Journal, June 24th, 1839.

3 Mrs H. Wyndham (editor), *Correspondence of Sarah Spencer, Lady Lyttelton* (1912), p. 286.

4 Journal, July 20th and August 24th, 1839.

5 Journal, September 8th, 1839.

6 Mrs H. Wyndham, op. cit., p. 292.

7 Journal, September 14th, 1839.

8 Journal, September 23rd, 1839.

9 Journal, September 23rd, 1839.

10 Journal, January 23rd, 1840.

11 Roger Fulford, *The Prince Consort* (1949), p. 44.

12 Journal, October 11th, 1839; *Girlhood* II.263.

13 *Letters* I.i.237, Queen Victoria to King Leopold, October 12th, 1839.

14 Journal, October 14th, 1839; *Girlhood* II.267.

15 Journal, October 15th, 1839; *Girlhood* II.268.

16 Journal, October 19th, 1839.

17 Journal, November 3rd, 1839.

18 Journal, November 12th, 1839.

19 *Greville*, November 26th, 1839.

20 Journal, January 27th, 1840.

21 Journal, February 2nd, 1840.

22 Journal, February 1st, 1840.

23 Journal, November 6th, 1839.

24 Journal, November 10th, 1839.

25 *Letters* I.i.269, Queen Victoria to Prince Albert, January 31st, 1840.

26 Journal, February 8th, 1840.

27 *Letters* I.i.273–4, Queen Victoria to Prince Albert, February 10th, 1840.

28 RA Z491, February 10th, 1840.

29 RA Z491, February 10th, 1840; Journal, February 10th, 1863.

CHAPTER XI

The Blotting Paper 1840

1 Journal, February 17th, 1840.

2 Journal, February 23rd, 1840.

3 Mrs H. Wyndham, op. cit., p. 306.

4 *Greville*, February 21st, 1840.

5 Mrs H. Wyndham, op. cit., p. 288.

6 Journal, February 28th, 1840.

7 Roger Fulford, op. cit., p. 55.

8 *Memoirs of Ernest II, Duke of Saxe-Coburg-Gotha* (1888), I.97, Prince Ernest to Prince Albert, June 6th, 1840.

9 *Letters* I.i.282, George Anson's memorandum, May 28th, 1840.

10 *Letters* I.i.283, George Anson's memorandum, May 28th, 1840.

11 *Greville*, February 13th, 1840.

12 Journal, December 11th, 1839.

13 Journal, June 10th, 1840.

14 Journal, June 11th, 1840.

15 Journal, July 2nd, 1840.

16 Journal, August 12th, 1840.

17 Journal, November 21st, 1840.

18 Journal, February 24th, 1841.

19 *Letters* I.i.321, Queen Vic-

toria to King Leopold, January 5th, 1841.

20 RA Z294/14, Duchess of Kent's Diary, May 14th, 1841.

21 Journal, December 3rd, 1841.

CHAPTER XII

'I Am Going' 1841–2

1 Journal, May 9th, 1841.

2 *Letters* I.i.428, Baron Stockmar's memorandum, October 6th, 1841.

3 *Letters* I.i.383, George Anson's memorandum, August 30th, 1841.

4 Journal, August 28th, 1841.

5 *Letters* I.i.381, George Anson's memorandum, August 29th, 1841.

6 Journal, October 10th, 1841.

7 RA Vic. Add. MSS, U2, 'Baroness Lehzen', Prince Albert to [Baron Stockmar], dated January 18th, 1842. The Prince's dating of this whole episode is confusing but the Queen's is clear. The Prince wrote on January 16th of 'what happened yesterday' and on the 18th of 'a scene like the one yesterday'. Yet in the same letter (January 18th) he wrote, 'On the 16th in the nursery . . .' Thus according to this dating there could have been three scenes: on the 15th, 16th and 17th. Queen Victoria, however, refers throughout to 'what happened on Sunday', the 16th. The undated note from Prince Albert to the Queen (see Reference Note 8 below) of which a copy was sent to Stockmar enclosed in the Prince's letter of January 18th, may have been sent to her on January 17th and provoked a second scene on that date. But there is no reference to such a scene in her letter to Stockmar of the 17th (see below); rather, she appears to be simmering down. Moreover, in the Prince's letter of January 18th describing what happened in the nursery, he concluded with the word, 'Later—', after which a word is missing from the text. This may be the word 'wrote'—i.e. he wrote the undated note mentioned above. A possible explanation of his chronology is that he wrote his dated letters on the nights of 16th–17th and 17th–18th, during the small hours. The story as told on pp. 199–201 of this book seems the most satisfactory.

8 RA Vic. Add. MSS, U2, Note, undated and unsigned (enclosed in letter from Prince Albert to [Baron Stockmar] on January 18th, 1842), probably Prince Albert to Queen Victoria, January 16th, 1842.

9 RA Vic. Add. MSS, U2, Queen Victoria to [Baron Stockmar], January 16th, 1842.

10 RA Vic. Add. MSS, U2, Prince Albert to [Baron Stockmar], dated January 16th, 1842.

11 RA Vic. Add. MSS, U2, Queen Victoria to [Baron Stockmar], evening of January 17th, 1842.

12 RA Vic. Add. MSS, U2,

Prince Albert to [Baron Stockmar], dated January 18th, 1842.

13 RA Vic. Add. MSS, U2, Queen Victoria to [Baron Stockmar], January 19th, 1842.

14 RA Vic. Add. MSS, U2, Baron Stockmar to Queen Victoria, January 19th, 1842.

15 RA Vic. Add. MSS, U2, Queen Victoria to [Baron Stockmar], January 19th, 1842.

16 RA Vic. Add. MSS, U2, Queen Victoria to [Baron Stockmar], January 20th, 1842.

17 RA Z159, Baroness Lehzen to Queen Victoria, September 28th, 1842.

18 *Letters* I.i.463, George Anson's memorandum, December 26th, 1841.

19 *Letters* I.i.322, George Anson's memorandum, I.1.322, January 15th, 1841.

CHAPTER XIII

A Safe Haven 1842–6

1 Journal, May 12th, 1839.

2 Vera Watson, *A Queen at Home* (1952), pp. 82 and 97–8.

3 Journal, April 6th, 1842.

4 Mrs H. Wyndham, op. cit., p. 322.

5 Journal, August 22nd, 1842.

6 Journal, March 7th, 1843.

7 RA Z491, Queen Victoria's 'Reminiscences', January 1862.

8 Journal, December 20th, 1843.

9 Journal, January 25th, 1842.

10 Baroness Bunsen (editor), *Memoirs of Baron Bunsen,* II.16.

11 Journal, June 17th and July 1st, 1842.

12 Journal, July 4th, 1842.

13 Journal, December 17th, 1842.

14 Journal, June 2nd, 1843.

15 Journal, March 3rd, 1844.

16 Journal, February 4th, 1844.

17 Journal, February 4th, 1844; Sir Theodore Martin, *Life of the Prince Consort* (1876–80), I.208.

18 E. E. P. Tisdall, *Restless Consort* (1952), p. 69.

19 Journal, April 11th, 1844.

20 Journal, August 3rd, 1843.

21 Journal, November 3rd, 1844.

22 Journal, August 30th, 1843.

23 Journal, September 9th, 1843.

24 Journal, January 19th, 1842.

25 Journal, December 3rd, 1842.

26 *Greville,* December 13th, 1844 and January 14th, 1845.

27 Journal, June 9th, 1844.

28 Journal, March 31st, 1845.

29 Journal, March 22nd, 1845.

30 Journal, August 20th, 1845.

31 Journal, February 20th, 1843.

32 Journal, April 21st, 1845.

33 Journal, June 9th, 1842.

34 Journal, February 18th, 1845.

35 Journal, August 2nd, 1845.

36 Journal, April 15th, 1845.

37 Journal, January 30th, 1845.

38 Journal, February 5th, 1845.

39 *Greville,* January 13th, 1846 and January 14th, 1848.

40 Journal, January 24th and March 14th, 1846.

41 Journal, June 8th, 1846.

42 *Letters* I.II.32, Queen Victoria to King Leopold, October 20th, 1844.

CHAPTER XIV

'Great Events Make Me Calm'
1846–8

1 Journal, July 22nd, 1846.
2 *Letters* I.II.III, Queen Victoria to Lord John Russell, August 3rd, 1846.
3 Journal, July 2nd, 1846.
4 Journal, September 7th, 1846.
5 Journal, September 23rd, 1846.
6 Journal, December 9th, 1849.
7 Journal, September 28th, 1846.
8 Journal, December 31st, 1846.
9 Journal, November 5th, 1847.
10 Journal, August 8th, 1849.
11 Cecil Woodham-Smith, *The Great Hunger* (1962), p. 406.
12 Journal, June 27th, 1850.
13 Journal, March 5th, 1848.
14 *Letters* I.II.197, Queen Victoria to King Leopold, April 4th, 1848.
15 Journal, April 8th, 1848.
16 *Letters* I.II.218, Queen Victoria to King Leopold, July 11th, 1848.

CHAPTER XV

The Devil's Son 1848–50

1 RA Y206, Sir James Clark's Diary, September 15th, 1848.
2 Journal, November 2nd, 1848.
3 Journal, January 22nd, 1849.

4 Frank Eyck, *The Prince Consort* (1959), p. 120.
5 Journal, January 24th, 1849.
6 Journal, January 24th, 1849.
7 Journal, February 7th and 19th, 1850.
8 Journal, May 16th, 1850.
9 Journal, May 20th, 1850.
10 Journal, March 2nd, 1850.
11 John Connell, *Regina v. Palmerston* (1962), p. 121.
12 Journal, August 15th, 1850.
13 Journal, September 9th, 1850.
14 Journal, October 18th, 1850.
15 Journal, October 29th, 1850.
16 Journal, December 17th, 1850.
17 Journal, February 23rd, 1851.
18 Journal, March 4th, 1851.
19 Journal, February 5th, 1852.
20 *Letters* I.II.423, Prince Albert's memorandum, December 27th, 1851.
21 Journal, December 24th, 1851.
22 Frank Eyck, op. cit., p. 53.

CHAPTER XVI

'Our Happy Home Life'
1846–51

1 Journal, October 10th, 1851.
2 Journal, August 1st, 1847.
3 Journal, August 22nd, 1850.
4 Journal, July 6th, 1849.
5 Journal, September 8th, 1848. This passage, as corrected by Sir Arthur Helps, appears in Queen Victoria's *Leaves from the Journal of Our Life in the Highlands*, (1868), p. 101.

6 Journal, September 22nd, 1848.

7 Journal, August 10th, 1848.

8 Journal, October 1st, 1848.

9 Baillie and Bolitho (editors), *Letters of Lady Augusta Stanley* (1927), p. 35.

10 Journal, October 3rd, 1850.

11 Journal, September 19th, 1850.

12 Journal, February 10th, 1852.

13 Journal, January 30th, 1848.

14 Sir Theodore Martin, op. cit., II.175.

15 *Greville*, January 22nd, 1848.

16 Journal, July 2nd, 1850.

17 Journal, November 12th, 1851.

18 Journal, January 24th, 1847.

19 Journal, November 21st, 1849.

20 Journal, February 22nd, 1850.

21 Asa Briggs, *Victorian People* (1954), p. 44.

22 Journal, June 30th, 1850.

23 Journal, April 14th, 1851.

24 RA F24, Lord John Russell to Prince Albert, April 19th, 1851.

25 Journal, June 1st, 1851.

26 *Letters* I.II.384, Queen Victoria to King Leopold, May 3rd, 1851.

27 *Letters*, I.II.438, Queen Victoria to King Leopold, February 3rd, 1852.

CHAPTER XVII

'Every Age Has Its Advantages'
1852–4

1 Journal, January 3rd, 1852.

2 Journal, February 26th, 1852.

3 Journal, February 23rd, 1852; Frank Eyck, op. cit., p. 191.

4 Journal, March 16th, 1852.

5 Journal, April 1st, 1852.

6 Journal, April 22nd, 1852.

7 *Letters* I.II.478, Queen Victoria to King Leopold, September 17th, 1853.

8 Journal, November 27th, 1852.

9 Journal, February 10th, 1852.

10 Journal, August 25th, 1852.

11 Journal, March 19th, 1853.

12 RA Z140, Prince Albert to Queen Victoria, May 9th, 1853.

13 Harvey Graham, *Eternal Eve* (1960), p. 319.

14 RA Z140, Prince Albert to Queen Victoria, May 9th, 1853.

15 Journal, November 2nd, 1853.

16 Journal, November 13th, 1853.

17 Sir Theodore Martin, op. cit., II.544 et seq., January 18th, 1854.

18 Journal, January 22nd, 1854.

19 Journal, February 10th, 1854.

CHAPTER XVIII

The Unsatisfactory War
1854–6

1 *Letters* I.III.25, Queen Victoria to Lord Aberdeen, April 1st, 1854.

2 Journal, October 9th, 1854.

3 Journal, October 11th, 1854.

4 Journal, November 13th 1854.

5 RA Z140, Prince Albert to Queen Victoria, January 3rd, 1855.

6 Journal, January 21st, 1855.

7 *Disraeli*, III.567.

8 Journal, February 5th, 1855.

9 Journal, February 7th, 1855.

10 Journal, August 21st, 1856.

11 Journal, November 18th, 1854.

12 Journal, December 8th, 1854.

13 Journal, June 13th, 1855.

14 Journal, October 4th, 1856.

15 Baillie and Bolitho, op. cit., p. 105.

16 Journal, March 3rd, 1855.

17 Journal, March 14th, 1855.

18 Journal, April 18th, 1855.

19 Lord Malmesbury, *Memoirs of an ex-Minister* (1885), p. 363; Christopher Hibbert, *The Destruction of Lord Raglan* (1961), p. 256.

20 Journal, April 20th, 1855.

21 Queen Victoria, *Leaves from a Journal*, edited by Raymond Mortimer (1961), p. 152.

22 *Greville*, September 5th, 1855.

23 Magdalen Ponsonby (editor), *Mary Ponsonby, a Memoir, some Letters, and a Journal* (1927), p. 26.

24 Journal, December 4th, 1855.

CHAPTER XIX

Dinner à Trois 1855–9

1 Joanna Richardson, *My Dearest Uncle* (1961), p. 196; Journal, June 30th, 1851.

2 Baillie and Bolitho, op. cit., p. 84–5.

3 RA Z140, Prince Albert to Queen Victoria, February 9th and November 16th, 1855.

4 Journal, September 14th, 1855.

5 *Further Letters*, p. 58, Queen Victoria to Princess Augusta of Prussia, October 22nd, 1855.

6 RA Y206, Sir James Clark's Diary, February 5th and 15th, 1856.

7 Journal, January 7th, 1856.

8 *Letters* I.III.321, Queen Victoria to Lord Clarendon, October 25th, 1857.

9 Journal, November 21st, 1857.

10 Journal, June 18th, 1856.

11 RA Z140, Prince Albert to Queen Victoria, October 1st and November 5th, 1856.

12 Journal, October 19th, 1857.

13 RA Y206, Sir James Clark's Diary, February 5th, 1856.

14 Journal, April 29th, 1857.

15 Journal, May 26th, 1857.

16 *Dearest Child*, p. 182, April 20th, 1859.

17 *Dearest Child*, p. 118, June 22nd, 1858.

18 *Dearest Child*, p. 50, February 19th, 1858.

19 *Dearest Child*, pp. 99 and 182, May 3rd, 1858 and April 20th, 1859.

20 Kronberg Letters; *Dearest Child*, p. 94, April 21st, 1858.

21 *Dearest Child*, p. 191, May 4th, 1859; Kronberg Letters, June 9th, 1858.

22 *Dearest Child*, p. 115, June 15th, 1858.

23 Kronberg Letters, October 4th, 1858.

24 Kronberg Letters, September 7th, 1858.
25 *Dearest Child*, p. 135, October 4th, 1858.
26 *Greville*, December 12th, 1858.
27 *Dearest Child*, p. 120, June 30th, 1858.

to Queen Victoria, June 6th, 1860.
20 *English Empress*, p. 56, June 15th, 1860.
21 Journal, November 10th, 1857.
22 *Dearest Child*, p. 211, September 26th, 1859.

CHAPTER XX

Last Years of Marriage 1855–60

1 Journal, July 5th, 1857.
2 RA Z444, Letter 9, F. W. Gibbs, December 1857.
3 Kronberg Letters, December 22nd, 1858.
4 RA Z444, Prince Consort to Prince of Wales, July 1858.
5 Journal, April 1st, 1857.
6 Journal, February 26th, 1858.
7 RA Z444, Letter 87, Rev. Tarver to Prince Consort, October, 1858.
8 Journal, August 7th, 1857.
9 *Ernest II*, op. cit., III.250.
10 Harold Kurtz, *The Empress Eugénie* (1964), p. 105.
11 Journal, November 21st, 1858.
12 Journal, March 22nd, 1858.
13 Journal, September 18th, 1858.
14 Journal, June 12th and 13th, 1859.
15 Journal, December 31st, 1860.
16 RA Z261, Queen Victoria, 'Remarks – Conversations – Reflections', February 10th, 1859.
17 *Dearest Child*, p. 205, August 10th, 1859.
18 RA Z140, Prince Consort to Queen Victoria, undated.
19 RA Z140, Prince Consort

CHAPTER XXI

'He Was My Life' 1861

1 *Dearest Child*, p. 354, October 1st, 1861.
2 RA Z4/21, Princess Royal to Prince Consort, June 7th, 1861; Hector Bolitho, *The Prince Consort and His Brother* (1933), p. 212; A. L. Kennedy (editor), *My Dear Duchess* (1956), p. 148, Lord Clarendon to Duchess of Manchester, April 14th, 1861.
3 RA Z140, Prince Consort to Queen Victoria, October 22nd, 1861.
4 *Dearest Child*, p. 370, November 30th, 1861.
5 Journal, December 2nd, 1861.
6 RA Z142, December 6th, 1861, 'Death of the Prince Consort', an account written by Queen Victoria in 1872 based on extracts from her Journal, November 9th to December 14th, 1861.
7 RA Z142, December 8th, 1861; Sir Theodore Martin, op. cit., p. 427, *et seq.*
8 Journal, July 9th, 1863; RA Z142, December 9th, 1861.
9 RA Z142, December 11th, 1861.
10 RA Z142, December 13th, 1861.

11 RA Z142, December 14th, 1861.

12 RA Z142, December 14th, 1861.

13 Baillie and Bolitho, op. cit., p. 245.

14 RA Z142, December 14th, 1861.

15 Stratfield Saye MSS, Dean Wellesley to Lord Cowley, December 16th, 1861.

PART TWO

CHAPTER XXII

Still December 1861–4

1 Journal, October 14th, 1852.

2 *Dearest Child,* p. 248, April 18th, 1860.

3 Kronberg Letters, May 6th, 1863.

4 Journal, January 25th, 1861.

5 Journal, June 24th, 1863.

6 Journal, July 16th, 1864.

7 Kronberg Letters, December 18th, 1861.

8 Kronberg Letters, December 27th, 1861.

9 Stratfield Saye MSS, Lady Augusta Bruce to Duchess of Wellington, December 30th, 1861.

10 RA Vic. Add. MSS A22/71 and 73, Duchess of Atholl to Mrs Thomas Biddulph, December 19th, 1861.

11 RA Vic. Add. MSS Z261, Queen Victoria, 'Remarks – Conversations – Reflections', January 1862.

12 RA Z491, Queen Victoria, 'Reminiscences', January 1862.

13 *Letters* II.1.20, Queen Victoria to Lord Derby, February 17th, 1862.

14 George Villiers, *A Vanished Victorian, The Life of Lord Clarendon by his Grandson* (1938), p. 310.

15 Journal, January 2nd, 1840.

16 Journal, July 3rd, 1836.

17 RA Vic. Add. MSS, U16, Lord Hertford's memorandum, February 1862.

18 Hughenden Papers, Disraeli's memorandum, 1862.

19 Journal, March 31st, 1863.

20 Sir Herbert Maxwell, *Life and Letters of Lord Clarendon* (1913), II.261–2; George Villiers, op. cit., p. 315–18.

21 RA Vic. Add. MSS, T4/23–6.

22 *English Empress,* p. 81, December 27th, 1861.

23 Kronberg Letters, January 15th and 18th, 1862.

24 Kronberg Letters, June 27th, 1862.

25 Kronberg Letters, December 27th, 1861.

26 Kronberg Letters, January 22nd and April 16th, 1862.

27 Kronberg Letters, June 26th, 1862.

28 Journal, September 18th, 1862, enclosure, Prince of Wales to Queen Victoria.

29 Kronberg Letters, November 12th, 1862.

30 Baillie and Bolitho, op. cit., p. 283; Journal, February 28th, 1863.

31 Kronberg Letters, November 14th, 1862.

32 Kronberg Letters, June 1st, 1863.

33 Journal, August 31st, 1863.

34 *Letters* II.i.189, Princess Royal to Queen Victoria, May 11th, 1864.

35 *Letters* II.i.187, Queen Victoria to King Leopold, May 12th, 1864; ibid. II.i.198, Queen Victoria to Earl Russell, May 27th, 1864.

36 Kronberg Letters, April 29th, 1863.

37 *English Empress*, p. 121, February 3rd, 1864.

38 Kronberg Letters, July 6th, 1864.

39 *Letters* II.i.207, Queen Victoria to Princess Royal, May 31st, 1864.

40 Journal, December 14th, 1864; June 16th, 1865.

41 *Greville*, Lord Clarendon to Queen Victoria, December 31st, 1851.

42 *Letters* II.i.218–19, King Leopold to Queen Victoria, June 15th, 1864.

43 Journal, June 21st, 1864; *Letters* II.i.233, Queen Victoria to King Leopold, June 30th, 1864.

44 Kronberg Letters, April 18th, 1864.

45 G. K. A. Bell, *Randall Davidson* (1935), I.82.

46 Journal, March 5th, 1863.

CHAPTER XXIII

Brown Eminence The 1860s

1 *Letters* II.i.279, Queen Victoria to King Leopold, October 20th, 1865.

2 Kronberg Letters, October 27th, 1865.

3 *Alice, Grand-Duchess of Hesse* (1885), p. 122.

4 Kronberg Letters, December 23rd, 1865.

5 Ponsonby Letters, Henry Ponsonby to his brother Arthur, March 19th, 1865.

6 *Letters* I.iii.587, Queen Victoria to King Leopold, October 21st, 1861.

7 E. E. P. Tisdall, *Queen Victoria's Private Life* (1961), p. 57.

8 Journal, October 26th, 1864.

9 RA Vic. Add. MSS, C3/2.

10 RA Vic. Add. MSS, C3/16.

11 RA Vic. Add. MSS, C3/7.

12 *Letters* II.i.255, Queen Victoria to King Leopold, November 24th, 1865.

13 Kronberg Letters, April 5th and 12th, 1865.

14 Kronberg Letters, July 12th, 1866; *Empress Frederick*, p. 60.

15 Ponsonby Letters, October 30th, 1866.

16 RA Vic. Add. MSS, A22/112, Queen Victoria to Lady Biddulph, December 26th 1866.

17 RA Vic. Add. MSS, J1363, Mrs M. A. Murray to Queen Victoria, 1867.

18 *Letters* II.i.434, Queen Victoria to Lord Charles Fitzroy, June 26th, 1867; ibid. II.i.449–50, Queen Victoria to Lord Charles Fitzroy, July 20th, 1867.

19 *Letters* II.i.540, Queen Victoria to Lord Charles Fitzroy, October 6th, 1868.

20 Ponsonby Letters, April 19th, 1870; Frederick Ponsonby, *Sidelights on Queen Victoria* (1930), Chap. 2.

21 Ponsonby Letters, October 27th and 29th, November 11th, 1870.

22 RA F23/1, October 25th, 1897.

23 *Further Letters*, p. 136.

24 Kronberg Letters, April 18th, 1863.
25 RA B24/40.
26 Journal, October 4th, 1888.
27 A. L. Kennedy, op. cit., pp. 188 and 191, Lord Clarendon to Duchess of Manchester, March 20th and 22nd, 1862.
28 *Dearest Child*, p. 356, October 7th, 1861.
29 G. K. A. Bell, op. cit., I. 82.
30 Kronberg Letters, October 2nd, 1888.
31 Journal, June 26th, 1864.
32 Journal, August 25th, 1872.
33 Journal, June 17th, 1862.
34 Arthur Ponsonby, *Life of Sir Henry Ponsonby* (1842), p. 119.
35 G. K. A. Bell, op. cit., I. 83.
36 Kronberg Letters, March 18th, 1865.
37 Lord Malmesbury, op. cit., June 5th, 1861.
38 Countess of Airlie, *Thatched with Gold* (1962), p. 96.

CHAPTER XXIV

Granite and Rock 1865–8

1 Journal, October 29th, 1865.
2 *Letters* II.i.296, Queen Victoria to Earl Russell, January 22nd, 1866.
3 Journal, January 15th, 1864.
4 *Further Letters*, p. 155.
5 Journal, May 20th, 1866.
6 *Letters* II.i.317, Queen Victoria to King of Prussia, April 10th, 1866.
7 Journal, June 26th, 1866.
8 Journal, June 28th, 1866.
9 Journal, October 9th, 1866.
10 Kronberg Letters, February 5th, 1867.
11 *Letters* II.i.451, Queen Victoria's Journal, July 24th, 1867.
12 Philip Magnus, *King Edward the Seventh* (1964), p. 73.
13 Kronberg Letters, December 18th, 1867.
14 Kronberg Letters, February 26th, 1868.
15 *Letters* II.ii.20–1, Queen Victoria's Journal, June 11th, 1870.
16 Kronberg Letters, May 30th, 1868.
17 Kronberg Letters, January 12th, 1870.
18 *Disraeli*, IV.591.
19 Journal, February 29th, 1868.
20 Journal, May 17th and 30th, 1868.
21 Journal, May 31st, 1868.
22 Journal, August 25th, 1868.
23 Ponsonby Letters, August 4th, 1868.
24 Baillie and Bolitho, *Later Letters of Lady Augusta Stanley* (1929), p. 77.
25 Journal, September 28th, 1868.
26 Journal, September 27th, 1868.
27 Philip Magnus, *Gladstone* (1954), p. 160.
28 Journal, November 15th, 1863.
29 Journal, November 24th, 1866.
30 Philip Magnus, *Gladstone*, p. 193.
31 *Letters* II.i.466, Queen Victoria's Journal, October 14th, 1867.
32 Journal, May 10th, 1866.
33 Journal, November 18th, 1867.
34 Kronberg Letters, November 6th, 1867.

35 Journal, November 23rd, 1867.

36 Journal, December 31st, 1867.

37 Journal, December 23rd, 1867.

38 Kronberg Letters, November 16th, 1867.

39 R. G. Wilberforce, *Life of Samuel Wilberforce* (1882), III.242.

40 Journal, July 25th, 1869.

41 Kronberg Letters, February 6th, 1869.

42 Journal, April 8th, 1869.

43 Journal, July 24th, 1869.

44 Kronberg Letters, September 25th, 1869.

45 Philip Guedalla, *The Queen & Mr Gladstone* (1933), I.47.

46 Journal, December 13th, 1868.

CHAPTER XXV

Head of all the Family 1865–9

1 Philip Magnus, *Edward the Seventh*, pp. 83–4; Kronberg Letters, April 28th, 1864.

2 Journal, April 12th, 1864.

3 Letters II.i.266, Queen Victoria to Mrs Lincoln, April 29th, 1865.

4 Kronberg Letters and Journal, July 13th, 1867.

5 Kronberg Letters, October 11th, 1864.

6 Kronberg Letters, November 19th, 1864.

7 Kronberg Letters, August 13th and November 14th, 1866.

8 RA Y206, Sir James Clark's Diary, December 1865.

9 Kronberg Letters, September 6th, 1868.

10 Journal, July 7th, 1867.

11 Ponsonby Letters, Henry Ponsonby to his brother Arthur, March 24th, 1866.

12 *Letters* II.i.190, Queen Victoria to Lord Clarendon, May 17th, 1864.

13 *Letters* II.i.369, Queen Victoria to Prince of Wales, October 16th, 1866.

14 *Letters* II.i.513, Queen Victoria to General Grey, March 7th, 1868.

15 Kronberg Letters, April 29th, 1868.

16 Kronberg Letters, August 12th, 1866.

17 Journal, May 24th, 1869.

18 Mary Howard McClintock, *The Queen Thanks Sir Howard* (1945), pp. 95 and 143.

19 Kronberg Letters, March 18th, 1868.

20 *Letters* II.i.633, Queen Victoria to Prince of Wales, November 29th, 1869.

21 Kronberg Letters, November 1st, 1870.

22 Ponsonby Letters, October 8th, 1870.

23 Ponsonby Letters, October 8th, 1870.

24 Ponsonby Letters, October 15th, 1870.

25 Kronberg Letters, September 23rd, 1864.

26 Kronberg Letters, September 11th, 1865.

27 Kronberg Letters, December 23rd, 1865.

28 Kronberg Letters, February 15th, 1867.

29 Kronberg Letters, January 15th, 1867.

30 Kronberg Letters, January 22nd, 1867.

31 *Alice, Grand-Duchess of Hesse,* p. 104.

743

32 Kronberg Letters, April 4th, 1863.

33 Kronberg Letters, November 14th, 1866.

34 James Pope-Hennessy, *Queen Mary* (1959), p. 38, Queen Victoria to the Princess Royal, April 21st, 1866.

35 Kronberg Letters, November 28th, 1866.

36 Kronberg Letters, August 8th and September 19th, 1868.

37 Philip Guedalla, op. cit., I.428, Queen Victoria to Gladstone, October 3rd, 1873.

38 Kronberg Letters, December 11th, 1867.

39 Mary Howard McClintock, op. cit., p. 85.

40 Baillie and Bolitho, *Later Letters of Lady Augusta Stanley*, p. 72.

CHAPTER XXVI

The Royalty Question 1870–4

1 Ponsonby Letters, February 23rd, 1870.

2 Kronberg Letters, March 2nd, 1870.

3 Kronberg Letters, March 9th, 1870.

4 Kronberg Letters, March 17th, 1870.

5 Journal, December 31st, 1870.

6 Kronberg Letters, August 1st, 1870 and March 1st, 1871; *English Empress*, pp. 171 and 183.

7 *Letters* II.II.64 and Journal, September 12th, 1870; Kronberg Letters, September 17th and October 8th, 1870.

8 Kronberg Letters, March 1st, 1871.

9 Kronberg Letters, March 4th, 1871.

10 Philip Guedalla, op. cit., I.52 and 180.

11 Ponsonby Letters, October 28th, 1870.

12 Kronberg Letters, November 10th, 1871.

13 Philip Guedalla, op. cit., I.66.

14 Journal, February 12th, 1871.

15 *Letters* II.II.131, Queen Victoria to Gladstone, April 23rd, 1871.

16 Journal, August 1st, 1871.

17 Journal, August 4th and 8th, 1871; Philip Guedalla, op. cit., I.297–8.

18 RA Vic. Add. MSS, AI/16; *English Empress*, p. 187.

19 Philip Guedalla, op. cit., I. 299–300, Queen Victoria to Lord Hatherley, August 10th, 1871.

20 Philip Guedalla, op. cit., ibid., Gladstone to Sir Henry Ponsonby, August 16th, 1871.

21 Ponsonby Letters, August 26th, 1871.

22 Philip Guedalla, op. cit., I.304, Gladstone to Sir Henry Ponsonby, September 6th, 1871; RA Vic. Add. MSS, AI/16.

23 *Letters* II.II.157 and 160–1; Journal, September 18th, 1871.

24 Ponsonby Letters, September 13th, 1871.

25 Ponsonby Letters, September 17th, 1871.

26 Ponsonby Letters, October 5th, 1871.

27 Ponsonby Letters, September 18th, 1871.

28 Philip Guedalla, op. cit., I.70 and 90, Gladstone to Gran-

ville, October 1st, 1871.

29 Ponsonby Letters, September 30th, 1871.

30 Ponsonby Letters, November 19th, 1871.

31 Ponsonby Letters, December 12th, 1871.

32 Journal, December 6th, 1871.

33 Baillie and Bolitho, *Later Letters of Lady Augusta Stanley*, p. 148.

34 Journal, December 14th, 1871.

35 Journal, December 15th, 1871.

36 Arthur Ponsonby, op. cit., p. 98.

37 Philip Guedalla, op. cit., I.326 and 330.

38 *Letters* II.ii.195; Journal, February 27th, 1872.

39 Journal, February 28th, 1872.

40 *Letters* II.ii.198; Journal, February 29th, 1872.

41 Journal, November 10th, 1872.

42 Ponsonby Letters, August 21st, 1871.

43 Ponsonby Letters, October 4th, 1871.

44 Ponsonby Letters, December 30th, 1872.

45 Kronberg Letters, March 13th, 1873.

46 Journal, March 13th, 1873.

47 Ponsonby Letters, April 23rd, 1873; Arthur Ponsonby, op. cit., p. 154.

48 Kronberg Letters, July 12th, 1873.

49 Egon Corti, *The Downfall of Three Dynasties*, p. 214.

50 Kronberg Letters, July 26th, 1873.

51 RA S27/129–30, Queen Victoria to Princess Alice, July 26th, 1874.

52 Kronberg Letters, April 8th, 1872.

53 Philip Guedalla, op. cit., I.227–8 and 229, Queen Victoria to Gladstone, May 6th, 1870, Gladstone to Queen Victoria, May 11th, 1870.

54 Journal, February 7th, 1874.

55 *Letters* II.ii.319, Lord Granville to Queen Victoria, February 17th, 1874.

CHAPTER XXVII

The Faery Queen 1874–8

1 Kronberg Letters, July 28th, 1875.

2 Ponsonby Letters, October 18th, 1874.

3 Kronberg Letters, October 25th, 1874.

4 Kronberg Letters, September 5th, 1875.

5 Ponsonby Letters, October 24th, 1874.

6 Kronberg Letters, November 18th, 1874.

7 *Letters* II.iii.451, Queen Victoria to Gladstone, October 30th, 1883.

8 *Disraeli*, V.339.

9 *Disraeli*, VI.463.

10 *Disraeli*, V.238–40.

11 *Disraeli*, V.251.

12 Ponsonby Letters, April 16th, 1875.

13 Robert Rhodes James, *Rosebery* (1963), p. 64.

14 *Disraeli*, VI.462.

15 Robert Rhodes James, op. cit., p. 112.

16 Ponsonby Letters, November 13th, 1873.

17 Journal, September 7th, 1874.

18 Ponsonby Letters, September 6th and 8th, 1874.

19 Ponsonby Letters, January 27th, 1873.

20 Ponsonby Letters, June 10th, 1875.

21 Journal, May 12th, 1876.

22 Ponsonby Letters, April 11th, 1876; Journal, May 7th, 1876.

23 Ponsonby Letters, February 1876.

24 Ponsonby Letters, August 14th, 1876.

25 Kronberg Letters, April 14th, 1877.

26 *Disraeli*, VI.217.

27 *Disraeli*, V.448.

28 *Letters* II.II.428, Queen Victoria to Theodore Martin, November 26th, 1875.

29 Journal, July 6th, 1876.

30 Ponsonby Letters, August 31st, 1876.

31 *Letters* II.II.480, Queen Victoria to Lord Beaconsfield, September 28th, 1876.

32 Ponsonby Letters, October 3rd, 1878.

33 Lord Redesdale, *Memories* (1915) II.650.

34 Journal, March 23rd, 1877.

35 Kronberg Letters, June 19th, 1877.

36 *Letters* II.II.550, Queen Victoria to Princess Royal, July 17th, 1877.

37 Kronberg Letters, July 17th, 1877: Letters II.III.229, Queen Victoria to Gladstone, August 7th, 1881.

38 Hughenden Papers, B/XIX/C/301 'The Wellesley Mission'; Ponsonby Letters, August 11th, 1877.

39 Kronberg Letters, February 15th, 1878.

40 *Disraeli*, VI.150.

41 *Disraeli*, VI.132–3.

42 *Disraeli*, VI.217.

43 Kronberg Letters, January 4th, 1878.

44 Journal, January 3rd, 1878.

45 Hughenden Papers, B/XIX/C/397, Prince Leopold to Queen Victoria, January 7th, 1878.

46 Journal, January 14th, 1878.

47 *Disraeli*, VI.233.

48 R. W. Seton Watson, *Disraeli, Gladstone and the Eastern Question* (1935), p. 203.

49 Journal, April 13th, 1878.

50 Kronberg Letters, July 10th, 1878.

51 Journal, June 13th, 1878.

52 Ponsonby Letters, July 16th, 1878.

53 Kronberg Letters, April 13th, 1878.

54 Kronberg Letters, August 8th, 1878.

CHAPTER XXVIII

'I Had No Alternative' 1878–80

1 Journal, September 27th, 1877.

2 Journal, April 11th, 1869.

3 Kronberg Letters, December 27th, 1873.

4 Journal, July 7th, 1876.

5 Ponsonby Letters, June 3rd, 1878.

6 Kronberg Letters, June 17th, 1878.

7 Ponsonby Letters, September 23rd, 1877.

8 Journal, June 26th, 1877.

9 Ponsonby Letters, November 14th, 1878.

10 Kronberg Letters, April 26th, 1876.

11 Kronberg Letters, May 20th, 1873.

12 Kronberg Letters, June 14th, 1875.

13 Kronberg Letters, May 26th, 1878.
14 Journal, March 2nd, 1878.
15 Kronberg Letters, August 30th, 1878.
16 Kronberg Letters, July 25th, 1877.
17 Kronberg Letters, March 6th, 1878.
18 Kronberg Letters, July 6th, 1878.
19 Kronberg Letters, January 9th, 1878.
20 Kronberg Letters, September 4th and 25th, 1877.
21 *Letters* II.ii.655, Queen Victoria's Journal.
22 Journal, December 14th, 1878.
23 Journal, May 15th, 1873.
24 Kronberg Letters, January 9th, 1879.
25 *Letters* II.iii.37–8, Queen Victoria to Lord Beaconsfield, July 28th, 1879.
26 Journal, July 26th, 1879.
27 Philip Magnus, *Gladstone*, p. 270.
28 Ponsonby Letters, October 23rd, 1879.
29 Arthur Ponsonby, op. cit., p. 184.
30 Arthur Ponsonby, op. cit., p. 185.
31 Arthur Ponsonby, op. cit., p. 186; Journal, April 6th, 1880.
32 *Letters* II.iii.75, Queen Victoria to Sir Henry Ponsonby, April 8th, 1880.
33 Ponsonby Letters, April 9th, 1880.
34 Arthur Ponsonby, op. cit., pp. 186–7.
35 Journal, April 18th, 1880.
36 *Letters* II.iii.80, Queen Victoria's Journal, April 22nd, 1880.
37 *Letters* II.iii.81, Queen Victoria's Journal, April 22nd, 1880.
38 *Letters* II.iii.82–3, Queen Victoria's memoranda, April 23rd, 1880.
39 *Letters* II.iii.84, Queen Victoria's memoranda, April 23rd, 1880.
40 Arthur Ponsonby, op. cit., p. 188.

CHAPTER XXIX

Among the Trumpets 1880–3

1 Journal, April 18th and 20th, 1880.
2 Journal, April 26th, 1880.
3 Kronberg Letters, May 2nd, 1880.
4 *Letters* II.iii.108, Queen Victoria to Lord Granville, June 5th, 1880.
5 *Letters* II.iii.143, Queen Victoria to Lord Beaconsfield, September 20, 1880.
6 Kronberg Letters, September 21st, 1880.
7 Arthur Ponsonby, op. cit., p. 185.
8 Hughenden Papers, B/XIX/B/1686, Queen Victoria to Lord Beaconsfield, April 26th, 1880.
9 Ponsonby Letters, June 11th, 1880.
10 *Letters* II.iii.179, Queen Victoria's Journal, January 3rd, 1881.
11 *Letters* II.iii.181, Lord Beaconsfield to Queen Victoria, January 11th, 1881.
12 Agatha Ramm, *Political Correspondence of Mr Gladstone and Lord Granville* (1962), I.67, Gladstone to Granville, January 5th, 1878.

13 Agatha Ramm, op. cit., I.178, Gladstone to Granville, September 19th, 1880.

14 Ponsonby, Letters, April 20th, 1884; Arthur Ponsonby, op. cit., p. 300.

15 Ponsonby Letters, June 18th, 1881.

16 Kronberg Letters, May 23rd, 1883.

17 Journal, July 30th, 1881.

18 Arthur Ponsonby, op. cit., p. 256.

19 Journal, June 15th, 1881.

20 Journal, July 14th, 1868.

21 Journal, December 4th, 1880.

22 Kronberg Letters, July 14th, 1880.

23 Journal, January 3rd, 1881.

24 *Letters* II.III.163, Queen Victoria to Lord Hartington, December 12th, 1880.

25 *Letters* II.III.166, Queen Victoria to W. E. Forster, December 25th, 1880.

26 Journal, April 8th, 1881.

27 Ponsonby Letters, June 18th, 1881.

28 *Letters* II.III.283, Queen Victoria's Journal, May 6th, 1882.

29 Journal, May 7th, 1882.

30 Journal, May 24th, 1882.

31 Kronberg Letters, March 6th, 1882.

32 Kronberg Letters, February 16th, 1881.

33 Kronberg Letters, May 23rd, 1881.

34 Kronberg Letters, November 29th, 1881.

35 Journal, March 19th, 1883.

36 Ponsonby Letters, July 7th, 1881.

37 *Letters* II.III.370, Queen Victoria to Lord Granville, December 12th, 1882.

38 Journal, November 29th, 1882.

39 Journal, December 12th, 1882.

CHAPTER XXX
The Bitter Cry 1883–4

1 Journal, January 19th and February 21st and 24th, 1883.

2 Ponsonby Letters, March 9th, 1883.

3 RA Z209–11.

4 Journal, August 27th, 1883.

5 G. St Aubyn, *Royal George,* p. 265.

6 Kronberg Letters, February 27th, 1884.

7 RA Vic. Add. MSS, A12/899.

8 RA Vic. Add. MSS, A12/900.

9 RA Vic. Add. MSS, A12/901.

10 Arthur Ponsonby, op. cit., p. 146.

11 RA Vic. Add. MSS, A12/903.

12 RA Vic. Add. MSS, A12/904.

13 RA Vic. Add. MSS, A12/905.

14 RA Vic. Add. MSS, A12/908.

15 G. K. A. Bell, op. cit., pp. 91 and 94.

16 RA Vic. Add. MSS, A12/909.

17 RA C3/57–8.

18 RA AA10 and 13.

19 Ponsonby Letters, November 11th, 1883.

20 Lady (Lintorn) Simmons's Diary.

21 Ponsonby Letters, September 6th, 1875.

22 Ponsonby Letters, May 19th, 1877.

23 Ponsonby Letters, November 11th, 1877.

24 Kronberg Letters, March 29th, 1884.

25 Kronberg Letters, May 30th, 1884.

26 *Letters* II.III.440, Queen Victoria to Lord Granville, September 18th, 1883.

27 *Letters* II.III.441, Queen Victoria to Gladstone, September 20th, 1883.

28 Kronberg Letters, October 2nd, 1883.

29 *Letters* II.III.442, Gladstone to Queen Victoria, September 22nd, 1883.

30 British Museum MSS, Hamilton Diary 48634–5.

31 Ponsonby Letters, January 2nd, 1884.

CHAPTER XXXI

Gordon and the Tup-Tupping 1884–5

1 Journal, March 5th, 1885.

2 Journal, February 14th, 1884.

3 *Letters* II.III.484, Queen Victoria to Sir Henry Ponsonby [March 14th, 1884].

4 *Letters* II.III.523, Queen Victoria to Gladstone, July 25th, 1884.

5 Journal, July 10th–12th, 1884.

6 Journal, August 24th, 1884.

7 Journal, September 14th, 1884.

8 Philip Magnus, *Gladstone,* p. 318.

9 Ponsonby Letters, September 17th, 1884.

10 Frederick Ponsonby, *Sidelights on Queen Victoria,* p. 195.

11 *Letters* II.III.554, Queen Victoria to Gladstone, October 22nd, 1884.

12 *Letters* II.III.577, Lord Granville to Queen Victoria, and Queen Victoria's Journal, November 18th, 1884.

13 Philip Magnus, *Gladstone,* p. 319.

14 Journal, November 22nd and 24th, 1884.

15 *Letters* II.III.581, Queen Victoria's Journal, November 27th, 1884.

16 *Letters* II.III.594–5, Queen Victoria to Sir Henry Ponsonby, January 24th, 1885.

17 Godfrey Elton (editor), *General Gordon's Khartoum Diary* (1961), p. 180.

18 *Letters* II.III.597, Queen Victoria to Gladstone, Granville and Hartington.

19 Kronberg Letters, February 7th, 1885.

20 Journal, February 20th, 1885.

21 *Letters* II.III.613, Queen Victoria to Lord Granville, February 26th, 1885.

22 *Letters* II.III.619, Queen Victoria to Lady Wolseley, March 3rd, 1885.

23 Kronberg Letters, May 28th, 1885.

24 *Letters* II.III.646, Queen Victoria to Lord Hartington, May 17th, 1885 and to Sir Henry Ponsonby, May 18th, 1885.

25 John Morley, *Life of Gladstone* (1903), III.194.

26 *Letters* II.III.652–5, Gladstone to Queen Victoria, May 23rd, 1885.

27 Journal, May 26th, 1885.

28 *Letters* II.III.662, Queen Victoria to Gladstone, June 11th, 1885.

29 Kronberg Letters, May 15th, 1884.

30 Ponsonby Letters, May 2nd, 1884.

31 Kronberg Letters, January 7th, 1885.

32 Kronberg Letters, July 25th, 1885.

33 Kronberg Letters, June 25th, 1883.

34 *English Empress*, p. 225, January 7th, 1885.

35 Kronberg Letters, February 13th, 1885.

36 *English Empress*, p. 226, January 19th, 1885.

37 *English Empress*, p. 227, July 8th, 1885.

38 Kronberg Letters, July 27th, September 30th, November 26th and 29th, 1884.

CHAPTER XXXII
Home Rule 1885–6

1 *Letters* II.III.695–6, Queen Victoria to Gladstone, October 2nd, 1885.

2 Kronberg Letters, June 17th, 1884.

3 Kronberg Letters, February 24th, 1886.

4 Ponsonby Letters, December 9th, 1885.

5 *Letters* II.III.713, Queen Victoria to G. J. Goschen, December 20th, 1885.

6 Journal, November 23rd, 1885.

7 Arthur Ponsonby, op. cit., p. 206.

8 Ponsonby Letters, January 29th, 1886.

9 *Letters* III.I.45, footnote, Queen Victoria's memoran-

dum, February 8th, 1886.

10 *Letters* III.I.111, Gladstone to Sir Henry Ponsonby, April 22nd, 1886.

11 Salisbury Papers, Queen Victoria to Lord Salisbury, May 20th, 1886.

12 *Letters* III.I.34, Queen Victoria's Journal, February 1st, 1886.

13 Salisbury Papers, Queen Victoria to Lord Salisbury, February 1st, 1886.

14 Kronberg Letters, February 3rd, 1886.

15 Kronberg Letters, February 15th, 1886.

16 Philip Magnus, *Gladstone*, p. 341.

17 Journal, October 28th, 1884 and March 23rd, 1886.

18 Journal, March 26th, 1886.

19 Robert Rhodes James, op. cit., p. 193.

20 Salisbury Papers, Queen Victoria to Lord Salisbury, May 9th and 10th, 1886; *Letters* III.I.128–30, Lord Salisbury's memorandum, May 15th, 1886.

21 Salisbury Papers, Queen Victoria to Lord Salisbury, May 16th, 1886.

22 Kronberg Letters, May 19th, 1886.

23 Salisbury Papers, Queen Victoria to Lord Salisbury, May 20th, 1886.

24 *Letters* III.I.143, Queen Victoria's Journal, June 8th, 1886.

25 Journal, June 14th, 1886.

26 Kronberg Letters, July 5th, 1886.

27 Kronberg Letters, July 5th, 1886.

28 G. St Aubyn, op. cit., p. 227.

29 Kronberg Letters, December 27th, 1886.

30 *Letters* III.I.179, 181, 191 and 196, Queen Victoria to Lord Salisbury, August 22nd and 23rd and September 1st, Queen Victoria to Lord Iddesleigh, August 27th, 1886.

31 Kronberg Letters, September 18th, 1886.

32 Journal, November 23rd, 1886.

33 Kronberg Letters, December 15th, 1886.

CHAPTER XXXIII

The Jubilee Bonnet 1887–91

1 Kronberg Letters, February 1st and 14th, 1887.

2 Salisbury Papers, Lord Salisbury to Queen Victoria, December 11th, 1887.

3 Journal, March 6th, 1887.

4 Salisbury Papers, Queen Victoria to Sir Henry Ponsonby, March 19th, 1887.

5 Ponsonby Letters, April 24th, 1887.

6 Journal, April 25th, 1887.

7 Salisbury Papers, Queen Victoria to Lord Salisbury, May 15th, 1887.

8 Kronberg Letters, May 31st, 1887.

9 *Letters* III.I.320, Queen Victoria's Journal, June 20th, 1887.

10 Kronberg Letters, December 12th, 1887.

11 Ponsonby Letters, August 27th, 1887 and March 30th, 1888; *Empress Frederick,* pp. 243–58.

12 *English Empress,* p. 259.

13 Kronberg Letters, February 16th and March 17th, 1888.

14 Kronberg Letters, March 31st, 1888.

15 Kronberg Letters, April 10th, 1888; *Empress Frederick,* p. 422, February 22nd, 1891.

16 Kronberg Letters, April 27th, 1888.

17 Kronberg Letters, May 2nd, 1888.

18 Kronberg Letters, June 15th, August 8th and 28th, 1888; *Empress Frederick,* pp. 319–27.

19 Kronberg Letters, October 23rd, 1888; *English Empress,* pp. 280–1.

20 Kronberg Letters, November 5th, 1888.

21 *Letters* III.I.440, Queen Victoria to Lord Salisbury, October 15th, 1888.

22 Kronberg Letters, September 4th, 1888.

23 *Letters* III.I.504, Emperor William II to Sir Edward Malet, June 14th, 1889.

24 Kronberg Letters, July 17th, 1889; *English Empress,* p. 325.

25 RA L20/124.

26 RA Vic. Add. MSS, A12/1667.

27 Arthur Ponsonby, op. cit., p. 131.

28 RA D10/187; India Office Library, MSS, Eur. D558/X/vol. I/No. 44, 45, Viceroy (Lord Lansdowne) to Queen Victoria, November 23rd and 26th, 1890.

29 Ponsonby Letters, December 22nd, 1888.

30 *Letters* III.II.54, Queen Victoria to Lord Cross, August 1st, 1891.

31 *Letters* III.II.69, Queen Victoria to Lady Harris,
751

September 10th, 1891.

32 Journal, April 1st, 1889.
33 Lord Ormathwaite, *When I was at Court* (1937), pp. 54–5.
34 Journal, July 27th, 1889.
35 Kronberg Letters, June 14th, 1890; James Pope-Hennessy (editor), *Queen Victoria at Windsor and Balmoral* (1959), pp. 31–41; *English Empress*, p. 335.
36 Kronberg Letters, June 2nd, 1891.
37 Kronberg Letters, April 10th, 1891.
38 Kronberg Letters, May 7th, 1889.
39 Kenneth Young, *Arthur James Balfour* (1963), pp. 122–3 and Appendix I; Kronberg Letters, June 2nd, 1891.
40 Kronberg Letters, December 6th, 1891.
41 *Letters* III.I.615, Queen Victoria to Lord Salisbury, June 12th, 1890.
42 Kronberg Letters, December 2nd, 1891.
43 Ponsonby Letters, November 28th, 1891.

CHAPTER XXXIV

'*Still Endure*' 1892–5

1 Journal, January 14th, 1892.
2 Journal, March 13th, 1892.
3 Ponsonby Letters, April 13th, 1892.
4 Kronberg Letters, June 2nd, 1891.
5 Kronberg Letters, June 27th, 1892.
6 Kronberg Letters, June 14th, 1892.
7 Kronberg Letters, June 22nd, 1892.
8 Kronberg Letters, June 29th, 1892.
9 Kronberg Letters, July 6th, 1892.
10 Journal, July 29th, 1892.
11 Lord Newton, *Life of Lansdowne* (1929), p. 100.
12 Arthur Ponsonby, op. cit., p. 399.
13 *Letters* III.II.145, Queen Victoria's Journal, August 15th, 1892.
14 Journal, August 7th, 1892.
15 Kronberg Letters, July 18th and 25th, 1892.
16 Journal, August 12th, 1892.
17 Kronberg Letters, November 30th, 1892.
18 G. St Aubyn, op. cit., p. 301.
19 *English Empress*, p. 346, May 30th, 1893.
20 Kronberg Letters, September 4th, 1893.
21 Journal, August 13th, 1893.
22 *Letters* III.II.370–1, Queen Victoria's Journal, March 3rd, 1894.
23 E. F. Benson, *Queen Victoria* (1935), p. 345.
24 *Letters* III.II.373, Queen Victoria to Gladstone, March 3rd, 1894.
25 Philip Guedalla, op. cit., II.75–6 and 82; Philip Magnus, *Gladstone*, p. 425.
26 Philip Guedalla, op. cit., II.76 and 82; Philip Magnus, *Gladstone*, pp. 425–6.
27 Ponsonby Letters, September 30th, 1884.
28 Ponsonby Letters, April 19th, 1875.
29 Frank Hardie, *The Political Influence of Queen Victoria*, (1935), p. 51.
30 Philip Magnus, *Gladstone*, p. 427.

31 Robert Rhodes James, op. cit., p. 325.

32 *Letters* III.ii.369, Queen Victoria to Lord Salisbury, March 2nd, 1894.

33 Journal, January 19th, 1894.

34 Ponsonby Letters, March 16th and 17th, 1894.

35 *Letters* III.ii.404, Queen Victoria to Lord Rosebery, June 8th, 1894.

36 *Letters* III.ii.441–2, Colonel Bigge to Sir Henry Ponsonby, November 3rd, 1894 and Sir Henry James's memorandum, November 5th, 1894.

37 Kronberg Letters, January 10th, 1894.

38 Kronberg Letters, November 25th, 1894.

39 Kronberg Letters, June 27th, 1894.

40 Ponsonby Letters, September 27th, 1894.

41 RA L16/87, Queen Victoria to Sir Henry Ponsonby, December 21st, 1894.

42 Journal, June 22nd, 1895.

43 Kronberg Letters, July 1st, 1895.

44 Kronberg Letters, July 30th, 1895.

CHAPTER XXXV

*The Labourer's Task
1892–1900*

1 Arthur Ponsonby, op. cit., p. 131.

2 RA C63/88.

3 RA Vic. Add. MSS, A12/2161.

4 Frederick Ponsonby, *Recollections of Three Reigns* (editor, Colin Welch, 1951), pp. 14–15.

5 Letters II.ii.502, Queen Victoria to Colonel Bigge, May 8th, 1895.

6 India Office Library, MSS, Eur. F84/126a, Frederick Ponsonby to Lord Elgin, January 16th, 1895; Munshi to Lord Elgin, November 30th, 1894; Sir Arthur Godley (Perm. Under Sec. of State) to Lord Elgin, March 8th, 1895.

7 India Office Library, ibid., Sir A. Godley to Lord Elgin, March 21st, 1895; C. S. Hayley to Sir Henry Babington-Smith (Priv. Sec. to Viceroy), September 14th, 1896; C. S. Hayley to Sir H. Babington-Smith, July 4th, 1896; Sir A. Godley to Lord Elgin, March 21st, 1895; Lord Elgin to Lord Sandhurst (Gov. of Bombay), March 14th, 1896; Lord George Hamilton to Lord Elgin, April 30th, 1897.

8 India Office Library, ibid., Lord George Hamilton to Lord Elgin, February 21st, 1896.

9 Kronberg Letters, April 27th, 1895.

10 RA A73/68, Lord Salisbury to Queen Victoria, March 6th, 1897.

11 James Pope-Hennessy, *Queen Mary*, p. 346.

12 India Office Library, ibid., Frederick Ponsonby to Sir H. Babington-Smith, April 27th, 1897.

13 India Office Library, ibid., Lord George Hamilton to Lord Elgin, April 30th and May 7th, 1897.

14 Salisbury Papers, Queen Victoria to Lord Salisbury, July 17th, 1897.

15 Salisbury Papers, Queen Victoria to Lord Salisbury, July 26th, 1897.

16 Salisbury Papers, Queen Victoria to Lord Salisbury, July 31st, 1897.

17 Salisbury Papers, Queen Victoria to Lord Salisbury, September 17th, 1897.

18 Salisbury Papers, Queen Victoria to Lord Salisbury, January 22nd, 1898.

19 Salisbury Papers, Queen Victoria to Lord Salisbury, June 6th, 1898.

20 Salisbury Papers, Queen Victoria to Lord Salisbury, March 11th, 1898.

21 Salisbury Papers, Queen Victoria to Lord Salisbury, August 3rd, 1898.

22 Salisbury Papers, Queen Victoria to Lord Salisbury, August 1898.

23 Salisbury Papers, Queen Victoria to Lord Salisbury, December 27th and 29th, 1898.

24 RA X14/29.

25 *Letters* III.III.20, Queen Victoria to Prince of Wales, January 11th, 1896; Journal, January 4th, 1896; Kronberg Letters, January 8th, 1896.

26 Kronberg Letters, May 3rd, 1899.

27 *Letters* III.III.378, Emperor William II to Queen Victoria, May 27th, 1899.

28 *Letters* III.III.239, Queen Victoria to A. J. Balfour, March 27th, 1898.

29 Kronberg Letters, November 25th, 1899.

30 James Pope-Hennessy, *Queen Mary*, p. 317.

31 Journal, March 4th, 1896.

32 Journal, July 4th, 1896.

33 Journal, May 5th, 1896.

34 Journal, November 30th, 1896.

35 *Letters* III.III.79, Queen Victoria's Journal, September 23rd, 1896.

36 Journal, February 23rd, 1897.

37 *Letters* III.III.127, Queen Victoria to Sir Arthur Bigge, January 30th, 1897.

38 James Pope-Hennessy, *Queen Mary*, p. 335.

39 *Letters* III.III.174, Queen Victoria's Journal, June 22nd, 1897.

40 Mary Lutyens (editor), *Lady Lytton's Court Diary* (1961), p. 114.

41 Lord Ormathwaite, op. cit., pp. 93–4.

42 RA F23/1.

43 *Letters* III.III.247, Queen Victoria to Mrs Gladstone, May 19th, 1898; Lord Esher, *Journals and Letters*, I.217.

44 *Letters* III.III.246, Queen Victoria's Journal, May 19th, 1898.

45 Kronberg Letters, May 31st, 1898.

46 Journal, December 4th, 1898.

47 *Letters* III.II.580, Queen Victoria's Journal, December 14th, 1895.

48 *Letters* III.III.298–9, Queen Victoria's Journal, October 25th, 1898.

49 Lady Gwendolen Cecil, *Life of Salisbury*, III.191.

50 Journal, May 16th, 1900.

51 Journal, March 14th, 1900.

52 Kronberg Letters, March 7th, 1900.

53 Journal, April 29th, 1900.

CHAPTER XXXVI

'Mother's Come Home' 1900–1

1 Journal, June 29th, 1900.
2 Princess Marie-Louise, *My Memories of Six Reigns* (1956), p. 112.
3 Journal, July 28th, 1900; *Letters* III.III.579–80, Queen Victoria's Journal, July 31st, 1900.
4 *Letters* III.III.592, Queen Victoria to G. J. Goschen, September 19th, 1900.
5 G. K. A. Bell, op. cit., p. 352.
6 Kronberg, January 21st, 1887.
7 RA Vic. Add. MSS, A8.
8 James Pope-Hennessy, *Queen Mary*, p. 353.
9 Journal, March 6th, 1873.
10 Journal, June 17th, 1880.
11 RA F23/1.
12 Journal, November 30th, 1864.
13 *Letters* II.I.491, Queen Victoria to Theodore Martin, January 16th, 1868.
14 Stratfield Saye MSS, Queen Victoria to Dean Wellesley, March 26th, 1861.
15 Kingsley Martin, *The Triumph of Lord Palmerston* (1963), p. 155.
16 Princess Marie-Louise, op. cit., p. 20.
17 RA Vic. Add. MSS, X2/211.
18 Ponsonby Letters, November 18th, 1871.
19 Ponsonby Letters, September 29th, 1878.
20 G. K. A. Bell, op. cit., p. 85.
21 Kronberg Letters, October 4th, 1892.
22 Kronberg Letters, August 27th, 1899.
23 James Pope-Hennessy, *Queen Mary*, p. 342.
24 Kronberg Letters, January 8th, 1870.
25 RA Vic. Add. MSS, A15/5153.
26 Kronberg Letters, February 17th, 1886.
27 Ponsonby Letters, August 28th, 1871.

INDEX

In this Index, V = Queen Victoria and A = Prince Albert
PR = Princess Royal, P of W = Prince of Wales

757

Albert—*continued*

honeymoon, 179–80; as dancer and horseman, 179–80; Royal family's hostility to, 180–1; so-called prudery, 181, 182; first signs of trouble, 184–7; 'husband, not master', 184–5; conflict with Lehzen, 186, 190, 193, 198–206, 212; V's supposed jealousy of, 186; and her first pregnancy, 187–8; appointed Regent, 190; V's increasing dependence on, 190; at first Council, 191; his 'Bed-chamber ladies' success, 195–6, 203; Melbourne's tribute to, 197; quarrel over PR's rearing, 199–202; and Lehzen's departure, 203; exaggerates V's deficiencies, 205; and her re-education, 206, 275–6, 328, 358, 381–2, 425, 525; his domestic reforms, 207–9; and Christmas tree, 210; and children's future, 215, 395, 396; father's death, 215–16; alleged coolness in love, 216; first train journey, 218; in the Highlands, 220–1, 265–7, 272; plans Osborne improvements, 221; V's favourite portrait of, 222; artistic interests, 223, 386; Chairman of Arts Commission, 223, 277; problem of constitutional position, 223, 259, 300, 333; first and last Parliamentary debate, 229; and Chartists, 244–5; differences with Palmerston, 248–9, 252, 256,

258–60; and domestic life, 262, 263–72; shooting, 266, 268, 275; anxiety over health, 269, 272, 306, 347, 362, 389; plans P of W's education, 270–1, 343, 346–8, 393; influence with manufacturers and artisans, 274, 276, 280, 283; intellectual tastes, 275–6, 525; and Great Exhibition, 277–83, 308; new-won popularity, 282–3; and moral standard of Court, 285; rejects post of C-in-C, 287, 305; his directives for Wellington's funeral, 287–8; and V's emotional crises, 293–4, 315, 322, 330–2, 341, 355–6, 365–6; slanders on, 298–9, 305; and Crimean War, 302–3, 305, 318, 323; alleged deficiencies as lover, 317; aims at Prussian alliance, 323, 324; and PR's instruction, 326–7, 329, 340; preoccupation in business, 330, 362, 364; devotion to PR, 331, 333, 339, 374; created Prince Consort, 333; and PR's wedding, 334, 336; as V's father-figure, 339, 382; and punishment of children, 340–1, 345; and Napoleon III's Austrian campaign, 352; advice on Conservative reform, 353; tired and worried, 356; V's increasing devotion, 358, 365; last visit to Germany, 359–60; carriage accident, 360; decline in health, 362–3, 364, 366–9; unremitting labours,

Brown, J.—*continued*
Royal family's dislike of, 484–5, 576; death, 566–7, 573; tributes and memorials to, 567; V's abortive plan to write memoir of, 570–4, 588; her greetings cards to, 572–3; *More Leaves* dedicated to, 574; his 'strong arm', 575; his services and disservices, 575–7; burial and growing fame, 577

Browning, Elizabeth Barrett, 76, 382

Browning, Robert, 425 *n*, 442

Bruce, Colonel (later General) Robert, 346, 373, 377, 393

Bruce (later Stanley), Lady Augusta, 267, 322 *n*, 363, 372, 375, 377, 383, 384, 442

Brunswick, Duke Charles of, 64, 68, 84, 313, 317–18

Bryce, Lord, 662

Buccleuch, Duchess of, 403

Buckingham, Richard Grenville, 2nd Duke of, 214

Buckingham Palace, 172, 175, 190, 224, 244–5, 246, 278, 457, 499, 530; V moves to, 90; dullness of Court, 114–15; ball in honour of Tsarevitch, 140–1; V's Declaration of Marriage in, 169; A's Household reforms, 207–9; nursery wing, 210; gas lighting in Chapel, 215; a 'domestic haven', 217; improvements to, 262, 287; garden parties, 435; Dickens at, 442; Golden Jubilee at, 626–7; Diamond Jubilee at, 689; a home for fallen women?, 713

Buckle, G. E., 609 *n*

Bulgarian atrocities, 465, 511–21

Bulgarian Horrors and the Question of the East, The (Gladstone), 512, 513

Buller, Sir Redvers, 696

Bulteel, Mary – *see* Ponsonby, Lady (Henry)

Burdett-Coutts, Angela, Baroness, 106

Burghersh, Lord, 303

Burke, Frederick, 560

Burney, Fanny, 205, 209

Burns, James, 418

Burns, John, 420

Butler, Bishop, 427

Cadiz, Francisco, Duke of, 234, 236

Caird, Dr John, 427, 452

Cairns, Lord, 446

Cambridge: A as Chancellor, 276; P of W at, 346, 367, 375

Cambridge, Adolphus, Duke of, 20, 21, 24, 177, 181, 240

Cambridge, George Frederick, Duke of, 24, 55, 64, 114, 170, 181, 308, 349, 434, 458, 488, 507, 564, 628, 630, 706; as C-in-C, 304, 478; opposes Army reforms, 478, 487, 553; conflict with Wolseley, 552–3; removal thwarted, 644; resigns at last, 670, 689

Cambridge, Princess Augusta of Hesse-Cassel, Duchess of, 21, 113, 569; supports Duchess of Kent against V, 114, 117; hostile to A, 180–1; death, 640

Camoys, Lord, 254

Conroy, Sir J.—*continued*
Progresses', 50–1, 52; and her confirmation, 58; rejected as private secretary, 61–2, 71; and Kensington 'system', 69–75; seeks Regency for Duchess, 70–1; tries again as private secretary, 71, 73; dismissed from V's Household, 79, 90; his exorbitant terms for retirement, 81–2; unbudgable, 105, 131; railroad accident, 107; and Flora Hastings affair, 119, 120, 126, 127, 130, 131; resigns and leaves country, 144–5, 148, 149, 155; his suspicious stewardship, 145–6; death, 146; evidence against immoral union with Duchess, 146–8

Conroy, Lady, 43, 48

Conroy, Sir Henry, 146

Conroy, Lady (Henry), 43

Conroy, Victoire, 35, 45, 71, 73

Constant, Benjamin, 694

Constantine I of Greece, 650

Constantinople, 244, 296, 304, 619, 676

Constitutional History (Hallam), 179, 711

Contagious Diseases, Royal Commission on, 442

Conyngham, Lord, 70, 74–5, 80, 94, 172

Conyngham, Lady, 31–2, 48

Cook, Thos. and Son, 582

Cooper, Fenimore, 53

Copenhagen, 583

Corelli, Marie, 707

Corn Laws, 226, 227, 228, 612

Cornwall, Duchy of, 92

Corry, Montagu (later Baron Rowton), 514, 515, 547, 548

Couper, Sir George, 145

Court Doctor Dissected, The (Murray), 153

Courtney, Corporal, 310

Coutts, Messrs, 92, 145

Coutts, Miss, 106

Cove (Cobh), 239

Cowell, Sir John, 434, 499, 655, 725 n

Cowes, 247, 385, 575, 631, 633, 682, 706

Cowley, Lord, 498, 712

Cranborne, Lord (later Salisbury), 440

Crathie, 426, 429, 505, 567, 576, 577, 654

Crawford, Lord, 560 n

Crawford, Virginia, 606 n

Creevey, Thomas, 96, 120

Crimean War, 283, 301, 302–6, 310–11, 312, 314, 318–20, 333, 343

Criminal Law Amendment Act (1885), 580

Croft, Sir Richard, 187 n

Croker, John Wilson, 169

Cromer, Sir Evelyn Baring, Lord, 651

Cross, Sir Richard (later Lord), 580, 622, 650

Crystal Palace, 277–83, 289, 297, 334

Cubitt, Thomas, 247

Cumberland, Ernest, Duke of (later King of Hanover), 20, 24, 77, 213; alleged plot against V, 44–6; refuses precedence to A, 170

Cumming, Sir William Gordon, 642

Currie, Sir Donald, 582
Curzon, Lord, 680

Daily Mail, 690–1
Daily News, 512
Daily Telegraph, 488, 632, 633
Dalhousie, Lady, 661
Darmstadt, 539, 599–600, 648, 667
Darwin, Charles, 297
Davidson, Archbishop Randall, 425, 427, 429, 571, 572, 644, 704, 705, 706, 708, 717, 718, 725
Davis, Dr David, 25 *n*
Davys, Rev. George, 37–8, 52, 205
Daybreak, The, 419
De L'Isle, Lord, 156
death duties, 670
Deceased Wife's Sister's Bill (1883), 546
Delane, John Thadeus, 514
Derby, Edward Stanley, 14th Earl of, 284–6, 288–9, 306–7, 391, 396, 449, 457; second Ministry, 351; defeat, 353; and Reform, 437; last Ministry, 440, 442
Derby, Edward Stanley, 15th Earl of, 550, 606, 712; and Bulgarian atrocities, 516, 517, 518–19
Derby, Frederick Stanley, 16th Earl of, 598
Devonshire, William Cavendish, 6th Duke of, 219
Devonshire, Spencer Compton Cavendish, 8th Duke of, 701. *See also* Hartington, Lord
Diamond Jubilee, 678, 683, 685–91

Dickens, Charles, 442
Dietz, 201
Dilke, Sir Charles, 488, 491, 538, 546, 565, 597, 606, 610, 618, 648, 720
Dillon, Miss, 97
Disestablishment, 450, 452–3, 666
Disraeli, Benjamin (later Lord Beaconsfield), 54, 77, 88, 102, 103, 226, 228, 307, 329, 391, 420, 423, 438, 493, 499, 500, 506, 522, 524, 531 *n*, 537, 545, 555, 567 *n*, 575, 582, 726; first meets V, 220; her comment on, 286, 444; his cribbed tribute to Wellington, 288; his flattery and flirtation, 317, 444–6, 502–3; his gibe on A's absolutism, 381; at P of W's wedding, 395–6; defence of dogma, 431; and Reform, 439–40, 444, 453, 526, 726; his 'two nations', 441; becomes Prime Minister, 442, 445; 'a man of the people', 443; V's most romantic relationship, 444–7, 502–3; A's dislike of, 444; Government defeat, 447; 'we authors, Ma'am', 470; and V's seclusion, 487; in power again, 497; first visit to Osborne as Premier, 502–3; his handling of V, 504, 506; and Royal Titles Bill, 508, 509; created Lord Beaconsfield, 509, 512; purchase of Suez Canal, 511; and Bulgarian atrocities, 511–21; 'Peace with Honour' from Berlin, 520, 521;

Disraeli, B.—*continued*
Gladstone's criticisms of, 535–6; defeat, 537, 539, 543; his advice on successor, 540–1; on ministerial responsibility, 547, 548; death, 548–9; V's debt to, 550; his pithy memoranda, 554; birthday as 'Primrose Day', 617; and party system, 712

Disraeli, Mrs, 220, 286, 395, 440, 444, 447, 493, 503, 509, 549

Dodgson, Rev. Charles (Lewis Carroll), 525

Dongola, 685

Douro, Lord, 360

Downey (photographer), 640

D'Oyly Carte Company, 639

Dreyfus, Colonel, 718

Dublin, 557, 559, 698

Duckworth, Canon, 414

Dufferin, Lord, 497, 521, 527

Dumas, Alexandre, 205

Duncannon, Lord, 92

Dundas, Admiral Sir James, 308

Dunraven, Lord, 425

Durham, John Lambton, 1st Earl of, 69

Eagle, Georgiana, 422

East India Company, 351

Eastern question, 185, 190, 232, 510–21

Ecclesiastical Titles Bill, 255, 282, 446

Eden, Emily, 504

Edgeworth, Maria, 53

Edinburgh, Prince Alfred, Duke of ('Affie'), 215, 240, 243, 266, 272, 344, 394, 460, 463, 469, 487, 488, 499, 528, 532, 648; birth, 214; naval training, 343; amorous escapade at Malta, 396, 465; and offer of Greek throne, 396; shot by Fenians, 451; marriage problem, 463, 465, 466, 467, 494; 'ruin' by Society, 464; row with Brown, 484; engagement and marriage to Marie of Russia, 494–6, 505, 507; and Bulgarian atrocities, 513; as Duke of Coburg, 667, 693; ill-health, 693; death, 701

Edinburgh, Prince Philip, Duke of, 604

Edinburgh, Marie of Russia, Duchess of (later Coburg), 465 *n*, 494–5, 507, 700, 704

Education Act (1870), 420

Edward VII (as Prince of Wales), 92, 203, 213, 217, 218, 240, 266, 275, 315, 316, 339 *n*, 360, 382, 388, 402, 448, 463, 475, 487, 524, 532, 534, 589, 648, 654 *n*, 686, 696; birth, 199, 210; backwardness, 214, 271, 343–4, 347; education, 215, 270–1, 343–8, 393; V's disappointment in, 271–2, 343, 347; told of his destiny, 271–2; inferiority complex, 272, 345; A's severity with, 340, 341, 344, 459; passion for teasing, 344, 365; rages, 341 *n*, 345; at Oxford and Cambridge, 346, 347, 367, 375; Curragh camp escapade, 348, 366, 391, 393; question of marriage, 357,

'Faithful Service Medal', 487

Faraday, Michael, 215, 331

'fashionables' (A's enemies), 230, 274, 278, 305

Fashoda, 695

Faust (Goethe), 276

Fawcett, Dame Millicent, 580, 625

Fawkes, Captain, 601

Fenians, 450–2, 469, 490, 557, 561

Feodore of Leiningen (later Hohenlohe), Princess, 19, 26, 32, 33, 35, 48, 64, 214, 399, 429, 491

Ferdinand of Bulgaria, 620

Ferdinand II of Portugal (Ferdinand of Saxe-Coburg-Kohary), 56, 63, 64, 157, 184, 236

Ferdinand of Roumania, 649

Ferdinand of Portugal, Prince, 366

Ferguson, Robert (accoucheur), 365 *n*

Fernanda, Infanta of Spain (Duchess of Montpensier), 233, 236, 243

Fife, Alexander Duff, 1st Duke of, 613, 641, 683

Fiji, 501

Finch, Lady Charlotte, 209

Fine Arts, Society of, 277, 363

Fisher, Dr John, Bishop of Salisbury, 29

Fitzclarence, Lord Adolphus, 182

Fitzclarence, Lord Augustus, 66

Fitzgerald, Hamilton, 122, 128

Fitzroy, Lord Charles, 412, 413, 414, 498

Florence, 634, 666

Florschütz, Herr (tutor), 161, 163

Forster, W. E., 478, 525, 555, 559, 593, 606

Fowler, Sir Henry, 1st Viscount Wolverhampton, 670, 675

Fowler, William, 43, 44

Francis, John, 212

Francis Joseph, Emperor, 256, 258, 352, 634, 636

Francis Joseph of Battenberg, Prince, 599 *n*, 620

Franco-Prussian War (1870–1871), 474–6, 478

Frazer, Peter, 220

Frederick, Empress – *see* Victoria Adelaide Mary Louise

Frederick the Noble (Mackenzie), 636

Frederick III of Prussia ('Fritz'), 215, 282, 330, 357, 474, 509; betrothed to PR, 324-6, 327, 328–9; marriage, 334–6, 351; opposition to Bismarck, 397; illness and death, 625–6, 627, 633, 635–6; becomes Emperor, 633; his war diary published, 636

Frederick VII of Denmark, 398

Frederick, Duke of Schleswig-Holstein-Augustenburg ('Fritz Holstein'), 398, 416

Frederick Charles of Hesse, Prince, 649 *n*

Frederick Charles of Prussia, Prince, 530, 534, 569

Frederick William IV of Prussia, 223, 225, 246, 258, 278, 362

Frederika of Hanover, Princess, 463, 467, 495

Free Trade, 226, 228, 278, 444

Frere, Sir Bartle, 593

Freytag, Gustav, 721

Frogmore, 211, 363, 462, 463, 531, 626; Mausoleum, 386, 388, 395, 401, 439, 534, 640, 688, 697, 707, 710

Froude, James Anthony, 442

Fry, Elizabeth, 225

Fulford, Roger, 198 *n*

Gallipoli, 516

Garibaldi, Giuseppe, 455–6

gas lighting, 215

Gatacre, Sir William Forbes, 696

George III, 19, 30, 111, 113, 115, 143, 258, 270, 341 *n*, 685

George IV, 30, 34, 38, 41, 42, 87, 89, 95, 98, 219, 221, 373, 500, 685; as Prince Regent, 18, 20, 23; at V's christening, 27–8; her childhood visit to, 32–3; and 'Cumberland plot', 44–5, 46

George V (as Duke of York), 522, 573, 646, 647, 649, 677, 693, 702; marriage to Princess May of Teck, 654, 679

George VI, 572, 693

George I of Greece, 582, 627, 647

George V of Hanover (Prince George of Cumberland), 24, 64, 463, 534

George of Denmark, Prince, 171, 190

Gibbs, Frederick Waymouth (tutor), 271–2, 344, 345, 346, 347

Gipsies' Advocate (Crabbe), 54

Gladstone, Herbert, 606

Gladstone, William Ewart, 197, 232, 296, 298, 300, 306, 308, 319, 329, 393, 400, 420, 448, 472, 509, 524, 534, 535, 622, 630, 645; first meets V, 220; resigns over Maynooth grant, 227; V's contempt for, 227; Derby considers 'unfit', 289, 449; opposes Palmerston's defence measures, 354; and V's claim to Liberalism, 433, 434; and the Irish, 455, 450, 453, 495, 555–60, 597; becomes Prime Minister, 447; 'the People's William', 447, 449, 537, 545, 663, 692; V's tribute to morals, 448, 661; her later distrust of, 449, 541; and Irish Church, 450, 452–3; not agreeable and 'talks so very much', 453; problem of V's seclusion, 476–7, 479–81, 487, 492; his Plan of Life for P of W, 491–2; fall of Government, 497; his internationalism, 502; treats V like a public department, 504; and Public Worship Bill, 505, 506; work among prostitutes, 506, 661–2; and Bulgarian atrocities, 510, 512–13, 518, 520, 521, 584; V's increased dislike of, 521; and Afghan war, 536; Midlothian election campaign, 536–8; defeats Disraeli, 538–42; V's dismay and search for alternative, 339–

Gladstone, W.—*continued*
41; first audience as Prime Minister, 543; her wishful thinking over his health, 544, 566; Cabinet appointments, 545; his uneasy tribute to Disraeli, 549, 693; predicts fall of monarchy, 553; unable to control colleagues, 554; his Land and Coercion Bills, 555, 557–8; slanders against, 562, 661; orders Alexandria bombardment, 563; and Brown, 567, 576; coolness over housing, 580, 581; dispute on Cabinet secrets, 582; visits Norway and Copenhagen, 582; decides to retire, 584; policy of abandoning Sudan, 585, 586–7, 684; and Gordon disaster, 588, 593–5, 692; and Reform Bill (1884), 589–92; shaken hold over Cabinet, 597; resigns on Budget defeat, 597; and Home Rule, 606, 607, 610, 611–16, 618, 656; returns to power, 608; difficulties with Household, 607; his letters to V shown to Salisbury, 607; Chamberlain's opposition to, 610, 611–12, 614, 656; V's plan to defeat, 616–17; refuses earldom on dissolution, 617; resigns, 618; at Golden Jubilee service, 628; suggests V's abdication, 644, 691; 'two dreadful speeches', 650; in power again, 650–2; increasing debility, 651, 653;

crisis over national defence, 656–7, 658; resigns, 658–60; failure of relations with V, 660–5; bitter discovery that he means nothing to her, 660; her dislike and jealousy, 662, 692; success with the masses, 664, 692; and Armenian atrocities, 676; death and V's reaction to it, 691–2; on her high qualities, 710; party loyalty, 712

Hartington, S.—*continued*
566, 597, 622; Minister for
War, 565; and Sudan, 586,
593, 594; and Reform, 591;
and Home Rule, 605, 610,
611, 612, 614, 615; Report
on Army, 644

Hastings, 2nd Marquess of,
124, 125, 127, 130, 150, 153,
154

Hastings, Dowager Marchioness of, 126, 127, 130, 150

Hastings, Lady Flora, 49, 53,
82, 85, 106, 107, 116, 132 n,
141, 172, 181, 490; appointed to Kent household, 54–5;
and Kensington 'system',
69; supports Conroy faction,
117; illness, 118, 370; suspected pregnancy, 119–22;
exonerated, 122–3; tells
brother of scandal, 124;
reconciled with V, 125; her
letter to uncle, 127–8; ostracized, 130; renewed illness,
143, 149; V visits, 151;
death, 152–3, 155, 560 n;
post-mortem, 151; renewed
scandal, 152–3; V's penitence, 154

Hastings, Lady Sophia, 152

Hatchard, John, 55

Haynau, General, 253

He Sing, 281

Heaven Our Home, 421, 426

Helen of Waldeck-Pyrmont,
Princess (Duchess of Albany), 561

Helena, Princess, later Princess Christian ('Lenchen'),
240, 264, 269, 295, 377,
394, 403, 461, 466, 563, 686,
716; birth, 215, 229; marriage, 435, 438, 462, 464,
466; idolizes Disraeli, 447;
nervous condition, 603

Hélène of Orleans, Princess,
643

Heligoland, 644

Helps, Sir Arthur, 392, 434,
480

Henry of Battenberg, Prince
('Liko'), 429, 599 n, 600–1,
620, 632, 681, 683, 707

Henry of Prussia, Prince, 468,
602, 623, 633, 649

Herschell, Farrer, Lord, 670

Hesse, Princess Elizabeth of
('Ella'), 468, 533, 539, 623

Hesse, Prince Ernest of (later
Grand Duke of Hesse-
Darmstadt), 533, 648, 667

Hesse, Prince Frederick
Charles of, 649 n

Hesse, Princess Irene of, 533,
623

Hesse-Darmstadt, Prince
Louis of – *see* Louis of
Hesse-Darmstadt

Heytesbury, Lord, 234

Hicks Beach, Sir Michael
(later Earl St Aldwyn), 539,
591

Hicks, William (Hicks Pasha),
585

Hildyard, Miss (governess),
265, 378

History of England (Macaulay),
218, 358

Hobbs, Mrs (nurse), 360

Hobhouse, Sir John, 94

Hogg, Quintin, 686

Hohenlohe-Langenburg,
Count, 34

Hohenthal, Countess Valerie,
719

Holland, Sir Eardley, 187 *n*

Holland, Sir Henry, 373, 427 *n*

Holland, Elizabeth Vassall, Lady, 98, 112–13

Home, Colonel, 565

Home, Daniel Dunglass, 349, 425, 592, 597, 606, 607, 610, 611–16, 617, 622, 654, 656

Hopetoun, Lord, 680

Housing, Royal Commission on (1884), 581

How, Bishop Walsham, 687

How the Ladies of the Future will make Love, 640

Howe, Lord, 417

Howlett's Tables, 38

Howley, Archbishop William, 74–5, 78, 99, 101, 102, 273

Hughenden, 487, 514, 548, 549

Humbert I of Italy, 701

Hume, Joseph, 88

Hunt, George Ward, 445

Hyde Park, 95, 411, 686, 688; V attacked in, 240–1; Great Exhibition at, 278–83; Jubilee celebrations, 629, 630

Hyères, 647

Iddesleigh, Sir Stafford Northcote, Lord, 622

Illustrated London News, 282

Imperial Institute, 630, 656

Impregnable Rock of Holy Scripture, The (Gladstone), 420

Improvement of the Conditions of the Working Classes, Society for the, 276

income tax, 197, 497

Indian Army, 251–2

Indian and Colonial Exhibition (1886), 613

Indian Mutiny, 350, 351–2

Ingestre, Lady Sarah, 150

Innocent, Mrs, 292

International Exhibition, 391; (1862), 406, 725; (1886) 614

Irene of Hesse, Princess, 533, 623

Irish Church, 449, 453

Irish Guards, formation of, 698

Irish Home Rulers, 544, 554, 592

Irish Industries Exhibition (1900), 702

Irish Nationalists, 606, 612, 622, 644,

Irish University Bill (1873), 493

Irving, Sir Henry, 639

Irving, Washington, 54

Isabella II of Spain, 231, 232–3, 235–6

Isandhlwana, 543

Jack the Ripper, 420

Jamaica Bill (1839), 134

James, Sir Henry, 667

James, Henry, 724

Jameson Raid, 681–3

Jane Eyre (Brontë), 359

Jenkinson, Lady Catherine, 74

Jenner, Dr (later Sir) William, 406, 424, 434, 438, 446, 465, 496, 506, 533, 567, 607, 625, 679, 717, 724; appointed Royal physician, 363; and A's fatal illness, 369, 371, 373, 375, 378; and Brown scandal, 416; and monarchy crisis, 477, 480–2, 485, 486, 487; on mortality of workers' children, 491; foresees nervous breakdowns of V, 500, 596, 642; on 'balmorality', 717

Morley, John, 611
Morning Chronicle, 280
Morning Post, 128, 130
Morse, Sydney, 640
Mulgrave, Lord, 99
Muller, William, 421
Mulock (journalist), 392
Mundella, Anthony John, 545
Munshi – *see* Abdul Karim
Munster, George Fitzclarence, Lord, 74
Munster, Countess of, 48
Murray, Sir Charles Augustus, 269 *n*
Murray, Dr John Fisher, 153
Murray, Mrs M. A., 411
Mystery of Pain, The (Hutton), 568

Napier, Sir Charles, 152
Napoleon I, 316, 620 *n*
Napoleon III, 284, 300, 327, 366, 399, 425, 587, 722; as Prince Louis Napoleon, 245; Palmerston supports, 256–7; and Crimean War, 302–3, 312, 314; visits Windsor, 312–15, 351; V's changed attitude to, 316–17; A's distrust of, 323; P of W's hero-worship of, 343; at Osborne, 349; Orsini's attempt on, 351; and Austrian campaign, 352–3; annexes Savoy and Nice, 354; defeat in Franco-Prussian War, 474–5, 478
Nautet, Mme Charlotte ('the Rubber'), 568, 578
Nemours, Princess Victoire, Duchess of, 157, 242, 243, 246, 358
Netley Hospital, 565, 576

New Lanark Mills, 28
New Philosophy, 426
New York Evening Post, 725
Newcastle, Henry Pelham, 5th Duke of, 304, 306, 308
Newman, Cardinal, 721
Newport, 171
Nice, 354, 720 *n*, 724
Nicholas I, Tsar, 154, 206, 220, 255, 256, 278–9, 388; and Crimean War, 296, 302, 312; death, 312
Nicholas II, Tsar, 655; marries Princess Alix, 667; visits Balmoral, 685; Coronation disaster, 689
Nield, John Camden, 286, 486
Nicolson, Sir Harold, 700 *n*
Nightingale, Florence, 283, 310–11, 451, 565, 625, 718, 721
Normanby, Sir Constantine Henry Phipps, 1st Marquis of, 188–9, 235, 257
Normanby, Lady, 196
Northanger Abbey (Austen), 359
Northcote, Sir Stafford (later Lord Iddesleigh), 508, 543, 550
Northern Whig, 421
Northumberland, Duchess of, 41, 53, 69, 72
Norton, Caroline, 83 *n*, 147, 150, 312

O'Brien, William Smith, 238, 616
O'Connell, Daniel, 226, 256
O'Connor, Arthur, 490–1
O'Connor, Feargus, 246
O'Shea, Captain William, 559, 644

Rhodes, Cecil, 587, 681, 683, 714
Richmond, Duke of, 500, 590
Richmond, Duchess of, 99
Richmond, George, 525
Ripon, George Robinson, Marquis of, 506, 611
Roberts, Lord, 696, 704
Roberts, Mrs (nurse), 199
Robertson, Dr (Balmoral factor), 414
Roebuck, John, 223, 306, 309, 510
Rolle, Lord, 102–3
Roman Catholics, 30, 227, 254, 446, 449, 505–6
Rosebery, Archibald Primrose, 5th Earl of, 503, 537, 582, 598, 606, 611, 657, 664, 666, 675, 697, 721; Foreign Secretary, 608, 652, 666; thinks bonnet unsuitable for Sovereign, 641, 627; V's liking for, 662, 671; Prime Minister, 665; and Disestablishment, 666; defeated, 670; and party system, 712; frightened only by V and Bismarck, 724
Rosebery, Hannah, Lady, 504, 610 n
Rosenau, the (A's birthplace), 162, 164, 222, 263, 371
Ross, Sir William Charles, 169, 243
Ross (piper), 456
Rosslyn, Lord, 150, 378
Rothschild, Lionel de, 443
Rothschild, Baron Meyer de, 610 n
Rowton, Montagu Corry, Baron, 547, 548, 550, 567, 570–1, 589, 609, 613 n, 630

Roxburgh, Duchess of, 574
Royal Titles Bill (1876), 507, 508–9
Ruskin, John, 568
Russell, Lord John (later Earl Russell), 120, 124, 134, 228–9, 266, 279, 280, 298, 307, 368, 390, 398, 448, 458, 582; becomes Prime Minister, 234; his 'littleness', 234; and V's Irish tour, 234, 239; argues on revolutions, 247, 248; mediation in campaign against Palmerston, 249, 250, 251, 252, 253, 256, 257, 261; and 'Papal aggression' and Reform, 254–5, 281; resigns, 284, 306; return to Foreign Office, 353, 354; and Schleswig-Holstein, 400; Prime Minister again, 433; and Reform, 437; defeated, 438; a party man, 711
Russell, Lady William, 490

Sadowa, 438, 463
Sahl, Hermann (librarian), 414, 475, 476, 512, 623
St Cyr, Gouvion, 288 n
St George's Chapel, Windsor, 211, 395–6, 534, 687, 708
St James's Gazette, 562, 563
St James's Palace, 49, 55, 58, 63, 65, 89, 173, 177, 457
St Laurent, Mlle (known as Madame) Julie de, 17–18, 20–22, 393
St Omer, 302
St Paul's Cathedral, 288, 378, 490, 687, 689
St Petersburg, 496
St Thomas's Hospital, 452, 479

786

Seymour, Colonel Francis, later Lord Hertford, 390–1
Shaftesbury, Lord, 86, 225, 281, 512
Shakespeare, 276, 382
Shah of Persia, 494, 522
Shore, Rev. Thomas Teignmouth, 581
Showers, Colonel, 422
Showers, Mary, 422
Sibthorp, Colonel Charles, 278
Sidmouth, 29
Siebold, Fraülein (midwife), 25, 26
Sigismund ('Siggie'), Prince, 408, 438
Silas Marner (Eliot), 370
Simmons, Lady (Lintorn), 430, 575
Simpson, Sir James Young, 291, 292
Singapore, 624
Singer, Fraülein (maid), 108
Sinope, 298
Skerrett (dresser), 203, 628
Slidell, John, 368
Smiles, Samuel, 277, 442, 527
Smith, Sydney, 196
Smith, W. H., 433, 518, 524, 645
Snow, Dr John, 291–2
social welfare, 224, 436, 491–2, 526–7, 579–81, 722–3
Sofia, 620
Solferino, 353
Somerset, Duchess of, 562
Somerset, Lady Augusta, 181
Somerset, Lady Geraldine, 181 n, 568
Sophia, Princess Augusta Sophia (daughter of George III), 31, 46–8, 66, 69, 74, 119, 145

Sophie of Prussia, Princess (later Queen of Hellenes), 641–2, 649
South Africa Company, 681, 683
South Kensington Museum, 436
Southey, Mrs, 192, 209
Späth, Baroness, 26, 47, 48
Spectator, 229
Spencer, Herbert, 427 n
Spencer, Lord, 544, 670
spiritualism, 418–26, 428–31, 572, 578
Spiritualist Magazine, 421
Spitalfields weavers, 224, 246
Spithead, 302, 383, 630
Stanley, Edward Smith (later 14th Earl of Derby), 228, 229
Stanley, Sir Frederick (later 16th Earl of Derby), 598
Stanley, Sir H. M., 527
Stanley, Dean Arthur, 100, 383, 408, 409, 453, 506, 515, 581, 722
Stanley, Lady Augusta (formerly Bruce), 442, 447, 470, 489, 496, 715
Stansfeld, Sir James, 491
Stead, W. T., 423, 579, 654 n, 656
Stephanie of Hohenzollern, Queen of Portugal, 321, 424
Stephen, Sir James, 345
Stephenson, Sir Benjamin, 71
Stirling, Lieutenant, 469
Stockmar, Baron, 29, 35, 69, 70, 72, 77, 79, 82, 128, 133, 143, 196, 215, 330, 340, 356, 367; as Leopold's agent, 79, 81, 156; career and character, 80–81; bad advice over

Trimmer, Mrs, 37
Trollope, Anthony, 359, 433, 554
Truth, 602, 651
Tryon, Admiral Sir George, 657
Tulloch, Principal John, 446, 526
Tyndall, Professor John, 382
typhoid, 366, 370, 372, 389, 391, 430, 489

Underwood, Lady Cecilia, 20
United Irishman, The, 698
Universe, 486
Uxküll, Count, 719

Vaughan, Cardinal, 688
Vavarescu, Mme Hélène, 429
Versailles, 316
Victoire of Saxe-Coburg-Kohary, Princess (later Duchess of Nemours), 157, 242, 243, 246, 358
Victor of Leiningen, Prince, 467
Victor Emmanuel II of Italy, 320, 343
Victoria, Queen: ancestry, 17–23; birth, 24–5; natural feeding, 25; vaccinated, 26; christened, 27; known as 'Drina', 28; first military review, 28; father's death, 28; search for father-figure, 30, 83, 88, 286, 339; early years at Kensington Palace, 31, 33, 44–6, 48, 51, 54, 55, 58, 137, 156, 363; first visit to George IV, 32; destined for A, 34, 63, 132, 155; family visits, 34–5; education, 35–8, 42, 53; has

Lehzen for governess, 35–7, 51, 54, 55, 92, 204–5, 206, 286; strict regime, 36; collection of dolls, 36–7; realizes nearness to throne, 39–40, 41; 'I will be good', 39, 271; alleged 'Cumberland plot' against, 44–6; and scandal of her mother and Conroy, 45, 47, 48, 50, 62, 66, 147–8; begins to hate him, 46, 62, 107; family friction over her upbringing, 47–9; source of her strong character, 49; her 'Royal Progresses', 50–53; carriage accident, 52–3; her reading, 53; additions to Household and social life, 54–5; visits from relations, 56–7, 63–6; animal companions, 56–7; predicts the next two important years, 58

battle against Conroy, 58, 61–2, 70–74, 105, 106; confirmed, 58; tour of North, 58–9; at Ramsgate with King Leopold, 59–60; attack of typhoid, 61–2; refuses to make Conroy private secretary, 62; and visit of A and Ernest, 63–6; her praise of A, 66; visits family tombs at Windsor, 67; suffers from Kensington 'system', 69–75; coolness towards mother, 69, 71–2; William IV's offer to, 71; refuses to compromise despite coercion, 72–3; hears of Accession, 75, 76; praised for her first Council, 77–8;

Victoria, Queen—*continued*

crowded first day as Queen, 78–9, 82; chooses Household, 79, 89; dismisses Conroy, 79; King Leopold's advice, 79–80; 'quite alone', 80, 137; her partnership with Melbourne, 83–8, 92, 98, 110, 116, 129, 150, 159, 163, 174, 212, 274, 382; political education, 84; her social conscience blunted, 85–6; proclaimed, 89; moves to Buckingham Palace, 90; increasing severance from mother, 90–91, 98, 105–7, 113, 126, 129; her income, 91–2; life at Windsor, 93–5; reviews troops, 95; Coronation, 96, 99–104, 163

her year's development, 98–9, 113; increasing criticisms and animosities, 105–8, 113–14; her love for Lehzen, 107–8; alleged foreign influences, 107–8; emancipation from King Leopold, 108–10; tolerates no interference from abroad, 110; worries over health and appearance, 110–12; jealousy over Melbourne, 112; 'unloved childhood', 114; dullness of Court, 114–15; and Lady Flora Hastings affair, 119–30, 135, 142, 149–54; considers marriage as alternative to life with mother, 131–3; decides to delay, 133, 134; and Melbourne's resignation, 134, 135; dislikes Peel, 136; conflict over Household

ladies, 137–43; new mood of pleasure, 143–4; and Conroy's departure, 145; mother's attempt at reconciliation, 149; hissed at Ascot, 150; need for new life, 154, 155; tries to postpone A's second visit, 155–6; renewal of Coburg family life, 158; A as her complement, 161; his inaccurate ideas about her, 163; his second visit, 164–8; decides to marry after all, 165–6; proposes to A, 166–7; objects to peerage for him, 168; her Declaration of Marriage, 168–9; and A's precedence and allowance, 169–71, 223–4; series of minor crises, 173–4; and ethics of love, 173; A's and Melbourne's struggle for her soul, 174; marriage, 170–8; and abuse of Court reputation, 181; difficulties of relationship with A, 183–6; her jealousy of him, 186; pregnancy, 187–8; escapes assassination, 188–9; increasing dependence on A, 190, 197, 224; birth of PR, 191

warned of falling revenue, 195; fresh Household crisis, 195–6; tours Whig houses, 198; trouble in nursery, 199–203; and Lehzen's departure, 203; feels inferior, 205, 206; A's re-education of, 206, 275–6, 328, 358, 381–2, 425, 525; money troubles, 208; birth of P of W, 210; two more attempts

Victoria, Queen—*continued*
320; relations with children, 321–42; and PR's betrothal to Frederick William of Prussia, 323–30; resents A's preoccupation with business, 330–1; creates him Prince Consort, 333; and PR's wedding, 334–6; uses daily letters to her for self-expression, 336–7, 339–40; sense of guilt over P of W's education, 343–8; concern over Palmerston, 348; agrees to cement French alliance, 349; and Indian Mutiny, 350; and reorganization of Indian Government, 352; on French and Austrian war, 352–3; agrees with Palmerston on defence, 354; worries over Princess Alice's future, 355–7; family and Household deaths, 357–8, 362; visits Germany, 359–60; first sees William II, 360; last Christmas with A, 361; death of mother, 363; heavy grief, and reports of unbalance, 363–4; and A's illness and death, 367–78

effect of his training, 381–2; her grief, 383–6, 388–92, 401, 408, 417; chooses spot for Mausoleum, 386; her seclusion, 389, 392; rumoured insanity, 391–2; blames P of W for A's illness, 393, 394, 457; and his marriage, 394–6; contest with Duke Ernest over Greek throne, 397; visits Germany and

seeks Prussian–Austrian accord, 347–8; argues for neutrality in Schleswig-Holstein problem, 398–9, 400–1; supports Russian suppression of Polish rising, 399; outcry against seclusion, 401–2, 410–11; gradual emergence, 402, 410, 434–5; deaths of Palmerston and K Leopold, 404, 433; begins to quote Brown, 404; his increasing influence, 405, 408–9, 413; brings him to Osborne, 407; myth of their marriage, 409–10, 417; lies and skits on, 412; her last will, 417; alleged spiritualism, 418–25, 428, 572, 578; opens Parliament for first time since widowhood, 434–5; hospital and prison visits, 436; and Reform crisis, 437–43; and Seven Weeks War, 438, 439, 463; pictures new Revolution, 441–3

factors in her recovery, 443; romantic relationship with Disraeli, 443–7, 502–3; sense of national unity, 446; first visit to Switzerland, 446; accepts Gladstone as Premier, 447; thinks him a humbug, 448; disapproves of his Irish Church policy, 450, 453; and alleged Fenian plots, 450–2; cannot find Gladstone agreeable, 453, 504; anxiety over family affairs, 454, 455–71, 498–9; 'royal' visits, 455–6; improved relations with P of

793

Victoria, Queen—*continued*
569; Brown's influence, 575–8; death of P Leopold, 578

interest in social problems, 579–81; disputes over Cabinet secrets, 582; disapproves of Gladstone's visit to Norway and Copenhagen, 582–3; and Gordon disaster, 586–8, 593–6; and Reform Bill, 589–92; and Princess Beatrice's marriage, 599–602; other family complications, 599–600; opens last Parliament, 607; unconstitutional correspondence with Salisbury during Gladstone's ministry, 609–10; and Home Rule, 612–16, 622, 656; Golden Jubilee, 622–31, 633; and illness of P Frederick William, 631, 633; visits him, 634–5; her attachment to the Munshi, 637–9, 672–80; failing health, 640, 700; renewed match-making for grandchildren, 640–3, 515, 649, 654, 667; death of D of Clarence, 646; and Gladstone's fourth ministry, 650–4; and Gladstone's resignation, 658–61; failure of their relationship, 660–4; chooses Rosebery to succeed, 665; more weddings, 667; pleasure at birth of Edward VIII, 668; death of Ponsonby, 669; and Jameson Raid, 681, 683; P Henry of Battenberg's death, 681, 683; Tsar's visit, 684; Diamond Jubilee, 685–91; curt reaction to Gladstone's death, 691–3; death of P Alfred, 693–4: and Boer War, 695–7; Irish tour, 698; deaths of D of Edinburgh and P Christian Victor, 701–2; death and funeral, 704–10; her achievement and character, 710–26

Appearance, 31, 34, 65, 94, 105, 112, 169, 319, 337, 487, 694, 721; inches, lack of, 85, 94, 316; weight, increasing, 105, 110, 111, 316; weight, loss of, 487

Character and characteristics, 22, 49, 53–4, 73, 76–7, 85, 98, 163, 195, 523–4, 712–26; accent, 25–6; beauty, susceptibility to, 158; children, attitude to, 192; contradictions in, 713–20; country, knowledge of, 51–2; death, horror of, 151; emotional crises, 293–4, 315, 322, 330–2, 341, 355, 365–6; Englishness, uncompromising, 328; family feeling, 456–68, 528–32, 561–2, 599–604, 620–1, 640–3, 646–7, 649–50, 654; father-figures, search for, 30, 83, 88, 286, 339, 716; good manners, 710; gossip, fondness for, 181; hard-heartedness, alleged, 181–2, 183; humility, 710; humour, 501, 561, 721; hysterics, 294, 370, 381; inquiring attitude, 426–8; intellect, 718; intellectual inferiority,

795

Victoria, Queen—*continued*
feeling of, 205–6; jealousy, 98, 112, 186, 319, 331, 663; kindness, 182; matriarchal feelings, 214, 456; memory, 205; 'military mania', 319; mimicry, gift for, 33; peremptoriness, 79, 535; possessiveness, 98, 112, 331; Protestant militancy, 505–6; romanticism, 54; self-criticism, 105, 347, 710; self-will, 381, 477; selfishness, 499; shyness, 382, 665; social conscience, 85, 89, 237; strength of, 80, 143, 185, 653; superstition, 424; temper, hot, 33, 98, 113, 133, 159, 184, 199, 201, 202, 206, 498, 677; thrift, 92; vocation, sense of, 550, 551; voice, 25–6, 77, 169, 721; wit, appreciation of, 504

Cultural interests: art, 206, 525; diary-writing, 51–2; drawing and painting, 38, 42, 52, 53; history, 36; languages, 38; literature, 53–4, 113, 205, 276, 358–9, 382, 525; music, 161; opera and ballet, 38, 55–6; poetry, 38; science, 382

Health, 110–11, 117, 395, 546, 640; in pregnancy, 187–8, 330–2; alleged mental instability, 326, 340, 365, 391, 485, 486, 487; nervous breakdown after mother's death, 303–5, 371; 'peculiarities' of system, 389; cold, fresh air necessary to, 389; shock due to A's

death, 383–6, 389–92; and monarchy crisis, 477, 480–4; rheumatic attacks, 566–7, 568, 578, 623, 658; failing sight, 700, 702; increasing debility, 701 *et seq.*

Interests: animals and pets, 56, 176; cultural – *see separate heading;* dolls, collection of, 36–7, 46; horsemanship, 94–5; psychology, 427; sanitation, 372, 449; sermons, 53, 426; social questions, 224–7, 237–8, 276, 311, 381, 436, 442, 491, 579–81, 722–3; spiritualism, alleged, 418–25, 427–30

Portraits: as a child, 31; at first Council, 78; Landseer's, 112; Winterhalter's, 222, 237; Angeli's, 498, 546; Constant's, 694

Views on: arranged marriages, 156; belief, 526; Britain's mission, 723; childbirth, 192, 291–2, 338, 339, 389, 467, 473; children, 192, 338, 403, 472–3, 569; cruelty to animals, 623; death, 151, 273, 387–8, 534, 579; duelling, 225, 455; education, 526–7; etiquette, 182; hereafter, 428–9; 'high tone', 502, 506, 511, 516; idleness, 382; immortality, 426–7; improvement, 726; John Brownism, 469; John Bullism, 469, 471; lady doctors, 25, 496; love, ethics of, 173; magnetism, 425; marriage, 328, 335, 338; moral-

Victoria, Queen—*continued*
  ity, 173–4; party system,
  712; penal system, 225;
  prostitution, 661; punishment, 189; punishment of
  children, 86, 271, 341, 348;
  racialism, 673, 697; religion,
  38, 80, 226–7, 254, 326–7,
  435–30, 450, 451–4, 505–6,
  526; republicanism, 478,
  479; revolution, 247, 248,
  257, 441–2; revolutionary
  Europe, 243–4, 247–8,
  259–61; Sabbatarians, 267;
  sanitation, 372; smoking,
  523–4; social classes, 441–2,
  468, 471, 478–9, 547; social
  customs, new, 531; social
  progress, 526, 726; vivisection, 510; women's
  rights, 496; working hours,
  225–6, 496
Victoria of Hesse (later Battenberg), Princess, 468, 533,
  539, 550, 599, 601, 603–4
Victoria of Prussia, Princess
  ('Young Vicky' or
  'Moretta'), 599, 603, 626,
  634, 641
Victoria Adelaide Mary
  Louise, Princess ('Vicky'),
  later Crown Princess of
  Prussia and Empress Frederick of Germany, 210, 213,
  217, 220, 221, 270, 315, 347,
  360, 362, 365, 369, 387,
  389, 395, 408, 413, 424, 438,
  452, 461, 463, 501, 510, 546,
  556, 599; birth, 191, 192–3;
  Lehzen's care of, 199–201,
  209; ill-health, 199, 209;
  precocity, 214, 271, 272;
  destined for Prussia, 215,

282, 323; a haemophilia
transmitter, 293; V's an-
xiety over development, 323,
325, 328; betrothed to P
Frederick William, 324–7;
confirmed, 326–7; question
of household, 328; courtship
and marriage preparations,
328–9; A's devotion to,
331, 333, 339, 374; grant to,
332; marriage, 334–6, 351;
V's constant letters and
advice to, 336–7, 339–40,
382, 383, 386, 392, 400, 404,
426, 430, 433, 442, 455, 457,
459, 465, 467–8, 472, 493,
500, 528, 530–1, 535, 600,
601, 603, 610, 619, 641, 642,
648, 653, 668, 670, 676,
692, 697, 706, 718; preg-
nancy, 339–40; difficult
birth of William II, 342;
birth of Princess Charlotte,
355; arranges meeting of
Princess Alexandra and P of
W, 364, 394; V's letters on
A's death, 383–4; opposed
to Bismarck, 397, 399, 400;
and Schleswig-Holstein,
399, 400; V's praise of
Brown to, 408, 430; alleged
immorality, 417, 631; stiffness in Society, 459; objects
to sisters' marriages, 461,
462; and Franco-Prussian
War, 475–6; and monarchy
crisis, 480, 481, 484, 487;
row with Brown, 484; quarrel with V over expensive
visits, 498–9; and Eastern
crisis, 516, 519; deepening
understanding with V,
531–2; difficulties with

William I—*continued*
474, 476, 478; shot at, 526;
death, 631, 633
William II, Kaiser, 599, 602,
623, 720; birth, 342; withered arm, 342, 360, 424,
705; V first sees, 360; at P
of W's wedding, 395; V's
advice on, 468, 534, 633,
655; arrogance, 532, 636;
promises to behave, 635;
visits Osborne, 637; as
matchmaker, 541, 667;
annual visits 'not quite
desirable', 655; Kruger telegram, 682; not asked to
Diamond Jubilee, 686; at
V's deathbed, 704, 705, 707
Williams, H. L., 576
Wilton, Lord, 99, 285
Windsor, Edward, Duke of,
668, 685
Windsor Castle, 30, 31, 35,
66, 93–6, 164, 180, 208,
211, 217, 218, 220, 221, 251,
448, 633, 649, 696, 702–3;
Closet, 93, 113, 136,
166–7; Corridor, 93, 157,
166, 377, 439, 598, 616; St
George's Chapel, 112,
395–6, 534, 687; A's visit
(1839), 164–8, 621; 'Paget
Club House', 172; honey-
moon at, 174, 178, 179;
Christmas entertainments,
211; drainage system, 224;
improvements, 264–5; fire
at, 290; Napoleon III at,
312–15, 351; A's last Christmas at, 361; his illness and
death at, 368–78; Blue

Room, 373–8, 388, 429, 431,
432, 533, 726; stone mark-
ing A's last shoot, 386;
V's fall downstairs, 566;
Ulster women's petition at,
616; Golden Jubilee at,
626–7, 629; Kaiser's last
visit to V at, 682; Diamond
Jubilee at, 687, 690; funeral
at, 708–10
Winterhalter, Franz, 222, 237,
276, 467
Wiseman, Cardinal, 254
Wolseley, Sir Garnet, 552–3,
564, 565, 582, 593, 594, 596,
598, 630, 684, 689, 695
Wolseley, Lady, 596
Women's Rights, 496
Wood, Sir Charles (later Lord
Halifax), 449
Woodroffe, Canon J. N. B.,
720 *n*
working hours, 225–6
World, The, 568
Wortley, Victoria, 383
Wreidt, Etta, 422, 423
Württemberg, Alexander of,
Prince, 56
Württemberg, Ernest of,
Prince, 56
Württemberg, Sophia of,
Princess, 156

Yates, Edmund, 413 *n*
York, Frederick, Duke of,
20, 31
'Young Ireland', 238

Zanzibar, 644
Zebehr (slave-trader), 587
Zulu War (1879), 536, 543